This book is based on NCERT syllabus prescribed by the Central Board of Secondary Education (CBSE) for Class X

Science for Tenth Class (Part – 3)

Biology

As per NCERT/CBSE Syllabus

Containing answers to NCERT book questions and value-based questions

LAKHMIR SINGH

And

MANJIT KAUR

This Book Belongs to:

Name..

Roll No...

Class.............................. Section...........................

School..

S. CHAND SCHOOL BOOKS
(An imprint of S. Chand Publishing)
A Division of S. Chand And Company Limited
(An ISO 9001 Certified Company)
7361, Ram Nagar, Qutab Road, New Delhi-110055
Phone: 23672080-81-82, 9899107446, 9911310888; Fax: 91-11-23677446
www.schandpublishing.com; e-mail : helpdesk@schandpublishing.com

Branches :

Ahmedabad	:	Ph: 27541965, 27542369, ahmedabad@schandpublishing.com
Bengaluru	:	Ph: 22268048, 22354008, bangalore@schandpublishing.com
Bhopal	:	Ph: 4274723, 4209587, bhopal@schandpublishing.com
Chandigarh	:	Ph: 2625356, 2625546, 4025418, chandigarh@schandpublishing.com
Chennai	:	Ph: 28410027, 28410058, chennai@schandpublishing.com
Coimbatore	:	Ph: 2323620, 4217136, coimbatore@schandpublishing.com (Marketing Office)
Cuttack	:	Ph: 2332580, 2332581, cuttack@schandpublishing.com
Dehradun	:	Ph: 2711101, 2710861, dehradun@schandpublishing.com
Guwahati	:	Ph: 2738811, 2735640, guwahati@schandpublishing.com
Hyderabad	:	Ph: 27550194, 27550195, hyderabad@schandpublishing.com
Jaipur	:	Ph: 2219175, 2219176, jaipur@schandpublishing.com
Jalandhar	:	Ph: 2401630, 5000630, jalandhar@schandpublishing.com
Kochi	:	Ph: 2809208, 2808207, cochin@schandpublishing.com
Kolkata	:	Ph: 23353914, 23357458, kolkata@schandpublishing.com
Lucknow	:	Ph: 4026791, 4065646, lucknow@schandpublishing.com
Mumbai	:	Ph: 22690881, 22610885, mumbai@schandpublishing.com
Nagpur	:	Ph: 6451311, 2720523, 2777666, nagpur@schandpublishing.com
Patna	:	Ph: 2300489, 2302100, patna@schandpublishing.com
Pune	:	Ph: 64017298, pune@schandpublishing.com
Raipur	:	Ph: 2443142, raipur@schandpublishing.com (Marketing Office)
Ranchi	:	Ph: 2361178, ranchi@schandpublishing.com
Sahibabad	:	Ph: 2771235, 2771238, delhibr-sahibabad@schandpublishing.com

First Published in 1980
Revised Edition 2014, 2016, 2017
This Edition 2018
Reprints 1981, 82, 83, 84, 85, 86, 87, 88, 89, 90, 91, 92, 93, 94, 95, 96, 97, 98, 99, 2000, 2001, 2002, 2003, 2004, 2005, 2006, 2007, 2008, 2009, 2010, 2011, 2012, 2013, 2015, 2016, 2017, 2018
First Impression 2019

ISBN : 978-93-5283-182-1 **Product code:** SCS3LKS100BIOAD17CBY

PRINTED IN INDIA

By Vikas Publishing House Pvt. Ltd., Plot 20/4, Site-IV, Industrial Area Sahibabad, Ghaziabad-201010
and Published by S. Chand And Company Limited, 7361, Ram Nagar, New Delhi -110 055.

ABOUT THE AUTHORS

LAKHMIR SINGH did his M.Sc. from Delhi University in 1969. Since then he has been teaching in Dyal Singh College of Delhi University, Delhi. He started writing books in 1980. Lakhmir Singh believes that book writing is just like classroom teaching. Though a book can never replace a teacher but it should make the student feel the presence of a teacher. Keeping this in view, he writes books in such a style that students never get bored reading his books. Lakhmir Singh has written more than 15 books so far on all the science subjects: Physics, Chemistry and Biology. He believes in writing quality books. He does not believe in quantity.

MANJIT KAUR did her B.Sc., B.Ed. from Delhi University in 1970. Since then she has been teaching in a reputed school of Directorate of Education, Delhi. Manjit Kaur is such a popular science teacher that all the students want to join those classes which she teaches in the school. She has a vast experience of teaching science to school children, and she knows the problems faced by the children in the study of science. Manjit Kaur has put all her teaching experience into the writing of science books. She has co-authored more than 15 books alongwith her husband, Lakhmir Singh.

It is the team-work of Lakhmir Singh and Manjit Kaur which has given some of the most popular books in the history of science education in India. Lakhmir Singh and Manjit Kaur both write exclusively for the most reputed, respected and largest publishing house of India : S.Chand And Company Limited.

AN OPEN LETTER

Dear Friend,

We would like to talk to you for a few minutes, just to give you an idea of some of the special features of this book. Before we go further, let us tell you that this book has been revised according to the NCERT syllabus prescribed by the Central Board of Secondary Education (CBSE). Just like our earlier books, we have written this book in such a simple style that even the weak students will be able to understand biology very easily. Believe us, while writing this book, we have considered ourselves to be the students of Class X and tried to make things as simple as possible.

The most important feature of this revised edition of the book is that we have included a large variety of different types of questions to assess the learning abilities of the students. This book contains :

(*i*) Very short answer type questions (including true-false type questions and fill in the blanks type questions),

(*ii*) Short answer type questions,

(*iii*) Long answer type questions (or Essay type questions),

(*iv*) Multiple choice questions (MCQs) based on theory,

(*v*) Questions based on high order thinking skills (HOTS),

(*vi*) Multiple choice questions (MCQs) based on practical skills in science,

(*vii*) NCERT book questions and exercises (with answers), and

(*viii*) Value based questions (with answers).

Please note that answers have also been given for the various types of questions, wherever required. All these features will make this book even more useful to the students as well as the teachers. "A picture can say a thousand words". Keeping this in mind, a large number of coloured pictures and sketches of various scientific processes, procedures, appliances and everyday situations involving principles of biology have been given in this revised edition of the book. This will help the students to understand the various concepts of biology clearly. It will also tell them how biology is applied in the real situations in homes, transport and industry.

Books by Lakhmir Singh and Manjit Kaur

1. Lakhmir Singh's Science for Class 1
2. Lakhmir Singh's Science for Class 2
3. Lakhmir Singh's Science for Class 3
4. Lakhmir Singh's Science for Class 4
5. Lakhmir Singh's Science for Class 5
6. Lakhmir Singh's Science for Class 6
7. Lakhmir Singh's Science for Class 7
8. Lakhmir Singh's Science for Class 8
9. Science for Ninth Class (Part 1) PHYSICS
10. Science for Ninth Class (Part 2) CHEMISTRY
11. Science for Tenth Class (Part 1) PHYSICS
12. Science for Tenth Class (Part 2) CHEMISTRY
13. Science for Tenth Class (Part 3) BIOLOGY
14. Science for Ninth Class (J & K Edition)
15. Science for Tenth Class (J & K Edition)
16. Science for Ninth Class (Hindi Edition) : PHYSICS and CHEMISTRY
17. Science for Tenth Class (Hindi Edition) : PHYSICS, CHEMISTRY and BIOLOGY
18. Self-Practice Book for Science for Ninth Class Part-1 Physics
19. Self-Practice Book for Science for Ninth Class Part-2 Chemistry
20. Self-Practice Book for Science for Tenth Class Part-1 Physics
21. Self-Practice Book for Science for Tenth Class Part-2 Chemistry
22. Self-Practice Book for Science for Tenth Class Part-3 Biology

We are sure you will agree with us that the facts of biology are just the same in all the books, the difference lies in the method of presenting these facts to the students. In this book, the various topics of biology have been explained in such a simple way that while reading this book, a student will feel as if a teacher is sitting by his side and explaining the various things to him. We are sure that after reading this book, the students will develop a special interest in biology and they would like to study biology in higher classes as well.

We think that the real judges of a book are the teachers concerned and the students for whom it is meant. So, we request our teacher friends as well as the students to point out our mistakes, if any, and send their comments and suggestions for the further improvement of this book.

Wishing you a great success,

Yours sincerely,

Lakhmir Singh

Manjit Kaur

396, Nilgiri Apartments,
Alaknanda, New Delhi-110019
E-mail : singhlakhmir@hotmail.com

CONTENTS

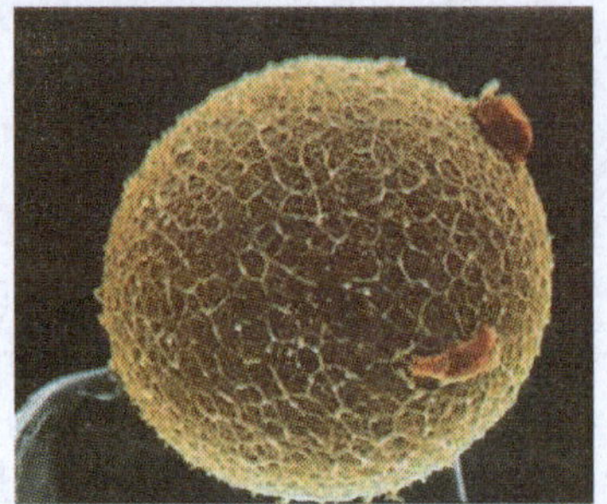

PHYSICS & CHEMISTRY BY SAME AUTHORS

Science for Tenth Class, Part 1 : PHYSICS

1. Electricity
2. Magnetic Effect of Electric Current
3. Sources of Energy
4. Reflection of Light
5. Refraction of Light
6. The Human Eye and the Colourful World

- Multiple Choice Questions (MCQs) Based on Practical Skills in Science (Physics)
- NCERT Book Questions and Exercises (with answers)
- Value Based Questions (with answers)

Science for Tenth Class, Part 2 : CHEMISTRY

1. Chemical Reactions and Equations
2. Acids, Bases and Salts
3. Metals and Non-Metals
4. Carbon and its Compounds
5. Periodic Classification of Elements

- Multiple Choice Questions (MCQs) Based on Practical Skills in Science (Chemistry)
- NCERT Book Questions and Exercises (with answers)
- Value Based Questions (with answers)

LATEST CBSE SYLLABUS, CLASS 10 SCIENCE (BIOLOGY PART – 3)

Life processes : "Living beings" ; Basic concept of nutrition, respiration, transport and excretion in plants and animals.

Control and coordination in animals and plants : Tropic movements in plants; Introduction to plant hormones ; Control and coordination in animals : nervous system ; voluntary, involuntary and reflex action, Chemical coordination : animal hormones.

Reproduction : Reproduction in animals and plants (asexual and sexual). Reproductive health–need for and methods of family planning, Safe sex vs HIV/AIDS, Child bearing and women's health.

Heredity and evolution : Heredity ; Mendel's contribution–Rules for inheritance of traits ; Sex determination : brief introduction ; Basic concepts of evolution.

Natural resources : Management of natural resources. Conservation and judicious use of natural resources. Forests and wildlife, coal and petroleum conservation. Examples of peoples' participation for conservation of natural resources. Big dams : advantages and limitations ; alternatives if any. Water harvesting. Sustainability of natural resources.

Our environment : Ecosystem, environmental problems, ozone depletion, waste production and their solutions. Biodegradable and non-biodegradable substances.

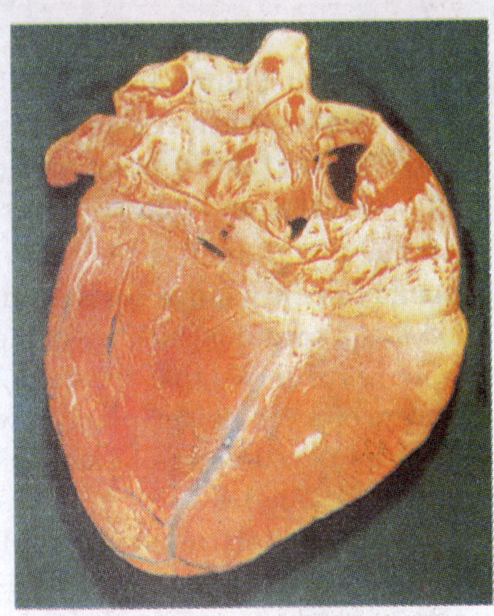

Life Processes

Something which is 'living' (not dead) is said to be 'alive'. In most simple terms, 'alive' means 'having life'. Alive is called *'jeevit'* or *'zinda'* in Hindi. We are alive and you are also alive. Those things which are alive are called 'living things'. **All the plants and animals (including human beings) are alive or living things.** Now, an important question arises : What criteria do we use to decide whether something is alive ? This is discussed below.

The most important criterion to decide whether something is alive (or not) is the movement. Movement is one of the most important signs of life in an organism. **All the living things (which are alive) move by themselves without any external help.** In some cases the movements of living things are quite fast which can be easily observed by us but in other cases the movements are very slow and hence observed with difficulty. For example, **the movements in most of the animals are fast and can be observed easily but**

(*a*) Frog jumping

(*b*) Birds flying

(*b*) Athletes running

Figure 1. Living things move. Movement is the most important sign of being alive. These pictures show the movement in animals (including human beings).

the movements in plants are usually slow and observed with difficulty. Animals and plants move in *different* ways. This will become clear from the following discussion.

Animals can move from one place to another or they can move their body parts. For example, a frog moves when it jumps into a pond, a bird moves when it flies in the sky, an athlete moves when he runs and a fish moves when it swims in water (see Figure 1). We move our hands when we clap and our chest moves up and down when we breathe. And a dog can wag its tail. All these movements show that a frog, bird, fish, dog and human beings are alive (or living things).

The plants are fixed in the soil at a place, so they cannot move like animals from place to place. **The plants can only move parts of their body such as leaves, flowers, shoots and roots.** The plant parts move *towards* a stimulus such as sunlight, gravity or water, etc. For example, the shoot, the leaves and flower of a sunflower plant move by bending towards the sun so as to face the sunlight (see Figure 2). The leaves of a *Mimosa pudica* plant (sensitive plant) move by folding up when touched with a finger. Plants also show movement by growing their roots and shoots bigger.

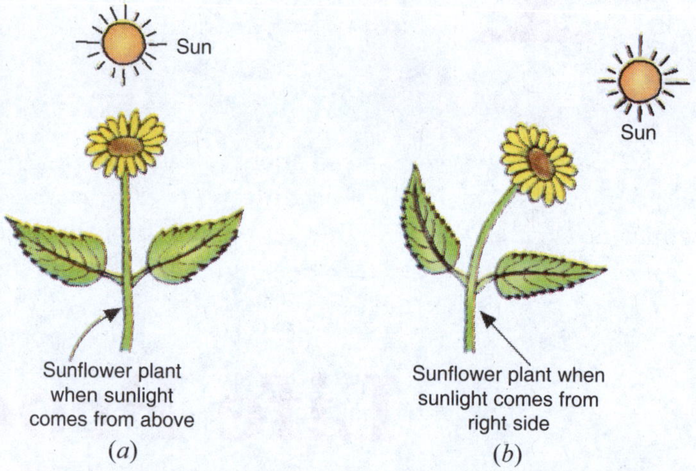

Figure 2. Plants are also living things. Since plants are fixed at a place, they can show movement only by bending their body parts in response to certain stimuli. This sunflower plant is showing movement by bending in response to sunlight.

Non-living things (which are not alive) cannot move by themselves. For example, a stone is a non-living thing which cannot move by itself from one place to another or show any other type of movement. We will have to move it by applying force from outside.

All the living things (plants and animals) are made up of tiny living units called cells. The cells themselves are made up of still smaller particles called molecules. **The movements over very small scale (as those in the molecules of living things) are invisible to the naked eye.** The invisible molecular movement is, however, necessary for the existence of life. In fact, viruses do not show any molecular movement in them (until they infect some cell) and this has created controversy about whether they are truly alive or not. In addition to movement, the living things also show some other characteristics. These are discussed below.

All the living things (which are alive) have some common characteristics (or features) which make them different from non-living things. **The characteristics of living things** are as follows :

(*i*) Living things can move by themselves.
(*ii*) Living things need food, air and water.
(*iii*) Living things can grow.
(*iv*) Living things can respond to changes around them. They are sensitive.
(*v*) Living things respire (release energy from food).
(*vi*) Living things excrete (get rid of waste materials from their body).
(*vii*) Living things can reproduce. They can have young ones.

What are Life Processes

All the organisms perform some basic functions to keep themselves alive. **The basic functions performed by living organisms to maintain their life on this earth are called life processes.** The basic life processes common to all the living organisms are : **Nutrition and Respiration; Transport and Excretion; Control and Coordination (Response to stimuli); Growth; Movement and Reproduction.** The process of nutrition involves the taking of food inside the body and converting it into smaller molecules which can be absorbed by the body. Respiration is the process which releases energy from the food absorbed by the body. Transport is the process in which a substance absorbed or made in one part of the body is moved to other parts of the body. Excretion is the process in which the waste materials produced in the cells of the body are removed from the body.

Control and coordination (or response to stimuli) is a process which helps the living organisms to survive in the changing environment around them. The process of growth involves the change from a small organism to a big organism (or an adult organism). In movement, the organism either moves from one place to another or moves its body parts while remaining at the same place. The process of reproduction involves the making of more organisms from the existing ones, so that organisms could live on this earth for ever.

Energy is Needed for the Life Processes

All the living organisms need energy to perform various life processes. They get this energy from food. **Food is a kind of fuel which provides energy to all the living organisms.** The living organisms use the chemical energy for carrying out various life processes. They get this chemical energy from food through chemical reactions. Actually, living organisms continuously need energy for their various life processes and other activities which they perform. For example, energy is required by an organism even during sleep. This is because when we are asleep, a number of biological processes keep on occurring in the body which require energy. Our heart beats non-stop even when we are asleep to pump blood throughout the body. And this beating of heart requires energy. Thus, the working of heart requires a continuous supply of energy.

The energy required by an organism comes from the food that the organism eats. Thus, food is the basic requirement of all the living organisms for obtaining energy. In this chapter we will first study the process of intake and utilisation of the food by an organism (called nutrition) and the liberation of energy from the food (called respiration). After that we will study the process of moving the digested food and other materials to the various parts of the body (called transport) and the removal of waste materials from the body (called excretion). Let us start with nutrition.

NUTRITION

Food is an organic substance. The simplest food is glucose. It is also called simple sugar. A more complex food is starch. Starch is made from glucose. The general name of substances like glucose (sugar)

Figure 3. This is glucose powder. Glucose is the simplest food. It is very easily absorbed by our body.

Figure 4. This is starch powder. Starch is a complex food. Most of our common foods like wheat, rice and potatoes contain a lot of starch.

and starch is 'carbohydrates'. Carbohydrates are the most common foods for getting energy. Fats and proteins are also foods. (A wider definition of food, however, also includes mineral salts, vitamins and water which are essential for the normal growth and development of an organism). The process of taking in food (consuming food) and utilising it is called nutrition. It is a process in which food is obtained in order to utilise it to provide energy for performing various metabolic activities of the organism. Actually, the term 'nutrition' comes from the word 'nutrient'. A nutrient is an organic or inorganic substance required for the maintenance of life and survival of a living organism. In most simple terms, a nutrient can be said to be a particular type of food. **A nutrient can be defined as a substance which an organism obtains from its surroundings and uses it as a source of energy or for the biosynthesis of its body constituents (like tissues and organs).** For example, **carbohydrates and fats are the nutrients** which are used by an organism mainly as a source of energy whereas **proteins and mineral salts are nutrients** used by an organism for the biosynthesis of its body constituents like skin, blood, etc.

The food taken in by an organism contains a large number of nutrients like carbohydrates, fats, proteins, minerals, vitamins and water, etc. We can now say that : **Nutrition is a process of intake of nutrients (like carbohydrates, fats, proteins, minerals, vitamins and water) by an organism as well as the utilisation of these nutrients by the organism.** We will now describe the various ways of procuring food (or obtaining food) by the different organisms. In other words, we will now describe the different modes of nutrition of the various organisms.

Modes of Nutrition

Modes of nutrition means methods of procuring food or obtaining food by an organism. All the organisms do not obtain their food in the same way. Different organisms have different methods of procuring food or obtaining food. In other words, organisms differ in their modes of nutrition. Depending on the mode (or method) of obtaining food, all the organisms can be classified into two groups: autotrophic and heterotrophic. Thus : **There are mainly two modes of nutrition :**

1. **Autotrophic,** and
2. **Heterotrophic.**

We will now discuss the autotrophic mode of nutrition and the heterotrophic mode of nutrition in detail, one by one.

1. Autotrophic Mode of Nutrition

The word 'auto' means 'self' and 'trophe' means 'nutrition'. Thus, autotrophic means 'self nutrition'. In autotrophic nutrition, the organism makes (or synthesizes) its own food from the inorganic raw materials like carbon dioxide and water present in the surroundings by using the sunlight energy. We can now say that : **Autotrophic nutrition is that mode of nutrition in which an organism makes (or synthesizes) its own food from the simple inorganic materials like carbon dioxide and water present in the surroundings (with the help of sunlight energy).** Please note that food is an organic material (like glucose, etc.). This means that, in autotrophic nutrition, organic material (food) is made (or synthesized) from inorganic materials

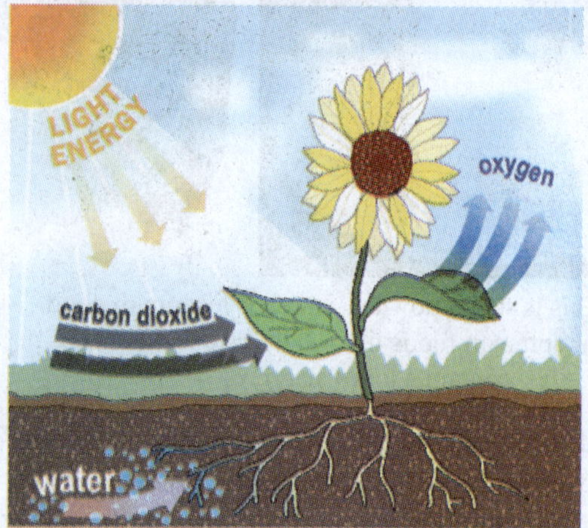

Figure 5. The green plants have autotrophic mode of nutrition. The green plants make their own food by combining carbon dioxide from air and water from ground in the presence of sunlight energy. This process is called photosynthesis.

Figure 6. Corn is a food. This corn cob has been made by corn plants by the process of photosynthesis.

Figure 7. Carrots are a food. These carrots have been made by carrot plants by the process of photosynthesis.

like carbon dioxide and water by utilizing the sunlight energy. **The green plants have an autotrophic mode of nutrition. The autotrophic bacteria also obtain their food by the autotrophic mode of nutrition** (though most bacteria are not autotrophic). The organisms having autotrophic mode of nutrition are called autotrophic organisms or just autotrophs.

Those organisms which can make their own food from carbon dioxide and water are called autotrophs. Carbon dioxide and water are inorganic substances. So, we can also say that : *Those organisms which can make their own food from the inorganic substances present in the environment, are called autotrophs.* **All the green plants are autotrophs** (because they can make their own food from inorganic substances like carbon dioxide and water present in the environment). Non-green plants are, however, not autotrophs. Certain bacteria called 'autotrophic bacteria' are also autotrophs.

The autotrophic organisms (or autotrophs) contain the green pigment called chlorophyll which is capable of trapping sunlight energy. This trapped sunlight energy is utilised by the autotrophs to make food by combining inorganic materials like carbon dioxide and water present in the environment by the process of photosynthesis. Thus, autotrophs make their own food by photosynthesis. So, autotrophs are the producers of food. The food produced by autotrophs (green plants) is also used by human beings and many, many other animals.

2. Heterotrophic Mode of Nutrition

The word 'heteros' means 'others' and 'trophe' refers to 'nutrition'. Thus, 'heterotrophic' means 'nutrition obtained from others'. In heterotrophic nutrition, the organism cannot make (or synthesize) its own food from the inorganic raw materials like carbon dioxide and water, and uses the food made by autotrophic organisms directly or indirectly. We can now say that : **Heterotrophic nutrition is that mode of nutrition in which an organism cannot make (or synthesize) its own food from simple inorganic materials like carbon dioxide and water, and depends on other organisms for its food.** A heterotrophic organism is a consumer which derives its nutrition from other organisms. That is, a heterotrophic organism has to eat other organisms for its nutrition. **All the animals have a heterotrophic mode of nutrition. Most bacteria and fungi also have heterotrophic mode of nutrition.** The organisms having heterotrophic mode of nutrition are called heterotrophic organisms or just heterotrophs.

(*a*) Deer eating plant leaves as food

(*b*) Tiger eating deer as food

(*c*) Brown bear about to eat fish as food

Figure 8. Deer, tiger and bear all have heterotrophic mode of nutrition.

Those organisms which cannot make their own food from inorganic substances like carbon dioxide and water, and depend on other organisms for their food are called heterotrophs. All the **animals are heterotrophs** (because they cannot make food from inorganic substances like carbon dioxide and water and obtain their food from other plants or animals.). Thus, man, dog, cat, deer, tiger, bear, lion, cow, etc., are all heterotrophs. **The non-green plants (like yeast) are also heterotrophs.** Heterotrophs depend on autotrophs and other heterotrophs for their food. In other words, **animals are heterotrophs which depend on plants or other animals for their food.**

From the above discussion we conclude that green plants make their own food. Non-green plants and animals cannot make their own food. They obtain food from plants and other animals. We will now discuss the various types of the heterotrophic mode of nutrition.

Types of Heterotrophic Nutrition

A heterotrophic organism (or heterotroph) can obtain its food from other organisms in three ways. So, the heterotrophic mode of nutrition is of three types :

1. **Saprotrophic nutrition,**
2. **Parasitic nutrition,** and
3. **Holozoic nutrition.**

We will now discuss the three types of heterotrophic nutrition in detail, one by one. Let us start with the saprotrophic nutrition.

1. Saprotrophic Nutrition (or Saprophytic Nutrition)

Saprotrophic nutrition is that nutrition in which an organism obtains its food from decaying organic matter of dead plants, dead animals and rotten bread, etc. 'Sapro' means 'rotten', so a saprotrophic organism draws its food from rotting wood of dead and decaying trees, rotten leaves, dead animals and household wastes like rotten bread, etc. The organisms having saprotrophic mode of nutrition are called saprophytes. We can now say that : **Saprophytes are the organisms which obtain their food from dead plants (like rotten leaves), dead and decaying animal bodies, and other decaying organic matter (like rotten bread).** Fungi (like bread moulds, mushrooms, yeast), and many bacteria are saprophytes. We know that fungi and bacteria are a kind of plants. So, we can also say that saprophytes are the plants which feed on dead and decaying organic matter. The saprophytes break down the complex organic molecules present in dead and decaying matter and convert them into simpler substances *outside* their body. These simpler substances are then absorbed by saprophytes as their food. Please note that saprotrophic nutrition is also known as saprophytic nutrition.

Figure 9. Mushroom (fungus) has saprophytic mode of nutrition. This picture shows mushrooms obtaining their food from the rotting wood of a dead tree.

2. Parasitic Nutrition

The parasitic nutrition is that nutrition in which an organism derives its food from the body of another living organism (called its host) without killing it. The organism which obtains the food is called a 'parasite', and the organism from whose body food is obtained is called the 'host'. We can now say that : **A parasite is an organism (plant or animal) which feeds on another living organism called its host.** A parasite receives its food from the host but gives no benefit to the host in return. A parasite usually harms the host. The host may be a plant or an animal. Most of the diseases which affect mankind, his domestic animals (like dogs and cattle) and his crops are caused by parasites. Parasitic mode of nutrition is observed in several fungi, bacteria, a few plants like *Cuscuta* (*amarbel*) and

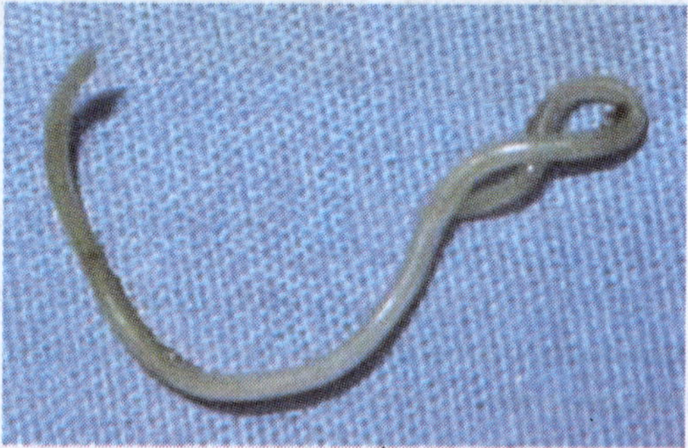

Figure 10. Roundworm has a parasitic mode of nutrition. Roundworm is a common intestinal parasite of man. Roundworms remain free in the intestine of infected man (host) and obtain their food from him.

some animals like *Plasmodium* and roundworms. Thus, the micro-organism '*Plasmodium*' (which causes malaria disease) is a parasite. Roundworm which causes diseases in man and domestic animals (like dogs and cattle) is also a parasite. Roundworms live inside the body of man and his domestic animals. Several fungi and bacteria, and plants like *Cuscuta* (*amarbel*) are also parasites. Some other examples of parasites are ticks, lice, leeches and tapeworms.

3. Holozoic Nutrition

'Holozoic nutrition' means 'feeding on solid food' (which may be a plant product or an animal product). Most of the animals (including human beings) take the solid food into their body by the process of ingestion. The ingested food is then digested (broken down) into simpler substances which are then absorbed into the cells of the body. And the undigested and unabsorbed waste materials are egested (thrown out) of the body. We can now say that : **The holozoic nutrition is that nutrition in which an organism takes the complex organic food materials into its body by the process of ingestion, the ingested food is digested and then absorbed into the body cells of the organism.** The undigested and unabsorbed part of the food is thrown out of the body of the organism by the process of egestion. The human beings and most of the animals have a holozoic mode of nutrition. In other words, man, cat, dog, cattle, deer, tiger, lion, bear, giraffe, frog, fish and *Amoeba*, etc., have the holozoic mode of nutrition.

Figure 11. Giraffe has a holozoic mode of nutrition. This picture shows a giraffe eating the leaves from a tree.

NUTRITION IN PLANTS

Just like other organisms, plants also require food which can supply energy for their various metabolic activities. Though animals can move from one place to another in search of food, plants just stand still at one place and make their own food. Green plants are autotrophic and synthesize their own food by the process of photosynthesis. 'Photo' means 'light' and 'synthesis' means 'to build', thus 'photosynthesis' means 'building up by light'. The plants use the energy in sunlight to prepare food from carbon dioxide and water in the presence of chlorophyll. Chlorophyll is present in the green coloured bodies called 'chloroplasts' inside the plant cells. In fact, the leaves of a plant are green because they contain tiny green coloured organelles called chloroplasts (which contain chlorophyll). Keeping these points in mind, we can now define the process of photosynthesis as follows :

Figure 12. This is chlorophyll. It has been extracted from the green leaves of plants.

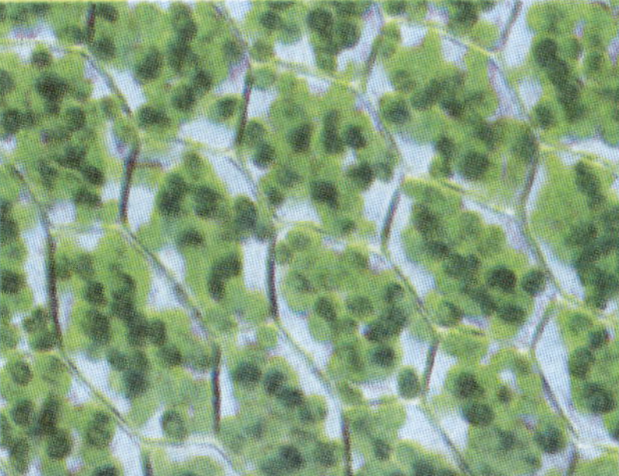

Figure 13. Chlorophyll is present in tiny organelles called chloroplasts inside the photosynthetic cells of leaves.

Figure 14. The green colour of plant leaves is due to the presence of chlorophyll in them.

The process by which green plants make their own food (like glucose) from carbon dioxide and water by using sunlight energy in the presence of chlorophyll, is called photosynthesis. Oxygen gas is released during photosynthesis. The process of photosynthesis can be represented as :

$$\underset{\text{(From air)}}{\underset{\text{Carbon dioxide}}{6CO_2}} + \underset{\text{(From soil)}}{\underset{\text{Water}}{6H_2O}} + \underset{\text{(From sun)}}{\text{Light energy}} \xrightarrow[\text{(Photosynthesis)}]{\text{Chlorophyll}} \underset{\text{(A food)}}{\underset{\text{Glucose}}{C_6H_{12}O_6}} + \underset{\text{Oxygen}}{6O_2}$$

The process of photosynthesis takes place in the green leaves of a plant. In other words, food is made in the green leaves of the plant. The green leaves of a plant make the food by combining carbon dioxide and water in the presence of sunlight and chlorophyll. This is shown clearly in Figure 15. The carbon dioxide gas required for making food is taken by the plant leaves from the air. This carbon dioxide enters the leaves through tiny pores in them called stomata. Water required for making food is taken from the soil. This water is transported to the leaves from the soil through the roots and stem. The sunlight provides energy required to carry out the chemical reactions involved in the preparation of food. The green pigment called chlorophyll present in green leaves helps in absorbing energy from sunlight. Oxygen gas is produced as a by-product during the preparation of food by photosynthesis. This oxygen gas goes into the air.

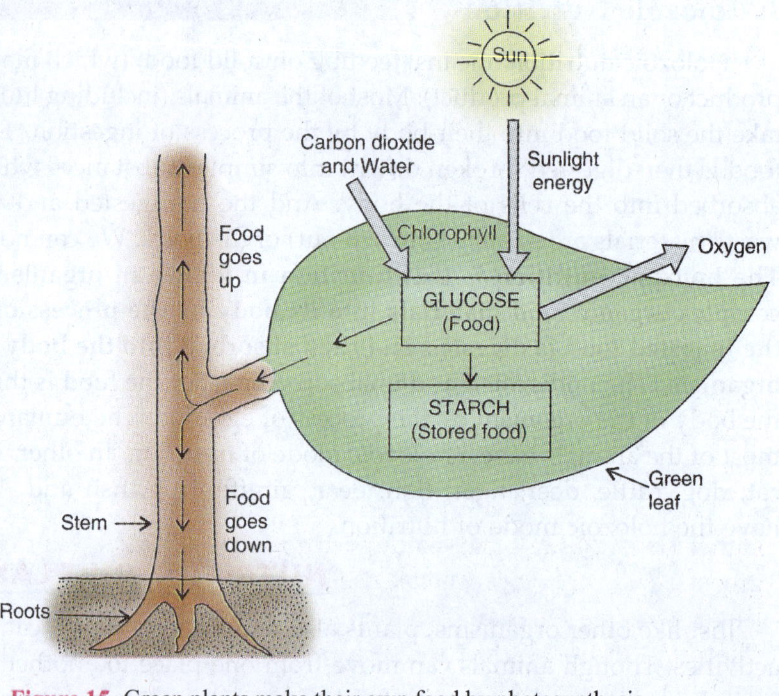

Figure 15. Green plants make their own food by photosynthesis.

The food prepared by the green leaves of a plant is in the form of a simple sugar called glucose. This glucose food made in the leaves is then sent to the different parts of the plant (see Figure 15). **The extra glucose is changed into another food called starch. This starch is stored in the leaves of the plant.** Glucose and starch belong to a category of foods called carbohydrates. The foods like carbohydrates prepared by photosynthesis contain chemical energy stored in them. Thus, **the green plants convert sunlight energy into chemical energy by making carbohydrates (foods).** The food prepared by photosynthesis provides all the energy to a plant which it needs to grow. And when we eat plant foods (like foodgrains, fruits and vegetables), the chemical energy stored in them is released in our body during respiration.

Figure 16. All these food items have been made by the plants by the process of photosynthesis.

We will now describe what actually happens during the process of photosynthesis. **The photosynthesis takes place in the following three steps :**

(*i*) Absorption of sunlight energy by chlorophyll.

(*ii*) Conversion of light energy into chemical energy, and splitting of water into hydrogen and oxygen by light energy.

(*iii*) Reduction of carbon dioxide by hydrogen to form carbohydrate like glucose by utilising the chemical energy (obtained by the transformation of light energy).

Please note that the three steps involved in photosynthesis need not take place one after the other immediately. They can take place at different times. For example, desert plants take up carbon dioxide at night and prepare an intermediate product which is acted upon by the sunlight energy absorbed by chlorophyll when the sun shines during the next day.

Conditions Necessary for Photosynthesis

It has been found by experiments that the presence of sunlight, chlorophyll, carbon dioxide and water is necessary for the process of photosynthesis. So, we can say that : The conditions necessary for photosynthesis to take place are :

1. **Sunlight,**
2. **Chlorophyll,**
3. **Carbon dioxide,** and
4. **Water.**

Please note that the conditions necessary for photosynthesis are also the conditions necessary for autotrophic nutrition. We will now describe some **experiments to show that sunlight, chlorophyll and carbon dioxide are necessary for photosynthesis by green plants.** These experiments will also show that leaves finally make 'starch' as food by photosynthesis.

The experiments on photosynthesis depend on the fact that **green leaves make starch as food.** And that **starch gives a blue-black colour with iodine solution.** Now, ordinarily all the plants have starch in their green leaves, so before we can use a plant in a photosynthesis experiment, the initial starch present in its leaves must be removed. In other words, **we should destarch the leaves of a plant before using it in a photosynthesis experiment.** The green leaves of a plant are destarched by keeping this plant in a completely dark place in a room for at least three days.

When the plant is kept in a dark place, it cannot make more starch (food) by photosynthesis because there is no sunlight. So, the plant kept in dark place uses the starch already stored in its leaves during respiration. **The plant will use up all the starch stored in its leaves in about three days' time.** So, after about three days, the plant leaves will not have any starch left in them. And we say that the leaves have been destarched. This plant with destarched leaves can now be used in the photosynthesis experiments. Please note that we will be using a plant growing in a pot in these experiments. The 'plant growing in a pot' is called 'potted plant'. Let us describe the experiments now.

1. Experiment to Show that Sunlight is Necessary for Photosynthesis

1. We take a potted plant having green leaves and place it in a completely dark place for about three days to destarch its leaves. So, in the beginning of the experiment, the leaves do not have any starch in them.
2. Take a thin strip of aluminium foil (or black paper) and wrap it in the centre of one leaf on both the sides (while the leaf is still attached to the plant) [see Figure 17(*a*)]. The aluminium foil should be fixed tightly to the leaf by using paper clips so that sunlight may not enter it from the sides. The aluminium foil should cover only a small part of the leaf so that the remaining part of the leaf remains uncovered and exposed to sunlight [see Figure 17(*a*)]. We have covered the centre part of the leaf with aluminium foil so that sunlight may not fall on this covered part of the leaf.
3. Keep this potted plant (with partially covered leaf) in bright sunshine for three to four days [see Figure 17(*a*)].
4. Pluck the partially covered leaf from the plant and remove its aluminium foil. Immerse this leaf in boiling water for a few minutes. This will break down the cell membranes of leaf cells and make the leaf more permeable to iodine solution (so that it may reach the starch present inside the leaf cells).This

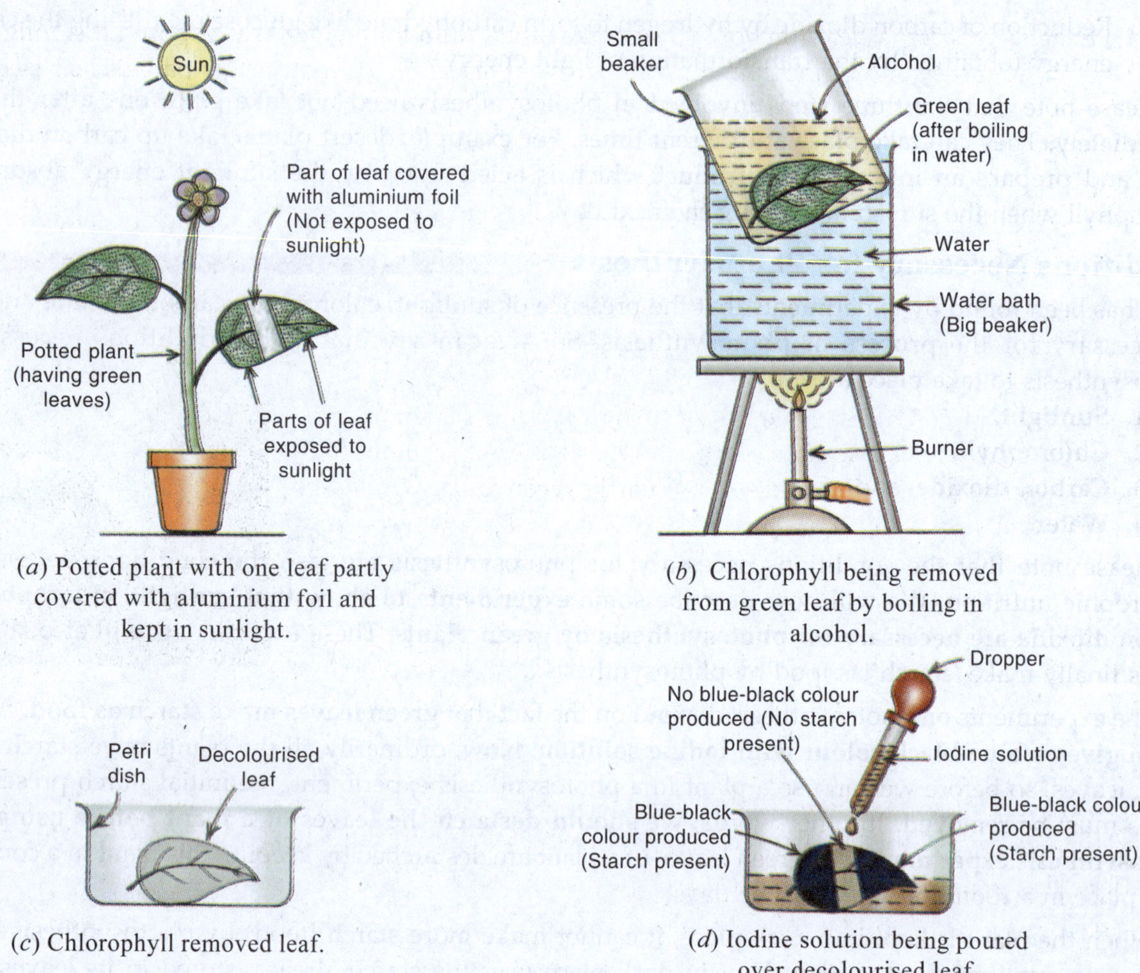

(*a*) Potted plant with one leaf partly covered with aluminium foil and kept in sunlight.

(*b*) Chlorophyll being removed from green leaf by boiling in alcohol.

(*c*) Chlorophyll removed leaf.

(*d*) Iodine solution being poured over decolourised leaf.

Figure 17. Experiment to show that sunlight is necessary for photosynthesis.

leaf is now to be tested for the presence of starch. But before testing for starch, chlorophyll has to be removed from the leaf. This is because chlorophyll interferes in the test for starch due to its green colour.

5. Put the plucked leaf in a beaker containing some alcohol. Place the beaker containing alcohol and leaf in a water bath (A water bath can be a bigger beaker containing water) [see Figure 17(*b*)]. A water bath is being used here for heating alcohol because alcohol is a highly inflammable liquid. So, if alcohol is heated directly over a flame, then it will catch fire at once.
6. Heat the water in the bigger beaker (or water bath). Then the alcohol in the smaller beaker will also get heated and start boiling soon. This boiling alcohol will extract (or remove) chlorophyll from the green leaf.
7. Boil the green leaf in alcohol till all its green pigment 'chlorophyll' is removed. The leaf will now become almost colourless or pale (and the alcohol will turn green).
8. Remove the colourless leaf from alcohol and wash it thoroughly with hot water to soften it and remove any chlorophyll which may be sticking to it.
9. Place the colourless leaf in a petri-dish [see Figure 17(*c*)]. Drop iodine solution over the decolourised leaf with the help of a dropper. Observe the change in colour of leaf.
10. The middle part of leaf which was covered with aluminium foil does not turn blue-black on adding iodine solution showing that no starch is present in this middle part of the leaf [see Figure 17(*d*)]. This is because sunlight could not reach the covered 'middle part' of the leaf due to which the covered 'middle part' of leaf could not do photosynthesis to make starch.

11. The uncovered part of leaf (on both sides of the aluminium foil) which was exposed to sunlight turns blue-black on adding iodine solution showing that starch is present in this part of leaf [see Figure 17(*d*)]. This means that the part of leaf which was exposed to sunlight could do photosynthesis to make starch.
12. Since the part of leaf which was covered and hidden from sunlight does not contain starch but the part of leaf which was exposed to sunlight contains starch, therefore, we conclude that **sunlight is necessary for photosynthesis (to make food like starch).**

From the above experiment, we actually get two conclusions. That :

(*i*) **sunlight is necessary for the process of photosynthesis,** and

(*ii*) **leaves make starch as food by photosynthesis.**

Most of the common plants have leaves which are totally green (because all the parts of such leaves contain the green pigment called chlorophyll). But there are some plants whose leaves are partly green and partly white. The green part of such a leaf contains chlorophyll but the white part of such a leaf does not contain chlorophyll. **The leaves which are partly green and partly white are called 'variegated leaves'.** The plants such as croton and *Coleus* have variegated leaves which are partly green and partly white. We will use a plant having variegated leaves in the next experiment to show that chlorophyll is necessary for the process of photosynthesis in plants.

Figure 18. Variegated leaves.

2. Experiment to Show that Chlorophyll is Necessary for Photosynthesis

1. We take a potted plant like croton whose leaves are partly green and partly white [see Figure 19(*a*)]. The green part of the leaf has chlorophyll but the white part of the leaf does not have chlorophyll.
2. Place this plant in a completely dark place for about three days to destarch its leaves.
3. Take out the potted plant from the dark place and keep it in bright sunshine for three to four days.

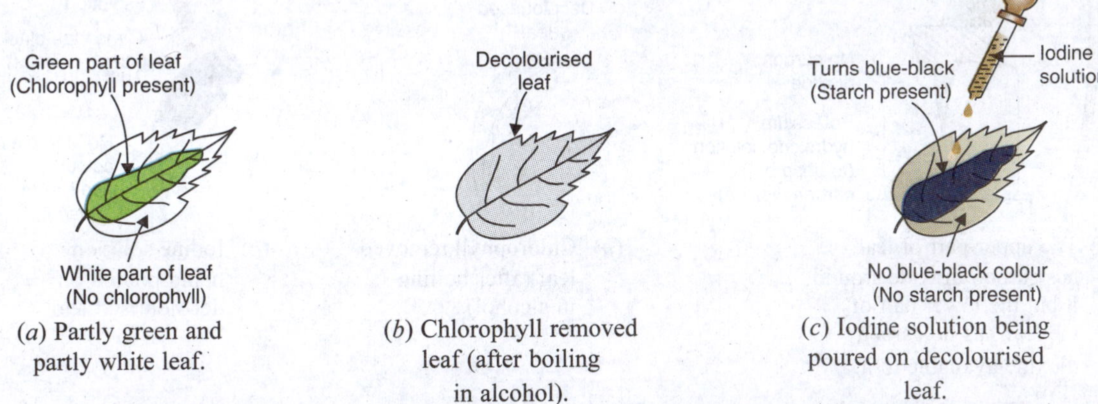

(*a*) Partly green and partly white leaf.

(*b*) Chlorophyll removed leaf (after boiling in alcohol).

(*c*) Iodine solution being poured on decolourised leaf.

Figure 19. Experiment to show that chlorophyll is necessary for photosynthesis.

4. Pluck the variegated leaf from the plant, boil it in water for a few minutes and then remove its green colour 'chlorophyll' by boiling it in alcohol. The green parts of the leaf get decolourised. So, we get decolourised leaf [see Figure 19(*b*)].
5. Wash the decolourised leaf with hot water to soften it and remove any chlorophyll which may be sticking to it.
6. Pour iodine solution over the colourless leaf and observe the change in colour of the leaf.
7. We will find that the outer part of leaf that was originally white (without chlorophyll) does not turn blue-black on adding iodine solution showing that no starch is present in this outer part of the leaf [see Figure 19(*c*)]. From this observation we conclude that the photosynthesis to make starch does not take place without chlorophyll.

8. The inner part of leaf which was originally green (contained chlorophyll) turns blue-black on adding iodine solution showing that starch is present in this inner part of the leaf [see Figure 19(*c*)]. From this observation we conclude that the photosynthesis to make starch takes place in the presence of chlorophyll. In other words, **chlorophyll is necessary for the process of photosynthesis to take place.**

3. Experiment to Show that Carbon Dioxide is Necessary for Photosynthesis

1. We take a potted plant having long and narrow leaves and place it in a completely dark place for about three days to destarch its leaves.
2. Take a glass bottle having a wide mouth and put some potassium hydroxide solution (KOH solution) in it. (This potassium hydroxide solution is to absorb the carbon dioxide gas from the air present in the glass bottle so that no carbon dioxide is left in the air inside the glass bottle).
3. Take a rubber cork which fits tightly into the mouth of the glass bottle and cut it into two halves.
4. Put a destarched leaf of the potted plant (while it is still attached to the plant), in-between the two halves of the cut cork and then fit the cork in the mouth of the glass bottle. The upper half of the leaf should remain outside the glass bottle and only the lower half of the leaf should be inside the glass bottle [as shown in Figure 20(*a*)].
5. The potted plant (with its one destarched leaf half inside the glass bottle containing potassium hydroxide solution) is kept in sunlight for 3 to 4 days. During this period, the upper half of the leaf (which is outside the glass bottle) gets carbon dioxide from the air but the lower half of the leaf (which is inside the glass bottle) does not get any carbon dioxide. This is because all the carbon dioxide of the air present in the glass bottle has been absorbed by potassium hydroxide solution. And no fresh air can come into the closed glass bottle.

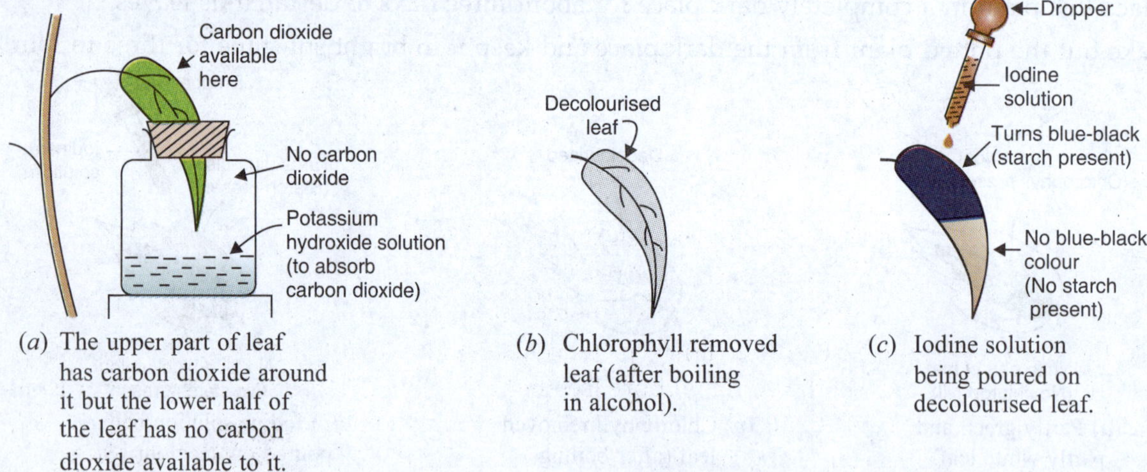

(*a*) The upper part of leaf has carbon dioxide around it but the lower half of the leaf has no carbon dioxide available to it.

(*b*) Chlorophyll removed leaf (after boiling in alcohol).

(*c*) Iodine solution being poured on decolourised leaf.

Figure 20. Experiment to show that carbon dioxide is necessary for photosynthesis.

6. Pluck the leaf from the plant and take it out from the glass bottle. Remove the green coloured chlorophyll from the leaf by boiling it in alcohol. In this way, we get a decolourised leaf [see Figure 20(*b*)].
7. Wash the decolourised leaf with water to remove any chlorophyll which may be sticking to it.
8. Pour iodine solution over the colourless leaf and observe the change in colour of the leaf.
9. We will find that the lower half part of the leaf (which was inside the glass bottle having no carbon dioxide around it), does not turn blue-black on adding iodine solution showing that no starch is present in this lower half of the leaf [see Figure 20(*c*)]. From this observation we conclude that **the photosynthesis to make starch in the leaf does not take place without carbon dioxide.**

10. The upper half part of the leaf (which was outside the glass bottle, having carbon dioxide around it) turns blue-black on adding iodine solution showing that starch is present in this upper half of the leaf [see Figure 20(*c*)]. From this observation we conclude that photosynthesis (to make starch) takes place in the presence of carbon dioxide. In other words, **carbon dioxide is necessary for the process of photosynthesis to take place.**

Raw Materials for Photosynthesis

The preparation of carbohydrates (food) by plants by the process of photosynthesis requires two materials (or substances) : carbon dioxide, and water. Thus, the raw materials for photosynthesis are :

(*i*) **Carbon dioxide,** and

(*ii*) **Water.**

We will now describe how these two raw materials become available to plants for photosynthesis.

1. How the Plants Obtain Carbon Dioxide

There are a large number of tiny pores called stomata on the surface of the leaves of plants (The singular of *stomata* is *stoma*). **The green plants take carbon dioxide from air for photosynthesis.** The carbon dioxide gas enters the leaves of the plant through the stomata present on their surface [see Figure 21(*a*)]. Each stomatal pore (or stoma) is surrounded by a pair of guard cells. The opening and closing of stomatal

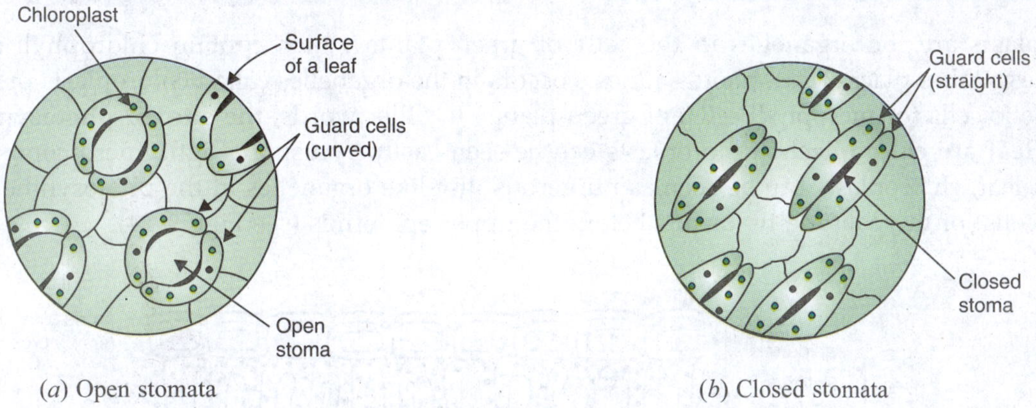

Figure 21. The plants take carbon dioxide required for photosynthesis from air through the stomata (tiny pores) present on the surface of a leaf.

pores is controlled by the guard cells. When water flows into the guard cells, they swell, become curved and cause the pore to open [see Figure 21(*a*)]. On the other hand, when the guard cells lose water, they shrink, become straight and close the stomatal pore [see Figure 21(*b*)]. A large amount of water is also lost from the cells of the plant leaves through open stomatal pores. So, when the plant does not need carbon dioxide and wants to conserve water, the stomatal pores are closed. The oxygen gas produced during photosynthesis also goes out through the stomatal pores of the leaves. Please note that in addition to leaves, the stomata are also present in the green stems (or shoots) of a plant. So, the green stems (or shoots) of a plant also carry out photosynthesis. It is clear from the above discussion that stomata allow the movement of gases in and out of plant cells. In other words, the gaseous exchange in plants takes place through the stomata in leaves (and other green parts). Please note that in most broad-leaved plants, the stomata occur only in the lower surface of the leaf but in narrow-leaved plants, the stomata are equally distributed on both the sides of the leaf. Another point to be noted is that the aquatic plants (or water plants) use the carbon dioxide gas dissolved in water for carrying out photosynthesis.

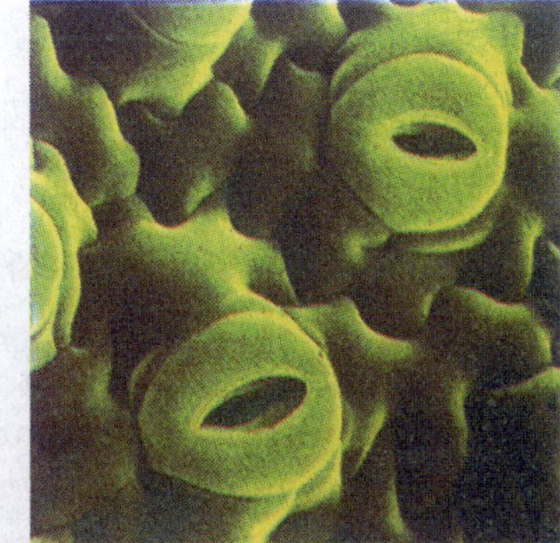

Figure 22. The stomata on the lower surface of a leaf as seen through a microscope.

2. How the Plants Obtain Water for Photosynthesis

The water required by the plants for photosynthesis is absorbed by the roots of the plants from the soil through the process of osmosis. The water absorbed by the roots of the plants is transported upward through the xylem vessels to the leaves where it reaches the photosynthetic cells and utilised in photosynthesis.

Figure 23. Water required for photosynthesis is absorbed by the roots of the plants from the soil.

The two raw materials, carbon dioxide and water, are required by the plants to prepare energy foods called carbohydrates (such as glucose and starch). But the plants also need other raw materials such as nitrogen, phosphorus, iron and magnesium, etc., for building their body. **The plants take materials like nitrogen, phosphorus, iron and magnesium, etc., from the soil.** For example, nitrogen is an essential element used by the plants to make proteins and other compounds. The plants take up nitrogen from the soil in the form of inorganic salts called nitrates (or nitrites), or in the form of organic compounds which are produced by bacteria from the atmospheric nitrogen.

Site of Photosynthesis : Chloroplasts

Chloroplasts are the organelles in the cells of green plants which contain chlorophyll and where photosynthesis takes place. Thus, photosynthesis occurs in the organelles called chloroplasts present in the photosynthetic cells (or mesophyll cells) of green plants. In other words, **the site of photosynthesis in a cell of the leaf are chloroplasts.** Chloroplasts can be seen easily by using a light microscope. In a cross-section of a leaf, chloroplasts can be seen as numerous disc-like organelles in the photosynthetic cells (or mesophyll cells) of the palisade tissue just below the upper epidermis (see Figure 24).

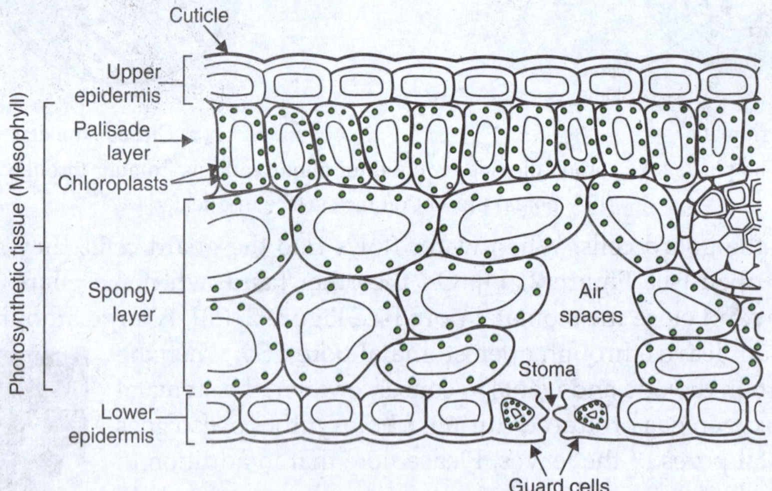

Figure 24. The structure of a leaf to show chloroplasts in it (The small green circles in the above diagram are all chloroplasts).

In the structure of a leaf shown in Figure 24, we can see that the middle layers in the leaf (palisade layer and spongy layer) contain photosynthetic cells called mesophyll cells. These cells contain more chlorophyll than other plant cells. A typical photosynthetic cell (or mesophyll cell) of a green leaf may contain 100 or more tiny chloroplasts in it, and a whole leaf may contain many thousands of photosynthetic cells. Carbon dioxide needed for photosynthesis enters from the air into the leaf through the stomata in its surface (see Figure 24), and then diffuses into the mesophyll cells and reaches the chloroplasts. Water is carried to the leaf by xylem vessels and passes into the mesophyll cells by diffusion and reaches the chloroplasts. There is a thin, waxy protective layer called cuticle above and below a leaf which helps to reduce the loss of water from the leaf.

NUTRITION IN ANIMALS

We have just studied the nutrition in plants. We have learnt that plants are autotrophic organisms which can manufacture their own food. So, plants don't have to look to others for getting their food. They are food producers themselves. But this is not so in the case of animals. Animals are heterotrophs and hence they depend on other organisms for their food. Thus, animals need an external source of food. We will now discuss how animals obtain their food.

Animals Obtain their Food from Plants or Other Animals

Since animals cannot make their own food, they depend on readymade food. This readymade food comes either from 'plants' or from 'other animals'. Thus, **animals obtain their food from plants or other animals (which they eat).** We (human beings) are also animals. We obtain the foods like wheat, rice, pulses (*dal*), fruits and vegetables from plants. And the foods like milk, curd, cheese and eggs are obtained from animals. Some people also eat meat, chicken and fish as food. These foods are also obtained from animals.

Many other animals obtain their food by eating the flesh of other animals. For example, the fish, birds, snakes and insects, all obtain their food from other animals. The big fish eats small fish; the birds eat worms and insects; the snake eats frogs and the insects eat dead bodies of animals. The non-green plants

(*a*) A fly sitting on the leaf of venus fly-trap plant

(*b*) The leaf of venus fly-trap plant folds up capturing the fly (which is its prey)

Figure 25. Even some of the plants can eat insects. Venus fly-trap plant is one such plant.

(which cannot make their own food by photosynthesis) also obtain their food from other plants and animals. Yeast plant is one such example. Even the plants can eat insects. For example, **the pitcher plant and the venus fly-trap are the two plants which eat insects.**

All the animals can be divided into three groups on the basis of their food habits (or eating habits). These are :

(*i*) **Herbivores,**

(*ii*) **Carnivores,** and

(*iii*) **Omnivores.**

We will now discuss herbivores, carnivores and omnivores in somewhat detail. Let us start with the herbivores.

1. Herbivores

Some animals eat only plants (or their products). **Those animals which eat only plants are called herbivores.** The herbivores may eat grasses, leaves, grains, fruits or the bark of trees. Some of the examples of herbivores are : Goat, Cow, Buffalo, Sheep, Horse, Deer, Camel, Ass, Ox, Elephant, Monkey, Squirrel,

Rabbit, Grasshopper and Hippopotamus. Cow is called a herbivore because it eats only plants as food. Thus, **herbivores are plant eaters.** Herbivores are also called herbivorous animals.

(*a*) Cow eats only plant food (like grass), so it is a herbivore

(*b*) Lion eats only meat (or flesh) of other animals, so it is a carnivore

(*c*) Humans eat plant food as well as meat, so they are omnivores

Figure 26. Herbivores, carnivores and omnivores.

2. Carnivores

Some animals eat only other animals. They do not eat plant food at all. **Those animals which eat only other animals as food are called carnivores.** Carnivores eat only the meat (or flesh) of other animals. So, we can also say that : *Those animals which eat only the meat (or flesh) of other animals are called carnivores.* Some of the examples of carnivores are : Lion, Tiger, Frog, Vulture, Kingfisher, Lizard, Wolf, Snake and Hawk. Lion is called a carnivore because it eats only the meat (or flesh) of other animals like deer, rabbit, goat, etc. Thus, **carnivores are meat eaters.** Carnivores are also called carnivorous animals.

3. Omnivores

Some animals eat both, plants as well as other animals as food. **Those animals which eat both, plants and animals, are called omnivores.** In other words, the omnivores eat plant food as well as the meat (or flesh) of other animals. Some of the examples of omnivores are : Man (Human beings), Dog, Crow, Sparrow, Bear, Mynah, and Ant. Man is called an omnivore because he eats the plant food (such as grains, pulses, fruits and vegetables) as well as the meat of animals (such as goat, chicken and fish). Thus, **omnivores are plant eaters as well as meat eaters.** Omnivores are also called omnivorous animals.

All the living things on earth actually depend on the sun for their food. This has been shown clearly in Figure 27 given below :

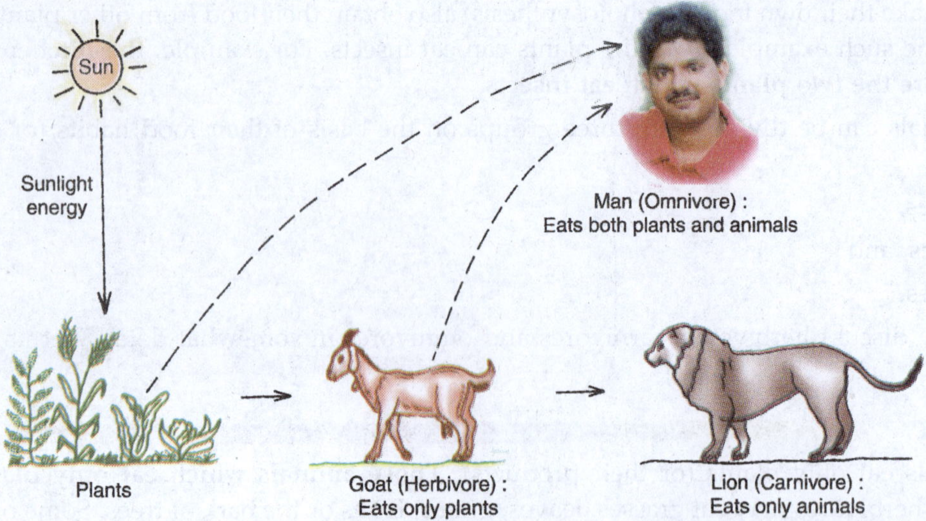

Figure 27. Diagram to show how all living things (plants and animals) depend on sun for their food.

Plants use the energy of sun and prepare food by photosynthesis. The plants utilise this food for maintaining their life. These plants (and their products) are also eaten up by herbivores and omnivores as food. And the carnivores eat herbivores as food. In this way, **it is the energy of the sun which provides food for plants, and animals (herbivores, carnivores and omnivores).** In Figure 27, the goat is a herbivore which eats plants; man is an omnivore who eats both, plants and meat of goat; and lion is a carnivore which eats the flesh of goat (The man usually does not get eaten up by lion because he is a very clever fellow !).

An organism either makes its own food from raw materials as green plants do or takes in readymade food as animals do. **The process of obtaining food and then using it for obtaining energy, growth and repair of the body, is called nutrition.** We will now discuss the animal nutrition in detail.

Different Steps in the Process of Nutrition in Animals

There are five main processes concerned with the use of food by animals. In other words, there are five steps in the process of nutrition in animals. These are : Ingestion, Digestion, Absorption, Assimilation and Egestion. All these steps are discussed below :

1. Ingestion

In order to provide the energy necessary for growth and carry on life's activities, we must 'eat food' or 'take food into the body'. **The process of taking food into the body is called ingestion.** In most simple terms, ingestion means 'eating of food' by the animal. When we put food into our mouth with hands, we are ingesting (the food).

2. Digestion

The food of most animals consists of large insoluble molecules which cannot be absorbed by the animal's body in this form. So, before the food can be used by the animal for various functions like getting energy or for growth, it must be broken down into small, water soluble molecules which can be absorbed by the body. **The process in which the food containing large, insoluble molecules is broken down into small, water soluble molecules (which can be absorbed by the body) is called digestion.** In most simple terms, digestion is the dissolving of the solid food. Digestion makes the food soluble so that it can be utilised by the animal's body. Most animals use both, physical and chemical methods for digesting (breaking up) the large food molecules. Physical methods include chewing and grinding the food in mouth and chemical methods include the addition of digestive juices (enzymes) to food by the body itself.

Figure 28. Our food contains very big molecules of carbohydrates (like starch), fats and proteins which cannot be absorbed in the body as such. They must be broken down into small, water soluble molecules which can be absorbed by the body. This happens in the process of digestion.

3. Absorption

After digestion, the food molecules become small and soluble. The soluble food molecules can pass through the walls of our intestine and go into blood. **The process in which the digested food passes through the intestinal wall into blood stream is called absorption.**

4. Assimilation

Blood carries the absorbed food to all the parts of the body. The food then enters each and every cell of the body where it is used for producing energy and for making materials for the growth and repair of the body. **The process in which the absorbed food is taken in by body cells and used for energy, growth and repair, is called assimilation.**

5. Egestion

The whole food which we eat is not digested by our body. A part of the food which we eat remains undigested (or insoluble) which cannot be used by the body. This undigested part of the food is then removed from the body in the form of faeces when we go to toilet. **The process in which the undigested food is removed from the body is called egestion.**

Nutrition in Simple Animals

Amoeba and *Paramecium* are two very simple animals. The body of each one of them consists of a single cell only. They are called unicellular animals. **In unicellular animals, all the processes of nutrition are performed by the single cell.** This point will become more clear from the following example of the nutrition in *Amoeba*.

NUTRITION IN *AMOEBA*

Amoeba is a unicellular animal. *Amoeba* eats tiny (microscopic) plants and animals as food which float in water in which it lives. The mode of nutrition in *Amoeba* is **holozoic.** The process of obtaining food by *Amoeba* is called **phagocytosis** ('Phagocytosis' means 'cell feeding'). The various steps involved in the nutrition of *Amoeba* are : ingestion, digestion, absorption, assimilation, and egestion. All the processes of nutrition are performed by the single cell of *Amoeba*. This is described below.

1. Ingestion

Amoeba has no mouth or a fixed place for the ingestion of food (intake of food). ***Amoeba* ingests food by using its pseudopodia.** When a food particle comes near *Amoeba*, then *Amoeba* ingests this food particle by forming temporary finger-like projections called pseudopodia around it [see Figure 29(*a*)]. The food is engulfed with a little surrounding water to form a food vacuole inside the *Amoeba*. This food vacuole can be considered to be a 'temporary stomach' of *Amoeba*.

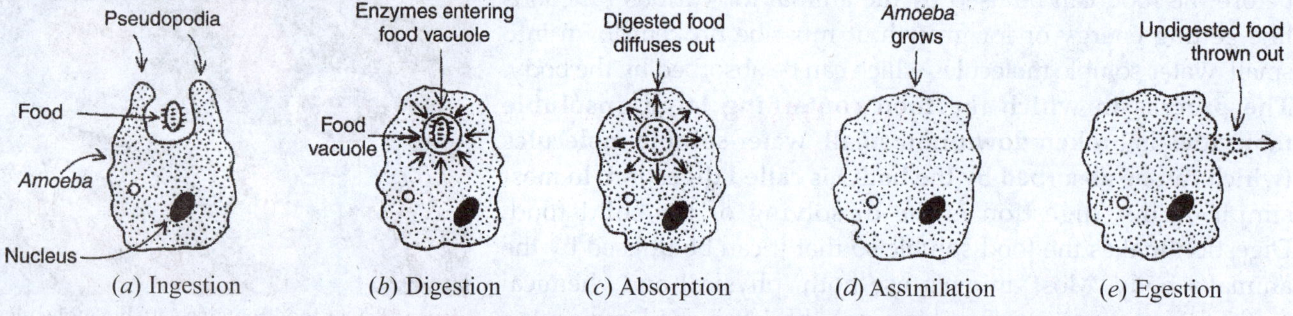

Figure 29. Different stages in the nutrition (feeding) of *Amoeba*.

2. Digestion

In *Amoeba*, food is digested in the food vacuole by digestive enzymes. The enzymes from surrounding cytoplasm enter into the food vacuole and break down the food into small and soluble molecules by chemical reactions [see Figure 29(*b*)]. Thus, digestion in *Amoeba* takes place inside the food vacuole due to which the food dissolves (or food becomes soluble).

3. Absorption

The digested food present in the food vacuole of *Amoeba* is absorbed directly into the cytoplasm of *Amoeba* cell by diffusion [see Figure 29(*c*)]. Since *Amoeba* consists of only one small cell, it does not require blood system to carry the digested food. The digested food just spreads out from the food vacuole into the whole of *Amoeba* cell. After absorption of food, the food vacuole disappears.

4. Assimilation

A part of the food absorbed in *Amoeba* cell is used to obtain energy through respiration. The remaining part of absorbed food is used to make the parts of *Amoeba* cell which lead to the growth of *Amoeba*. Thus, on assimilating food *Amoeba* grows in size [see Figure 29(*d*)]. And then *Amoeba* can reproduce by dividing into two daughter cells.

5. Egestion

Amoeba has no fixed place (like anus) for removing the undigested part of food. When a considerable amount of undigested food collects inside *Amoeba*, then its cell membrane suddenly ruptures at any place and the undigested food is thrown out of the body of *Amoeba* [see Figure 29(*e*)].

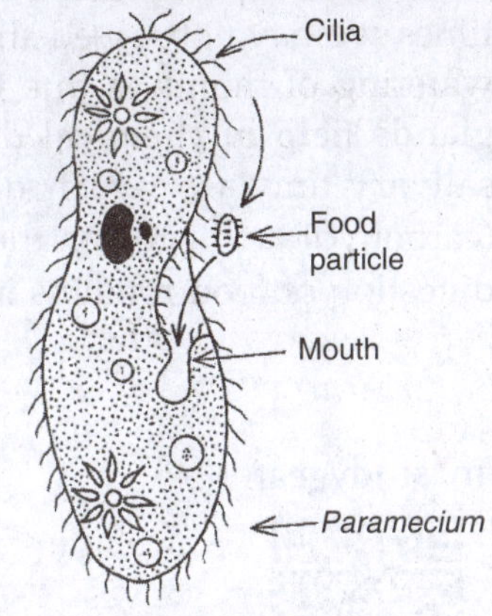

Figure 30. *Paramecium* puts the food particle into its mouth with the help of cilia.

Paramecium is also a tiny unicellular animal which lives in water. ***Paramecium* uses its hair like structures called cilia to sweep the food particles from water and put them into its mouth** (see Figure 30). The *Paramecium* has thin, hair-like cilia all over its body. The cilia move back and forth rapidly in water. When the cilia present around the mouth region of *Paramecium* move back and forth, they sweep the food particles present in water into the mouth of *Paramecium* (see Figure 30). This is the first step in the nutrition of *Paramecium* which is called ingestion. Ingestion is followed by other steps such as digestion, absorption, assimilation and egestion (as explained in the case of *Amoeba*).

Nutrition in Complex Multicellular Animals

In the complex multicellular animals like man (humans), grasshopper, fish and frog, etc., all the processes involved in nutrition are performed by a combination of digestive organs. This combination of digestive organs is called digestive system. We will now describe all the processes in the nutrition of complex multicellular animals by taking the example of nutrition in human beings. Please note that **a long tube running from mouth to anus of a human being (or other animals) in which digestion and absorption of food takes place is called alimentary canal**. Alimentary canal is also called 'gut'. Let us now study the nutrition in human beings.

NUTRITION IN HUMAN BEINGS
(Human Digestive System)

The nutrition in human beings (or man) takes place through human digestive system. The human digestive system consists of the alimentary canal and its associated glands. **The various organs of the human digestive system in sequence are : Mouth, Oesophagus (or Food pipe), Stomach, Small intestine and Large intestine. The glands which are associated with the human digestive system and form a part of the human digestive system are : Salivary glands, Liver and Pancreas.** The human alimentary canal which runs from mouth to anus is about 9 metres long tube. The ducts of various glands open into the alimentary canal and pour the secretions of the digestive juices into the alimentary canal. The human digestive system is shown in Figure 32. We will now describe the various steps of nutrition in human beings (or man).

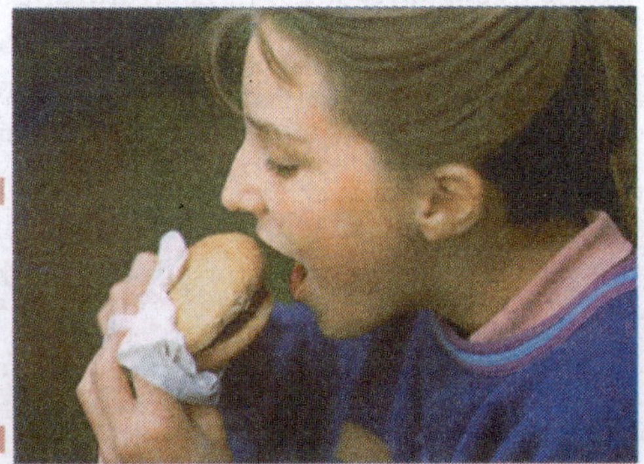

Figure 31. The digestion of food starts as soon as we put food in our mouth.

1. Ingestion

The human beings have a special organ for the ingestion of food. It is called mouth. So, in human beings, food is ingested through the mouth. The food is put into the mouth with the help of hands.

2. Digestion

In human beings, the digestion of food begins in the mouth itself. In fact, the digestion of food starts as soon as we put food in our mouth. This happens as follows : The mouth cavity (or buccal cavity) contains teeth, tongue, and salivary glands. The teeth cut the food into small pieces, chew and grind it. So, **the teeth help in physical digestion.** The salivary glands in our mouth produce saliva. Our tongue helps in mixing this saliva with food. Saliva is a watery liquid so it wets the food in our mouth. The wetted food can be swallowed more easily. Many times we have observed that when we see or eat a food which we really like, our mouth 'waters'. This watering of mouth is due to the production of saliva by the salivary glands in the mouth. The **salivary glands help in chemical digestion by secreting enzymes.** The human saliva contains an enzyme called salivary amylase which digests the starch present in food into sugar. Thus, the digestion of starch (carbohydrate) begins in the mouth itself. Since the food remains in the mouth only for a short time, so the digestion of food remains incomplete in mouth.

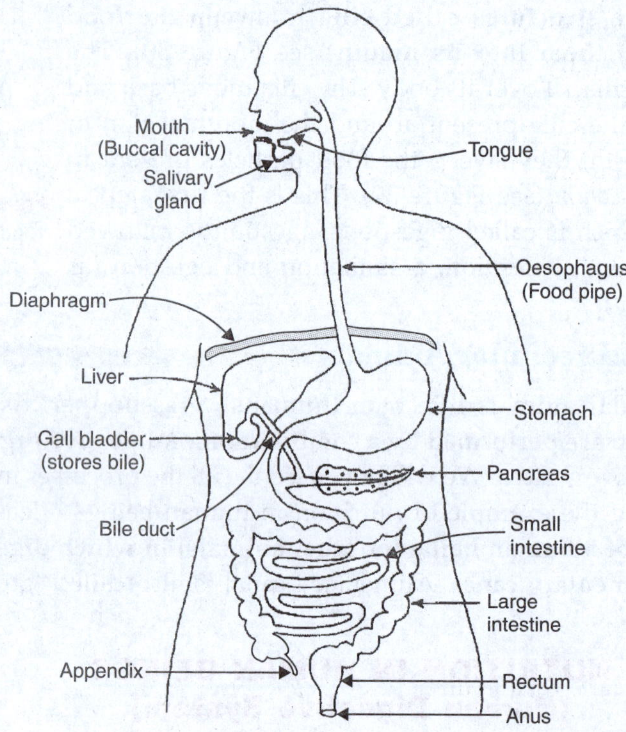

Figure 32. The human digestive system.

The slightly digested food in the mouth is swallowed by the tongue and goes down the food pipe called oesophagus (see Figure 32). The oesophagus carries food to the stomach. This happens as follows : The walls of food pipe have muscles which can contract and expand alternately. When the slightly digested food enters the food pipe, the walls of food pipe start contraction and expansion movements. The contraction and expansion movement of the walls of food pipe is called **peristaltic movement.** This peristaltic movement of food pipe (or oesophagus) pushes the slightly digested food into the stomach (In fact, the peristaltic movement moves the food in all the digestive organs throughout the alimentary canal).

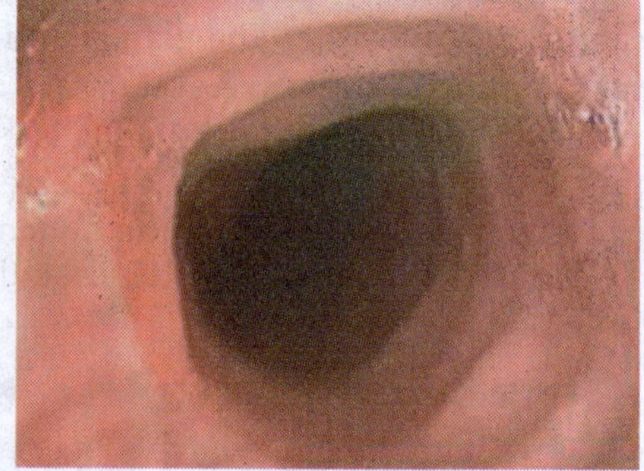

Figure 33. The inner side of food pipe (or oesophagus) as viewed by an endoscope.

The stomach is a J-shaped organ present on the left side of the abdomen (see Figure 32). The food is further digested in the stomach. The food is churned in the stomach for about three hours. During this time, the food breaks down into still smaller pieces and forms a semi-solid paste. The stomach wall contains three tubular glands in its walls. The glands present in the walls of the stomach secrete gastric juice. **The gastric juice contains three**

substances : hydrochloric acid, the enzyme pepsin and mucus. Due to the presence of hydrochloric acid, the gastric juice is acidic in nature. In the acidic medium, **the enzyme pepsin begins the digestion of proteins present in food to form smaller molecules**. Thus, the protein digestion begins in the stomach. Please note that the protein digesting enzyme pepsin is active only in the presence of an acid. So, the function of hydrochloric acid in the stomach is to make the medium of gastric juice acidic so that the enzyme pepsin can digest the proteins properly. Another function of hydrochloric acid is that it kills any bacteria which may enter the stomach with food. The mucus helps to protect the stomach wall from its own secretions of hydrochloric acid. If mucus is not secreted, hydrochloric acid will cause the erosion of inner lining of stomach leading to the formation of ulcers in the stomach. The partially digested food then goes from the stomach into the small intestine. The exit of food from stomach is regulated by a 'sphincter muscle' which releases it in small amounts into the small intestine.

From the stomach, the partially digested food enters the small intestine. The small intestine is the largest part of the alimentary canal. It is about 6.5 metres long in an adult man. Though the small intestine is very long, it is called small intestine because it is very narrow. The small intestine is arranged in the form of a coil in our belly (see Figure 32). Please note that the length of the small intestine differs in various animals depending on the type of food they eat. For example, cellulose is a carbohydrate food which is digested with difficulty. So, the herbivorous animals like cow which eat grass need a longer 'small intestine' to allow the cellulose present in grass to be digested completely. On the other hand, meat is a food which is easier to digest. So, the carnivorous animals like tigers which eat meat have a shorter 'small intestine'.

The small intestine in human beings is the site of complete digestion of food (like carbohydrates, proteins and fats). This happens as follows :

(*a*) The small intestine receives the secretions of two glands : liver and pancreas. Liver secretes bile. Bile is a greenish yellow liquid made in the liver which is normally stored in the gall bladder. Bile is alkaline, and contains salts which help to emulsify or break the fats (or lipids) present in the food. Thus, bile performs two functions : (*i*) makes the acidic food coming from the stomach *alkaline* so that pancreatic enzymes can act on it, and (*ii*) bile salts *break* the fats present in the food into small globules making it easy for the enzymes to act and digest them. Pancreas is a large gland which lies parallel to and beneath the stomach (see Figure 32). Pancreas secretes pancreatic juice which contains digestive enzymes like pancreatic amylase, trypsin and lipase. The enzyme amylase breaks down the starch, the enzyme trypsin digests the proteins and the enzyme lipase breaks down the emulsified fats.

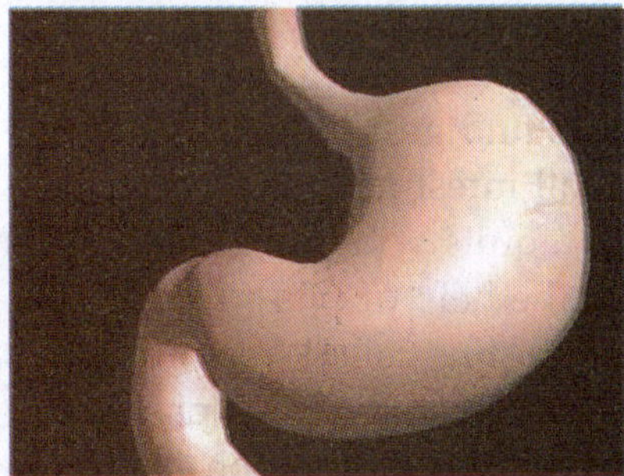

Figure 34. The glands in the walls of the stomach secrete gastric juice containing hydrochloric acid, enzyme pepsin and mucus.

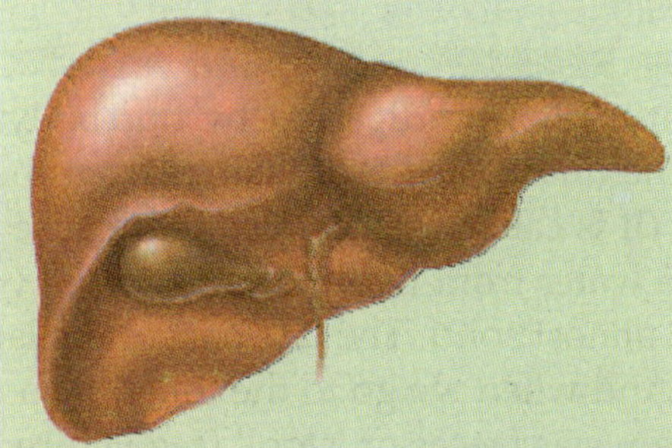

Figure 35. Liver secretes bile into the small intestine. We can also see the gall bladder in this picture which stores bile.

Figure 36. Pancreas secretes pancreatic juice into the small intestine which contains three digestive enzymes : pancreatic amylase, trypsin and lipase.

(*b*) The walls of small intestine contain glands which secrete intestinal juice. The intestinal juice contains a number of enzymes which complete the digestion of complex carbohydrates into glucose, proteins into amino acids and fats into fatty acids and glycerol. Glucose, amino acids, fatty acids and glycerol are small, water soluble molecules. In this way, the process of digestion converts the large and insoluble food molecules into small, water soluble molecules. The chemical digestion of food is brought about by biological catalysts called *enzymes*.

3. Absorption

After digestion, the molecules of food become so small that they can pass through the walls of the small intestine (which contain blood capillaries) and go into our blood. This is called absorption. **The small intestine is the main region for the absorption of digested food.** In fact, the small intestine is especially adapted for absorbing the digested food. The inner surface of small intestine has millions of tiny, finger-like projections called villi. The presence of villi gives the inner walls of the small intestine a very large surface area. And the large surface area of small intestine helps in the rapid absorption of digested food. The digested food which is absorbed through the walls of the small intestine, goes into our blood.

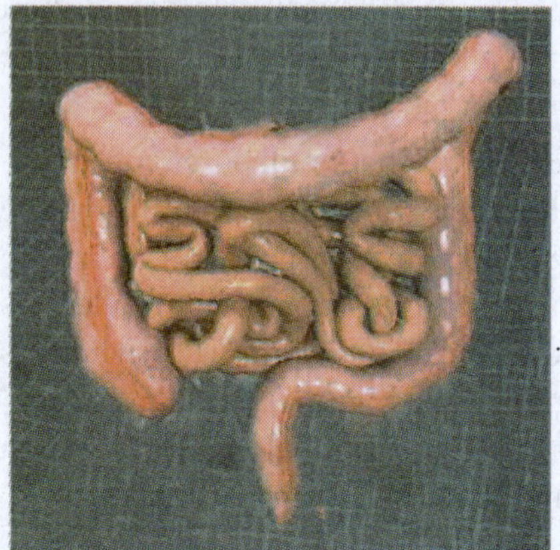

Figure 37. The narrow tube in this picture is the small intestine whereas the wider tube is the large intestine.

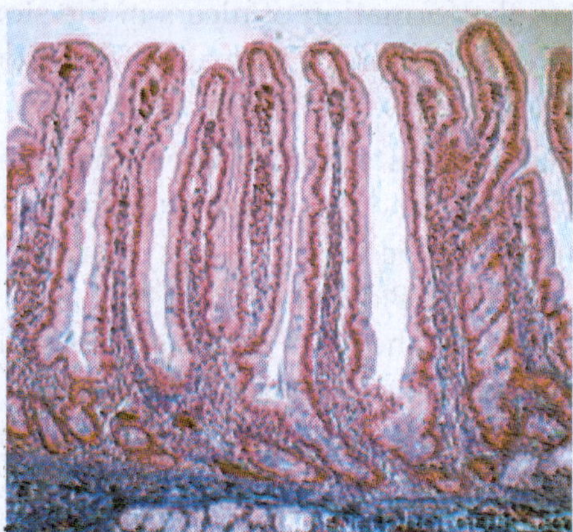

Figure 38. Villi are present on the inner surface of small intestine. They help in absorbing digested food into the blood of a person.

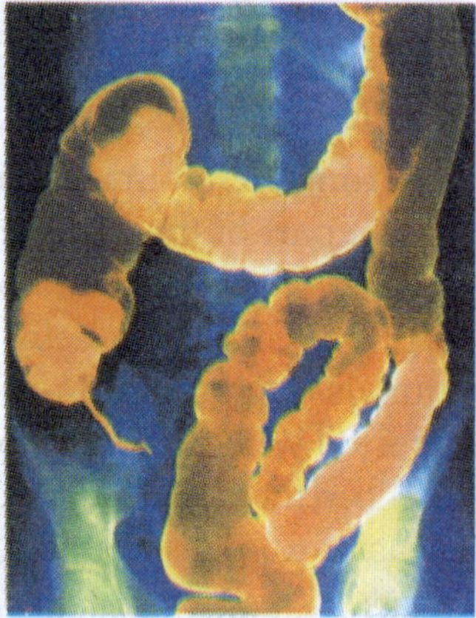

Figure 39. The X-ray photograph of large intestine taken after the person had been given a barium meal.

4. Assimilation

The blood carries digested and dissolved food to all the parts of the body where it becomes assimilated as part of the cells. This assimilated food is used by the body cells for obtaining energy as well as for growth and repair of the body. The energy is released by the oxidation of assimilated food in the cells during respiration. The digested food which is not used by our body immediately is stored in the liver in the form of a carbohydrate called 'glycogen'. This stored glycogen can be used as a source of energy by the body as and when required.

5. Egestion

A part of the food which we eat cannot be digested by our body. This undigested food cannot be absorbed in the small intestine. So, the undigested food passes from the small intestine into a wider tube called large intestine (see Figure 32) (It is called large intestine because it is a quite wide tube). The walls of large intestine absorb most of the water from the undigested food (with the help of villi). Due to this, the undigested part of food becomes almost solid. The last part of the large intestine called 'rectum' stores this undigested food for some time. And when we go to the toilet, then this undigested food is passed out (or egested) from our body through anus as faeces or 'stool' (see Figure 32). The act of expelling the faeces is called **egestion** or **defecation.** The exit of faeces is controlled by the anal sphincter.

Let us solve one problem now.

Sample Problem. 1 mL of very dilute starch solution (1% starch solution) is taken in a test-tube and 1 mL of saliva is added to it. After keeping this mixture for half an hour, a few drops of dilute iodine solution are added to the test-tube. There is no change in colour on adding iodine solution. What does this tell you about the action of saliva on starch ?

Answer. When a mixture of dilute starch solution and saliva is kept in a test-tube for half an hour, it does not produce a blue-black colour with iodine solution showing that no starch is left in the test-tube. This tells us that the action of saliva has broken down starch into some other substance which does not

substances : hydrochloric acid, the enzyme pepsin and mucus. Due to the presence of hydrochloric acid, the gastric juice is acidic in nature. In the acidic medium, **the enzyme pepsin begins the digestion of proteins present in food to form smaller molecules**. Thus, the protein digestion begins in the stomach. Please note that the protein digesting enzyme pepsin is active only in the presence of an acid. So, the function of hydrochloric acid in the stomach is to make the medium of gastric juice acidic so that the enzyme pepsin can digest the proteins properly. Another function of hydrochloric acid is that it kills any bacteria which may enter the stomach with food. The mucus helps to protect the stomach wall from its own secretions of hydrochloric acid. If mucus is not secreted, hydrochloric acid will cause the erosion of inner lining of stomach leading to the formation of ulcers in the stomach. The partially digested food then goes from the stomach into the small intestine. The exit of food from stomach is regulated by a 'sphincter muscle' which releases it in small amounts into the small intestine.

From the stomach, the partially digested food enters the small intestine. The small intestine is the largest part of the alimentary canal. It is about 6.5 metres long in an adult man. Though the small intestine is very long, it is called small intestine because it is very narrow. The small intestine is arranged in the form of a coil in our belly (see Figure 32). Please note that the length of the small intestine differs in various animals depending on the type of food they eat. For example, cellulose is a carbohydrate food which is digested with difficulty. So, the herbivorous animals like cow which eat grass need a longer 'small intestine' to allow the cellulose present in grass to be digested completely. On the other hand, meat is a food which is easier to digest. So, the carnivorous animals like tigers which eat meat have a shorter 'small intestine'.

The small intestine in human beings is the site of complete digestion of food (like carbohydrates, proteins and fats). This happens as follows :

(*a*) The small intestine receives the secretions of two glands : liver and pancreas. Liver secretes bile. Bile is a greenish yellow liquid made in the liver which is normally stored in the gall bladder. Bile is alkaline, and contains salts which help to emulsify or break the fats (or lipids) present in the food. Thus, bile performs two functions : (*i*) makes the acidic food coming from the stomach *alkaline* so that pancreatic enzymes can act on it, and (*ii*) bile salts *break* the fats present in the food into small globules making it easy for the enzymes to act and digest them. Pancreas is a large gland which lies parallel to and beneath the stomach (see Figure 32). Pancreas secretes pancreatic juice which contains digestive enzymes like pancreatic amylase, trypsin and lipase. The enzyme amylase breaks down the starch, the enzyme trypsin digests the proteins and the enzyme lipase breaks down the emulsified fats.

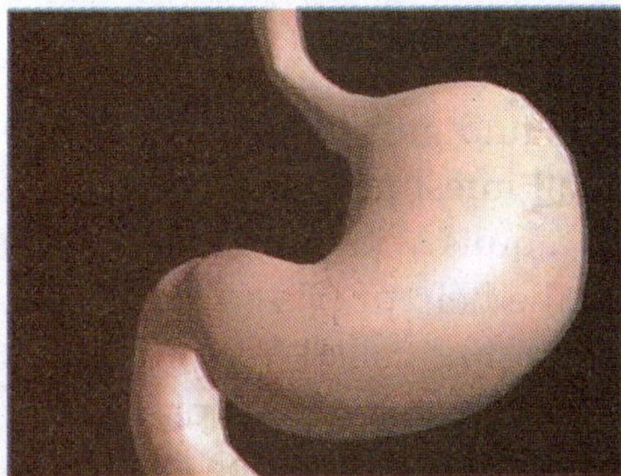

Figure 34. The glands in the walls of the stomach secrete gastric juice containing hydrochloric acid, enzyme pepsin and mucus.

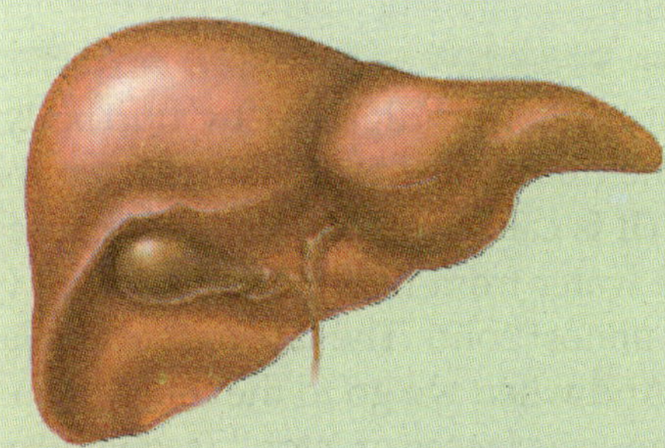

Figure 35. Liver secretes bile into the small intestine. We can also see the gall bladder in this picture which stores bile.

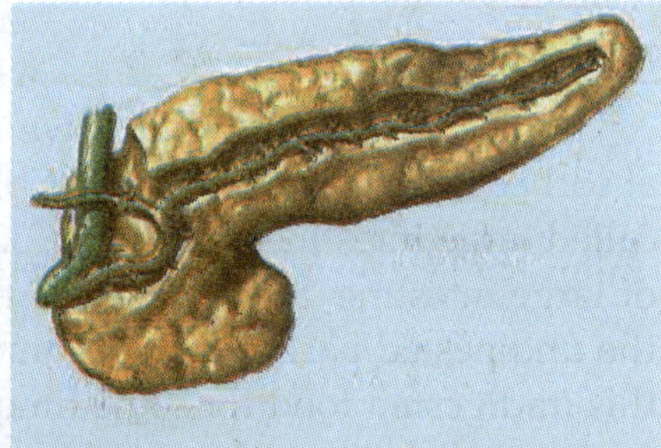

Figure 36. Pancreas secretes pancreatic juice into the small intestine which contains three digestive enzymes : pancreatic amylase, trypsin and lipase.

(*b*) The walls of small intestine contain glands which secrete intestinal juice. The intestinal juice contains a number of enzymes which complete the digestion of complex carbohydrates into glucose, proteins into amino acids and fats into fatty acids and glycerol. Glucose, amino acids, fatty acids and glycerol are small, water soluble molecules. In this way, the process of digestion converts the large and insoluble food molecules into small, water soluble molecules. The chemical digestion of food is brought about by biological catalysts called *enzymes*.

3. Absorption

After digestion, the molecules of food become so small that they can pass through the walls of the small intestine (which contain blood capillaries) and go into our blood. This is called absorption. **The small intestine is the main region for the absorption of digested food.** In fact, the small intestine is especially adapted for absorbing the digested food. The inner surface of small intestine has millions of tiny, finger-like projections called villi. The presence of villi gives the inner walls of the small intestine a very large surface area. And the large surface area of small intestine helps in the rapid absorption of digested food. The digested food which is absorbed through the walls of the small intestine, goes into our blood.

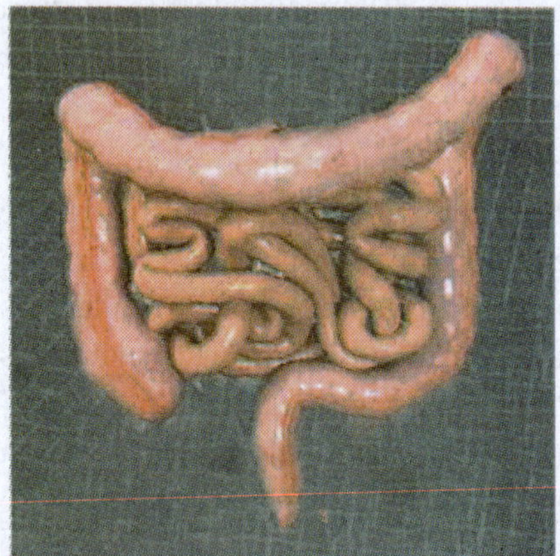

Figure 37. The narrow tube in this picture is the small intestine whereas the wider tube is the large intestine.

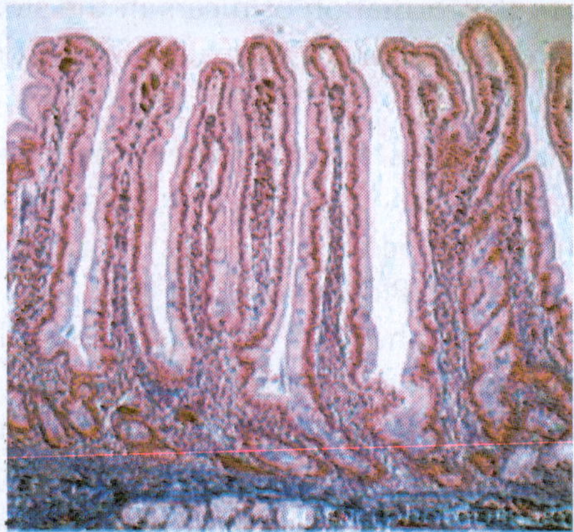

Figure 38. Villi are present on the inner surface of small intestine. They help in absorbing digested food into the blood of a person.

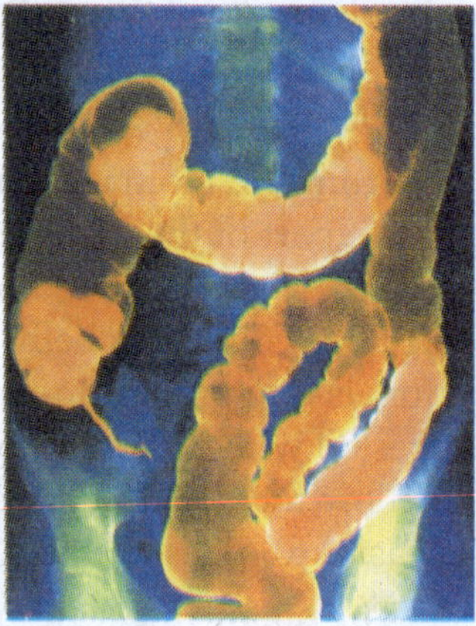

Figure 39. The X-ray photograph of large intestine taken after the person had been given a barium meal.

4. Assimilation

The blood carries digested and dissolved food to all the parts of the body where it becomes assimilated as part of the cells. This assimilated food is used by the body cells for obtaining energy as well as for growth and repair of the body. The energy is released by the oxidation of assimilated food in the cells during respiration. The digested food which is not used by our body immediately is stored in the liver in the form of a carbohydrate called 'glycogen'. This stored glycogen can be used as a source of energy by the body as and when required.

5. Egestion

A part of the food which we eat cannot be digested by our body. This undigested food cannot be absorbed in the small intestine. So, the undigested food passes from the small intestine into a wider tube called large intestine (see Figure 32) (It is called large intestine because it is a quite wide tube). The walls of large intestine absorb most of the water from the undigested food (with the help of villi). Due to this, the undigested part of food becomes almost solid. The last part of the large intestine called 'rectum' stores this undigested food for some time. And when we go to the toilet, then this undigested food is passed out (or egested) from our body through anus as faeces or 'stool' (see Figure 32). The act of expelling the faeces is called **egestion** or **defecation.** The exit of faeces is controlled by the anal sphincter.

Let us solve one problem now.

Sample Problem. 1 mL of very dilute starch solution (1% starch solution) is taken in a test-tube and 1 mL of saliva is added to it. After keeping this mixture for half an hour, a few drops of dilute iodine solution are added to the test-tube. There is no change in colour on adding iodine solution. What does this tell you about the action of saliva on starch ?

Answer. When a mixture of dilute starch solution and saliva is kept in a test-tube for half an hour, it does not produce a blue-black colour with iodine solution showing that no starch is left in the test-tube. This tells us that the action of saliva has broken down starch into some other substance which does not give any colour with iodine solution. Actually, saliva contains an enzyme 'amylase' which converts starch into a sugar.

Dental Caries

The hard, outer covering of a tooth is called enamel (see Figure 40). Tooth enamel is the hardest material in our body. It is harder than even bones. The part of tooth below enamel is called dentine. Dentine is similar to bone. Inside the dentine is pulp cavity. The pulp cavity contains nerves and blood vessels. **The formation of small cavities (or holes) in the teeth due to the action of acid-forming bacteria and improper dental care is called dental caries.** This happens as follows.

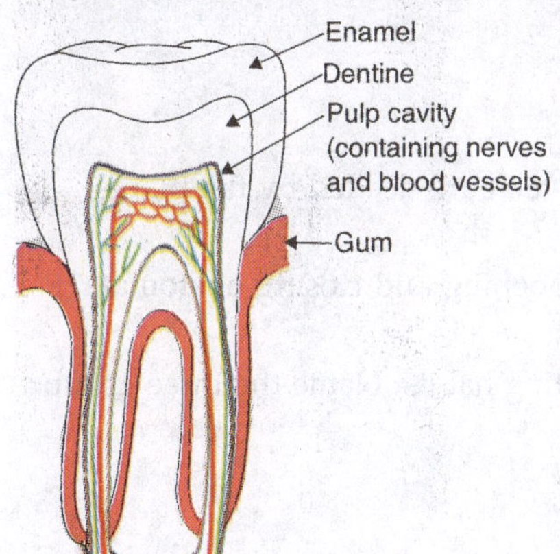

Figure 40. Parts of a tooth.

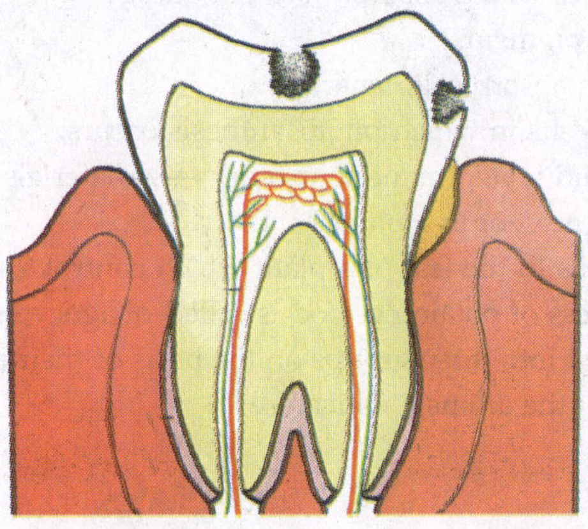

Figure 41. Tooth decay starts on the top of large back teeth and where one tooth touches another.

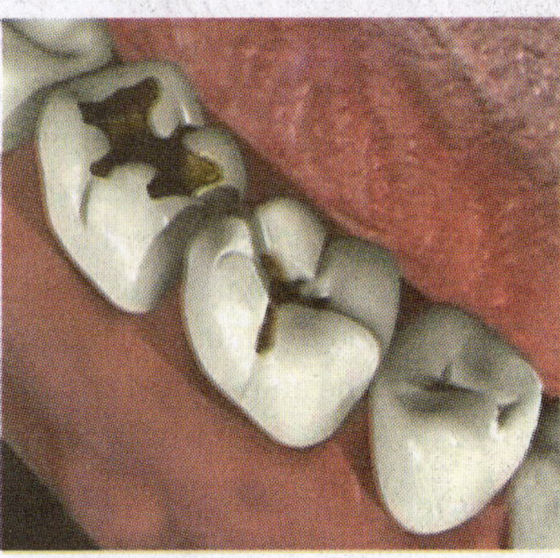

Figure 42. This picture shows badly kept teeth of a person having dental caries.

When we eat sugary food, the bacteria in our mouth act on sugar to produce acids. These acids first dissolve the calcium salts from the tooth enamel and then from dentine forming small cavities (or holes) in the tooth over a period of time. The formation of cavities reduces the distance between the outside of the tooth and the pulp cavity which contains nerves and blood vessels. The acids produced by bacteria irritate the nerve endings inside the tooth and cause toothache. If the cavities caused by dental decay are not cleaned and filled by a dentist, the bacteria will get into the pulp cavity of tooth causing inflammation and infection leading to severe pain.

If the teeth are not cleaned regularly, they become covered with a sticky, yellowish layer of food particles and bacteria cells called 'dental plaque'. Since plaque covers the teeth forming a layer over them, the alkaline saliva cannot reach the tooth surface to neutralise the acid formed by bacteria and hence tooth decay sets in. Brushing the teeth regularly, after eating food, removes the plaque before bacteria produces acids. This will prevent dental caries or tooth decay. Before we go further and discuss respiration, **please answer the following questions :**

Very Short Answer Type Questions

1. Which is the basic requirement of living organisms for obtaining energy ?
2. Which of the following type of energy is used by living organisms to perform vital life processes ?
   Kinetic energy, Chemical energy, Potential energy, Nuclear energy
3. Which of the following is an autotroph ?
   Green plant or Man
4. Name two inorganic substances which are used by autotrophs to make food.
5. What is the mode of nutrition in fungi ?
6. Name one organism each having saprophytic, parasitic and holozoic modes of nutrition.
7. Name the process by which plants make food.

8. In addition to carbon dioxide and water, state two other conditions necessary for the process of photosynthesis to take place.
9. Apart from sunlight and chlorophyll, what other things are required to make food by photosynthesis ?
10. (*a*) Name a gas used in photosynthesis.
    (*b*) Name a gas produced in photosynthesis.
11. The leaves of a plant first prepare food *A* by photosynthesis. Food *A* then gets converted into food *B*. What are *A* and *B* ?
12. Which substance is used to remove chlorophyll from a green leaf during photosynthesis experiments ?
13. Why do we boil the leaf in alcohol when we are testing it for starch ?
14. (*a*) Name the pigment in leaves which absorbs sunlight energy.
    (*b*) What is the colour of this pigment ?
15. Name the pigment which can absorb solar energy.
16. Name the organelle of plant cells in which photosynthesis occurs.
17. Apart from carbon dioxide and water, name four other raw materials which are needed by the plants.
18. Where is chlorophyll mainly present in a plant ?
19. What is the name of those cells in the leaf of a plant which control the opening and closing of stomata?
20. Name an animal whose process of obtaining food is called phagocytosis.
21. All the animals can be divided into three groups on the basis of their eating habits. Name the three groups.
22. What is the scientific name of the animals which are :
    (*i*) only meat eaters ?
    (*ii*) only plant eaters ?
    (*iii*) both, plant and meat eaters ?
23. Name the green pigment present in the leaves of a plant.
24. Arrange the following processes involved in the nutrition in animals in the correct order (in which they take place) :
    Assimilation, Egestion, Ingestion, Absorption, Digestion
25. How does *Amoeba* engulf the food particle ?
26. What substances enter into the food vacuole in *Amoeba* to break down the food ?
27. From which part of the body, undigested food is egested in *Amoeba* ?
28. Name a unicellular animal which uses cilia to move food particles into its mouth.
29. Name the enzyme present in human saliva. What type of food material is digested by this enzyme ?
30. Which of the organs perform the following functions in humans ?
    (*i*) Absorption of food
    (*ii*) Absorption of water
31. What moves the food in the digestive organs ?
32. What is the other name of food pipe ?
33. What substance is mixed with food in the mouth during chewing by the teeth ?
34. What is the name of tiny projections on the inner surface of small intestine which help in absorbing the digested food ?
35. In which part of the digestive system is water absorbed ?
36. What is the name of the opening in the human body through which undigested food is thrown out ?
37. Where is digested food absorbed into blood in human body ?
38. Name the biological catalysts which bring about chemical digestion of food.
39. Fill in the following blanks with suitable words :
    (*a*) All green plants are..................
    (*b*) All non-green plants and animals are ....
    (*c*) Heterotrophs depend on.............and other................... for food.
    (*d*) Green plants use............,................and...............to make food.
    (*e*) Iodine turns blue-black on reacting with.......................

Short Answer Type Questions

40. (*a*) What is chlorophyll ? What part does chlorophyll play in photosynthesis ?
(*b*) (*i*) Which simple food is prepared first in the process of photosynthesis ?
(*ii*) Name the food which gets stored in plant leaves.

41. (*a*) What criteria can be used to decide whether something is alive ?
(*b*) What is meant by life processes ? Name the basic life processes common to all living organisms which are essential for maintaining life.

42. (*a*) What are autotrophs ? Give one example of autotrophs.
(*b*) What are the conditions necessary for autotrophic nutrition ?

43. (*a*) What are heterotrophs ? Give one example of heterotrophs.
(*b*) What is the difference between autotrophic nutrition and heterotrophic nutrition ?

44. (*a*) Define a nutrient. Name four important nutrients present in our food.
(*b*) What are the various types of heterotrophic nutrition ?

45. (*a*) Photosynthesis converts energy X into energy Y. What are X and Y ?
(*b*) State the various steps involved in the process of photosynthesis.

46. (*a*) How do plants obtain food ?
(*b*) Why do plants need nitrogen ? How do plants obtain nitrogen ?

47. Define (*i*) saprophytic nutrition (*ii*) parasitic nutrition, and (*iii*) holozoic nutrition. Give one example of each type.

48. Define (*i*) saprophyte, and (*ii*) parasite. Name two saprophytes and two parasites.

49. (*a*) How does carbon dioxide from the air enter the leaves of a plant to be used in photosynthesis ?
(*b*) How does water from the soil reach the leaves of a plant to be used in photosynthesis ?

50. What substances are contained in gastric juice ? What are their functions ?

51. What substances are contained in pancreatic juice ? What are their functions ?

52. (*a*) What is the role of hydrochloric acid in our stomach ?
(*b*) What is the function of enzymes in the human digestive system ?

53. (*a*) Which part of the body secretes bile ? Where is bile stored ? What is the function of bile ?
(*b*) What is trypsin ? What is its function ?

54. What are the functions of liver and pancreas in the human digestive system ?

55. Match the organisms given in column I with the processes given in column II :

Column I	*Column II*
(*i*) Leech	(*a*) Holozoic nutrition
(*ii*) *Amoeba*	(*b*) Autotrophic nutrition
(*iii*) Mushroom	(*c*) Parasitic nutrition
(*iv*) Green plant	(*d*) Saprophytic nutrition

56. Name the following :
(*a*) The process in plants which converts light energy into chemical energy.
(*b*) Organisms that cannot prepare their own food.
(*c*) Organisms that can prepare their own food.
(*d*) The cell organelle where photosynthesis occurs.
(*e*) The cells which surround a stomatal pore.
(*f*) An enzyme secreted by gastric glands in stomach which acts on proteins.

57. Match the terms in column I with those in column II :

Column I	*Column II*
(*i*) Trypsin	(*a*) Liver
(*ii*) Amylase	(*b*) Gastric glands
(*iii*) Bile	(*c*) Pancreas
(*iv*) Pepsin	(*d*) Saliva

58. (*a*) What is common for *Cuscuta*, ticks and leeches ?
(*b*) Name the substances on which the following enzymes act in the human digestive system :
(*i*) Trypsin (*ii*) Amylase (*iii*) Pepsin (*iv*) Lipase
(*c*) Why does absorption of digested food occur mainly in the small intestine ?

59. (*a*) Why is small intestine in herbivores longer than in carnivores ?
(*b*) What will happen if mucus is not secreted by the gastric glands ?
(*c*) What causes movement of food inside the alimentary canal ?

60. (*a*) How do guard cells regulate opening and closing of stomatal pores ?
(*b*) Two similar green plants are kept separately in oxygen free containers, one in dark and the other in continuous light. Which one will live longer ? Give reasons.

61. (*a*) What would happen if all the green plants disappear from the earth ?
(*b*) If a plant is releasing carbon dioxide and taking in oxygen during the day, does it mean that there is no photosynthesis occurring ? Justify your answer.

62. (*a*) Leaves of a healthy potted plant were coated with vaseline. Will this plant remain healthy for long ? Give reason for your answer.
(*b*) What will happen to the rate of photosynthesis in a plant under the following circumstances ?
(*i*) cloudy day in morning but bright sunshine in the afternoon
(*ii*) no rainfall in the area for a considerable time.
(*iii*) gathering of dust on the leaves

Long Answer Type Questions

63. (*a*) What is photosynthesis ?
(*b*) Write a chemical equation to show the process of photosynthesis in plants.
(*c*) Explain the mechanism of photosynthesis.

64. (*a*) Name the raw materials required for photosynthesis. How do plants obtain these raw materials ?
(*b*) What are the various conditions necessary for photosynthesis ?
(*c*) Name the various factors which affect the rate of photosynthesis in plants.

65. (*a*) Define nutrition. Why is nutrition necessary for an organism ?
(*b*) What are the different modes of nutrition ? Explain with one example of each mode of nutrition.
(*c*) Name the mode of nutrition in (*i*) roundworm, and (*ii*) *Plasmodium*.

66. (*a*) What are herbivores, carnivores and omnivores ? Give two examples of each.
(*b*) Classify the following into herbivores, carnivores and omnivores :
Lion, Man, Dog, Goat, Crow, Elephant, Snake, Hawk, Rabbit, Deer
(*c*) Name the five steps which occur in the process of nutrition in animals.

67. (*a*) Describe the process of nutrition in *Amoeba*. Draw labelled diagrams to show the various steps in the nutrition in *Amoeba*.
(*b*) What is the mode of nutrition in *Amoeba* known as ?
(*c*) What is the process of obtaining food by *Amoeba* called ? What does it mean ?

68. (*a*) Draw a labelled diagram of the human digestive system. With the help of this diagram, describe the process of digestion of food in man (humans).
(*b*) Describe one way in which the small intestine is adapted for the absorption of digested food.
(*c*) What is the special name of the contraction and expansion movement which pushes the food further in our digestive tract (or alimentary canal) ?

69. (*a*) Describe the parts of our tooth with the help of a labelled diagram.
(*b*) What is meant by dental caries ? How are they caused ?
(*c*) What is dental plaque ? What harm can it do ? How can the formation of plaque be prevented ?

70. (*a*) Name the main organs of the human digestive system. Also name the associated glands.
(*b*) How do carbohydrates, fats and proteins get digested in human beings ?

Multiple Choice Questions (MCQs)

71. Which of the following has the longest small intestine ?
(*a*) carnivore (*b*) omnivore (*c*) herbivore (*d*) autotroph
72. The process of obtaining food by *Amoeba* is known as :
(*a*) dialysis (*b*) cytokinesis (*c*) phagocytosis (*d*) amoebiasis
73. The organism having parasitic mode of nutrition is :
(*a*) *Penicillium* (*b*) *Plasmodium* (*c*) *Paramecium* (*d*) Parrot
74. One of the following organisms has a saprophytic mode of nutrition. This organism is :
(*a*) mushroom (*b*) malarial parasite (*c*) leech (*d*) lice
75. The length of small intestine in a human adult is about :
(*a*) 4.5 m (*b*) 1.5 m (*c*) 3.5 m (*d*) 6.5 m
76. The process of digestion of food in humans begins in :
(*a*) stomach (*b*) food pipe (*c*) mouth (*d*) small intestine
77. The process of digestion in humans is completed in :
(*a*) oesophagus (*b*) small intestine (*c*) stomach (*d*) large intestine
78. In human digestive system, bile is secreted by :
(*a*) pancreas (*b*) liver (*c*) kidneys (*d*) stomach
79. Two of the following organisms have a holozoic mode of nutrition. These organisms are :
(*a*) *Paramecium* and *Plasmodium* (*b*) *Plasmodium* and Parakeet
(*c*) Parakeet and *Paramecium* (*d*) *Paramecium* and Parasite
80. The autotrophic mode of nutrition requires :
(*a*) carbon dioxide and water (*b*) chlorophyll (*c*) sunlight (*d*) all of the above
81. The correct order of steps occurring in nutrition in animals is :
(*a*) Ingestion ⟶ Absorption ⟶ Digestion ⟶ Assimilation ⟶ Egestion
(*b*) Ingestion ⟶ Digestion ⟶ Assimilation ⟶ Absorption ⟶ Egestion
(*c*) Ingestion ⟶ Digestion ⟶ Absorption ⟶ Assimilation ⟶ Egestion
(*d*) Ingestion ⟶ Assimilation ⟶ Digestion ⟶ Absorption ⟶ Egestion
82. In human digestive system, the enzymes pepsin and trypsin are secreted respectively by :
(*a*) pancreas and liver (*b*) stomach and salivary glands
(*c*) pancreas and gall bladder (*d*) stomach and pancreas
83. When carrying out the starch test on a leaf, why is it important to boil the leaf in alcohol ?
(*a*) to dissolve the waxy cuticle (*b*) to make the cells more permeable to iodine solution
(*c*) to remove the chlorophyll (*d*) to stop chemical reactions in the cells.
84. Pancreatic juice contains enzymes which digest :
(*a*) proteins and carbohydrates only (*b*) proteins and fats only
(*c*) fats and carbohydrates only (*d*) proteins, fats and carbohydrates
85. Which of the following is the correct statement regarding bile ?
(*a*) secreted by bile duct and stored in liver (*b*) secreted by gall bladder and stored in liver
(*c*) secreted by liver and stored in bile duct (*d*) secreted by liver and stored in gall bladder
86. Where are proteins first digested in the alimentary canal ?
(*a*) small intestine (*b*) oesophagus (*c*) mouth (*d*) stomach
87. The inner lining of stomach is protected by one of the following from the harmful effect of hydrochloric acid. This is :
(*a*) pepsin (*b*) mucus (*c*) saliva (*d*) bile
88. Which part of alimentary canal receives bile from the liver ?
(*a*) oesophagus (*b*) small intestine (*c*) stomach (*d*) large intestine
89. Which of the following component of our food is digested by an enzyme which is present in saliva as well as in pancreatic juice ?
(*a*) proteins (*b*) fat (*c*) minerals (*d*) carbohydrate

90. If the saliva is lacking in salivary amylase, then which of the following processes taking place in the buccal cavity will be affected ?
(*a*) proteins breaking down into amino acids (*b*) starch breaking down into sugars
(*c*) fats breaking down into fatty acids and glycerol (*d*) intestinal layer breaking down leading to ulcers

91. Which of the following are the correct functions of two components of pancreatic juice trypsin and lipase ?
(*a*) trypsin digests proteins and lipase carbohydrates
(*b*) trypsin digests emulsified fats and lipase proteins
(*c*) trypsin digests starch and lipase fats
(*d*) trypsin digests proteins and lipase emulsified fats

92. The oxygen liberated during photosynthesis by green plants comes from :
(*a*) glucose (*b*) water (*c*) carbon dioxide (*d*) chlorophyll

93. Which of the following is an incorrect statement ?
(*a*) energy is essential for life processes
(*b*) organisms grow with time
(*c*) movement of molecules does not take place among cells
(*d*) organisms must repair and maintain their body

94. The internal energy (cellular energy) reserve in autotrophs is :
(*a*) proteins (*b*) fatty acids (*c*) glycogen (*d*) starch

95. Which of the following events does not occur in photosynthesis ?
(*a*) conversion of light energy into chemical energy
(*b*) reduction of carbon dioxide to carbohydrates
(*c*) oxidation of carbon to carbon dioxide
(*d*) absorption of light energy by chlorophyll

96. The opening and closing of the stomatal pores depends upon :
(*a*) oxygen (*b*) water in guard cells
(*c*) temperature (*d*) concentration of CO_2 in stomata

97. Most of the plants absorb nitrogen in one of the following forms. This is :
(*a*) proteins (*b*) nitrates and nitrites (*c*) urea (*d*) atmospheric nitrogen

98. The first enzyme to mix with food in the digestive tract is :
(*a*) pepsin (*b*) cellulose (*c*) amylase (*d*) trypsin

99. Which of the following is the correct statement ?
(*a*) heterotrophs synthesise their own food
(*b*) heterotrophs utilize solar energy for photosynthesis
(*c*) heterotrophs do not synthesise their own food
(*d*) heterotrophs are capable of converting carbon dioxide and water into carbohydrates

100. In which of the following groups of organisms the food material is broken down outside the body and then absorbed ?
(*a*) Mushroom, Green plants, *Amoeba* (*b*) Yeast, Mushroom, Bread mould
(*c*) *Paramecium*, *Amoeba*, *Cuscuta* (*d*) *Cuscuta*, Lice, Tapeworm

101. Which of the following is the correct sequence of parts as they occur in the human alimentary canal ?
(*a*) Mouth → Stomach → Small intestine → Oesophagus → Large intestine
(*b*) Mouth → Oesophagus → Stomach → Large intestine → Small intestine
(*c*) Mouth → Stomach → Oesophagus → Small intestine → Large intestine
(*d*) Mouth → Oesophagus → Stomach → Small intestine → Large intestine

Questions Based on High Order Thinking Skills (HOTS)

102. When a person eats sugary food, then organisms A present in his mouth act on sugar to produce a substance B. The substance B first dissolves the calcium salts from the top part C of the tooth and then from its middle part D forming holes E. These holes ultimately reach the part F in the lower part of tooth which contains nerves and blood vessels. The substance B irritates the nerve endings inside the tooth causing toothache.

(*a*) What are (*i*) organisms A, and (*ii*) substance B ?
(*b*) What are (*i*) part C, and (*ii*) part D, of tooth known as ?
(*c*) By what name are the holes E in the tooth known ?
(*d*) Name the part F of the tooth.
(*e*) What will happen if organisms A reach part F of the tooth ?

103. If the teeth are not cleaned regularly, they become covered with a sticky yellowish layer W of food particles and bacteria. Since layer W covers the teeth, the alkaline liquid X secreted by glands Y inside the mouth cannot reach the teeth surface to neutralise the acid formed by the action of organisms Z on sugary food, and hence tooth decay sets in.
(*a*) What is W known as ?
(*b*) What is (*i*) X, and (*ii*) Y ?
(*c*) What are organisms Z ?
(*d*) State one way of removing layer W from the teeth.

104. When a person puts food in his mouth, then teeth cut it into small pieces, chew and grind it. The glands A in the mouth secrete a substance B which is mixed with the food by tongue. The substance B contains an enzyme C which starts the digestion of food in the mouth. The slightly digested food from the mouth goes down a tube D. The special type of movements E in the walls of tube D push the food into stomach for further digestion. The stomach wall secretes gastric juice containing three substance F, G and H. One of the functions of F is to kill bacteria which may enter the stomach with food. The substance G protects the inside layer of stomach from the damaging effect of substance F whereas substance H is an enzyme for digestion. The partially digested food then enters into small intestine for further digestion.
(*a*) What is (*i*) gland A (*ii*) substance B, and (*iii*) enzyme C ?
(*b*) Name the tube D.
(*c*) What is the movement E known as ?
(*d*) What are (*i*) F (*ii*) G, and (*iii*) H ?

105. The partially digested food coming from the stomach of a person enters a long and narrow organ A in his body. The organ A receives the secretions of two glands : liver and pancreas. Liver secretes a greenish-yellow liquid B which is normally stored in the organ C. Pancreas secretes pancreatic juice which contains three digestive enzymes D, E and F. The intestinal juice completes the process of digestion of food. The inner wall of organ A has millions of tiny finger-like projections G which help in the rapid absorption of digested food into blood stream. The undigested part of food then passes into wider tube H which absorbs most of the water from undigested food. The last part of tube H called I stores this undigested food (or waste) for some time. The undigested food is then passed out though opening J as faeces in the process known as K.
(*a*) Name the organ A.
(*b*) Name (*i*) liquid B, and (*ii*) organ C.
(*c*) What are the digestive enzymes D, E and F ?
(*d*) Name the projections G present on the inner wall of organ A.
(*e*) Name (*i*) tube H (*ii*) part I (*iii*) opening J, and (*iv*) process K.

106. A unicellular animal P having no fixed shape ingests a food particle by forming temporary finger-like projections Q. The food particle is engulfed with a little surrounding water to form a temporary stomach R inside it. The chemicals S from surrounding cytoplasm enter into R and break down food into small and soluble molecules by chemical reactions. The digested food is absorbed directly into cytoplasm by the process T. The undigested food is thrown out of the body by the rupture of a cell organelle U in a process called V.
(*a*) Name the unicellular animal P.
(*b*) What are (*i*) Q, and (*ii*) R ?
(*c*) Name (*i*) chemical S, and (*ii*) process T.
(*d*) Name (*i*) organelle U, and (*ii*) process V.

107. There are four organisms A, B, C and D. The organism A eats only the flesh of other animals as food. The organism B can eat grains, fruits and vegetables as well as meat and fish. The organism C can make the food itself from simple inorganic substances present in the environment by utilising sunlight energy. On the other hand, organism D eats only plants and their products as food.
(*a*) Which organism is (*i*) omnivore (*ii*) herbivore, and (*ii*) carnivore ?

(*b*) Which organism is an autotroph ?
(*c*) Which organism is/are heterotroph(s) ?
(*d*) Which organism can be a producer ?
(*e*) Which organism is/are consumer (s) ?
(*f*) Give one example each of organisms which could be like (*i*) A (*ii*) B (*iii*) C, and (*iv*) D

108. The organisms A, B and C can obtain their food in three different ways. Organism A derives its food from the body of another living organism which is called its D, without killing it. The organism B takes in the solid food by the process of ingestion, digests a part of this food and throws out undigested food in the process called E. The organism C obtains its food from dead and decaying plants.
(*a*) What is the mode of nutrition of (*i*) organism A (*ii*) organism B, and (*iii*) organism C ?
(*b*) What is the organism like D called ?
(*c*) Name the process E.
(*d*) Give one example each of organisms like (*i*) A (*ii*) B, and (*ii*) C.
(*e*) What is the general name of three modes of nutrition exhibited by organisms A, B and C ?

109. An organism A which cannot move from one place to another, makes a simple food B from the substances C and D available in the environment. This food is made in the presence of a green coloured substance E present in organs F in the presence of light energy in a process called G. Some of the simple food B also gets converted into a complex food H for storage purposes. The food H gives a blue-black colour with dilute iodine solution.
(*a*) What is (*i*) organism A (*ii*) food B, and (*iii*) food H ?
(*b*) What are C and D ?
(*c*) Name (*i*) green coloured substance E, and (*ii*) organ F.
(*d*) What is the process G ?

110. X is a wild animal which eats only the flesh of other animals whereas Y is a domestic animal which feeds mainly on green grass.
(*a*) What are animals like X known as ?
(*b*) What are animals like Y known as ?
(c) Which animal, X or Y, has a longer small intestine ? Why ?
(*d*) Name one animal which is like X.
(*e*) Name one animal which is like Y.

ANSWERS

1. Food **2.** Chemical energy **3.** Green plant **10.** (*a*) Carbon dioxide (*b*) Oxygen **11.** A is glucose ; B is starch **19.** Guard cells **20.** *Amoeba* **31.** Peristaltic movement **39.** (*a*) autotrophs (*b*) heterotrophs (*c*) plants ; animals (*d*) carbon dioxide, water, sunlight (*e*) starch **40.** (*b*) (*i*) Glucose (*ii*) Starch **45.** (*a*) X : Light energy ; Y : Chemical energy **55** (*i*) *c* (*ii*) *a* (*iii*) *d* (*iv*) *b* 56 (*a*) Photosynthesis (*b*) Heterotrophs (*c*) Autotrophs (*d*) Chloroplast (*e*) Guard cells (*f*) Pepsin **57.** (*i*) *c* (*ii*) *d* (*iii*) *a* (*iv*) *b* **58.** (*a*) Parasitic mode of nutrition (*b*) (*i*) Proteins (*ii*) Starch (*iii*) Proteins (*iv*) Fats (*c*) Due to the presence of a large number of villi **60.** (*b*) Plant kept in continuous light will live longer because it will be able to produce oxygen required for its respiration by the process of photosynthesis **61.** (*a*) Green plants are the source of food for all the organisms. If all the green plants disappear from the earth, then all the organisms (herbivores, carnivores and omnivores) will die due to starvation (*b*) When photosynthesis occurs during the day, the carbon dioxide released by plants by respiration is all used up and not released. Similarly, some of the oxygen produced during photosynthesis is used up in respiration. Since the plant here is releasing carbon dioxide and taking in oxygen even during the day, it means that no photosynthesis is taking place **62.** (*a*) This plant will not remain healthy for long because vaseline coating closes the stomatal pores on the leaves due to which (*i*) plant will not get oxygen for respiration (*ii*) plant will not get carbon dioxide for photosynthesis, and (*iii*) plant will not get water (and minerals) due to stoppage of transpiration (*b*) (*i*) Decreases in morning but increases in the afternoon (*ii*) Decreases (*iii*) Decreases **71.** (*c*) **72.** (c) **73.** (*b*) **74.** (*a*) **75.** (*d*) **76.** (*c*) **77.** (*b*) **78.** (*b*) **79.** (*c*) **80.** (*d*) **81.** (*c*) **82.** (*d*) **83.** (*c*) **84** (*d*) **85.** (*d*) **86.** (*d*) **87.** (*b*) **88.** (*b*) **89.** (*d*) **90.** (*b*) **91.** (*d*) **92.** (*b*) **93.** (*c*) **94.** (*d*) **95.** (*c*) **96.** (*b*) **97.** (*b*) **98.** (*c*) **99.** (*c*) **100.** (*b*) **101.** (*d*) **102.** (*a*) (*i*) Bacteria (*ii*) Acid (*b*) (*i*) Enamel (*ii*) Dentine (*c*) Dental caries (*d*) Pulp cavity (*e*) Inflammation and infection will occur leading to severe pain **103.** (*a*) Dental plaque (*b*) (*i*) Saliva (*ii*) Salivary glands (*c*) Bacteria (*d*) Brushing the teeth regularly after eating food

104. (*a*) (*i*) Salivary gland (*ii*) Saliva (*iii*) Salivary amylase (*b*) Oesophagus (*c*) Peristaltic movement (*d*) (*i*) Hydrochloric acid (*ii*) Mucus (*iii*) Enzyme pepsin **105.** (*a*) Small intestine (*b*) (*i*) Bile (*ii*) Gall bladder (*c*) Pancreatic amylase, Trypsin and Lipase (*d*) Villi (*e*) (*i*) Large intestine (*ii*) Rectum (*iii*) Anus (*iv*) Egestion **106.** (*a*) *Amoeba* (*b*) (*i*) Pseudopodia (*ii*) Food vacuole (*c*) (*i*) Enzymes (*ii*) Diffusion (*d*) (*i*) Cell membrane (*ii*) Egestion **107.** (*i*) B (*ii*) D (*iii*) A (*b*) C (*c*) A, B and D (*d*) C (*e*) A, B and D (*f*) (*i*) Lion (*ii*) Human (Man) (*iii*) Green plant (*iv*) Cow **108.** (*a*) (*i*) Parasitic (*ii*) Holozoic (*iii*) Saprophytic (*b*) Host (*c*) Egestion (*d*) (*i*) Tapeworm (*ii*) Man (*iii*) Mushroom (*e*) Heterotrophic nutrition **109.** (*a*) (*i*) Green plant (*ii*) Glucose (*iii*) Starch (*b*) Carbon dioxide and Water (*c*) (*i*) Chlorophyll (*ii*) Green leaf (*d*) Photosynthesis **110.** (*a*) Carnivores (*b*) Herbivores (*c*) Animal Y has a longer small intestine. The animal Y is a herbivore which eats grass (and other green plants). The grass contains a carbohydrate called cellulose which is digested with difficulty. A longer small intestine allows the cellulose present in grass to be digested completely. (*d*) Tiger (*e*) Cow

RESPIRATION

We have just studied that digested food is assimilated into the body of the living organisms. The assimilated food is used mainly for two purposes :

1. **Assimilated food is used as a fuel to get energy for various life processes,** and
2. **Assimilated food is used as a material for the growth and repair of the body.**

We will now describe how energy is released from the food which is absorbed and assimilated in the cells of the body. Please note that **food is the 'fuel' for energy production in cells.** Let us see how energy is actually obtained.

Most living things need oxygen (of air) to obtain energy from food. This oxygen reacts with the food molecules (like glucose) present in the body cells and burns them slowly to release energy. The energy thus released is stored in ATP molecules in the cells. The body can use this stored energy whenever it wants to do so.

The process of releasing energy from food is called respiration. When oxygen burns the food in the cells of the body to release energy, then carbon dioxide and water are produced as waste products which are to be eliminated from the body (see Figure 43). **The process of respiration involves taking in oxygen (of air) into the cells, using it for releasing energy by burning food, and then eliminating the waste products (carbon dioxide and water) from the body.** The process of respiration can be written in the form of a word equation as follows :

$$\text{Food} + \text{Oxygen} \longrightarrow \text{Carbon dioxide} + \text{Water} + \text{Energy}$$

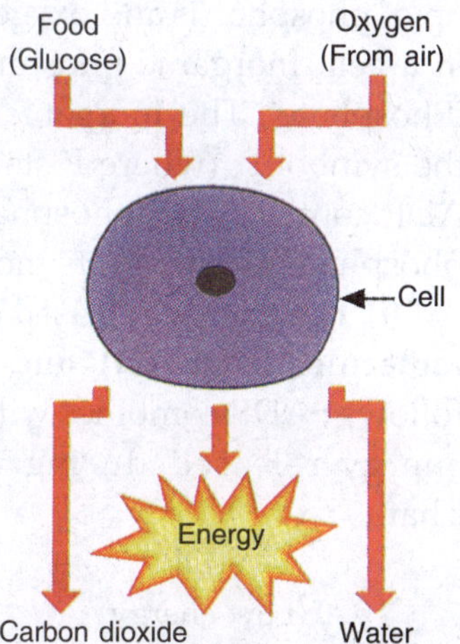

Figure 43. Respiration takes place in every cell in our body (and those of other organisms). Respiration produces energy from food (like glucose).

The process of respiration which releases energy takes place inside the cells of the body. So, it is also known as cellular respiration. The process of cellular respiration is common to all the living organisms. It provides energy to the cells. There are two by-products of cellular respiration : carbon dioxide and water. Out of these only carbon dioxide is considered the real waste product of respiration because its accumulation in the body is harmful to the organism. Water produced during respiration is not harmful to the body. It is rather beneficial for the body. Please note that **respiration is essential for life because it provides energy for carrying out all the life processes which are necessary to keep the organisms alive.**

Breathing and Respiration

The mechanism by which organisms obtain oxygen from the air and release carbon dioxide is called breathing. Respiration is a more complex process. Respiration includes breathing as well as the oxidation of food in the cells of the organism to release energy. Breathing is a physical process whereas respiration also includes biochemical process of oxidation of food. The process of breathing involves the lungs of the organism whereas the process of respiration also involves the mitochondria in the cells where food is oxidised to release energy.

Respiration is actually a biochemical process which occurs in stages and requires many enzymes. **The main purpose of respiration is the release of energy from the oxidation of simple food molecules like glucose.** The energy released during respiration is used for carrying out the biological functions which are necessary for the maintenance of life and survival of an organism. Please note that **respiration is just opposite of photosynthesis.** This is because *photosynthesis makes food* (like glucose) by using carbon dioxide, water and sunlight energy, and releasing oxygen; whereas *respiration breaks food* (like glucose) by using oxygen, and releasing carbon dioxide, water and energy.

How Energy Released During Respiration is Stored

All the energy released during respiration is not used immediately by an organism (plant or animal). **The energy produced during respiration is stored in the form of ATP molecules in the cells of the body** and used by the organism as and when required. In order to understand this we should first know the meaning of ADP, ATP and inorganic phosphate. These are given below.

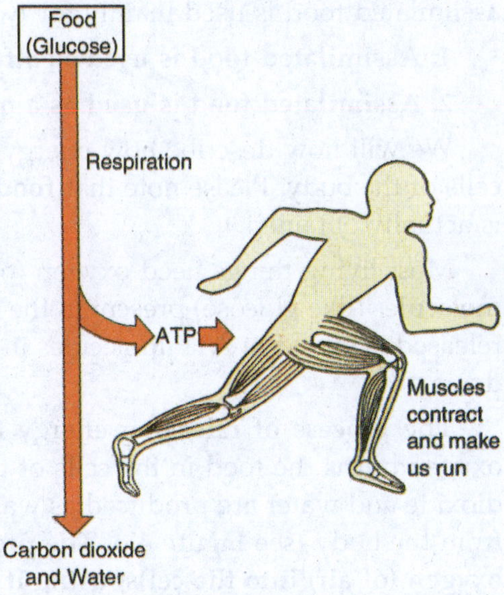

ADP is a substance called Adenosine Di-Phosphate. The molecules of ADP are present in a cell. ADP has low energy content. **ATP is a substance called Adenosine Tri-Phosphate.** It is also present inside a cell. ATP has a high energy content. Inorganic phosphate is a substance which contains a phosphate group made up of phosphorus and oxygen. Inorganic phosphates are also present in a cell. Inorganic phosphate can be represented by writing just 'Phosphate'. The inorganic phosphate can also be represented by the symbol P_i (where P stands for phosphate and i for inorganic). ADP contains two phosphate groups whereas ATP contains three phosphate groups in its molecule.

Food (Glucose)
Respiration
ATP
Muscles contract and make us run
Carbon dioxide and Water

Figure 44. The energy produced from food like glucose during respiration is stored in the form of ATP molecules in the cells of the body. This stored energy can be utilised by the body for various purposes (say, like the contraction of muscles to make us walk or run).

(*i*) The energy released during respiration is used to make ATP molecules from ADP and inorganic phosphate. This happens as follows : ADP combines with inorganic phosphate by absorbing the energy released during respiration to form ATP molecules. That is :

$$\underset{\text{(Low energy)}}{\text{ADP}} + \text{Phosphate} + \underset{\text{(From respiration)}}{\text{Energy}} \longrightarrow \underset{\text{(High energy)}}{\text{ATP}}$$

Thus, energy is stored in the cells in the form of ATP.

(*ii*) When the cell needs energy, then ATP can be broken down using water to release energy. Thus :

$$\text{ATP} \longrightarrow \text{ADP} + \text{Phosphate} + \underset{\text{(For use in cells)}}{\text{Energy}}$$

The energy equivalent to 30.5 kJ/mole is released in this process. The energy released by ATP is used to carry out all the endothermic reactions taking place in the cells.

Please note that ADP can be converted to ATP by absorbing energy produced during respiration, and ATP can be converted back to ADP releasing energy to be used by the cells, again and again. This ensures a continuous supply of energy to the organism.

Just as a battery can provide electrical energy for different purposes such as lighting, heating, running radio and computer, etc., in the same way, **the energy stored in ATP is used by the body cells for various purposes like contraction of muscles, conduction of nerve impulses, synthesis of proteins, and many other activities related to the functioning of cells.** In fact, ATP is known as the energy currency of cells.

An Important Discussion

In most of the cases, the organisms (plants and animals) carry out respiration by using oxygen (called aerobic respiration). There are, however, some organisms which carry out respiration without using oxygen (called anaerobic respiration). Before we describe aerobic respiration and anaerobic respiration, we should keep the following points in mind which will help us in understanding the two types of respiration.

1. **Glucose is $C_6H_{12}O_6$. It is a six carbon atom compound.** It is the simple food which is oxidised in the cells of organisms during respiration.
2. **The oxidation of glucose to pyruvic acid (or pyruvate) is called glycolysis.** It occurs in the cytoplasm of a cell and not in mitochondria. The oxidation of glucose to pyruvic acid does not require oxygen. One molecule of glucose on glycolysis produces two molecules of pyruvic acid (or pyruvate).
3. **Pyruvic acid is a three carbon atom compound. It is also called pyruvate.** The formula of pyruvic acid or pyruvate is $CH_3{-}\underset{\underset{O}{\parallel}}{C}{-}COOH$. It is a ketonic carboxylic acid.
4. The fate of pyruvate formed during respiration depends on whether oxygen is present in the cells or not. If oxygen is present in the cells, then pyruvate is completely oxidised to carbon dioxide and water, and a lot of energy is produced (in the form of ATP). If, however, oxygen is not present in the cells (that is, in the absence of oxygen), pyruvate is converted to either 'ethanol and carbon dioxide' or 'lactic acid' depending on whether such a process is taking place in a plant cell or an animal cell. Much less energy is released in this case.
5. **Lactic acid is also a three carbon atom compound.** It is also called lactate. The formula of lactic acid or lactate is $CH_3{-}\underset{\underset{OH}{|}}{CH}{-}COOH$. It is a hydroxy carboxylic acid.

TYPES OF RESPIRATION

So far we have studied that respiration takes place in the presence of oxygen (of air). Respiration can, however, also take place in the absence of oxygen (of air), though it is very rare. This means that oxidation of food to obtain energy can occur in the *presence* of oxygen as well as in the *absence* of oxygen. Based on this, we have two types of respiration : **aerobic respiration** and **anaerobic respiration.**

1. Aerobic Respiration

The respiration which uses oxygen is called aerobic respiration. It is called aerobic respiration because it uses air which contains oxygen ('aerobic' means 'with air'). In aerobic respiration, the glucose food is completely broken down into carbon dioxide and water by oxidation. Aerobic respiration produces a considerable amount of energy for use by the organism which gets stored in the ATP molecules. The breaking down of glucose (food) during aerobic respiration (which is carried out by most of the organisms) can be represented as follows :

$$\underset{\text{(1 molecule)}}{\text{Glucose}} \xrightarrow[\text{(in cytoplasm)}]{\text{Glycolysis}} \underset{\substack{\text{(Pyruvic acid)}\\ \text{(2 molecules)}}}{\text{Pyruvate}} \xrightarrow[\text{(in mitochondria)}]{\text{Oxygen (Kreb's cycle)}} \underset{\substack{\text{Carbon}\\ \text{dioxide}}}{6CO_2} + \underset{\text{Water}}{6H_2O} + \underset{\text{Energy}}{38\text{ ATP}}$$

Please note that during aerobic respiration (shown above), 1 molecule of glucose (food) produces 38 energy-rich ATP molecules (Please do not worry about the name 'Kreb's cycle' written in the above equation. We will study this in higher classes). All the organisms which obtain energy by aerobic respiration, cannot live without oxygen (of air). This is because if there is no oxygen, they cannot get energy from the food which they eat. **Mitochondria are the sites of aerobic respiration in the cells** (see Figure 45). Thus, the breakdown of pyruvate to give carbon dioxide, water and energy takes place in mitochondria.

The energy released during aerobic respiration is used by the organism. **Most of the living organisms carry out aerobic respiration (by using oxygen of air).** For example, humans (man), dogs (see Figure 46), cats, lions, elephants, cows, buffaloes, goat, deer, birds, lizards, snakes, earthworms, frogs, fish, and insects (such as cockroach, grasshopper, houseflies, mosquitoes and ants, etc.) and most of the plants carry out aerobic respiration by using oxygen of air (to obtain energy)

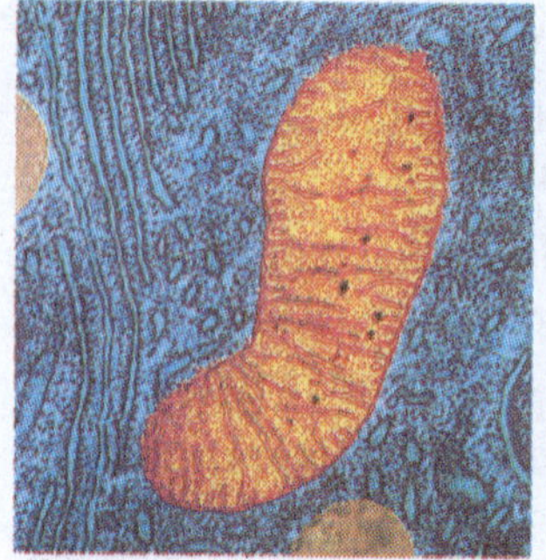

Figure 45. The orange organelle in this picture is mitochondrion where aerobic respiration in a cell takes place.

Figure 46. The dog obtains energy from its food through aerobic respiration (by using oxygen of air).

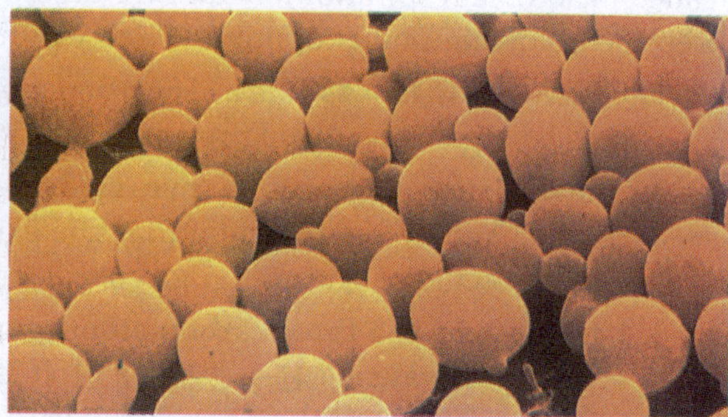

Figure 47. Yeast (single-celled fungus) obtains energy through anaerobic respiration (without using oxygen of air). This picture shows a large number of yeast cells.

2. Anaerobic Respiration

The respiration which takes place without oxygen is called anaerobic respiration. It is called anaerobic respiration because it takes place without air which contains oxygen ('anaerobic' means 'without air'). The microscopic organisms like yeast and some bacteria obtain energy by anaerobic respiration (which is called fermentation). **In anaerobic respiration, the micro-organisms like yeast break down glucose (food) into ethanol and carbon dioxide, and release energy.** This energy is then used by the micro-organisms. Anaerobic respiration produces much less energy which gets stored in the ATP molecules. The breaking down of glucose (food) during anaerobic respiration carried out by yeast (plants) can be represented as follows :

$$\underset{\text{(1 molecule)}}{\text{Glucose}} \xrightarrow[\text{(in cytoplasm)}]{\text{Glycolysis}} \underset{\substack{\text{(Pyruvic acid)}\\ \text{(2 molecules)}}}{\text{Pyruvate}} \xrightarrow[\substack{\text{(Yeast)}\\ \text{(Fermentation)}}]{\text{In absence of oxygen}} \underset{\text{Ethanol}}{2C_2H_5OH} + \underset{\substack{\text{Carbon}\\ \text{dioxide}}}{2CO_2} + \underset{\text{Energy}}{2\text{ ATP}}$$

Please note that during anaerobic respiration (shown above), 1 molecule of glucose (food) produces only 2 energy-rich ATP molecules. A few organisms such as yeast plants and certain bacteria (called anaerobic bacteria) can obtain energy from food in the absence of oxygen by the process of anaerobic respiration. Please note that all the organisms which obtain energy by anaerobic respiration can live without oxygen (of air). For example, the single-celled, non-green plant called 'yeast' can live without oxygen because it obtains energy by the process of anaerobic respiration (see Figure 47). From this discussion we conclude that *all the cells do not use oxygen to produce energy.* Energy can be produced in cells even without oxygen. Please note that the whole process of anaerobic respiration takes place in the cytoplasm of cells.

We can carry out the fermentation of sugar by using the anaerobic respiration of yeast as follows : Take some sugar solution (or fruit juice) in a test-tube and add a little of yeast to it. Close the mouth of the test-tube with a cork and allow it to stand for some time. Now, open the cork and smell. A characteristic smell of ethanol (ethyl alcohol) is obtained from the test-tube. A gas is also evolved during this process. When this gas is passed through lime-water, the lime-water turns milky showing that it is carbon dioxide gas. This experiment tells us that the products of fermentation of sugar brought about by yeast are ethanol and carbon dioxide.

We (the human beings) obtain energy by aerobic respiration. But anaerobic respiration can sometimes take place in our muscles (or the muscles of other animals). For example, **anaerobic respiration takes place in our muscles during vigorous physical exercise when oxygen gets used up faster in the muscle cells than can be supplied by the blood.** When anaerobic respiration takes place in human muscles (or animal muscles), then glucose (food) is converted into lactic acid with the release of a small amount of energy. The breaking down of glucose (food) during anaerobic respiration in muscles can be represented as follows :

$$\underset{\text{(1 molecule)}}{\text{Glucose}} \xrightarrow[\text{(in cytoplasm)}]{\text{Glycolysis}} \underset{\substack{\text{(Pyruvic acid)} \\ \text{(2 molecules)}}}{\text{Pyruvate}} \xrightarrow[\text{(muscle tissue)}]{\text{In absence of oxygen}} \text{2 Lactic acid} + \underset{\text{Energy}}{\text{2ATP}}$$

The sudden build up of lactic acid in our muscles during vigorous physical activity can cause muscular 'cramps'. (The painful contractions of muscles are called cramps). Let us discuss this in a little more detail. During heavy physical exercise (or any other heavy physical activity), most of the energy in our muscles in produced by aerobic respiration. Anaerobic respiration in muscles provides only some extra energy which is needed under the conditions of heavy physical activity (like running very fast or running for a long time) (see the people running a long distance race in Figure 48). The anaerobic respiration by muscles brings about partial breakdown of glucose (food) to form lactic acid. This lactic acid accumulates in the muscles. **The accumulation of lactic acid in the muscles causes muscle cramps.** Thus, muscle cramps occur due to the accumulation of lactic acid in muscles when the muscles respire anaerobically (without oxygen) while doing hard physical exercise. **We can get relief from cramps in muscles caused by heavy exercise by taking a hot water bath or a massage.** Hot water bath (or massage) *improves* the circulation of blood in the muscles. Due to improved blood flow, the supply of oxygen to the muscles increases. This oxygen breaks down lactic acid accumulated in muscles into carbon dioxide and water, and hence gives us relief from cramps. The anaerobic respiration does not take place only in the muscles of human beings, it also takes place in the muscles of other animals such as lion, tiger, cheetah, deer, and many other animals when they run very fast and require much more energy than normal. This means that even the animals like

Figure 48. During vigorous physical exercise (such as running a long distance race) leg muscles respire anaerobically (without oxygen) to produce extra energy. The man on the right side in the above picture has just got a cramp in the leg due to the accumulation of lactic acid in the leg muscles produced by the anaerobic respiration which took place in leg muscles during marathon (a long-distance running race).

Figure 49. Just imagine what would happen if the fast running deer trying to escape from the clutches of cheetah gets a leg cramp at this very moment (due to accumulation of lactic acid in its leg muscles produced during anaerobic respiration). The cheetah is sure to get enough lunch or dinner !

lion, tiger, cheetah and deer, etc., can get leg cramps due to the accumulation of lactic acid in leg muscles if they run very fast for a considerable time. Please note that :

(*a*) the anaerobic respiration in plants (like yeast) produces ethanol and carbon dioxide as end products.

(*b*) the anaerobic respiration in animal muscle tissue produces lactic acid as the end product.

The similarity between aerobic respiration and anaerobic respiration is that in both the cases, energy is produced by the breakdown of food like glucose. The main differences between aerobic respiration and anaerobic respiration are given below.

Differences between Aerobic and Anaerobic Respiration

Aerobic respiration	*Anaerobic respiration*
1. Aerobic respiration takes place in the *presence* of oxygen.	1. Anaerobic respiration takes place in the *absence* of oxygen.
2. Complete breakdown of food occurs in aerobic respiration.	2. Partial breakdown of food occurs in anaerobic respiration.
3. The end products in aerobic respiration are carbon dioxide and water.	3. The end products in anaerobic respiration may be ethanol and carbon dioxide (as in yeast plants), or lactic acid (as in animal muscles).
4. Aerobic respiration produces a considerable amount of energy.	4. Much less energy is produced in anaerobic respiration.

Let us answer one question now.

Sample Problem. The breakdown of pyruvate to give carbon dioxide, water and energy takes place in :
(*a*) cytoplasm (*b*) mitochondria (*c*) chloroplast (*d*) nucleus **(NCERT Book Question)**

Answer. (*b*) mitochondria

RESPIRATION IN PLANTS

Like animals, plants also need energy. The plants get this energy by the process of respiration. Plants also use oxygen of air for respiration and release carbon dioxide. Thus, the respiration in plants also involves the exchange of oxygen and carbon dioxide. So, *oxygen and carbon dioxide are called respiratory gases.* **The respiration in plants differs from that in animals in three respects :**

1. All the parts of a plant (like root, stem and leaves) perform respiration individually. On the other hand, an animal performs respiration as a single unit.
2. During respiration in plants, there is a little transport of respiratory gases from one part of the plant to the other. On the other hand, respiratory gases are usually transported over long distances inside an animal during respiration.
3. The respiration in plants occurs at a slow rate. On the other hand, the respiration in animals occurs at a much faster rate.

Plants get Oxygen by Diffusion

Plants have a branching shape, so they have quite a large surface area in comparison to their volume. Therefore, diffusion alone can supply all the cells of the plants with as much oxygen as they need for respiration. Diffusion occurs in the roots, stems and leaves of plants.

1. Respiration in Roots

Air is present in-between the particles of soil. The roots of a plant take the oxygen required for respiration from the air present in-between the soil particles by the process of diffusion. The extensions of the epidermal cells of a root are called root hair. The root hair are in contact with the air in the soil. Oxygen (from air in the soil particles) diffuses into root hairs and reaches all the other cells of the root for respiration. Carbon dioxide gas produced in the cells of the root during respiration moves out through the same root hairs by the process of diffusion. Thus, the respiration in roots occurs by the diffusion of respiratory gases (oxygen and carbon dioxide) through the root hairs (see Figure 50). It has been found that the land plants die if their roots remain waterlogged for a considerable time. This is because too much water expels all the air from in-between the soil particles. Due to this, oxygen is not available to the roots for aerobic respiration. Under these conditions, the roots will respire anaerobically, producing alcohol. This may kill the plant.

In order to understand the respiration in stems of plants we should remember that the soft stems of small, herbaceous plants have *stomata* in them whereas the hard and woody stems of large plants and trees have *lenticels* in them. Lenticel is a small area of bark in a woody stem where the cells are loosely packed allowing the gaseous exchange to take place between the air and the living cells of the stem.

2. Respiration in Stems

The stems of herbaceous plants (or herbs) have stomata. So, the exchange of respiratory gases in the stems of herbaceous plants takes place through stomata. The oxygen from air diffuses into the stem of a herbaceous plant through stomata and reaches all the cells for respiration. The carbon dioxide gas produced during respiration diffuses out into the air through the same stomata. The hard and woody stems of big plants or trees do not have stomata. In woody stems, the bark (outer covering of stem) has lenticels for gaseous exchange (see Figure 51). The oxygen from air diffuses into the stem of a woody plant through lenticels and reaches all the inner cells of the stem for respiration. The carbon dioxide gas produced in the cells of the stem during respiration diffuses out into the air through the same lenticels.

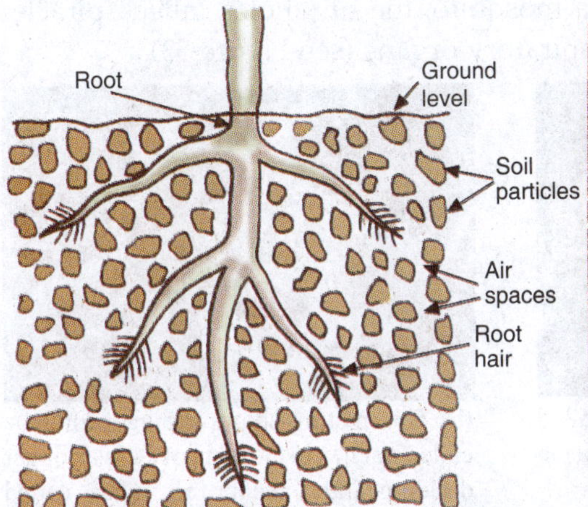

Figure 50. Roots absorb oxygen from air present in-between the soil particles through the root hair.

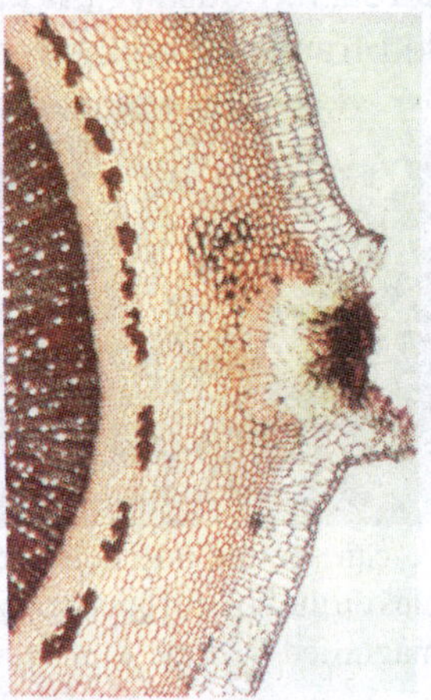

Figure 51. Woody stems of plants (or trees) have lenticels for the exchange of respiratory gases.

Figure 52. The exchange of respiratory gases in leaves takes place through tiny pores called stomata.

3. Respiration in Leaves

The leaves of a plant have tiny pores called stomata (see Figure 52). The exchange of respiratory gases in the leaves takes place by the process of diffusion through stomata. Oxygen from air diffuses into a leaf through stomata and reaches all the cells where it is used in respiration. The carbon dioxide produced during respiration diffuses out from the leaf into the air through the same stomata.

It should be noted that **respiration in leaves occurs during the day time as well as at night.** On the other hand, **photosynthesis occurs only during the day time** (no photosynthesis occurs at night). Due to this, **the net gaseous exchange in the leaves of a plant is as follows :**

(*i*) During day time, when photosynthesis occurs, oxygen is produced. The leaves use some of this oxygen for respiration and the rest of oxygen diffuses out into air. Again, during day time, carbon dioxide produced by respiration is all used up in photosynthesis by leaves. Even more carbon dioxide is taken in from air. Thus, **the net gas exchange in leaves during day time is : O_2 diffuses out ; CO_2 diffuses in.**

(*ii*) At night time, when no photosynthesis occurs and hence no oxygen is produced, oxygen from air diffuses into leaves to carry out respiration. And carbon dioxide produced by respiration diffuses out into air. So, **the net gas exchange in leaves at night is : O_2 diffuses in; CO_2 diffuses out.**

RESPIRATION IN ANIMALS

Different animals have different modes of respiration. For example :

(*i*) In simple unicellular animals like *Amoeba*, respiration takes place by the simple diffusion of gases through the cell membrane.

Most of the animals have, however, specific organs for respiration.

(*ii*) The animals like earthworms which live in the soil use their skin to absorb oxygen from air and remove carbon dioxide. So, the respiratory organ in the earthworm is the skin.

(*iii*) The aquatic animals like fish, prawns and mussels have gills as the respiratory organs which extract oxygen dissolved in water and take away carbon dioxide from the body.

(*iv*) In the insects like grasshopper, cockroach, housefly and a mosquito, the tiny holes called spiracles on their body and the air tubes called tracheae are the respiratory organs (see Figure 53).

(*a*) This is a grasshopper. It is an insect

(*b*) We can see the tiny holes called spiracles on the body of grasshopper in this magnified picture

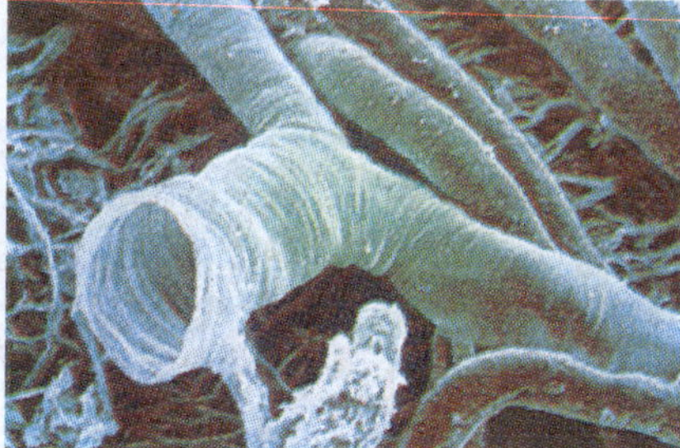

(*c*) This picture shows a bigger air tube called trachea in the body of a grasshopper dividing into smaller air tubes called tracheoles

Figure 53. Grasshopper (an insect) breathes and respires through tiny holes called spiracles, air tubes called tracheae and their branches called tracheoles.

(*v*) The respiratory organs of the land animals such as man (humans), birds, lizard, dog, and frog, etc., are the lungs. (Frogs, however, breathe both by lungs and skin).

Once the air (containing oxygen) enters the skin or lungs, blood absorbs the oxygen and transports it to various tissues of the animal. Blood also picks up the carbon dioxide from the tissues and brings it back to the skin or lungs for throwing it out into the air. Please note that **all the respiratory organs (whether skin, gills, trachea or lungs) have three common features** :

1. All the respiratory organs have a large surface area to get enough oxygen.
2. All the respiratory organs have thin walls for easy diffusion and exchange of respiratory gases.
3. All the respiratory organs like skin, gills and lungs have a rich blood supply for transporting respiratory gases (only in the tracheal system of respiration, air reaches the cells directly).

The animals which live in water (aquatic animals) use the oxygen dissolved in water to carry out respiration. Since the amount of dissolved oxygen in water is low as compared to the amount of oxygen in the air, therefore, **the rate of breathing in aquatic animals in much faster than in terrestrial animals** (or land animals). A faster rate of breathing provides *more* oxygen to the aquatic animal. The terrestrial animals (or land animals) use the oxygen of air or atmosphere for breathing and respiration. Thus, a terrestrial animal has an advantage over an aquatic animal in regard to obtaining oxygen for respiration that it is surrounded by an oxygen-rich atmosphere from where it can take any amount of oxygen. We will now describe the process of respiration in *Amoeba*, earthworm, fish and human beings.

Respiration In *Amoeba*

Amoeba is a single-celled animal. ***Amoeba* depends on simple diffusion of gases for breathing.** The diffusion of gases takes place through the thin cell membrane of *Amoeba*. In other words, the exchange of gases in *Amoeba* takes place through its cell membrane. Let us discuss this in somewhat detail. *Amoeba* lives in water. This water has oxygen gas dissolved in it. The oxygen from water diffuses into the body of *Amoeba* through its cell membrane (see Figure 54). Since the *Amoeba* is very small in size, so the oxygen spreads quickly into the whole body of *Amoeba*. This oxygen is used for respiration (energy release) inside the *Amoeba* cell. The process of respiration produces carbon dioxide gas continuously. This carbon dioxide gas diffuses out through the membrane of *Amoeba* into the surrounding water (see Figure 54). Thus, the breathing surface (or respiratory surface) of *Amoeba* is its cell surface membrane. In addition to *Amoeba*, other simple animals like *Paramecium* and *Planaria* also depend on the simple diffusion of gases for breathing and respiration. Thus, ***Amoeba, Paramecium* and *Planaria* all breathe through their cell membranes.**

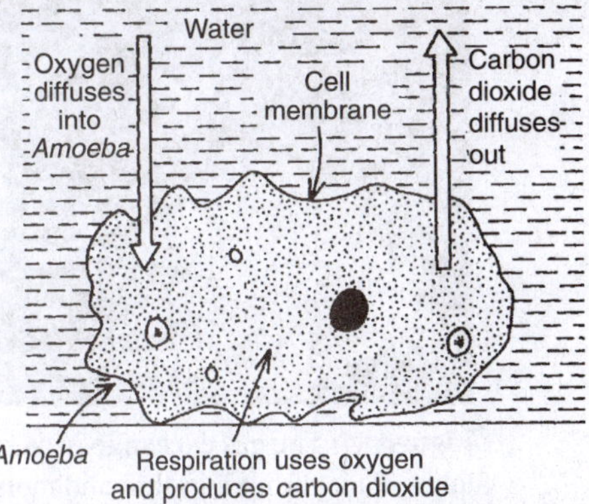

Figure 54. Diagram to show the process of breathing (gaseous exchange) in *Amoeba*.

In the small, single-celled animals such as *Amoeba*, the volume of their body is so small that oxygen can be introduced quickly into the whole body by the process of diffusion. This is because due to the smallness of *Amoeba* cell, the oxygen does not have to go far. But this is not so in larger animals like earthworms, grasshopper, fish and man (humans), etc. In large animals, the volume of body is so big that oxygen cannot diffuse into all the cells of the body quickly. This is because in these cases the oxygen has to travel a very large distance to reach each and every cell of the body. So, **in large animals, there is a blood circulatory system to carry oxygen to all the parts of the body quickly (and remove carbon dioxide).** The blood contains respiratory pigments which take up oxygen from air and carry it to the body cells. This will become more clear from the following example.

Diffusion is insufficient to meet the oxygen requirements of large multicellular organisms like humans because the volume of human body is so big that oxygen cannot diffuse into all the cells of the human body quickly. This is because oxygen will have to travel large distances inside the human body to reach each and every cell of the body. Diffusion being a very slow process will take a lot of time to make oxygen available to all the body cells. For example, it has been estimated that if diffusion were to provide oxygen in our body, then it would take about 3 years for a molecule of oxygen from our lungs to reach our toes by the process of diffusion. On the other hand, the blood circulatory system in humans carries oxygen to all the parts of the body quickly (and removes carbon dioxide). Actually, **human blood contains a respiratory pigment called haemoglobin which carries the oxygen from the lungs to all the body cells very efficiently.** Haemoglobin is present in red blood corpuscles. We will now discuss the process of breathing and respiration in some large animals like earthworm, fish and humans.

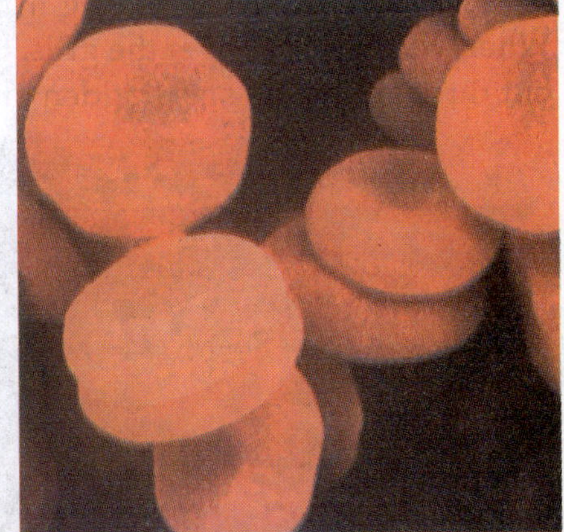

Figure 55. These are red blood cells (RBCs). They contain a red pigment called haemoglobin. Haemoglobin is a respiratory pigment in blood which carries oxygen from the lungs to all the body cells very effectively.

Respiration in Earthworm

The earthworm exchanges the gases through its skin (see Figure 56). This means that the respiratory surface of an earthworm is its skin. The skin of an earthworm is quite thin and moist, and has a good blood supply. So, **the earthworm absorbs the oxygen needed for respiration through its moist skin.** This oxygen is then transported to all the cells of the earthworm by its blood where it is used in respiration. The carbon dioxide produced during respiration is carried back by the blood. This carbon dioxide is expelled from the body of the earthworm through its skin. Thus, in earthworm, gaseous exchange takes place through the skin which is thin and moist. Just like earthworms, the leeches also absorb the oxygen needed for respiration through their skin (see Figure 57). And carbon dioxide produced inside the leeches (during respiration) also goes out through the skin.

Figure 56. The gas exchange in an earthworm takes place through its thin and moist skin.

Figure 57. The gas exchange in a leech also occurs through its skin.

Respiration in Fish

The fish has special organs of breathing called 'gills'. The fish has gills on both the sides of its head (see Figure 60). The gills are covered by gill covers so they are not visible from outside. The fish lives in water and this water contains dissolved oxygen in it. For breathing, the fish uses the oxygen which is dissolved in water. This happens as follows.

The fish breathes by taking in water through its mouth and sending it over the gills (see Figure 60). **When water passes over the gills, the gills extract dissolved oxygen from this water.** The water then goes out through the gill slits (hidden under the gill cover). Thus, the dissolved oxygen is extracted from water by the fish when it flows over the gills. The extracted oxygen is absorbed by the blood and carried to all the parts of the fish. The carbon dioxide produced by respiration is brought back by the blood into the gills for expelling into the surrounding water. The fish has no lungs like us, the gaseous exchange in fish takes place in the gills. So, the respiratory surface of a fish is the surface of its gills. It is a common observation that when a fish is taken out from water it dies soon (even though there is a lot of oxygen in the air around

Figure 58. Fish in water.

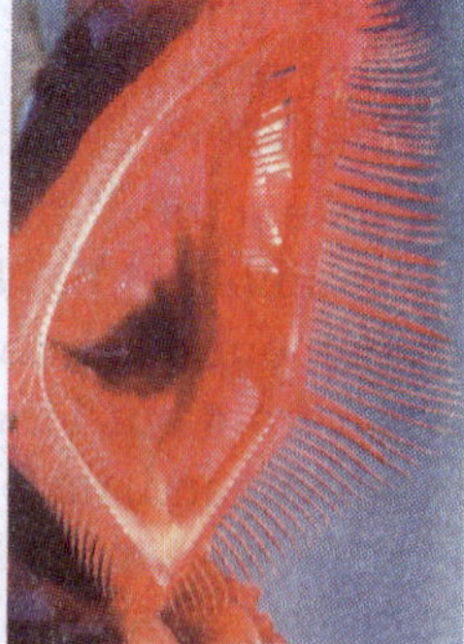

Figure 59. Gill of fish.

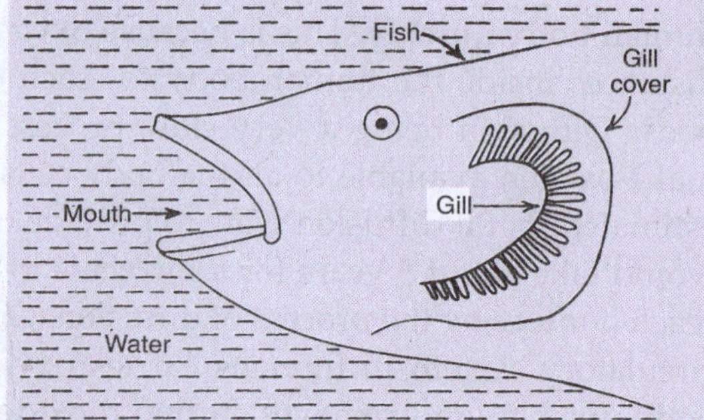

Figure 60. Diagram to show the gills in fish which extract dissolved oxygen from water.

it). This is because a fish does not have lungs to utilise the oxygen of air for breathing and respiration. The fish has gills which can extract only dissolved oxygen from water and provide it to fish. Gills cannot take in the oxygen from air on land. Since fish does not get oxygen for breathing when taken out of water, it dies. In addition to fish, many other aquatic animals like prawns and mussels also have special organs called 'gills' for breathing and respiration.

Please note that the fish and earthworm do not exchange the gases during respiration in the same way. The fish exchanges the gases by using its special organs called 'gills' whereas the earthworm exchanges the gases through its thin and moist 'skin'.

Respiration in Humans

Like other land animals, human beings are air breathers. Air contains oxygen. The human beings need oxygen to stay alive. We get this oxygen by breathing in air. The oxygen helps to break down the food absorbed in the body to release energy. This energy is used for maintaining our life. **The process by which energy is released from food in our body is called respiration.** Carbon dioxide and water are the two by-products of respiration. The process of respiration takes place inside the cells of our body. It involves our respiratory system. **The function of respiratory system is to breathe in oxygen for respiration (producing energy from food), and to breathe out carbon dioxide produced by respiration.** The breathing organs of human beings are lungs (see Figure 61). It is in the lungs that the gases are exchanged between the blood and air. **The gases exchanged between blood and air are oxygen and carbon dioxide.** We will now describe

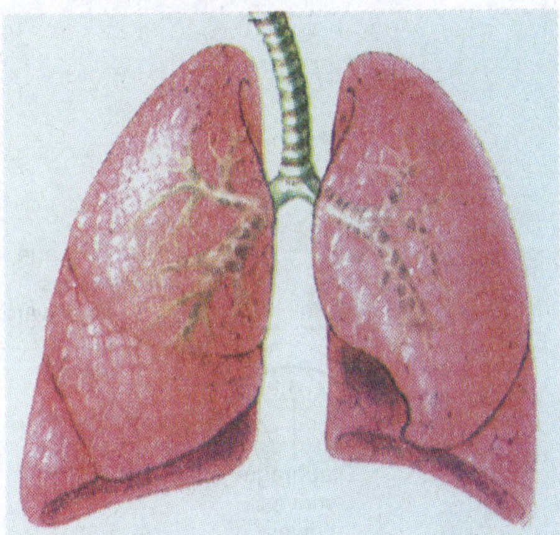

Figure 61. Human beings breathe through their lungs.

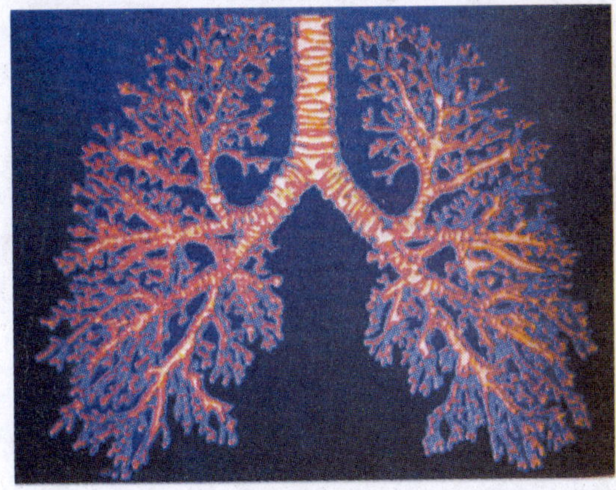

Figure 62. A resin cast of the human lungs.

the human respiratory system in detail. Before we go further and describe the human respiratory system in detail, it is necessary to learn the process of breathing which is an important part of respiration. This is discussed below.

We can live without food and water for many days but we cannot live for more than a few minutes without air. This is because air is necessary for breathing. During breathing, we take air into our lungs through the nose, and then expel it. The ordinary air which we take into the lungs is rich in oxygen but the air expelled from the lungs is rich in carbon dioxide. We can now define breathing as follows : **Breathing is the process by which air rich in oxygen is taken inside the body of an organism and air rich in carbon dioxide is expelled from the body (with the help of breathing organs).** The breathing in human beings takes place through the organs called lungs.

The taking in of air rich in oxygen into the body during breathing is called *'inhalation'* and giving out (or expelling) the air rich in carbon dioxide is called *'exhalation'*. Both, inhalation and exhalation take place regularly during breathing. **A breath means 'one inhalation plus one exhalation'.** We know that air contains oxygen. So, when we breathe in air, it is actually the oxygen gas present in air which is utilised by our body (to break down food and produce energy). Thus, we *'breathe in' air to supply oxygen to the cells of our body (for* *the breakdown of food to release energy), and we 'breathe out' to remove waste product carbon dioxide from our body (which is produced during the breakdown of food in the cells).* Breathing is a continuous process which goes on all the time throughout our life.

We will now learn the mechanism of breathing. That is , we will now learn how air from outside is sucked into our lungs during *inhaling* (breathing in), and how air from our lungs is pushed out during *exhaling* (breathing out). The process of breathing takes place in our lungs. Lungs are connected to our nostrils (holes in the nose) through nasal passage (or nasal cavity) and windpipe. When we inhale air, it enters our nostrils , passes through nasal passage and windpipe, and reaches our lungs. Our two lungs hang in an airtight space in our body called 'chest cavity'. Around the sides of the chest cavity is the **rib cage** with sheets of muscles between the ribs. The rib cage encloses the lungs in it [see Figure 63(*a*)]. At the bottom of the chest cavity is a curved sheet of muscle called diaphragm [see Figure 63(*a*)]. Diaphragm forms the floor of chest cavity. **Breathing involves the movements of the rib cage and the diaphragm.** This happens as follows :

(*a*) Breathing in. When we breathe in (or inhale), then two things happen at the same time : (*i*) the muscles between the ribs contract causing the rib cage to move *upward and outward*, and (*ii*) the diaphragm contracts and moves *downward* [see Figure 63(*a*)]. The upward and outward movement of rib cage, as well as the downward movement of diaphragm, both *increase the space in the chest cavity* and make it *larger* [see Figure 63(*a*)]. **As the chest cavity becomes larger, air is sucked in from outside into the lungs.** The lungs get filled up with air and expand.

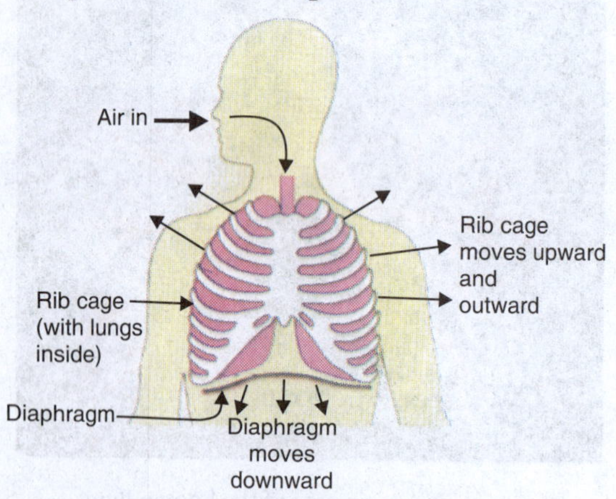

(*a*) Breathing in : chest cavity becomes bigger, air is sucked into lungs

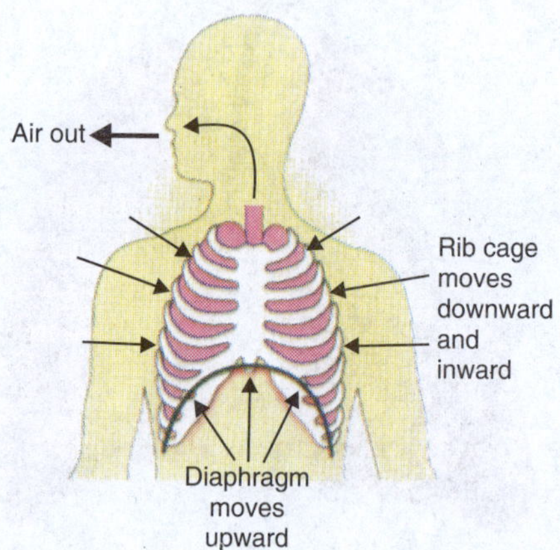

(*b*) Breathing out : chest cavity becomes smaller, air is pushed out of lungs

Figure 63. The mechanism of breathing.

(*b*) Breathing out. When we breathe out (or exhale), even then two things happen at the same time : (*i*) the muscles between the ribs relax causing the rib cage to move *downward and inward*, and (*ii*) the diaphragm relaxes and moves *upward* [see Figure 63(*b*)]. The downward and inward movement of rib cage, as well as the upward movement of diaphragm, both *decrease the space in our chest cavity* and make it *smaller* [see Figure 63(*b*)]. **As the chest cavity becomes smaller, air is pushed out from the lungs.**

RESPIRATORY SYSTEM IN HUMANS (OR MAN)

In human beings, many organs take part in the process of respiration. We call them organs of respiratory system. **The main organs of human respiratory system are : Nose, Nasal passage (or Nasal cavity), Trachea, Bronchi, Lungs and Diaphragm.** The human respiratory system is shown in Figure 64.

The human respiratory system begins from the nose. Our nose has two holes in it which are called nostrils (see Figure 64). There is a passage in the nose behind the nostrils which is called nasal passage (or nasal cavity). **The air for respiration is drawn into our body through the nostrils present in the nose.** This air then goes into nasal passage. The nasal passage is separated from the mouth cavity (buccal cavity

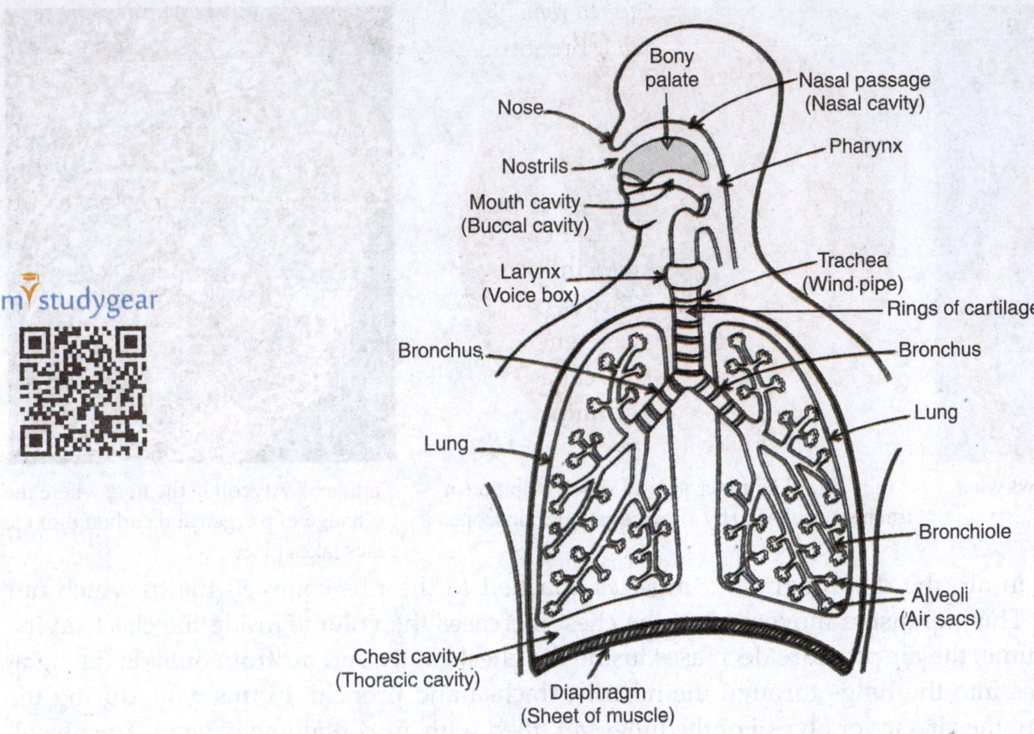

Figure 64. The human respiratory system.

or oral cavity) by a hard, bony palate so that we can breathe in air even when we are eating food (and the mouth cavity is filled with food). The nasal passage is lined with fine hair and mucus (Mucus is secreted by the glands inside the nasal passage). When air passes through the nasal passage, the dust particles and other impurities present in it are trapped by nasal hair and mucus so that clean air goes into the lungs. The part of throat between the mouth and wind pipe is called pharynx. From the nasal passage, air enters into pharynx and then goes into the wind pipe (or trachea) (see Figure 64).

The trachea is a tube which is commonly known as wind pipe. The air coming from the nostrils during breathing passes through trachea. Trachea does not collapse even when there is no air in it because it is supported by rings of soft bones called cartilage. The upper end of trachea has a voice box called larynx. The trachea runs down the neck and divides into two smaller tubes called 'bronchi' at its lower end (see Figure 64). (The singular of bronchi is bronchus). The two bronchi are connected to the two lungs. The lungs lie in the chest cavity or thoracic cavity which is separated from abdominal cavity by a muscular partition called diaphragm. The lungs are covered by two thin membranes called pleura. The lungs are enclosed in a 'rib cage' made of bones called 'ribs'. We have not shown the rib cage in Figure 64 to keep the diagram simple.

Each bronchus divides in the lungs to form a large number of still smaller tubes called 'bronchioles'. The smallest bronchioles have tiny air-sacs at their ends (see Figure 64). The pouch-like air-sacs at the ends of the smallest bronchioles are called 'alveoli' (singular alveolus). The walls of alveoli are very thin and they are surrounded by very thin blood capillaries. It is in the alveoli that oxygen is taken into the body and carbon dioxide is eliminated. In other words, **it is in the alveoli that gaseous exchange takes place.** The human lungs have been designed to maximise the exchange of gases as follows : There are millions of alveoli in the lungs. The presence of millions of alveoli in the lungs provides a very large area for the exchange of gases. And the availability of large surface area maximises the exchange of gases. For example, if all alveoli from the two human lungs are unfolded, they would give an area of about 80 square metres (which is nearly the size of a tennis court !). The diaphragm is a sheet of muscle below the lungs (see Figure 64). It helps in 'breathing in' and 'breathing out'. The muscles of chest also help in breathing in and breathing out.

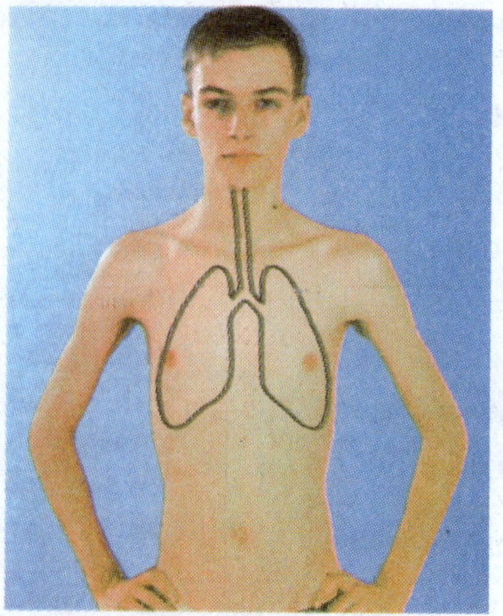

Figure 65. This picture shows where in the body our lungs are.

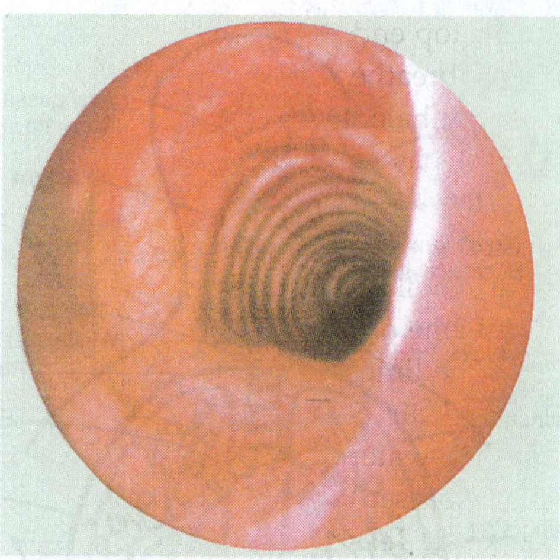

Figure 66. The inner side of our windpipe (or trachea) as viewed by a device called endoscope.

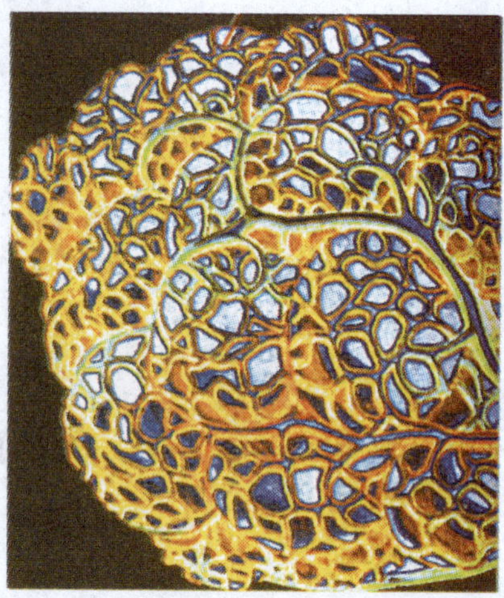

Figure 67. Alveoli in the lung where the exchange of oxygen and carbon dioxide gases takes place.

When we breathe in air, the diaphragm and muscles attached to the ribs contract due to which our chest cavity expands. This expansion movement of the chest increases the volume inside the chest cavity. Due to increase in volume, the air pressure decreases inside the chest cavity and air from outside (being at higher pressure) rushes into the lungs through the nostrils, trachea and bronchi. In this way, during the process of 'breathing in' the air sacs or alveoli of the lungs get filled with air containing oxygen. The alveoli are surrounded by very thin blood vessels called capillaries carrying blood in them. So, the oxygen of air diffuses out from the alveoli walls into the blood. The oxygen is carried by blood to all the parts of the body (This oxygen is carried by a red pigment called haemoglobin present in blood). **As the blood passes through the tissues of the body, the oxygen present in it diffuses into the cells (due to its higher concentration in the blood).** This oxygen combines with the digested food (glucose) present in the cells to release energy. Carbon dioxide gas is produced as a waste product during respiration in the cells of the body tissues. **This carbon dioxide diffuses into the blood (due to its higher concentration in body tissues).** Blood carries the carbon dioxide back to the lungs where it diffuses into the alveoli. When we breathe out air, the diaphragm and the muscles attached to the ribs relax due to which our chest cavity contracts and becomes smaller. This contraction movement of the chest pushes out carbon dioxide from the alveoli of the lungs into the trachea, nostrils and then out of the body into air. In this way the process of gaseous exchange is completed in the human respiratory system.

Please note that during the breathing cycle, when air is taken in (or inhaled) and let out (or exhaled), the lungs always contain a certain *residual volume* of air so that there is sufficient time 'for the oxygen to be absorbed' into the blood and 'for the carbon dioxide to be released' from the blood. Another point to be noted is that carbon dioxide is more soluble in water (than oxygen), so it is mostly transported in the dissolved form in our blood.

Experiment to Show That Carbon Dioxide is Produced During Respiration

We know that carbon dioxide gas turns lime-water milky. The fact that carbon dioxide is produced during respiration can be shown by demonstrating the effect of inhaled air and exhaled air on lime-water. The apparatus to demonstrate the effect of inhaled air and exhaled air on lime-water is shown in Figure 68. The apparatus consists of two boiling tubes *A* and *B* fitted with two-holed corks. The boiling tubes *A* and *B* are connected through a special type of glass tube *C*. The left arm of glass tube *C* is short which goes in the boiling tube *A*. The right arm of glass tube *C* is long and dips in lime-water in boiling tube *B* (see Figure 68). The boiling tube *A* has another bent glass tube *D* whose longer side dips in lime-water contained in it. The boiling tube *B* has also another short, bent tube *E* in it which does not dip in lime-water.

To perform the experiment, we put the top end of the tube *C* in mouth and 'breathe in' and 'breathe out' gently. When we breathe in, then the inhaled air (fresh air) enters the glass tube *D* and passes through the lime-water in boiling tube *A*. And when we breathe out, then the exhaled air (coming from our lungs) passes through the lime-water in boiling tube *B*. We continue to breathe in and breathe out for about five minutes. We will find that the lime-water in boiling tube *A* (in which inhaled air is passed) turns milky only slightly but the lime-water in boiling tube *B* (in which exhaled air is passed) turns milky appreciably. This shows that **less carbon dioxide is present in inhaled air but much more carbon dioxide is present in exhaled air.** From this observation we conclude that **carbon dioxide is produced during respiration (which comes out in exhaled air).**

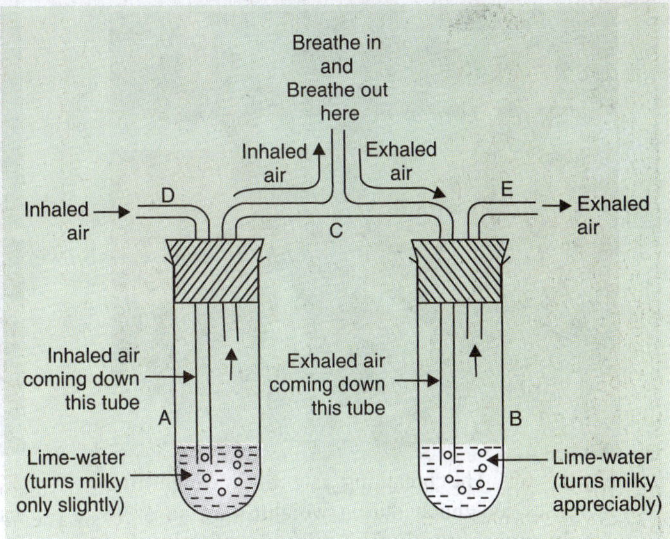

Figure 68. Testing inhaled air and exhaled air for carbon dioxide.

The air which we 'inhale' is a mixture of gases and the air which we 'exhale' is also a mixture of gases. **The only difference in the inhaled air and exhaled air is that they contain different proportions of oxygen, carbon dioxide and water vapour. (The proportion of nitrogen gas in the inhaled air and exhaled air remains the same, 78 per cent, because it is neither used up in respiration nor produced during respiration).** The proportions of oxygen, carbon dioxide and water vapour in 'inhaled air' and 'exhaled air' are given below :

Inhaled Air	
Oxygen	: **21%**
Carbon dioxide	: **0.04%**
Water vapour	: **A little**

Exhaled Air	
Oxygen	: **16.4%**
Carbon dioxide	: **4.4%**
Water vapour	: **A lot**

We can see from the above figures that the air which we inhale contains a greater proportion (21 per cent) of oxygen. Now, some of the oxygen of inhaled air is used up in breaking down glucose food during respiration, so the exhaled air which comes out after the process of respiration contains a lower proportion (16.4 per cent) of oxygen. The air which we inhale contains a lower proportion (0.04 per cent) of carbon dioxide. Now, during respiration, when oxygen breaks down glucose food, then a lot of carbon dioxide is produced, so the exhaled air which comes out after respiration contains a much higher proportion (4.4 per cent) of carbon dioxide. Again, the air which we inhale contains only a little of water vapour. Now, when glucose food is broken down by oxygen during respiration, then water is also produced (alongwith carbon dioxide). So, the exhaled air contains a lot more water vapour than inhaled air.

Rate of Breathing

The process of breathing pumps in oxygen into our body (and removes carbon dioxide). Breathing occurs involuntarily (on its own) but the rate of breathing is controlled by the respiratory system of brain. **The average breathing rate in an adult man at rest is about 15 to 18 times per minute.** This breathing rate increases with increased physical activity. For example, if we do some physical exercise (like sit-up exercise), then our breathing rate goes up considerably. This is because when we do some physical exercise, then our body needs more energy. And to produce more energy through respiration, our body requires more oxygen gas. **Rapid breathing supplies more oxygen to body cells for producing more energy required for doing physical exercise.** Thus, we breathe faster after exercise so as to produce more energy to compensate the loss of energy suffered by our body in doing exercise.

Figure 69. The breathing rate of a weightlifter increases too much during weightlifting so as to supply oxygen rapidly for the speedy breakdown of food to provide extra energy (required for lifting heavy weights).

Figure 70. Human beings do not have gills like the fish which can extract dissolved oxygen from water and utilise it for breathing. So, a deep sea diver carries an oxygen gas cylinder for breathing when he goes deep under the sea water.

We all breathe through nose. We can, however, not breathe inside water when we are diving. This is because water does not have free air or oxygen for us to breathe (and we do not have gills like the fish to utilise oxygen dissolved in water). So, the deep sea divers carry oxygen gas cylinders with them for breathing when they go under the sea.

We have just studied that oxygen required for breathing and respiration (release of energy) is carried by haemoglobin present in our blood. The normal range of haemoglobin in the blood of a healthy adult person is from 12 to 18 grams per decilitre (12 to 18 g/dL) of blood. **The deficiency of haemoglobin in the blood of a person reduces the oxygen-carrying capacity of blood resulting in breathing problems, tiredness and lack of energy.** The person looks pale and loses weight.

Many times we have heard of **carbon monoxide poisoning.** This happens as follows. Carbon monoxide gas (CO) is formed whenever a fuel burns in an insufficient supply of air. For example, if coal (or charcoal) is burned in a closed space (like a room with closed doors and windows), then a lot of carbon monoxide is formed. Carbon monoxide is also produced when petrol burns in a car engine. Now, we know that haemoglobin present in our blood carries oxygen to all the parts of our body. Haemoglobin has more affinity (or attraction) for carbon monoxide than oxygen, So, if carbon monoxide gas is inhaled by a person, then this **carbon monoxide binds very strongly with haemoglobin in the blood and prevents it from carrying oxygen to the brain and other parts of the body.** Due to lack of oxygen, the person cannot breathe properly. If carbon monoxide is inhaled for a long time, then the person becomes unconscious and can even die due to oxygen starvation.

The persons having breathing problems (or respiratory problems) are given oxygen masks to facilitate breathing. In serious cases, the patient is put on a machine called 'ventilator' in which a tube is inserted directly into the trachea (or wind pipe) of the patient to help him in breathing comfortably. Before we go further and describe the transport of materials in plants and animals, **please answer the following questions :**

Very Short Answer Type Questions

1. Do all cells use oxygen to produce energy ?
2. Name one substance which is produced in anaerobic respiration by an organism but not in aerobic respiration.
3. Name one organism which can live without oxygen.
4. In which type of respiration, aerobic or anaerobic, more energy is released ?
5. Name the substance whose build up in the muscles during vigorous physical exercise may cause cramps.
6. Which part of roots is involved in the exchange of respiratory gases ?

7. Name the process by which plant parts like roots, stems, and leaves get oxygen required for respiration.
8. Name the pores in a leaf through which respiratory exchange of gases takes place.
9. Name the areas in a woody stem through which respiratory exchange of gases takes place.
10. What is the name of the extensions of the epidermal cells of a root which help in respiration ?
11. Out of photosynthesis and respiration in plants, which process occurs :
    (*a*) all the time ?
    (*b*) only at daytime ?
12. Name the organs of breathing in fish.
13. Name an animal which absorbs oxygen through its moist skin.
14. Name an animal which depends on simple diffusion of gases for breathing.
15. Name two animals which breathe through gills.
16. The trachea divides into two tubes at its lower end. What is the name of these tubes ?
17. Where does the blood absorb oxygen in the human body ?
18. Name the red pigment which carries oxygen in blood.
19. Which gases are exchanged in your lungs ?
20. Where in the lungs does gas exchange take place ?
21. What is the name of tiny air-sacs at the end of smallest bronchioles in the lungs ?
22. What is the other name of wind-pipe ?
23. What organs are attached to the two bronchi ?
24. In the lungs :
    (*a*) what substance is taken into the body ?
    (*b*) what substance is removed from the body ?
25. State whether the following statements are true or false :
    (*a*) During respiration, the plants take CO_2 and release O_2.
    (*b*) Energy can be produced in cells without oxygen.
    (*c*) Fish and earthworm exchange gases during respiration in the same way.
26. Fill in the following blanks with suitable words :
    (*a*) The organs of respiration in man are the.................
    (*b*) The actual exchange of gases takes place in the................of the lungs.
    (*c*) ....in the lungs provide a very large surface area for gaseous exchange.
    (*d*) Yeast undergoes.................respiration whereas *Amoeba* undergoes..................respiration.
    (*e*) Gills are the breathing organs in................

Short Answer Type Questions

27. Explain why, a land plant may die if its roots remain waterlogged for a long time.
28. What are the differences between aerobic and anaerobic respiration ? Name some organisms that use anaerobic mode of respiration.
29. Name the final product/products obtained in the anaerobic respiration, if it takes place :
    (*a*) in a plant (like yeast).
    (*b*) in an animal tissue (like muscles).
30. What type of respiration takes place in human muscles during vigorous physical exercise ? Give reason for your answer.
31. Name the type of respiration in which the end products are :
    (*a*) C_2H_5OH and CO_2
    (*b*) CO_2 and H_2O
    (*c*) Lactic acid
    Give one example of each case where such a respiration can occur.
32. Define breathing. State the differences between breathing and respiration.
33. What are the different ways in which glucose is oxidised to provide energy in various organisms ? Give one example of each.

34. Explain why, when air is taken in and let out during breathing, the lungs always contain a residual volume of air.

35. Explain why, it is dangerous to inhale air containing carbon monoxide.

36. Describe the process of respiration in *Amoeba*. State whether it is anaerobic respiration or aerobic respiration.

37. State the three common features of all the respiratory organs like skin, gills and lungs.

38. Describe the process of respiration in fish.

39. What would be the consequences of deficiency of haemoglobin in our bodies ?

40. Describe the process of respiration in the following parts of a plant :
(*a*) Root (*b*) Stem (*c*) Leaves

41. (*a*) What is meant by aquatic animals and terrestrial animals ?
(*b*) From where do the aquatic animals and terrestrial animals obtain oxygen for breathing and respiration ?

42. Why do fishes die when taken out of water ?

43. Why is the rate of breathing in aquatic organisms much faster than in terrestrial organisms ?

44. Name the energy currency in the living organisms. When and where is it produced ?

45. Explain why, plants have low energy needs as compared to animals.

46. Explain how, it would benefit deep sea divers if humans also had gills.

Long Answer Type Questions

47. (*a*) What is the function of the respiratory system ?
(*b*) What are the major organs of respiratory system in man (or humans) ?
(*c*) Draw a labelled diagram of the human respiratory system.

48. (*a*) Explain how, the air we breathe in gets cleaned while passing through the nasal passage.
(*b*) Why do the walls of trachea not collapse when there is less air in it ?
(*c*) How are oxygen and carbon dioxide exchanged in our body during respiration ?
(*d*) How are lungs designed in human beings to maximise the exchange of gases ?

49. (*a*) Give the main points of difference between respiration in plants and respiration in animals.
(*b*) Describe the exchange of gases which takes place in the leaves of a plant (*a*) during daytime, and (*b*) at night.
(*c*) Which contains more carbon dixoide : exhaled air or inhaled air ? Why ?

50. (*a*) "Respiration is a vital function of the body". Justify this statement.
(*b*) What is the main difference between aerobic respiration and anaerobic respiration ? Give one example of each.
(*c*) What type of repiration takes place (*i*) in yeast, and (*ii*) in humans ?

51. (*a*) Why is diffusion insufficient to meet the oxygen requirements of large multicellular organisms like humans ?
(*b*) What type of arrangement exists in the bodies of large animals to meet their oxygen requirements adequately ?
(*c*) What advantage a terrestrial animal has over an aquatic animal with regard to obtaining oxygen for respiration ?

Multiple Choice Questions (MCQs)

52. Which of the following is not produced during anaerobic respiration in unicellular fungus ?
(*a*) C_2H_5OH (*b*) H_2O (*c*) CO_2 (*d*) ATP

53. One of the following organisms can live without oxygen of air. This organism is :
(*a*) *Amoeba* (*b*) Yak (*c*) Yeast (*d*) Leech

54. During respiration, the exchange of gases takes place in :
(*a*) bronchi (*b*) alveoli (*c*) bronchioles (*d*) trachea

55. In one of the following organisms, the gaseous exchange during repiration does not take place through cell membrane/skin. This organism is :
(*a*) Electric eel (*b*) Leech (*c*) Earthworm (*d*) *Amoeba*

56. Which of the following is correct for the process of anaerobic respiration ?

	Carbon dioxide always produced	A lot of energy released
(a)	No	Yes
(b)	No	No
(c)	Yes	No
(d)	Yes	Yes

57. Which of the following increases in muscle cells when they are lacking in oxygen ?
(a) carbon dioxide (b) lactose (c) lactic acid (d) uric acid

58. Internal respiration may be defined as :
(a) breathing in and releasing of oxygen in the tissue
(b) the oxidation of food substances to release energy
(c) the building up (synthesis) of complex substances
(d) getting rid of carbon dixode that would accumulate in the tissues.

59. When air is blown from mouth into a test-tube containing lime water, the lime water turns milky due to the presence of :
(a) oxygen (b) carbon dioxide (c) nitrogen (d) water vapour

60. Which of the following is the correct sequence of air passage during inhalation ?
(a) nostrils ⟶ larynx ⟶ pharynx ⟶ trachea ⟶ lungs
(b) nasal passage ⟶ trachea ⟶ pharynx ⟶ larynx ⟶ alveoli
(c) larynx ⟶ nostrils ⟶ pharynx ⟶ lungs
(d) nostrils ⟶ pharynx ⟶ larynx ⟶ trachea ⟶ alevoli

61. Lack of oxygen in muscles often leads to cramps in the legs of sprinters. This is due to conversion of pyruvate to :
(a) ethanol (b) carbon dioxide (c) acetic acid (d) lactic acid

62. During the deficiency of oxygen in tissues of human beings, pyruvic acid is converted into lactic acid in :
(a) cytoplasm (b) chloroplast (c) mitochondria (d) golgi body

63. Which of the following statements are correct ?
(i) pyruvate can be converted into ethanol and carbon dioxide by yeast
(ii) fermentation takes place in the case of aerobic bacteria
(iii) fermentation takes place in mitochondria
(iv) fermentation is a form of anaerobic respiration
(a) (i) and (iii) (b) (ii) and (iv) (c) (i) and (iv) (d) (ii) and (iii)

64. Which of the following statements are true about respiration ?
(i) during inhalation, ribs move inward and diaphragm is raised.
(ii) the gaseous exchange takes place in the alveoli.
(iii) haemoglobin has greater affinity for carbon dioxide than oxygen.
(iv) alveoli increase surface area for the exchange of gases
(a) (i) and (iv) (b) (ii) and (iii) (c) (i) and (iii) (d) (ii) and (iv)

65. Which of the following is known as the energy currency of cells in biology ?
(a) DTP (b) PDP (c) ATP (d) DDT

66. The two organisms which breathe only through their moist skin are :
(a) fish and frog (b) frog and earthworm
(c) leech and earthworm (d) fish and earthworm

67. One of the following animals does not use tracheae as the respiratory organs. This animal is :
(a) grasshopper (b) prawn (c) mosquito (d) cockroach

68. The photosynthesis in a plant is not taking place during the day time if the plant is releasing :
(a) water vapour (b) oxygen (c) carbon dioxide (d) all the above

69. The breathing and respiration in woody stem of a plant takes place through :
(a) root hair (b) lenticels (c) closed stomata (d) open stomata

70. One of the following organism does not depend on simple diffusion of gases for breathing and respiration. This organism is :
(*a*) Amoeba (*b*) Prawn (*c*) Planaria (*d*) Bryophyllum

71. During marathon, we sometimes get painful contractions of leg muscles due to the accumulation of one of the following in leg muscles. This is :
(*a*) carbon dioxide (*b*) alcohol (*c*) lactose (*d*) lactic acid

72. In cockroaches, air enters the body through :
(*a*) lungs (*b*) gills (*c*) spiracles (*d*) skin

73. Which of the following is most likely to have a much higher breathing rate ?
(*a*) man (*b*) fish (*c*) dog (*d*) sparrow

Questions Based on High Order Thinking Skills (HOTS)

74. During the respiration of an organism A, 1 molecule of glucose produces 2 ATP molecules whereas in the respiration of another organism B, 1 molecule of glucose produces 38 ATP molecules.
(*a*) Which organism is undergoing aerobic respiration ?
(*b*) Which organism is undergoing anaerobic respiration ?
(*c*) Which type of organism, A or B, can convert glucose into alcohol ?
(*d*) Name one organism which behaves like A.
(*e*) Name two organisms which behave like B.

75. A, B and C are three living organisms. The organism A is a unicellullar fungus which can live without air. It is used in the commercial production of an organic compound P from molasses. The organism B is a unicellular animal which lives in water and feeds and moves by using pseudopodia. It breathes through an organelle Q. The organism C is a tiny animal which acts as a carrier of malarial parasite. It breathes and respires through a kind of tiny holes R and air-tubes S in its body.
(*a*) What are organisms (*i*) A (*ii*) B, and (*iii*) C ?
(*b*) Name (*i*) P (*ii*) Q (*iii*) R, and (*iv*) S.
(*c*) Which organism/organisms undergo aerobic respiration ?
(*d*) Which organism/organisms undergo anaerobic respiration ?

76. There are five animals P, Q, R, S and T. The animal P always lives in water and has gills for breathing. The animal Q can stay in water as well as on land and can breathe both, through moist skin and lungs. The animal R lives in soil and breathes only through its skin. The animal S lives on land and breathes through spiracles and tracheae. And animal T lives in water and breathes through its cell membrane.
(*a*) Which of the animals could be *Amoeba* ?
(*b*) Which of the animals could be frog ?
(*c*) Which animal could be fish ?
(*d*) Which animal could be grasshopper ?
(*e*) Which animal could be earthworm ?

77. Some sugar solution is taken in a test-tube and a little of substance X in powder form is added to it. The mouth of test-tube is closed with a cork and allowed to stand for sometime. On opening the cork, a characteristic smell of substance Y is obtained and a gas Z is also observed to be formed. The gas Z extinguishes a burning matchstick.
(*a*) What could be (*i*) X, (*ii*) Y, and (*iii*) Z ?
(*b*) What is the process of converting sugar into substance Y by the action of X known as ?
(*c*) What type of respiration is exhibited by X in the above process ?

78. Consider the following chemical reactions which take place in different organisms/tissues under various conditions :
(*i*) Glucose $\xrightarrow{\text{Respiration}}$ Ethanol + Carbon dioxide + Energy
(*ii*) Glucose $\xrightarrow{\text{Respiration}}$ Carbon dioxide + Water + Energy
(*iii*) Glucose $\xrightarrow{\text{Respiration}}$ Lactic acid + Energy
(*a*) Name one organism which respires according to equation (*i*) above.
(*b*) Name one organism which respires according to equation (*ii*) above.

(*c*) When and where does respiration represented by equation (*iii*) above take place ?

(*d*) Which equation/equations represent aerobic respiration ?

(*e*) Which equation/equations represent anaerobic respiration ?

(*f*) Which of the above reactions produces the maximum amount of energy ?

79. When a person breathes in air, the air enters into his body through an organ A having two holes B in it. The air then passes through pharynx and larynx and enters into a tube C. The tube C divides into two smaller tubes D at its lower end. The two smaller tubes are attached to two respiratory organs E. Each smaller tube divides inside the organs E to form a large number of still smaller tubes called F. The smallest tubes F have air-sacs G at their ends in which gaseous exchange takes place in the body of the person. What are A, B, C, D, E, F and G ?

80. An organism X having breathing organs A lives on land. When organism X goes under water, it cannot survive for a long time unless carrying an oxygen cylinder. On the other hand, the organism Y having breathing organs B always lives in water and if taken out of water, it dies after a short while. A third organism Z having breathing organs C and D which lives on the banks of ponds, lakes and rivers can survive on land as well as in water equally well.

(*a*) What could organism X be ? Name the breathing organs A.

(*b*) What could organism Y be ? Name the breathing organs B.

(*c*) What could organism Z be ? Name the breathing organs C and D.

(*d*) Out of X, Y and Z, which organism is (*i*) amphibian, (*ii*) aquatic, and (*iii*) terrestrial ?

ANSWERS

1. No **2.** Ethanol **5.** Lactic acid **7.** Diffusion **10.** Root hair **11.** (*a*) Respiration (*b*) Photosynthesis **17.** Alveoli in lungs **24.** (*a*) Oxygen (*b*) Carbon dioxide **25.** (*a*) False (*b*)True (*c*) False **26.** (*a*) lungs (*b*) alveoli (*c*) Alveoli (*d*) anaerobic; aerobic (*e*) fish **31.** (*a*) Anaerobic respiration in yeast (*b*) Aerobic respiration (*c*) Anaerobic respiration in muscle tissue of animals **44.** ATP **46.** The deep sea divers could remain under sea water even without carrying oxygen cylinders for breathing (because they could then extract dissolved oxygen from water for breathing purpose just like fish) **52.** (*b*) **53.** (*c*) **54.** (*b*) **55.** (*a*) **56.** (*b*) **57.** (*c*) **58.** (*b*) **59.** (*b*) **60.** (*d*) **61.** (*d*) **62.** (*a*) **63.** (*c*) **64.** (*d*) **65.** (*c*) **66.** (*c*) **67.** (*b*) **68.** (*c*) **69.** (*b*) **70.** (*b*) **71.** (*d*) **72.** (*c*) **73.** (*b*) **74.** (*a*) B (*b*) A (*c*) A (*d*) Yeast (*e*) Man, Dog **75.** (*a*) (*i*) Yeast (*ii*) *Amoeba* (*iii*) Mosquito (*b*) (*i*) Ethanol (*ii*) Cell membrane (*iii*) Spiracles (*iv*) Tracheae (*c*) B and C (*d*) A **76.** (*a*) T (*b*) Q (*c*) P (*d*) S (*e*) R **77.** (*a*) (*i*) Yeast (*ii*) Ethanol (*iii*) Carbon dioxide (*b*) Fermentation (*c*) Anaerobic respiration **78.** (*a*) Yeast (*b*) Man (*c*) In animal's muscles ; When the animal needs extra energy for doing heavy physical activity (*d*) (*ii*) (*e*) (*i*) and (*iii*) (*f*) (*ii*) **79.** A = Nose; B = Nostrils ; C = Trachea (or Windpipe) ; D = Bronchi ; E = Lungs ; F = Bronchioles ; G = Alveoli **80.** (*a*) Man; Lungs (*b*) Fish ; Gills (*c*) Frog ; Lungs and Skin (*d*) (*i*) Z (*ii*) Y (*iii*) X

TRANSPORT

The body of every organism (plant or animal) is made up of cells. A large organism has millions and millions of cells in its body. In order that the organism may be able to maintain its life and survive, all its cells must be supplied with essential substances like food, oxygen, water, etc. So, **some arrangement is required inside an organism which can carry the essential substances to all its parts so that they reach each and every cell of its body.**

In everyday language, 'transport' means 'to carry things from one place to another'. **In biology, transport is a life process in which a substance absorbed (or made) in one part of the body of an organism is carried to other parts of its body.** Large organisms (large plants and animals) need transport systems in their bodies to supply all their cells with food, oxygen, water, and other materials. In fact, special tissues and organs are needed for the transport of substances in plants and animals because these tissues and organs can pick up the essential substances like food, oxygen, water, etc., at one end of their body and carry them to all other parts.

We will now study the transport system of plants and of human beings, and describe the parts which make up these systems. In other words, we will learn how plants and animals carry substances from one part of their body to another.

TRANSPORT IN PLANTS

Transport system in plants is less elaborate than in animals (including human beings). Plants are less active, so their cells do not need to be supplied with materials so quickly. Also, due to the branching shape of a plant, all the cells of a plant can get oxygen for respiration and carbon dioxide for photosynthesis directly from the air by diffusion. So, the only substances which are to be supplied to a plant through a transport system are water and minerals (which they can't get from the air). Another job of the transport system of plants is to transport food prepared in the leaves to the various parts of the plant like stems, roots, etc. The plants have two types of conducting tissues called xylem and phloem. Xylem tissues carry water and minerals whereas phloem tissues carry the food prepared by the plants (see Figure 71). We can now say that :

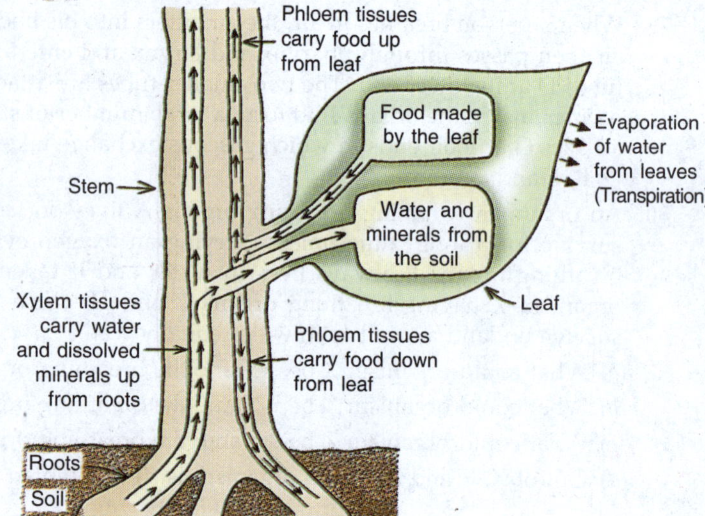

Figure 71. Diagram to show the transport system in plants.

The plants have two transport systems :

1. **Xylem** which carries water and minerals, and
2. **Phloem** which carries the food materials which the plant makes (Phloem also carries the hormones made by the plants in their root and shoot tips).

The transport of materials in a plant can be divided into two parts :

(*i*) Transport of water and minerals in the plant, and
(*ii*) Transport of food and other substances (like hormones) in the plant.

We will now discuss both the parts of the transport system in plants in detail, one by one. Let us start with the transport of water and minerals in the plants.

Transport of Water and Minerals

Plants require water for making food by photosynthesis. Plants also need mineral salts for various purposes (such as making proteins, etc.). Water and minerals are absorbed from the soil by the roots of the plant and transported to the various parts of the plant like stem, leaves and flowers. In the leaves, water is used in making food by photosynthesis. The water and minerals dissolved in it move from the roots of the plant to its leaves through the two kinds of elements of the xylem tissue called **xylem vessels** and **tracheids.** Xylem vessels and tracheids are both non-living conducting tissues which have thick walls. Let us discuss xylem vessels and tracheids in a little more detail.

1. Xylem Vessels

The xylem vessel is a non-living, long tube which runs like a drainpipe through the plant [see Figure 72(*a*)]. A xylem vessel is made of many hollow, dead cells (called vessel elements), joined end to end. The end walls of the cells have broken down so a long, open tube is formed. Xylem vessels run from the roots of the plant right up through the stem and reach the leaves. The xylem vessels branch into every leaf of the plant.

Xylem vessels do not contain the cytoplasm or nuclei. The walls of xylem vessels are made of cellulose and lignin. Lignin is a very hard and strong substance, so xylem vessels also provide strength to the stems and help to keep the plant upright. Wood is made almost entirely of lignified xylem vessels. Xylem vessels have pits in their thick cell walls. Pits are not open pores. Pits are the thin areas of the cell wall where no

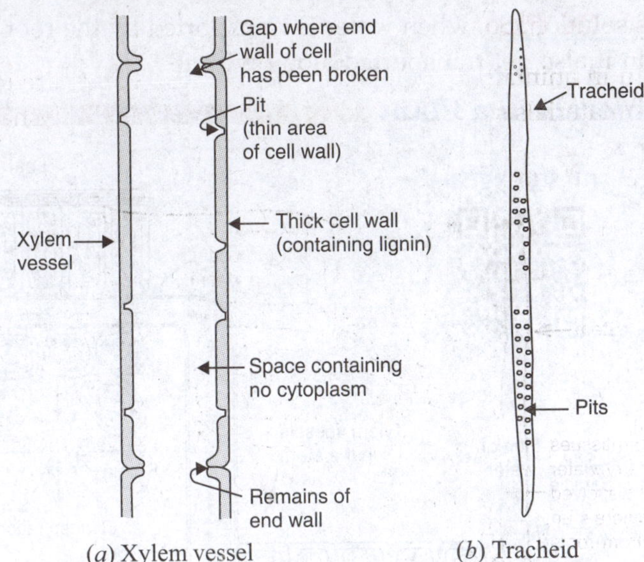

Figure 72. The structure of xylem vessels and tracheids.

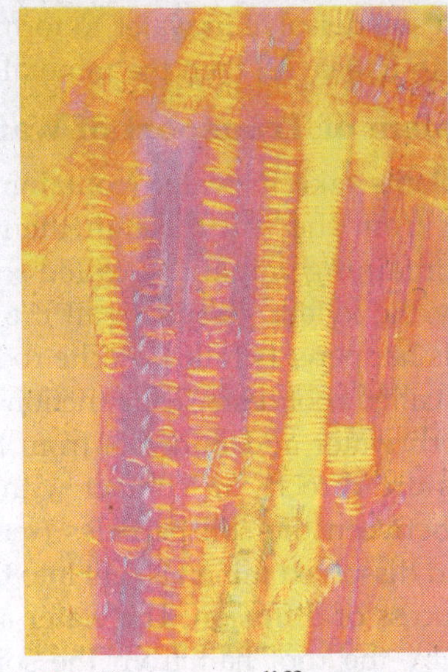

Figure 73. We can see different types of xylem vessels in this micrograph (Micrograph is a photograph taken using a microscope).

lignin has been deposited. Pits have unthickened cellulose cell wall. **In flowering plants, either only xylem vessels transport water or both xylem vessels and tracheids transport water.**

2. Tracheids

Tracheids are long, thin, spindle shaped cells with pits in their thick cell walls [see Figure 72(*b*)]. Water flows from one tracheid to another through pits. Tracheids are dead cells with lignified walls but they do not have open ends, so they do not form vessels. They are elongated cells with tapering ends. Even though their ends are not completely open, tracheids have pits in their walls, so water can pass from one tracheid to another through these pits. **Although all the plants have tracheids, they are the only water conducting tissue in non-flowering plants.**

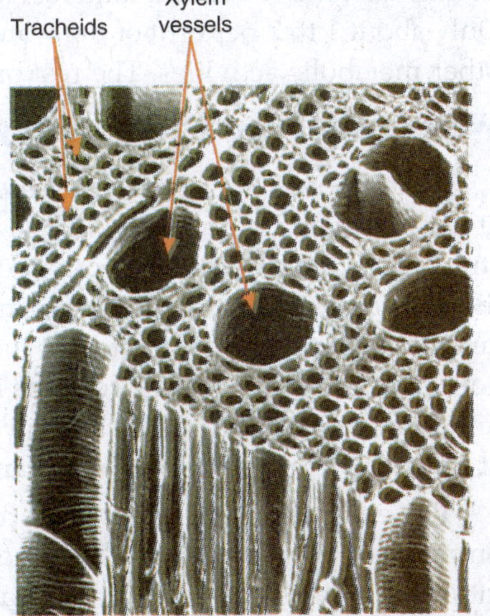

Figure 74. This is the scanning electron micrograph of the xylem tissues in the stem of a plant. We can see the xylem vessels and tracheids which taken together form the xylem tissue (Scanning electron micrograph is a highly magnified photograph taken by scanning electron microscope which uses an electron beam instead of light to produce highly magnified images).

Before we describe the mechanism of the transport of water from the roots of a plant to the leaves, we should know the meanings of the terms epidermis, endodermis, root cortex and root xylem. The outer layer of cells in the root is called epidermis. Epidermis is only one cell thick. The layer of cells around the vascular tissues (xylem and phloem) in the root is called endodermis (It is the innermost layer of cortex). The part of root between the epidermis and endodermis is called root cortex. And the xylem tissue present in roots is called root xylem. Please note that in a root, the root hair are at its outer edge but the root xylem vessels (which carry water to the other parts of plant) are at the centre of the root. And in-between the root hair and root xylem are epidermis, root cortex and endodermis. So, before water absorbed by root hair from the soil reaches the root xylem, it has to pass through the epidermis, root cortex and endodermis.

Another point to be noted is that the minerals needed by the plants are taken up by the plants in inorganic form such as nitrates and phosphates. These minerals are present in the soil. The minerals present in soil dissolve in water to form an aqueous solution. So, when water is transported by the root of the plant to its leaves, then the minerals dissolved in it also get transported along with it.

Mechanism of Transport of Water and Minerals in a Plant

The plants take in water (containing dissolved minerals) from the soil through their roots. This water (containing minerals) called xylem sap is carried by the xylem vessels to all the parts of the plant. This happens as follows : The roots of a plant have hair called root hairs. The function of root hairs is to absorb water and minerals from the soil. The root hairs are directly in contact with the film of water in-between the soil particles (see Figure 75). Water (and dissolved minerals) get into the root hairs by the process of diffusion. The water and minerals absorbed by the root hair from the soil pass from cell to cell by osmosis through the epidermis, root cortex, endodermis and reach the root xylem (see Figure 75).

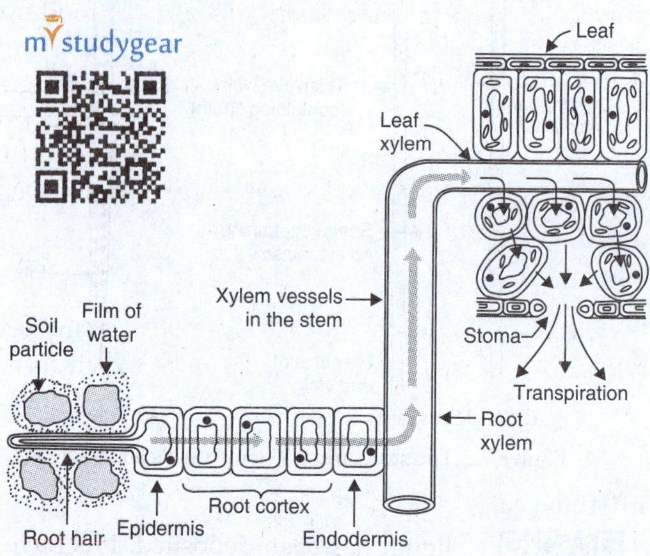

Figure 75. Diagram to show how water (and dissolved minerals) are transported from the soil up to the leaf of a plant.

The xylem vessels of the root of the plant are connected to the xylem vessels of its stem. So, the water (containing dissolved minerals) enters from the root xylem vessels into stem xylem vessels. The xylem vessels of the stem branch into the leaves of the plants. So, the water and minerals carried by the xylem vessels in the stem reach the leaves through the branched xylem vessels which enter from the petiole (stalk of the leaf) into each and every part of the leaf. In this way, the water and minerals from the soil reach through the root and stem to the leaves of the plant. Only about 1 to 2 per cent of the water absorbed by the plant is used up by the plant in photosynthesis and other metabolic activities. The rest of water is lost as water vapour to the air through transpiration.

Water is Sucked Up by the Xylem Vessels

Water moves up into xylem vessels in the same way that a cold drink moves up a straw when we suck at the upper end of the straw. Now, when we suck a straw, we are reducing the pressure at the top of the straw. The cold drink at the bottom of the straw is at a higher pressure (which is atmospheric pressure), so the cold drink flows up the straw into our mouth. The same thing happens with the water in the xylem vessels. The pressure at the top of the xylem vessels (in the leaves) is lowered whereas the pressure at the bottom of the xylem vessels remains high. Due to this water flows up the xylem vessels into the leaves. An important question now arises : How is the pressure at the top of the xylem vessels reduced ? **The pressure at the top of xylem vessels in a plant is reduced due to transpiration.** This is discussed below :

The evaporation of water from the leaves of a plant is called transpiration. The leaves of a plant have tiny pores on their surface which are called stomata. A lot of water from the leaves keeps on evaporating into the air through the stomata. This loss of water (as water vapour) from the leaves of a plant is called transpiration. Since the cells of the leaf are losing water by transpiration, so water from the xylem vessels in the leaf will travel to the cells by osmosis to make up this loss of water. Thus, water is constantly being taken away from the top of the xylem vessels in the leaves to supply it to the cells in the leaves. This reduces the effective pressure at the top of the xylem vessels, so that water flows up into them (from the soil). Thus, **the continuous evaporation of water (or transpiration) from the cells of a leaf creates a kind of suction which pulls up water through the xylem vessels.** In this way, the process of transpiration helps in the upward movement of water (and dissolved minerals) from the roots to the leaves through the stem.

Transport of Food and Other Substances

Leaves make food by the process of photosynthesis. The food made by leaves is in the form of simple sugar (glucose). Other types of substances called plant hormones are made in the tips of roots and shoots. Now, every part of the plant needs food. So, food made in the leaves of a plant has to be transported (or carried) to all the parts of the plant like branches, stem and roots, etc. The food manufactured by the leaves of a plant is transported to its all other parts through a kind of tubes called phloem (which are present in all the parts of a plant). **The transport of food from the leaves to other parts of the plant is called translocation.** Thus, phloem translocates the food (or sugar) made in the leaves. The movement of food materials (and other substances like hormones) through phloem depends on the action of living cells called sieve tubes.

Phloem Contains Sieve Tubes

Like xylem vessels, phloem is made of many cells joined end to end to form long tubes (see Figure 76). However, the end walls of the cells which form phloem are not completely broken down. The end walls of cells in the phloem form sieve plates, which have small holes in them. These holes in the sieve plates allow the food to pass along the phloem tubes. The cells of phloem are called sieve tubes (or sieve elements). **Sieve tubes which form phloem are living cells which contain cytoplasm but no nucleus.** The sieve tube cells do not have lignin in their walls. **Each sieve tube cell has a companion cell next to it** (see Figure 76). The companion cell has a nucleus and many other organelles. Companion cells supply the sieve tubes with some of their requirements.

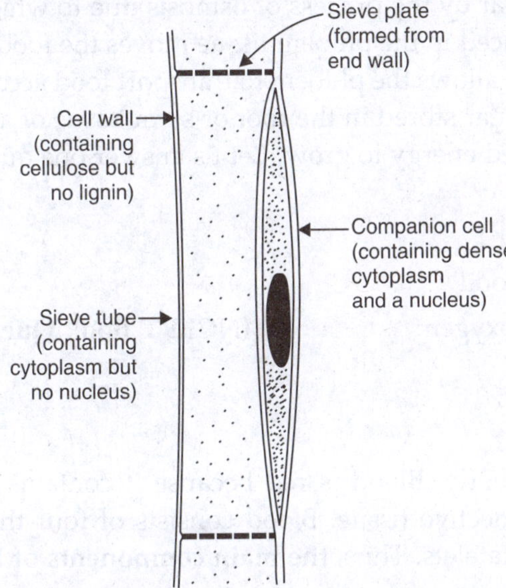

Figure 76. The structure of phloem (made of sieve tubes).

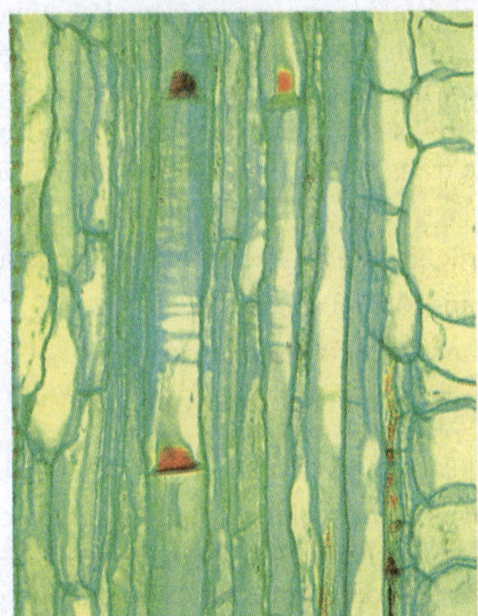

Figure 77. This is the micrograph of a longitudinal section through phloem tissue of a plant made up of sieve tubes (alongwith their companion cells). The red triangles in the above micrograph are the places where sieve plates existed.

The food is made in the mesophyll cells (or photosynthetic cells) of a leaf. The food (like sugar) made by the mesophyll cells of a leaf enters into the sieve tubes of the phloem. Interconnected phloem tubes are present in all the parts of the plant. So, once the food (like sugar) enters the phloem tubes in the leaves, it is transported (or carried) to all other parts of the plant by the

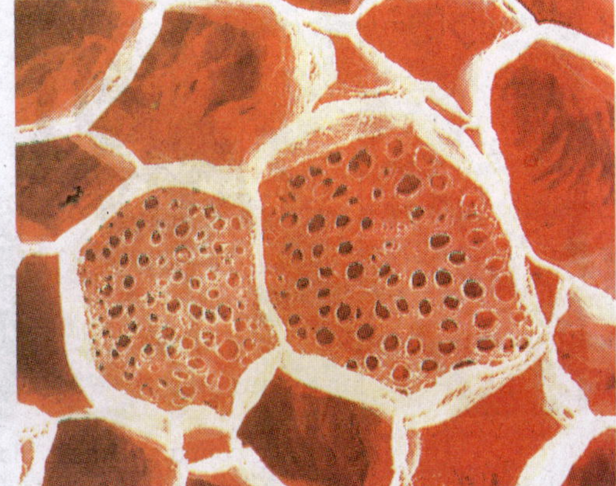

Figure 78. We can see the sieve plates and sieve tubes clearly in this transverse section of phloem.

network of phloem tubes present in all the parts of the plant like stem and roots. The translocation (transport of food from leaves to other parts of the plant) is necessary because every part of the plant needs food for obtaining energy, for building its parts and maintaining its life. Please note that when food is transported in a plant through a network of phloem tubes, then other substances made by the plant (like hormones) are also carried by the phloem tubes from one part of the plant to its other parts.

We have already studied that **the movement of water (and dissolved salts) in xylem is always upwards (from soil to leaves)** and it is caused by the suction of water at the top because of low pressure created by transpiration from leaves. **The movement of food in phloem can be, however, upwards or downwards** depending on the needs of the plant. We will now describe how food moves in the phloem tissue of a plant.

Mechanism of Transport of Food in a Plant

The movement of food in phloem (or translocation) takes place by utilising energy. This happens as follows : The sugar (food) made in leaves is loaded into the sieve tubes of phloem tissue by using energy from ATP. Water now enters into sieve tubes containing sugar by the process of osmosis due to which the pressure in the phloem tissue rises. This high pressure produced in the phloem tissue moves the food to all the parts of the plant having less pressure in their tissues. This allows the phloem to transport food according to the needs of the plant. For example, in spring, even the sugar stored in the root or stem tissue of a plant would be transported through phloem to the buds which need energy to grow. Let us answer one question now.

Sample Problem. The xylem in plants are responsible for :

(*a*) transport of water (*b*) transport of food

(*c*) transport of amino acids (*d*) transport of oxygen **(NCERT Book Question)**

Answer. (*a*) transport of water.

BLOOD

Blood is a red coloured liquid which circulates in our body. Blood is red because it contains a red pigment called haemoglobin in its red cells. Blood is a connective tissue. Blood consists of four things : plasma, red blood corpuscles, white blood corpuscles and platelets. Thus, **the main components of blood are :**

1. Plasma,
2. Red Blood Corpuscles (or Red Blood Cells),
3. White Blood Corpuscles (or White Blood Cells), and
4. Platelets.

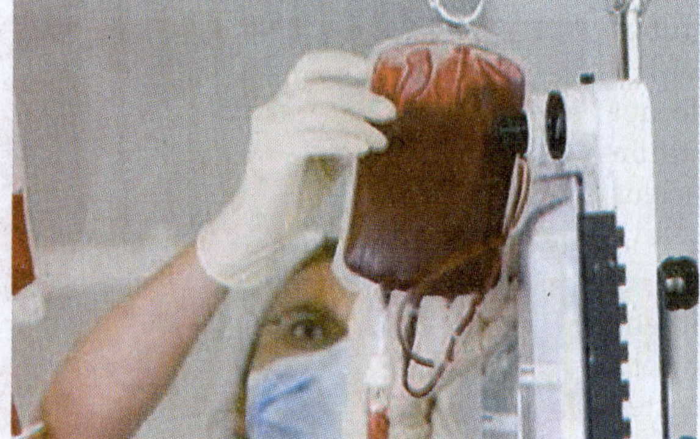

Figure 79. This plastic bag contains human blood. The blood comes from donors. It is sent to hospitals in plastic packs.

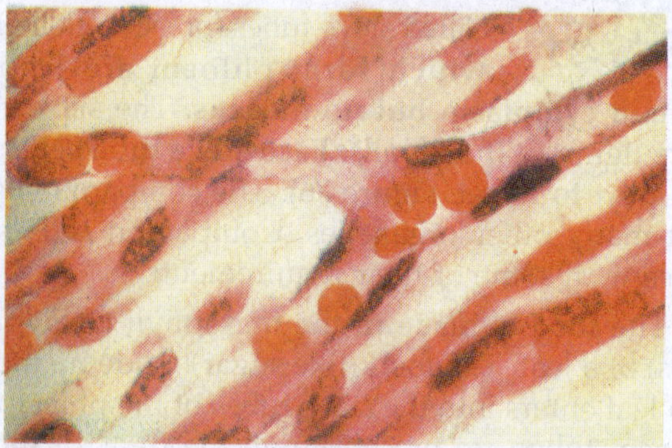

Figure 80. There are about 5 million red cells in one drop of blood. This micrograph shows red blood cells moving through a capillary.

Plasma is a liquid (which is also called fluid matrix) and the three types of cells, red blood cells, white blood cells and platelets keep floating in it. We can now define blood as follows : **Blood is a liquid (or fluid matrix) called plasma with red cells, white cells and platelets floating in it.** We will now describe all the four components of blood in a little more detail.

Plasma

The liquid part (or fluid part) of blood is called plasma. Plasma is a colourless liquid which consists mainly of water with many substances dissolved in it. Plasma contains about 90 per cent water. Plasma also contains dissolved substances such as proteins, digested food, common salt, waste products (like carbon dioxide and urea), and hormones. Plasma carries all these dissolved substances from one part to another part in the body. Red blood cells, white blood cells and platelets are immersed in this liquid called plasma.

Red Blood Cells

Red blood cells are red in colour due to the presence of a red pigment called haemoglobin inside them (see Figure 81). Red blood cells (RBC) are carriers of oxygen. **Red blood cells carry oxygen from the lungs to all the cells of the body.** It is actually the haemoglobin present in red blood cells which carries oxygen in the body. Haemoglobin performs a very important function of carrying oxygen from lungs to body tissues. Haemoglobin also carries some of the carbon dioxide from body tissues to the lungs (most of carbon dioxide is carried by plasma of blood in the dissolved form). Red blood cells are circular in shape. **Red blood cells do not have nuclei.** Red blood cells have to be made quickly because they do not live for very long. Each red blood cell lives for about four months. One reason for the short life of red blood cells is that they do not have nuclei. It has been estimated that about three million red blood cells of the human blood die everyday but four times that number are made in the bone marrow everyday. So, **when we donate blood to save the life of a person, then the loss of blood from our body can be made up very quickly, within a day.** This is because red blood cells are made very fast in our bone marrow. Please note that most of the cells in blood are red blood cells.

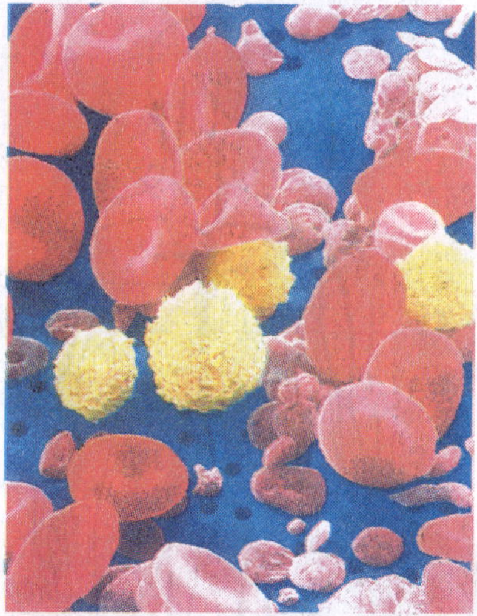

Figure 81. This micrograph shows the different types of cells in blood : red cells, white cells and platelets (small pink cells).

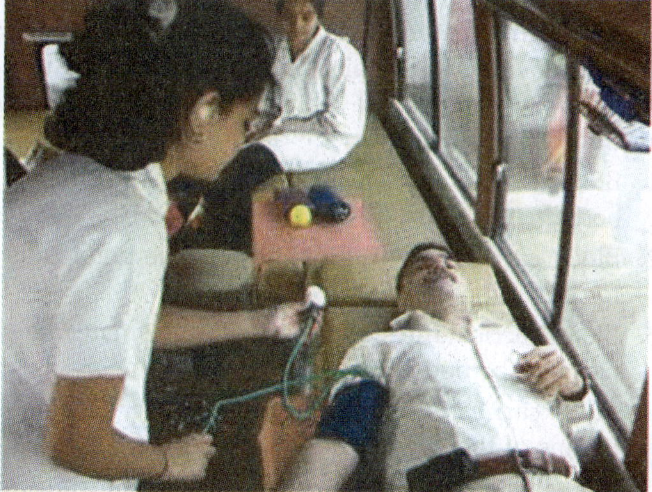

Figure 82. This person is donating blood. Our body can make up the loss of this blood very quickly. Blood donation saves other peoples' lives who have met with an accident or are seriously ill. We should make it a habit to donate blood periodically. Remember : '*Rakt daan*' is '*jeevan daan*'.

White Blood Cells

White blood cells fight infection and protect us from diseases (see Figure 81). This is because white blood cells help to fight against germs and other foreign bodies which cause diseases. Some white blood cells can eat up the germs (like bacteria) which cause diseases. Other white blood cells make chemicals known as 'antibodies' to fight against infection. In other words, white blood cells manufacture antibodies which are responsible for providing immunity in our body (due to which we are protected from disease and infection). In fact, **white blood cells are called soldiers of the body.** This is because they protect the body from the attack of disease-causing germs (pathogens) and other harmful foreign materials. White blood cells are either spherical in shape or irregular in shape. All the white blood cells have a nucleus though the shape of nucleus is different in different types of white blood cells. White blood cells (WBC) in the blood are much smaller in number than red blood cells.

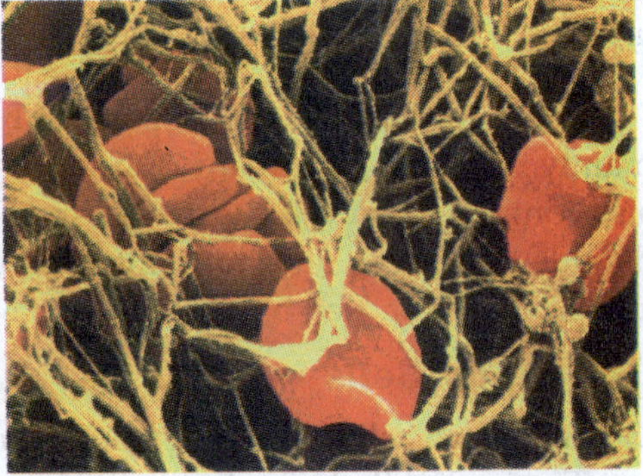

Figure 83. When we get a cut anywhere on our body, then blood starts coming out. Platelets present in blood produce a mesh of fine threads which trap the red blood cells forming a clot that blocks the cut and stops bleeding.

Platelets

Platelets are the tiny fragments of special cells formed in the bone marrow (see Figure 81). Platelets do not have nuclei. **Platelets help in the coagulation of blood (or clotting of blood) in a cut or wound.** For example, when a cut or wound starts bleeding, then platelets help clot the blood (make the blood semi-solid) due to which further bleeding stops (see Figure 83). All the blood cells are made in the bone marrow from the cells called stem cells.

Functions of Blood

Blood has three main functions in the human body. These are : Transport of substances (like respiratory gases, oxygen and carbon dioxide; digested food or nutrients; waste products; hormones; enzymes and ions) from one part of the body to the other, Protection against disease, and Regulation of body temperature. We can now say that : **The important functions of blood in our body are as follows :**

1. Blood carries **oxygen** from the lungs to different parts of the body.
2. Blood carries **carbon dioxide** from the body cells to the lungs for breathing out.
3. Blood carries **digested food** from the small intestine to all the parts of the body.
4. Blood carries **hormones** from the endocrine glands to different organs of the body (where they are needed).
5. Blood carries a waste product called **urea** from the liver to the kidneys for excretion in urine.
6. Blood **protects** the body from diseases. This is because white blood cells kill the bacteria and other germs which cause diseases.
7. Blood regulates the body temperature. This is because the blood capillaries in our skin help to keep our body temperature constant at about 37°C.

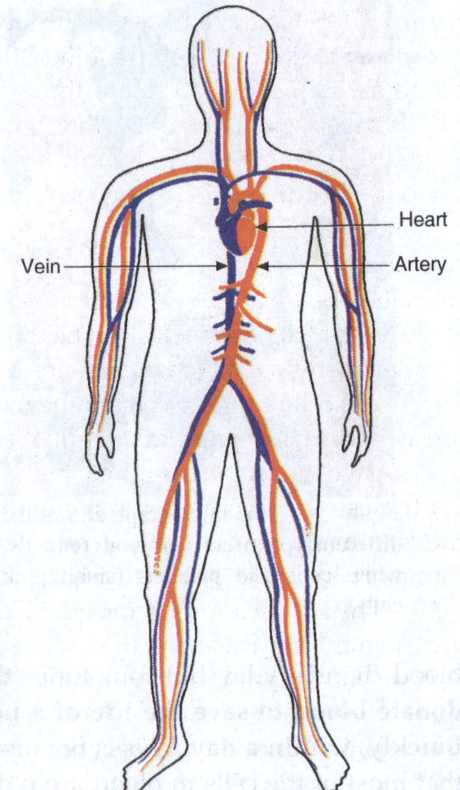

Figure 84. Blood circulatory system in humans (Arteries are shown in red colour and veins in blue colour. Capillaries which join arteries to veins are not shown).

Transport in Humans

The main transport system in human beings (or man) is the 'blood circulatory system' (which is sometimes called just 'circulatory system' for the sake of convenience). In the human circulatory system, blood carries oxygen, digested food and other chemicals like hormones and enzymes to all the parts of the body. It also takes away the waste products (or excretory products) like carbon dioxide and urea produced in the body cells. **The human blood circulatory system consists of the heart (the organ which pumps and receives the blood) and the blood vessels (or tubes) through which the blood flows in the body.** In blood circulatory system, the blood flows through three types of blood vessels :

(*i*) **arteries,**
(*ii*) **veins,** and
(*iii*) **capillaries.**

The blood vessels of the circulatory system are present in each and every part of the human body due to which the blood reaches all the parts of the body (see Figure 84).

In addition to the **blood circulatory system** for the transport in human beings, there is another system called **lymphatic system** which also helps in the transport of materials in the human body. The liquid which circulates and carries materials in the lymphatic system is called lymph. Thus, **in human beings, the various substances are transported through two liquids called 'blood' and 'lymph'.** We will first describe the blood circulatory system which is the main transport system in humans.

HUMAN CIRCULATORY SYSTEM

The organ system of human beings (and other animals) which is responsible for the transport of materials inside the body is called circulatory system. **The various organs of the circulatory system in humans are : Heart, Arteries, Veins and Capillaries.** Blood is also considered a part of the circulatory system. So, **the human circulatory system consists of the heart, arteries, veins, capillaries, and blood.** In the circulatory system, the heart acts as a pump to push out blood. The arteries, veins and capillaries act as pipes (or tubes) through which the blood flows. These tubes which carry blood are called blood vessels. Thus, there are three types of blood vessels in the human body : *arteries, veins* and *capillaries*. We will now describe all the parts of the circulatory system in detail.

The heart is roughly triangular in shape. It is made of special muscle called cardiac muscle. The size of our heart is about the same as our 'clenched fist'. The heart has four compartments called 'chambers' inside it (see Figure 85). The upper two chambers of heart are called atria (singular atrium), and the lower two chambers of heart are called ventricles. The two atria receive blood from the two main veins. And the two ventricles transport blood to the entire body and the lungs. The left atrium is connected to the left ventricle through a valve V_1 (see Figure 85). Similarly, the right atrium is connected to the right ventricle through another valve V_2. These valves prevent the backflow of blood into atria when the ventricles contract to pump blood out of the heart to the rest of the body. This is because when the ventricles contract, the valves V_1 and V_2 close automatically so that the blood may not go back into atria. **The job of heart is to pump blood around our body**. All the atria and ventricles of the heart contract and relax (expand) at appropriate times and make the heart behave like a

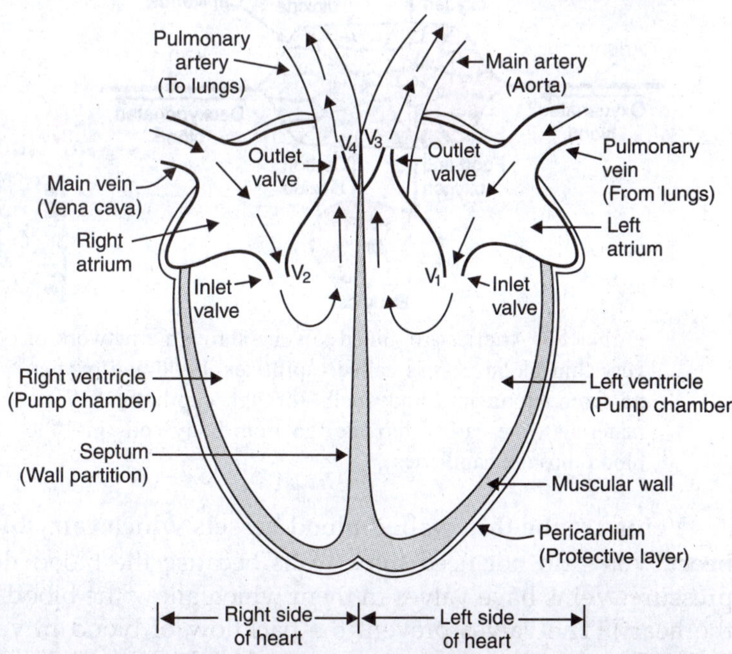

Figure 85. Diagram to show the inside structure of human heart.

pump. Since ventricles have to pump blood into various organs with high pressure, they have thicker walls than atria. A sheath of tissue called 'pericardium' protects the muscular heart (see Figure 85). The chambers of the heart are separated by a partition called septum.

The arteries, veins and capillaries are a kind of thin pipes (or tubes) through which blood flows in the body. Arteries, veins and capillaries are called blood vessels. **Arteries are the thick walled blood vessels which carry blood from the heart to all the parts of the body.** Arteries have thick walls because blood emerges from the heart under high pressure. Arteries are found in the whole of our body. The main artery (called aorta) is connected to the left ventricle of the heart through a valve V_3 (see Figure 85). The main artery carries *oxygenated* blood from the left ventricle to all the parts of the body (except the lungs). Another artery called pulmonary artery is connected to the right ventricle of the heart through another valve V_4 (see Figure 85). The pulmonary artery carries *deoxygenated* blood from the right ventricle to the lungs (see Figure 85).

The capillaries are thin walled and extremely narrow tubes or blood vessels which connect arteries to veins. Thus, the capillaries are in-between the arteries and veins (see Figure 86). The blood from arteries enters the capillaries in the body. Every living cell of our body is close to a capillary. The walls of capillaries are only one-cell thick. The various dissolved substances (like oxygen, food, etc.) present in blood pass into the body cells through the thin walls of the capillaries (see Figure 86). At the same time, the waste substances (like carbon dioxide) formed in the cells enter into capillaries. Thus, **the exchange of various materials like oxygen, food, carbon dioxide, etc., between the blood and the body cells takes place through capillaries.** The other end of capillaries is joined to some wider tubes called veins. The deoxygenated blood (or dirty blood) coming from the capillaries enters into veins.

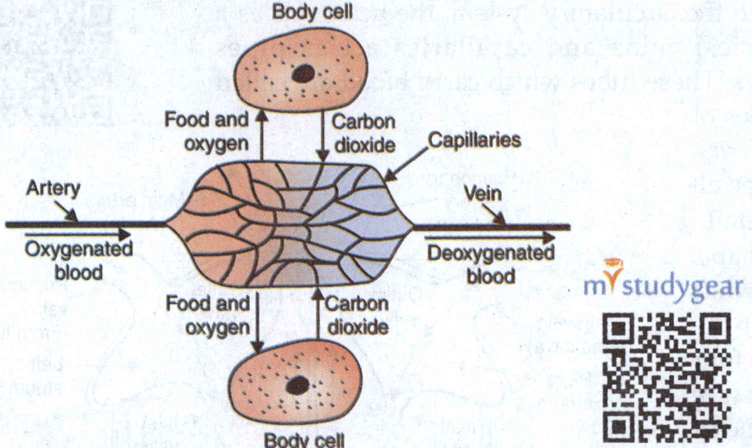

Figure 86. Arteries are joined to veins through a network of very thin blood vessels called capillaries. Food and oxygen go from blood into body cells through capillaries. Waste materials (like carbon dioxide) go from body cells into the blood through capillaries.

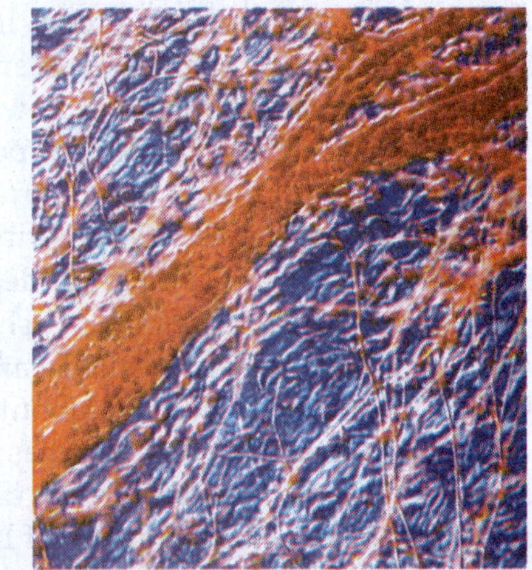

Figure 87. This photo of capillaries was taken by using a modern microscope. See how thin the capillaries are.

Veins are the thin walled blood vessels which carry blood from all the parts of the body back to the heart. Veins do not need thick walls because the blood flowing through them is no longer under high pressure. Veins have valves in them which allow the blood in them to flow in only one direction (towards the heart). The valves prevent the backflow of blood in veins. Veins are also found in the whole of our body. The pulmonary vein is connected to the left atrium of the heart (see Figure 85). The pulmonary vein carries *oxygenated* blood from lungs back to the heart. There is also a main vein (called vena cava). The main vein is connected to the right atrium of the heart (see Figure 85). The main vein carries *deoxygenated* blood from all the parts of the body (except lungs), back to the heart. Please note that **the main difference between an artery and a vein is that an artery carries blood from the heart to the body organs whereas a vein carries blood from the body organs back to the heart.**

We have just studied that the heart is a kind of pump which pumps blood around our body continuously, without stopping. Actually, heart is not a single pump. **Heart is really a double pump.** The left side of heart (left atrium and left ventricle) acts as one pump which pumps blood into the whole body, except the lungs. The right side of heart (right atrium and right ventricle) acts as another pump which pumps blood only into the lungs. We can see from Figure 85 that the left side of heart is completely separated from the right side by a partition called septum. So, **the two pumps in the heart work independently**. The separation of left and right sides of the heart is necessary to prevent the mixing of the oxygenated blood on the left side with the deoxygenated blood on the right side.

Before we describe the circulation of blood in the human body with the help of a diagram, we should keep the following two points in mind : First that the blood circulates in our body in two forms : oxygenated blood and deoxygenated blood. **The blood carrying oxygen in it is called oxygenated blood.** We get oxygenated blood in the lungs where the fresh oxygen of air passes into the blood. **The blood having no oxygen in it is called deoxygenated blood.** The deoxygenated blood is formed in all the organs of the body (except the lungs). This is because when the oxygenated blood passes through the organs of the body, the body cells use up its oxygen and make it deoxygenated. **The deoxygenated blood, however, carries carbon dioxide in it** (which is produced during respiration in body cells). The second point to remember is that when blood circulates in the body, then it supplies oxygen, digested food and other chemicals (like hormones) to all the cells of the body. It also carries back waste products like carbon dioxide, etc., from the body cells.

The heart beats non-stop all the time. The heart beat is due to the rhythmic contraction and relaxation of the heart muscles which make up the atria and the ventricles. Please note that the two atria (left atrium and right atrium) contract together and relax together. Similarly, the two ventricles (left ventricle and right ventricle) contract together and relax together. The contraction of two atria is immediately followed by the contraction of the two ventricles.

The heart beats (or beating of heart) circulates the blood in the human body. We will now describe the circulation of blood in the human body with the help of a highly simplified diagram (see Figure 88)

1. When the muscles of all the four chambers of the heart are relaxed, the pulmonary vein brings the oxygenated blood (oxygen-carrying blood) from the lungs into the left atrium of the heart (see step 1 in Figure 88).

2. When the left atrium contracts, the oxygenated blood is pushed into the left ventricle through the valve V_1 (see step 2 in Figure 88).

3. When the left ventricle contracts, the oxygenated blood is forced into the main artery called 'aorta' (see step 3 in Figure 88). This main artery then branches into smaller arteries which go into different body organs (except the lungs). The smaller arteries (called arterioles) further branch into capillaries (The smaller arteries and capillaries have not been shown in Figure 88 to keep the diagram simple).

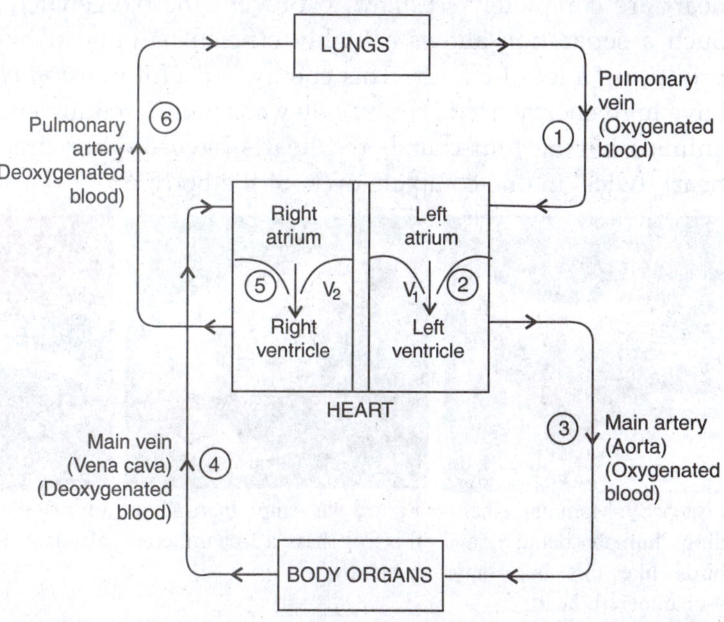

Figure 88. Diagram to show blood circulation in human body.

4. The main artery carries blood to all the organs (or parts) of the body like head, chest, arms, stomach, intestines, liver, kidney, trunk and legs (except the lungs). When the oxygenated blood passes through the capillaries of the body organs, then it gives oxygen to the body cells. Since the blood loses oxygen here, we

say that the blood has been deoxygenated. The blood also gives the digested food and other dissolved materials to the body cells. At the same time, carbon dioxide produced as a waste material during respiration enters into the blood. The deoxygenated blood (carrying carbon dioxide) from the body organs enters into the main vein called vena cava. The main vein carries the deoxygenated blood to the right atrium of the heart (see step 4 in Figure 88).

5. When the right atrium contracts, deoxygenated blood is pushed into the right ventricle through the valve V_2 (see step 5 in Figure 88).

6. And when the right ventricle contracts, the deoxygenated blood is pumped into the lungs through the pulmonary artery (see step 6 in Figure 88). In the lungs, deoxygenated blood releases its carbon dioxide and absorbs fresh oxygen from air. So, the blood becomes oxygenated again. This oxygenated blood is again sent to the left atrium of heart by pulmonary vein for circulation in the body.

This whole process is repeated continuously. In this way, the blood keeps on circulating in our body without stopping due to which all the body parts keep on getting oxygen, digested food and other materials all the time. The blood circulation also keeps on removing waste products formed in the cells of the body.

The blood circulatory system in human beings is an example of double circulation. This can be explained as follows : **A circulatory system in which the blood travels twice through the heart in one complete cycle of the body is called double circulation.** In the human circulatory system the pathway of blood from the heart to the lungs and back to the heart is called **pulmonary circulation**; and the pathway of blood from the heart to the rest of the body and back to the heart is called the **systemic circulation.** These two types of circulation taken together make double circulation.

The animals such as mammals (including human beings), and birds have four-chambered heart (which consists of two atria and two ventricles). In a four-chambered heart, the left side and right side of the heart are completely *separated* to prevent the oxygenated blood from mixing with deoxygenated blood. Such a separation allows a highly efficient supply of oxygen to the body cells which is necessary for producing a lot of energy. This energy is useful in *warm-blooded* animals (like mammals and birds) which have high energy needs because they constantly require energy to maintain their body temperature. All the animals having four-chambered hearts have **double circulation** in which the blood passes through the heart 'twice' in one complete cycle of the body.

Figure 89. Mammals (including human beings) and birds like this hen) have 4-chambered heart.

Figure 90. Amphibians (like this frog) have a 3-chambered heart.

Figure 91. Reptiles (like this lizard) also have a 3-chambered heart.

Figure 92. Fish has a 2-chambered heart.

The animals such as amphibians and many reptiles are *cold-blooded* animals whose body temperature depends on the temperature in the environment. They do not need energy to maintain their body temperature and hence their requirement of energy is less. **The amphibians (like frogs) and reptiles (like lizards) have a three-chambered heart (which consists of two atria and one ventricle).** Due to incomplete division within their heart, the oxygenated and deoxygenated bloods mix to some extent in amphibians and reptiles. This reduces the production of energy. The amphibians and reptiles have, however, a **double circulation** that delivers blood to the lungs and the rest of the body, respectively.

The fish has a two-chambered heart (which consists of one atrium and one ventricle). The fish does not have lungs, it has gills to oxygenate blood. In a fish, the heart pumps deoxygenated blood to the gills. Oxygenation of blood takes place in the gills. The oxygenated blood from the gills is supplied to the body parts of the fish where oxygen is utilised and carbon dioxide enters into it making it deoxygenated. This deoxygenated blood returns to the heart to be pumped into gills again. The flow of blood in a fish is called **single circulation** because the blood passes through the heart of fish only once in one complete cycle of the body.

Heart Beats

The heart pumps blood into our arteries by contracting. When the heart contracts, it becomes smaller in size and pushes the blood into main artery with a great force. Then the heart relaxes (comes back to its original size) and gets filled up with blood from pulmonary vein. In this way, the heart keeps on contracting and relaxing again and again to pump blood into the body continuously. **One complete contraction and relaxation of the heart is called a heart beat.** The heart usually beats about 70 to 72 times in a minute when we are resting. This means that the heart pumps out blood to the arteries about 70 to 72 times per minute.

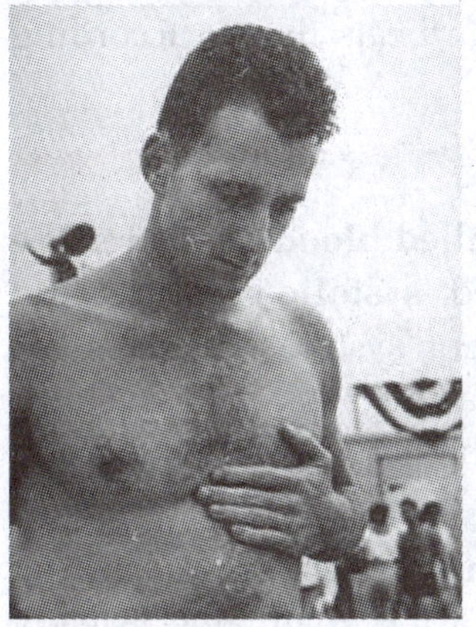

Figure 93. We can feel our heartbeats if we place our hand on the chest, just above the heart region.

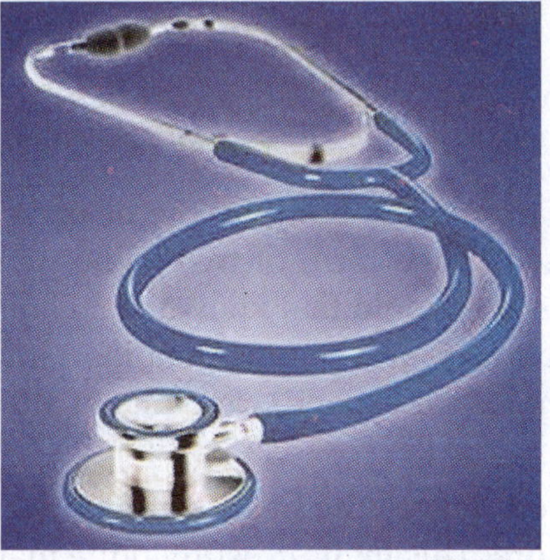

Figure 94. A stethoscope magnifies the sound of heartbeats so that they can be heard clearly.

Figure 95. A doctor listens to our heartbeats by using a stethoscope. This gives the doctor an idea of the condition of our heart.

We can feel our heart beats if we place our hand on the chest just above the heart region (see Figure 93). A doctor listens to our heart beats by using an apparatus called stethoscope (see Figures 94 and 95). The stethoscope magnifies the sound of heart beats so that the doctor can hear the heart beats clearly.

Though the average number of heart beats of a person at rest is about 70 to 72 per minute but the number of heart beats increases too much after a physical exercise or when a person is excited. For example, if we count our heart beats after running for a while, we will find it to be more than 100 per minute. **The heart beats faster during and after an exercise because the body needs more energy under these conditions.** The faster beating of heart pumps blood more rapidly to the body organs which supplies more oxygen to the body cells for rapid respiration to produce more energy. The heart beats can be counted easily by counting the pulse.

Pulse

Every time the heart beats, blood is *forced* into arteries. This blood makes the arteries expand a little. **The expansion of an artery each time the blood is forced into it, is called pulse**. Each heartbeat generates one pulse in the arteries, so *the pulse rate of a person is equal to the number of heartbeats per minute*. Since the heart beats about 70 to 72 times per minute, therefore, **the pulse rate of an adult person while resting is 70 to 72 per minute**. Thus, the pulse rate is the *same* as the heart rate. Just like heartbeats, the pulse rate of a person is higher after a physical exercise or when a person is excited.

Most of our arteries lie deep inside our body and hence cannot be used to feel the pulse. But at some places in our body like the wrist, temple and neck, the arteries are close to the surface of skin and pass over bones. So, we can feel the pulse at wrist, temple and neck by pressing the artery lightly with our finger tips. **The pulse is traditionally taken above the wrist**. We can feel our own pulse and find the pulse rate as follows :

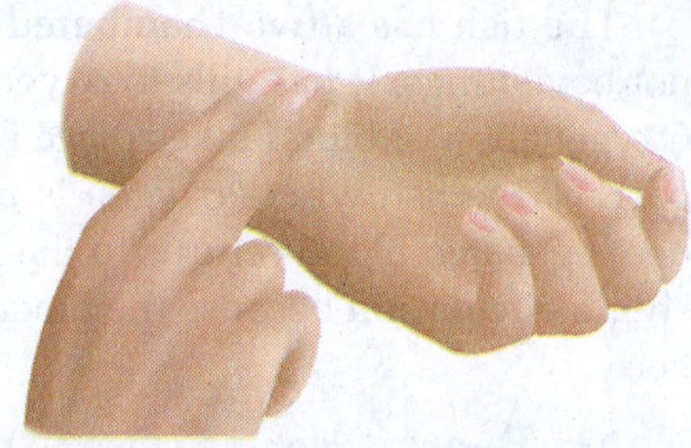

Figure 96. Feeling the pulse in the wrist.

The pulse can be felt with fingers placed gently on arteries at the wrist. We place the first two fingers (index finger and middle finger) of our right hand on the inner side of our left wrist and press it gently (see Figure 96). We will feel some waves touching our fingers. These waves are the pulse. We can count the number of such waves (or thumpings) in one minute by using a watch. This will give us the pulse rate (per minute).

We usually see the doctor taking the pulse rate of a patient by keeping his fingers on the wrist of the patient and at the same time looking into his watch. Doctors can tell by counting the pulse rate and listening to heartbeats whether a person is well or not. This is because the pulse rate and heartbeats change according to the condition of our heart.

Blood Pressure

The pressure at which blood is pumped around the body by the heart is called blood pressure. The blood pressure of a person is always expressed in the form of two values called '**systolic pressure**' and '**diastolic pressure**'. In order to understand this, we should first know the meaning of 'systole' and 'diastole'. The phase of the heart beat when the heart contracts and pumps the blood into arteries is called 'systole'. And the phase of heart beat when the heart relaxes (or expands) and allows the chambers to fill with blood is called 'diastole'.

The maximum pressure at which the blood leaves the heart through the main artery (aorta) during contraction phase, is called the systolic pressure. This high pressure in the main artery maintains a steady flow of blood in all the arteries towards the capillaries. **The minimum pressure in the arteries during the relaxation phase of heart is called the diastolic pressure.** The value of diastolic pressure is always *lower* than that of the systolic pressure. The blood pressure of a person is expressed in terms of millimetres of mercury (which is written as mm Hg). **The normal blood pressure values are :**

Systolic pressure : 120 mm Hg
Diastolic pressure : 80 mm Hg
This is usually written as 120/80

The blood pressure values vary from person to person and from time to time. They also vary with age. For example, a young person may have blood pressure of 110/75 but at the age of 60 years it could be 145/90. **High blood pressure is called hypertension.** High blood pressure is caused by the constriction (narrowing) of very small arteries (called arterioles) which results in *increased* resistance to blood flow. Very high blood pressure can lead to rupture of an artery and internal bleeding.

How to Measure Blood Pressure

Blood pressure is measured by using an instrument called sphygmomanometer. Two readings of blood pressure are taken : **systolic pressure** (when the heart is contracting and pumping out blood), and **diastolic pressure** (when the heart relaxes and fills with blood). The various steps in measuring the blood pressure of a person are as follows :

(*i*) A rubber cuff (which is a flat rubber tube) is wrapped around the person's arm [see Figure 97(*a*)]. The rubber cuff is inflated by pumping air into it to give a pressure of about 200 mm Hg to the brachial artery (which runs down the arm). This pressure can be seen on the scale of the instrument sphygmomanometer. If a stethoscope is now placed on the artery of the arm, no sound is heard through it.

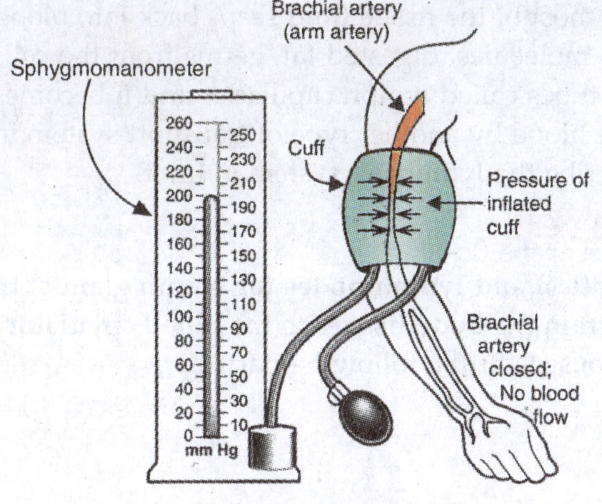

(*a*) No sound heard in stethoscope : cuff pressure is greater than systolic pressure

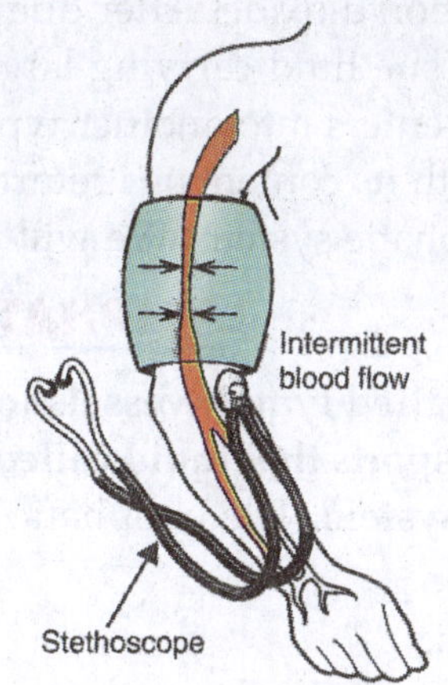

(*b*) When tapping sound first heard : cuff pressure is equal to systolic pressure

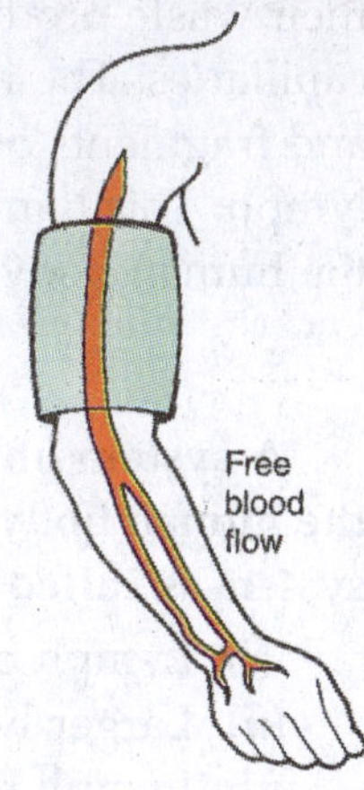

(*c*) When tapping sound just disappears : cuff pressure is equal to diastolic pressure

Figure 97. Measuring of blood pressure by using a mercury sphygmomanometer.

(*ii*) With stethoscope still placed on artery, the cuff pressure is reduced gradually by deflating it. The cuff pressure when the heart beat is *first heard* as a soft tapping sound through the stethoscope gives us the systolic pressure [see Figure 97(*b*)]

(*iii*) The cuff pressure is reduced further by deflating it more and more. The cuff pressure when the tapping sound in stethoscope *just disappears,* gives us the diastolic pressure [see Figure 97(*c*)].

The above observations can be explained as follows : When a high pressure of about 200 mm Hg is applied to the arm by the cuff, then the brachial artery gets closed fully and hence no blood flows in it [see Figure 97(*a*)]. Since no blood flows in the brachial artery at this stage, therefore, no tapping sound is heard in the stethoscope. When the cuff pressure is reduced and becomes equal to the systolic pressure, then the brachial artery opens up slightly and there is an intermittent blood flow in it due to which a soft tapping sound just begins to be heard in the stethoscope [see Figure 97(*b*)]. And finally, when the cuff pressure is reduced further and it becomes equal to diastolic pressure, then the brachial artery opens up fully, the blood flow in it is fully restored and hence the tapping sound just disappears [see Figure 97(*c*)].

Figure 98. A doctor measuring the blood pressure of a patient by using a sphygmomanometer.

How do Food and Oxygen Reach Body Cells

We have studied that blood carries food and oxygen around the body. But blood never comes in contact with body cells. So, how do food and oxygen get from the blood to the body cells where they are needed ? This happens with the help of plasma which leaks from the blood capillaries around the body cells. This plasma which leaks out from the blood capillaries is called tissue fluid. We can now say that : **The liquid from the blood which is forced out through the capillary walls and moves between all the body cells (providing them with food and oxygen, and removing carbon dioxide) is called tissue fluid.**

Actually, the walls of blood capillaries are very thin. So, when blood flows through the capillaries, a liquid called tissue fluid leaks from the blood capillaries and goes into tiny spaces between the various body cells in the tissues. The tissue fluid carries food and oxygen from the blood to the cells, and picks up their waste products like carbon dioxide. After doing its job, most of the tissue fluid seeps back into blood capillaries. The remaining tissue fluid carrying large protein molecules, digested fat, germs from the cells and fragments of dead cells, enters into another type of tiny tubes called lymph capillaries and it becomes lymph. This lymph (alongwith its contents) is returned to the blood by another type of transport system in the human body called lymphatic system. We will now describe the lymphatic system in brief.

LYMPHATIC SYSTEM

A system of tiny tubes called lymph vessels (or lymphatics) and lymph nodes (or lymph glands) in the human body which transports the liquid called lymph from the body tissues to the blood circulatory system is called lymphatic system. The lymphatic system consists of the following parts :

(*i*) Lymph capillaries,
(*ii*) Larger lymph vessels,
(*iii*) Lymph nodes (or Lymph glands), and
(*iv*) Lymph.

Lymph capillaries are tiny tubes which are present in the whole body (just like blood capillaries) (see Figure 99). Lymph capillaries, however, differ from blood capillaries in two ways : lymph capillaries are closed ended (the end of lymph capillaries in the tissues of the body is closed), and the pores in the walls of lymph capillaries are bigger in size (than that of blood capillaries). Since the ends of the lymph capillaries in the body tissues are closed, so the tissue fluid can only seep into the walls of the lymph capillaries present in the body tissues. Moreover, since the pores in the walls of the lymph capillaries are somewhat bigger, so even large protein molecules present in the tissue fluid can enter into lymph capillaries (which could not pass into blood capillaries).

The lymph capillaries join to form larger lymph vessels. The lymph vessels have lymph nodes (or lymph glands) at intervals (see Figure 99). The lymph nodes contain special type of cells called lymphocytes. Lymph nodes containing lymphocytes are involved in the cleaning of lymph and protecting the body from disease. The lymph vessels are connected to large veins of the blood circulatory system (see Figure 99).

Lymph is a light yellow liquid which is somewhat similar in composition to blood plasma. Lymph is not red like blood because it does not contain red blood cells. Lymph contains large protein molecules and digested food (which come into it from the tissue fluid between the cells). It also contains germs from the cells and fragments of dead cells. **Lymph is another medium of circulation in the human body.** But lymph flows in only **one direction** – from body tissues to the heart. Since lymph is derived from the tissue fluid which remains outside the cells of the body, so it is also called extracellular fluid. **Lymph contains a special type of white blood cells called lymphocytes which help in fighting infection and disease.**

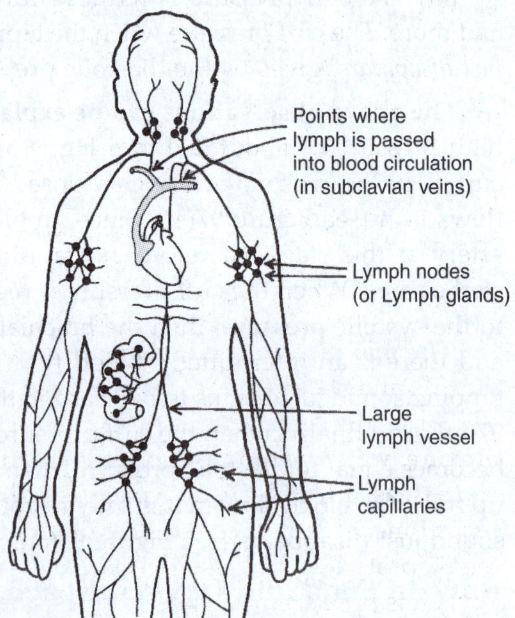

Figure 99. Diagram of human lymphatic system

Lymph containing large protein molecules, digested fat, germs and fragments of dead cells from the tissue fluid around the body cells seeps into the lymph capillaries present throughout the body. From lymph capillaries, lymph passes into larger lymph vessels containing lymph nodes. **In the lymph nodes, lymph is cleaned by white blood cells called lymphocytes.** These white blood cells eat the germs and

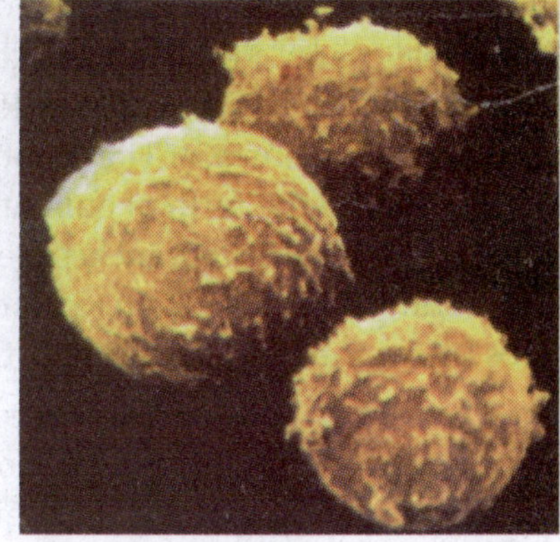

Figure 100. Lymphocytes are special type of white blood cells. In this micrograph, lymphocytes have been stained (coloured with a dye) so that they can be seen clearly.

dead cells, and also make antibodies for protecting the body from disease. The cleaned lymph containing large protein molecules, digested fat and other useful materials is transported by lymph vessels to the large veins (called subclavian veins) which run just beneath the collar bone. These veins carry the lymph to the heart. In this way, the circulation of lymph from the body tissues to the heart is completed.

The Functions of Lymph (or Lymphatic System)

1. Lymph (or lymphatic system) takes part in the nutritive process of the body. For example, it puts into circulation large protein molecules by carrying them from the tissues into the blood stream (which could not be absorbed by blood capillaries due to their large size). Lymph also carries digested fat for the nutritive process.
2. Lymph (or lymphatic system) protects the body by killing the germs drained out of the body tissues with the help of lymphocytes contained in the lymph nodes, and by making antibodies.
3. Lymph (or lymphatic system) helps in removing the waste products like fragments of dead cells, etc.

EXCRETION

All the organisms (plants and animals) are made up of cells. These cells work all the time for sustaining the life of the organism. Most of the work of the cells is in the form of biochemical reactions which they carry out all the time. The biochemical reactions taking place in the cells of an organism may produce toxic wastes (poisonous wastes) in the body. The accumulation of toxic wastes in the body harms an organism. So, for an organism to lead a normal life, the toxic wastes being produced in its body must be removed continuously. **The process of removal of toxic wastes from the body of an organism is called excretion.** Excretion takes place in plants as well as in animals.

EXCRETION IN PLANTS

Like animals, plants also produce a number of waste products during their life processes. As compared to animals, the plants produce waste products very slowly and in very small amounts. The plants have no special organs for waste removal like the animals. The plants remove their waste products by different methods. Some of the important plant wastes and the methods by which they are removed are described below.

The main waste products produced by plants are carbon dioxide, water vapour and oxygen. Carbon dioxide and water vapour are produced as wastes during respiration by plants whereas oxygen is produced as a waste during photosynthesis. **The gaseous wastes of respiration and photosynthesis in plants (carbon dioxide, water vapour and oxygen) are removed through the 'stomata' in leaves and 'lenticels' in stems and released to the air.** The plants excrete carbon dioxide produced as a waste during respiration only at night time. This is because the carbon dioxide produced during respiration in day time is all used up by the plant itself in photosynthesis. The plants excrete oxygen as a waste only during the day time (because oxygen is produced by photosynthesis only during the day time when the sunlight is there). Water vapour produced as a waste by respiration is, however, excreted by plants all the time (day as well as night). This waste water is got rid of by transpiration.

The plants also store some of the waste products in their body parts. For example, some of the waste products collect in the leaves, bark and fruits of the plants (or trees). **The plants get rid of these wastes by shedding of leaves, peeling of bark and felling of fruits.** So, when the dead leaves, bark and ripe fruits fall off from a tree, then the waste products contained in them are got rid of (see Figure 101). Some of the plant wastes get stored in the fruits of the plant in the form of solid bodies called **raphides.** These wastes are removed when the fruits get detached from the plant. For example, the fruit called 'yam' (*zamikand*) has needle-shaped raphides on its surface. The plants secrete their wastes in the form of gum and resins from their stems and branches (see Figure 102). The plants also excrete some waste substances into the soil around them.

Figure 101. The plants store some of their waste products in old leaves which fall in autumn.

Figure 102. The stem of this tree is secreting some of its waste products in the form of gum.

From the above discussion we conclude that the various methods used by the plants to get rid of their waste products are the following :

(*i*) The plants get rid of gaseous waste products through stomata in leaves and lenticels in stems.
(*ii*) The plants get rid of stored solid and liquid wastes by the shedding of leaves, peeling of bark and felling of fruits.
(*iii*) The plants get rid of wastes by secreting them in the form of gums and resins.
(*iv*) Plants also excrete some waste substances into the soil around them.

EXCRETION IN ANIMALS

Different animals have different arrangements (or organs) for excretion, which depend on the constitution of the animal. For example :

1. In *Amoeba* (and other single celled animals), the waste material carbon dioxide is removed by diffusion through the cell membrane, but nitrogenous wastes (like ammonia) and excess water are removed by the contractile vacuole.
2. In earthworm, the tubular structures called nephridia are the excretory organs. In addition to nephridia, the moist skin of earthworm also acts as an excretory organ.
3. In human beings, the microscopic thin tubules form nephron, which functions as excretory unit. About 1 million nephrons taken together form the excretory organ of human beings called kidney.

Figure 103. This cow is excreting carbon dioxide, and urea (in the form of urine), as waste products. Carbon dioxide is being excreted by the lungs of the cow (while 'exhaling') and urea is being excreted by the kidneys in the form of urine.

Removal of Waste Products in Humans

All the time (even when we are asleep), our body produces waste substances. **The major wastes produced by the human body are : Carbon dioxide and Urea.** Carbon dioxide is produced as a waste by the oxidation of food during the process of respiration. Urea is produced as a waste by the decomposition of unused proteins in the liver. Our body must get rid of these waste materials because their accumulation in the body is poisonous and harms us. **Waste removal is called excretion.**

The human body has different organs for the removal of wastes from the body. These are our lungs and kidneys. **Our lungs excrete carbon dioxide. Our kidneys excrete urea.** The kidneys are the main excretory organs of the human body. So, the main excretory system in human beings involves the kidneys. We will first describe how lungs excrete carbon dioxide and then study the main excretory system of human body.

The lungs remove respiratory waste carbon dioxide. This happens as follows : Carbon dioxide is produced as a waste product in the body by the oxidation of food during respiration. This carbon dioxide enters from the body tissues into the blood stream by diffusion. Blood carries this carbon dioxide to the lungs. When we breathe out, then the lungs excrete carbon dioxide which goes into the air through nostrils. Thus, **our lungs act as the excretory organs for removing the waste product carbon dioxide from the body.**

Figure 104. This is the waste product urea produced by the decomposition of unused proteins in our liver.

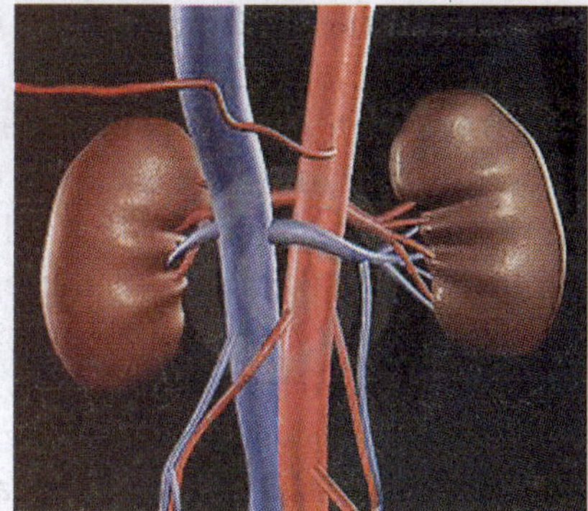

Figure 105. The waste product urea is removed from our blood continuously by our kidneys in dissolved form through urine.

EXCRETION IN HUMANS

The excretory system of human beings collects the liquid wastes of the body and helps it get rid of them. **The excretory system of human beings consists of the following main organs : Two kidneys, Two ureters, Bladder and Urethra** (see Figure 107). The kidneys are bean shaped organs towards the back of our body just above the waist (see Figure 106). Every person has two kidneys. The blood in our body is constantly passing through our kidneys. The renal artery (or kidney artery) brings in the dirty blood (containing waste substances) into the kidneys. **The function of kidneys is to remove the poisonous substance urea, other waste salts and excess water from the blood and excrete them in the form of a yellowish liquid called urine.** Thus, kidneys clean our blood by filtering it to remove unwanted substances present in it. The cleaned blood is carried away from the kidneys by the renal vein (or kidney vein). The ureters (or excretory tubes), one from each kidney, opens into urinary bladder (see Figure 107). Ureters are the tubes which carry urine from the kidneys to the bladder. Urine is stored in the bladder. The bladder is a bag which stores urine till the time we go to the toilet. The urethra is a tube. The urine collected in the bladder is passed out from the body through the urethra (see Figure 107). We will now describe a kidney in detail.

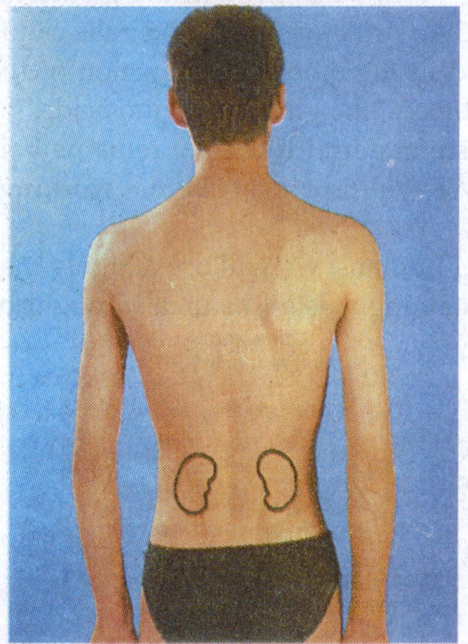

Figure 106. This picture shows where in the body our kidneys are.

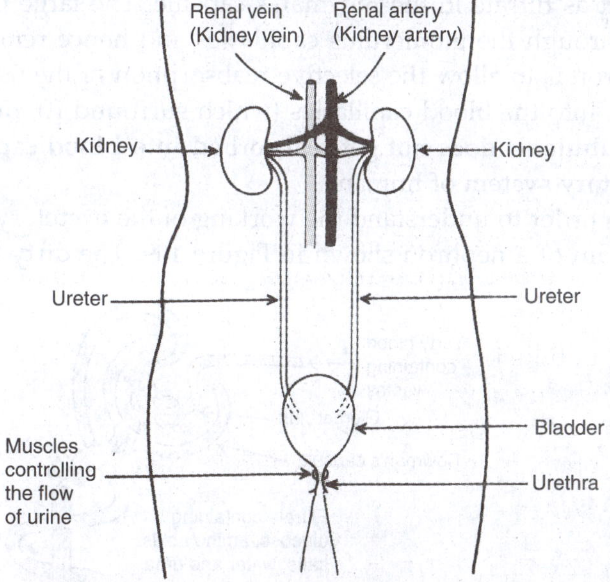

Figure 107. The human excretory system (or urinary system).

Figure 108 shows a kidney which has been cut open to show the inner structure. **Each kidney is made up of a large number of excretory units called nephrons** (We have shown only one nephron to make things simple). The nephron has a cup-shaped bag at its upper end which is called Bowman's capsule. The lower end of Bowman's capsule is tube-shaped and it is called a tubule. **The Bowman's capsule and the tubule taken together make a nephron.** One end of the tubule is connected to the Bowman's capsule and its other end is connected to a urine-collecting duct of the kidney. The Bowman's capsule contains a bundle of blood capillaries which is called glomerulus (plural glomeruli). One end of the glomerulus is attached to the renal artery which brings the dirty blood containing the urea waste into it (see Figure 108). The other end of glomerulus comes out of Bowman's capsule as a blood capillary, surrounds the tubule of nephron and finally joins a renal vein (putting urea-free clean blood into it).

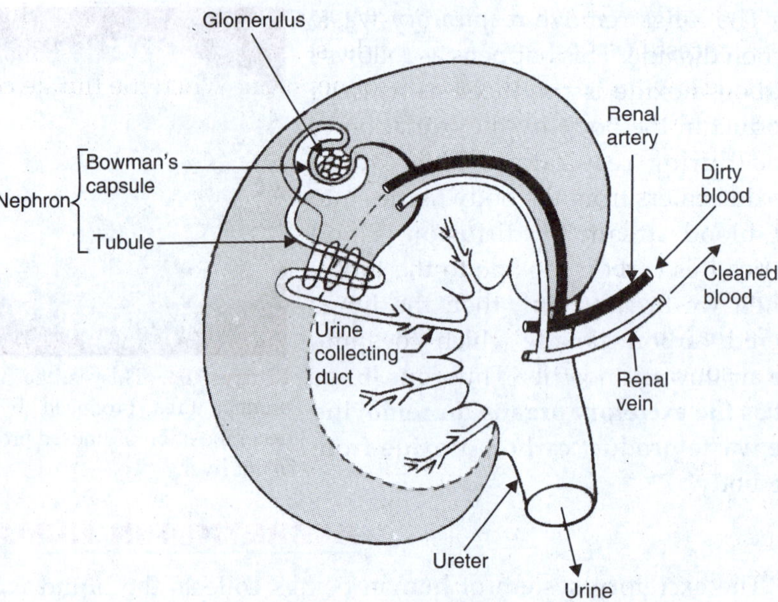

Figure 108. The structure of a kidney.

The function of glomerulus is to filter the blood passing through it. Only the small molecules of substances present in blood like glucose, amino acids, salts, urea and water, etc., pass through the glomerulus and collect as filtrate in the Bowman's capsule. The large molecules like proteins and blood cells cannot pass out through the glomerulus capillaries and hence remain behind in the blood. The function of tubule of nephron is to allow the selective reabsorption of the useful substances like glucose, amino acids, salts and water into the blood capillaries (which surround it). But **the waste material like urea remains behind in the tubule. It does not get reabsorbed into blood capillaries.** We will now describe the **working of the excretory system** of humans.

In order to understand the working of the excretory system of humans, we will use a highly magnified diagram of a nephron shown in Figure 109. The dirty blood containing waste like urea (brought by renal

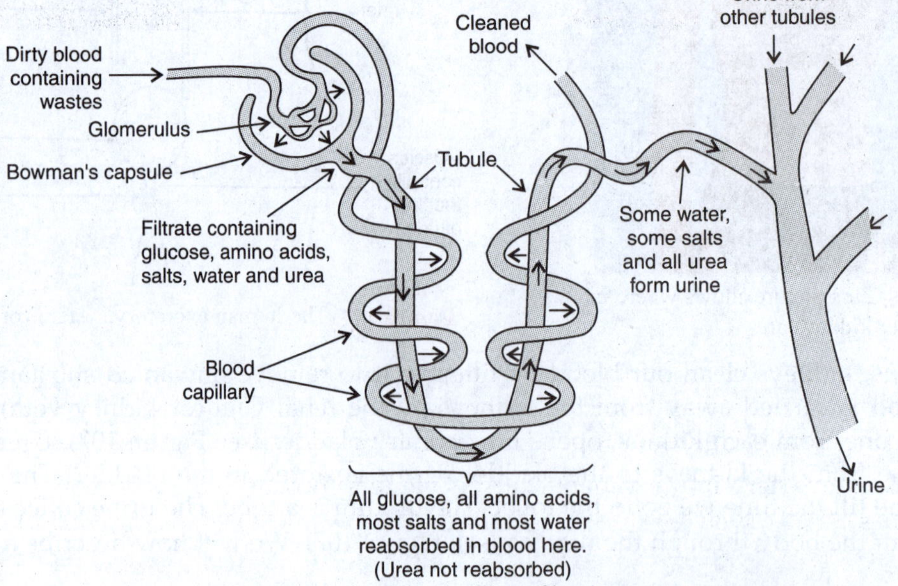

Figure 109. Diagram to show the working of human excretory system.

artery) enters the glomerulus (see Figure 109). The glomerulus filters this blood. During filtration, the substances like glucose, amino acids, salts, water and urea, etc., present in the blood pass into Bowman's capsule and then enter the tubule of nephron. When the filtrate containing useful substances as well as the waste substances passes through the tubule, then the useful substances like all glucose, all amino acids, most salts, and most water, etc., are reabsorbed into the blood through blood capillaries surrounding the tubule. Only the waste substances urea, some unwanted salts and excess water remain behind in the tubule. The liquid left behind in the tubule of nephron is urine. The nephron carries this urine into the collecting duct of the kidney from where it is carried to ureter. From the ureter, urine passes into urinary bladder. Urine is stored in the bladder for some time and ultimately passed out of the body through urethra. Please note that the human urine contains water, some salts and nitrogenous substances, most of which is urea (and some uric acid).

Renal Failure (Kidney Failure) and the Technology for Survival

Sometimes, a person's kidneys may stop working. An infection in the kidneys, an injury to kidneys, very high blood pressure, very high blood sugar or restricted blood flow to the kidneys, can damage the kidneys due to which they stop working. **Complete failure of the kidneys allows the urea and other waste products to build up in the blood.** Even the amount of water in the body is not regulated. This will cause death if the patient is not given immediate treatment.

The best long term solution for kidney failure is the kidney transplant. The damaged kidney is removed and a matching kidney donated by a healthy person is transplanted in its place by a surgical operation (see Figure 110). If a kidney transplant is not possible due to some reasons, **then the patient with**

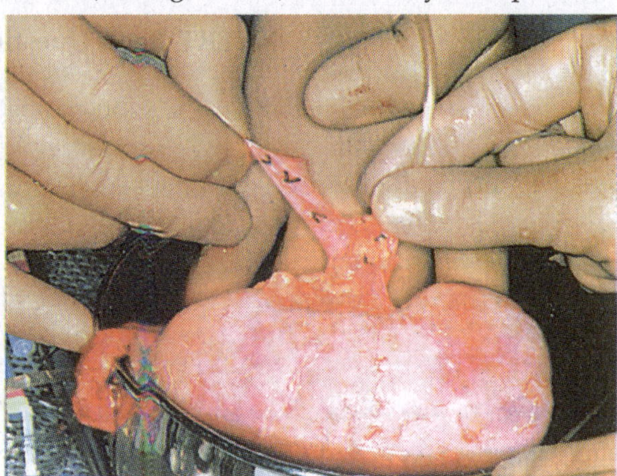

Figure 110. A kidney being prepared for a transplant operation.

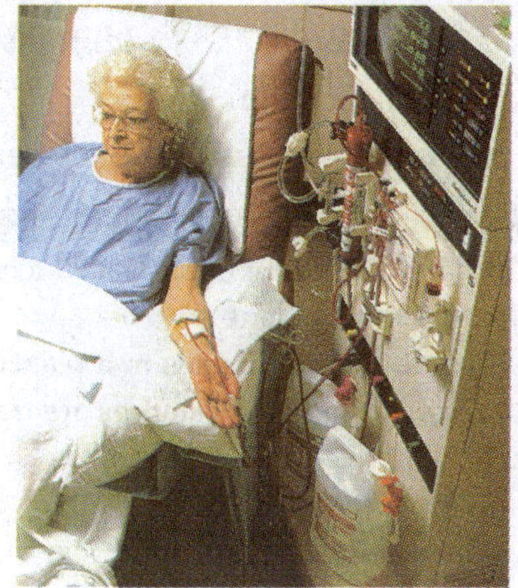

Figure 111. This woman having damaged kidneys has been put on kidney dialysis machine to filter her blood and remove urea.

kidney failure is treated periodically on a kidney machine (by a procedure called dialysis) (see Figure 111). This is because a kidney machine can do the work of damaged kidneys. The kidney machine is sometimes called 'artificial kidney'. An artificial kidney is a device to remove nitrogenous waste products from the blood through dialysis.

Dialysis

The blood of a person having kidney failure can be cleaned regularly by using a kidney machine (or dialysis machine). **The procedure used for cleaning the blood of a person by separating the waste substance (urea) from it is called dialysis.** The principle of dialysis is explained below.

The blood from an artery in the patient's arm is made to flow into the dialyser of a dialysis machine made of long tubes of selectively permeable membrane (like cellulose) which are coiled in a tank containing dialysing solution (see Figure 112). The dialysing solution contains water, glucose and salts

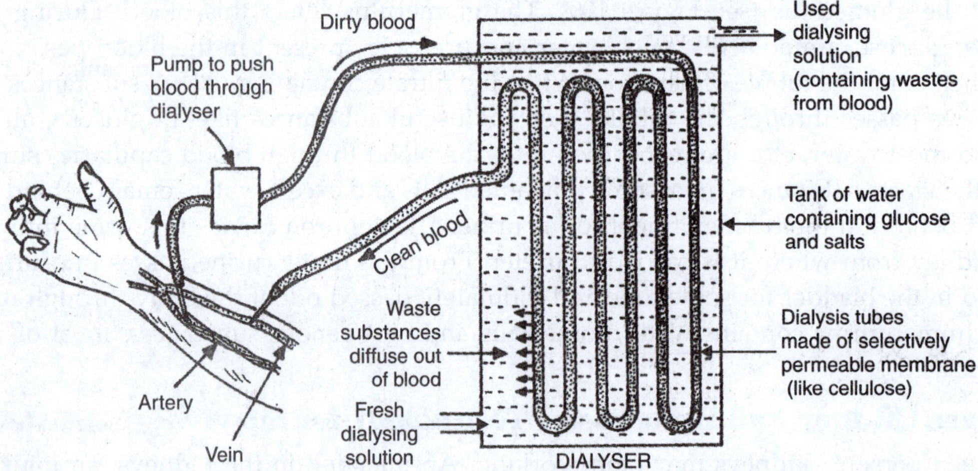

Figure 112. The principle of the kidney dialysis machine

in similar concentrations to those in normal blood. As the patient's blood passes through the dialysing solution, most of the wastes like urea present in it pass through the selectively permeable cellulose tubes into the dialysing solution. The clean blood is pumped back into a vein of the patient's arm.

Sample Problem. The kidneys in human beings are a part of the system for :

(*a*) nutrition (*b*) respiration

(*c*) excretion (*d*) transportation **(NCERT Book Question)**

Answer. (*c*) excretion.

We are now in a position to **answer the following questions :**

Very Short Answer Type Questions

1. What is the name of tissues which transport :
   (*a*) food in a plant ?
   (*b*) water and minerals in a plant ?
2. What substance/substances are transported in plants by :
   (*a*) xylem vessels and tracheids ?
   (*b*) sieve tubes (or phloem) ?
3. Which organ acts as a pump in the circulatory system ?
4. Veins and arteries carry blood. Which of these carry blood :
   (*a*) away from the heart ?
   (*b*) back to the heart ?
5. Where does blood absorb oxygen ?
6. What stops blood from flowing backwards through the heart ?
7. Name (*i*) largest artery, and (*ii*) largest vein, in our body.
8. What gaseous waste products are excreted by plants ?
9. Where is the dirty blood in our body filtered ?
10. Name the procedure used in the working of artificial kidney.
11. From the following terms, choose one term which includes the other four :
    Plasma, Platelets, Blood, RBC, WBC
12. What are the components of the transport system in highly organised plants ?
13. Out of xylem and phloem, which one carries materials :
    (*a*) upwards as well as downwards ?
    (*b*) only upwards ?

14. Name two liquids which help in the transport of substances in the human body.
15. What is the other name of main vein ?
16. Name the conducting tissue of plants which is made of sieve tubes alongwith companion cells.
17. Name the conducting tissue in plants which is made of (*a*) living cells, and (*b*) dead cells.
18. State the term used for the transport of food from leaves to other parts of plant.
19. Which process in a plant is accomplished by utilising energy from ATP : transport of water and minerals or transport of food ?
20. Name the two types of transport systems in the human beings.
21. Name a waste gas released by the plants (*a*) only during the day time, and (*b*) only during the night time.
22. Name one animal having single circulation of blood and another having double circulation.
23. State whether the following statements are true or false :
    (*a*) Some organisms store wastes in body parts.
    (*b*) The value of systolic pressure is always lower than that of diastolic pressure.
24. Name the two parts of a plant through which its gaseous waste products are released into the air.
25. What happens to the glucose which enters the nephron tubule alongwith the filtrate ?
26. Name the two waste products of the human body which are produced in the body cells.
27. What is the role of glomerulus in the kidney ?
28. What is the the other name of 'high blood pressure' ?
29. Fill in the following blanks with suitable words :
    (*a*) Gums and resins are the .... products of plants.
    (*b*) Bowman's capsule and tubule taken together make a..................
    (*c*) The organs which extract the nitrogenous wastes from the blood are ....
    (*d*) The extracellular fluid which always flows from body tissues to the heart is called.................
    (*e*) The ....blood cells make antibodies whereas................ blood cells help in respiration.

Short Answer Type Questions

30. What is xylem tissue ? Name the two kinds of cells in xylem tissue. State whether these cells are living or dead.
31. What is phloem tissue ? Phloem contains two types of cells joined side by side. Name these two types of cells. State whether these cells are living or dead.
32. (*a*) What is transpiration ?
    (*b*) What do you mean by 'translocation' with respect to transport in plants ?
    (*c*) Which plant tissue is involved in translocation : xylem or phloem ?
33. (*a*) Draw a labelled diagram of (*i*) a xylem vessel, and (*ii*) a sieve tube (or phloem).
    (*b*) What are the differences between the transport of materials in xylem and phloem ?
34. Match the terms in column I with their uses in column II

Column I	*Column II*
(*i*) Heart	(*a*) Pipes for transport in humans
(*ii*) Arteries and Veins	(*b*) Clotting of blood
(*iii*) Xylem vessels	(*c*) Pumping organ
(*iv*) RBC	(*d*) Water transport in plants
(*v*) Platelets	(*e*) Carrier of oxygen

35. Define excretion. Name the excretory unit of a kidney.
36. (*a*) What job is done by the kidneys ?
    (*b*) What do kidneys excrete ?
    (*c*) What is the name of the tubes which connect the kidneys to bladder ?
    (*d*) What does the bladder in our body do ?
37. Why do some people need to use a dialysis machine ? What does the machine do ?
38. What is the liquid part of the blood called ? What is the function of platelets in the blood ?

39. (*a*) How many types of blood vessels are there in the human body ? Name them.
(*b*) Why does the heart need valves ?

40. A dialysis machine contains long tubes coiled in a tank containing dialysing solution :
(*i*) Of what substance are the tubes made ?
(*ii*) What does the dialysing solution contain ?
(*iii*) Name the main waste which passes into the dialysing solution.

41. State the differences between artery, vein and capillary.

42. (*a*) What are the upper parts of the heart called ?
(*b*) What are the lower parts of the heart called ?
(*c*) What is the name of blood vessels which connect arteries to veins ?
(*d*) (*i*) Which side of the heart pumps blood into the lungs ?
(*ii*) Which side of the heart pumps blood into entire body (except the lungs) ?

43. (*a*) What are the methods used by plants to get rid of their waste products ?
(*b*) How are waste products excreted in *Amoeba* ?

44. (*a*) What is lymph ? State two major functions of lymph.
(*b*) What is meant by saying that the blood pressure of a person is 120/80 ?

45. What is hypertension ? Why is it caused ? What harm can it do ?

46. What are the various components of blood ? State their functions.

47. With which human organ systems (or human systems) are the following associated ?
(*i*) vena cava (*ii*) glomerulus (*iii*) alveoli (*iv*) villi

48. What is meant by 'systolic pressure' and 'diastolic pressure' ? What are their normal values ?

49. (*a*) What is meant by 'heart beat' ? What is the usual heart beat rate at rest ?
(*b*) What change occurs in heart beats if a person runs for a while ? Why ?

Long Answer Type Questions

50. (*a*) What is blood ? Why is it red ?
(*b*) State the functions of blood in our body.
(*c*) Name a circulatory fluid in the human body other than blood.

51. (*a*) What is meant by human circulatory system ? Name the organs of the circulatory system in humans.
(*b*) Draw a diagram of the human heart and label its parts.
(*c*) What is meant by the terms 'single circulation' and 'double circulation' ?

52. Describe the working of human blood circulatory system with the help of a suitable diagram which shows all the steps involved.

53. (*a*) Name the red pigment which carries oxygen in the blood.
(*b*) Why is it necessary to separate oxygenated and deoxygenated blood in mammals and birds ?
(*c*) How many chambers are there in the heart of : (*i*) an amphibian, (*ii*) a mammal, and (*iii*) a fish ?
(*d*) Describe the circulatory system in a fish.

54. (*a*) What is lymphatic system ? What are its functions ?
(*b*) What is blood pressure ? What are the two factors used to express the blood pressure of a person ?
(*c*) Name the main nitrogenous waste in the human blood. How is it removed from the blood ?

55. (*a*) Name the various organs of the human excretory system.
(*b*) Draw a neat labelled diagram of the human excretory system.
(*c*) What is the function of excretory system in humans ?

56. (*a*) Describe the mechanism of urine formation in human excretory system. Draw a labelled diagram to illustrate your answer.
(*b*) Where is urine carried through ureters ?
(*c*) What is urethra ?

57. (*a*) What is meant by dialysis ? What type of patients are put on dialysis ?
(*b*) Explain the principle of dialysis with the help of a labelled diagram.

58. (*a*) Why is transport of materials necessary in an organism (plant or animal) ?
(*b*) What is the need of special tissues or organs for transport of substances in plants and animals ?
(*c*) How are water and minerals transported in plants ?
(*d*) How is food transported in plants ?

Multiple Choice Questions (MCQs)

59. One of the following does not have a nucleus. This one is :
(*a*) red blood cell (*b*) white blood cell (*c*) guard cell (*d*) epidermal cell
60. The component of blood which makes chemicals known as antibodies is :
(*a*) platelets (*b*) white blood cells (*c*) red blood cells (*d*) plasma
61. An animal in which the oxygenation of blood does not take place in the lungs is :
(*a*) cow (*b*) fish (*c*) frog (*d*) fox
62. Which of the following carries substances upwards as well as downwards in a plant ?
(*a*) xylem (*b*) companion cells (*c*) phloem (*d*) tracheids
63. One of the following is not a constituent of blood. This one is :
(*a*) red blood cells (*b*) white blood cells (*c*) sieve plates (*d*) platelets
64. If a patient is put on dialysis, he is most likely suffering from a severe ailment of the :
(*a*) circulatory system (*b*) respiratory system (*c*) excretory system (*d*) digestive system
65. Water absorption through roots can be increased by keeping the potted plants :
(*a*) in the shade (*b*) in dim light
(*c*) under the fan (*d*) covered with a polythene bag
66. A blood vessel which carries blood back to the heart is :
(*a*) artery (*b*) vein (*c*) capillary (*d*) platelet
67. Blood is pumped from the heart to the entire body by the :
(*a*) lungs (*b*) ventricles (*c*) atria (*d*) nerves
68. The blood leaving the tissues becomes richer in :
(*a*) carbon dioxide (*b*) water (*c*) haemoglobin (*d*) oxygen
69. What prevents the backflow of blood inside the heart during contraction ?
(*a*) thick muscular walls of ventricles (*b*) valves
(*c*) thin walls of atria (*d*) all of the above
70. Which of the following is the correct path taken by urine in our body ?
(*a*) kidney $\longrightarrow$ ureter $\longrightarrow$ urethra $\longrightarrow$ bladder
(*b*) kidney $\longrightarrow$ bladder $\longrightarrow$ urethra $\longrightarrow$ ureter
(*c*) kidney $\longrightarrow$ ureter $\longrightarrow$ bladder $\longrightarrow$ urethra
(*d*) bladder $\longrightarrow$ kidney $\longrightarrow$ ureter $\longrightarrow$ urethra
71. In which of the following vertebrate group/groups, heart does not pump oxygenated blood to different parts of the body ?
(*a*) pisces and amphibians (*b*) amphibians and reptiles
(*c*) amphibians only (*d*) pisces only
72. Which vein brings clean blood from the lungs into the heart ?
(*a*) renal vein (*b*) pulmonary vein (*c*) vena cava (*d*) hepatic vein
73. Which blood vessel does not carry any carbon dioxide ?
(*a*) pulmonary artery (*b*) vena cava (*c*) hepatic vein (*d*) pulmonary vein
74. It has been found that people living in very high mountains have many more red corpuscles in their blood than people living in plains. Which one of the following best accounts for this phenomenon ?
(*a*) the cold climate stimulates the production of red corpuscles to keep the body warm
(*b*) people of high mountains breathe more quickly
(*c*) the low air pressure requires more red corpuscles to supply the body cells with oxygen.
(*d*) the low air pressure in high mountains speeds up the blood circulation so that more red corpuscles are needed
75. The phloem tissue in plants is responsible for the transport of :
(*a*) water (*b*) water and minerals (*c*) sugar (*d*) all of the above
76. Which of the following has a three-chambered heart ?
(*a*) pigeon (*b*) lizard (*c*) fish (*d*) lion

77. In which of the following are the largest amounts of nitrogen excreted from a mammalian body ?
(*a*) breath (*b*) sweat (*c*) urine (*d*) faeces

78. Which one of the following has cytoplasm but no nucleus :
(*a*) xylem vessel (*b*) sieve tube (*c*) tracheid (*d*) companion cell

79. The process of carrying food from the leaves to other parts of a plant is called :
(*a*) transpiration (*b*) transportation (*c*) translocation (*d*) transformation

80. Which of the following is the only conducting tissue in non-flowering plants ?
(*a*) xylem vessels (*b*) sieve tubes (*c*) companion cells (*d*) tracheids

81. Which of the following helps in the upward movement of water and dissolved minerals from the roots to the leaves through the stem ?
(*a*) transportation (*b*) translocation (*c*) tropic movement (*d*) transpiration

82. Which one of the following does not have valves ?
(*a*) heart (*b*) arteries (*c*) capillaries (*d*) veins

83. Which of the following is accomplished in a plant by utilising the energy stored in ATP ?
(*a*) transport of food (*b*) transport of water and minerals
(*c*) transport of oxygen (*d*) transport of water, minerals and food

84. Coagulation of blood in a cut or wound is brought about by :
(*a*) plasma (*b*) platelets (*c*) WBC (*d*) RBC

85. The blood vessel which carries oxygenated blood from the lungs to the heart is :
(*a*) main artery (*b*) pulmonary artery (*c*) main vein (*d*) pulmonary vein

86. The instrument for measuring blood pressure is called :
(*a*) manometer (*b*) sphygmomanometer (*c*) barometer (*d*) potentiometer

87. The excretory unit in the human excretory system is called :
(*a*) nephron (*b*) neuron (*c*) nephridia (*d*) kidneyon

88. The substance which is not reabsorbed into the blood capillaries surrounding the tubule of a nephron is mainly :
(*a*) glucose (*b*) amino acid (*c*) urea (*d*) water

89. The procedure of cleaning the blood of a person by using a kidney machine is known as :
(*a*) ketolysis (*b*) hydrolysis (*c*) dialysis (*d*) photolysis

90. The excretory organs in an earthworm are :
(*a*) nephridia (*b*) nephrons (*c*) raphides (*d*) ureters

91. The cells in our blood which destroy disease-causing germs, are :
(*a*) platelets (*b*) skin cells (*c*) RBCs (*d*) WBCs

92. The wave of expansion of an artery when blood is forced into it is called :
(*a*) flow (*b*) heart beat (*c*) pulse (*d*) ticking

93. In autotrophs, water is transported through :
(*a*) root hair (*b*) phloem (*c*) stomata (*d*) xylem

94. An animal having double circulation in a three-chambered heart is :
(*a*) fish (*b*) snake (*c*) deer (*d*) sparrow

Questions Based on High Order Thinking Skills (HOTS)

95. The transport system in plants consists of two kinds of tissues X and Y. The tissue X is made up of living cells and consists of two components A and B. The component A has tiny pores in its end walls and contains only cytoplasm but no nucleus. On the other hand, component B has cytoplasm as well as nucleus. The tissue Y is made up of dead cells and consists of two components C and D. The component C has open ends whereas component D does not have open ends. In flowering plants, either only C or both C and D transport water but D is the only water conducting tissue in non-flowering plants.
(*a*) What is (*i*) tissue X (*ii*) component A, and (*iii*) component B ?
(*b*) What is (*i*) tissue Y (*ii*) component C, and (*iii*) component D ?

96. Water and dissolved minerals get into the root hair of a plant by a process called A and enter the conducting tissue B. The process C helps the water and dissolved minerals to move up through the tissue B in roots and stem, and reach the leaves of a plant. In the leaves food is made by a process D. This food is then transported to all the parts of a plant through tissue E. The process of distributing food made in the leaves to all the parts of the plant is called F.

(*a*) What are (*i*) A (*ii*) B (*iii*) C (*iv*) D (*v*) E, and (*vi*) F ?

(*b*) Which tissue is made up of living cells : B or E ?

(*c*) Which tissue, B or E, contains sieve tubes ?

(*d*) Which tissue, B or E, contains tracheids ?

97. The liquid connective tissue A circulates in our body continuously without stopping. This tissue contains a pigment B which imparts it a colour C. The tissue A consists of four components D, E, F and G. The component D fights infection and protects us from diseases. The component E helps in the clotting of tissue A if a person gets a cut. The component F is a liquid which consists mainly of water with many substances dissolved in it and component G carries oxygen from the lungs to all the parts of the body.

(*a*) What is (*i*) tissue A (*ii*) pigment B, and (*iii*) colour C ?

(*b*) Name (*i*) D (*ii*) E (*iii*) F, and (*iv*) G.

(*c*) Name one substance (other than oxygen) which is transported by tissue A in the human body.

(*d*) Which two components of tissue A are the cells without nucleus ?

(*e*) Name any two organisms (animals) which do not have liquid like A in their body.

98. The human body has an organ A which acts as a double pump. The oxygenated blood coming from the lungs through a blood vessel B enters the upper left chamber C of the double pump. When chamber C contracts, then blood goes into lower left chamber D. The contraction of chamber D forces the blood to go into a blood vessel E which supplies oxygenated blood to all the organs of the body (except the lungs). The deoxygenated blood coming out of the body organs is taken by a blood vessel F to the right upper chamber G of pumping organ. Contraction of chamber G forces the deoxygenated blood into right lower chamber H. And finally the contraction of chamber H sends the deoxygenated blood into lungs through a blood vessel I.

(*a*) What is organ A ?

(*b*) Name the blood vessel (*i*) B (*ii*) E (*iii*) F, and (*iv*) I.

(*c*) What are chambers (*i*) C, and (*ii*) D ?

(*d*) What are chambers (*i*) G and (*ii*) H ?

99. A liquid X of colour Y circulates in the human body only in one direction : from body tissues to the heart. Among other things, liquid X contains germs from cells and dead cells. The liquid X is cleaned of germs and dead cells by a special type of white blood cells called Z. This cleaned liquid is then put into blood circulatory system in subclavian veins.

(*a*) What is (*i*) liquid X, and (*ii*) colour Y ?

(*b*) What are Z ?

(*c*) The liquid X is somewhat similar to a component of blood. Name this component.

(*d*) Why is liquid X not red ?

100. There is a pair of bean-shaped organs P in the human body towards the back, just above the waist. A waste product Q formed by the decomposition of unused proteins in the liver is brought into organ P through blood by an artery R. The numerous tiny filters S present in organ P clean the dirty blood by removing the waste product Q. The clean blood goes into circulation through a vein T. The waste substance Q, other waste salts, and excess water form a yellowish liquid U which goes from organ P into a bag-like structure V through two tubes W. This liquid is then thrown out of the body through a tube X.

(*a*) What is (*i*) organ P, and (*ii*) waste substance Q ?

(*b*) Name (*i*) artery R, and (*ii*) vein T.

(*c*) What are tiny filters S known as ?

(*d*) Name (*i*) liquid U (*ii*) structure V (*iii*) tubes W, and (*iv*) tube X.

101. The organs A of a person have been damaged completely due to which too much of a poisonous waste material B has started accumulating in his blood, making it dirty. In order to save this person's life, the blood from an artery in the person's arm is made to flow into long tubes made of substance E which are kept in coiled form in a tank containing solution F. This solution contains three materials G, H and I in similar proportions to those in normal blood. As the person's blood passes through long tubes of substance E, most of the wastes present in it go into solution. The clean blood is then put back into a vein in the arm of the person for circulation.

(*a*) What are organs A ?

(*b*) Name the waste substance B.

(*c*) What are (*i*) E, and (*ii*) F ?

(*d*) Name G, H and I.

(*e*) What is the process described above known as ?

ANSWERS

4. (*a*) Arteries (*b*) Veins **6.** Valves **7.** (*i*) Aorta (*ii*) Vena cava **11.** Blood **13.** (*a*) Phloem (*b*) Xylem **14.** Blood and Lymph **15.** Vena cava **16.** Phloem **17.** (*a*) Phloem (*b*) Xylem **18.** Translocation **19.** Transport of food **21.** (*a*) Oxygen (*b*) Carbon dioxide **23.** (*a*) True (*b*) False **24.** Lenticels and Stomata **25.** It is reabsorbed into the blood through blood capillaries surroundings the tubule **26.** Carbon dioxide and Urea **28.** Hypertension **29.** (*a*) waste (*b*) nephron (*c*) kidneys (*d*) lymph (*e*) white ; red **34.** (*i*) *c* (*ii*) *a* (*iii*) *d* (*iv*) *e* (*v*) *b* **40.** (*i*) Cellulose (*ii*) Water, glucose and salts in similar concentrations to those in normal blood (*iii*) Urea **42.** (*a*) Atria (*b*) Ventricles (*c*) Capillaries (*d*) (*i*) Right side (*ii*) Left side **47.** (*i*) Circulatory system (*ii*) Excretory system (*iii*) Respiratory system (*iv*) Digestive system **50.** (*c*) Lymph **59.** (*a*) **60.** (*b*) **61.** (*b*) **62.** (*c*) **63.** (*c*) **64.** (*c*) **65.** (*c*) **66.** (*b*) **67.** (*b*) **68.** (*a*) **69.** (*b*) **70.** (*c*) **71.** (*d*) **72.** (*b*) **73.** (*d*) **74.** (*c*) **75.** (*c*) **76.** (*b*) **77.** (*c*) **78.** (*b*) **79.** (*c*) **80.** (*d*) **81.** (*d*) **82.** (*c*) **83.** (*a*) **84** (*b*) **85.** (*d*) **86.** (*b*) **87.** (*a*) **88.** (*c*) **89.** (*c*) **90.** (*a*) **91.** (*d*) **92.** (*c*) **93.** (*d*) **94.** (*b*) **95.** (*a*) (*i*) Phloem (*ii*) Sieve tube (*iii*) Companion cell (*b*) (*i*) Xylem (*ii*) Xylem vessel (*iii*) Tracheids **96.** (*a*) (*i*) Diffusion (*ii*) Xylem (*iii*) Transpiration (*iv*) Photosynthesis (*v*) Phloem (*vi*) Translocation (*b*) E (*c*) E (*d*) B **97.** (*a*) (*i*) Blood (*ii*) Haemoglobin (*iii*) Red (*b*) (*i*) White blood cells (*ii*) Platelets (*iii*) Plasma (iv) Red blood cells (*c*) Digested food (*d*) E (Platelets) and G (Red blood cells) (*e*) *Amoeba* and Grasshopper **98.** (*a*) Heart (*b*) (*i*) Pulmonary vein (*ii*) Aorta (*iii*) Vena cava (*iv*) Pulmonary artery (*c*) (*i*) Left atrium (*ii*) Left ventricle (*d*) (*i*) Right atrium (*ii*) Right ventricle **99.** (*a*) (*i*) Lymph (*ii*) Light yellow (*b*) Lymphocytes (*c*) Plasma (*d*) It does not contain red blood cells having the red pigment haemoglobin **100.** (*a*) (*i*) Kidneys (*ii*) Urea (*b*) (*i*) Renal artery (*ii*) Renal vein (*c*) Nephrons (*d*) (*i*) Urine (*ii*) Bladder (*iii*) Ureters (*iv*) Urethra **101.** (*a*) Kidneys (*b*) Urea (*c*) (*i*) Cellulose (*ii*) Dialysing solution (*d*) Water, Glucose and Salts (*e*) Dialysis.

Control and Coordination

All the living organisms (plants and animals) respond and react to changes in the environment around them. **The changes in the environment to which the organisms respond and react are called stimuli** (singular of stimuli is stimulus). The living organisms show response to stimuli such as light, heat, cold, sound, smell, taste, touch, pressure, pain, water, and force of gravity, etc. **The response of organisms to a stimulus is usually in the form of some movement of their body part.** For example, if a man touches a very hot utensil accidently, he quickly pulls his hand away from the hot utensil. Here, heat is the stimulus and the man reacts by moving his hand away from the hot utensil. Similarly, when the sun is bright, we close our eyes. In this case, light is the stimulus and we react by closing the eyes.

(*a*) This father lion is responding to the bite he has received from his cub

(*b*) These are the leaves of sensitive plant (*Mimosa pudica)* about to be touched with a pencil

(*c*) When touched with pencil (or fingers), the sensitive plant responds by folding up its leaves

Figure 1. All the living things (animals and plants) respond to stimuli acting on them.

When we are frightened by a dog, we run away as fast as we can. Here, fear (of dog) is the stimulus and we react by running away. If we prick an earthworm with a needle, then the earthworm withdraws (moves back). In this case, pain (produced by pin prick) is the stimulus and the earthworm reacts by withdrawing. We know that a sunflower always faces the sun. Here, sunlight is the stimulus and sunflower reacts by bending (or moving) towards the sun. We eat food when we are hungry (and need energy). In this case, hunger is the stimulus and we react by eating food. From the above discussion we conclude that **the reaction to stimuli is a characteristic property of the living organisms**. Another word which is also used in place of 'reaction' is 'response'. So, we can also say that **the response to stimuli is a characteristic property of the living organisms.**

Both, plants and animals react (or respond) to various stimuli around them. But the method of reacting to stimuli is not similar in plants and animals. They react to stimuli in different ways. For example, plants bend towards light but animals do not bend towards light. The animal *Amoeba* reacts to the presence of food by moving towards the food particle. Similarly, *Amoebae* tend to aggregate (collect together) in moderately warm water which is their reaction to the stimulus called heat. *Amoeba* and other protozoa react to the mechanical obstacles by avoiding them. We find that the *Amoeba* (which is an animal) can react to different stimuli in different ways. **The animals can react to stimuli in many different ways** because they have a nervous system and an endocrine system involving hormones. **The plants, however, react to stimuli in a very limited way.** This is because the plants do not have a nervous system like the animals have. The plants use only the hormones for producing reaction to external stimuli.

From all the above examples we conclude that when a stimulus acts on our body, then we react (or respond) in a manner which is in the best interest of our body. The reaction (or response) which we give to the stimulus involves many organs of our body. It is, therefore, necessary that all the concerned organs should work with one another in a systematic manner so as to produce the required reaction. In other words, the various organs should co-operate with one another to provide proper reaction to the stimulus. **The working together of the various organs of an organism in a systematic manner so as to produce a proper response to the stimulus, is called coordination.** We will now discuss the control and coordination in plants, animals and human beings, one by one. Let us start with control and coordination in plants.

CONTROL AND COORDINATION IN PLANTS

The plants do not have a nervous system and sense organs like eyes, ears, or nose, etc., like the animals, but they can still sense things. The plants can sense the presence of stimuli like light, gravity, chemicals, water, and touch, etc., and respond to them. The plants can sense things like light, gravity, chemicals, water, and touch, etc., by the action of hormones in them. The stimuli like light, gravity, chemicals, water, and touch, etc., are called environmental changes. So, we can also say that **the plants coordinate their behaviour against environmental changes by using hormones.** The hormones in plants do not act the same way as in animals. The hormones in plants coordinate their behaviour by affecting the growth of a plant. And the effect on growth of the plant can result in the movement of a part of the plant like shoot (stem) or root, etc.

Figure 2. The sunflowers always face the sun. Here sunlight is the stimulus and the sunflower plants respond by bending (or moving) towards the sun.

Animals use both nervous system and hormones for coordination of their activities. **Plants have *no* nervous system, so plants use *only* hormones for coordination.** Thus, the reaction (or response) of plants to different stimuli like light, gravity, chemical substances, water, and touch etc., is due to the effect of hormones. Please note that animals *can* respond quickly because they have a nervous system. Plants *cannot* respond quickly because they have no nervous system. **The plants respond to various stimuli very slowly by growing.** So, in most of the cases, the response of a plant to a stimulus cannot be observed immediately. It usually takes a considerable time to observe the effect of a stimulus on a plant.

From the above discussion we conclude that **the function of control and coordination in plants is performed by the chemical substances called plant hormones**. Please note that the plant hormones are also called phytohormones ('phyto' means 'plant'). Before we discuss the various types of plant hormones, we should know the meanings of 'dormancy' and 'breaking of dormancy'. A resting, inactive condition in which metabolism almost stops is called dormancy. The seed of a plant is inactive or dormant. It has dormancy. A seed must have certain conditions like water, warmth, air and hormones to break dormancy and germinate to form a seedling (which then grows into a plant). Another part of a plant having dormancy is the bud. The bud is a young, undeveloped shoot of a plant which on breaking dormancy can form a branch, a leaf or a flower depending on its position in the plant. The breaking of dormancy of a bud also requires certain plant hormones. Keeping these points in mind, we will now discuss the various types of plant hormones.

Plant Hormones (or Phytohormones)

The control and coordination in plants is done by plant hormones (or phytohormones). The plant hormones coordinate the activities of the plant by controlling one or the other aspect of the growth of the plant. So, the plant hormones are also known as plant growth substances. The growth of a plant can be divided into three stages : cell division, cell enlargement and cell differentiation (or cell specialisation), and these stages have particular locations in a plant. These three stages of plant growth as well as promotion of dormancy, breaking of dormancy, stomata control, falling of leaves, fruit growth, ripening of fruits and ageing in plants are controlled by the various plant hormones.

There are four major types of plant hormones (or phytohormones) which are involved in the control and coordination in plants. These are :

1. **Auxins,**
2. **Gibberellins,**
3. **Cytokinins,** and
4. **Abscisic acid (ABA).**

Auxins, gibberellins and cytokinins are the plant hormones which *promote* growth of plants. On the other hand, abscisic acid is a plant hormone which *inhibits* (or prevents) the growth. The detailed functions of the various plant hormones are given below.

Figure 3. These pictures show the effect of gibberellin plant hormones on the growth of plants. The plants on the left side in the above picture have low levels of gibberellin hormones so their growth is less. When synthetic gibberellin hormones are applied, the plants grow much more rapidly as shown on the right hand side in the above picture.

(*i*) Auxins are the plant hormones which **promote cell enlargement and cell differentiation** in plants. Auxins also **promote fruit growth.** Auxin hormone controls a plant's response to light and gravity. In other words, auxin hormone is responsible for the phototropic and geotropic responses of plants. Auxin is made by cells at the tip of stems and roots. Auxin moves away from light, and towards gravity. Auxin has opposite effect on the growth of stem and roots. Auxin speeds up growth in stem but it slows down growth in roots. Synthetic auxins are applied in agriculture and horticulture.

(*ii*) Gibberellins are plant hormones which **promote cell enlargement and cell differentiation in the presence of auxins.** Gibberellins **help in breaking**

the dormancy in seeds and buds. They also **promote growth in fruits**. Gibberellin hormone is involved mainly in shoot extensions. Gibberellin stimulates elongation of shoots of various plants (see Figure 3).

(*iii*) Cytokinins are the plant hormones which **promote cell division** in plants. Cytokinins also **help in breaking the dormancy of seeds and buds**. They **delay the ageing in leaves.** Cytokinins **promote the opening of stomata.** They also **promote fruit growth.**

(*iv*) Abscisic acid is a plant hormone which functions mainly as a growth inhibitor. Abscisic acid **promotes the dormancy in seeds and buds** (this is the opposite of breaking of dormancy). It also **promotes the closing of stomata.** Abscisic acid **promotes the wilting and falling of leaves** (which is called abscission). It also causes the detachment of flowers and fruits from the plants.

Plant Movements

The plants are fixed at a place with their roots in the ground, so they cannot move from one place to another. That is, plants do not show locomotion (movement of the entire body). However, movements of the individual parts or organs of a plant (like shoot, root, leaves, etc.) are possible when they are subjected to some external stimuli like light, force of gravity, chemical substances, water, and touch, etc. These **movements of the plant part are usually caused by an unequal growth in its two regions by the action of plant hormones, under the influence of the stimulus.** For example, the auxin hormone is made and secreted by the meristematic tissue at the tip of stem (or tip of shoot). The auxin hormone speeds up the growth in stems. So, **if one side of a stem has more auxin than the other side, then the side of stem having more auxin hormone will grow faster than the other side** (having less auxin hormone). **This will cause the stem to bend.** And when the stem bends to one side, we say that the stem is showing movement. This movement (or bending) of the stem has been caused by its growth. So, we can say that the bending of a stem (or shoot) (when exposed to light from one side) is a growth movement. In fact, **the movement in any part of a plant is usually a growth movement.** Please note that when a plant part shows movement, it remains attached to the main body of the plant. It does not get detached from it. We will now discuss tropism in which the part of a plant shows movement in response to various stimuli.

Figure 4. A young grass seedling bends towards the light (coming from the candle). This bending has been caused by the action of plant hormone called auxin.

The plant movements made in response to external stimuli fall into two main categories : **tropisms** and **nasties.** Though all the tropisms are growth movements but nasties may be growth movements or growth-independent movements. **In tropisms, the direction of stimulus determines the direction of movement of the plant part but in nasties the direction of movement is not determined by the direction of stimulus.**

TROPISMS (OR TROPIC MOVEMENTS)

A growth movement of a plant part in response to an external stimulus in which the direction of stimulus determines the direction of response is called tropism. Thus, tropism is a **directional movement** of the part of a plant caused by its growth. The growth of a plant part in response to a stimulus can be towards the stimulus (in the direction of stimulus) or away from the stimulus (against the direction of stimulus) due to which we can have a positive tropism or negative tropism, respectively. So :

1. **If the growth (or movement) of a plant part is towards the stimulus, it is called *positive* tropism,** and
2. **If the growth (or movement) of a plant part is away from the stimulus, then it is called *negative* tropism.**

We will now give an example of tropism. When a growing plant is exposed to light from only one side, then it responds by bending its stem (or shoot) towards the light. This is an example of phototropism (which is caused by the 'light' acting as 'stimulus'. 'Photo' stands for 'light'). The bending of the plant stem (or shoot) towards light is actually *positive* phototropism.

Types of Tropisms

There are five common stimuli in the environment : light, gravity, chemicals, water and touch (or contact). These five stimuli give us five types of tropisms : phototropism, geotropism, chemotropism, hydrotropism and thigmotropism. In phototropism, the stimulus is light ; in geotropism the stimulus is gravity, in chemotropism the stimulus is a chemical, in hydrotropism the stimulus is water, and in thigmotropism the stimulus is touch (of a solid surface). It is obvious that the tropisms are named according to the stimulus. This will become clear from the following table.

Stimulus	*Type of tropism*
Light	Phototropism
Gravity	Geotropism
Chemical	Chemotropism
Water	Hydrotropism
Touch	Thigmotropism

We will now give the definitions of all the five types of tropisms.

(*i*) The movement of a plant part in response to light is called phototropism. In other words, the response of a plant to light is called phototropism. If the plant part moves towards light, it is called positive phototropism. On the other hand, if the plant part moves away from light, then it is called negative phototropism. The stem (or shoot) of a growing plant bends towards light, so the stem (or shoot) of a plant shows positive phototropism (see Figure 5). On the other hand, the roots of a plant move away from light, so the roots of a plant show negative phototropism.

Figure 5. The shoots of this potted plant kept near the window of a room bend towards sunlight coming from outside the window (on the left side). This is *positive* phototropism.

Figure 6. The roots of this potted plant bend downward in the direction of force of gravity. They show *positive* geotropism.On the other hand, the shoot (or stem) of this plant bends upwards, showing *negative* geotropism.

(*ii*) The movement of a plant part in response to gravity is called geotropism. In other words, the response of a plant to gravity is called geotropism. If the plant part moves in the direction of gravity, it is called positive geotropism. On the other hand, if the plant part moves against the direction of gravity, it is negative geotropism (Please note that the force of gravity acts in the downward direction). Now, the roots of a plant move downwards in the direction of gravity, so the roots of a plant show positive geotropism (see Figure 6). On the other hand, the stem (or shoot) of a plant moves upwards against the direction of gravity, so the stem (or shoot) of a plant shows negative geotropism (see Figure 6).

(iii) **The movement of a plant part in response to a chemical stimulus is called chemotropism.** In other words, the response of a plant to chemical stimulus is called chemotropism. If the plant part shows movement (or growth) towards the chemical, it is called positive chemotropism. On the other hand, if the plant part shows movement (or growth) away from the chemical, then it is called negative chemotropism. The growth of pollen tube towards the ovule during the process of fertilisation in a flower is an example of chemotropism (It is actually positive chemotropism). In this case the pollen tube grows towards the sugary substance (chemical) secreted by the ripe stigma of carpel in the flower.

(iv) **The movement of a plant part in response to water is called hydrotropism.** In other words, the response of a plant part to water is called hydrotropism. If the plant part moves towards water, it is called positive hydrotropism. On the other hand, if the plant part moves away from water, then it is called negative hydrotropism. The roots of a plant always go towards water, so roots are positively hydrotropic (see Figure 7).

Figure 7. The roots of a plant always go towards water. They show *positive* hydrotropism.

Figure 8. The tendrils of a plant always grow towards any support which they happen to touch. They show *positive* thigmotropism.

Figure 9. This cucumber plant is climbing on a support with the help of its climbing organs called tendrils.

(v) **The directional growth movement of a plant part in response to the touch of an object is called thigmotropism.** The climbing parts of the plants such as tendrils grow towards any support which they happen to touch and wind around that support. So, tendrils of plants are positively thigmotropic (see Figures 8 and 9).

We will now describe a plant's response to light, gravity, chemicals, water and touch with the help of diagrams.

Response of Plants to Light : Phototropism

Plants need sunlight, so the stems (or shoots) respond to sunlight by growing towards it. The plants also turn their leaves to face the sun. This makes sure that the leaves get as much sunlight as possible. When a plant is grown in the open ground with the sunlight coming from above, then the stem of plant grows straight up. If, however, the plant is grown with sunlight coming from one side, then the stem of plant bends towards the direction from which the sunlight comes. The root of plant, however, bends away from the direction from which the sunlight comes. We will now describe an experiment to show the response of plant parts to light.

We take a potted plant growing in a transparent glass jar. When this potted plant is kept in the open space, the sunlight falls from above due to which the stem of plant grows straight up towards the source of light 'sun' [see Figure 10(*a*)]. The root of plant also grows straight but in the downward direction.

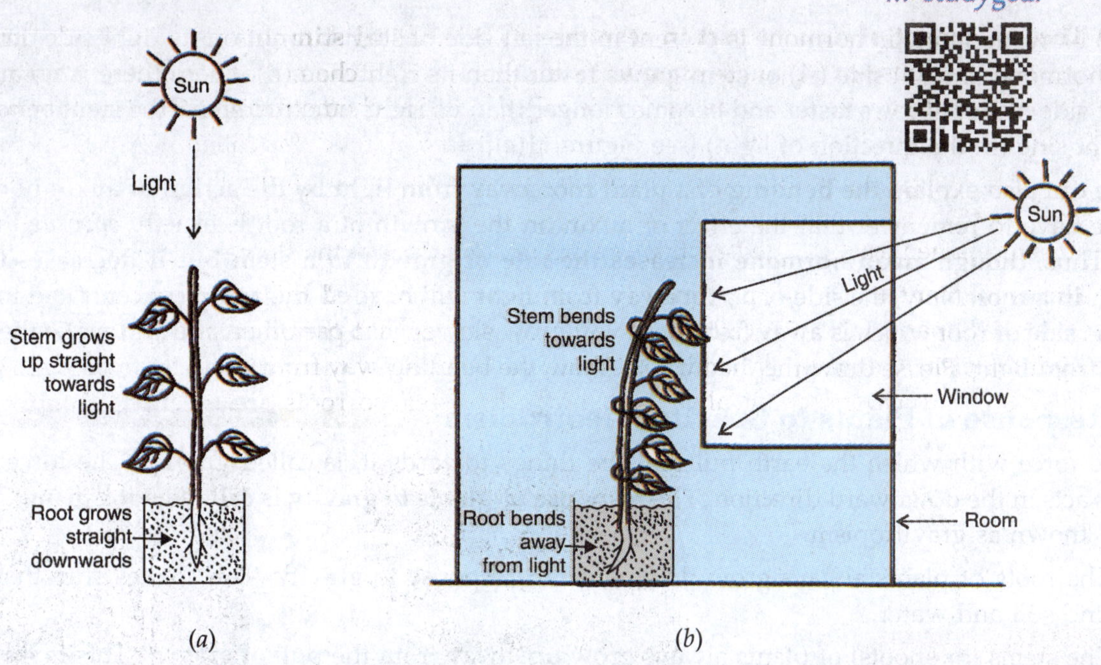

Figure 10. Diagrams to show the response of a plant to light (or phototropism).

Let us now keep the potted plant having straight stem and straight root near the window in a dark room so that sunlight falls on it from the right side (through the window) only. After some days we will see that the stem of the plant bends towards the right side from where the light is coming [see Figure 10(*b*)]. This observation shows that **the stem of plant responds to light and bends towards it.** Even the leaves of the plant turn towards the sun so as to obtain the maximum sunlight. Thus, the stem (and leaves) of a plant are *positively* phototropic. Now, if we look at the root of the plant in Figure 10(*b*), we find that the root bends to the left side away from the light. This observation shows that the root of plant responds to light by growing away from it. Thus, the root of plant is *negatively* phototropic.

We will now explain the bending of a plant stem towards sunlight. **The plant stem responds to light and bends towards it due to the action of 'auxin hormone'.** This happens as follows :

(*i*) When sunlight comes from above, then the auxin hormone present in the tip of the stem spreads uniformly down the stem [see Figure 11(*a*)]. Due to the equal presence of auxin, both the sides of the stem (*A* and *B*) grow equally rapidly [see Figure 11(*a*)]. And the stem grows straight up.

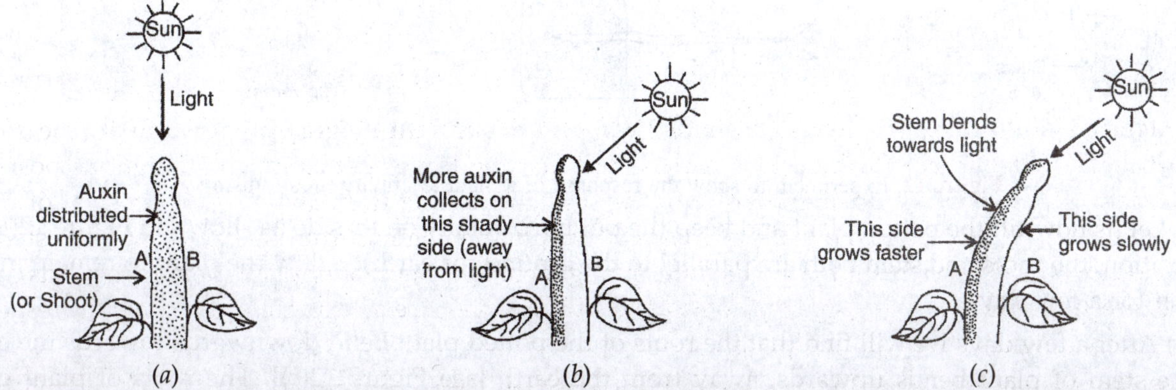

Figure 11. Diagrams to explain the bending of a plant stem (or shoot) towards light by the action of 'auxin' hormone.

(*ii*) When the light falls only on the right side of the stem [side *B* in Figure 11(*b*)], then the auxin hormone collects in the left side (shady side *A*) of the stem, away from light. This is because **auxin hormone prefers to stay in shade.**

(*iii*) Now, more auxin hormone is present in the left side of stem but not on its right side. Due to more auxin hormone, the left side (*A*) of stem grows faster than its right side (*B*) where there is no auxin. Since the left side of stem grows faster and becomes longer than its right side, therefore, the stem bends towards the right side (in the direction of light) [see Figure 11(*c*)].

We can also explain the bending of a plant root away from light by the action of auxin hormone. For this we have to remember that the effect of auxin on the growth of a root is exactly *opposite* to that on a stem. Thus, **though auxin hormone increases the rate of growth in a stem but it decreases the rate of growth in a root.** Now, the side of a root away from light will have all the auxin concentrated in it. Due to this, the side of root which is away from light will grow slower than the other side and make the root bend away from light. Please draw the diagram to show the bending of plant root away from light yourself.

The Response of Plants to Gravity : Geotropism

The force with which the earth pulls all the things towards it, is called gravity. The force of gravity always acts in the downward direction. **The response of plants to gravity is called geotropism.** Geotropism is also known as gravitropism.

(*i*) The roots of plants always grow downward in response to gravity. This makes sure that they will find soil and water.

(*ii*) The stems (or shoots) of plants always grow up, away from the pull of gravity. This makes sure that they will get light.

The movement of plant roots towards the earth and that of stem away from earth, both are cases of geotropism. Since the roots grow down towards the pull of gravity, so the downward growth (or downward movement) of roots is called *positive* geotropism. The stem (or shoot) grows upwards, away from the pull of gravity, so the upward growth (or upward movement) of stem or shoot is called *negative* geotropism. The response of plants to gravity (or geotropism) will become more clear from the following experiment.

(*i*) We take a potted plant growing in a transparent glass jar. When this potted plant is kept in the normal position, we can see that its roots are growing downwards and its stem is growing upwards [see Figure 12(*a*)].

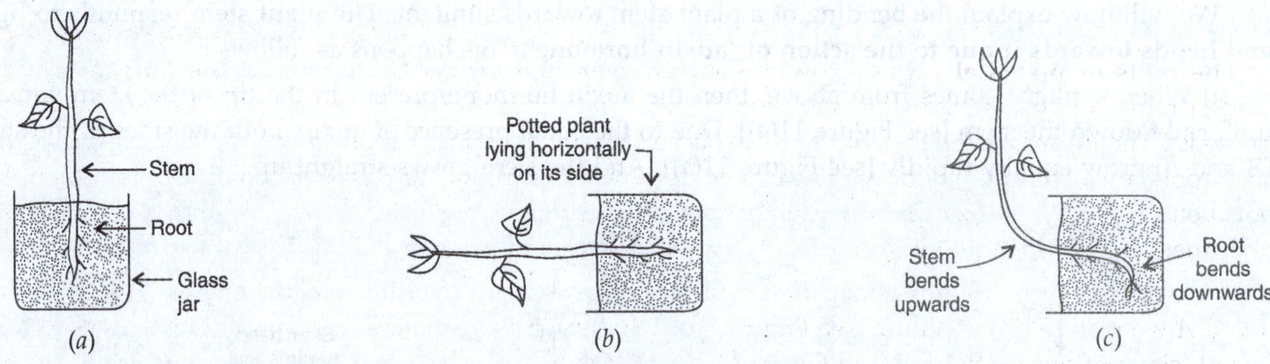

Figure 12. Experiment to show the response of a plant to gravity (geotropism).

(*ii*) Let us now tilt the potted plant and keep the pot horizontally on its side as shown in Figure 12(*b*). In this position, the roots and stem both are parallel to the ground (or earth). Allow the plant to remain in this position for a few days.

(*iii*) After a few days we will find that the roots of the potted plant bend downwards towards the earth and the stem of plant bends upwards, away from the earth [see Figure 12(*c*)]. The roots of plant grow downwards in response to the pull of gravity. The stem of plant responds to gravity in the opposite way, by growing upwards (away from the pull of gravity).

Response of Plants to Chemicals : Chemotropism

The growth (or movement) of a plant part due to chemical stimulus is known as chemotropism. The growth (or movement) of a pollen tube towards the ovule induced by a sugary substance as stimulus, is an example of chemotropism. This can be explained as follows : The ripe stigma in the carpel of a flower secretes a chemical substance (which is a sugary substance) into the style towards the ovary (see Figure 13).

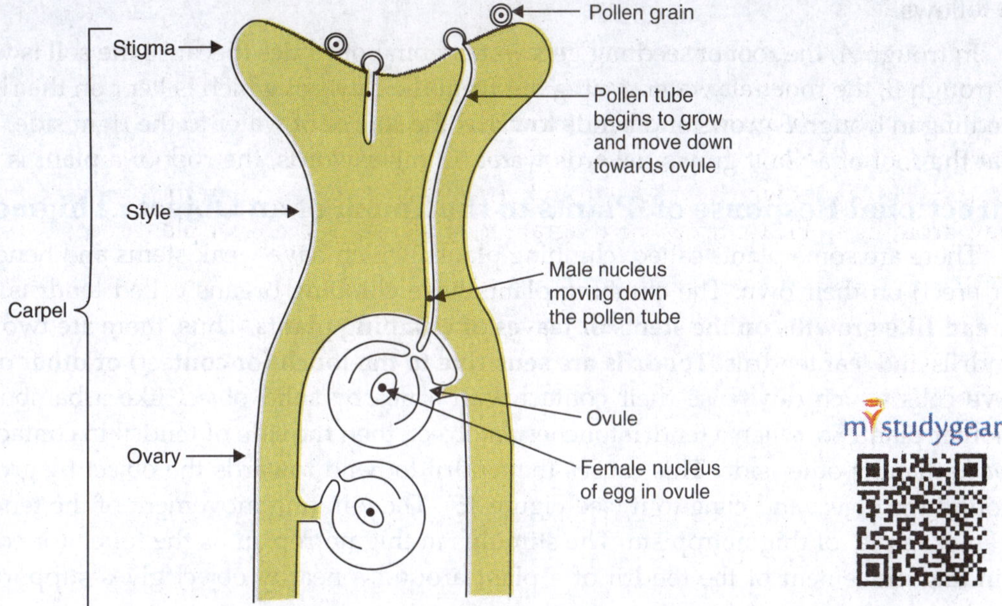

Figure 13. Diagram to show the response of a plant part 'pollen' to chemical secreted by stigma (or chemotropism).

This sugary substance acts as a stimulus for the pollen grains which fall on the stigma of the carpel. The pollen grain responds to this stimulus by growing a pollen tube in the downward direction into the style of the carpel and reaches the ovule in the ovary of the flower for carrying out fertilisation. This growth of the pollen tube in response to a chemical substance secreted by the stigma of a flower is an example of chemotropism.

Response of Plants to Water : Hydrotropism

The roots of plants always go towards water, even if it means going against the pull of gravity. Though roots normally grow downwards but in order to reach water, they can grow sideways or even upwards ! The roots grow in the direction of source of water so as to obtain water for the developing plant. Since roots always grow (or move) towards water, therefore, roots are positively hydrotropic. When the roots bend by growing towards water, it appears that they move towards water. We will now describe an experiment to demonstrate hydrotropism. This will show us the response of roots to water.

We take two glass troughs *A* and *B* and fill each one of them two-thirds with soil (see Figure 14). In trough *A* we plant a tiny seedling [see Figure 14(*a*)]. In trough *B* we plant a similar seedling and also place a small 'clay pot' inside the soil [see Figure 14(*b*)]. Water the soil in trough *A* daily and uniformly. Do *not* water the soil in trough *B* but put some water in the clay pot buried in the soil. Leave both the troughs for a few days.

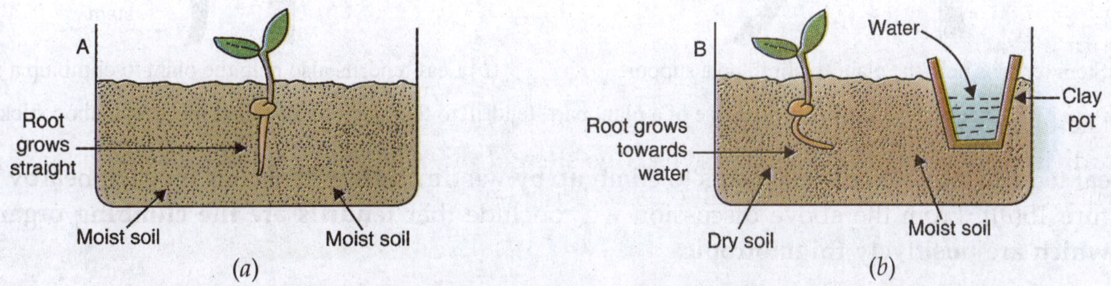

Figure 14. Experiment to show the response of a plant to water (hydrotropism).

Now, dig up the seedlings carefully from both the troughs without damaging their roots. We will find that the root of seedling in trough *A* is straight. On the other hand, the root of seedling in trough *B* is found to be bent to the right side (towards the clay pot containing water) [see Figure 14(*b*)]. This can be explained as follows.

In trough *A*, the root of seedling gets water from both sides (because the soil is watered uniformly). But in trough *B*, the root gets water oozing out from the clay pot which is kept on the right side. So, the root of seedling in trough *B* grows and bends towards the source of water to the right side. This experiment shows that the root of a plant grows towards water. In other words, the root of a plant is positively hydrotropic.

Directional Response of Plants to the Touch of an Object : Thigmotropism

There are some plants called 'climbing plants' which have weak stems and hence cannot stand upright (or erect) on their own. The climbing plants have climbing organs called tendrils. **Tendrils are the thin, thread-like growths on the stems or leaves of climbing plants.** Thus, there are two types of tendrils : stem tendrils and leaf tendrils. **Tendrils are sensitive to the touch (or contact) of other objects.** That is, tendrils have cells which can sense their contact with a nearby solid object like a bamboo stick, or the stem of another plant. So, when a tendril touches an object, then the side of tendril in contact with the object grows *slowly* than its other side. This causes the tendril to bend towards the object by growing towards it, wind around the object and cling to it (see Figure 15). The winding movement of the tendril of a climbing plant is an example of thigmotropism. The stimulus in thigmotropism is the touch (or contact) of an object. The winding movement of the tendril of a plant around a nearby object gives support to the plant having a weak stem.

Thigmotropism is often seen in plants having tendrils. **Tendrils are positively thigmotropic which means that they grow towards things they happen to touch.** The plants having stem tendrils or leaf tendrils which are positively thigmotropic climb up artificial supports, other plants or fences very easily. The plants such as bitter gourd (*karela*), bottle gourd (*lauki*), grape vine and passion flower have stem tendrils which are positively thigmotropic and make these plants to climb up by winding around various types of supports [see Figure 15(*a*)]. The plants such as peas and glory lily have leaf tendrils which are positively thigmotropic.

(*a*) Stem tendrils help the plant to climb up a support (*b*) Leaf tendrils also help the plant to climb up a support

Figure 15. Diagrams to show the response of a plant part 'tendril' to the touch of an object (here a bamboo stick).

These leaf tendrils also make their plants to climb up by winding around various types of nearby supports [see Figure 15(*b*)]. From the above discussion we conclude that **tendrils are the climbing organs of the plants which are positively thigmotropic.**

The Usefulness of Tropic Movements

The various types of tropic movements help the plants to survive. For example, even if a seed is planted upside down, its root will still grow downwards into earth because it is positively geotropic (see Figure 16). The root will also grow towards water because it is positively hydrotropic. Similarly, the shoot of such a seed will grow upwards because it is negatively geotropic and towards light because it is positively phototropic. These tropic movements help the plants to obtain water and nutrients from soil and light from the sun, which are necessary for their growth and survival.

Figure 16. Whichever way up a seed is planted, its root always grows downwards into the soil. This is *positive* geotropism in seeds.

NASTIES (OR NASTIC MOVEMENTS)

We have just studied that in tropism, a plant part either moves towards the stimulus or away from the stimulus. However, in some plants, the movement of the plant part is neither towards the stimulus nor away from the stimulus. That is, the movement of plant part in some plants is not in a particular direction with respect to stimulus. **The movement of a plant part in response to an external stimulus in which the direction of response is not determined by the direction of stimulus is called nastic movement.** Nastic movements of plants are also called nasties. The nastic movements of plants are induced by stimuli such as heat, light, touch (or contact), etc. **The main difference between tropic and nastic movements is that tropic movement is a directional movement of a plant part but nastic movement is not a directional movement of the plant part with respect to the stimulus.** The direction of nastic movement is *not* determined by the direction from which the stimulus is applied. In nastic movement, from whichever direction the stimulus is applied, it affects all the parts of the organ of a plant equally and they always move in the same direction. Nastic movements are mostly exhibited by the flat organs of the plants like 'leaves' and 'petals of flowers'. Some of the examples of the nastic movements of plants (or nasties) are given below :

(*i*) The folding up of the leaves of a sensitive plant (*Mimosa pudica*) on touching is an example of *nastic* movement. Here the stimulus is *touch*.

(*ii*) The opening up of the petals of dandelion flowers in morning in bright light and closing in the evening when the light fades is an example of *nastic* movement. In this case the stimulus is *light*.

(*iii*) The closing of the petals of moonflower in the morning in bright light and opening at dark when the light fades is also an example of *nastic* movement. In this case also the stimulus is *light*.

Please note that though all tropisms are growth movements but all nasties (or nastic movements) are not growth movements. Nastic movements may or may not be growth movements. For example, **the folding up of the leaves of a sensitive plant on touching is not a growth movement** but **the opening and closing of petals of flowers by the action of sunlight is a growth movement.**

We have just said that most of the movements of the plant parts are caused by their growth. Now, since the growth of a plant part is usually a slow process, therefore, **most of the movements of plant parts are very slow.** There are, however, some exceptions. **We will now describe the movement of a plant part (leaves) which is unusually fast and takes place almost immediately.** It is the folding up of the leaves of a sensitive plant when touched with a finger (or any other object). This is discussed below under the topic on thigmonasty.

Thigmonasty

The non-directional movement of a plant part in response to the touch of an object is called thigmonasty. In other words, thigmonasty is the nastic movement of a plant part in response to touch. Thus, the stimulus in thigmonasty is the *'touch'*. An example of the nastic movement in plants caused by touch (or thigmonasty) is provided by the sensitive plant (*Mimosa pudica*) which is also known as touch-me-not plant. It is called *chhui-mui* in Hindi. If we touch the leaves (or rather leaflets) of the sensitive plant with our fingers, then its leaves fold up and droop almost immediately. The folding up of the leaves of sensitive plant on touching, is an example of nastic movements in plants (in which the stimulus is the 'touch' of our fingers).

Figure 17. Diagrams to show the nastic movements in the leaves of sensitive plant (*Mimosa pudica*) caused by 'touch'.

Figure 17(*a*) shows the open leaves of a sensitive plant. When we touch the leaves of this sensitive plant with our fingers, then these leaves of sensitive plant fold up at once as shown in Figure 17(*b*). In this case, the 'touch' of our fingers is the stimulus and the leaves respond by 'folding up'. Please note that the folding of leaves of a sensitive plant is not a case of tropism (like thigmotropism) because in this case the direction of movement of leaves does not depend on the direction of stimulus (touch). We will now describe how the leaves of a sensitive plant fold up when touched.

The sensitive plant has pad-like swellings called 'pulvini' at the base of each leaf [see Figure 18(*a*)] (The singular of *pulvini* is *pulvinus*). The pulvini contain a lot of water in their cells. Due to the internal 'water pressure' in them (called turgor), all the pulvini are very firm and hold the leaves above them upright [see Figure 18(*a*)]. The pulvini have also large intercellular spaces (empty spaces) between their cells. **The folding up of the leaves of a sensitive plant on touching is due to the sudden loss of water from pad-like swellings called 'pulvini' present at the base of all leaves of the sensitive plant which make the pulvini lose their firmness causing the leaves to droop and fall.** This happens as follows.

When the leaves of sensitive plant (having pulvini at their base) are touched with a finger, then an electrical impulse is generated which travels through ordinary cells (because there are no nerve cells in

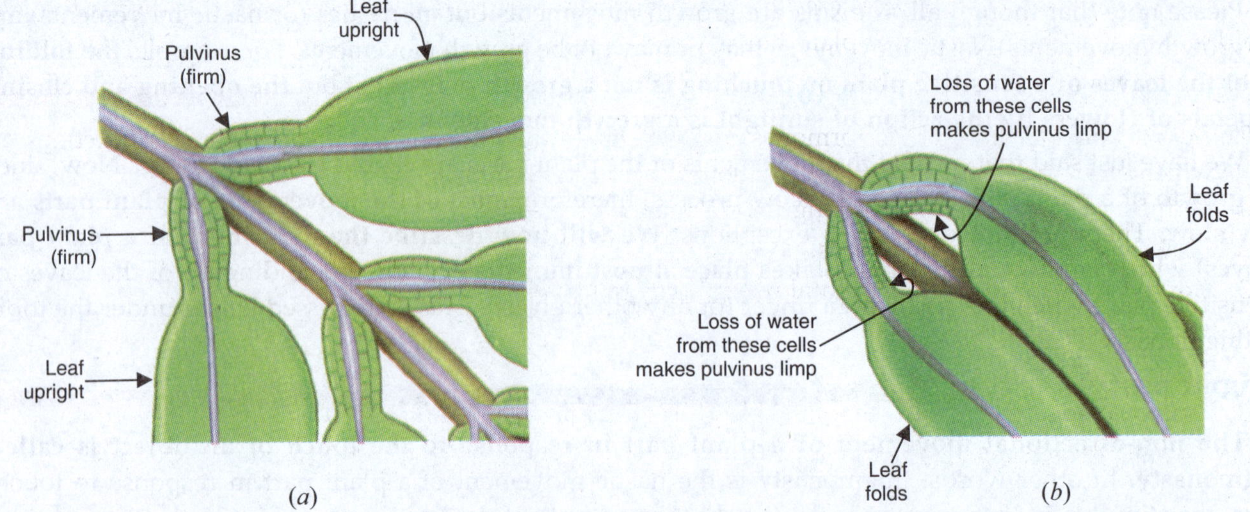

Figure 18. The leaves of sensitive plant fold due to the loss of water from pulvinus at their base.

sensitive plant or other plants). This electrical impulse acts on a plant hormone. The plant hormone makes the water migrate from the cells of one half of a pulvinus to the intercellular spaces in the other half of pulvinus. This loss of water from half of pulvinus causes the pulvinus to lose its firmness making the leaf to fold [see Figure 18(*b*)]. Similarly, all the pulvini lose firmness and become limp due to which all the leaves above them collapse and fold up.

At a gap of 15 to 30 minutes after the leaves have folded, water usually diffuses back into same cells of pulvinus from which it left, and the leaf returns to its original position.

Photonasty

The non-directional movement of a plant part (usually petals of flowers) in response to light is called photonasty. In other words, photonasty is the nastic movement of a plant part (like petals of flowers) in response to light. Thus, the stimulus in photonasty is *light*. A dandelion flower opens up in the morning in bright light but closes in the evening when the light fades and it gets dark (see Figure 19). The opening

(*a*) Dandelion flower opens the petals in bright light during the daytime

(*b*) Dandelion flower closes the petals at dusk (or night) when it gets dark

Figure 19. Nastic movements of petals of dandelion flower in response to light. This is an example of photonasty.

(*a*) Moonflower closes the petals during the daytime when there is bright light

(*b*) Moonflower opens the petals at dusk (or night) when it gets dark and there is no light

Figure 20. Nastic movements of petals of moonflower in response to light. Another example of photonasty.

and closing of petals of dandelion flowers in response to the intensity of light is an example of nastic movement in which the stimulus is light. In other words, it is an example of photonasty. The moonflower behaves exactly *opposite* to that of dandelion flowers in respect of response to light. The petals of moonflower close during the day when there is bright light but open up at night when it is dark and there is no light (see Figure 20). This is also an example of photonasty.

Please note that **the opening and closing of flowers in response to light (or photonasty) are growth movements.** Petals open when their *inner surfaces grow more* than their outer surfaces. On the other hand, petals close when their *outer surfaces grow more* than their inner surfaces. Before we end this discussion, we would like to give the functions of plant hormones.

Functions of Plant Hormones (or Phytohormones)

The plant hormones (or phytohormones) regulate many functions in plants. The various functions in plants which are regulated by the plant hormones (or phytohormones) are :

1. Germination of seeds (or Breaking the dormancy of seeds),
2. Growth of root, stem and leaves,
3. Movement of stomata (or stomatal movement) in leaves,
4. Flowering of plants,
5. Ripening of fruits, and
6. Phototropism, geotropism, chemotropism, hydrotropism, thigmotropism and nastic movements.

Let us answer some questions now.

Sample Problem 1. Which of the following is a plant hormone ?

(*a*) Insulin (*b*) Thyroxine (*c*) Oestrogen (*d*) Cytokinin **(NCERT Book Question)**

Answer. (*d*) Cytokinin.

Sample Problem 2. How do auxins promote the growth of a tendril around a support ? **(NCERT Book Question)**

Answer. When the tip of a tendril touches a support, then the auxins (plant hormones) present in its tip move to that side of tip which is away from the support. Auxins promote growth. So, due to more auxins in it, the side of tendril away from the support grows faster (and becomes longer) than the side which is in contact with the support, and makes the tendril curve (or bend) towards the support. This 'curving' tendril can then encircle the support and wind around it.

Sample Problem 3. How is the movement of the leaves of the sensitive plant different from the movement of a shoot towards light ? **(NCERT Book Question)**

Answer. The main differences between the movement of the leaves of a sensitive plant and the movement of a shoot towards light are as follows :

Movement of leaves of sensitive plant	*Movement of a shoot towards light*
1. It is a nastic movement which does not depend on the direction of stimulus applied	1. It is a tropic movement which depends on the direction of stimulus applied.
2. The stimulus is 'touch'.	2. The stimulus is 'light'.
3. It is caused by the sudden loss of water from the swellings at the base of leaves	3. It is caused by the unequal growth on the two sides of the shoot.
4. It is not a growth movement.	4. It is a growth movement.

Sample Problem 4. What is the difference between the manner in which movement takes place in a sensitive plant and the movement in our legs ? **(NCERT Book Question)**

Answer. The movement in the leaves of a sensitive plant takes place due to the sudden loss of water in the pad-like swellings (called pulvini) at the base of all the leaves. The loss of water makes the pulvini limp leading to drooping and folding of leaves. On the other hand, the movement in our legs takes place when the leg muscles pull on the leg bones.

Before we go further and discuss control and coordination in animals (including human beings), **please answer the following questions :**

Very Short Answer Type Questions

1. What is the general name of chemical substances which bring about control and coordination in plants ?
2. Which plant hormone is responsible for the wilting and falling of leaves ?
3. Which plant hormone makes a stem (or shoot) bend towards light ?
4. Where is the auxin hormone made in a plant stem ?
5. What is the scientific name of sensitive plant ?
6. Name one plant hormone that promotes growth and another plant hormone which inhibits growth.
7. Name one example of the movement of a plant part which is very quick and can be observed easily.
8. Name the type of chemical substances that control the growth in plants.
9. What is the stimulus in : (*a*) phototropism ? (*b*) geotropism ? (*c*) chemotropism ? (*d*) hydrotropism ? (*e*) thigmotropism ?
10. Give the scientific terms used to represent the following :
    (*a*) Bending of a shoot towards light.
    (*b*) Growing of roots towards the earth.
    (*c*) Growth of a pollen tube towards ovule.
    (*d*) Bending of roots towards water.
    (*e*) Winding of tendril around a support.

11. Give one example of the movement of a plant part which is caused by the loss of water (or migration of water).
12. Give one example each of a plant part :
    (*a*) which is positively hydrotropic as well as positively geotropic.
    (*b*) which is positively phototropic but negatively geotropic.
13. Which of the following is a growth movement and which is not ?
    (*a*) folding up of leaves of sensitive plant on touching with hand.
    (*b*) folding up of petals of dandelion flower when light fades.
14. Name the plant part :
    (*a*) which bends in the direction of gravity but away from light
    (*b*) which bends towards light but away from the force of gravity
15. To which directional stimuli do :
    (*a*) roots respond ?
    (*b*) shoots respond ?
16. Fill in the following blanks :
    (*a*) A plant's response to light is called ....
    (*b*) A plant's response to gravity is called ....
    (*c*) Plant shoot grows upward in response to ....
    (*d*) Plant roots grow downward in response to ....
    (*e*) Tendrils wind around a support in response to ....
    (*f*) Plant roots grow towards....... and in the direction of force of ....
    (*g*) A root of a plant grows downward. This is known as ....
    (*h*) ...... is the hormone that causes phototropism in plants
    (*i*) The response of leaves to the sunlight is called ....

Short Answer Type Questions

17. Plant parts show two types of movements, one dependent on growth and the other independent of growth. Give one example of the movement in plant parts :
    (*a*) which depends on growth
    (*b*) which does not depend on growth
18. What is a plant hormone ? Name four plant hormones. State one function of each.
19. (*a*) What does a root do in response to gravity ? What is this phenomenon known as ?
    (*b*) What does a stem (or shoot) do in response to light ? What is this phenomenon known as ?
20. (*a*) What does a stem (or shoot) do in response to gravity ? What is this phenomenon known as ?
    (*b*) What does a root do in response to light ? What is this phenomenon known as ?
21. (*a*) What does a *Mimosa pudica* plant do in response to touch ? What is this phenomenon known as ?
    (*b*) What happens to the dandelion flower (*i*) during daytime, and (*ii*) at night ? What is this phenomenon known as ?
22. (*a*) What does a plant root do in response to water ? What is this phenomenon known as ?
    (*b*) What happens to the moonflower (*i*) during daytime, and (*ii*) at night ? What is this phenomenon known as ?
23. What is a tendril ? Name the two types of tendrils. What does a tendril do in response to the touch of a support ? What is this phenomenon known as ?
24. Name the five types of tropisms. How are tropic movements helpful to plants ? Explain with an example.
25. Define chemotropism. Give one example of chemotropism. State whether this example is of positive chemotropism or negative chemotropism.
26. Distinguish between tropic movements and nastic movements in plants. Give examples to illustrate your answer.
27. (*a*) What is meant by nastic movements in plants ? Give one example of nastic movements in plants.
    (*b*) What is the difference between photonasty and thigmonasty ?

28. A potted plant is kept horizontally for a considerable time. The three positions of the parts A and B of the potted plant are shown in the following figures :

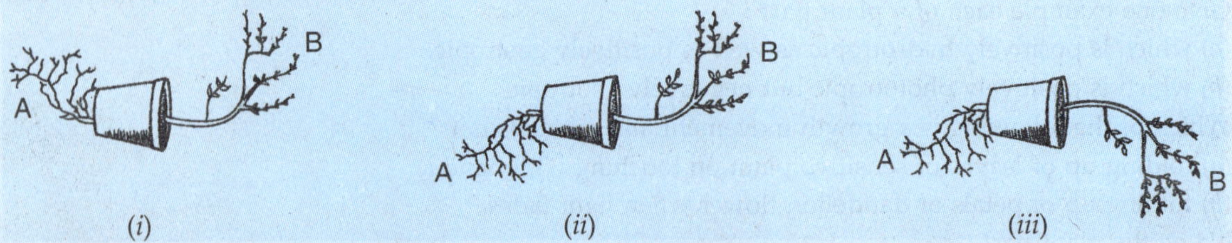

(*i*) (*ii*) (*iii*)

(*a*) Which figure shows the correct position taken by the parts A and B of the plant ?
(*b*) What type of phenomenon is exhibited by the figure chosen in (*a*) above ?

29. Name the plant hormones which are responsible for the following effects :
(*a*) falling of leaves (*b*) opening of stomata
(*c*) bending of stem towards light (*d*) closing of stomata

30. Name the plant organs which are :
(*a*) positively phototropic (*b*) positively geotropic
(*c*) negatively geotropic (*d*) positively hydrotropic

31. Why is the folding up of the leaves of a sensitive plant on touching with a finger not a tropism ?

32. Why is the closing of a dandelion flower at dusk (when it gets dark) not a tropism ?

Long Answer Type Questions

33. (*a*) What is meant by 'tropisms' (or tropic movements) ? Explain with an example.
(*b*) What are the different types of tropisms ? Define each type of tropism. Write the name of stimulus in each case.
(*c*) How do tropisms differ from nasties (or nastic movements) ?

34. (*a*) Define phototropism. Give one example of phototropism.
(*b*) How does phototropism occur in a plant stem (or shoot) ? Explain with the help of labelled diagrams.
(*c*) What is meant by positive phototropism and negative phototropism ? Give one example of each type.

35. (*a*) Define geotropism. Give one example of geotropism.
(*b*) What is meant by 'positive geotropism' and 'negative geotropism ? Give one example of each type. Draw a labelled diagram to illustrate your answer indicating the plant part which shows positive geotropism and the plant part which shows negative geotropism.
(*c*) Name one plant part which exhibits positive thigmotropism.

36. (*a*) How does control and coordination take place in plants ? How does it differ from that in animals ?
(*b*) Name five stimuli which act on plants. Name the type of tropism produced by each one of these stimuli.
(*c*) Define hydrotropism. Give one example of hydrotropism. State whether this example is of positive hydrotropism or negative hydrotropism. Illustrate your answer with the help of labelled diagram.

37. (*a*) What is meant by positive tropism and negative tropism ? Explain with examples.
(*b*) Define thigmotropism. Give one example of thigmotropism.
(*c*) What is the difference between thigmotropism and thigmonasty ? Name one plant which exhibits thigmotropism and one plant which exhibits thigmonasty. What behaviour (or responses) of these plants make you think that they exhibit thigmotropism and thigmonasty respectively ?

Multiple Choice Questions (MCQs)

38. Which of the following is not a plant hormone ?
(*a*) auxin (*b*) ascorbic acid (*c*) cytokinin (*d*) abscisic acid

39. One of the following plant hormones is responsible for the phenomenon of phototropism in plants. This is :
(*a*) gibberellin (*b*) eltroxin (*c*) cytokinin (*d*) auxin

40. The movement of a plant part in response to the force of attraction exerted by the earth is called :
(*a*) hydrotropism (*b*) geotropism (*c*) chemotropism (*d*) phototropism

41. The movement of sunflower in accordance with the path of the sun is due to :
(*a*) photonasty (*b*) phototropism (*c*) hydrotropism (*d*) chemotropism

42. The plant part which exhibits negative geotropism is :
(*a*) root (*b*) stem (*c*) branch (*d*) leaves

43. A big tree falls in a forest but its roots are still in contact with the soil. The branches of this fallen tree grow straight up (vertically). This happens in response to
(*a*) water and light
(*b*) water and minerals
(*c*) gravity and water
(*d*) light and gravity

The branches of this fallen tree are growing straight up in response to two stimuli. What are those two stimuli ? (see question 43).

44. Which of the following is not caused by a growth movement ?
(*a*) bending of the shoot of a plant in response to light
(*b*) closing up of leaves of a sensitive plant on touching with an object
(*c*) climbing up of a plant on an object by using tendrils
(*d*) movement of the root of a plant towards a source of water

45. The root of a plant is :
(*i*) positively phototropic but negatively geotropic
(*ii*) positively geotropic but negatively phototropic
(*iii*) negatively phototropic but positively hydrotropic
(*iv*) negatively hydrotropic but positively phototropic
(*a*) (*i*) and (*ii*) (*b*) (*ii*) and (*iii*) (*c*) (*iii*) and (*iv*) (*d*) (*i*) and (*iv*)

46. The main function of the plant hormone called abscisic acid is to :
(*a*) increase the length of cells (*b*) promote cell division
(*c*) inhibit growth (*d*) promote growth of stem and roots

47. The growth of tendrils in pea plants is due to the :
(*a*) effect of sunlight on the tendril cells facing the sun
(*b*) effect of gravity on the part of tendril hanging down towards the earth
(*c*) rapid cell division and elongation in tendril cells that are away from the support
(*d*) rapid cell division and elongation in tendril cells in contact with the support

48. Which of the following phytohormone is not associated with the promotion of growth in plants ?
(*a*) auxin (*b*) abscisic acid (*c*) gibberellin (*d*) cytokinin

49. The plant hormone which triggers the fall of mature leaves and fruits from the plant body is :
(*a*) auxin (*b*) gibberellin (*c*) abscisic acid (*d*) cytokinin

50. Which of the following terms denotes the movement of the root of a plant towards moisture in the soil ?
(*a*) thigmotropism (*b*) chemotropism (*c*) hydrotropism (*d*) geotropism

51. The growth of a pollen tube towards the ovule caused by a sugary substance as stimulus is an example of :
(*a*) phototropism (*b*) chlorotropism (*c*) gravitropism (*d*) chemotropism

52. The bending of the shoot of a plant in response to light is called :
(*a*) geotropism (*b*) phototropism (*c*) thigmotropism (*d*) photonasty

53. The stimulus in the process of thigmotropism is :
(*a*) touch (*b*) gravity (*c*) light (*d*) chemical

54. A growing seedling is kept in a dark room. A burning candle is placed near it for a few days. The top part of seedling bends towards the burning candle. This is an example of :
(*a*) chemotropism (*b*) hydrotropism (*c*) phototropism (*d*) geotropism

55. Which of the following acts as a stimulus in the process of hydrotropism ?
(*a*) hydrocarbon (*b*) hydrogen oxide (*c*) hydrogen chloride (*d*) hydrogen peroxide

56. The growth movement of a plant part in response to the touch of an object is called :
(*a*) thigmonasty (*b*) hydrotropism (*c*) thigmotropism (*d*) geotropism

57. The climbing organs of plants like tendrils grow towards any support which they happen to touch and wind around the support. This is an example of :
(*a*) chemotropism (*b*) nastic movement (*c*) thigmotropism (*d*) geotropism

58. The rate of growth in roots is decreased by one of the following plant hormones. This plant hormone is :
(*a*) gibberellin (*b*) auxin (*c*) cytokinin (*d*) ethene

59. When the leaves of a *Mimosa pudica* plant are touched with a finger, they fold up quickly. This is an example of :
(*a*) chemotropism (*b*) thigmonasty (*c*) photonasty (*d*) thigmotropism

60. Dandelion flowers open the petals in bright light during the daytime but close the petals in dark at night. This response of dandelion flowers to light is called :
(*a*) phototropism (*b*) thigmonasty (*c*) chemotropism (*d*) photonasty

61. To which of the following directional stimulus roots of a plant do not respond ?
(*a*) moisture (*b*) candle light (*c*) touch (*d*) gravity

62. One of the following is not caused by the growth related movement of the concerned plant part. This is :
(*a*) phototropism (*b*) photonasty (*c*) thigmonasty (*d*) thigmotropism

63. The bending of the root of a plant away from a source of light is caused by a plant hormone called :
(*a*) cytokinin (*b*) gibberellin (*c*) abscisic acid (*d*) auxin

64. Most of the plant hormones promote plant growth. A plant hormone which inhibits growth is :
(*a*) abscisic acid (*b*) ethene (*c*) ascorbic acid (*d*) cytokinin

65. The movement of a shoot towards light is :
(*a*) geotropism (*b*) hydrotropism (*c*) chemotropism (*d*) phototropism

66. The bending of the stem of a plant towards a source of light is caused by the action of a phytohormone known as :
(*a*) abscisic acid (*b*) auxin (*c*) gibberellins (*d*) cytokinin

67. Which of the following plant part exhibits negative phototropism ?
(*a*) root (*b*) branch (*c*) leaves (*d*) stem

68. Which of the following are not tropisms ?
(*i*) growing of pollen tube in response to a sugary substance
(*ii*) folding up of leaves of sensitive plant in response to touch
(*iii*) winding of tendril around a support in response to touch
(*iv*) opening up of the leaves of a daisy flower in response to light
(*a*) (*i*) and (*ii*) (*b*) (*ii*) and (*iii*) (*c*) (*i*) and (*iv*) (*d*) (*ii*) and (*iv*)

Questions Based on High Order Thinking Skills (HOTS)

69. The chemical substance P is made and secreted by the meristematic tissue at the tip of stem (or shoot) of a plant. The chemical substance P is responsible for a phenomenon Q in plants in which the stem bends towards a source of light. The same chemical substance P has an opposite effect on the root of a plant. It causes the root of a plant to bend away from the source of light in a process called R.
(*a*) What is the chemical substance P ?
(*b*) State whether P prefers to remains in the sunlit side of a stem or in shade.
(*c*) What is the effect of substance P on the rate of growth of (*i*) a root, and (*ii*) a stem ?
(*d*) What is the name of process (*i*) Q, and (*ii*) R ?
(*e*) What is the general name of chemical substances like P ? Name another substance which belongs to this class of chemical substances.

70. A potted plant is growing in a transparent glass jar. In this plant, X and Y are the two growing parts having a lot of meristematic tissue. It is observed that the part X of this plant exhibits positive geotropism but negative phototropism. On the other hand, part Y of this plant exhibits negative geotropism but positive phototropism.
(*a*) Name the part X of plant.
(*b*) Name the part Y of plant.
(*c*) Which part of the plant, X or Y, will exhibit positive hydrotropism ?
(*d*) Which part of the plant, X or Y, can have tendrils on it ?

(e) Which phytohormone causes the part X to exhibit negative phototropism ?

71. There are three plants A, B and C. The flowers of plant A open their petals in bright light during the day but close them when it gets dark at night. On the other hand, the flowers of plant B open their petals at night but close them during the day when there is bright light. The leaves of plant C fold up and droop when touched with fingers or any other solid object.

(a) Name the phenomenon shown by the flowers of (i) plant A, and (ii) plant B.
(b) Name one flower each which behaves like the flower of (i) plant A, and (ii) plant B.
(c) Name the phenomenon exhibited by the leaves of plant C.
(d) Name a plant whose leaves behave like those of plant C.
(e) Which plant/plants exhibit the phenomenon based on growth movements ?

72. While conducting experiments to study the effect of various stimuli on the plants, it was observed that the roots of a plant X grow and bend towards two stimuli A and B but bend away from a third stimulus C. The stem of the plant X, however, bends away from stimuli A and B but bends towards the stimulus C. The stimulus B is known to act on the roots due to too much weight of the earth. Keeping these points in mind, answer the following questions :

(a) What could stimulus A be ?
(b) Name the stimulus B.
(c) What could stimulus C be ?
(d) The branches of a fallen tree in a forest grow straight up in response to two stimuli. What could be these two stimuli out of A, B and C ? Also name these two stimuli.

73. P and Q are two types of plants having weak stems which cannot stand upright on their own. The plants P and Q have organs R and S respectively which can grow towards any support which they happen to touch and wind around that support. It is observed that organ R originates from the leaves of the plant whereas organ S originates directly from the stem of the plant.

(a) What is (i) R, and (ii) S ?
(b) What is the name of growth movement exhibited by the organs R and S ?
(c) Name the stimulus involved in this case.
(d) State whether the behaviour of organs R and S is a tropic movement or a nastic movement.
(e) Name one plant like P and another plant like Q.

74. The top part A of the flask-shaped reproductive organ X in the flower of a plant secretes a surgery substance into its lower part B which goes towards the bottom part C of the flask-shaped organ. When a tiny grain D coming from the top part E of another reproductive organ Y in the flower falls on part A, it grows a long tube F through the organ X in response to the sugary substance and reaches the bottom part C of flask-shaped organ to carry out fertilisation.

(a) What is (i) organ X, and (ii) organ Y, inside the flower ?
(b) Name parts (i) A (ii) B, and (iii) C, of flask-shaped organ.
(c) Name (i) grain D, and (ii) part E of organ Y.
(d) Name the tube F.
(e) What is the phenomenon of growing a long tube in response to a sugary substance in the process of fertilisation in a flower known as ?

75. P, Q, R and S are four major types of phytohormones. P is a phytohormone which functions mainly as a growth inhibitor. It promotes the wilting and falling of leaves. Q, R and S are phytohormones which all promote growth of plants in various ways. Q is responsible for the phenomenon of phototropism in plants. R is involved mainly in shoot extensions. The phytohormone S helps in breaking the dormancy of seeds and buds. What are P, Q, R and S ? Give one reason each for your choice.

76. A potted plant having straight parts A and B was placed horizontally on its side as shown in Figure (i). After a few days it was observed that the parts A and B of the plant acquire new positions as shown in Figure (ii).

(a) Name the phenomenon exhibited by the position of plant parts A and B in Figure (ii)
(b) Name the stimulus (other than sunlight) which causes plant part A to grow and bend upwards, and plant part B to bend downwards.

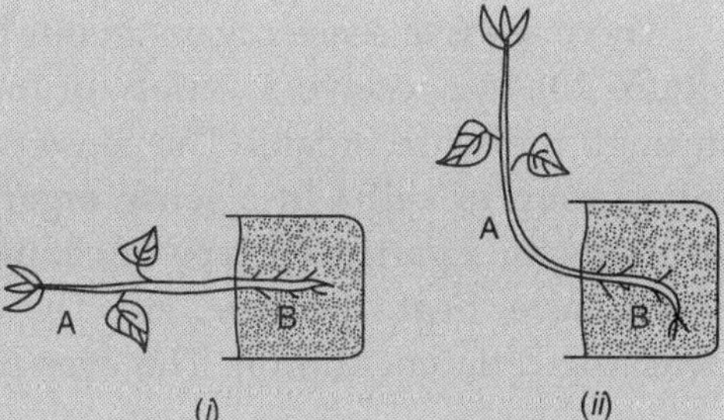

(i) (ii)

77. When the leaves of a sensitive plant are touched with a finger, they fold up and when light fades at dusk, the petals of a dandelion flower close.
(*a*) State one way in which the above two processes are similar.
(*b*) State two ways in which the above two processes differ.

ANSWERS

1. Phytohormones (or Plant hormones) **2.** Abscisic acid **3.** Auxin **4.** In the tip of plant stem **5.** *Mimosa pudica* **6.** Promotes growth : Gibberellin ; Inhibits growth : Abscisic acid **7.** Folding up of the leaves of a sensitive plant on touching **8.** Plant hormones **11.** Folding up of the leaves of a sensitive plant on touching **12.** (*a*) Root (*b*) Stem (or Shoot) **13.** (*a*) Not a growth movement (*b*) It is a growth movement **14.** (*a*) Root (*b*) Stem (or Shoot) **15.** (*a*) Light, Gravity and Water (*b*) Light and Gravity **16.** (*a*) phototropism (*b*) geotropism (*c*) sunlight (*d*) gravity (*e*) touch (*f*) water ; gravity (*g*) positive geotropism (*h*) Auxin (*i*) phototropism **17.** (*a*) Bending of stem (or shoot) towards light (*b*) Folding up of the leaves of a sensitive plant on touching **19.** (*a*) Root bends downwards in the direction of gravity ; Positive geotropism (*b*) Stem (or shoot) bends towards the light; Positive phototropism **20.** (*a*) Stem (or shoot) grows upward against the direction of gravity ; Negative geotropism (*b*) Root bends away from light ; Negative phototropism **28.** (*a*) Figure (*ii*) (*b*) Geotropism **29.** (*a*) Abscisic acid (*b*) Cytokinin (*c*) Auxin (*d*) Abscisic acid **30.** (*a*) Stem (or Shoot) (*b*) Root (*c*) Stem (or Shoot) (*d*) Root **35.** (*c*) Tendril **38.** (*b*) **39.** (*d*) **40.** (*b*) **41.** (*b*) **42.** (*b*) **43.** (*d*) **44.** (*b*) **45.** (*b*) **46.** (*c*) **47.** (*c*) **48.** (*b*) **49.** (*c*) **50.** (*c*) **51.** (*d*) **52.** (*b*) **53.** (*a*) **54.** (*c*) **55.** (*b*) **56.** (*c*) **57.** (*c*) **58.** (*b*) **59.** (*b*) **60.** (*d*) **61.** (*c*) **62.** (*c*) **63.** (*d*) **64.** (*a*) **65.** (*d*) **66.** (*b*) **67.** (*a*) **68.** (*d*) **69.** (*a*) P is auxin hormone (*b*) In shade (*c*) (*i*) Decreases the rate of growth of root (*ii*) Increases the rate of growth of stem (*d*) (*i*) Positive phototropism (*ii*) Negative phototropism (*e*) Plant hormones ; Gibberellin **70.** (*a*) Root (*b*) Stem (or Shoot) (*c*) X (*d*) Y (*e*) Auxin **71.** (*a*) (*i*) Photonasty (*ii*) Photonasty (*b*) (*i*) Dandelion flower (*ii*) Moonflower (*c*) Thigmonasty (*d*) Sensitive plant (*Mimosa pudica*) (*e*) A and B **72.** (*a*) Water (*b*) Gravity (*c*) Light (*d*) B and C ; Gravity and Light (or Sunlight) **73.** (*a*) (*i*) Leaf tendril (*ii*) Stem tendril (*b*) Thigmotropism (*c*) Touch (of support) (*d*) Tropic movement (*e*) Organs like P (leaf tendrils) : Pea plant ; Organs like Q (stem tendrils) : Bitter gourd plant **74.** (*a*) (*i*) Carpel (*ii*) Stamen (*b*) (*i*) Stigma (*ii*) Style (*iii*) Ovary (*c*) (*i*) Pollen grain (*ii*) Anther (*d*) Pollen tube (*e*) Chemotropism **75.** P is abscisic acid ; Q is auxin ; R is gibberellin ; S is cytokinin **76.** (*a*) Geotropism (*b*) Gravity **77.** (*a*) Both are nasties (or nastic movements) (*b*) In the folding of leaves of sensitive plant, stimulus is touch but in the folding of petals of dandelion flower, stimulus is light ; Folding of leaves of a sensitive plant is not a growth movement but the closing of petals of a dandelion flower is a growth movement

COORDINATION IN ANIMALS

The multicellular animals (except sponges) have specialised cells called nerve cells (or neurons) to respond to stimuli and coordinate their activities. **A system made up of nerve cells is called nervous system.** The coordination in simple multicellular animals takes place through **nervous system** only. For example, *Hydra* is a simple multicellular animal. The nervous system of *Hydra* consists of a network of nerve cells joined to one another and spread throughout its body (see Figure 21). **The control and coordination in higher animals called vertebrates (including human beings) takes place through nervous system as well as hormonal system called endocrine system.** Before we describe the control and coordination in humans, it will be good to know something about sense organs, receptors and effectors. These are described below.

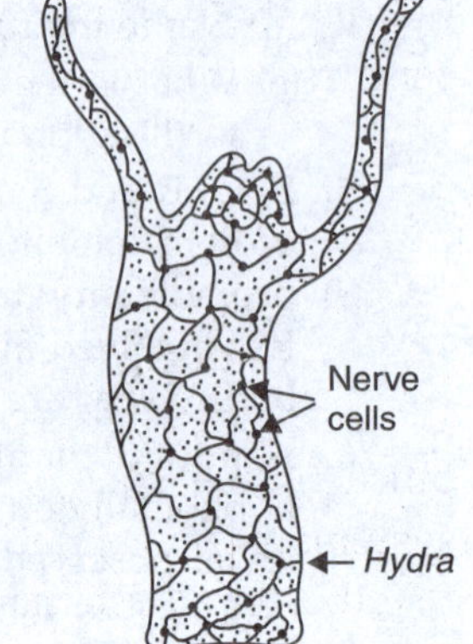

Figure 21. Nervous system of *Hydra*. (Please note the network of nerve cells throughout the body of *Hydra*).

There are five sense organs in our body : eyes, ears, nose, tongue and skin (see Figure 22). We receive a variety of information from the environment around us through the sense organs. The sense organs contain receptors. **A receptor is a cell (or a group of cells) in a sense organ which is sensitive to a particular type of stimulus (or a particular type of change in the environment) such as light, sound, smell, taste, heat, pressure, etc.** The different sense organs contain receptors for detecting different stimuli. The eyes have light receptors (which can detect light), ears have sound receptors (which can detect sound), nose has smell receptors (which can detect smell), tongue has taste receptors (which can detect taste) whereas skin has receptors for detecting touch, pressure, heat (or cold) and pain, etc. The common type of receptors also have special names such as photoreceptors, phonoreceptors, olfactory receptors, gustatory receptors and thermoreceptors. **Photoreceptors detect light** (they are present in eyes), **phonoreceptors detect sound** (they are present in inner ears), **olfactory receptors detect smell** (they are present in nose), **gustatory receptors detect taste** (they are present in tongue) whereas **thermoreceptors detect heat or cold** (they are present in skin).

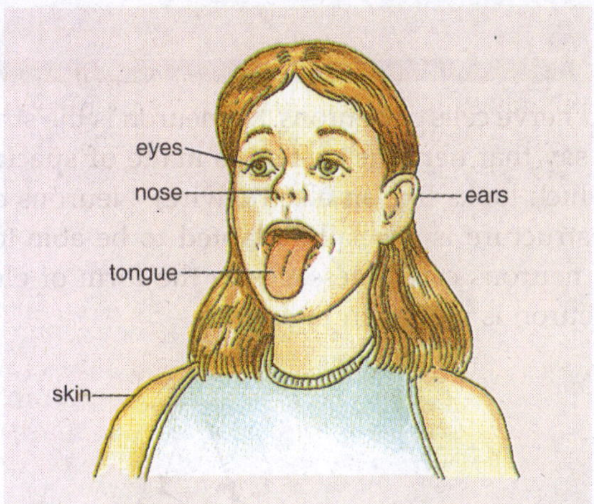

Figure 22. Eyes, ears, nose, tongue and skin are sense organs. They contain different receptors which can detect different stimuli in the environment.

Figure 23. Just like us, a dog has also five sense organs. A dog has an excellent sense of smell. Due to this, dogs are used as detectives to trace criminals and detect bombs.

A stimulus is a kind of energy such as light, sound, smell, taste, heat, or mechanical pressure, etc. Receptors contain groups of cells which are sensitive to the energy provided by the stimulus. At a receptor, the energy provided by a stimulus sets off a chemical reaction which converts the energy of stimulus into an electrical signal called 'electrical impulse' (nerve impulse or just impulse). So, **all the receptors in the sense organs receive stimuli from the surrounding environment and send the message conveyed by them to the spinal cord and brain in the form of electrical impulses through the sensory nerves**. Another type of nerves called motor nerves transmit the response from the brain and spinal cord to the 'effectors', again in the form of electrical impulses. **An effector is a part of the body which can respond to a stimulus according to the instructions sent from the nervous system (spinal cord and brain).** The effectors are mainly the **muscles** and **glands** of our body. All our muscles and glands respond to electrical impulses sent from the nervous system through motor nerves.

Control and Coordination in Humans

There are two systems of coordination of activities in humans. These are :

(*i*) **Nervous system,** and

(*ii*) **Endocrine system** (or Hormonal system).

In human beings, nervous system and endocrine system work together to control and coordinate all our activities such as our physical actions, our thinking processes and our emotional behaviour. Both the systems of coordination, nervous system and endocrine system, consist of a number of organs working together in a systematic way. We will now describe the nervous system and endocrine system in humans in detail, one by one. Let us discuss the nervous system first.

HUMAN NERVOUS SYSTEM

The function of nervous system is to coordinate the activities of our body. It is the control system for all our actions, thinking and behaviour. **The nervous system helps all other systems of our body to work**

together. The nervous system is like a manager inside our body. Its job is to control and coordinate the parts of our body so that they work together, doing their job at the right time. Our nervous system coordinates muscles so that we can do things which need thinking like reading, writing, cycling or dancing. The nervous system also coordinates things which we don't have to think about, like heart beat and breathing. **The human nervous system receives information from the surroundings, processes it, interprets it and then responds accordingly.** The nervous system also passes information from one internal system to another. For example, as soon as we put food in our mouth, it immediately causes the release of saliva from the salivary glands.

The Unit of Nervous System : Neuron

The units which make up the nervous system are called nerve cells or neurons. So, neuron is the structural and functional unit of the nervous system. We can now say that **nervous system is made of special cells called neurons.** Neuron is the *largest* cell in the body (which looks like an electric wire). Neurons contain the same basic parts as any other animal cell but their structure is specially adapted to be able to carry messages over large distances in the body quickly. The neurons carry messages in the form of electrical signals called electrical impulses or nerve impulses. A neuron is shown in Figure 24.

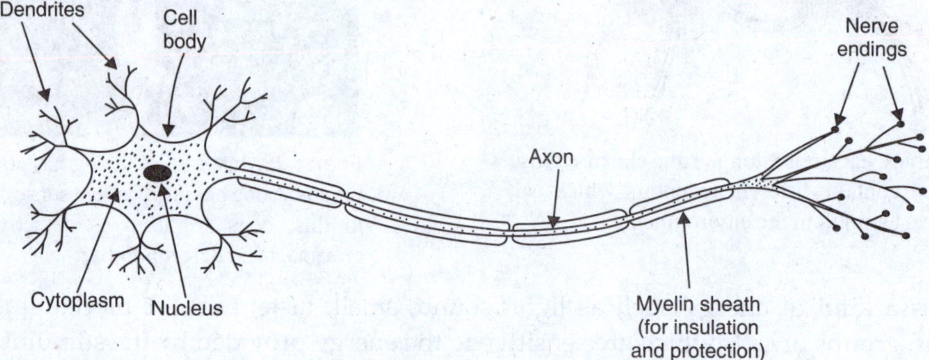

Figure 24. A neuron (or nerve cell).

A neuron (or nerve cell) has three components :

(*i*) Cell body,
(*ii*) Dendrites, and
(*iii*) Axon.

The cell body of a neuron is like a typical animal cell which contains cytoplasm and a nucleus (see Figure 24). A number of long and thin fibres are stretching out from the cell body of a neuron. They are called nerve fibres. The shorter fibres on the body of a neuron are called **dendrites.** The longest fibre on the cell body of a neuron is called **axon.** The axon has an insulating and protective sheath (or cover) of myelin around it (Myelin is made of fat and protein). It is clear that both dendrites and axon arise from the cell body of a neuron.

The messages which the neurons transmit in the nervous system are in the form of electrical impulses called nerve impulses (or just impulses). The dendrites pick up the nerve impulses (or messages) from receptors. They pass the impulses to the cell body and then along the axon. The axon passes the impulse (or message) to another neuron through a junction called synapse. Neurons are of three types : sensory neurons, motor neurons and relay neurons.

(*i*) Sensory neurons transmit impulses from the sensory cells (or receptors) towards the central nervous system (spinal cord and brain).

(*ii*) Motor neurons transmit impulses from the central nervous system (spinal cord and brain) towards the muscle cells (or effectors).

(*iii*) Relay neurons occur in the central nervous system (brain and spinal cord) where they serve as links between other neurons.

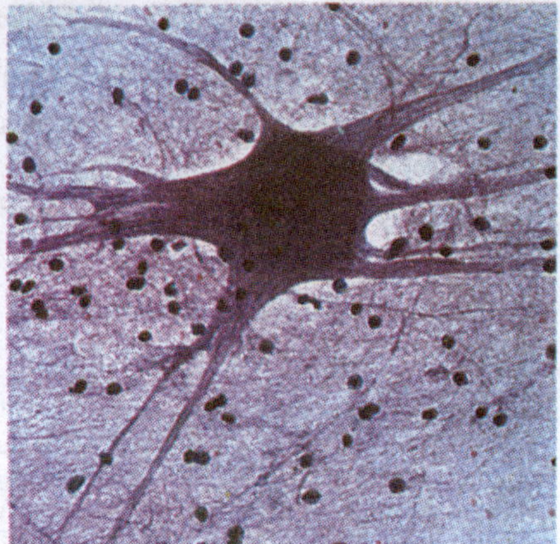

Figure 25. Nerve cells have long thin fibres which carry 'messages' around our body.

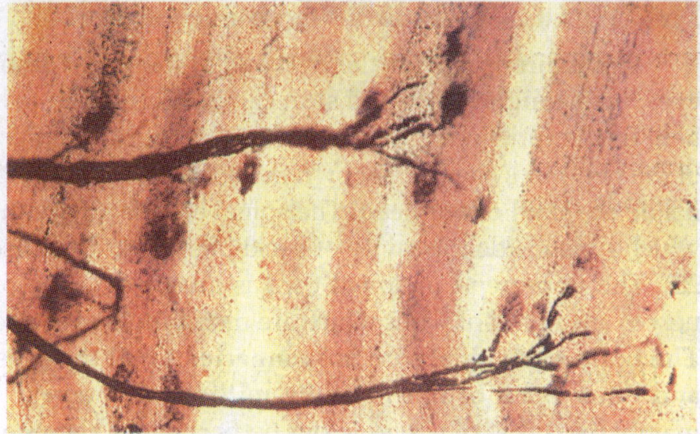

Figure 26. This picture shows a highly enlarged photograph of motor nerve endings (or motor neuron endings) attached to muscle.

We will now explain how nerve impulses (or messages) are transferred from one neuron to another in the nervous system. Any two neurons in the nervous system do not join to one another completely. There is always a very, very small gap between the two neurons (where they join). This gap is called a synapse. The nerve impulses are carried over this small gap between a pair of neurons by means of a chemical substance called neurotransmitter substance. We can now say that : **A microscopic gap between a pair of adjacent neurons over which nerve impulses pass when going from one neuron to the next is called a synapse.** Thus, synapses connect neurons (though it looks surprising that even gaps can connect two things !). We will now understand the conduction of electrical nerve impulses through synapse with the help of a diagram.

Suppose there are two neurous (or nerve cells) *A* and *B* near each other (see Figure 27). Let *A* be a sensory neuron which is directly connected to the receptor. There is an extremely small, microscopic gap between the end of the axon of neuron *A* and the dendrite of the next neuron *B* which is called a synapse (see Figure 27). We will now explain how the electrical impulse travels through the gap (synapse) between the two neurons.

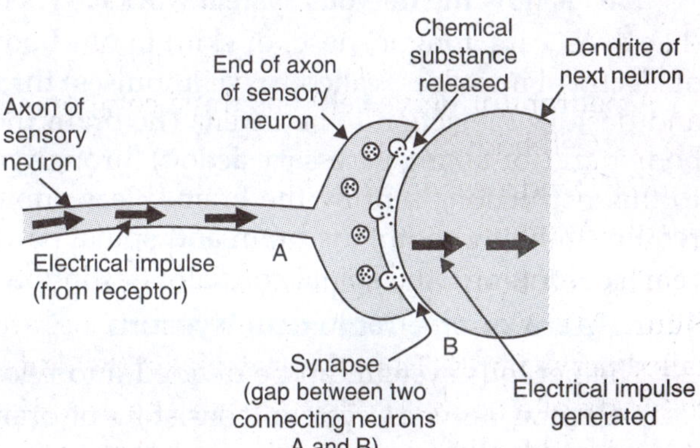

Figure 27. Diagram to show how electrical impulses (or nerve impulses) are conducted from one neuron to another across synapses (gaps) between them by the release of a chemical substance (called a neuro-transmitter substance).

The receptor in a sense organ is in touch with the dendrites of sensory neuron. When a stimulus acts on the receptor, a chemical reaction is set off which produces an electrical impulse in it. This impulse travels from the dendrite of sensory neuron *A* to its cell body and then along its axon. At the end of axon of sensory neuron *A*, the electrical impulse releases tiny amount of a chemical substance into the synapse (or gap). This chemical substance crosses the gap (or synapse) and starts a similar electrical impulse in the dendrite of the next neuron *B* (see Figure 27). From the dendrite, this electrical impulse is carried to the cell body and then to the end of axon of the second neuron. It can then be transferred to a third neuron in a similar way. This process goes on till the electrical impulse reaches the relay neurons in spinal cord and brain. The relay neurons and motor neurons connect in a similar way to bring electrical impulses from the brain and spinal cord to the effectors like muscles and glands.

Synapses actually act like one-way valves. This is because the chemical substance is present on only one side of the gap. Due to this, the nerve impulses (or messages) through a particular set of neurons can go across only from one side (which contains the chemical substance). In this way, **synapses ensure that nerve impulses travel in only one direction (through a particular set of neurons).**

The Organs of Human Nervous System

The main organs of the nervous system are : Brain, Spinal cord and Nerves. The sense organs like **eyes, ears, tongue, nose and skin** can be considered to be other organs of the nervous system because they help in the functioning of the nervous system. The main organs of the nervous system are shown in Figure 28. The brain is located inside the skull of our head. The spinal cord is a very thick nerve which runs inside the cavity of backbone in our body (see Figure 28). The upper end of spinal cord is attached to the brain. The nerves are a kind of wires which are distributed all over our body. **The brain and spinal cord are connected to all the sense organs and other parts of our body by millions of nerves.** There are mainly two types of nerves in our body : cranial nerves and spinal nerves. The cranial nerves connect all the parts in the head directly to brain. The spinal nerves connect all the remaining parts of the body (like muscles and skin, etc.) to the spinal cord (see Figure 28). There is also a third type of nerves called visceral nerves. Most of the visceral nerves connect the internal organs of the body to spinal cord though some also connect to brain (Visceral nerves have not been shown in Figure 28 to keep the diagram simple and avoid confusion). The cranial nerves, spinal nerves and visceral nerves are also of two types : sensory nerves and motor nerves. *The nerves which carry messages from the body parts to the brain (or spinal cord) are called sensory nerves.* And *the nerves which carry message from the brain (or spinal cord) to the body parts for action are called motor nerves.*

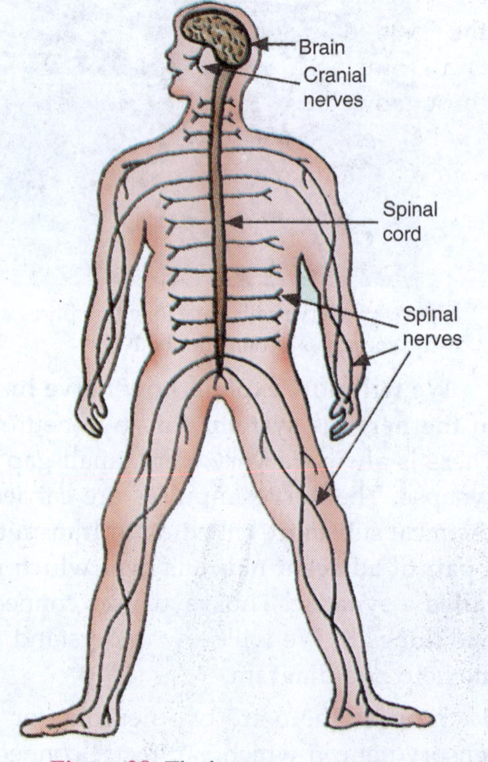

Figure 28. The human nervous system.

This is how the nervous system works : When the sense organ (like eyes, ears, tongue, nose, or skin) in our body is affected, it sends the message to the brain in the form of electrical impulses (called nerve impulses) through the sensory neurons. The brain analyses this message and decides the action to be taken. The brain then sends out instructions to the muscles of the concerned body part (for taking necessary action) through motor nerves. The concerned body part then acts according to the instructions sent by the brain. Please note that in the processing of complicated responses (which require thinking) both, the brain and spinal cord are involved, but in the simple responses (which do not require thinking), the spinal cord alone is involved.

The Parts of the Nervous System

The nervous system can be divided into two main parts :

1. **Central nervous system** (consisting of brain and spinal cord), and
2. **Peripheral nervous system** (consisting of all the nerves of the body like cranial nerves, spinal nerves and visceral nerves).

The peripheral nervous system can be further divided into two parts :

(*i*) Voluntary nervous system (which is under voluntary control from the brain), and
(*ii*) Autonomic nervous system (which operates automatically or involuntarily).

The classification of nervous system into various parts is given in the following chart :

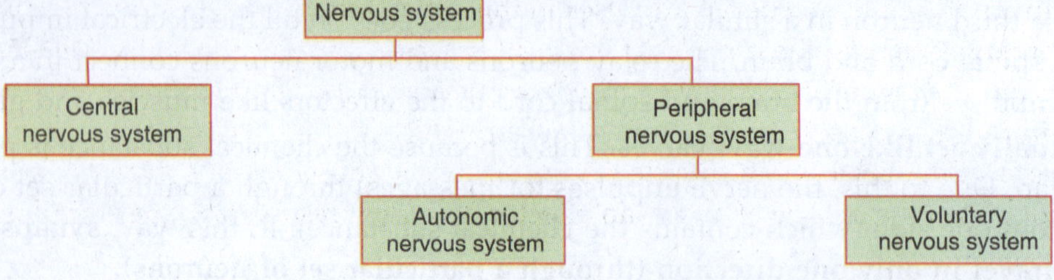

THE PERIPHERAL NERVOUS SYSTEM

All the nerves of the body together make up the peripheral nervous system (PNS). They all enter or leave the central nervous system. The three types of nerves which make up the peripheral nervous system are spinal nerves, cranial nerves and visceral nerves. Spinal nerves arise from the spinal cord along most of the length of the spinal cord and spread throughout the body (except the head). They all carry both sensory and motor neurons and are described as mixed nerves. Cranial nerves arise from the brain and spread throughout the head. They also carry both sensory and motor neurons. The visceral nerves are a special kind of nerves which mostly arise from the spinal cord (though some also arise from the brain). They are connected to the internal organs of the body. Visceral nerves also carry both sensory and motor neurons.

Reflex Action and Reflex Arcs

The simplest form of response in the nervous system is reflex action. This is a rapid, automatic response to a stimulus which is not under the voluntary control of the brain. It is described as an involuntary action. Thus, **a reflex action is one which we perform automatically.** It is a comparatively simple form of behaviour in which the same stimulus produces the same response every time.

If we unknowingly touch a hot plate, we immediately move our hand away from it. So, **moving our hand away on touching a hot plate is an example of reflex action.** Similarly, moving our foot away when we step on something sharp, is also an example of reflex action. A knee jerk, movement of diaphragm

(*a*) Yawning

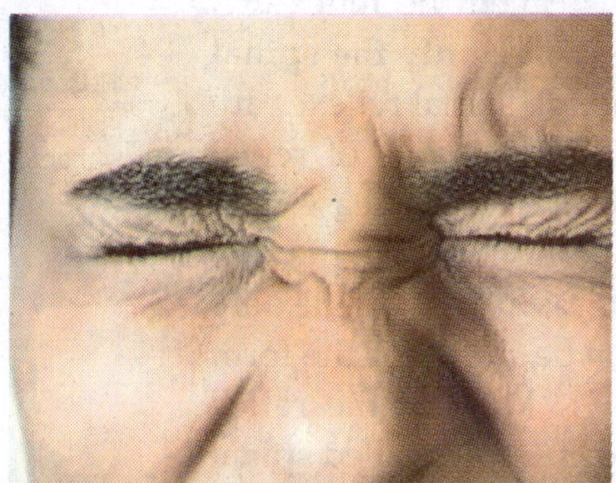

(*b*) Blinking of eyes

(*c*) Sneezing

Figure 29. Yawning, blinking of eyes and sneezing are all reflex actions (which are performed by us unknowingly).

(during respiration), coughing, yawning, blinking of eyes and sneezing are all reflex actions. In a reflex action, we are unaware that anything is going to happen to us. Reflex actions are the actions which we do without thinking to protect ourselves. For example, coughing is a reflex action which clears our windpipe. The pupils of our eyes get smaller in bright light. This reflex action protects the retina of our eyes from damage due to too much light. The pupils of our eyes get bigger in dim light so as to help us see properly even in dim light.

The pathway (or route) taken by nerve impulses in a reflex action is called the reflex arc. Reflex arcs allow rapid response. We will explain the meaning of a reflex arc by taking an example.

A reflex action is an automatic response to a stimulus. An example of the way in which we respond to a stimulus is our reaction to touching a hot object (like a hot plate). Very quickly, and without thinking about it, we pull our hand away. This sort of very fast, automatic response is called the reflex action. Figure 30 shows the pathway taken by the nerve impulses in this reflex action. The stimulus here is the heat which we feel in our hand on touching the hot plate. This heat is sensed by a heat receptor (or thermoreceptor) in our hand. The receptor triggers an impulse in a sensory neuron, which transmits the message to the spinal cord. Here, the impulse is passed on to a relay neuron, which in turn, passes it to a motor neuron. The motor neuron passes the impulse to a muscle in our arm. The muscle then contracts and pulls our hand away from the hot plate. The muscle of arm is an effector because it responds to the stimulus. This pathway

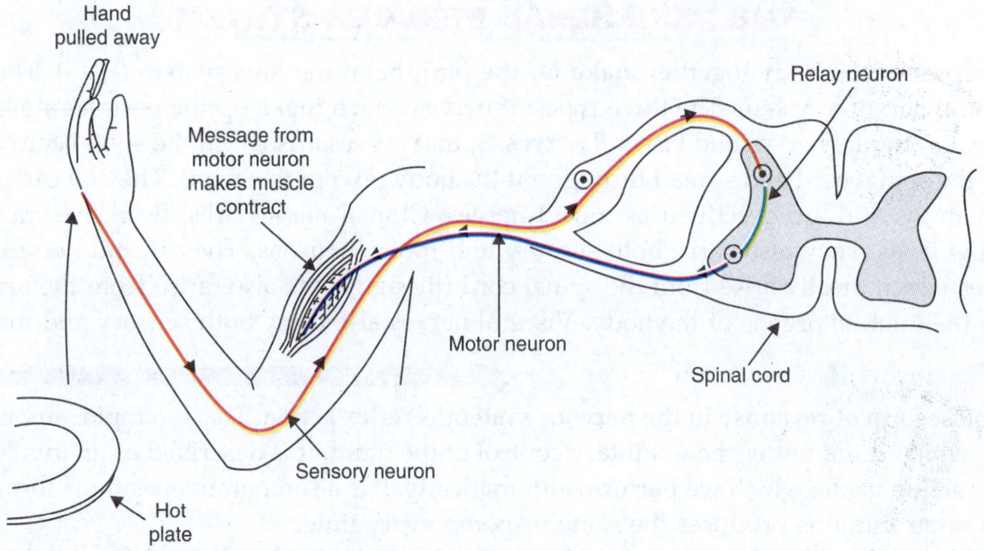

Figure 30. Diagram to show the reflex action and its path (which is called reflex arc).

along which the impulse travels is called the reflex arc. **The reflexes of this type which involve only the spinal cord are called spinal reflexes.** Though spinal reflexes are produced in the spinal cord but the message of reflex action taken also goes on to reach the brain. Please note that when we lift a hot plate, then alongwith *heat*, the *pain* produced by heat also acts as a 'stimulus'. The reflex arc described in the above example can be shown in the form of a flow-chart given in Figure 31. Most of the reflex actions involve only the spinal cord. They are called spinal reflexes. The reflex action which we have shown in Figure 30 is actually a spinal reflex. And the reflex arc given in Figure 31 is actually a spinal reflex arc. Some reflex actions, however, involve the brain rather than the spinal cord. Such reflex actions are known as cerebral reflexes. This is described below.

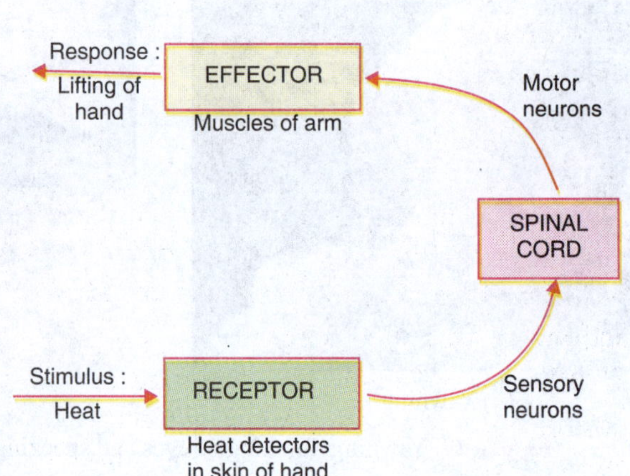

Figure 31. A reflex arc (This is actually a spinal reflex arc).

Those reflex actions which involve brain are called cerebral reflexes. Cerebral reflexes occur in the organs present in the head because these organs are directly connected to the brain. This will become clear from the following example. Our eyes are present in the head. In dim light, the pupil (a hole in the front of eye) is large so that more light can enter into the eye and make us see properly even in dim light (see Figure 32). Now, when a bright light shines into our eye, then the pupil of our eye automatically becomes smaller (and prevents the damage to the retina of eye from too much light) (see Figure 33). **The contraction of pupil of our eye automatically in the presence of bright light is an example of cerebral reflex.** This cerebral reflex action can be explained as follows :

When a bright light falls on the eye, the light receptors in the eye produce impulses in the sensory nerves. The sensory nerves carry this message of bright light in the form of electrical impulses to the brain. The brain produces the response (that the amount of light entering the eye must be reduced). The response produced by the brain is carried by motor nerves to the circular muscles of the iris of the eye. The circular muscles of the iris of the eye contract and reduce the size of the pupil (or hole) of the eye. As the size of pupil becomes smaller, the amount of light entering the eye is reduced. All this happens very, very quickly.

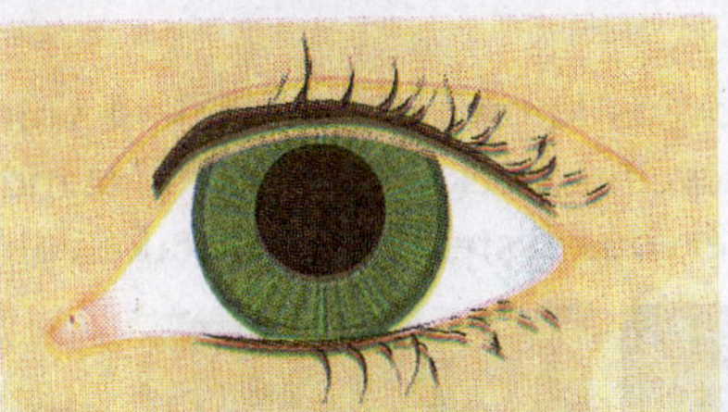

Figure 32 In dim light, the pupil of eye is large so that more light can enter into the eye.

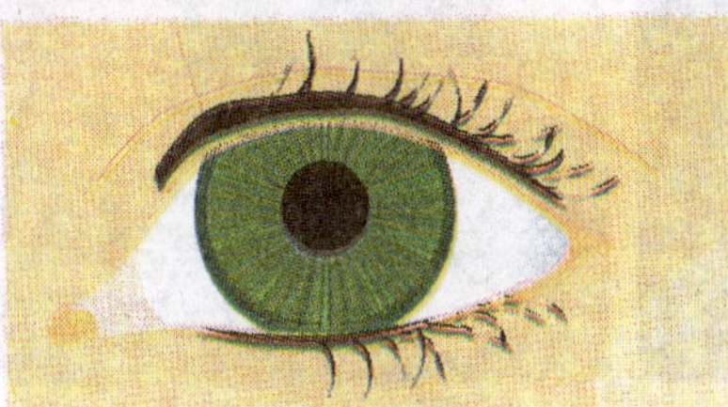

Figure 33. In bright light, a speedy reflex action makes the pupil smaller. This reduces the light entering the eye.

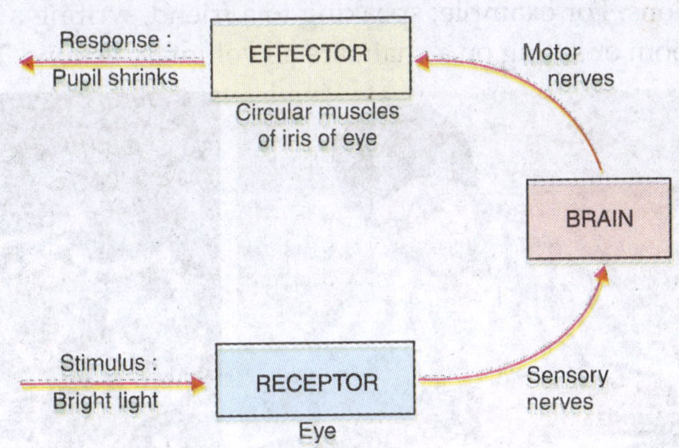

Figure 34. A reflex arc showing cerebral reflex action

This cerebral reflex action can be shown by drawing a reflex arc given in Figure 34. Please note that though the pupil is a circular opening (or hole) in the centre of the iris of the eye but it appears to be dark because no light is reflected from it (see Figures 32 and 33).

How the Effectors (or Muscles) Cause Action or Movement

When a motor nerve impulse sent by the spinal cord (or brain) reaches the effector organs (which are muscles), then the muscles cause action or movement (such as lifting the hand away from a hot plate). **We will now describe how muscles are able to move in response to electrical nerve impulses and cause action.**

Muscles are made up of muscle cells. Muscle cells contain special proteins which can change their arrangement when stimulated by electrical impulses, causing the muscle cells to change shape and contract. When the muscle cells contract, the muscles also contract (and become shorter). When the muscles contract, they pull on the bones of the body part and make it move. For example, when electrical impulses sent by the spinal cord (or brain) stimulate the biceps muscle of the upper arm, they make biceps muscle to contract. And when the biceps muscle contracts, it pulls on a bone of the lower arm and makes it move (lifting the hand away from the hot plate). Please note that the contraction of muscles (or muscle cells) caused by the action of electrical impulses is a reversible process.

The Autonomic Nervous System

The term 'autos' means 'self' and 'nomos' means 'governing', so **'autonomic nervous system' means 'self governing nervous system'.** The autonomic nervous system is that part of the peripheral nervous system which controls the activities of the organs *inside* our body automatically even without our thinking about them. The autonomic nervous system is a specific network of nerves in the body which controls the processes like breathing, heart beat, digestion, sweating, etc., that maintain our life and keep us alive. The nerves of the autonomic nervous system are attached to the smooth muscles of the various internal organs of the human body like head, heart, blood vessels, alimentary canal, lungs, kidneys, urinary bladder, glands and skin, etc. Thus, **the autonomic nervous system controls and regulates the functions of the internal organs of our body involuntarily (on its own).**

Voluntary Nervous System

Those actions which need thinking and which are performed by us knowingly are called voluntary actions. For example, speaking to a friend, writing a letter, dancing, cycling, kicking a football, standing in a room or sitting on a chair, are all voluntary actions. **The voluntary nervous system helps us take voluntary**

(*a*) Writing a letter (*b*) Dancing

(*c*) Kicking a football

Figure 35. Writing a letter, dancing, and kicking a football are all voluntary actions (which are performed by us knowingly).

actions which are under the conscious control of the brain. We will now give an example to understand the working of voluntary nervous system.

Suppose we are walking down to school at a slow pace. After covering some distance, we look at our watch and find that we are getting late. So, we start walking very fast. We can do this because of our voluntary nervous system as follows :

(*i*) When our eyes see time on the watch, they send this information to the brain through the sensory nerves.

(*ii*) The brain analyses this information and decides that since there is risk of being late to school, so we should walk faster.

(*iii*) The brain sends the instructions to walk faster to the muscles of our legs through the motor nerves.

(*iv*) The muscles of the legs act accordingly and make us walk faster.

This is an example of voluntary action and the decision to take this voluntary action has been made by the voluntary nervous system.

CENTRAL NERVOUS SYSTEM

The central nervous system (CNS) consists of the brain and the spinal cord. Like a telephone exchange with ingoing and outgoing wires, it is responsible for the coordination and control of the activity of the

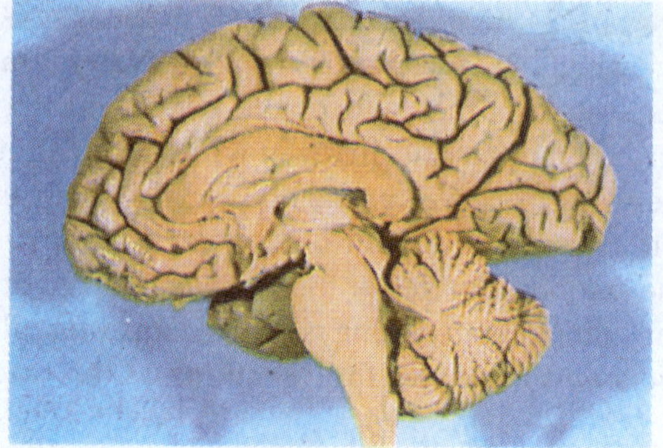

(*a*) The human brain

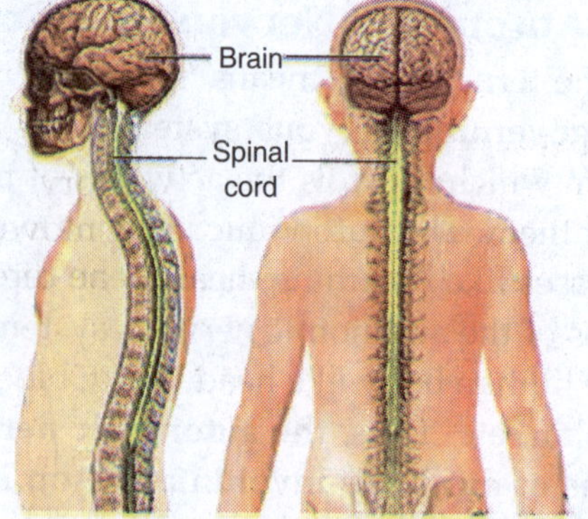

(*b*) The human brain with spinal cord attached to it

Figure 36. The central nervous system consists of the brain and the spinal cord.

nervous system. The work of central nervous system is to direct incoming messages to the motor neurons that are connected to the part of the body which will respond to a stimulus. In complicated responses, the brain and spinal cord are both involved. That is, in complicated responses, central nervous system is involved. The central nervous system enables a person to give a more appropriate and more intelligent response to various situations. By using the central nervous system, a person can vary his behaviour according to the changing situations. This point will become more clear from the following example.

If we pick up a very hot plate in the kitchen (without knowing that it is very hot), then our reflex action produced by the spinal cord alone says that we should pull away our hand (so that our hand is saved from burns). But if we pull away our hand, then the plate would drop and break into pieces (and our mother will definitely scold us for breaking the plate!). Now, it is here that the central nervous system involving brain steps in. When the message from our fingers saying that the 'plate is too hot' arrives at our central nervous system, there is already another message saying 'but don't drop it' (This is due to the intelligence of the brain). The central nervous system will consider the two messages together. It may then decide to send a message to our muscles to tell them to put down the plate gently and not drop it. This intelligent response has been made possible only due to the central nervous system.

The job of the central nervous system is to collect all the information from all the receptors in our body. This information is added together before messages are sent out to the effectors. In this way, the best action can be taken in a particular set of circumstances. We will now describe the two organs of the central nervous system, brain and spinal cord in detail.

Brain

Brain is the highest coordinating centre in the body. The brain is located inside the skull of our body (at the top of the spinal cord). It is protected by a bony box in the skull called **cranium** (see Figure 37). The brain is surrounded by three membranes called **meninges**, which help to protect it. The space between the membranes (or meninges) is filled with a **cerebro spinal fluid** which protects the brain from mechanical shocks. Pairs of cranial nerves arise from the brain.

The brain is broadly divided into three regions : forebrain, midbrain and hindbrain (see Figure 37). The forebrain consists mainly of **cerebrum.** The midbrain does not have any further divisions. The hindbrain consists of three centres called **pons, cerebellum and medulla** (see Figure 37). We will now discuss the functions of the forebrain, midbrain and hindbrain. Let us start with cerebrum which is in the forebrain.

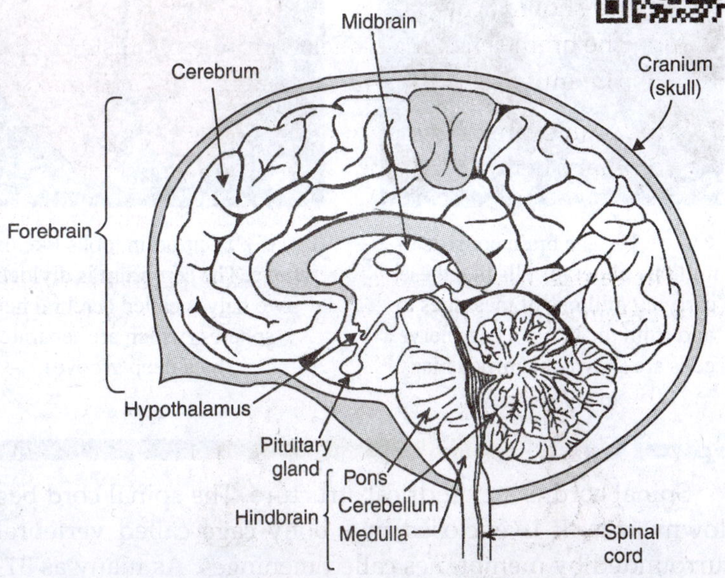

Figure 37. The human brain.

The cerebrum (or forebrain) is the main thinking part of the brain. It is the site of our faculties such as learning, reasoning, intelligence, personality and memory. All our thoughts, sensations, actions and movements are controlled by the cerebrum. The cerebrum has *different* areas for performing *different* functions. There are association areas in cerebrum which control thinking and memory. These association areas also store information and experiences. There are sensory areas where information is received from the sense organs like eyes, ears, nose, tongue and skin, and give us the 'sensation' or 'feeling'. Similarly, cerebrum has motor areas from which instructions are sent to muscles to do various types of jobs.

All the voluntary actions of the body are coordinated by the cerebrum. This happens as follows: The cerebrum receives sensory information through the receptors of sense organs. The cerebrum interprets this information in the light of previous experiences and takes a decision which it thinks is right. It then sends out instructions to the motor area (which controls the movement of voluntary muscles) so as to make voluntary muscles move to bring about the appropriate responses.

We will now describe the **functions of midbrain**. The midbrain controls reflex movements of the head, neck and trunk in response to visual and auditory stimuli. It also controls the reflex movements of the eye muscles, changes in pupil size and shape of the eye lens.

We will now describe the **functions of the parts of the hindbrain** which are pons, cerebellum and medulla. The **pons** takes part in regulating respiration. The **cerebellum** helps in maintaining posture and balance of the body. It also enables us to make precise and accurate movements. The cerebellum coordinates smooth body movements such as walking, dancing, riding a bicycle and picking up a pencil, etc. **Medulla** controls various involuntary actions such as heart beat (blood circulation), breathing, blood pressure and peristaltic movements of alimentary canal. Medulla is also the controlling centre for reflexes such as swallowing, coughing, sneezing, secretion of saliva and vomiting.

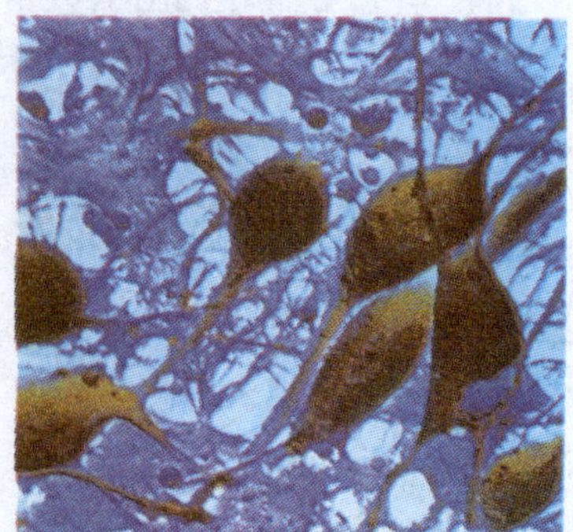

Figure 38. The brain consists of millions of nerve cells like these, carrying millions of messages to and from the brain. These nerve cells are shown magnified many many times.

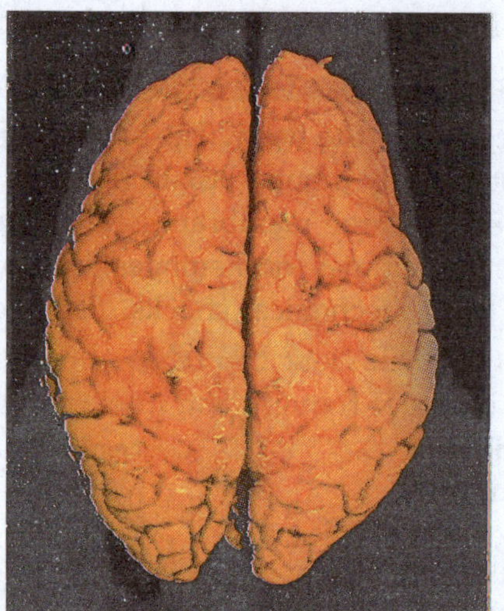

Figure 39. Our brain looks like this from above. The cerebrum is divided into two halves called cerebral hemispheres (which are separated by a deep groove).

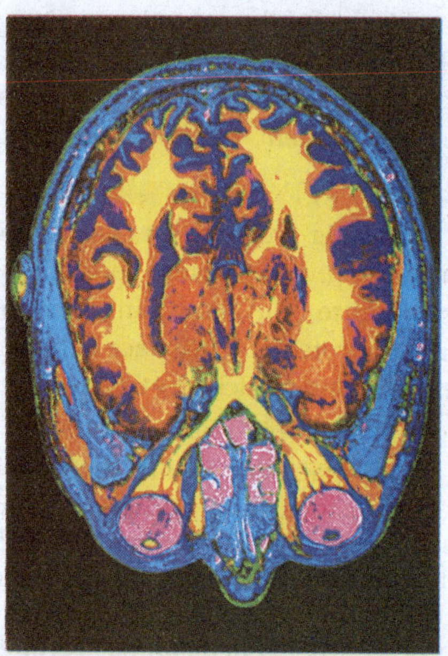

Figure 40. Computer Tomography Scan (CT scan) of a healthy brain, showing both halves of the brain enclosed within the cranium. CT scan is used to detect abnormalities (like injury, etc.) in the human brain.

Spinal Cord

Spinal cord is a cylindrical structure. The spinal cord begins in continuation with medulla and extends downwards. It is enclosed in a bony cage called vertebral column (see Figure 41). Spinal cord is also surrounded by membranes called meninges. As many as 31 pairs of nerves arise from the spinal cord (see Figure 42). The spinal cord is concerned with spinal reflex actions and the conduction of nerve impulses to and from the brain.

Before we end this discussion, we would like to give the various functions of brain. The various **functions of brain** are as follows :

1. The brain receives information-carrying nerve impulses from all the sensory organs of the body.

Figure 41. This sketch shows spinal cord enclosed in a bony cage called vertebral column. The spinal cord is connected to brain at the upper end.

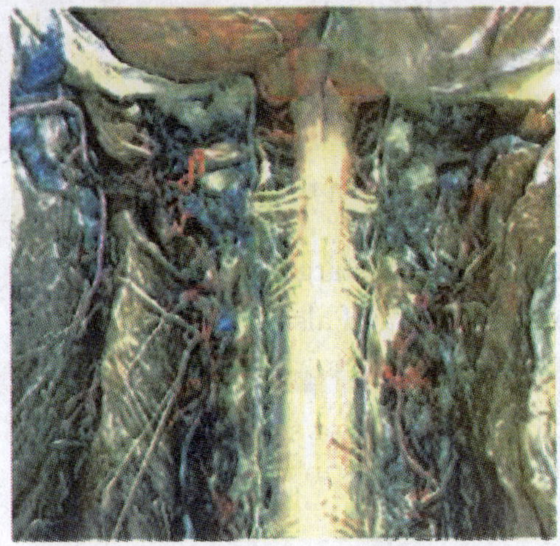

Figure 42. This is a highly enlarged view of the spinal cord in the body of a person. Pairs of spinal nerves can be seen extending from the spinal cord.

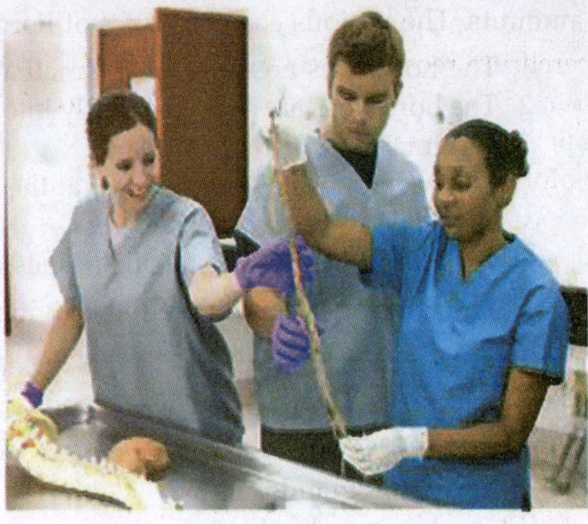

Figure 43. The thin rope like object held in the hands in this picture is a real human spinal cord.

2. The brain responds to the impulses brought in by sensory organs by sending its own instructions (through motor nerves) to the muscles and glands causing them to function accordingly.
3. The brain correlates the various stimuli from different sense organs and produces the most appropriate and intelligent response.
4. The brain coordinates the body activities so that the mechanisms and chemical reactions of the body work together efficiently.
5. The brain stores 'information' so that behaviour can be modified according to the past experience. This function makes the brain the organ of thought and intelligence.

Let us answer some questions now.

Sample Problem 1. The gap between two neurons is called a :

(*a*) dendrite (*b*) synapse (*c*) axon (*d*) impulse **(NCERT Book Question)**

Answer. (*b*) synapse.

Sample Problem 2. The brain is responsible for :

(*a*) thinking (*b*) regulating the heart beat

(*c*) balancing the body (*d*) all of the above **(NCERT Book Question)**

Answer. (*d*) all of the above.

Before we describe the hormonal system or endocrine system for the coordination in human beings, we should know the meanings of two terms : hormones and endocrine glands. So, let us first discuss hormones and endocrine glands.

Hormones

Hormones are chemical substances secreted in very small amounts by specialised tissues in the body called endocrine glands. These hormones coordinate the activities of living organisms and also their growth. So, we can now say that : **Hormones are the chemical substances which coordinate the activities of living organisms and also their growth.** Hormones are made inside the body of an organism in very small amounts. The various characteristics of hormones are given below :

1. The hormones are secreted in small amounts by the endocrine glands.
2. The hormones are poured directly into the blood and carried throughout the body by blood circulatory system.
3. The hormones have their effect at the sites different from the sites where they are made. So, they are also called chemical messengers.
4. The hormones act on specific tissues or organs (called target organs).
5. The hormones coordinate the activities of the body and also its growth.

Endocrine Glands

A gland is a structure which secretes a specific substance (or substances) in the body. A gland is made up of a group of cells or tissue. There are two types of glands in the body :

(*i*) **exocrine glands,** and
(*ii*) **endocrine glands.**

A gland which secretes its product into a duct (or tube) is called an exocrine gland. For example, the salivary gland secretes the saliva into a duct called salivary duct, therefore, salivary gland is an exocrine gland. Thus, **exocrine glands are the glands having ducts** (see Figure 44). A gland which does not have a duct and secretes its product directly into the blood stream is called an endocrine gland. Thus, **endocrine glands are ductless glands.** An endocrine gland secretes a chemical substance called hormone. We can now say that : **A structure (group of cells or tissue) which makes hormones in the body is called an endocrine gland.** The various endocrine glands present in the human body are shown in Figure 45. The endocrine glands do not have ducts to secrete their hormones, so they are also called ductless glands. The endocrine glands release hormones directly into the blood of a person. These hormones reach the concerned body part through the blood and act on it. **Hormones are a kind of chemical messengers.** A hormone is produced in *one* part of the body but it acts on some *other* part of the body. The hormones are of different types and perform different functions.

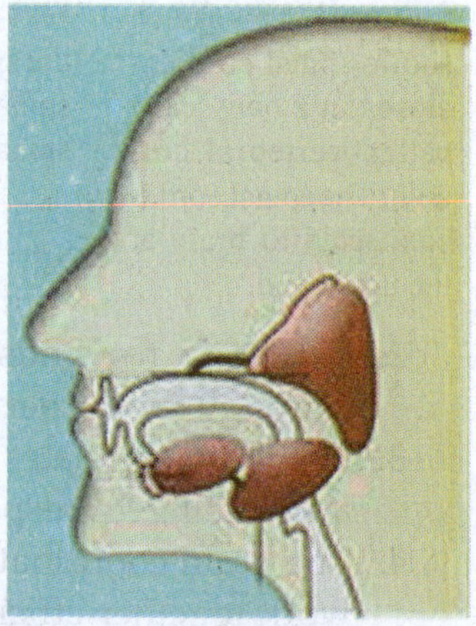

Figure 44. Salivary glands are exocrine glands (having ducts). This picture shows the location of salivary glands in the human body.

Some of the glands in our body have both exocrine and endocrine functions. The pancreas, testes and ovary are such glands. For example, pancreas acts as an endocrine gland and secretes the hormone insulin. It also acts as an exocrine gland and secretes pancreatic juice containing digestive enzymes into the pancreatic duct that leads to the alimentary canal. The testes are glands which act as endocrine glands and secrete the hormone called testosterone. They act as exocrine glands and release sperms (male sex cells) into the duct. Similarly, ovaries are glands which act as endocrine glands and secrete the hormones oestrogen (read as 'estrogen') and progesterone. They act as exocrine glands and release ova or eggs (female sex cells) into the duct.

THE ENDOCRINE SYSTEM

A group of endocrine glands which produces various hormones is called an endocrine system. The endocrine system is also called **hormonal system.** We will now discuss the endocrine system in humans in detail.

In addition to nervous system, the endocrine system also helps in coordinating the activities of our body. The endocrine system in our body consists of a number of glands (or tissues) which make, store, and release chemicals called hormones. There are a large number of endocrine glands in the human body. **The endocrine glands present in the human body are : Pineal gland ; Hypothalamus gland ; Pituitary gland ; Thyroid gland ; Parathyroid glands ; Thymus ; Pancreas ; Adrenal glands ; Testes (only in males) and Ovaries (only in females).** The positions of all these endocrine glands in the human body are shown in

Figure 45. The endocrine glands are located in different parts of the body. As we can see from Figure 45, the endocrine glands are located in the head, neck and trunk of our body. Different endocrine glands make different types of hormones which act on different organs of our body. The working of endocrine glands is controlled by our nervous system. **The hormones produced by endocrine glands act as messengers between the nervous system and the organs of our body.** We will now take the example of adrenal glands to show how the endocrine system (or hormonal system) coordinates our body activities.

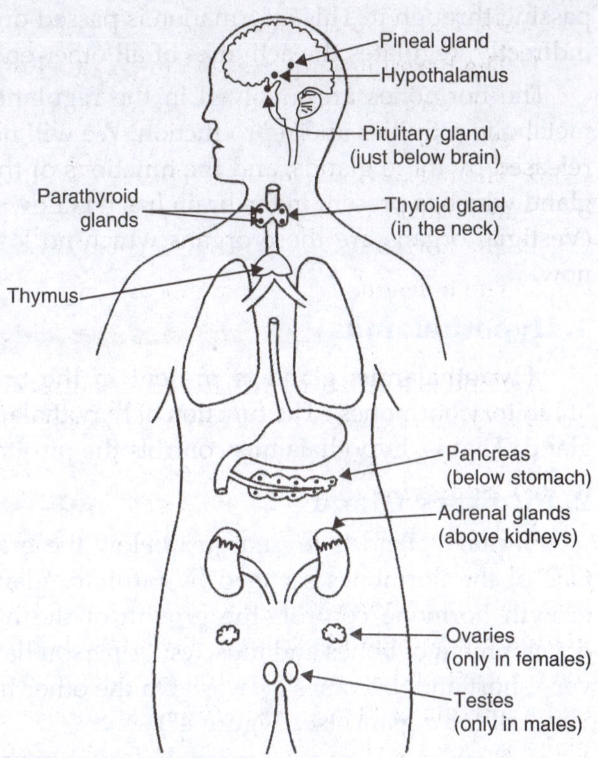

Figure 45. The positions of endocrine glands in the human body.

There are two adrenal glands in our body, one on top of each kidney (see Figure 45). The adrenal glands make adrenaline hormone. **The adrenaline hormone prepares our body to function at maximum efficiency during emergency situations like danger, anger, excitement, etc.** This happens as follows : When we are faced with a dangerous situation (like being chased by a ferocious dog), then our nervous system stimulates the adrenal glands to secrete more adrenaline hormone into our blood. This adrenaline hormone increases our 'heart beats', 'breathing rate', 'blood flow into muscles' and causes liver 'to put more stored glucose into our blood'. All these actions of adrenaline hormone produce a lot of energy in our body very, very quickly. And this energy helps us to run away very fast from the dog to save ourselves. In this way, **the adrenaline hormone**

Figure 46. It is the adrenaline hormone (secreted by adrenal glands) which has prepared the body of this person to run away very fast from a ferocious dog.

prepares our body to run away very fast from a frightening object. Similarly, **it is the adrenaline hormone which prepares our body to fight an enemy** (say, a burglar in our house) by providing us a lot of energy in a very short time. A lot of adrenaline hormone is also secreted by adrenal glands when we are 'angry' or 'excited'. The rapid output of energy thus caused helps us to cope with these extreme emotional situations.

The complete coordination in the human body is achieved by the nervous system and endocrine system working together. The main centres in the body for the coordination of the two systems of control (nervous system and the endocrine system) are the **hypothalamus** and **pituitary gland.** The hypothalamus plays an important role in collecting information from other regions of the brain and from blood vessels passing through it. This information is passed on to pituitary gland which by its own secretions, directly or indirectly, regulates the activities of all other endocrine glands.

The hormones are involved in the regulation of several functions in the human body like growth, metabolic activities and reproduction. We will now give the names of the endocrine glands, the hormones released by these glands, and the functions of these hormones in the human body. Please note that pineal gland which is present in the brain has no known function. Pineal gland is supposed to be a vestigial organ (Vestigial organs are those organs which no longer function). Let us discuss the other endocrine glands now.

1. Hypothalamus

Hypothalamus gland is present in the brain. Hypothalamus produces 'releasing hormones' and 'inhibitory hormones'. The function of hypothalamus is to regulate the secretions of hormones from pituitary gland. That is, hypothalamus controls the pituitary hormones.

2. Pituitary Gland

Pituitary gland is present just below the brain. The pituitary gland secretes a number of hormones. One of the hormones secreted by pituitary gland is growth hormone (or human growth hormone). The growth hormone controls the growth of the human body. For example, growth hormone controls the development of bones and muscles. A person having a deficiency of growth hormone in childhood remains very short and becomes a dwarf. On the other hand, a person having too much growth hormone becomes very tall (or a giant) (see Figure 47).

Figure 47. An improperly functioning pituitary gland can produce either too little or too much growth hormone. Too little growth hormone makes a person dwarf whereas too much growth hormone makes a person a giant.

Figure 48. If a person does not get enough iodine from diet or drinking water, the thyroid gland cannot make sufficient thyroxine hormone. Due to the deficiency of thyroxine hormone, the thyroid gland in the neck enlarges, causing the neck to swell too much. This condition is called goitre. Please note the swollen neck of the woman shown in the above picture. She is suffering from goitre disease.

Figure 49. Iodised salt can provide all the iodine needed by thyroid gland to make sufficient thyroxine hormone for our body so that goitre does not develop.

3. Thyroid Gland

Thyroid gland is attached to the wind pipe in our body. Thyroid gland makes a hormone called thyroxine (which contains iodine). The function of thyroxine hormone is to control the rate of metabolism of carbohydrates, fats and proteins in the body. **Iodine is necessary for the making of thyroxine hormone by thyroid gland, therefore, a deficiency of iodine in the diet can cause a deficiency of thyroxine hormone in the body.** The deficiency of iodine in the diet of a person produces less thyroxine hormone and causes a disease known as **goitre**. The main symptom of goitre is that the neck of the person appears to be swollen (due to the enlargement of thyroid gland located in the neck). People are advised to use iodised salt for cooking food so as to prevent goitre disease. This can be explained as follows : Iodine is required by the thyroid gland to make thyroxine hormone. Iodised salt contains appropriate amount of iodine compounds (such as potassium iodide). Iodised salt can provide all the iodine needed by thyroid gland to make sufficient thyroxine for our body (see Figure 49). Since there will be no deficiency of thyroxine in the body, goitre cannot develop.

4. Parathyroid Glands

There are four small parathyroid glands which are embedded in the thyroid gland (see Figure 45). Parathyroid glands secrete a hormone called parathormone. The function of parathormone hormone is to regulate calcium and phosphate levels in the blood.

5. Thymus Gland

Thymus gland lies in the lower part of the neck and upper part of chest. Thymus gland secretes thymus hormone which plays a role in the development of the immune system of the body. Thymus gland is large in young children but shrinks after puberty (or sexual maturity).

6. Pancreas

The pancreas is just below the stomach in the body. Pancreas secretes the hormone called insulin. **The function of insulin hormone is to lower the blood sugar level (or blood glucose level).** Deficiency of insulin hormone in the body causes a disease known as diabetes. Diabetes disease is characterised by large quantities of sugar in the blood (and even urine). The insulin hormone controls the metabolism of sugar. If, due to some reason, pancreas does not produce and secrete sufficient amount of insulin into blood, then the sugar level in the blood rises. The high sugar level in the blood can cause many harmful effects to the body of a person. The person having high sugar level in blood (or diabetes) is called a diabetic. Diabetic

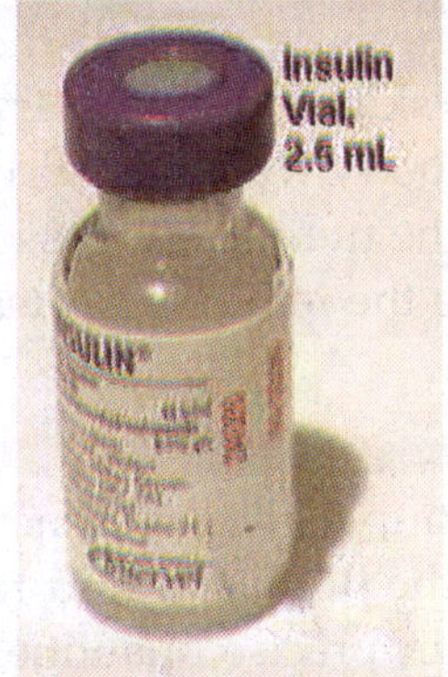

Figure 50. This bottle contains insulin (in the form of a colloidal solution).

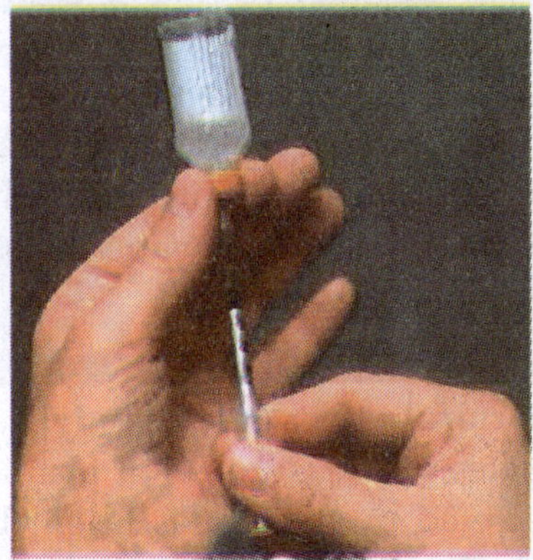

Figure 51. Insulin solution being filled in a syringe through the injection needle.

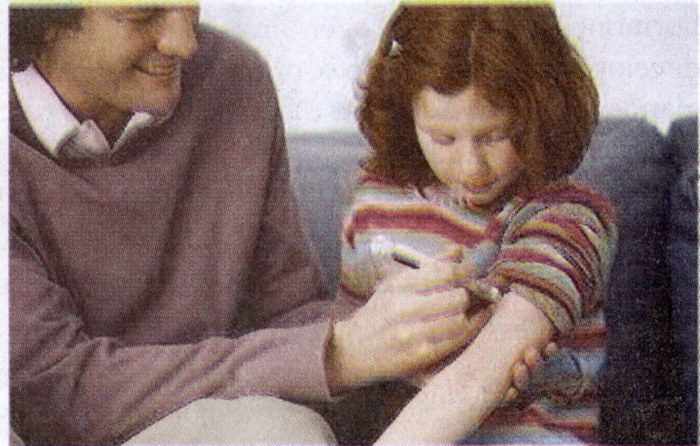

Figure 52. A child suffering from diabetes is being given an insulin injection.

persons are advised by doctors to take less sugar in their diet. Common diabetes can be controlled by controlling diet, reducing weight, doing regular physical exercise and taking medicines. The persons having severe diabetes are treated by giving injections of insulin.

7. Adrenal Glands

There are two adrenal glands which are located on the top of two kidneys (see Figure 53). The adrenal glands secrete adrenaline hormone. The function of adrenaline hormone is to regulate heart rate, breathing rate, blood pressure and carbohydrate metabolism. Adrenaline hormone is secreted in small amounts all the time but in large amounts when a person is frightened or excited. When adrenaline is secreted in large amounts it prepares our body for action (see Figure 54). It speeds up heart beat and breathing, raises blood pressure and allows more glucose (carbohydrate) to go into the blood to give us a lot of energy quickly to fight or flight (run away). Adrenal glands are often called 'glands of emergency'.

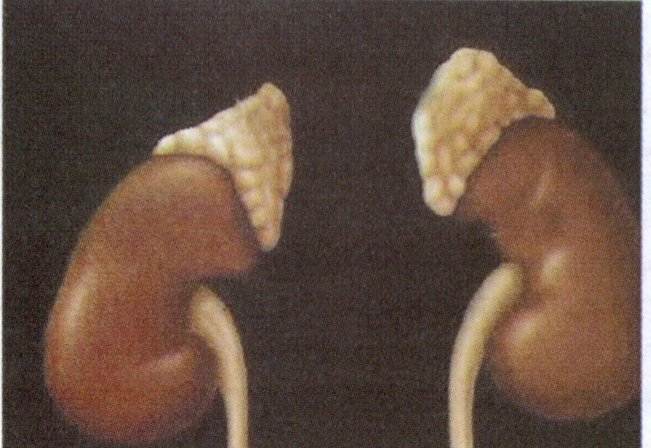

Figure 53. The two adrenal glands are located on the top of two kidneys in our body. They make and secrete adrenaline hormone.

Figure 54. This picture shows how the adrenaline hormone prepares the body for action.

8. Testes

Testes are the glands which are present only in males (men). Testes make male sex hormones called testosterone. The function of testosterone hormone is to control the development of male sex organs and male features such as deeper voice, moustache, beard, and more body hair (than females). All these changes caused by testosterone are associated with male puberty which the boys attain at an age of 13 to 14 years. The testes also make the male gametes called sperms.

9. Ovaries

Ovaries are the glands which are present only in females (women). Ovaries make two female sex hormones called oestrogen and progesterone. The function of oestrogen hormone is to control the development of female sex organs, and female features such as feminine voice, soft skin and mammary glands (breasts). All these changes caused by oestrogen are associated with female puberty which the girls attain at an age of 10 to 12 years. The function of progesterone hormone is to control the uterus changes in menstrual cycle. It also helps in the maintenance of pregnancy. The ovaries also make the female gametes called ova (or eggs).

Feedback Mechanism

The excess or deficiency of hormones has a harmful effect on our body. For example, the deficiency of insulin hormone results in a disease called diabetes whereas excess of insulin in the body can lead to coma. So, it is necessary that the hormones are secreted by the glands in our body in precise quantities which are required for the normal functioning of the body. This means that there should be some 'mechanism' to regulate the production and release of hormones in the body. **The timing and amount of hormones released by various glands are controlled by the 'feedback mechanism' which is in-built in our body.** For example, if the sugar level in the blood rises too much, they are detected by the cells of pancreas which respond by producing and secreting more insulin into blood. And as the blood sugar falls to a certain level, the secretion of insulin is reduced automatically.

Before we end this discussion we would like to give **a comparison of the nervous system and endocrine system (or hormonal system)** for the control and coordination in humans (and other higher animals).

Nervous system	*Endocrine system (Hormonal system)*
1. Made of neurons (nerve cells)	1. Made of secretory cells (or glands)
2. Messages transmitted in the form of electrical impulses	2. Messages transmitted in the form of chemicals called hormones
3. Messages transmitted along nerve fibres	3. Messages transmitted through blood stream
4. Messages travel very quickly	4. Messages travel more slowly
5. Effect of message usually lasts for a very short while	5. Effect of message usually lasts longer

We are now in a position to **answer the following questions :**

Very Short Answer Type Questions

1. Name the two systems of control and coordination in higher animals.
2. What are the two parts of the vertebrate nervous system ?
3. If we happen to touch a hot object unknowingly, we immediately pull back our hand. What is this type of action known as ?
4. Name the three components of a neuron (or nerve cell).
5. (*a*) What are the short fibres of a neuron known as ?
   (*b*) What is the long fibre of a neuron known as ?
6. Name the most important part of the human brain.
7. Which part of the brain maintains posture and balance of the body ?
8. State one function each of cerebellum and pons.
9. Name one hormone secreted by the pituitary gland.
10. Where are hormones made in the human body ?
11. What is the name of the system of glands which produces hormones ?
12. Which gland secretes the growth hormone ?
13. Name the hormones secreted by (*a*) testes, and (*b*) ovaries
14. What are the scientific names for the following receptors in animals ?
   (*a*) receptors for light (*b*) receptors for heat (*c*) receptors for sound
   (*d*) receptors for smell (*e*) receptors for taste
15. Name the disease caused by the deficiency of insulin hormone in the body.
16. Name the disease caused by the deficiency of thyroxine hormone in the body.
17. Which halogen element is necessary for the making of thyroxine hormone by the thyroid gland ?
18. Why are some patients of diabetes treated by giving injections of insulin ?
19. What is the name of in-built 'arrangement' in our body which controls the timing and amount of hormones released by various endocrine glands in the body ?
20. Name one gland each :
   (*a*) which acts only as an endocrine gland.
   (*b*) which acts only as an exocrine gland.
   (*c*) which acts both as an endocrine gland as well as an exocrine gland.
21. What part does the diet play in helping us to have a healthy thyroid gland ?
22. If sugar is detected in the urine of a person, name the disease he is suffering from.
23. Name two parts of the body which contain receptors of chemical stimuli.
24. Which part of the eye contains cells which are sensitive to light ?
25. What are the two main communications systems in an animal's body ?
26. Which one term in each of the following includes the other three ?
   (*a*) thyroid, ductless gland, thymus, pituitary, ovary
   (*b*) adrenalin, insulin, hormone, thyroxine, estrogen
27. Which parts of the body form the central nervous system ?
28. Give three examples of reflex actions.
29. Why do you need iodine in your diet ?
30. State whether coughing is a voluntary action or reflex action.
31. Fill in the following blanks with suitable words :
   (*a*) The two examples of effectors are ....and ....
   (*b*) Our..................system allows us to react to our surroundings. Information from receptors passes along................neurons to our brain. Our brain sends impulses along..........neurons to our muscles.
   (*c*) A neuron which carries an impulse to the brain is called a .... neuron.
   (*d*) The neuron which carries a message for action to a muscle or gland is known as a................... neuron.

Short Answer Type Questions

32. (*a*) What are the various sense organs in our body ?
    (*b*) What is meant by receptors and effectors ? Give two examples of each.
33. (*a*) What is spinal cord ? What is its main function ?
    (*b*) Give the functions of medulla.
34. (*a*) Name the three types of nerves which constitute the peripheral nervous system.
    (*b*) What is the difference between a reflex action and walking ?
    (*c*) How do we detect the smell of an incense stick (*agarbatti*) ?
35. (*a*) What substances are made by endocrine glands ?
    (*b*) What is the function of receptors and effectors in our body ?
36. (*a*) Name the hormones secreted by the following endocrine glands :
    (*i*) Thyroid gland (*ii*) Parathyroid glands (*iii*) Pancreas (*iv*) Adrenal glands
    (*b*) Write the functions of testosterone and oestrogen hormones.
37. (*a*) Write the names of the regions in hindbrain. Give one function of each region.
    (*b*) Name the functions of cerebrum.
38. (*a*) The human brain can be broadly divided into three regions. Name these three regions.
    (*b*) What is cranium ? What is its function ?
39. (*a*) How does chemical coordination take place in human beings ?
    (*b*) Why is the use of iodised salt advisable ?
40. What is the function of insulin hormone ? What type of patients are given insulin injections ?
41. Compare the nervous system and endocrine system (hormonal system) for control and coordination in humans.
42. State the functions of the following hormones :
    (*a*) Thyroxine (*b*) Adrenaline (*c*) Growth hormone
43. Write the names of all the major endocrine glands present in the human body. Which of these glands also function as exocrine glands ?
44. Match the hormones given in column I with their functions given in column II :

Hormones	*Functions*
(*i*) Thyroxine	(*a*) Causes breasts to develop in females
(*ii*) Adrenaline	(*b*) Causes the male to start producing sperms
(*iii*) Insulin	(*c*) Prepares the body for an emergency
(*iv*) Estrogen	(*d*) Controls the metabolic rate
(*v*) Testosterone	(*e*) Regulates the amount of sugar in blood

45. A person walks across a room in barefeet and puts his foot on a drawing pin lying on the floor. He lets out a cry. Explain what happens in his nervous system in bringing about this response.
46. In what ways are puberty and adolescence result of the activity of some glands in the human body ?
47. List three ways in which neurons are similar to other cells.
48. Explain the difference between each of the following pairs of terms :
    (*a*) receptor and effector (*b*) cerebrum and cerebellum
49. What is the difference between a voluntary and an involuntary action ? Which kind of action is digestion ? Explain your choice.
50. What does CNS stand for ? Which part of CNS : (*a*) consists of two cerebral hemispheres, and (*b*) has spinal nerves attached to it ?
51. Which hormone :
    (*a*) prepares the body for action ?
    (*b*) controls the amount of glucose in blood ?
    (*c*) gives boys a deep voice ?
    (*d*) gives girls soft skin ?

52. When you smell a favourite food your mouth begins to water (that is, you secrete saliva). Write down what the following are examples of :

(*a*) the smell of the food

(*b*) the cells in your nasal passages which perceive the smell

(*c*) the gland which is stimulated to secrete saliva.

Long Answer Type Questions

53. (*a*) Name the structural and functional unit of nervous system.

(*b*) Draw a flow chart to show the classification of nervous system into various parts.

(*c*) What is autonomic nervous system ? What is its function ?

(*d*) What is voluntary nervous system ? Explain the working of voluntary nervous system with an example.

54. (*a*) What is a reflex action ? Explain with the help of an example.

(*b*) Define reflex arc. Give the flow chart of a spinal reflex arc.

(*c*) How are involuntary actions and reflex actions different from each other ?

55. (*a*) What is the function of our nervous system ?

(*b*) What are the main organs of the human nervous system ? Draw a labelled diagram to show the main organs of the human nervous system.

(*c*) How does the human nervous system work ? Explain.

56. (*a*) What is a neuron ? Draw a labelled diagram of a neuron.

(*b*) What is a synapse ? What happens at the synapse between two neurons ? How are the messages carried across a synapse ? Explain with the help of a labelled diagram.

57. (*a*) Name two systems which taken together perform the functions of control and coordination in human beings.

(*b*) What does the central nervous system in humans consist of ? What is the job of the central nervous system ?

(*c*) Give the various functions of brain.

58. (*a*) Write the names of five endocrine glands found in the human body. Name the hormones secreted by each gland.

(*b*) How do hormones reach the organs they control ?

(*c*) Name the gland which controls the secretion of hormones from the pituitary.

(*d*) How does our body respond when adrenaline is secreted in large amounts into the blood ?

(*e*) Name the disease which occurs in adults due to the deficiency of iodine in the diet. What is the main symptom of this disease ?

Multiple Choice Questions (MCQs)

59. A cell (or group of cells) in a sense organ which is sensitive to a particular type of stimulus is called :

(*a*) interceptor (*b*) effector (*c*) receptor (*d*) acceptor

60. Which of the following cannot be considered a receptor ?

(*a*) ear (*b*) nose (*c*) muscle (*d*) eye

61. One of the following acts as an endocrine gland as well as an exocrine gland. This one is :

(*a*) salivary gland (*b*) pancreas (*c*) pituitary (*d*) parathyroid

62. Which of the following helps in maintaining posture and balance of the human body ?

(*a*) cerebellum (*b*) cerebrum (*c*) medulla (*d*) pons

63. The number of pairs of nerves which arises from the spinal cord is :

(*a*) 21 (*b*) 31 (*c*) 41 (*d*) 51

64. Cerbellum, medulla and pons are the parts of :

(*a*) mid-brain (*b*) hind-brain (*c*) forebrain (*d*) spinal cord

65. Which of the following are cerebral reflexes ?

(*i*) a person pulls away his hand on touching a hot object

(*ii*) a person spits out immediately when a fly enters his mouth while talking

(*iii*) A person walking bare foot lifts his foot at once on stepping on to a nail
(*iv*) A person's pupil contracts at once in the presence of bright light
(*a*) (*i*) and (*ii*) (*b*) (*ii*) and (*iii*) (*c*) (*iii*) and (*iv*) (*d*) (*ii*) and (*iv*)

66. Iodine is necessary for the synthesis of which of the following hormone ?
(*a*) adrenaline (*b*) auxin (*c*) thyroxine (*d*) insulin

67. Which of the following is a mis-matched pair ?
(*a*) adrenaline : pituitary gland (*b*) estrogen : ovary
(*c*) pancreas : insulin (*d*) progesterone : ovary

68. One of the following is an incorrect statement about insulin. This is :
(*a*) it is produced in pancreas
(*b*) it regulates growth and development of the body
(*c*) it regulates blood glucose level in the blood
(*d*) its deficiency in the body will cause diabetes

69. The spinal cord orginates from :
(*a*) cerebrum (*b*) cerebellum (*c*) medulla (*d*) pons

70. The involuntary actions in the body are controlled by :
(*a*) medulla in forebrain (*b*) medulla in hindbrain
(*c*) medulla in spinal cord (*d*) medulla in midbrain

71. Which of the following is not an involuntary action ?
(*a*) vomiting (*b*) chewing (*c*) heart beat (*d*) salivation

72. Which of the following hormone prepares our body for action in emergency situations ?
(*a*) testosterone (*b*) growth hormone (*c*) adrenaline (*d*) insulin

73. One of the following controls the peristaltic movements of alimentary canal. This one is :
(*a*) cerebrum (*b*) cerebellum (*c*) pons (*d*) medulla

74. The hormone which is associated with male puberty is called :
(*a*) oestrogen (*b*) adrenaline (*c*) testosterone (*d*) progesterone

75. Which of the following endocrine gland does not occur as a pair in the human body ?
(*a*) adrenal (*b*) pituitary (*c*) testis (*d*) ovary

76. The junction between two adjacent neurons is called :
(*a*) nerve junction (*b*) sensory junction (*c*) synapse (*d*) neuro-muscular joint

77. The life processes in humans are controlled and regulated by :
(*a*) reproductive and endocrine systems (*b*) respiratory and nervous systems
(*c*) endocrine and digestive systems (*d*) nervous and endocrine systems

78. A doctor advised a person to take injection of insulin because :
(*a*) his blood pressure was high
(*b*) his heart beat was high
(*c*) his blood sugar was high
(*d*) his thyroxine level in blood was high

79. All the voluntary actions of our body are controlled by :
(*a*) cerebrum (*b*) cerebellum (*c*) pons (*d*) medulla

80. One of the following statements is not true about thyroxine. This is :
(*a*) Thyroid gland requires iron to synthesise thyroxine
(*b*) It regulates carbohydrate, protein and fat metabolism
(*c*) Iodine is essential for the synthesis of thyroxine
(*d*) Thyroid gland can enlarge due to lack of thyroxine

81. Which of the following does not act as an endocrine gland as well as an exocrine gland ?
(*a*) testis (*b*) ovary (*c*) pituitary (*d*) pancreas

82. The part of brain which controls the involuntary actions such as heart beat, breathing, blood pressure, etc. is :
(*a*) pons (*b*) medulla (*c*) cerebrum (*d*) cerebellum

83. Dwarfism results due to :
(*a*) excessive secretion of thyroxine hormone
(*b*) excessive secretion of growth hormone
(*c*) less secretion of adrenaline hormone
(*d*) less secretion of growth hormone

84. The dramatic changes in body features associated with puberty are mainly because of the secretions of :
(*a*) estrogen from testes and testosterone from ovary
(*b*) estrogen from adrenal gland and testosterone from pituitary gland
(*c*) testosterone from testes and estrogen from ovary
(*d*) testosterone from thyroid gland and estrogen from pituitary gland

85. Which of the following statements is correct about receptors ?
(*a*) gustatory receptors detect taste while olfactory receptors detect smell
(*b*) both gustatory and olfactory receptors detect smell
(*c*) auditory receptors detect smell and olfactory receptors detect taste
(*d*) olfactory receptors detect taste and gustatory receptors detect smell

86. The part of brain which takes part in regulating respiration in the human body is :
(*a*) medulla (*b*) pons (*c*) cerebellum (*d*) cerebrum

87. Electrical impulse travels in a neuron from :
(*a*) dendrite ⟶ axon ⟶ axon end ⟶ cell body
(*b*) cell body ⟶ dendrite ⟶ axon ⟶ axon end
(*c*) dendrite ⟶ cell body ⟶ axon ⟶ axon end
(*d*) axon end ⟶ axon ⟶ cell body ⟶ dendrite

88. In a synapse, chemical signal is transmitted from :
(*a*) axon to cell body of the same neuron
(*b*) cell body to axon end of the same neuron
(*c*) dendrite end of one neuron to axon end of adjacent neuron
(*d*) axon end of one neuron to dendrite end of adjacent neuron

89. In a neuron, the conversion of electrical signal to a chemical signal occurs at/in :
(*a*) dendrite end (*b*) cell body (*c*) axon end (*d*) myelin sheath

90. One of the following gives the correct sequence of the components in a reflex arc. This is :
(*a*) Receptors ⟶ Muscle ⟶ Sensory neuron ⟶ Motor neuron ⟶ Spinal cord
(*b*) Receptors ⟶ Motor neuron ⟶ Spinal cord ⟶ Sensory neuron ⟶ Muscle
(*c*) Receptors ⟶ Spinal cord ⟶ Sensory neuron ⟶ Motor neuron ⟶ Muscle
(*d*) Receptors ⟶ Sensory neuron ⟶ Spinal cord ⟶ Motor neuron ⟶ Muscle

91. Which of the following statements are true ?
(*i*) sudden action in response to something in the environment is called reflex action
(*ii*) sensory neurons carry electrical signals from spinal cord to muscles in a reflex action
(*iii*) motor neurons carry signals from receptors to spinal cord in a reflex action
(*iv*) the pathway of transmitting signals from a receptor to a muscle is a reflex action
(*a*) (*i*) and (*ii*) (*b*) (*i*) and (*iii*) (*c*) (*i*) and (*iv*) (*d*) (*i*), (*ii*) and (*iii*)

92. The gustatory receptors of our body are in one of the following organs. This organ is :
(*a*) ear (*b*) nose (*c*) tongue (*d*) skin

93. The olfactory receptors in humans are located in :
(*a*) eyes (*b*) tongue (*c*) ears (*d*) nose

94. The contraction of pupil of the eye in the presence of bright light is an example of :
(*a*) Voluntary reflex (*b*) Spinal reflex (*c*) Cerebral reflex (*d*) Adrenal reflex

95. The faulty functioning of an endocrine gland can make a person very short or very tall. This gland is :
(*a*) thyroid (*b*) pineal (*c*) adrenal (*d*) pituitary

96. The underactive endocrine gland which causes goitre is :
(*a*) pancreas (*b*) thyroid (*c*) adrenal (*d*) pituitary

97. The endocrine gland whose malfunctioning causes diabetes disease is :
(*a*) pituitary (*b*) pineal (*c*) parathyroid (*d*) pancreas

98. The use of iodised salt is recommended to prevent :
(*a*) diabetes (*b*) gonorrhoea (*c*) dysentery (*d*) goitre

99. Which of the following are often called glands of emergency ?
(*a*) thyroid (*b*) pituitary (*c*) adrenal (*d*) pancreas

Questions Based on High Order Thinking Skills (HOTS)

100. P is a cell (or group of cells) in the human body which is sensitive to a particular type of stimulus and conveys the messages to CNS through nerves Q. On the other hand, R is a part of the human body which can respond to a stimulus according to the instructions sent from the CNS through nerves S.
(*a*) What is P ? Name five organs which contain cells (or group of cells) like P.
(*b*) Name the nerves Q.
(*c*) What is R ? Give two examples of R.
(*d*) Name nerves S.
(*e*) How do messages travel through the nerves Q and S ?

101. The human body contains a large number of cells A which are very long and branched, and look like electric wires. The longest branch of this cell is B whereas there are many small branches C. Any two A cells do not join to one another completely in the human body. There is a microscopic gap D between every pair of adjacent A cells through which electric impulses can pass by the release of a chemical substance.
(*a*) What are cells A ?
(*b*) What is the name of (*i*) branch B, and (*ii*) branches C ?
(*c*) What is the microscopic gap D known as ?
(*d*) What is the function of cells like A in the human body ?
(*e*) The cells A are of three types. Name the three types.

102. When we touch a hot plate unknowingly, then this heat is sensed by a receptor P present in our fingers. The receptor triggers an impulse in neuron Q which transmits the message to an organ R which is a part of the central nervous system. Here the impulse is passed on to a neuron S which in turn passes it to a yet another neuron T. The neuron T passes the impulse to a tissue U in our arm. The tissue U then contracts and pulls our hand away from the hot plate.
(*a*) What is the name of (*i*) receptor P (*ii*) neuron Q, and (*iii*) organ R ?
(*b*) What is (*i*) neuron S, and (*ii*) neuron T ?
(*c*) Name the tissue U.
(*d*) What name is given to the phenomenon in which hand is pulled away quickly from the hot plate ?
(*e*) Name the effector in this whole process.

103. The gland X which is located just below the brain in the human head secretes a chemical substance Y which controls the development of bones and muscles in the body of a person. Secretion of too little of substance Y as well as the secretion of too much of substance Y by the gland X leads to abnormal development of the body of a person.
(*a*) Name the gland X.
(*b*) What is the chemical substance Y ?
(*c*) What happens if too little of substance Y is secreted ?
(*d*) What happens if too much of substance Y is secreted ?
(*e*) Name the system of glands in the human body of which gland X is a part.

104. A and B are the two systems of control and coordination in the human body. The messages in system A are transmitted in the form of chemical substances C which travel comparatively slowly through the blood stream. The substances C are made in tissues D present in the head and trunk of human body. The messages in system B are transmitted very quickly in the form of electrical impulses through fibres E. The effect of messages transmitted by system B usually lasts for a much shorter time as compared to those transmitted by system A.
(*a*) Name the system A. What does system A consist of ?

(*b*) Name the chemical susbtance C.
(*c*) What is tissue D ? Name any five such tissues in the human body.
(*d*) Name the system B. What does system B consist of ?
(*e*) Name the fibres E.
(*f*) State whether system A controls the working of system B or system B controls the working of system A.

105. A cylindrical structure P in our body begins in continuation with medulla and extends downwards. It is enclosed in a bony cage Q and surrounded by membranes R. As many as x pairs of nerves arise from the structure P. The structure P is involved in the reflex actions of our body and conduction of nerve impulses to and from another organ S of our body with which it forms CNS.
(*a*) Name the structure P.
(*b*) Name (*i*) bony cage Q, and (*ii*) membranes R.
(*c*) How much is x ?
(*d*) Name the organ S.
(*e*) What are the reflexes involving structure P only known as ?

106. The pancreas is made up of two parts A and B. The part A secretes insulin whereas part B secretes pancreatic juice.
(*a*) Which part is functioning as an endocrine gland ? Why ?
(*b*) What is insulin and what effect does it have in the body ?
(*c*) Name the disease which can be treated by giving insulin injections.
(*d*) What does pancreatic juice contain ? Where does pancreatic juice go ?
(*e*) Name the life process in which pancreatic juice is made use of.

107. The gland A is attached to the wind pipe in the human body. The gland A makes and secretes a hormone B which controls the metabolism of carbohydrates, fats and proteins in the body. The non-metal element C is necessary for the formation of hormone B. The deficiency of C in the diet can cause a deficiency of hormone B in the body leading to a disease D in which the neck of a person appears to be swollen. People are advised to use salt E in cooking food so as to avoid disease D.
(*a*) Name (*i*) gland A, and (*ii*) hormone B.
(*b*) What is the element C ?
(*c*) Name one type of food which can provide sufficient C in the diet of a person.
(*d*) Name (*i*) disease D, and (*ii*) salt E.

108. A piece of thread was tied tightly around an animal's pancreatic duct. The animal subsequently had difficulty in digesting food but did not get diabetes. Explain.

109. Which is the target organ of both adrenaline and insulin ?
(*a*) heart (*b*) kidney (*c*) liver (*d*) pancreas

110. A gland W is located just below the stomach in the human body. The gland W secretes a hormone X. The deficiency of hormone X in the body causes a disease Y in which the blood sugar level of a person rises too much. The person having high blood sugar is called Z.
(*a*) Name (*i*) gland W, and (*ii*) hormone X.
(*b*) What is the function of hormone X ?
(*c*) Name (*i*) disease Y, and (*ii*) person Z.
(*d*) What advice would you like to give to a person who is suffering from disease Y due to faulty life-style ?

111. There are two similar glands P which are located on the top of two similar organs Q in the human body. The glands P are often called glands of emergency and they secrete a hormone R into the blood stream. The hormone R is secreted in large amounts when a person is frightened. It brings about temporary changes in the body which allow a lot of substance S from the liver to go into blood so as to provide a lot of energy in a very short time. This helps the person concerned to fight back or run away from the frightening situation. What are P, Q, R and S ?

112. The two glands A and B which occur in pairs, are present in the endocrine system of humans. The pair of glands A is found only in females whereas the pair of glands B occurs only in males. The glands A make and secrete two hormones C and D whereas glands B make and secrete only one hormone E. In addition to hormones, glands A make gametes F whereas glands B make gametes G.
(*a*) What are glands A ?
(*b*) What are hormones C and D ?
(*c*) What are glands B ? Name the hormone E.

(*d*) What are gametes (*i*) F, and (*ii*) G ?

(*e*) Which event in the life of males and females is associated with the secretion of hormones C, D and E ?

113. The organ A which is located inside the skull of our body is protected by a bony box B and it is surrounded by three membranes C. The space between the membranes is filled with a liquid D which protects the organ A from mechanical shocks. The organ A in combination with another organ E makes up the central nervous system.

(*a*) What is organ A ?

(*b*) What are (*i*) B (*ii*) C, and (*iii*) D ?

(*c*) Name the organ E.

(*d*) While walking barefooted, if we happen to step on a sharp piece of stone, we immediately lift our foot up. Which of the two organs, A or E, is directly involved in this action ?

(*e*) If we step out from a darkened room into bright sunshine, we close our eyes for a moment. Which of the two organs, A or E, is directly involved in this action ?

114. Write down the following in the correct order for a simple reflex arc :

(*a*) impulse travels in motor fibre

(*b*) impulse travels in sensory fibre

(*c*) effector organ stimulated

(*d*) impulse crosses synapse

115. Explain why, the tongue may be considered to be both a receptor and an effector organ.

ANSWERS

3. Reflex action **11.** Endocrine system **17.** Iodine **19.** Feedback mechanism **21.** Diet provides iodine for making thyroxine hormone which keeps the thyroid gland healthy **23.** Nose and Tongue **24.** Retina **26.** (*a*) ductless gland (*b*) hormone **31.** (*a*) muscle; glands (*b*) nervous ; sensory ; motor (*c*) sensory (*d*) motor **44.** (*i*) *d* (*ii*) *c* (*iii*) *e* (*iv*) *a* (*v*) *b* **47.** Both types of cells have a cell membrane, cytoplasm and a nucleus **49.** Involuntary action **52.** (*a*) Stimulus (*b*) Receptors (Olfactory receptors) (*c*) Effector (Salivary gland) **59.** (*c*) **60.** (*c*) **61.** (*b*) **62.** (*a*) **63.** (*b*) **64.** (*b*) **65.** (*d*) **66.** (*c*) **67.** (*a*) **68.** (*b*) **69.** (*c*) **70.** (*b*) **71.** (*b*) **72.** (*c*) **73.** (*d*) **74.** (*c*) **75.** (*b*) **76.** (*c*) **77.** (*d*) **78.** (*c*) **79.** (*a*) **80.** (*a*) **81.** (*c*) **82.** (*b*) **83.** (*d*) **84.** (*c*) **85.** (*a*) **86.** (*b*) **87.** (*c*) **88.** (*d*) **89.** (*c*) **90.** (*d*) **91.** (*c*) **92.** (*c*) **93.** (*d*) **94.** (*c*) **95.** (*d*) **96.** (*b*) **97.** (*d*) **98.** (*d*) **99.** (*c*) **100.** (*a*) P is a receptor ; Eyes, Ears, Nose, Tongue and Skin (*b*) Sensory nerves (*c*) Effector ; Muscles and Glands (*d*) Motor nerves (*e*) In the form of electrical impulses **101.** (*a*) Neurons (*b*) (*i*) Axon (*ii*) Dendrites (*c*) Synapse (*d*) Transmit messages to and from the central nervous system (*e*) Sensory neurons, Motor neurons and Relay neurons **102.** (*a*) (*i*) Thermoreceptor (*ii*) Sensory neuron (*iii*) Spinal cord (*b*) (*i*) Relay neuron (*ii*) Motor neuron (*c*) Muscle (*d*) Reflex action (*e*) Muscle (of arm) **103.** (*a*) Pituitary gland (*b*) Human growth hormone (*c*) The person remains very short and becomes a dwarf (*d*) The person grows very tall and becomes a giant (*e*) Endocrine system **104.** (*a*) Endocrine system ; Glands (*b*) Hormones (*c*) Endocrine glands ; Pituitary, Thyroid, Pancreas, Adrenals, Testes (*d*) Nervous system ; Brain , Spinal cord and Nerves (*e*) Nerve fibres (*f*) System B (Nervous system) controls the working of system A (Endocrine system) **105.** (*a*) Spinal cord (*b*) (*i*) Vertebral column (*ii*) Meninges (*c*) 31 (*d*) Brain (*e*) Spinal reflexes **106.** (*a*) Part A; It is secreting a hormone called insulin (*b*) Insulin is a hormone ; It controls the blood sugar level (*c*) Diabetes (*d*) Pancreatic juice contains digestive enzymes like pancreatic amylase, tryspin and lipase ; Small intestine (*e*) Digestion **107.** (*a*) (*i*) Thyroid gland (*ii*) Thyroxine (*b*) Iodine (*c*) Sea-food (like fish) (*d*) (*i*) Goitre (*ii*) Iodised salt **108.** When a piece of thread is tied tightly around the animal's pancreactic duct, then the pancreatic duct gets closed due to which pancreatic juice containing digestive enzymes cannot go into small intestine. In the absence of pancreatic juice, the animal has difficulty in digesting food. The pancreas however, releases insulin hormone directly in the blood due to which the animal does not get diabetes, **109.** (*c*) liver **110.** (*a*) (*i*) Pancreas (*ii*) Insulin (*b*) Hormone X (insulin) controls the blood sugar level (*c*) (*i*) Diabetes (*ii*) Diabetic person (*d*) Control diet , Reduce weight, Do regular physical exercise ; Take medicines regularly **111.** P : Adrenal glands ; Q : Kidneys ; R : Adrenaline hormone ; S : Glucose **112.** (*a*) Ovaries (*b*) Oestrogen and Progesterone (*c*) Testes ; Testosterone (*d*) (*i*) Ova (or Eggs) (*ii*) Sperms (*e*) Puberty **113.** (*a*) Brain (*b*) (*i*) Cranium (Skull) (*ii*) Meninges (*iii*) Cerebro spinal fluid (*c*) Spinal cord (*d*) Organ E (Spinal cord) (*e*) Organ A (Brain) **114.** (*b*) $\longrightarrow$ (*d*) $\longrightarrow$ (*a*) $\longrightarrow$ (*c*) **115.** Tongue is considered a receptor because it has taste buds which act as receptors for tastes ; Tongue can be considered to be an effector because it is a muscular organ having muscles which can respond to a stimulus.

How Do Organisms Reproduce

In the previous Chapters, we have studied those life processes which help an organism (plant or animal) to keep 'alive'. Now, all the living organisms grow old with time and ultimately die. In fact, every living organism remains alive on this earth for a limited period of time and then dies. So, new organisms have to be produced in place of those who die. **The production of new organisms from the existing organisms of the same species is known as reproduction.** In most simple words we can say that *reproduction is the creation of new living things (from the existing living things)*. Actually, one of the most important characteristics of living organisms is their ability to reproduce more members of their species. **Reproduction is essential for the survival of a species on this earth.** So, living organisms produce more organisms of their kind to maintain the life of their species on this earth.

The process of reproduction ensures continuity of life on earth. For example, human beings reproduce by giving birth to babies (sons and daughters). These babies grow and ultimately become adults. So, when the old parents die, their sons and daughters keep living on this earth. These sons and daughters also

(*a*) Humans reproduce by giving birth to babies

(*b*) Dogs reproduce by giving birth to puppies

(*c*) Most of the plants reproduce by producing seeds to grow more plants

Figure 1. The process of reproduction ensures continuity of life for various species.

reproduce by giving birth to more babies, and this process goes on and on. Thus, **reproduction by human beings ensures that the human species will continue to exist on this earth for all the time to come.**

Similarly, cats reproduce by giving birth to kittens so that their species may live for ever. And dogs reproduce by giving birth to puppies so that their species may continue to live on this earth. Most of the plants reproduce by producing seeds to grow more plants so that their species may continue to live on this earth.

It is clear from the above discussion that for a species of a plant or an animal to continue living on this earth, it must reproduce itself. **Reproduction gives rise to more organisms with the same basic characteristics as their parents.** For example, human beings always produce human babies; cats always produce kittens; and sunflower seeds always produce sunflower plants. If, however, some species of the living organisms cannot reproduce due to certain reasons, then the organisms of this species will gradually die out and disappear from this earth one day. In this chapter we will discuss the various methods of reproduction in plants and animals.

Please note that the existing organism or organisms are called parents and the new organisms produced by them are called offsprings. For example, our father and mother are parents and we (their children) are the offsprings. The parent or parents of organisms can be animals as well as plants. Sometimes, the word daughter (or daughter cells) is also used for the offsprings of an organism.

Types of Reproduction

There are many different ways in which new organisms are produced from their parents. Some organisms like *Amoeba* just split into two parts to produce new *Amoebae*; some organisms like *Hydra* and yeast grow out of the parent's body in the form of a bud; some organisms like birds and snakes hatch out of the eggs

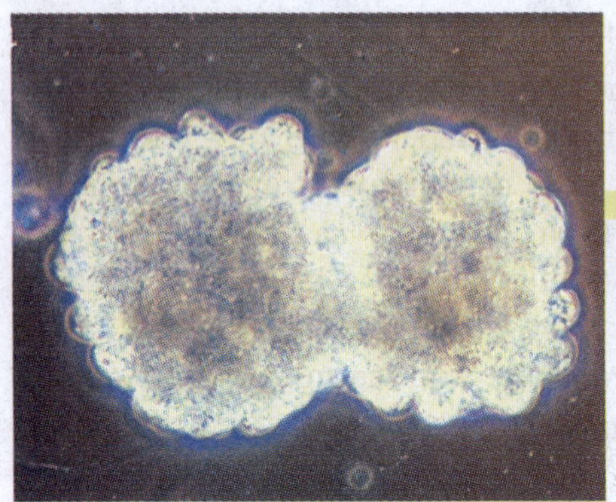

(*a*) An *Amoeba* reproduces just by splitting into two parts to form two *Amoebae*

(*b*) Chicken is hatched from the egg

(*c*) Tiger cubs are born from their mother tigress

Figure 2. There are many different ways in which new organisms are produced from their parents.

laid by their parents; whereas some organisms like human babies, cubs, kittens and puppies are born from their mother. This means that each species of organisms reproduces in a different way. All the different ways of reproduction can be divided into two main groups : asexual reproduction and sexual reproduction. Thus, **there are two main methods of reproduction in living organisms :**

(*i*) asexual reproduction, and

(*ii*) sexual reproduction.

We can now say that the living organisms reproduce mainly by two methods : 'asexual reproduction' and 'sexual reproduction'. This means that new living organisms (new plants and animals) can be made either by the method of 'asexual reproduction' or by the method of 'sexual reproduction'. We will now discuss the meaning of asexual reproduction and sexual reproduction. In order to understand this, please keep in mind that certain organisms contain **'reproductive cells'** (called **'sex cells', 'gametes'** or **'germ cells'**) in their bodies whereas some other organisms do not contain 'reproductive cells' ('sex cells', 'gametes' or 'germ cells') in their bodies.

1. Asexual Reproduction

In asexual reproduction, the offspring arises from a single parent. **The production of a new organism from a single parent without the involvement of sex cells (or gametes) is called asexual reproduction.** It is called asexual reproduction because it does not use special cells called 'sex cells' (or gametes) for producing a new organism. In asexual reproduction, a part of the parent organism separates off and grows into a new organism. Thus, *in asexual reproduction, only one parent is needed to produce a new organism.* But no sex cells are involved in asexual reproduction. **Some of the examples of asexual reproduction are : binary fission in *Amoeba*; budding in *Hydra*; spore formation in *Rhizopus* fungus (or bread mould); regeneration *in Planaria* (flatworm) ; fragmentation in *Spirogyra* and vegetative propagation in flowering plants (like rose plants).**

Please note that asexual reproduction is the simplest method of reproduction. It takes place mainly in those organisms whose bodies have a simple structure. So, the simple animals, simple plants and micro-organisms (like bacteria) reproduce by asexual reproduction methods. Actually, asexual reproduction takes place in unicellular animals and plants, micro-organisms (like bacteria) and simple multicellular animals (like *Hydra* and *Planaria*) and some multicellular plants (like *Bryophyllum* and rose plants, etc.).

Figure 3. *Hydra* is a tiny animal which lives in freshwater. *Hydra* grows a bud on its side which then separates off and becomes a new *Hydra*. Only one parent (only one *Hydra*) is needed in this asexual reproduction by budding.

2. Sexual Reproduction

In sexual reproduction, the offspring arises from two parents of different sexes : a male sex and a female sex. The male parent contains male sex cells (or male gametes) and the female parent contains female sex cells (or female gametes). **The production of a new organism from two parents by making use of their sex cells (or gametes) is called sexual reproduction.** In sexual reproduction, the sex cell of one parent fuses with the sex cell of the other parent to form a new cell called 'zygote'. This zygote then grows and develops to form a new organism. Thus, *in sexual reproduction, two parents are needed to produce a new organism.* The two parents which are involved in sexual reproduction are called male and female. Our father is a male and our mother is a female. The male and female parents have special organs in them which produce male sex cells and female sex cells respectively (which are required in sexual reproduction). **The humans, fish, frogs, hens, cats, dogs, cows, horses, deer, rabbits, lions and tigers all reproduce by the method of sexual reproduction. Most of the flowering plants also reproduce by sexual reproduction.** As we will study after a while, some organisms use both the methods (asexual and sexual) for reproduction whereas other organisms use only one of these methods for reproduction.

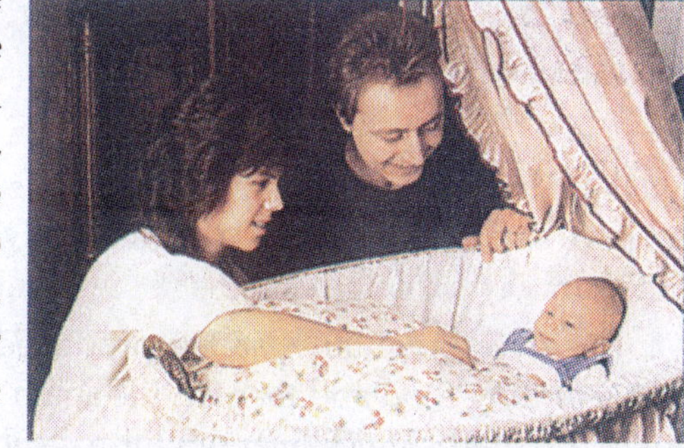

Figure 4. Two parents called male and female (man and woman or father and mother) are involved in the sexual reproduction of a human being (or baby).

The basic difference between asexual and sexual reproduction is that only one parent is needed in asexual reproduction whereas two parents are needed in sexual reproduction. Another difference is that no sex cells (or gametes) are involved in asexual reproduction but sex cells (or gametes) take part in sexual reproduction. We will now study the asexual reproduction and sexual reproduction in detail, one by one. Let us start with asexual reproduction.

ASEXUAL REPRODUCTION

In the asexual reproduction method, certain body cells of the parent organism undergo repeated mitotic cell divisions to form two (or more) new organisms of the same kind. Asexual reproduction takes place by six different methods. These are :

1. Fission 2. Budding 3. Spore formation 4. Regeneration
5. Fragmentation 6. Vegetative propagation

We will now describe all these methods of asexual reproduction in detail, one by one. Let us start with fission.

1. FISSION

Many single-celled organisms like protozoa and bacteria just split (or break) into two identical halves during cell division, leading to the creation of new organisms. This is called fission. In biology, fission is the process of reproduction in unicellular organisms such as protozoa (like *Amoeba*, *Paramecium*, *Leishmania*, etc.) and many bacteria. **In the process of fission, a unicellular organism splits (or divides) to form two (or more) new organisms.** Fission is of two types : binary fission and multiple fission, depending on whether the parent organism splits to form two new organisms or more than two organisms. The two types of fission are discussed below :

(*i*) Binary Fission

Binary fission is an asexual method of reproduction of organisms. **In binary fission, the parent organism splits (or divides) to form two new organisms.** When this happens, the parent organism ceases to exist and two new organisms come into existence. The unicellular organisms like *Amoeba*, *Paramecium*, *Leishmania*, bacteria, etc., reproduce by binary fission. This is described below.

Amoeba reproduces by binary fission by dividing its body into two parts. This happens as follows : When the *Amoeba* cell has reached its maximum size of growth, then first the nucleus of *Amoeba* lengthens and divides into two parts. After that the cytoplasm of *Amoeba* divides into two parts, one part around each

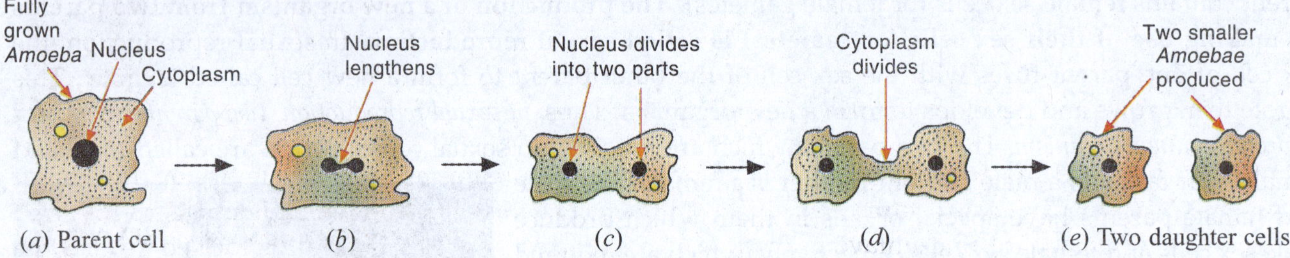

Figure 5. *Amoeba* reproducing by binary fission.

nucleus. In this way, one parent *Amoeba* divides to form two smaller *Amoebae* (called daughter *Amoebae*). And we say that one *Amoeba* produces two *Amoebae*. The reproduction in *Amoeba* by binary fission is shown in Figure 5.

The two daughter *Amoebae* produced here grow to their full size by eating food and then divide again to produce four *Amoebae*, and so on. In the unicellular organisms such as *Amoeba*, the splitting of the parent cell during fission (or cell division) can take place in any plane.

Paramecium is a unicellular animal having short thread-like structures called cilia over its surface (see Figure 6). *Paramecium* also reproduces by the method of binary fission. A fully grown *Paramecium* divides its body into two parts to form two smaller *Paramecia*. This happens by the division of nucleus followed by the division of cytoplasm.

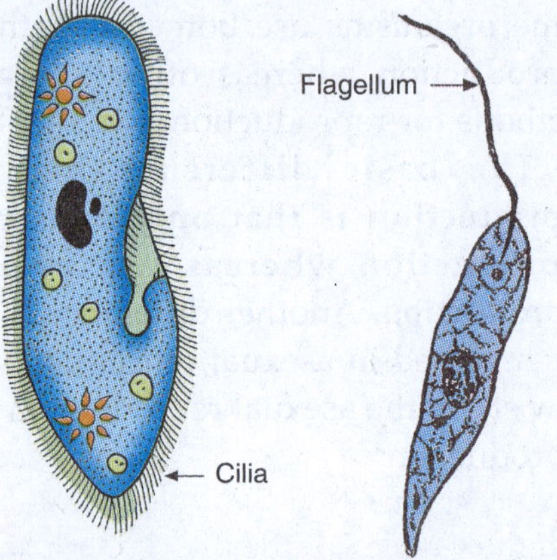

Figure 6. *Paramecium* **Figure 7.** *Leishmania*

Leishmania is a unicellular animal (which is a protozoan)

(see Figure 7). It is a parasite which causes the disease known as *kala-azar* (or black fever). *Kala-azar* is also known as leishmaniasis. *Leishmania* has a greater degree of organisation in its body, having a whip-like structure called flagellum at its one end (see Figure 7). *Leishmania* reproduces by the process of binary fission. In *Leishmania,* the splitting of parent cell during fission (or cell division) takes place in a definite plane (longitudinally) with respect to flagellum at its end. In this respect *Leishmania* differs from *Amoeba* (in which fission can take place in any plane).

From the above discussion we conclude that the simple animals like *Amoeba, Paramecium* and *Leishmania* reproduce by binary fission. The micro-organisms like bacteria also reproduce by the method of binary fission. Please note that the word 'binary' means 'two' and the word 'fission' means 'splitting'. So, the term 'binary fission' means 'splitting into two'.

We can observe the binary fission of *Amoeba* or *Paramecium* under a microscope. This can be done as follows : Collect some water from a pond or any other stagnant water body (especially where weeds, hay and husk are dumped). Put a few drops of this pond water on a clean slide and observe first under low magnification and then under high magnification of microscope. We will see the *Amoeba* or *Paramecium* dividing (or reproducing) by the method of binary fission.

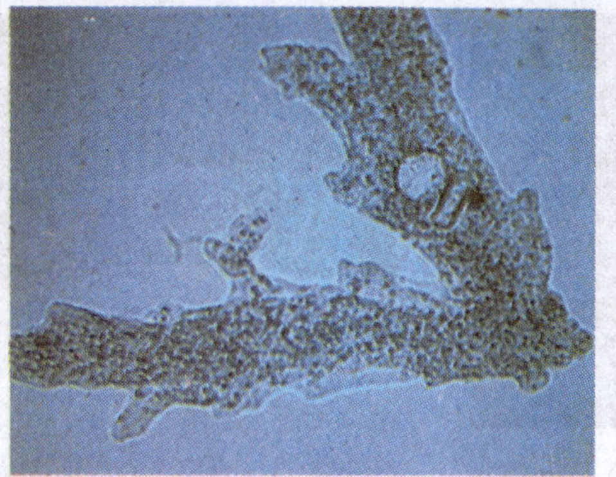

(*a*) An *Amoeba* dividing to give two *Amoebae*

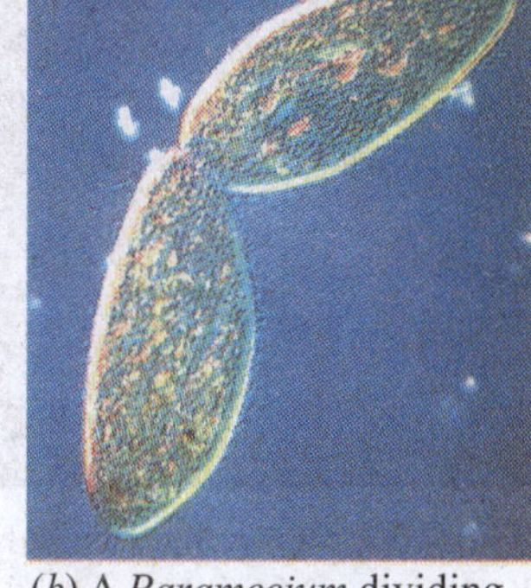

(*b*) A *Paramecium* dividing to give two *Paramecia*

Figure 8. *Amoeba* and *Paramecium* reproducing by binary fission (as seen under the high magnification of microscope).

The term 'multiple' means 'many' or 'several'. So, multiple fission means 'splitting into many' or 'splitting into several'. Let us discuss the multiple fission now.

(*ii*) Multiple Fission

Multiple fission is also an asexual method of reproduction in organisms. **In multiple fission, the parent organism splits (or divides) to form many new organisms at the same time.** This happens as follows : Sometimes (particularly during unfavourable conditions), a cyst or protective wall is formed around the cell of a single-celled organism (like that of *Plasmodium*) [see Figure 9(*a*)].

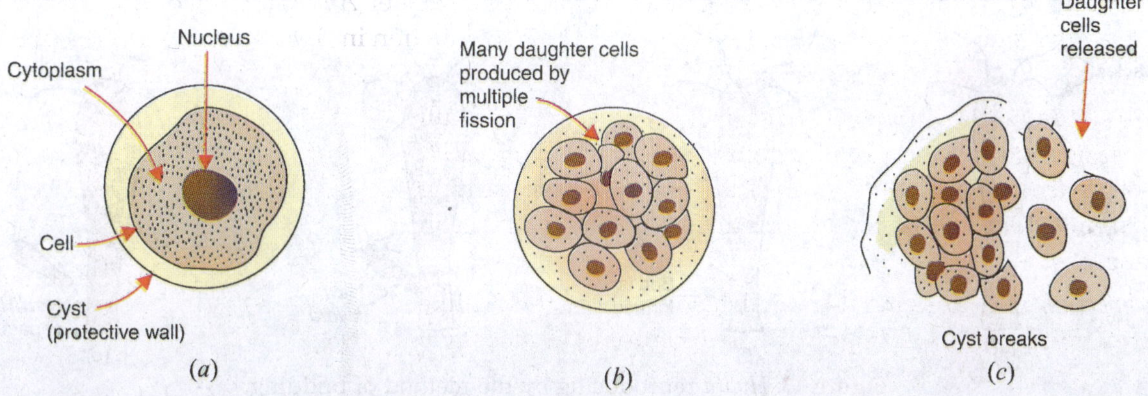

Figure 9. Reproduction by multiple fission.

Inside the cyst, the nucleus of cell splits (or divides) several times to form many smaller nuclei called daughter nuclei. Little bits of cytoplasm collect around each daughter nuclei and thin membranes are formed around them. In this way, many new daughter cells are formed from a single parent cell within the cyst [see Figure 9(*b*)]. In fact, as many daughter cells are formed as the number of daughter nuclei produced by the divisions of the parent nucleus. When the favourable conditions arrive, the cyst breaks open and the many daughter cells present in it are released, each forming a new organism [see Figure 9(*c*)]. In this way, a single celled parent undergoes multiple fission to reproduce many daughter cells at the same time. *Plasmodium* is a protozoan (a microscopic, single-celled animal) which reproduces by the asexual method of multiple fission. About 1000 daughter cells are produced by the multiple fission of one *Plasmodium* cell. *Plasmodium* is the malarial parasite which produces malaria disease in human beings. Malarial parasite *Plasmodium* is carried by female *Anopheles* mosquitoes from one person to another thereby spreading the malaria disease.

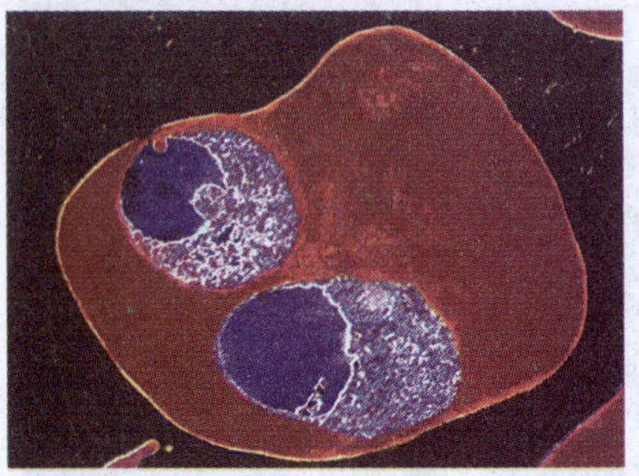

Figure 10. This is a highly enlarged photograph of the red blood cell of a person suffering from malaria disease. This red blood cell contains two *Plasmodium* cells which have been coloured blue.

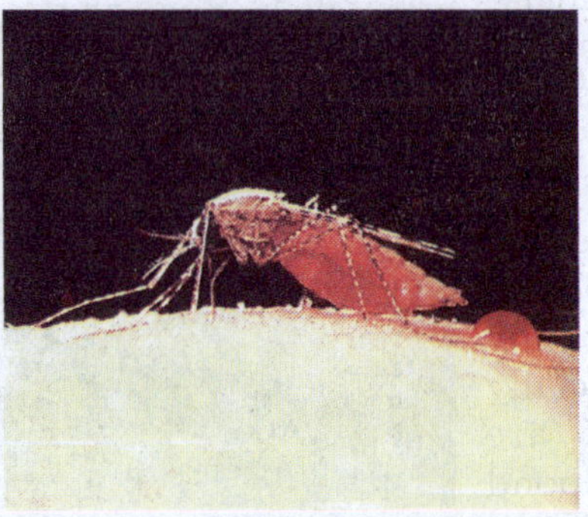

Figure 11. The female *Anopheles* mosquito carries the parasite of malaria disease called *Plasmodium.* So, it transmits malaria.

Figure 12. A health department worker is fumigating homes to remove mosquitoes so as to prevent malaria disease.

Before we discuss the next asexual method of reproduction called budding, we should know the meaning of the term 'bud'. The 'bud' here means a 'small outgrowth' from the body of a living organism. Let us discuss the method of 'budding' now.

2. BUDDING

Budding is an asexual method of reproduction. **In budding, a small part of the body of the parent organism grows out as a 'bud' which then detaches and becomes a new organism.** The asexual reproduction by budding is observed in *Hydra* and yeast. This is described below.

Hydra is a simple multicellular animal [see Figure 13(*a*)]. *Hydra* reproduces by the process of budding (by using its regenerative cells). This happens as follows : In *Hydra*, first a small outgrowth called 'bud' is

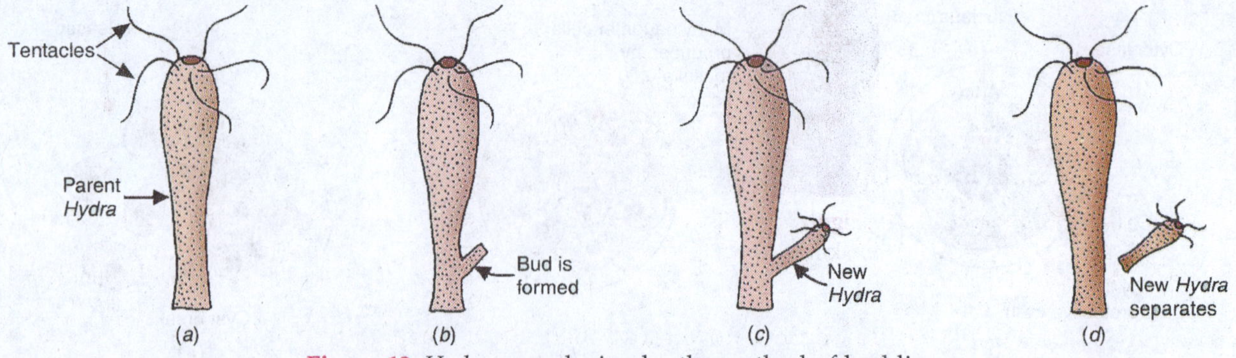

Figure 13. *Hydra* reproducing by the method of budding.

formed on the side of its body by the repeated mitotic divisions of its cells [see Figure 13(*b*)]. This bud then grows gradually to form a small *Hydra* by developing a mouth and tentacles [see Figure 13(*c*)]. And finally the tiny new *Hydra* detaches itself from the body of parent *Hydra* and lives as a separate organism [see Figure 13(*d*)]. In this way, the parent *Hydra* has produced (or created) a new *Hydra*. Thus, *Hydra* reproduces asexually by growing buds from its body. This is called budding. Please note that the bud formed in a *Hydra* is not a single cell. It is a group of cells.

We will now describe the reproduction in yeast plant by the process of budding. Please note that each single cell of yeast is a complete plant in itself.

Yeast is tiny, unicellular, non-green plant (which is a fungus). Yeast reproduces by budding. Figure 14(*a*) shows a parent yeast cell (which is a complete plant). In yeast, first a bud appears on the outside of the cell wall [Figure 14(*b*)]. The nucleus of parent yeast cell then divides into two parts and one part of the nucleus moves into the bud [Figure 14(*b*)]. Ultimately, the bud separates off from the parent yeast cell and forms a new yeast cell (or new yeast plant) [Figure 14(*c*)]. The budding in yeast, however, often takes place so fast that the first buds start forming their own buds and all of them remain attached to the parent yeast cell forming a chain of yeast cells [Figure 14(*d*)]. After some time, all the yeast cells of the chain separate from one another and form individual yeast plants.

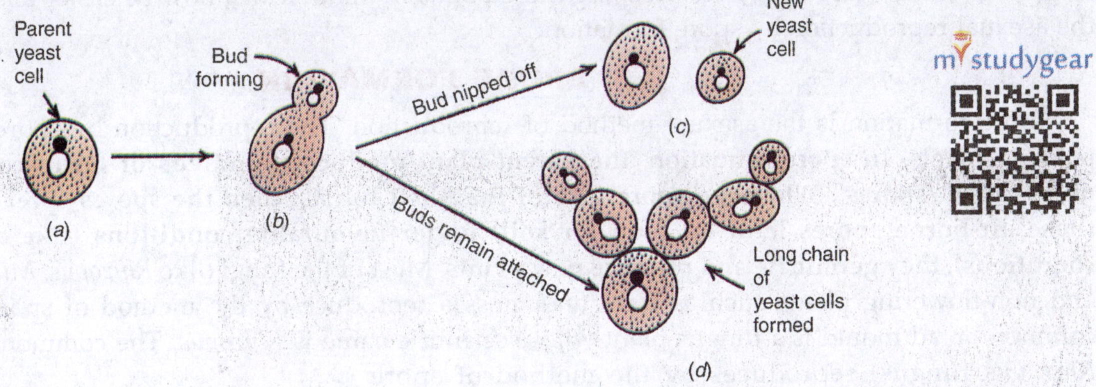

Figure 14. Yeast reproducing by the method of budding.

We can study the process of asexual reproduction in yeast by budding in the laboratory as follows: Take 100 mL of water in a conical flask and dissolve 10 grams of sugar in it. Then add 5 grams of yeast powder (or yeast granules) to this sugar solution and stir it well with a glass rod. Put a cotton plug in the neck of the conical flask. This conical flask containing sugar solution and yeast mixture is kept aside in a warm place for 3 to 5 days. When froth is observed in the flask, the yeast culture is ready for examination.

Take out a small quantity of the yeast culture solution from near the bottom of the conical flask with the help of a dropper and place a drop of this culture solution on a clean slide. Add a very little of iodine solution over the culture solution drop to stain it. Place a coverslip over the slide. Keep the slide under the microscope and observe it first under low power and then under the high power of the microscope. Note the formation of buds on the yeast cells and how they separate from the parent cell (see Figure 16).

Figure 15. This is yeast powder. It is used for making yeast culture solution in the laboratory.

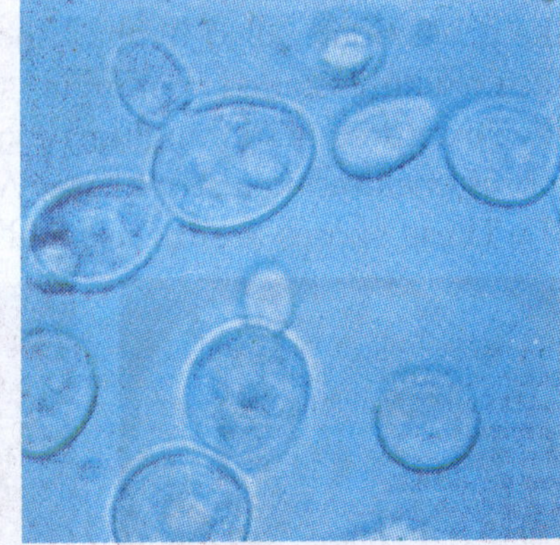

Figure 16. Yeast cells reproducing by budding (as seen in yeast culture solution under the high power of microscope).

In some organisms like sponges and corals, the buds remain attached to the parent organism permanently. These buds then grow and produce buds of their own. In this way, **a colony of sponges or corals is formed.**

Before we discuss the next asexual method of reproduction called 'spore formation', we should know something about 'spores'. **Spores are the microscopic 'asexual reproductive bodies' which are covered by**

a hard protective coat. This coat enables them to survive under unfavourable conditions like lack of food, lack of water and extreme temperatures. But when the conditions are favourable (food and water is available, and temperature is suitable), then the spores grow to produce new plants. Thus, **spores are a kind of seeds of plants.** These spores are very light and keep floating in air all around us. They are so small that we cannot see them with naked eyes. Keeping these points in mind, it will now be easier for us to understand the asexual reproduction by spore formation.

3. SPORE FORMATION

Spore formation is the asexual method of reproduction. The reproduction by spore formation takes place in plants. **In spore formation, the parent plant produces hundreds of microscopic reproductive units called 'spores'. When the spore case of the plant bursts, then the spores spread into air. When these air-borne spores land on food (or soil) under favourable conditions (like damp and warm conditions), they germinate and produce new plants**. Most of the fungi (like *Rhizopus*, *Mucor*, etc.), bacteria and non-flowering plants such as ferns and mosses reproduce by the method of spore formation. The common bread mould is a fungus plant whose scientific name is *Rhizopus*. The common bread mould (or *Rhizopus* fungus) reproduces by the method of spore formation. This is described below.

The tiny spores of 'bread mould' (a fungus plant) are almost always present in the air. If we keep a moist slice of bread aside for a few days, then the spores of bread mould plant present in air settle on the moist bread and germinate to form new fungus plants. The bread mould plants first look like a white cottony mass covering the bread slice which later on turns black. If we observe the surface of this slice of bread through a magnifying glass, then the bread mould plant growing on it will appear to be like that shown in Figure 17.

Sporangium
Spore case bursts
Spores being dispersed into air
Stem
Hyphae

Figure 17. This is a common bread mould plant (or *Rhizopus* fungus). It reproduces by forming spores.

The common bread mould plant consists of fine, thread-like projections called hyphae and thin stems having knob-like structures called sporangia (see Figure 17). Each knob-like structure (or sporangium) contains hundreds of minute spores enclosed in a spore case. When the spore case bursts, the tiny spores are dispersed in air (see Figure 17). These spores are the asexual reproductive units which can produce more bread mould plants under

Figure 18. Bread mould (*Rhizopus* fungus) growing on a slice of bread.

Figure 19. Bread mould fungus as seen through a magnifying glass. The white threads are 'hyphae'. Each black dot is a 'sporangium' which contains thousands of tiny spores.

Figure 20. This is *Penicillium* fungus. It also reproduces by forming spores.

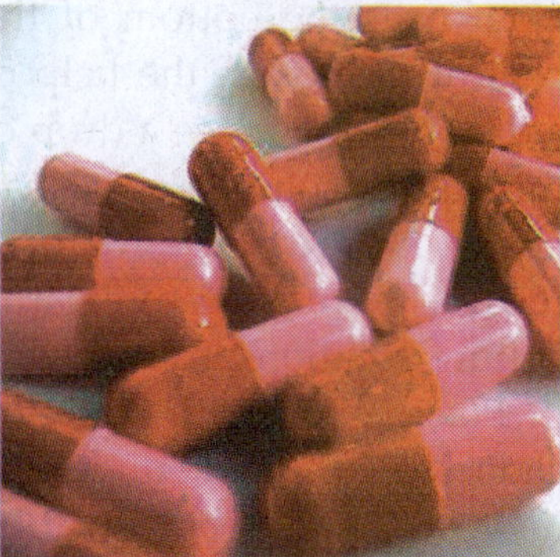

Figure 21. The antibiotic drug called penicillin is made from *Penicillium* fungus.

suitable conditions. Actually, it was one such air-borne spore which grew on the moist slice of bread kept aside by us for a few days. If we remove one sporangium from the bread mould, keep it on a slide, put a coverslip over it and observe this slide through a microscope, we can see the spores.

The spore formation method of asexual reproduction is used by unicellular organisms as well as by multicellular organisms. For example, bacteria are the unicellular organisms which reproduce by spore formation whereas fungi such as *Rhizopus* (bread mould) and *Mucor*, and non-flowering plants such as ferns and mosses are multicellular organisms which reproduce by spore formation method.

4. REGENERATION

In some organisms (plants as well as animals) small cut parts of their body can grow (or regenerate) to form whole new organisms complete in all respects. **The process of getting back a full organism from its body parts is called regeneration.** The simple animals like *Hydra* and *Planaria* show regeneration. This means that in these organisms, whole new organisms can be reproduced from their cut body parts. In other words, if *Hydra* or *Planaria* somehow get cut into a number of pieces, then each body piece can grow into a complete organism. This point will become more clear from the following example.

Planaria is a flatworm which is found in freshwater ponds and slow-moving streams. *Planaria* possesses great power of regeneration. If the body of *Planaria* somehow gets cut into a number of pieces, then each body piece can regenerate into a complete *Planaria* by growing all the missing parts. This is shown in Figure 22.

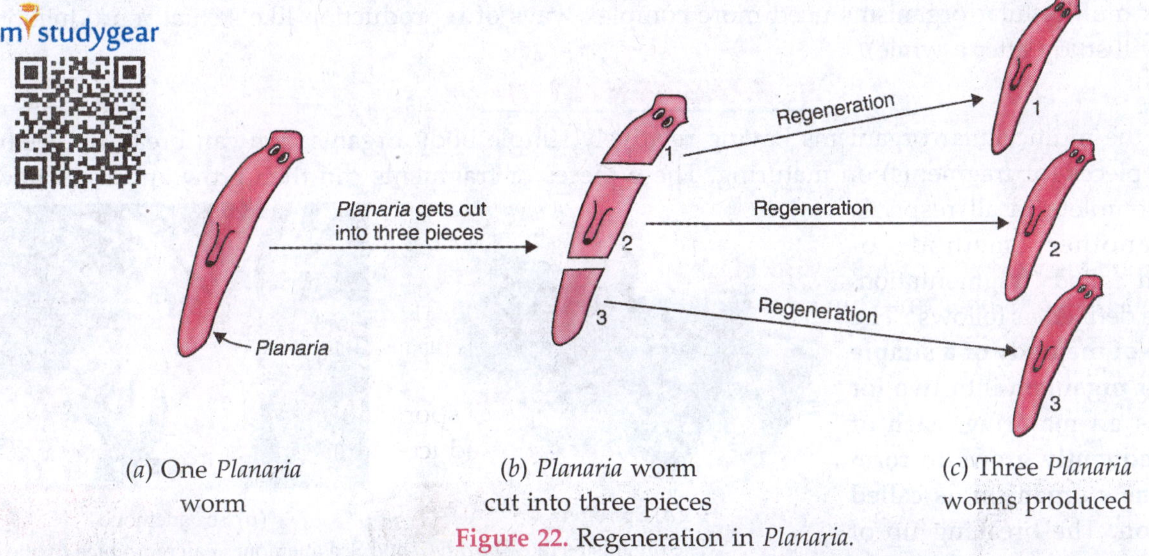

(*a*) One *Planaria* worm

(*b*) *Planaria* worm cut into three pieces

(*c*) Three *Planaria* worms produced

Figure 22. Regeneration in *Planaria*.

Figure 22(*a*) shows one *Planaria* worm. This *Planaria* worm somehow gets cut into three pieces [see Figure 22(*b*)]. After a certain time, each cut piece of the body of *Planaria* worm grows into a complete *Planaria* worm [see Figure 22(*c*)]. In this way, three *Planaria* worms are produced from just one *Planaria* worm. Similarly, if the body of a *Hydra* gets cut into a number of pieces, then each body piece of *Hydra* can grow into a complete *Hydra*. Please note that regeneration is *not* exactly the same as reproduction because most simple animals would not depend on being cut into pieces to be able to reproduce.

The regeneration of an organism from its cut body part occurs by the process of **growth and development.** This happens as follows : The cells of cut body part of the organism divide rapidly to make a 'ball of cells'. The cells present in the 'ball of cells' move to their proper places within the ball where they have to form various organs and body parts of the organism. The cells then change their shapes (or become specialised) to form different types of tissues. These different tissues form various organs and body parts of the organism. In this way a complete organism is regenerated.

The organisms like *Planaria* and *Hydra* are simple multicellular organisms which can be regenerated from their cut body parts to form complete organisms. **We will now explain why the complex multicellular organisms (like mammals) cannot give rise to complete individuals from their cut body parts through the process of regeneration.**

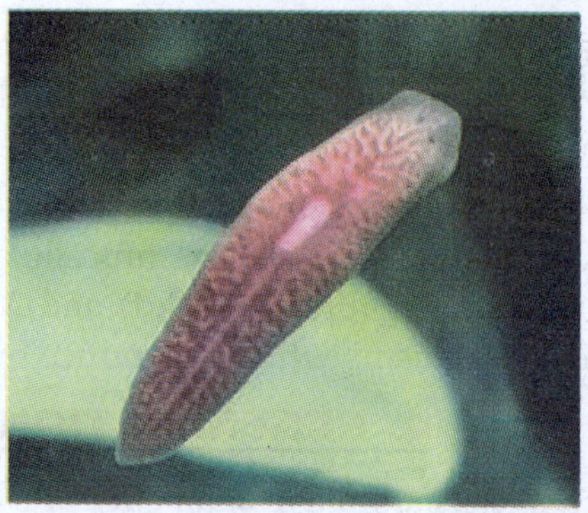

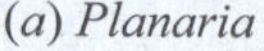

(*a*) *Planaria*

(*b*) *Hydra*

Figure 23. *Planaria* and *Hydra* are simple multicellular animals which can be regenerated from their cut body parts.

Regeneration can be used to reproduce only those organisms which have relatively simple body organisation consisting of only a few specialised cells (or tissues). In complex multicellular organisms, specialised cells make up tissues; tissues make up organs; organs make up organ systems; and finally organ systems make up organisms. Since complex multicellular organisms have a very high degree of organisation in their body, they cannot be reproduced from their cut body parts by the process of regeneration. For example, a dog is a complex multicellular organism which cannot be regenerated from its cut body part say, a cut tail. This is because the cells present in the cut tail of a dog cannot produce dog's organs like heart, brain, lungs, stomach, intestines and limbs, etc, needed for the making of a complete dog. The complex multicellular organisms need more complex ways of reproduction like sexual reproduction (which we will study after a while).

5. FRAGMENTATION

Some of the multicellular organisms having relatively simple body organisation can break up easily into smaller pieces (or fragments) on maturing. These pieces or fragments can then grow and form new organisms complete in all respects. This is another method of reproduction called 'fragmentation' which can be defined as follows : **The breaking up of the body of a simple multicellular organism into two (or more) pieces on maturing, each of which subsequently grows to form a complete new organism, is called fragmentation.** The breaking up of the body of an organism in fragmentation to form new organisms occurs naturally (on its own) when the parent organism matures. Fragmentation is an asexual method of reproduction. The reproduction by fragmentation method can occur in simple multicellular plants as well as animals. **The organisms like *Spirogyra* and sea anemones can reproduce by the method of fragmentation.** Please note that *Spirogyra* is a plant whereas sea anemones are marine animals. Let us discuss the reproduction in *Spirogyra* in a little more detail.

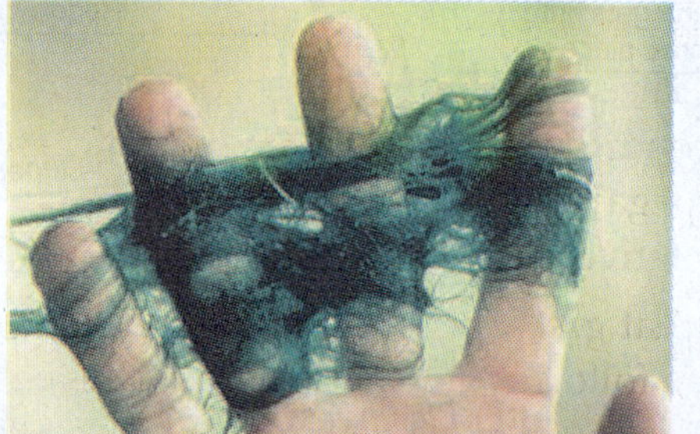

(*a*) Spirogyra

(*b*) Sea anemone

Figure 24. The organisms like *Spirogyra* and Sea anemones can reproduce by the method of fragmentation.

Spirogyra is a green, filamentous alga plant which is found in ponds, lakes and slow moving streams. *Spirogyra* filament simply breaks into two or more fragments on maturation, and each fragment then grows into a new *Spirogyra*. This break up of the filament of a mature *Spirogyra* on its own brings about asexual reproduction. Thus, ***Spirogyra* reproduces by the asexual method of fragmentation**. This is shown in Figure 25. In Figure 25, a mature *Spirogyra* filament is undergoing fragmentation to produce three new *Spirogyra*. These three *Spirogyra* will mature in due course of time and break again to produce even more *Spirogyra*. And this process of reproduction goes on and on.

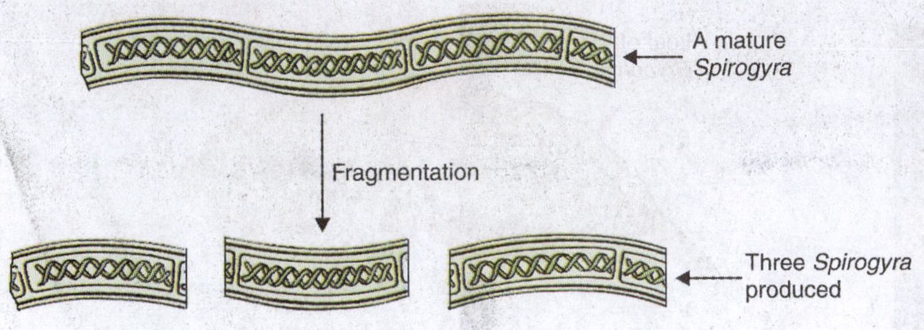

Figure 25. *Spirogyra* (a filament-type green alga plant) reproduces by the method of fragmentation.

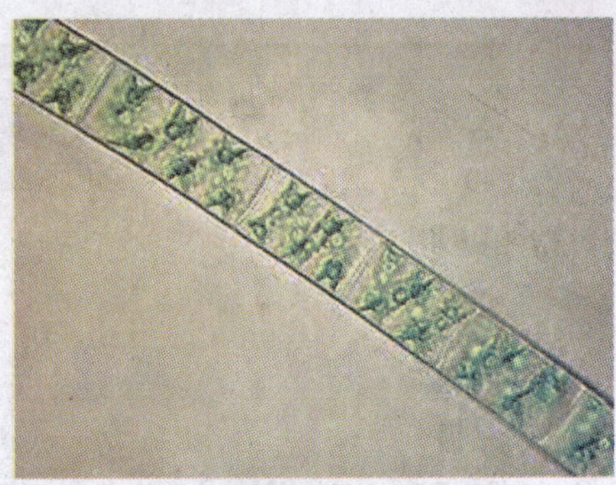

Figure 26. *Spirogyra* as seen under the microscope.

We can study *Spirogyra* in the laboratory as follows : Collect some water from a pond (or lake) which appears dark green and contains long filament-type (thread-type) structures. Take out the green coloured mass from the pond water sample and separate its threads or filaments by using two needles. Place one filament on a clean slide, put a drop of glycerine over it and cover it with a coverslip. Keep this slide under the microscope and see it first under the low power and then under the high power of microscope. Observe the detailed structure of the green filament of *Spirogyra* and draw a diagram accordingly.

Please note that **the main difference between fission and fragmentation is that in fission, a unicellular organism breaks up to form two (or more) daughter organisms, whereas in fragmentation, a multicellular organism breaks up to form two (or more) daughter organisms.**

6. VEGETATIVE PROPAGATION

Vegetative propagation is an asexual method of reproduction. The reproduction by vegetative propagation occurs only in plants. **In vegetative propagation, new plants are obtained from the parts of old plants (like stems, roots and leaves), without the help of any reproductive organs.** Vegetative propagation usually involves the growth and development of one (or more) buds present on the old part of the plant to form a new plant. These buds are in the dormant state (inactive state) in the old part of the plant. When provided suitable conditions (like moisture, warmth, etc.), these buds grow to form new plants. Please note that vegetative propagation is also called vegetative reproduction. Here is an example of the vegetative propagation (or vegetative reproduction) in grass.

It is a common observation that green grass plants spring up in dry fields after the rains. This happens due to vegetative propagation as follows : The fields have dry stems of the old grass plants all over them. These dry stems have buds which are in the inactive state. By getting rain water, the buds present on dry grass stems get activated and grow to produce new grass plants. Thus, **the green grass grows in the fields after rains from the dry, old stems of grass plants present in the fields, by the method of vegetative propagation.**

Buds are present on the stems as well as the leaves of the *Bryophyllum* plant which can develop into new plants. So, ***Bryophyllum* plants can be reproduced by vegetative propagation by using either a piece of its stem or its leaves.** For example, if we plant a broken piece of the stem of a *Bryophyllum* plant in the ground, we will get a new *Bryophyllum* plant growing from it in a week's time. Even the leaves of a *Bryophyllum* plant can produce new plants. This happens as follows : The leaves of a *Bryophyllum* plant have special type of buds in their margins (or edges) [see Figure 27(*a*)]. These buds may get detached from the leaves, fall to the ground and then grow to produce new *Bryophyllum* plants. The buds can also drop to the ground together with the leaf and then grow to produce new plants. Sometimes even before a leaf drops off from a *Bryophyllum* plant, we can see new plantlets already growing on it [see Figure 27(*b*)]. When such a mature leaf of the *Bryophyllum* plant falls on the ground, then each plantlet can grow into a

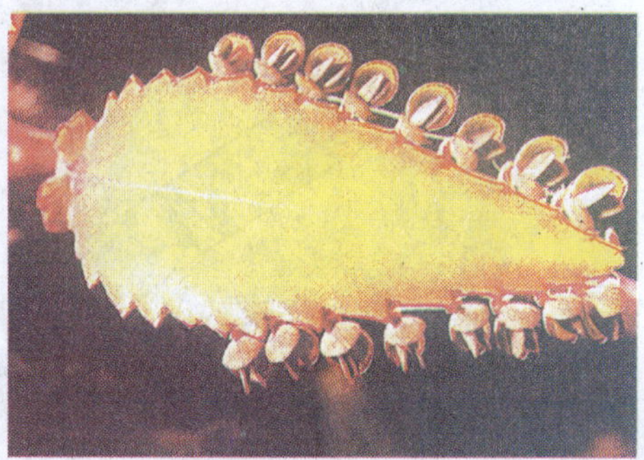

(*a*) A leaf of *Bryophyllum* plant with buds in its margin (or edges)

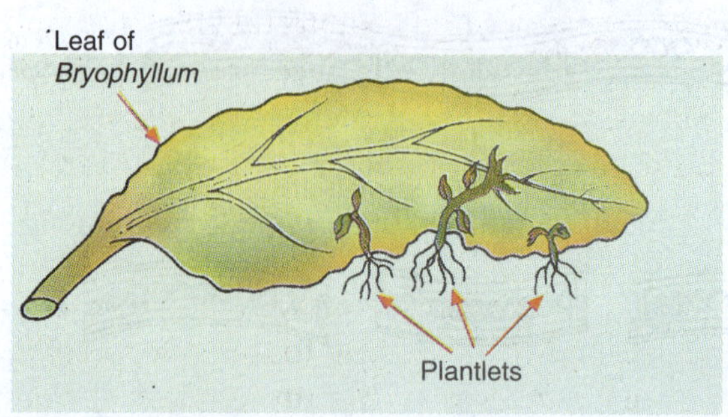

(*b*) Plantlets growing in the margin of *Bryophyllum* leaf

Figure 27.

new plant. Thus, the leaves of *Bryophyllum* plant can produce new plants. Another plant called *Begonia* also reproduces by vegetative propagation through its leaves.

Money plant can also be grown by vegetative propagation by using a piece of its stem as follows : Cut a piece of stem of money plant in such a way that it contains at least one leaf on it (The point on stem where a leaf is attached is called a node). Dip one end of this stem in water. After a few days we will find that new roots appear at the point where leaf was attached. The piece of stem will gradually grow into a new money plant. Please note that if we cut the stem of money plant in between two leaves, then it will not grow into a new plant. This is because it does not have a growing point (here a node) in it.

We will now describe the vegetative propagation of plants by using tubers which are the modified, underground stems (or roots). **A tuber is the thickened, underground stem (or root) of a plant which is swollen with stored food**. The tuber has a number of 'buds' (called 'eyes'). Each bud (or eye) of the tuber grows into a new plant when the old tuber is planted in the soil in the next growing season.There are two types of tubers : stem tubers and root tubers. Potato is a stem tuber whereas sweet potato is a root tuber. We will now describe how vegetative reproduction in potato takes place by using tubers.

Potato tuber is an underground stem of the potato plant. **Potato tuber can be used for the vegetative reproduction of potato plants.** Each potato tuber can produce more than one plant. This happens as follows : A potato tuber has many buds (called eyes) on its body (see Figure 28). These buds act as organs for vegetative reproduction. When a potato tuber is planted in the soil, then the various buds of the potato tuber start growing to form new potato plants. In Figure 28, we have shown the new potato plants growing

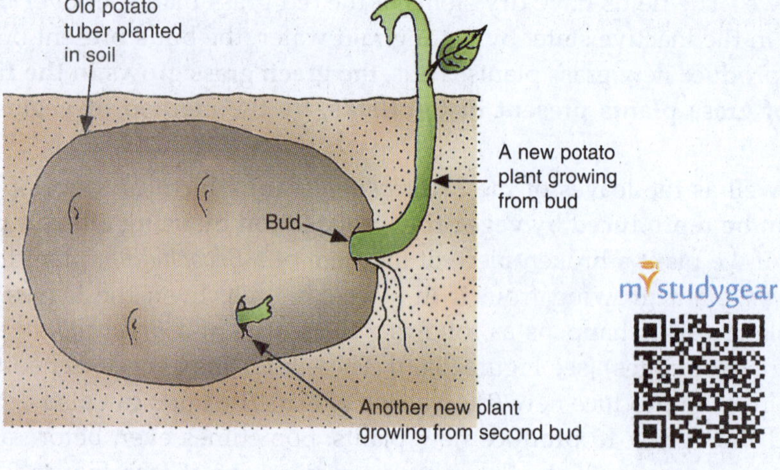

Figure 28. Vegetative propagation (reproduction) of potato plant from a potato tuber. A new potato plant grows from each bud on the old potato.

Figure 29. A potato plant with tubers.

from only two buds of the potato tuber. Other buds can also do the same.

Please note that **it is not necessary to plant the whole potato tuber in the ground to produce new potato plants.** We can even plant 'cut pieces' of a potato tuber in the ground to obtain new potato plants. But all these cut pieces of potato tuber should have a bud (or eye) on them. So, if we cut a potato tuber into a number of pieces in such a way that every piece has a bud (or eye) on it and plant them in the ground, then each cut piece of potato tuber will produce a new potato plant in due course of time.

Each potato plant produces more than one tuber and each tuber has more than one bud (which produce more than one new plant). Due to this, **the vegetative propagation method of producing potato plants by tubers is much faster than the production of potato plants from seeds.**

We can study the vegetative propagation of potatoes as follows : Take a potato and cut it into small pieces in such a way that some pieces contain a bud (or eye) in them. Place the potato pieces having buds on wet cotton kept in a tray. Keep the tray aside for a few days (but sprinkle water on the cotton daily to keep it wet). We will see that green shoots and roots appear from the buds of the potato pieces. These are the new potato plants. If, however, we take potato pieces without buds in this experiment, then no new potato plants will grow from them.

The roots of a guava plant have buds which can develop into new guava plants. In fact, a large number of plants can be reproduced by the method of vegetative propagation. Some of the examples of the plants which can be reproduced by vegetative propagation are : *Bryophyllum*, Guava, Potato, Onion, Banana, Garlic, Water hyacinth, Tulip, Mint, Strawberry and Lily. We will now describe the artificial propagation of plants.

ARTIFICIAL PROPAGATION OF PLANTS

We can grow many plants from one plant by using the man-made methods. **The process of growing many plants from one plant by man-made methods is called artificial propagation of plants.** A number of methods of artificial propagation of plants are used in agriculture (for raising crops), and horticulture (cultivation of vegetables, fruits and flowers). The three common methods for the artificial propagation of plants are :

1. **Cuttings,**
2. **Layering,** and
3. **Grafting.**

We will now describe all these methods, one by one. Let us start with the cuttings method for the artificial propagation of plants.

1. Cuttings

A small part of a plant which is removed by making a cut with a sharp knife is called a 'cutting'. A cutting may be a piece of stem, root or even a leaf. While making a cutting, care should to taken to see that there are some buds on it.

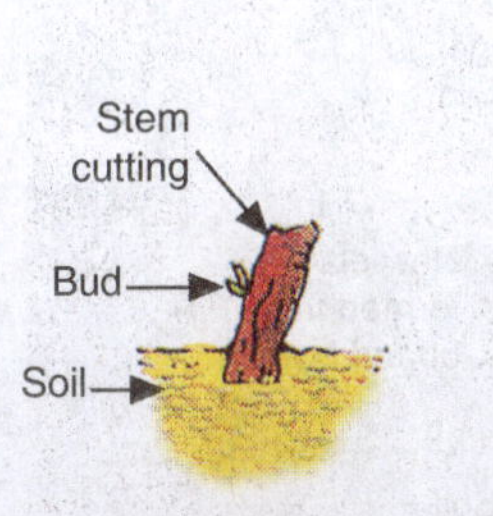

(*a*) A stem cutting (with bud) planted in soil

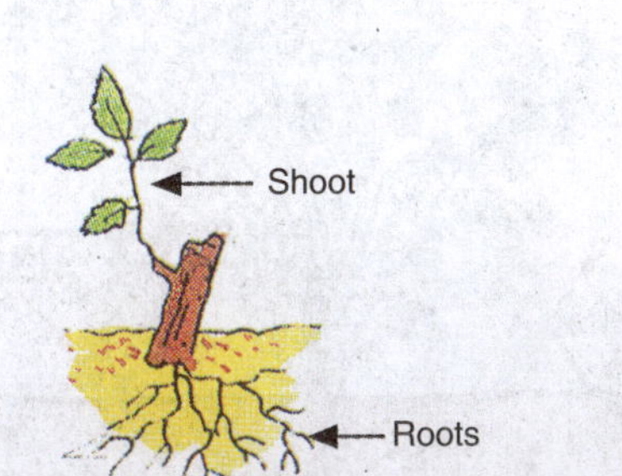

(*b*) Stem cutting develops roots and shoot

(*c*) A new plant is formed

Figure 30. The propagation of plants by 'cuttings' method.

In this method, a cutting of the parent plant (say, of stem or shoot) having some buds on it is taken and its lower part is buried in the moist soil [see Figure 30(*a*)]. After a few days, the cutting develops roots and shoot, and grows into a new plant [see Figures 30(*b*) and (*c*)]. Cuttings are a means of asexual reproduction in plants. The new plant formed from a cutting is exactly similar to the parent plant.

The plants like rose, *Bougainvillea*, *Chrysanthemum*, grapes, sugarcane, bananas, and cactus, etc., can be grown by means of cuttings. For example, rose plants are propagated (or reproduced) by means of cuttings from stems (or shoots) as follows : A piece of stem (or side shoot) having bud is cut from an existing rose plant with the help of a knife. The lower part of this cutting is buried in moist soil. After a few days, the end of cutting buried in soil develops roots and later on grows to become a new rose plant. An advantage of cuttings method is that by using this method we can produce many new plants from just one plant quickly, without waiting for flowers and seeds.

Figure 31. The cutting from a plant kept in a jar of water. See how new roots have grown.

Figure 32. Rose plants are grown by cuttings method.

Figure 33. Sugar cane plants are grown by cuttings method.

Figure 34. Banana plants are also grown by cuttings method.

2. Layering

In this method, a branch of the plant is pulled towards the ground and a part of it is covered with moist soil leaving the tip of the branch exposed above the ground. After some time, new roots develop from the part of the branch buried in the soil. The branch is then cut off from the parent plant. The part of the branch which has developed roots grows to become a new plant (just like the parent plant). Jasmine plant (*chameli*) is propagated or produced by the layering method as shown in Figure 35.

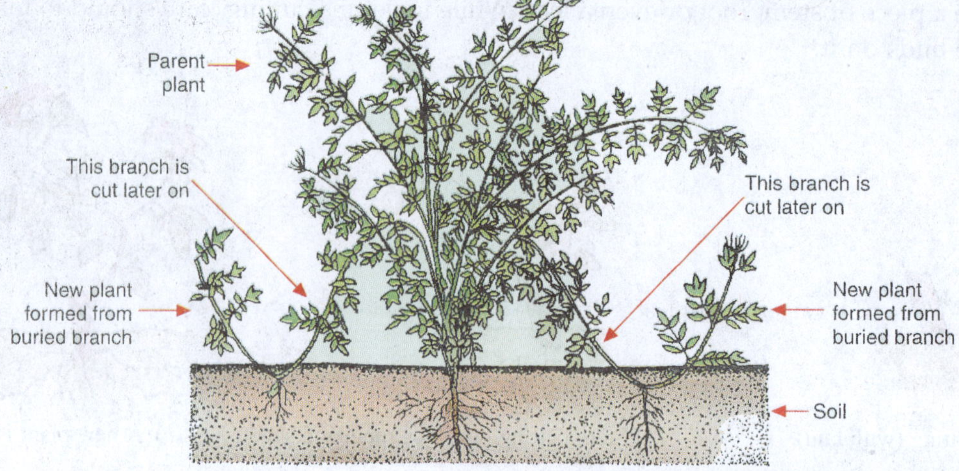

Figure 35. The propagation of jasmine plants (*chameli*) by the layering method.

We can see from Figure 35 that one left side branch and one right side branch of the parent jasmine plant have been buried in moist soil. The parts of branches which are buried in soil grow their own roots (see Figure 35). When this happens, the branches of the parent plant connecting the newly formed plants are cut off so that the newly formed plants may grow on their own and develop into mature plants (like the parent plant).

Many plants like strawberry and raspberry are propagated by the natural layering method. The natural layering occurs because these plants form runners (which are soft horizontal stems running above the ground). Wherever the ends of such runners touch the ground, new plants are formed at those places. In this way, many more strawberry or raspberry plants are formed from the parent plant in a natural way.

The layering method is used for the propagation (or reproduction) of plants like : Jasmine, Strawberry, Raspberry, Lemon, Guava, *Hibiscus* (China rose), *Bougainvillea* and many slender ornamental plants.

3. Grafting

Grafting is a method in which the cut stems of two different plants (one with roots and other without roots) are joined together in such a way that the two stems join and grow as a single plant. This new plant will have the characteristics of both the original plants.

(*i*) **The cut stem of a plant (or tree) having roots (and fixed in soil) is called stock.** Stock is the lower part of a plant (or tree) having the roots.

(*ii*) **The cut stem of another plant (without roots) is called scion.** Scion is the upper part of a plant which may have leaves on it (but no roots).

In carrying out grafting, two plants (or trees) are chosen which are to be used as scion and stock. First, the stem (or branch) is removed from the plant chosen to be made scion (for its desirable characteristics) by making a slanting cut. This gives us the scion with a slanting cut [see Figure 36 (*a*)]. The stem of second plant (or tree) to be used in grafting is also cut in a slanting way. The lower part of this plant (or tree) is stock. It has also a slanting cut [see Figure 36(*a*)].

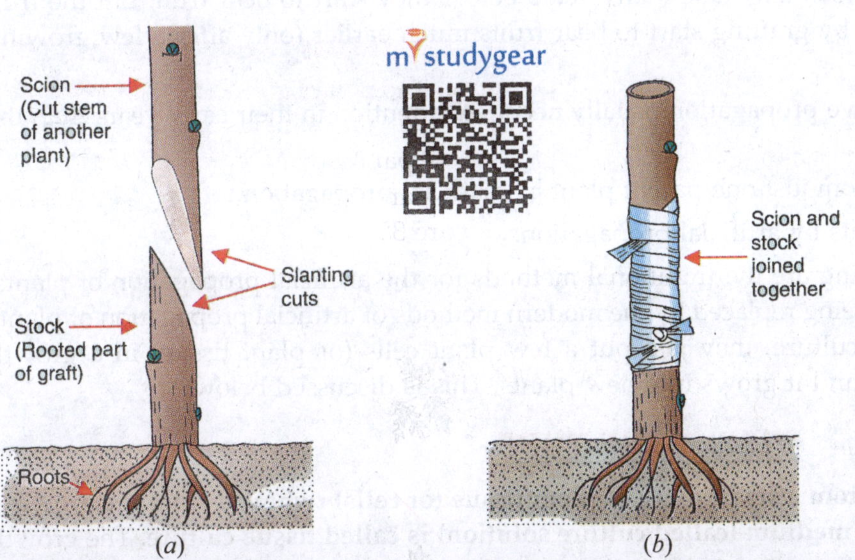

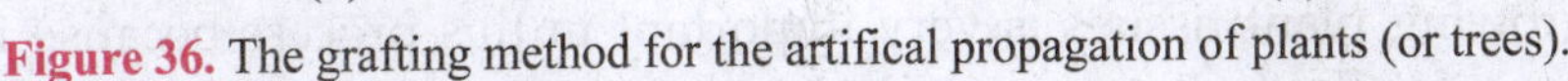
Figure 36. The grafting method for the artifical propagation of plants (or trees).

Figure 37. Grafting was used to grow this apple tree.

The scion is placed over the stock [see Figure 36(*b*)]. The cut surfaces of the scion and stock are fitted together and bound tightly with a piece of cloth and covered properly with polythene sheet (so as to prevent harmful infection by bacteria or fungus, and loss of water and plant sap from the cut and joined ends of stock and scion). While joining the scion to the stock, care should be taken to make sure that the cambium layer of scion is in contact with the cambium layer of stock (because the cambium layer in the stem is responsible for growth). The cut soon heals and the stock and scion of two plants grow together and become one plant. The scion continues to produce its original leaves, flowers and fruits but it gets water and minerals for making food from the chosen stock. So, the fruits will have the characteristics of both the plants (from which scion and stock have come).

Grafting is used to breed fruit trees and flowering bushes. **Apple, peach, apricot and pear trees are often grafted**. We will now describe some of the **advantages of the grafting method of artificial propagation**.

(*i*) Grafting enables us to combine the most desirable characteristics of the two plants (scion and stock) in its flowers and fruits.

(*ii*) By grafting method, a very young scion (shoot part of a plant) can be made to flower and produce fruits quite fast when it is grafted to the stock (stem having roots) of a mature plant.

(*iii*) It enables us to obtain flowers and fruits having different desired characteristics by grafting scions from different varieties of plants on the same stock. Many varieties of mango have been produced by grafting method.

(*iv*) Grafting can be used to produce varieties of seedless fruits.

Artificial vegetative propagation is usually used for the propagation (or reproduction) of those plants which produce either very few seeds or do not produce viable seeds. Some examples of such plants which are reproduced by artificial vegetative propagation methods are : Banana, Pineapple, Orange, Grape, Rose, etc.

Advantages of Artificial Vegetative Propagation

The artificial propagation of farm and garden plants has several advantages. Some of the important advantages of the artificial vegetative propagation of plants are given below :

1. The new plants produced by artificial vegetative propagation will be exactly like the parent plants. Any desirable features of the parent plant will be replicated in the new plants.
2. The fruit trees grown from seeds may take many years before they start to bear fruit. But the fruit trees grown from cuttings or by grafting start to bear fruits much earlier (only after a few growing seasons).
3. The plants grown by vegetative propagation usually need less attention in their early years than the plants grown from seeds.
4. Many plants can be grown from just one parent plant by artificial propagation.
5. We can also get seedless plants by artificial propagation.

The cuttings, layering and grafting are the traditional methods for the artificial propagation of plants. For commercial purposes, they are being replaced by the modern methods of artificial propagation of plants involving tissue culture. In tissue culture, they just put a few plant cells (or plant tissue) in a growth medium with plant hormones in it and it grows into new plants. This is discussed below.

TISSUE CULTURE

The production of new plants from a small piece of plant tissue (or cells) removed from the growing tips of a plant in a suitable growth medium (called culture solution) is called tissue culture. The growth medium (or culture solution) used for growing plant tissues is very important in this process because it contains various plant nutrients in the form of 'jelly' (called *agar*) and plant hormones which are necessary for plant growth. The process of tissue culture for producing new plants is carried out as follows :

1. A small piece of plant tissue is taken from the growing point of the plant (tip of the plant) and placed on a sterile jelly which contains nutrients and plant hormones. The hormones make the cells in the plant tissue divide rapidly producing many cells which form a shapeless lump of mass called 'callus'.

2. The callus is then transferred to another jelly containing suitable plant hormones which stimulate the callus to develop roots.
3. The callus with developed roots is then put on a yet another jelly containing different hormones which stimulate the development of shoots.
4. The callus having roots and shoots separates into tiny plantlets . In this way, many tiny plantlets are produced from just a few original plant cells (or tissue).
5. The plantlets thus produced are transplanted into pots or soil where they can grow to form mature plants.

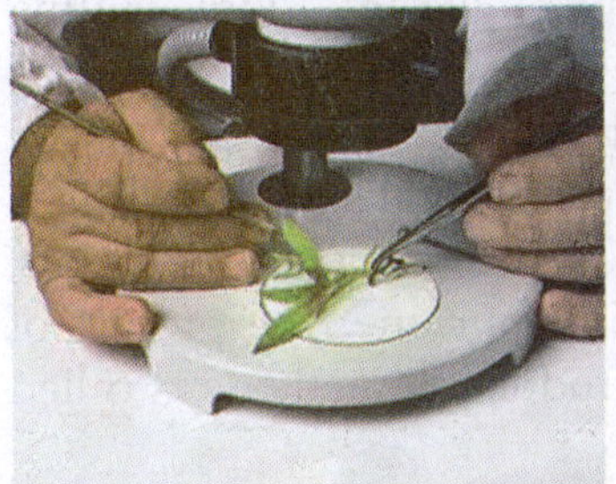
(*a*) A small piece of plant tissue being taken from the growing point (tip) of a plant

(*b*) Plant tissue grows to form callus

(*c*) Callus develops roots and shoots

(*d*) Many plantlets are produced. These can be transplanted into pots or soil

Figure 38. The tissue culture technique of producing new plants.

The tissue culture technique is being used increasingly for the production of ornamental plants like orchids, dahlia, carnation, *Chrysanthemum*, etc. The production of plants by the method of **tissue culture** is also known as **micropropagation** (due to the extremely small amount of plant material used).

Advantages of Tissue Culture

1. Tissue culture is a very fast technique. Thousands of plantlets can be produced in a few weeks' time from a small amount of plant tissue.
2. The new plants produced by tissue culture are disease free.
3. Tissue culture can grow plants round the year, irrespective of weather or season.
4. Very little space is needed for developing new plants by tissue culture.

Do Organisms Create Exact Copies of Themselves in Asexual Reproduction

Asexual reproduction usually results in the production of genetically identical offsprings, the only genetic variation arises as a result of occasional inaccuracies in DNA replication (or DNA copying) at the time of cell division. This will become clear from the following discussion.

The material which carries genetic information from the parents to the offsprings is DNA–Deoxyribo Nucleic Acid (which is present in the form of chromosomes in the nuclei of all the cells). The basis of asexual reproduction is mitosis. This is the division of a nucleus into two identical daughter nuclei (see Figure 39). Each daughter nucleus has the same genetic make up because of the replication of DNA (or

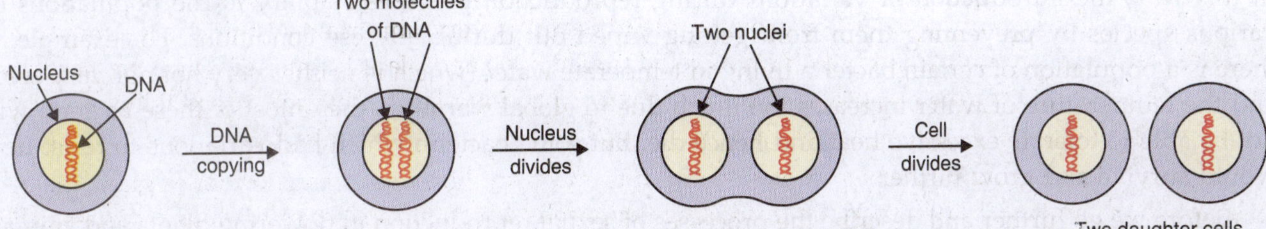

Figure 39. The process of asexual reproduction.

copying of DNA) of the parent cell. After the division of the nucleus, the rest of parent cell divides to form two genetically identical daughter cells. The daughter cells can then form two offsprings. From this we conclude that all the offsprings produced by one parent as a result of asexual reproduction are usually genetically identical.

The new organisms (or offsprings) produced by one parent through asexual reproduction (which are genetically identical to the parent) are called clones. The clones possess exact copies of the DNA (or genes) of their parent and hence show remarkable similarity to the parent and to one another. Thus, asexual reproduction produces genetically identical offsprings called clones. For example, when a parent *Hydra* reproduces by the asexual method of budding, the new *Hydrae* (or offsprings) formed are clones (which are genetically identical to the parent *Hydra* as well as to one another). Similarly, when we are using a cutting to grow a new plant, we are making a clone. The cutting of a plant contains the same DNA (or genes) as the original plant (or parent plant). This cutting will grow into an exact copy of the original plant. So, a clone is formed. The clones of plants can be produced by the asexual methods of reproduction such as cuttings, layering, grafting, tissue culture, etc. These days techniques have been developed to clone even animals. Dolly the sheep hit the headlines in 1997 as the first successfully produced animal clone. The process of producing genetically identical new organisms (or offsprings) by asexual reproduction methods is called cloning.

We will now explain **how slight variations are introduced in asexual reproduction.** The replication (or copying) of DNA in the cell is done by certain biochemical reactions which synthesize more of genetic material. No biochemical reaction can reproduce 100 per cent same results. So, when the DNA already present in the nucleus of the parent cell is replicated (or copied) by making more DNA at the time of asexual reproduction, then slight variations come in the two copies formed. Due to this, the two DNA molecules formed by replication will be similar but may not be exactly identical to the original DNA. These slight variations in the replication of DNA molecule will lead to slight variations in the offsprings produced by asexual reproduction.

From the above discussion we conclude that the **importance of DNA replication** (or DNA copying) in asexual reproduction is that slight variations may arise in the offsprings in respect to the parent organism. So, although the offsprings produced by asexual reproduction are said to be genetically the same as the parent organism, but still they have occasional variations. This means that the organisms *do not* always create exact copies of themselves in asexual reproduction. Please note that the importance of DNA copying in asexual reproduction is that the characteristics of the parent organisms are transmitted to its offsprings and at the same time some occasional variations are also produced in the offsprings. We will now describe the importance of variations introduced in reproduction.

The importance of variations in organisms introduced during reproduction is that it helps the species of various organisms to survive and flourish even in adverse environment. This will become clear from the following discussion. There may be some drastic changes like excessive heat or cold or shortage of water (drought), etc., in the habitat of a species of organisms. Now, if all the organisms of a population living in that habitat are exactly identical, then there is danger that all of them may die and no one would survive under those conditions. This will eliminate the species from that habitat completely. However, if some variations are present in some individual organisms to tolerate excessive heat or cold or survive on meagre water supply, then there is a chance for them to survive and fluorish even in adverse environment. In this way, the introduction of variations during reproduction provides stability to the populations of various species by preventing them from getting wiped out during adverse conditions. For example, if there is a population of certain bacteria living in temperate water (which is neither very hot nor very cold) and the temperature of water increases too much due to global warming, then most of these bacteria will not be able to tolerate excessive heat and hence die. But some bacteria which had variations to resist heat would survive and grow further.

Before we go further and describe the processes of sexual reproduction in flowering plants and animals (including human beings), **please answer the following questions :**

Very Short Answer Type Questions

1. Which life process ensures that a plant or animal species will not disappear from this earth ?
2. What is the name of the reproductive process :
   (*a*) which involves two parents ?
   (*b*) which involves only one parent ?
3. State whether the following statement is true or false :
   Spores produced by the bread mould plant are actually its seeds.
4. Most of the plants reproduce by sexual method. Name two plants which can reproduce asexually.
5. Which type of reproduction :
   (*a*) involves gametes ?
   (*b*) does not involve gametes ?
6. State whether human beings reproduce by sexual method or asexual method.
7. (*a*) Name two animals which reproduce sexually.
   (*b*) Name two animals which reproduce asexually.
8. Name one organism which reproduces by spore formation.'
9. Name the method by which *Paramecium* reproduces. Is this method sexual or asexual ?
10. Name two plants :
    (*a*) which can be grown from their broken stems.
    (*b*) which can be grown from their leaves.
11. Name the asexual method of reproduction in yeast.
12. Name the asexual method of reproduction in (*a*) *Hydra*, and (*b*) *Plasmodium*.
13. What is the name of asexual reproduction method in :
    (*i*) *Spirogyra*, and (*ii*) *Leishmania* ?
14. Name the artificial propagation mehod used for the propagation of (*a*) rose plants, and (*b*) apple trees.
15. Which artificial propagation method is used for the production of jasmine plants ?
16. Name the natural method by which strawberry plants are propagated.
17. Name two plants which are propagated by layering method.
18. Name any two plants which are propagated by cuttings method.
19. Write down the different methods of asexual reproduction.
20. Why are budding, fragmentation and regeneration, all considered to be asexual type of reproduction ?
21. Fill in the following blanks with suitable words :
    (*a*) The process of..............ensures continuity of life on earth.
    (*b*) *Plasmodium* reproduces by the process of .... fission whereas *Paramecium* reproduces by the process of .... fission.
    (*c*) Rose plants and sugar cane crop are usually grown by the .... method.
    (*d*) Vegetative reproduction of potato plants is done by using ....
    (*e*) Strawberry plants are propagated by the natural........................ method.

Short Answer Type Questions

22. (*a*) What is the basic difference between asexual reproduction and sexual reproduction ?
    (*b*) Which of the following organisms reproduce by sexual method and which by asexual method ?
    Amoeba, Cats, Humans, *Hydra*, Birds
23. (*a*) What is meant by regeneration ? Name two animals which can regenerate fully from their cut body parts.
    (*b*) Explain why, more complex multicellular organisms cannot give rise to new organisms through regeneration.
24. Explain vegetative propagation with the help of two examples. List two advantages of vegetative propagation.
25. (*a*) What is meant by the term 'artificial propagation of plants' ?
    (*b*) Name three common methods which are used for the artificial propagation of plants.
    (*c*) Name two plants which are usually propagated by artificial propagation methods. Name the method of artificial propagation used in each case.

26. Describe the layering method for the artificial propagation of plants. Illustrate your answer with the help of a labelled diagram. Name any five plants which are propagated by the layering method.

27. (*a*) What is meant by the term 'fission' as used in biology ?
(*b*) How does binary fission differ from multiple fission ?
(*c*) Name one organism which reproduces by binary fission and another which reproduces by multiple fission.
(*d*) State whether the above named organisms are animals or plants.

28. (*a*) Can you consider cell division as a type of reproduction in unicellular organisms ? Give reason.
(*b*) What is a clone ? Why do offsprings formed by asexual reproduction exhibit remarkable similarity ?

29. (*a*) The yeast cells fail to multiply in water but they multiply rapidly in sugar solution. Give one reason for it.
(*b*) Why does bread mould grow profusely on a moist slice of bread but not on a dry slice of bread ?

30. (*a*) What is a tuber ? Name one stem tuber and one root tuber.
(*b*) What is name of the organ of propagation present in a tuber ?
(*c*) Name one commonly used vegetable which is propagated by using tubers.

31. (*a*) What is meant by vegetative propagation ?
(*b*) Vegetative propagation involves the growth and development of 'something' present in the old part of the plant to form a new plant. What is this 'something' ?
(*c*) Why do green grass plants spring up in dry fields on their own after the rains ?

32. (*a*) Explain how, new *Bryophyllum* plants can be produced from the leaves of the old plant ? Illustrate your answer with the help of a labelled diagram.
(*b*) How can you grow money plant by vegetative propagation ?

33. Match the organisms given in column I with the methods of reproduction/propagation given in column II :

Column I	*Column II*
(*i*) *Plasmodium*	(*a*) Spore formation
(*ii*) *Spirogyra*	(*b*) Leaves
(*iii*) Jasmine	(*c*) Regeneration
(*iv*) Apple tree	(*d*) Budding
(*v*) *Bryophyllum*	(*e*) Binary fission
(*vi*) Potatoes	(*f*) Layering
(*vii*) *Rhizopus*	(*g*) Fragmentation
(*viii*) *Hydra*	(*h*) Tubers
(*ix*) *Planaria*	(*i*) Cuttings
(*x*) *Leishmania*	(*j*) Multiple fission
(*xi*) Sugar cane	(*k*) Grafting
(*xii*) Rose	

Long Answer Type Questions

34. (*a*) What is meant by reproduction ?
(*b*) What are the two general methods of reproduction in organisms ?
(*c*) How does an *Amoeba* reproduce ? Describe the process of reproduction in *Amoeba* with the help of labelled diagrams of different stages in its reproduction process.
(*d*) What is the name of the process by which *Amoeba* reproduces ?
(*e*) Name two organisms which reproduce by the same asexual process as that of *Amoeba*.

35. (*a*) What is the difference between the two asexual methods of reproduction : fission and fragmentation ?
(*b*) Name one organism which reproduces by fission and another which reproduces by fragmentation.
(*c*) What is meant by multiple fission ? Name one organism which reproduces by the process of multiple fission.
(*d*) Describe the process of reproduction in *Hydra* with the help of labelled diagrams. What is the name of this process of reproduction ?
(*e*) Name one unicellular organism which reproduces by the same asexual process as *Hydra*.

36. (*a*) Name the method by which bread mould (*Rhizopus* fungus) reproduces. Is this method sexual or asexual ?
(*b*) What is yeast ? Describe the process of reproduction in yeast with the help of labelled diagrams.
(*c*) Name a tiny fresh-water animal which reproduces by the same method as that of yeast ? What is this method known as ?
(*d*) Name two marine organisms which also reproduce by the same method as yeast but form colonies.
37. (*a*) What is meant by 'grafting' as a means of propagation in plants ?
(*b*) Define 'stock' and 'scion'.
(*c*) Describe the grafting method for the artificial propagation of plants with the help of labelled diagrams.
(*d*) Name two fruit trees which are usually propagated by grafting method.
(*e*) State two advantages of grafting method of artificial propagation of plants.
(*f*) What is the difference between the cuttings method and grafting method for the artificial propagation of plants ?
38. (*a*) What is tissue culture ?
(*b*) Name any four types of ornamental plants which are being produced by tissue culture technique.
(*c*) What is the importance of DNA copying in reproduction ? Explain with an example.
(*d*) How does reproduction help in providing stability to populations of species ?
(*e*) Why is variation during reproduction beneficial to the species but not necessarily for the individual ?
39. (*a*) What is a 'cutting' in respect of plants for propagation purposes ?
(*b*) What care should be taken while making a cutting from a plant ?
(*c*) Describe the cuttings method for the artificial propagation of plants. Illustrate your answer with the help of labelled diagrams.
(*d*) Name any two plants which are usually propagated by the cuttings method.

Multiple Choice Questions (MCQs)

40. Asexual reproduction is :
(*a*) a fusion of specialised cells
(*b*) a method by which all types of organisms reproduce
(*c*) a method producing genetically identical offspring
(*d*) a method in which more than one parent are involved
41. One of the following organisms does not reproduce by binary fission. This is :
(*a*) *Amoeba* (*b*) *Plasmodium* (*c*) *Leishmania* (*d*) *Paramecium*
42. The micro-organism which reproduces by multiple fission is the one which causes the disease known as :
(*a*) *Kala-azar* (*b*) marasmus (*c*) malaria (*d*) amoebiasis
43. The protozoan having a flagellum at its one end is :
(*a*) *Amoeba* (*b*) *Paramecium* (*c*) *Hydra* (*d*) *Leishmania*
44. In the list of organisms given below, those which reproduce by the asexual method are :
(*i*) banana (*ii*) yak (*iii*) yeast (*iv*) *Amoeba*
(*a*) (*ii*) and (*iv*) (*b*) (*i*), (*iii*) and (*iv*) (*c*) (*i*) and (*iv*) (*d*) (*ii*), (*iii*) and (*iv*)
45. One of the following organisms does not reproduce by budding . This is :
(*a*) Sponge (*b*) Yeast (*c*) *Hydra* (*d*) *Planaria*
46. The disease *kala-azar* is caused by a micro-organism known as :
(*a*) *Planaria* (*b*) Leech (*c*) *Leishmania* (*d*) *Plasmodium*
47. Reproduction is essential for living organisms in order to :
(*a*) keep the individual organ alive (*b*) fulfil their energy requirements
(*c*) maintain growth (*d*) continue the species for ever
48. The unicellular organism which reproduces by budding is :
(*a*) *Spirogyra* (*b*) *Hydra* (*c*) *Planaria* (*d*) Yeast
49. A multicellular organism which reproduces by budding is :
(*a*) *Amoeba* (*b*) Yeast (*c*) *Leishmania* (*d*) *Hydra*

50. The offsprings formed by asexual reproduction method have greater similarity among themselves because :
(*i*) asexual reproduction involves only one parent
(*ii*) asexual reproduction involves two parents
(*iii*) asexual reproduction involves gametes
(*iv*) asexual reproduction does not involve gametes
(*a*) (*i*) and (*ii*) (*b*) (*i*) and (*iii*) (*c*) (*ii*) and (*iv*) (*d*) (*i*) and (*iv*)

51. A simple multicellular animal having tentacles which lives in freshwater usually reproduces by the asexual process of :
(*a*) binary fission (*b*) spore formation (*c*) budding (*d*) fragmentation

52. One of the following does not reproduce by spore formation method. This is :
(*a*) *Rhizopus* fungus (*b*) *Penicillium* fungus (*d*) Yeast fungus (*d*) *Mucor* fungus

53. The factors responsible for the rapid spreading of bread mould on slices of bread are :
(*i*) presence of large number of spores in air
(*ii*) presence of large number of thread-like branched hyphae
(*iii*) presence of moisture and nutrients
(*iv*) formation of round shaped sporangia
(*a*) (*i*) and (*iii*) (*b*) (*ii*) and (*iv*) (*c*) (*i*) and (*ii*) (*d*) (*iii*) and (*iv*)

54. One of the following reproduces by forming spores. This in :
(*a*) Fern (*b*) *Planaria* (*c*) *Spirogyra* (*d*) Potato

55. Asexual reproduction through budding takes place in :
(*i*) *Amoeba* and Yeast (*ii*) Yeast and *Hydra* (*iii*) *Hydra* and *Plasmodium* (*iv*) Corals and Sponges
(*a*) (*i*) and (*ii*) (*b*) only (*ii*) (*c*) (*i*) and (*iii*) (*d*) (*ii*) and (*iv*)

56. A feature of reproduction that is common to *Amoeba*, Yeast and *Bacterium* is that :
(*a*) they are all multicellular (*b*) they are all unicellular
(*c*) they reproduce only sexually (*d*) they reproduce asexually

57. One of the following organisms does not reproduce by fission. This is :
(*a*) *Amoeba* (*b*) *Leishmania* (*c*) *Planaria* (*d*) *Plasmodium*

58. An organism which may be considered to be a kind of plant and reproduces by budding is :
(*a*) *Paramecium* (*b*) Bread mould (*c*) *Hydra* (*d*) Yeast

59. An animal which reproduces by the process of budding is :
(*a*) *Plasmodium* (*b*) yeast (*c*) *Hydra* (*d*) *Planaria*

60. In *Spirogyra,* asexual reproduction takes place by :
(*a*) division of a cell into two cells (*b*) breaking up of filaments into smaller bits
(*c*) division of a cell into many cells (*d*) formation of a large number of buds

61. The ability of a cell to divide into several cells during reproduction in *Plasmodium* is called :
(*a*) budding (*b*) fragmentation (*c*) binary fission (*d*) multiple fission

62. In *Rhizopus* fungus, the fine thread-like structures spread on the whole surface of slice of bread are called :
(*a*) rhizoids (*b*) stems (*c*) roots (*d*) hyphae

63. Vegetative propagation refers to the formation of new plants from the following existing organs of the old plants :
(*a*) stems, roots and flowers (*b*) stems, roots and leaves
(*c*) stems, flowers and fruits (*d*) stems, leaves and flowers

64. The two organisms which can regenerate fully from their cut body parts are :
(*a*) *Paramecium* and *Hydra* (*b*) *Hydra* and *Amoeba* (*c*) *Planaria* and *Leishmania* (*d*) *Hydra* and *Planaria*

65. The two types of organisms which produce colonies by the process of budding are :
(*a*) *Hydra* and Corals (*b*) Yeast and Sponges (*c*) Corals and Sponges (*d*) *Hydra* and Yeast

66. Spore formation is the most common asexual method of reproduction in :
(*a*) protozoa (*b*) tubers (*c*) fungi (*d*) algae

67. An alga which reproduces by the asexual reproduction method called fragmentation is :
(*a*) *Rhizopus* (*b*) *Salmonella* (*c*) *Plasmodium* (*d*) *Spirogyra*

68. The organisms which can reproduce by fragmentation are :
(*a*) Corals and Sponges (*b*) Corals and *Spirogyra*
(*c*) Sea anemone and *Spirogyra* (*d*) Sponges and Sea anemones

69. Binary fission describes the type of reproduction where the organism divides to form :
(*a*) many spores (*b*) two daughters (*c*) many buds (*d*) two hyphae

70. The cut part of a plant stem (without roots) which is used in grafting is called :
(*a*) stock (*b*) stump (*c*) scion (*d*) graft

71. The cut part of plant stem (having roots and fixed to ground) which is used in the process of grafting is known as :
(*a*) stock (*b*) scion (*c*) cutting (*d*) bud

72. Multiple fission occurs in one of the following. This is :
(*a*) bread mould (*b*) *kala-azar* parasite (*c*) flatworm (*d*) malaria parasite

73. An organism having a whip-like structure at one end which reproduces by the process of binary fission is :
(*a*) *Hydra* (*b*) *Paramecium* (*c*) *Leishmania* (*d*) *Plasmodium*

74. A tiny animal having tentacles which reproduces by growing buds on the sides of its body is :
(*a*) *Planaria* (*b*) Yeast (*c*) *Amoeba* (*d*) *Hydra*

75. An organism which can reproduce by two asexual reproduction methods one similar to the reproduction in yeast and the other similar to the reproduction in *Planaria* is :
(*a*) *Spirogyra* (*b*) *Bryophyllum* (*c*) *Hydra* (*d*) Sea anemone

76. Stock and scion are involved in the artificial propagation method known as :
(*a*) tissue culture (*b*) layering (*c*) grafting (*d*) cuttings

77. In asexual reproduction, two offsprings having the same genetic material and the same body features are called :
(*a*) callus (*b*) twins (*c*) clones (*d*) chromosomes

78. The method of asexual reproduction in plants in which callus is produced is :
(*a*) micropropagation (*b*) vegetative propagation (*c*) regeneration (*d*) fragmentation

79. A *Planaria* worm is cut horizontally in the middle into two halves P and Q such that the part P contains the whole head of the worm. Another *Planaria* worm is cut vertically into two halves R and S in such a way that both the cut pieces R and S contain half head each. Which of the cut pieces of the two *Planaria* worms could regenerate to form the complete respective worms ?
(*a*) only P (*b*) only R and S (*c*) P, R and S (*d*) P, Q, R and S

Questions Based on High Order Thinking Skills (HOTS)

80. There are four tiny organisms A, B, C and D. The organism A is a parasitic protozoan which causes a disease known as *kala-azar*. The organism B is a microscopic single-celled animal which causes malaria disease in human beings. The organism C is a unicellular animal which can change its body shape according to need, it has no fixed shape. The organism D is also a unicellular animal which is slipper-shaped having a large number of tiny hair all around its body.
(*a*) Name the organisms A, B, C and D
(*b*) Name one characteristic body feature of organism A.
(*c*) Name the insect which carries organism B and transmits it from one person to another.
(*d*) What name is given to the asexual method of reproduction of (*i*) organism A, and (*ii*) organism B ?
(*e*) Where do organisms C and D live ?

81. Two very small organisms X and Y both reproduce by the method of budding. Organism X is industrially very important because it is used in making alcohol from sugar. It is also used in making bread. Organism Y lives in freshwater. If organism Y gets cut into a number of parts accidently, each cut part can grow to form complete organism.
(*a*) What are organisms X and Y ?
(*b*) What is the name of the process in which X converts sugar into alcohol ?

(*c*) To which class of organisms does X belong ?
(*d*) Name an important body feature of organism Y.
(*e*) Which organism is multicellular and which one is unicellular ?

82. When a moist slice of bread was kept aside for a few days then some organism grew on it to form a white cottony mass which later turned black. When this slice of bread was observed through a magnifying glass, then fine thread-like projections and thin stems having bulb-like structures at the top were seen.
(*a*) What is the common name and scientific name of the organism which grew on the moist slice of bread ?
(*b*) How did this organism grow on the moist slice of bread automatically ?
(*c*) What are the fine, thread-like projections on the surface of slice of bread known as ?
(*d*) What name is given to the knob-like structures and what do they contain ?
(*e*) What is the name of this method of reproduction ?
(*f*) Name one unicellular organism which reproduces by this method.
(*g*) Name two non-flowering plants which reproduce by this method.

83. A scientist removed some cells from the growing point of a plant and placed it in a suitable medium leading to the formation of a shapeless lump of mass X. X is then transferred to another medium which stimulates it to develop roots. When X with developed roots is placed in a yet another medium, then it develops shoots to form tiny plantlets. These plantlets can then be transplanted in pots or soil where they can grow to form mature plants.
(*a*) What is the shapeless lump of mass X known as ?
(*b*) What name is given to this method of producing new plants ?
(*c*) The growth medium used in this method contains plant nutrients in the form of a 'jelly'. Name this jelly.
(*d*) What is the general name of chemicals used to stimulate the growth of plant cells and development of roots and shoots ?
(*e*) Name any two plants which are produced by this method.
(*f*) State any two advantages of this method of producing plants.
(*g*) What is the other name of this method [other than that given in (*b*) above] ?

84. The stem of a fruit tree X fixed in soil is cut in a slanting way. The upper part of stem of another fruit tree Y of different variety of same species is also cut in a slanting way. The cut stem of tree Y, without roots but having some leaves, is placed over the rooted cut stem of tree X in such a way that their cut surfaces fit together properly. While joining the two cut stems, care is taken to make sure that the layer Z of one cut stem is in contact with layer Z of the other cut stem. The joint of cut stem is bound tightly with a piece of cloth and covered properly with polythene. Soon the cut heals and the two stems grow together and become one fruit tree producing leaves, flowers and fruits.
(*a*) What is the name of this method of producing plants or trees ?
(*b*) What name is given to the cut stem of tree X having roots ?
(*c*) What name is given to the cut stem of tree Y which has no roots but has some leaves ?
(*d*) Name the layer Z.
(*e*) Why should the layer Z of one cut stem be in contact with the layer Z of the other cut stem ?
(*f*) Name any four fruit trees which are usually bred by this technique.
(*g*) State any one advantage of producing fruit trees by this technique.

85. A small part of the shoot of a plant is removed with a sharp knife. When the lower end of this small part of the shoot is buried in moist soil, it gradually develops roots and shoots and grows to become a new plant.
(*a*) What is the name of this method of propagating plants ?
(*b*) What care should be taken while removing a small part of the shoot from the parent plant with a knife ?
(*c*) Name any two plants which provide us with food directly or indirectly and are grown by this method.
(*d*) Give one advantage of this method of producing new plants.
(*e*) State whether it is a sexual method of reproduction or an asexual method. Why ?
(*f*) What special name can be given to the genetically identical new plants produced by this technique ?

86. When the branches of a plant growing in the field are pulled towards the ground and a part of them is covered with moist soil (leaving the tips of the branches exposed above the ground), then after some time new roots develop from the parts of branches buried in the soil. On cutting these branches from the parent plant, new plants are produced from the cut parts of branches which had developed roots.

(*a*) What is this method of propagation of plants known as ?

(*b*) What type of branches should a plant have to be able to be propagated by this method ?

(*c*) Name any two plants which are grown for their flowers and propagated by this method.

(*d*) Name any two plants which are grown for their fruits and propagated by this method

(*e*) Name one plant which gets propagated by this method naturally by forming runners (soft horizontal stems running above the ground).

87. A worm X found in freshwater and slow-moving streams has been accidently cut into three pieces. It was observed that in due course of time, each cut piece of the worm develops to become a complete worm by growing all the missing parts.

(*a*) Name the worm X which can exhibit this phenomenon of making complete worm from its cut body parts.

(*b*) Name another organism Y which possesses the same characteristic of growing fully from its cut body parts.

(*c*) What is the name of this process in which a complete organism is formed from its cut body part.

(*d*) State whether X and Y are unicellular and/or multicellular organisms.

(*e*) Can a dog be produced completely from its cut body part (say, a cut tail) just like organisms X and Y ? Why ?

88. A thickened underground stem X of a plant which is swollen with stored food has a number of points Y on its surface. When the old stem X is planted in the soil of a field in the next growing season, then each point Y present on its surface grows into a new plant.

(*a*) What is the general name of the underground stems like X ?

(*b*) Give one example of X.

(*c*) What are points Y present on X known as ?

(*d*) Is it necessary to plant the whole of stem X in the ground to obtain its new plants ? Explain your answer.

(*e*) What is the name of this method of reproduction of plants ?

(*f*) What is the advantage of growing new plants from the underground stems like X ?

89. A filamentous alga X is found in ponds, lakes and slow-moving streams. The filament of this alga simply breaks into two (or more) pieces on maturing and each piece then grows to become a complete new alga.

(*a*) Name an alga which X is likely to be.

(*b*) What is the colour of X ?

(*c*) What is the method of forming new algae by the breaking of parent alga known as ?

(*d*) An *Amoeba* also breaks up to form two daughter *Amoebae*. What is the difference in the splitting of *Amoeba* and splitting of this alga as a method of reproduction ?

(*e*) Name one marine animal which reproduces in the same way as alga X.

90. When a broken piece of the stem of a plant X is planted in the soil, a new plant grows from it in a week's time. The leaves of plant X also have many small entities Y in their margins which can fall to the ground alone or alongwith leaves and grow into new plants.

(*a*) Name a plant which X could be.

(*b*) What are the entities Y present on the leaves of X known as ?

(*c*) Name a plant other than X which can be reproduced from its leaves.

(*d*) Name a common plant grown in many homes which can be propagated from its broken stems like plant X.

(*e*) Name a kind of dormant organs present in dry stems of old grass plants lying in the fields which get activated and produce green grass plants after the rains.

ANSWERS

1. Reproduction **2.** (*a*) Sexual reproduction (*b*) Asexual reproduction **3.** False **4.** Ferns and Mosses **5.** (*a*) Sexual reproduction (*b*) Asexual reproduction **6.** Sexual method **7.** (*a*) Dogs and Cows (*b*) *Amoeba* and *Hydra* **8.** Bread mould (*Rhizopus* fungus) **9.** Binary fission ; Asexual method **10.** (*a*) *Bryophyllum* and Money plant (*b*) *Bryophyllum* and *Begonia* **20.** Because in all these methods of reproduction, new organisms (offsprings) are obtained from a single parent without the use of sex cells or gametes **21.** (*a*) reproduction (*b*) multiple ; binary (*c*) cuttings (*d*) tubers (*e*) layering **22.** (*b*) Sexual method : Cats, Humans, Birds ; Asexual method : *Amoeba, Hydra* **23.** (*a*) *Planaria* and *Hydra* **27.** (*c*) Binary fission : *Amoeba* ; Multiple fission : *Plasmodium* (*d*) Microscopic animals **28.** (*a*) Yes, because it leads to the formation of two daughter cells **29.** (*a*) Water does not provide any energy to yeast cells. So, yeast cells fail to multiply in water due to inadequate energy in its cells. Sugar provides energy to yeast cells to carry out reproduction by multiplying rapidly (*b*) Moisture is necessary for the growth of bread mould. The moist slice of bread provides both moisture and nutrients due to which bread mould grows profusely. On the other hand, the dry slice of bread provides nutrients but no moisture. So, in the absence of moisture, bread mould does not grow on the dry slice of bread **30.** (*a*) Stem tuber : Potato ; Root tuber : Sweet potato (*b*) Buds (or Eyes) (*c*) Potatoes **31.** (*b*) Buds **33.** (*i*) *j* (*ii*) *g* (*iii*) *f* (*iv*) *k* (*v*) *b* (*vi*) *h* (*vii*) *a* (*viii*) *d* (*ix*) *c* (*x*) *e* (*xi*) *i* (*xii*) *i* **34.** (*d*) Binary fission (*e*) *Paramecium* and *Leishmania* **35.** (*b*) By fission : *Amoeba* ; By fragmentation : *Spirogyra* (*c*) *Plasmodium* (*d*) Budding (*e*) Yeast **36.** (*a*) Spore formation ; Asexual method (*c*) *Hydra* ; Budding (*d*) Sponges and Corals **40.** (*c*) **41.** (*b*) **42.**(*c*) **43.** (*d*) **44.** (*b*) **45.** (*d*) **46.** (*c*) **47.** (*d*) **48.** (*d*) **49.** (*d*) **50.** (*d*) **51.** (*c*) **52.** (*c*) **53.** (*a*) **54.** (*a*) **55.** (*d*) **56.** (*d*) **57.** (*c*) **58.** (*d*) **59.** (*c*) **60.** (*b*) **61.** (*d*) **62.** (*d*) **63.** (*b*) **64.** (*d*) **65.** (*c*) **66.** (*c*) **67.** (*d*) **68.** (*c*) **69.** (*b*) **70.** (*c*) **71.** (*a*) **72.** (*d*) **73.** (*c*) **74.** (*d*) **75.** (*c*) **76.** (*c*) **77.** (*c*) **78.** (*a*) **79.** (*d*) **80.** (*a*) A is *Leishmania*, B is *Plasmodium*, C is *Amoeba* and D is *Paramecium* (*b*) Organism A (*Leishmania*) has a whip-like structure called flagellum at its one end (*c*) Female *Anopheles* mosquito (*d*) (*i*) Binary fission (*ii*) Multiple fission (*e*) In pond water **81.** (*a*) X is yeast and Y is *Hydra* (*b*) Fermentation (*c*) Fungi (*d*) Y has tentacles (*e*) Y is multicellular whereas X is unicellular **82.** (*a*) Bread mould ; *Rhizopus* (*b*) Spores of bread mould plant are always present around us. One such spore landed on moist slice of bread and finding the conditions favourable (presence of moisture, nutrients and warmth, etc.) grew into bread mould (*c*) Hyphae (*d*) Sporangia ; Spores (*e*) Spore formation (*f*) Bacteria (*g*) Ferns and Mosses **83.** (*a*) Callus (*b*) Tissue culture (*c*) *Agar* (*d*) Plant hormones (*e*) Dahlia and Carnation (*f*) See page 139 (*g*) Micropropagation **84.** (*a*) Grafting (*b*) Stock (*c*) Scion (*d*) Cambium layer (*e*) Because the layer Z (called cambium layer) in the stem is responsible for growth (*f*) Apple, peach, apricot and pear trees (*g*) It enables us to combine the most desirable characteristics of the two plants in fruits **85.** (*a*) Cuttings method (*b*) The cutting should have one (or more) bud on it (*c*) Sugar cane and Banana plants (*d*) By using the cuttings method, we can produce many new plants from just one plant quickly, without waiting for flowers and seeds (*e*) Asexual method of reproduction ; Because new plants are produced from a single parent plant without the involvement of sex cells (or gametes) of the plant (*f*) clones **86.** (*a*) Layering (*b*) Slender branches (Thin branches) (*c*) Jasmine and China rose (*d*) Lemon and Guava (*e*) Strawberry **87.** (*a*) *Planaria* (Flatworm) (*b*) *Hydra* (*c*) Regeneration (*d*) Simple multicellular organisms (*e*) No ; Because dog is a complex multicellular organism **88.** (*a*) Stem tubers (*b*) Potato tuber (*c*) Eyes or Buds (*d*) No ; Even cut pieces of X can be planted in the soil to obtain new plants provided each cut piece has an eye or bud on it (*e*) Vegetative propagation by tubers (*f*) The vegetative propagation method of growing new plants from tubers like X is much faster than the production of new plants from their seeds **89.** (*a*) *Spirogyra* (*b*) Green (*c*) Fragmentation (*d*) The binary fission in *Amoeba* is a reproduction process which takes place in unicellular organisms ; Fragmentation in alga is a reproduction process which takes place in simple multicellular organisms (*e*) Sea anemone **90.** (*a*) *Bryophyllum* (*b*) Buds (*c*) *Begonia* (*d*) Money plant (*e*) Buds.

SEXUAL REPRODUCTION

Sexual reproduction takes place by the combination of special reproductive cells called 'sex cells'. Sex cells are of two types : male sex cells and female sex cells (which come from two different parents : a male and a female). The sex cells are commonly known as gametes. Thus, **the cells involved in sexual reproduction are called gametes.** Gametes are of two types : male gametes and female gametes. **In sexual reproduction, a male gamete fuses with a female gamete to form a new cell called *'zygote'*. This zygote then grows and develops into a new organism in due course of time.** Please note that the sex cells or **gametes are also sometimes called germ cells.** And there are two types of germ cells : male germ cells and female germ cells. In this chapter we will be mostly using the term 'gamete'. The students are, however, free to use the term 'germ cell' (in place of gamete).

SEXUAL REPRODUCTION IN FLOWERING PLANTS

The plants in which the sex organs are carried within the flowers and the seeds are enclosed in a fruit are called angiosperms. Angiosperms are commnly known as flowering plants. **The flowering plants reproduce by 'sexual reproduction' method.** This means that two sexes (male and female) are involved in reproduction in flowering plants. Like human beings, plants have also male and female sex organs, though they are different in form from humans. **The sex organs (or reproductive organs) of a plant are in its**

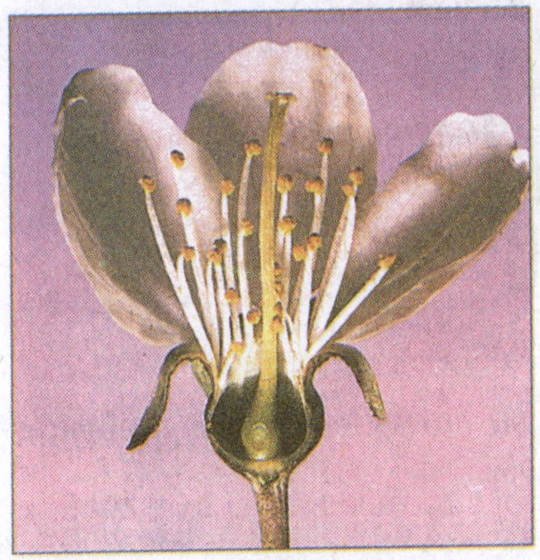

Figure 40. Flowers contain the sexual reproductive organs of a plant (This flower has been cut open to show the sexual reproductive organs inside). Flowers make fruits which contain seeds. These seeds can produce new plants.

Figure 41. Apples, oranges, lemons and tomatoes, etc., are all fruits. They contain the seeds of their plants inside them. These seeds can be sown in the soil to grow more plants.

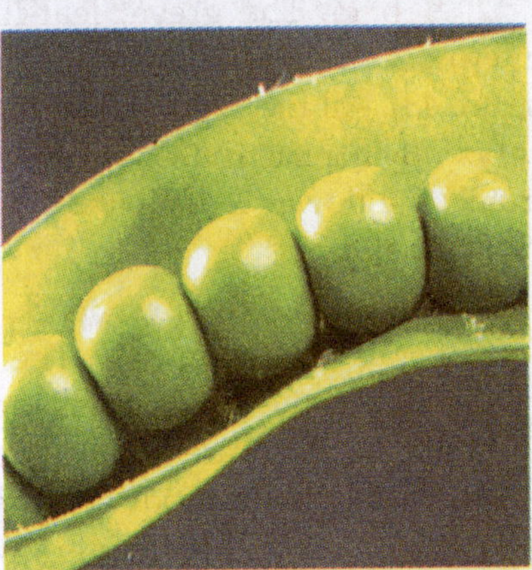

Figure 42. Pea pods are also fruits. The peas inside them are seeds of the pea plant. These peas (or seeds) can be sown in the soil to grow new pea plants.

flowers. In other words, flowers contain the sexual reproductive organs of a plant (see Figure 40). In most of the plants, the same flower contains the male organ as well as the female organ. In other words, the majority of plants are bisexual having the male and female reproductive organs in the same plant (or same flower). In fact, the reproductive part of higher plants is the flower. **The function of a flower is to make male and female gametes and to ensure that fertilisation will take place to make new seeds for the reproduction of plant** (see Figures 41 and 42). Sexual reproduction is the most common method of reproduction in flowering plants. From all this discussion we conclude that flowers are for sexual reproduction in plants. A flower makes both male and female gametes needed for sexual reproduction in plants.

The sexual reproduction in plants takes place in the following steps :

1. The male organ of flower called 'stamen' makes the male gametes (male sex cells) of the plant. These male gametes are present in pollen grains.
2. The female organ of a flower called 'carpel' makes the female gametes (female sex cells) of the plant. These female gametes are present in ovules. The female gametes present in ovules are also called 'ova', 'egg cells' or just 'eggs'.
3. The male gametes present in pollen grains fertilise the female gametes or egg cells present in ovules.
4. The fertilised egg cells grow within ovules and become seeds.
5. The seeds produce new plants on germination (under suitable conditions of water, warmth, air and light, etc.).

We will now describe the various parts of a flower including the sexual reproductive organs. And then we will discuss the sexual reproduction in plants in detail.

The main parts of a flower are : Receptacle, Sepals, Petals, Stamen and Carpel. These main parts of a flower are shown in Figure 43.

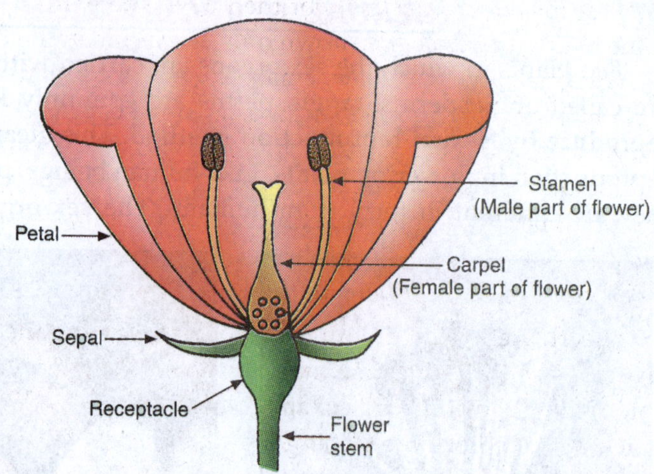

Figure 43. Diagram to show the parts of a flower.

1. Receptacle. The base of a flower to which all the parts of a flower are attached is called receptacle (see Figure 43).

2. Sepals. The green, leaf-like parts in the outermost circle of a flower are called sepals (see Figure 43). All the sepals taken together are called **'calyx'**. The function of sepals (or calyx) is to protect the flower in its initial stages when it is in the form of a bud.

3. Petals. The colourful parts of a flower are called petals (see Figure 43). The petals lie inside the sepals. All the petals taken together are called **'corolla'**. The petals are usually scented. The function of petals (or corolla) is to attract insects (for pollination) and to protect the reproductive organs which are at the centre of the flower.

4. Stamen. The little stalks with swollen tops just inside the ring of petals in a flower are called stamens. **Stamen is the male reproductive organ of the plant** (see Figure 44). Stamen produces pollen grains. The stamen is made of two parts : a filament and an anther (see Figure 44). The stalk of stamen is called filament and the swollen top of stamen is called anther. It is actually the anther of a stamen which makes the pollen grains and stores them (The pollen grains appear to be yellow, powder-like substance to us). Pollen grains contain the male gametes (or male sex cells) of the plant. It is clear from this discussion that **the male gametes of a plant are made in the anther of stamen.** Another point to be noted is that a flower usually has a number of stamens in it.

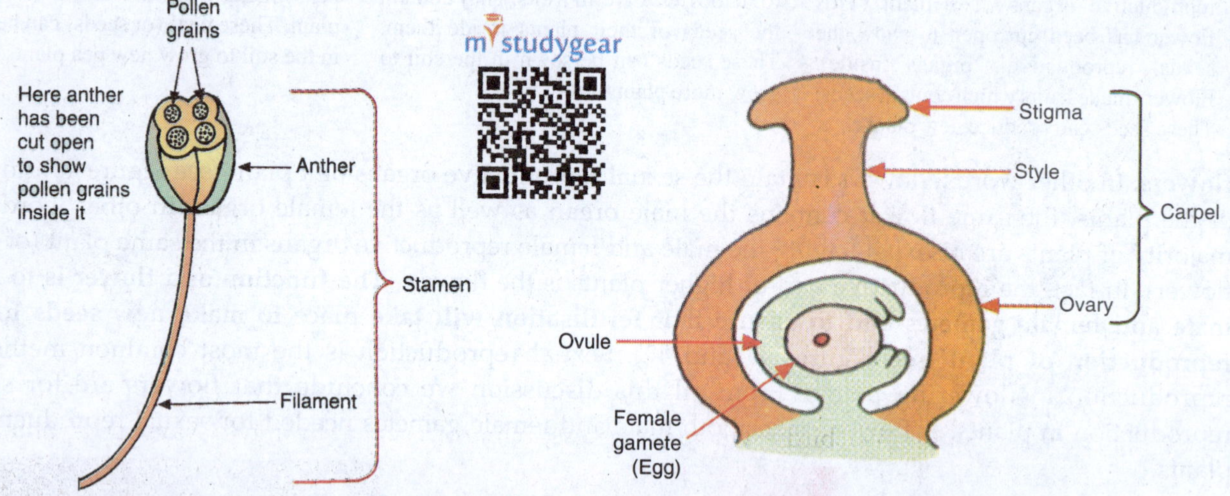

Figure 44. Stamen : Male reproductive organ of a plant

Figure 45. Carpel : Female reproductive organ of a plant (Carpel is also called Pistil).

5. Carpel. In the centre of a flower, there is a flask-shaped organ called carpel. **Carpel is the female reproductive organ of the plant** (see Figure 43). A carpel is made of three parts : stigma, style and ovary (see Figure 45). The top part of carpel is called stigma. Stigma is for receiving the pollen grains from the anther of stamen (during pollination). Stigma is sticky so that pollen can stick to it. The middle part of carpel is called style. Style is a tube which connects stigma to the ovary. The swollen part at the bottom of a carpel is called ovary (see Figure 45). The ovary makes ovules and stores them. Ovules contain the female gametes (or female sex cells) of the plant. There are usually many ovules in the ovary (but we have shown only one ovule in the ovary in Figure 45). Each ovule contains only one female gamete of the plant. The female gamete (or female sex cell) of the plant which is present inside the ovule is called 'ovum' or 'egg'. It is clear from this discussion that **the female gametes of a plant are made in the ovary of carpel**. Please note that **the female organ of a plant is known by two names : carpel and pistil.** Another point to be noted is that the female organ called carpel is surrounded by a number of male organs called stamens in the flower (see Figure 46).

Figure 46. This picture shows the carpel of a tulip flower surrounded by many brown stamens.

The flowers which contain only one sex organ, either stamens or carpels, are called unisexual flowers. The flowers of papaya and watermelon plants are unisexual flowers. On the other hand, **the flowers which contain both the sex organs, stamens as well as carpel, are called bisexual flowers.** The flowers of *Hibiscus* and mustard plants are bisexual flowers.

A new seed of the plant is formed when the male gamete present in a pollen grain unites with the female gamete present in the ovule. This happens in two steps : pollination and fertilisation.

1. Pollination

For the male gamete to be able to combine with the female gamete, it is necessary that first the pollen grains from the anther of stamen should be carried to the stigma of carpel. **The transfer of pollen grains from the anther of a stamen to the stigma of a carpel is called pollination.** Thus, pollination is said to take place when pollen grains are carried from the anther to the stigma of the flower. Pollination is done by insects (like bees and butterflies), birds, wind, and water. Pollination can occur in two ways : self-pollination and cross-pollination. **When the pollen grains from the anther of a flower are transferred to the stigma of the same flower (or another flower on the same plant), it is called self-pollination** [see Figure 47(*a*)].

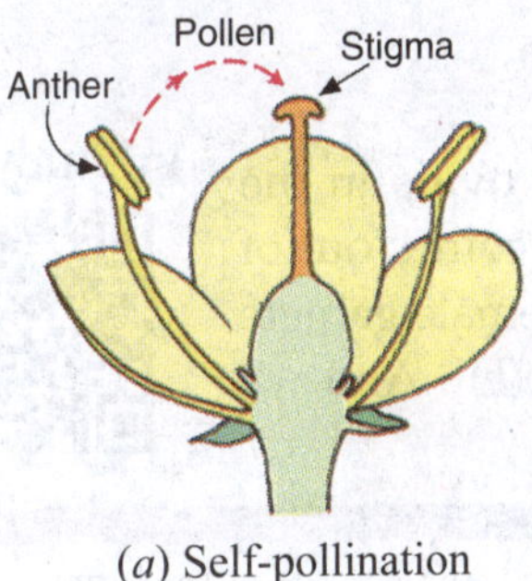

(*a*) Self-pollination

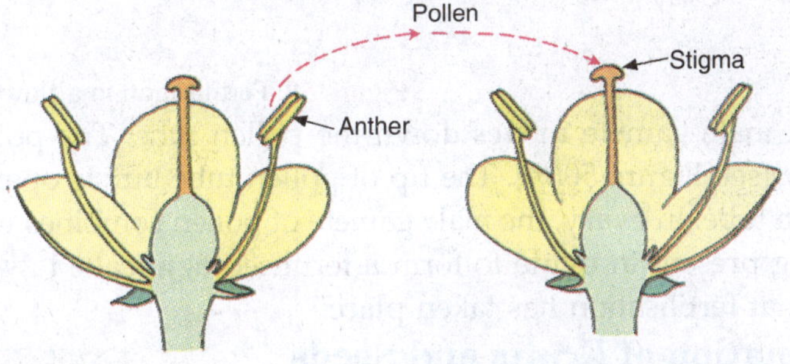

(*b*) Cross-pollination

Figure 47. Pollination.

When the pollen grains from the anther of a flower on one plant are transferred to the stigma of a flower on another similar plant, it is called cross-pollination [see Figure 47(*b*)]. Insects help in cross-pollination as follows :

Figure 48. Insects (such as this bee) which sit on different flowers to suck nectar, help in pollination by transferring pollen from the anther of one flower to the stigma of another flower.

Figure 49. The male flowers in this picture are shedding a dust of their pollens into the air. These pollens are then carried away by wind to the stigma of another flower for pollination.

When an insect sits on the flower of a plant for sucking nectar, then the pollen grains from the anther of this flower stick to its body. And when this insect now sits on another flower of another similar plant, then the pollen grains sticking to its body are transferred to the stigma of this second flower (see Figure 48). In this way the insect transfers the pollen grains from the anther of flower in one plant to the stigma of flower in another plant and causes cross-pollination. The blowing wind also carries pollen grains from one flower to another flower and helps in cross pollination (see Figure 49).

2. Fertilisation

After a pollen grain falls on the stigma, the next step is fertilisation. **Fertilisation occurs when the male gamete present in pollen grain joins with the female gamete (or egg) present in ovule**. This happens as follows. When a pollen grain falls on the stigma of the carpel, it bursts open and grows a pollen tube downwards through the style towards the female gamete in the ovary [see Figure 50(*a*)].

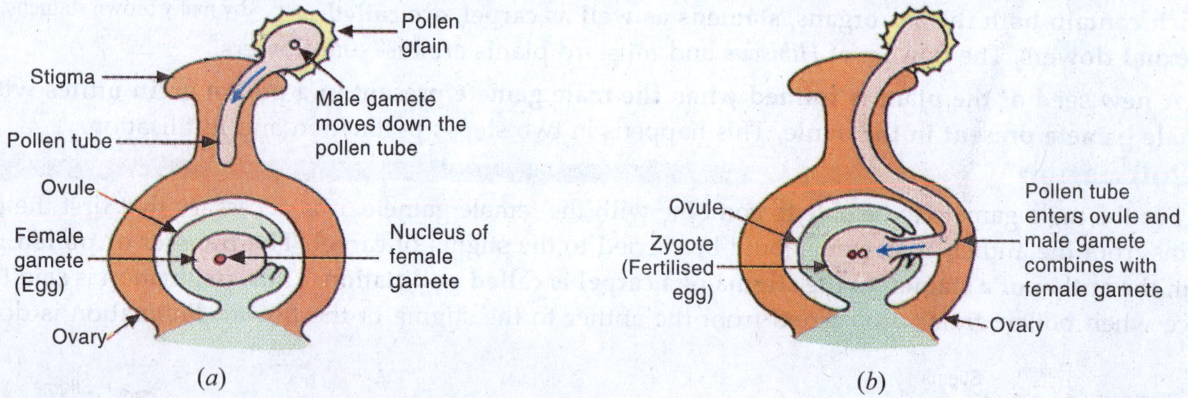

Figure 50. Fertilisation in a flower.

A male gamete moves down the pollen tube. The pollen tube enters the ovule in the ovary [see Figure 50(*b*)]. The tip of pollen tube bursts open and male gamete comes out of pollen tube. In ovary, the male gamete of pollen combines with the nucleus of female gamete or egg present in ovule to form a fertilised egg (called zygote) [see Figure 50(*b*)]. And we say that fertilisation has taken place.

Formation of Fruits and Seeds

The fertilised egg (or zygote) divides several times to form an embryo within the ovule. The ovule develops a tough coat around it and is gradually converted into a seed (containing the baby plant). In fact, all the eggs in the ovules present in the ovary of a flower get fertilised by male gametes from pollen grains and grow to become seeds. **The ovary of flower develops and becomes a fruit (with seeds inside it)**. The

(*a*) An apple is a fruit. It has seeds of apple tree in it.

(*b*) A pea pod is a fruit. It has seeds of pea plant inside it.

Figure 51. A fruit contains seeds of the plant inside it.

other parts of flower like sepals, petals, stamens, stigma and style dry up and fall off. Only the ovary is left behind. So, at the place on plant where we had a flower originally, we now have a fruit (which is the ovary of the flower containing seeds). A fruit protects the seeds (see Figure 51). Some fruits are soft, sweet and juicy like mangoes and oranges. But some fruits are hard, dry and woody like the peanuts and almonds, etc.

A seed is the reproductive unit of a plant (which can be used to grow a new plant). The seed contains

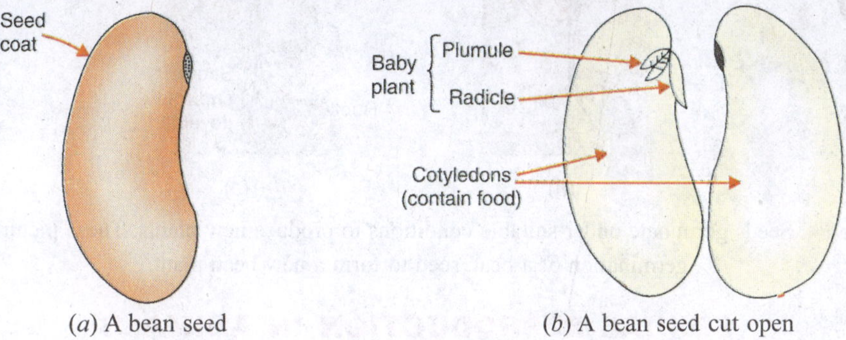

(*a*) A bean seed (*b*) A bean seed cut open

Figure 52. Parts of a seed.

a baby plant (or embryo) and food for the baby plant (see Figure 52). The part of baby plant in seed which develops into shoot with leaves is called plumule and the part which develops into root is called radicle. The part of seed which contains stored food for the baby plant is called cotyledon. The wheat grains, gram (*chana*), corn, peas, and beans, are all seeds (see Figure 53). The baby plant present inside a seed is in the

(*a*) Wheat seeds (*b*) Bengal gram seeds (*c*) Corn (or maize) seeds (*d*) Bean seeds

Figure 53. These pictures show seeds of some common food crop plants. All these seeds can be used to grow new crop plants under suitable conditions.

inactive state (called dormant state). When the seed gets suitable conditions like water, air and warmth, etc., it germinates and a new plant grows out of the seed. In this way, **the parent plant reproduces more plants like itself by forming seeds through flowers.**

Germination of Seeds

The seeds obtained from a plant are usually very dry. In this dry state, the seeds can remain alive but inactive for long periods. They are said to be dormant. When a seed gets water, air and warmth, etc., it begins to grow. When a seed begins to grow, it is said to germinate. Thus, **the beginning of the growth of seeds is called germination of seeds**. Germination begins when the seed absorbs water, swells and bursts through the seed coat. The water helps the enzymes to function in the seed. The enzymes digest the stored food in cotyledons and make it soluble. This soluble food makes the radicle and plumule present in the seed to grow. The germination of a bean seed is shown in Figure 54.

The radicle of the seed grows first to form the root [see Figure 54(*a*)]. The root pushes down into the soil and begins to absorb water and minerals from the soil. After this the plumule grows upwards to form the shoot [see Figure 54(*b*)]. The shoot and root grow further [see Figure 54(*c*)]. When the shoot comes up above the ground, it develops green leaves [see Figure 54(*d*)]. The green leaves of the shoot begin to synthesise own food in the presence of sunlight. This seedling grows gradually and ultimately becomes a new plant.

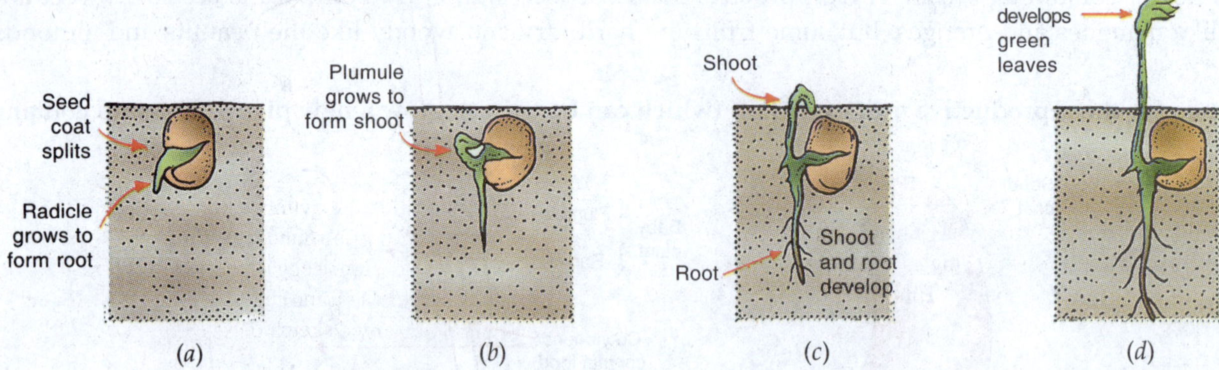

Figure 54. Seeds germinate under suitable conditions to produce new plants. These pictures show the germination of a bean seed to form a new bean plant.

SEXUAL REPRODUCTION IN ANIMALS

In order to understand sexual reproduction, we should know the meanings of some important terms like male sex, female sex, gametes, sperms, ova (or eggs), fertilisation, zygote and embryo, which are involved in sexual reproduction. These are discussed below :

Male and Female

Our father is a male and our mother is a female. We can also say that our father has male sex and our mother has female sex. Now, our father is a man and our mother is a woman. This means that **a man is male** whereas **a woman is female.** Thus, a man is said to have male sex and a woman is said to have female sex. Similarly, a boy has a male sex and a girl has a female sex. Just like us human beings, other

(*a*) A man

(*b*) A woman

Figure 55. A man is male whereas a woman is female.

animals also have male and female sexes. Even the plants have male and female sexes. As we will learn after a while, being male or female depends on the type of sex cells present in one's body. **An animal having male sex cells called 'sperms' in its body is called male.** On the other hand, **an animal having female sex cells called 'ova' (or 'eggs') in its body is called female.** We will now discuss gametes.

Gametes

Sexual reproduction takes place by the combination of special reproductive cells called 'sex cells'. These sex cells are also known by another name which is 'gamete'. We can now say that : **The cells involved in sexual reproduction are called gametes.** In other words, gametes are the sexual reproductive cells (or sex cells). Gametes are of two types : male gametes, and female gametes. **The male gamete in animals is called 'sperm'** and **the female gamete in animals is called 'ovum' or 'egg'** (see Figures 56 and 57). Sperms

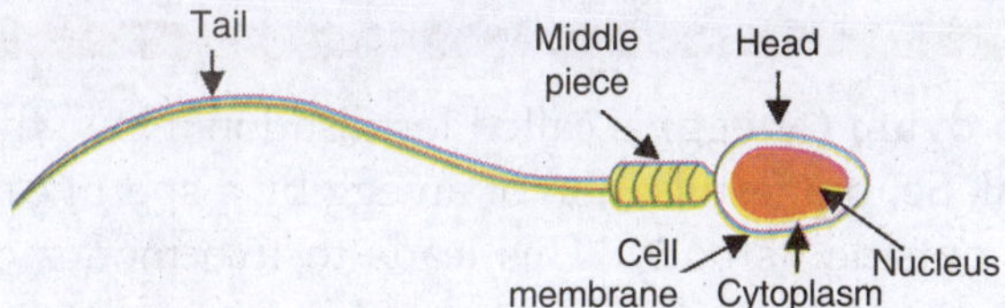

Figure 56. A human sperm (male gamete). A sperm is about 0.05 mm long. A sperm has a head, a middle piece and a tail. A sperm is a single cell with nucleus, cytoplasm and cell membrane. This figure is a highly enlarged sketch of a sperm.

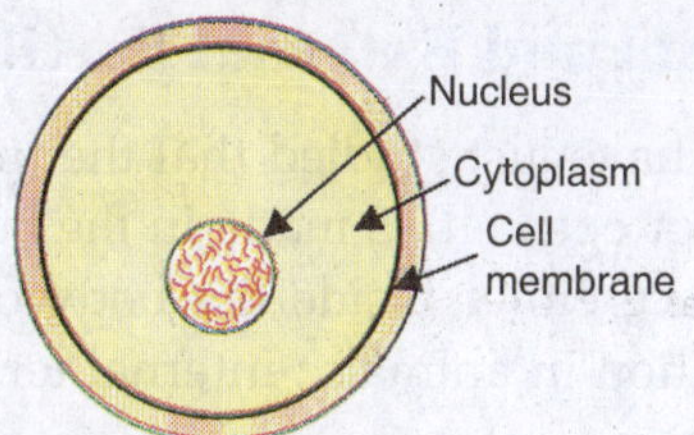

Figure 57. A human ovum or egg (female gamete). An ovum or egg is round and about 0.15 mm in diameter. The ovum or egg is also a single cell having a nucleus, cytoplasm and cell membrane. This figure is a highly enlarged sketch of an ovum or egg.

and ova (or eggs) are extremely small cells which can be seen only with the help of a high power microscope. Please note that a female gamete (or female sex cell) is usually known by two names : ovum and egg. So, whether we use the term 'ovum' or 'egg', it will mean the same thing. Another point to be noted is that the plural of ovum is ova. The ovum or egg contains water and stored food. The important part of ovum or egg is its nucleus (see Figure 57). The sperm cell is hundreds or even thousands of times smaller than the ovum or egg and it has a long tail (see Figure 56). The sperms are motile which can move independently with the help of their tails. The nuclei of the sperm and ovum (or egg) contain chromosomes which carry the genes.

It is clear from the above discussion that sperms are the male gametes of animals. And ova (or eggs) are the female gametes of animals. In other words, sperms are the male sex cells of animals and ova (or eggs) are the female sex cells of the animals. As we will study after a short while, **fusion of gametes gives rise to a single cell called zygote.** We can also say that **the cell which is formed by the fusion of a male gamete and a female gamete is called zygote.** In most simple words, *zygote is a 'fertilised ovum' or 'fertilised egg'*. All the multicellular animals start their life from a single cell called zygote through sexual reproduction. The process of fusion of gametes is called fertilisation. This is discussed below.

Fertilisation

For sexual reproduction to occur, a male gamete must combine (or fuse) with a female gamete. **The fusion of a male gamete with a female gamete to form a zygote during the sexual reproduction, is called fertilisation.** Since the male gamete of an animal is called sperm and the female gamete of an animal is called ovum (or egg), therefore, we can also say that : **The fusion of a sperm with an ovum (or egg) to form a zygote during sexual reproduction, is called fertilisation.** It is clear that the process of fertilisation produces a new cell called zygote. The zygote is actually 'fertilised ovum' or 'fertilised egg'. The zygote (or fertilised egg) grows and develops to form a new baby. The unborn baby in the uterus in the early stages of development (when its body parts are not much developed) is called an embryo. On the other hand, the unborn baby in the uterus in the later stages of development (when all its body parts are well developed and can be identified) is called a foetus (The word 'foetus' is pronounced as 'fetus').

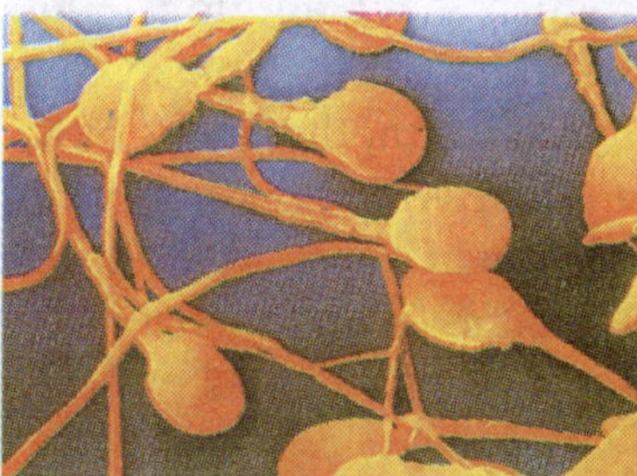

Figure 58. This picture shows a number of sperms (greatly magnified).

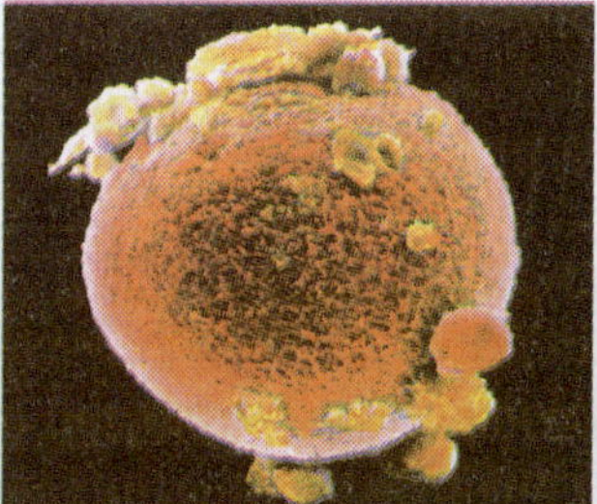

Figure 59. This picture shows an ovum or egg (greatly magnified).

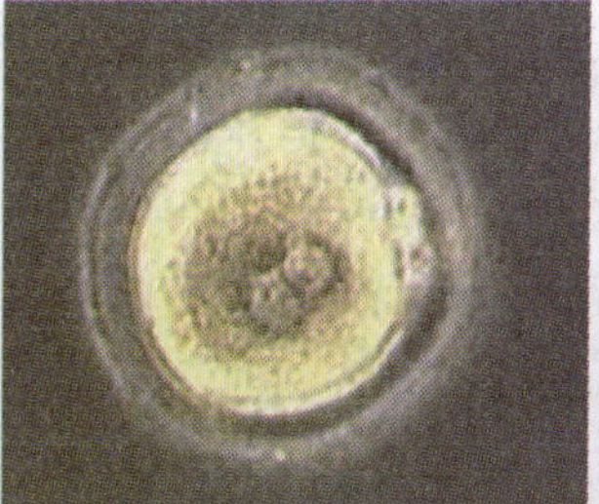

Figure 60. This is a zygote (or fertilised egg) formed by the fusion of a sperm with an ovum or egg.

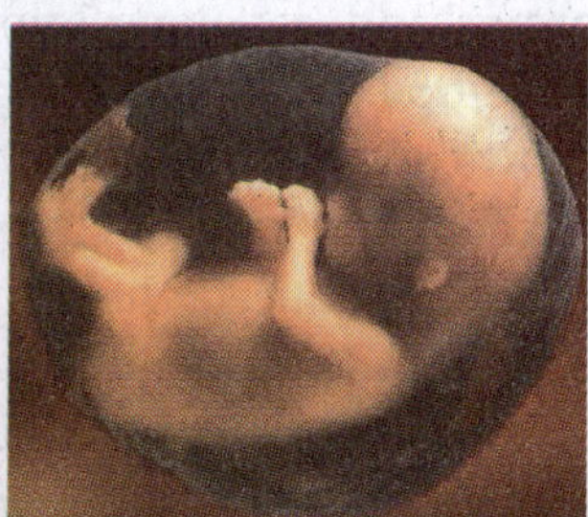

Figure 61. This is the foetus formed from a zygote (or fertilised egg). It will grow further and become a baby.

Internal and External Fertilisation

We have just studied that the fusion of a sperm with an ovum (or egg) is called fertilisation. Now, the ovum (or egg cell) is made in the body of the female animal. So, the fertilisation of an egg by a sperm can take place either inside the body of the female animal or outside its body. This leads to two modes of fertilisation in animals : internal fertilisation and external fertilisation.

The fertilisation which occurs inside the female body is called internal fertilisation. In internal fertilisation, the female animal's eggs are fertilised by sperms inside her body. In mammals (including human beings), birds and reptiles, the fertilisation occurs inside the female body. In other words, **internal fertilisation takes place in mammals (including human beings), birds and reptiles.** In internal fertilisation, the male animal puts his sperms into the female animal's body. This transfer of sperms from the testes of the male animal into female animal's body occurs at the time of copulation (or mating). Copulation is the act by which the male animal transfers his sperms into the female animal's body. During copulation, very large number of sperms are discharged into the female body. These sperms fertilise the eggs inside her body. For example, during copulation a man puts his sperms inside a woman's body through an organ called penis. These sperms then fertilise the egg inside the woman's body. So, this is a case of internal fertilisation.

The fertilisation which occurs outside the female body is called external fertilisation. In external fertilisation, the female animal's eggs are fertilised by sperms outside its body. In amphibians (like frogs and toads) and fishes, the fertilisation of eggs occurs outside the female animal's body. In other words, **in amphibians (like frogs and toads) and fishes, external fertilisation takes place.** In external fertilisation, the male and female animals release their sperms and eggs in water where fertilisation takes place by collisions between sperms and eggs. For example, the males and females of frogs and fishes release their sperms and eggs in water in which they live. The sperms then collide with the eggs and fertilise them outside the body of female frog or fish (see Figure 62).

Figure 62. As the female frog lays eggs in water, the male frog releases its sperms. The collisions between sperms and eggs leads to fertilisation. This is an example of external fertilisation.

From the above discussion we conclude that **there are two different modes of fertilisation in nature : internal fertilisation and external fertilisation.** The fertilisation in humans, cats, dogs and birds are the examples of internal fertilisation. The fertilisation in frogs and fishes are the examples of external fertilisation.

We know that the new cell which is formed by fertilisation is called 'zygote'. And this zygote then grows and develops into a full organism (or baby animal). **The method in which a zygote grows and develops into a full organism also varies in different animals.** For example, in human beings the zygote grows and develops into a baby inside the female body (mother's body). And then the mother gives birth to the baby. Just like humans, the animals like cats and dogs also give birth to their young ones. But the process is entirely different in the animals (like birds) which lay eggs. For example, a hen sits on its fertilised eggs for a considerable time to give them warmth. During this period, the zygote grows and develops to form a complete chick. This chick then comes out of the egg by breaking its shell. It is clear from this discussion that *all the organisms do not give birth to individuals like humans do.*

The Advantages of Sexual Reproduction

The sexual reproduction has many advantages over asexual reproduction. In asexual reproduction, the offsprings are almost identical to their parent because they have the same genes as their parent. So, **much genetic variation is not possible in asexual reproduction**. This is a disadvantage of asexual reproduction because it inhibits the further evolution of the organism.

In sexual reproduction the offsprings, although similar to their parents, are not identical to them or to one another. This is because the offsprings receive some genes from the mother and some from the father. Because of the mixing of genes of mother and father in various different combinations, all the offsprings have genetic variations. In this way, **sexual reproduction leads to a greater variety in population.** This means that a species (animal or plant) can adapt more quickly to changes in its surroundings (or environment). This is because there are always likely to be some individuals which are more suited to the changes than others, and these individuals will survive and reproduce themselves.

From the above discussion we conclude that sexual reproduction promotes diversity of characters in the offsprings by providing **genetic variation.** Sexual reproduction plays an important role in the **origin of new species** having different characteristics. This genetic variation leads to the continuous **evolution** of various species to form better and still better organisms. All this is not possible in the case of asexual reproduction.

Why the Amount of DNA Does Not Get Doubled During Sexual Reproduction

In sexual reproduction, though the genetic material DNA (in the form of chromosomes) from two gametes, male and female gametes, combines together to form a new cell 'zygote' but the amount of DNA in zygote does not get doubled. This can be explained as follows : **The gametes are special type of cells called reproductive cells which contain only half the amount of DNA (or half the number of chromosomes) as compared to the normal body cells of an organism.** So, when a male gamete combines with a female gamete during sexual reproduction, then the new cell 'zygote' will have the normal amount of DNA (or normal number of chromosomes in it). For example, the human sperm has 23 chromosomes and the human egg (or ovum) has also 23 chromosomes. So, when a sperm and an egg fuse together during fertilisation, then the zygote formed will have 23 + 23 = 46 chromosomes, which is the normal number of chromosomes.

How Sexual Reproduction in Animals Takes Place

Sexual reproduction is the most common method of reproduction in animals (including human beings). The sexual reproduction in animals takes place in the following steps :

1. The male parent produces male gametes (male sex cells) called sperms. The sperm is a small cell with a long tail (flagellum) for movement [see Figure 63(*a*)].
2. The female parent produces female gametes (female sex cells) called ova (or eggs). The ovum (or egg) is a much bigger cell than the sperm, having a lot of cytoplasm [see Figure 63(*a*)].

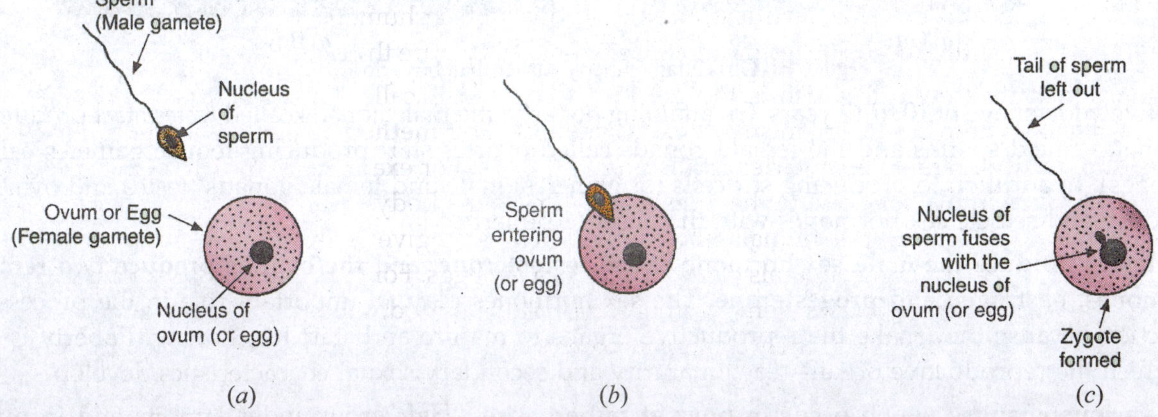

Figure 63. Fertilisation of an ovum (or egg) by a sperm to form a zygote.

3. The sperm enters into the ovum (or egg) and fuses with it to form a new cell called 'zygote' [see Figures 63(*b*) and (*c*)]. This process is called fertilisation. So, the zygote is a fertilised ovum (or fertilised egg).

4. The zygote then divides again and again to form a large number of cells (all of which remain together). And ultimately zygote grows and develops to become a new baby.

From the above discussion we conclude that **the whole process of sexual reproduction in animals involves the formation of sperms and eggs; joining together of sperm and egg to form a zygote; and then the growth and development of zygote to form a baby animal.** In complex multicellular animals (like human beings) there are special reproductive organs to make sperms and eggs; to bring together sperms and eggs for fertilisation; and for the growth and development of zygote into a baby. We will study all this in the human reproductive system. Before we describe the human reproductive system, we should know the meaning of the term 'puberty'. This is discussed below.

Puberty

When a child is small, sometimes it becomes difficult to tell from appearance whether it is a boy or a girl (see Figure 65). This is because small boys and girls have the same body shape. A time of rapid growth and body changes starts in the early teens which makes the boy and the girl appear different and also behave differently (see Figure 66). These changes start earlier in girls than in boys. We call the time between childhood and adulthood 'adolescence.' The production of male and female 'sex hormones' in the bodies of boys and girls increases dramatically at this stage and causes a wide-ranging changes in their bodies. The testes (in boys) and ovaries (in girls) make different hormones, so the boys and girls develop in different ways. Ultimately the boys and girls become sexually mature and their reproductive systems start functioning.

The age at which the sex hormones (or gametes) begin to be produced and the boy and girl become sexually mature (able to reproduce) is called puberty. Puberty tends to start earlier in females (girls) than in males (boys). Generally boys attain puberty at the age of 13 to 14 years while girls reach puberty at a comparatively lower age of 10 to 12 years. On attaining puberty, the male gonads called testes start producing male gametes called sperms and the female gonads called ovaries start producing female gametes called ova (or eggs). In addition to producing sex cells (or gametes) male and female gonads (testes and ovaries) also produce and secrete sex hormones with the onset of puberty.

(*a*) Girls

(*b*) Boys

Figure 64. Girls attain puberty earlier than boys do.

The testes produce the male sex hormone called testosterone, and the ovaries produce two female sex hormones, oestrogen and progesterone. The sex hormones play an important role in the process of reproduction because they make the reproductive organs to mature and start functioning. Puberty is the age at which the reproductive organs reach maturity and secondary sexual characteristics develop.

The various changes which occur in boys at puberty are : Hair grow under armpits and in pubic regions (genital area) between the thighs. Hair also grow on other parts of the body like chest and face (moustache, beard, etc.) (see Figure 66). Body becomes more muscular due to the development of muscles. The voice deepens (or cracks). Chest and shoulders broaden. The penis and testes become larger. The testes start to make sperms. Feelings and sexual drives associated with adulthood begin to develop. All these changes in boys are brought about by the male sex hormone *'testosterone'* made in testes.

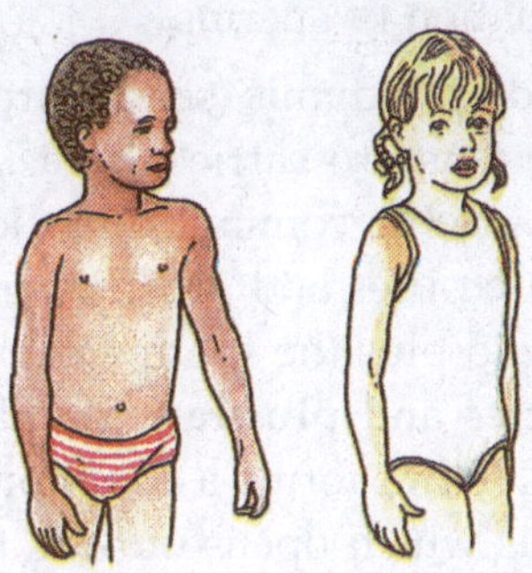

Figure 65. Small boys and girls have the same body shape. So, they look alike.

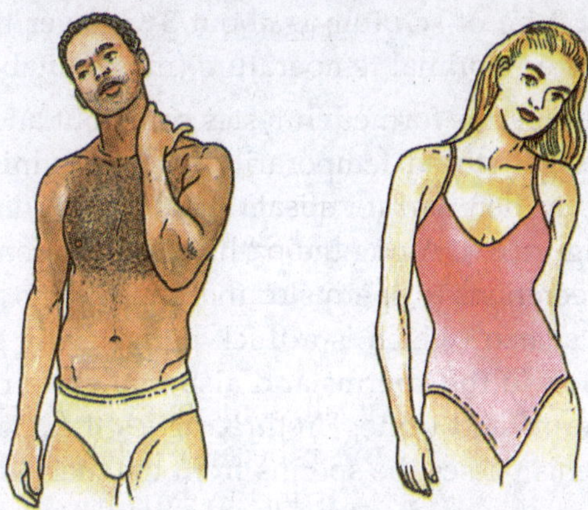

Figure 66. Grown up boys and girls have different body shapes. So, they look different.

The various changes which occur in girls at puberty are : Hair grow under armpits and pubic region (This change is the same as in boys). Mammary glands (or breasts) develop and enlarge. The hips broaden (see Figure 66). Extra fat is deposited in various parts of the body like hips and thighs. Fallopian tubes, uterus and vagina enlarge. Ovaries start to release eggs. Menstruation (monthly periods) start. Feelings and sexual drives associated with adulthood begin to develop. All these changes in girls are brought about by the female sex hormones *'oestrogen'* and *'progesterone'* made in ovaries. Please note that the hormone 'oestrogen' is also written and spoken as 'estrogen'.

Human Reproductive System

The humans use sexual mode of reproduction. The organs associated with the process of reproduction in human males (men) and human females (women) are different, so the reproductive systems in males and females are different which are known as male reproductive system and female reproductive system, respectively. **The reproductive systems in human beings become functional (or start functioning) at a definite age called puberty.** We will now describe the human male reproductive system and female reproductive system in detail, one by one.

THE MALE REPRODUCTIVE SYSTEM

The human male reproductive system consists of the following organs : Testes, Scrotum, Epididymis, Vas deferens (or Sperm duct), Seminal vesicles, Prostrate gland and Penis. The human male reproductive system is shown in Figure 67. Since the human male is called man, so we can also say that it is the reproductive system of man.

Testes are the oval shaped organs which lie outside the abdominal cavity of a man (see Figure 67). A man has two testes (singular of testes is testis). **Testes are the primary reproductive organs in man (or males).** The function of testes is to make the male sex cells (or male gametes) called sperms and also to make the male sex hormone called testosterone. Please note that the testes of a man make the sex gametes (or sperms) from puberty onwards, throughout his life. The testes of a man lie in small muscular pouch called scrotum, outside the abdominal cavity (see Figure 67). The testes are

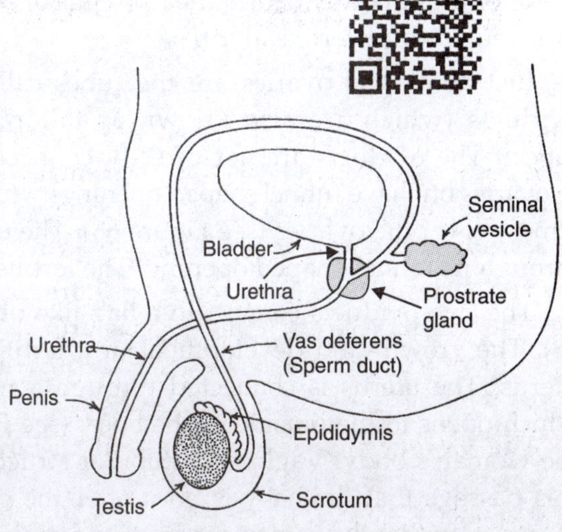

Figure 67. The male reproductive system in humans (side view).

outside the abdominal cavity of the body (and not deep inside the body), because the sperm formation requires a lower temperature than the normal body temperature. Being outside the abdominal cavity, the temperature of scrotum is about 3°C lower than the temperature inside the body. In this way, the testes provide an optimal temperature (most suitable temperature) for the formation of sperms.

The sperms formed in testes come out and go into a coiled tube called epididymis (see Figure 67). The sperms get stored temporarily in epididymis. From epididymis, the sperms are carried by a long tube called vas deferens (or sperm duct) which joins with another tube called urethra coming from the bladder (see Figure 67). Along the path of vas deferens, the glands called seminal vesicles and prostrate gland add their secretions to sperms so that the sperms are now in a liquid. This liquid plus the sperms it contains is called semen (which is a thick liquid). **The secretions of seminal vesicles and prostrate gland provide nutrition to the sperms and also make their further transport easier.** Urethra forms a common passage for sperms and urine. Urethra carries the sperms to an organ called penis which opens outside the body. The penis passes the sperms from the man's body into vagina in the woman's body during mating for the purpose of reproduction. Please note that in man (or human male) there is only one opening for the urine and sperms to pass out of the body.

THE FEMALE REPRODUCTIVE SYSTEM

The human female reproductive system consists of the following organs : Ovaries, Oviducts (which are also called Fallopian tubes), Uterus, and Vagina. The human female reproductive system is shown in Figure 68. Since the human female is called woman, so we can also say that it is the reproductive system of woman.

Ovaries are the oval shaped organs which are inside the abdominal cavity of a woman near the kidneys (see Figure 68). A woman has two ovaries. **Ovaries are the primary reproductive organs in a woman (or female).** The function of ovaries is to make mature female sex cells (or female gametes) called 'ova' or 'eggs', and also to make the female sex hormones (called oestrogen and progesterone). Each ovary is composed of several thousand follicles (which are a kind of unripe eggs or unripe ova). At puberty these follicles mature to form the ripe eggs or ripe ova (required for fertilisation).

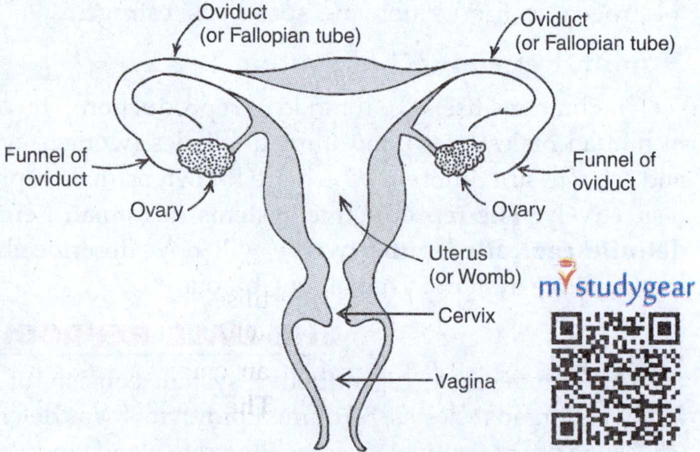

Figure 68. The female reproductive system in humans (front view).

Just above the ovaries are the tubes called oviducts (which are also known as fallopian tubes). The oviducts are not directly connected to ovaries but have funnel shaped openings which almost cover the ovaries (see Figure 68). The ovum (or egg cell) released by an ovary goes into the oviduct through its funnel-shaped opening. The fertilisation of egg (or ovum) by a sperm takes place in the oviduct.

The two oviducts connect to a bag like organ called uterus (or womb) at their other ends (see Figure 68). The growth and development of a fertilised ovum (or fertilised egg) into a baby takes place in the uterus. The uterus is connected through a narrow opening called cervix to another tube called vagina which opens to the outside of the body (see Figure 68). Vagina receives the penis for putting sperms into the woman's body. Vagina is a tubular structure. Vagina is also called 'birth canal' because it is through this passage that the baby is born after the completion of development inside the uterus of the mother. Please note that in woman (or human female) the opening for passing out urine (called urethra) and the vaginal opening are separate.

It is obvious from the above discussion that the female reproductive system in humans is more complex than that of the male reproductive system. The complexity in structure and function of the female reproductive system is necessary for the union of sperms and ovum (or eggs) inside the female body and the development of the baby in the mother's uterus.

Fertilisation

In human beings, internal fertilisation takes place. The sperms (or male gametes) made in the testes of man are introduced into the vagina of the woman through penis during copulation (or mating). In this way, millions of sperms are released into the vagina at one time. The sperms are highly active and mobile (moving). The sperms move up through cervix into the uterus. From uterus, the sperms pass into the oviducts (see Figure 69).

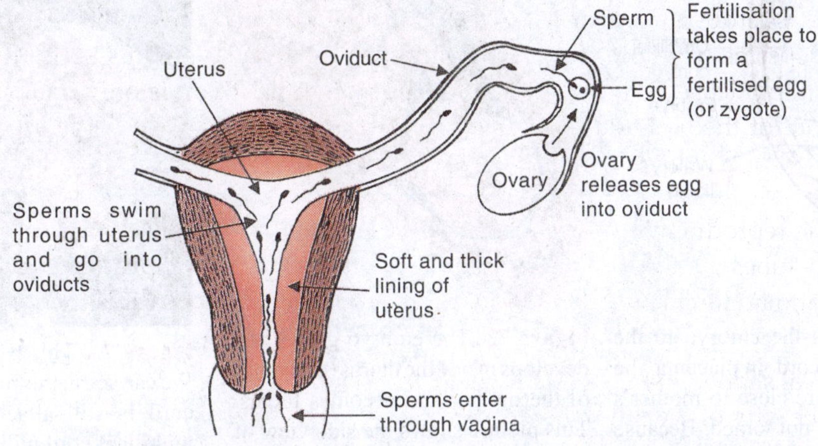

Figure 69. Fertilisation in human to form a zygote (fertilised egg).

One of the oviducts contains an ovum (or egg cell) released by the ovary during ovulation. Only one sperm fuses with the ovum (or egg) in the oviduct to form a zygote. This is called fertilisation. Thus, **the fertilisation of the ovum (or egg) takes place in the oviduct.**

Development of Embryo

When the ovum (or egg) is fertilised in the oviduct, then a zygote is formed. The zygote divides rapidly by mitosis as it moves down slowly in the oviduct and forms a hollow ball of hundreds of cells. This hollow ball of cells, now called an embryo, sinks into the soft and thick lining of the uterus and gets embedded in it (see Figure 70). **The embedding of embryo in the thick lining of the uterus is called implantation.**

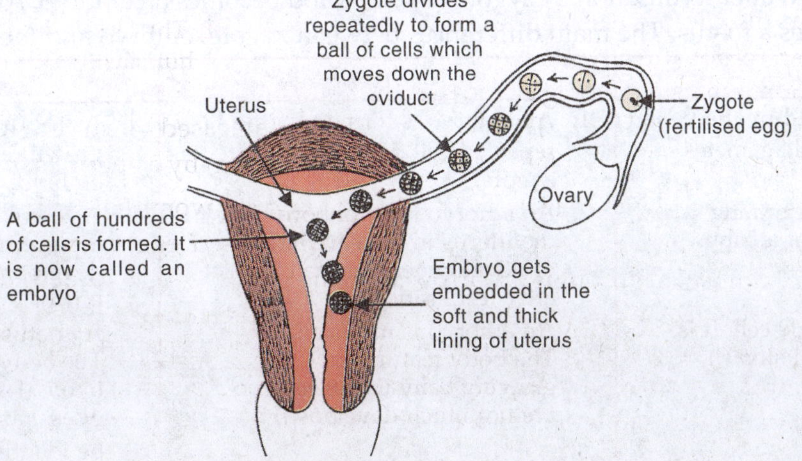

Figure 70. Implantation of embryo in the uterus.

After implantation, a disc-like special tissue develops between the uterus wall (called uterine wall) and the embryo (or foetus), which is called **placenta** (see Figure 71) (The foetus is connected to placenta in mother's body through umbilical cord). It is through the placenta that all the requirements of the developing foetus like nutrition, respiration, and excretion, etc., are met from the mother's body. In other words, **the exchange of nutrients, oxygen and waste products between the embryo and the mother takes place through the placenta.**

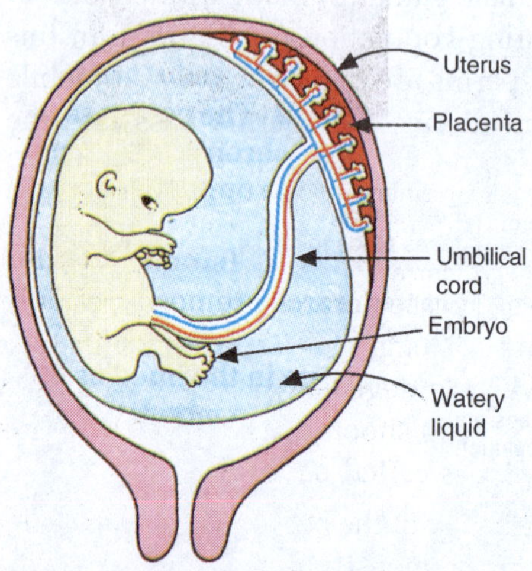

Figure 71. Placenta links the embryo to the mother through umbilical cord. In placenta, the embryo's blood vessels are close to mother's blood vessels but they are not joined. Because the two sets of blood vessels are close to each other, substances (like oxygen, nutrients and wastes) can pass between the two blood supplies.

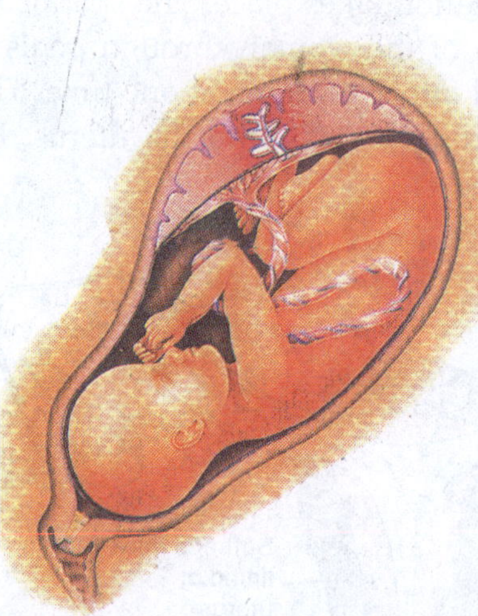

Figure 72. The embryo grows and develops inside the uterus (or womb) of the mother and becomes foetus. This picture shows the side view of developing foetus a few weeks before birth.

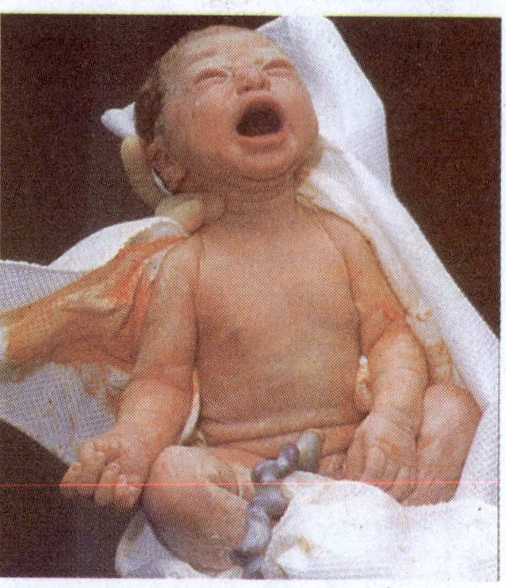

Figure 73. This baby has just been born. We can see in this picture that the umbilical cord is still attached to the baby. The umbilical cord will be just tied and cut to separate the new born baby from the mother.

The time period from the fertilisation up to the birth of the baby is called gestation. The average gestation period in humans (or the average duration of human pregnancy) is about nine months (or about 38 weeks). During the gestation period, the foetus grows to become a baby (see Figure 72). Birth begins when the strong muscles in the walls of the uterus start to contract rhythmically. The rhythmic contraction of uterus muscles gradually pushes the baby out of the mother's body through vagina. This is how a baby is born (see Figure 73). All of us were born from our mother in this way.

Differences Between Zygote, Embryo and Foetus

A zygote is formed after fertilisation. A zygote develops and becomes an embryo. And finally, an embryo develops and becomes a foetus. The main differences between zygote, embryo and foetus are given below :

Zygote	*Embryo*	*Foetus*
1. A zygote is formed by the fusion of male and female gametes (sperm and egg)	1. An embryo is formed by the repeated cell division of a zygote.	1. A foetus is formed by the growth and development of an embryo.
2. A zygote is the beginning of the formation of a baby.	2. An embryo is an unborn baby in the uterus in the early stages of development (up to 8 weeks after fertilisation)	2. A foetus is an unborn baby in the uterus in the later stages of development (after 8 weeks till birth).
3. A zygote is a single cell. It is smaller than a full stop (.)	3. An embryo is multicellular. The body features of growing baby in the embryo are not much developed.	3. A foetus is also multicellular. The body features of developing baby (like hands, legs, head, eyes and ears, etc.) can be identified.

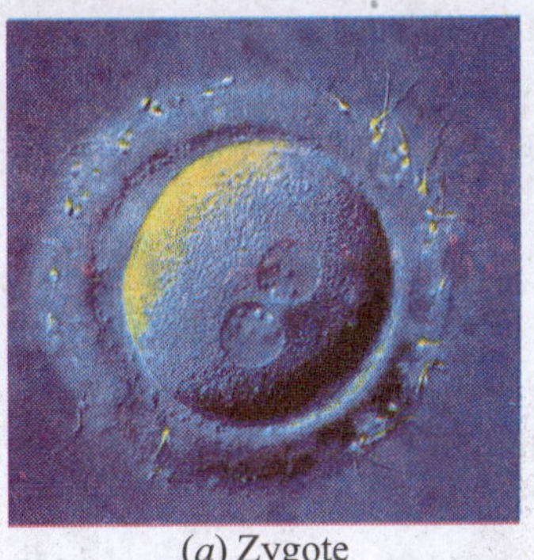
(*a*) Zygote

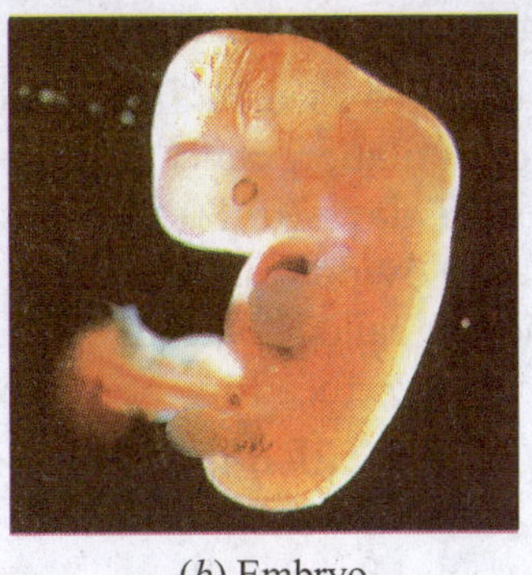
(*b*) Embryo

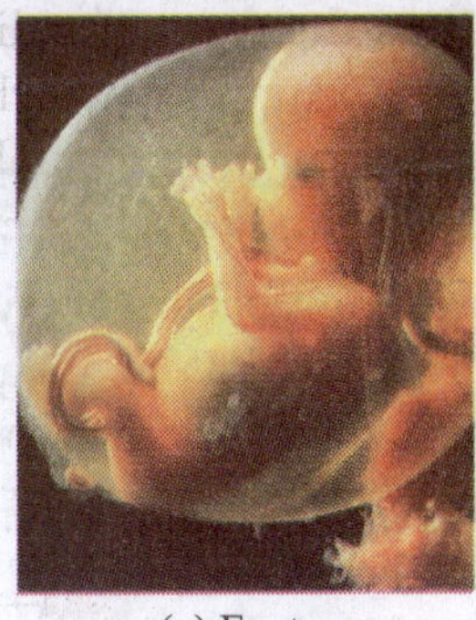
(*c*) Foetus

Figure 74. These pictures show the difference between a human zygote, an embryo and a foetus.

Sexual Cycle in Females : Menstruation

We will now describe the sexual cycle in human females (or women). Please note that when a girl child is born, her ovaries already contain many thousands of immature ova (or eggs) which are contained in immature follicles. When a girl reaches the age of puberty, then one follicle develops at a time to form a mature ovum (or egg). On maturing, the follicle bursts and the ovum (or egg) shoots out of the ovary. This is called ovulation. Thus, **the release of an ovum (or egg) from an ovary is called ovulation.**

In a normal, healthy girl (or woman), ovulation takes place on the 14th day of the beginning of menstrual cycle of 28 days. This means that ovulation takes place in the middle of the menstrual cycle (because 14th day is the middle of 28 days). **In human females (or girls), the ovaries start releasing ovum or egg (female gamete) once every 28 days from the age of puberty.** That is, in girls ovulation starts when they attain puberty. Please note that ovulation does not take place every day after puberty. It takes place after a period of every 28 days (which is almost once a month).

Before every ovulation, the inner lining of the uterus becomes thick and soft with lot of blood capillaries (or blood vessels) in it (see Figure 75). These changes in the uterus are necessary because in case the ovum (or egg) released by the ovary gets fertilised by the sperm, then the uterus has to keep this fertilised ovum

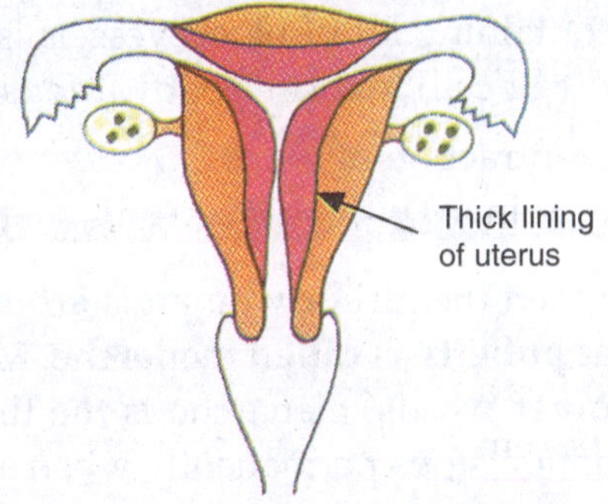

Figure 75. A thick lining grows in the uterus to receive the fertilised egg cell (if any).

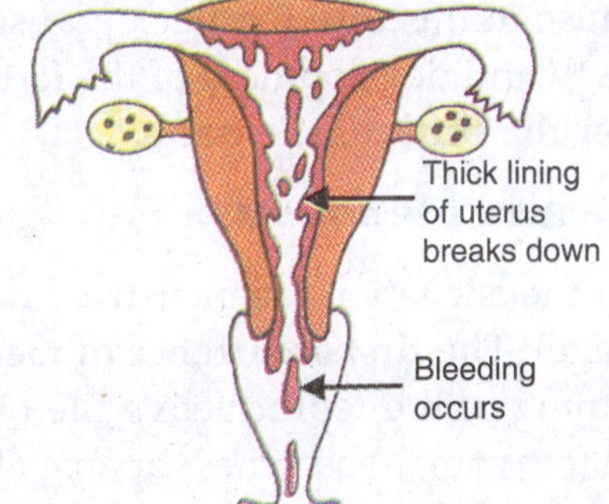

Figure 76. In case the egg cell is not fertilised, the thick uterus lining breaks down leading to bleeding. This is called menstruation (or periods).

(or egg) for further development and supply it with food and oxygen, etc., so that it may grow into a baby in due course of time. If, however, a sperm is not available at the time of ovulation, then fertilisation of ovum (or egg) does not take place. Since the ovum (or egg) is not fertilised, so the thick and soft uterus lining having lot of blood capillaries in it is not required. Thus, the unfertilised ovum (or egg) dies within a day and the uterus lining also breaks down. Since the thick and soft uterus lining contains a lot of blood vessels, so the breaking (or disintegration) of the uterus lining produces blood alongwith other tissues. This blood and other tissues come out of the vagina in the form of 'bleeding' (see Figure 76). We can now say that **the breakdown and removal of the inner, thick and soft lining of the uterus alongwith its blood**

vessels in the form of vaginal bleeding is called menstrual flow or menstruation.

Menstruation occurs if an ovum (or egg) released by the ovary of a woman does not get fertilised due to non-availability of sperm at the time of ovulation. Since the process of menstruation in a woman occurs again and again after a fixed period of 28 days (to 30 days), so it is also known as menstrual cycle. **Menstruation occurs every 28 days because ovulation (release of ovum or egg by ovary) occurs every 28 days.** In everyday language, menstruation is called 'periods'. We will now describe the menstruation (or menstrual cycle) point-wise which can be reproduced in the examination.

The sexual cycle in females (or women) is called menstruation or menstrual cycle. This is described below :

1. When a girl reaches puberty at the age of about 10 to 12 years, the sex hormones released into her blood cause some of the ova (or egg cells) in her ovaries to become mature (or ripe).
2. Usually one mature ovum (or egg) is released from the ovary into the oviduct once every 28 days. This is called ovulation.
3. Before ovulation (or release of ovum), the inner lining of uterus becomes thick and spongy, and full of tiny blood vessels (or blood capillaries), and prepares itself to receive the fertilised ovum or egg (in case it gets fertilised by sperm).
4. If the ovum (or egg) does not get fertilised (due to non-availability of sperm in the female body) then the thick and soft inner lining of uterus is no longer needed and hence it breaks. So, the thick and soft inner lining of uterus alongwith the blood vessels and the dead ovum (or egg) comes out of the vagina in the form of a bleeding called menstruation.
5. Menstruation usually occurs 14 days after ovulation and usually lasts for about 3 to 5 days.
6. After menstruation is over, the inner lining of the uterus starts building up again so that it may become ready to receive the next ovum (or egg) in case it gets fertilised.
7. If the ovum (or egg) does not get fertilised even now, then menstruation takes place again. This cycle of menstruation is repeated again and again in women after every 28 days (till the time ovum gets fertilised). **The menstrual cycle is controlled by hormones.**

Menstruation stops temporarily when the ovum (or egg) gets fertilised and the woman gets pregnant. This is because in this case the thick and soft lining of the uterus containing lot of blood vessels is needed for the growth and development of the fertilised ovum (or fertilised egg cell) to form a baby. **Menstruation restarts after the birth of the baby.**

Menarche and Menopause

The first menstruation (or menstrual flow) begins at puberty (when the girl or woman is around 10 to 12 years of age). **The first occurrence of menstruation (or periods) at puberty is called menarche**. Menarche is the beginning of the reproductive life of a girl (or woman). In other words, menarche is the time from which a girl (or woman) becomes capable of having a baby. Menstruation stops permanently when a woman reaches the age of about 45 to 50 years. With the permanent stoppage of menstruation, a woman loses her ability to bear children. She becomes infertile. **The permanent stoppage of menstruation (or periods) in a woman is called menopause.** Menopause occurs in women at the age of about 45 to 50 years. A woman stops ovulating at menopause and can no longer become pregnant. Menopause is the end of the reproductive life of a woman. We can now say that *the reproductive life of a woman starts at menarche and ends at menopause.*

BIRTH CONTROL

The population of our country is increasing rapidly day by day (see Figure 77). Though our country has sufficient food resources but still many people do not get sufficient food for their large families (having many children) due to poverty. So, every year it is becoming very difficult for our Government to provide sufficient food, adequate clothing, good housing and proper education to every citizen of the country. It is, therefore, very important for the couples (husbands and wives) who are in the reproductive stage of their lives to control the size of their families by having fewer children by practising family planning through birth control measures. Family planning enables a couple to decide on the number of children it wants to have and when to have them. If a couple has less number of children, it can provide good food, good clothes, and good education to each child. This will make the parents as well as the children happy. So, a **small family is a happy family** (see Figure 78). It should be noted that having fewer children also keeps the mother in good health. We should remember that to keep the size of our family small by having less number of children is in our own interest as well as in the interest of our Nation.

Figure 77. The population is increasing at a very rapid rate. We can see crowds of people everywhere.

Figure 78. A small family is a happy family. Having just one or two kids is the best option. Parents can then provide good food, good clothes and good education to each child.

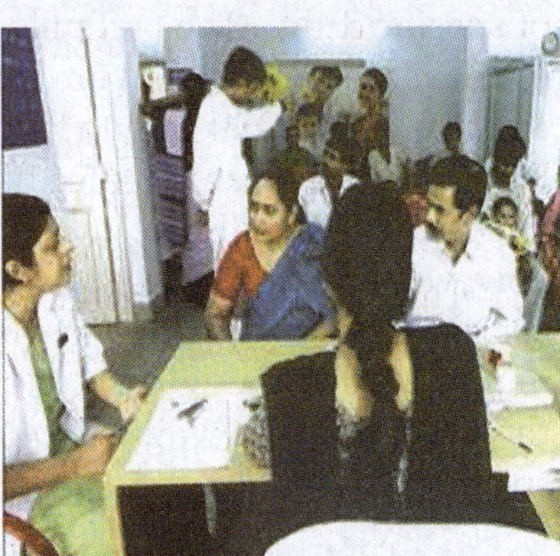

Figure 79. This is a Family Planning Centre where people can obtain free advice and contraceptive devices for the various birth control measures. Our Government has opened such Family Planning Centres throughout the country.

Family planning can be done by practising birth control measures. **Birth control can be done by preventing pregnancy in females (or women).** And pregnancy can be prevented by adopting a method or procedure by which sperms produced during copulation between man and his wife can be prevented from meeting the ovum (or egg) and fertilising it. It is possible to prevent fertilisation (and hence prevent pregnancy) because the ovum is available for fertilisation only for a short period. Since frequent pregnancies have a very bad effect on the mother's health, and also add to our already exploding population, so a number of techniques or methods have been developed to prevent pregnancies in women. We can call them birth control measures, family planning measures or population control measures. These are discussed below.

BIRTH CONTROL METHODS

The prevention of pregnancy in women (by preventing fertilisation) is called contraception. And any device or chemical (drug) which prevents pregnancy in woman is called a contraceptive. All the birth control methods can be broadly divided into three categories :

1. Barrier methods,
2. Chemical methods, and
3. Surgical methods.

We will now discuss all these methods of contraception (or preventing pregnancies) in women briefly.

1. Barrier Methods

In the barrier methods of preventing pregnancy, the physical devices such as condoms and diaphragm (or cap) are used. Condoms are used by males (by putting them as a covering on the penis). Condom is called *'nirodh'* in Hindi. Diaphragm (or cap) is used by females (by putting it in the vagina to cover the cervix). Condom as well as diaphragm prevent the sperms from meeting the ovum (or egg) by acting as a barrier between them. **An important benefit in the use of condom is that it protects a person from the sexually transmitted diseases such as gonorrhoea, syphilis and AIDS.** No other method of contraception provides protection against sexually transmitted diseases.

2. Chemical Methods

In the chemical methods of preventing pregnancy, the females use two types of pills : oral pills and vaginal pills, which are made of specific drugs. The oral pills contain hormones which stop the ovaries from releasing ovum (or eggs) into the oviduct. Oral pills are also called Oral Contraceptives (written in short as OC) (see Figure 80). This is a very effective method of preventing pregnancy so long as the pills are taken at the right time. Some women, however, do experience unpleasant side effects on taking oral pills because they change the hormonal balance in the body. So, it is important that the women on pills have regular check-ups with their doctor. The vaginal pills contain the chemicals called spermicides which kill the sperms.

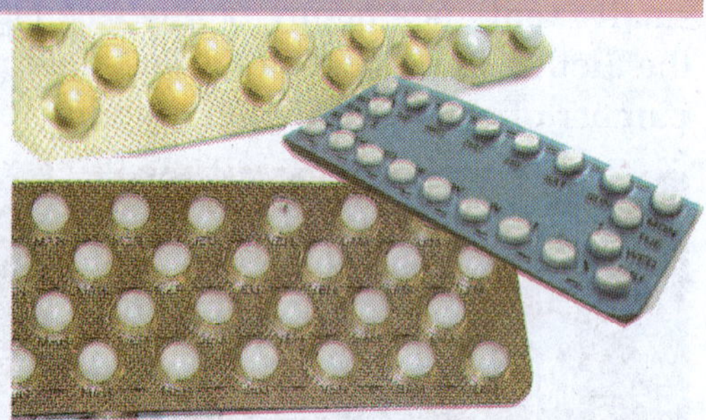

Figure 80. Some women choose Oral Pills as contraceptive for birth control. The oral contraceptive pills are popular in India by the name *Mala* D.

3. Intra-Uterine Contraceptive Device (IUCD)

The use of intrauterine contraceptive device called Copper-T is also very effective in preventing pregnancy. A Copper-T is placed inside the uterus by a doctor or a trained nurse. The IUCD or Copper-T prevents the implantation of fertilised egg in the uterus. If a woman uses a Copper-T as a method of contraception for avoiding unwanted pregnancies, then Copper-T cannot protect her from acquiring sexually transmitted diseases (if her partner has such a disease).

4. Surgical Methods

Surgical methods of birth control are available for males as well as females. In males, a small portion of the sperm duct (or vas deferens) is removed by surgical operation and both the cut ends are ligated (or tied) properly. This prevents the sperms from coming out. **The surgical procedure carried out in males is called 'vasectomy'.** In females, a small portion of the oviducts is removed by surgical operation and the cut ends are ligated (or tied). This prevents the ovum (or egg) from entering into the oviducts. **The surgical procedure carried out in females is called tubectomy.**

Stop Female Foeticide !

Surgical operations can also be used for the termination of pregnancies in women particulary after eight weeks of conception. Such surgical termination of pregnancy (or abortion) is allowed by law only in certain circumstances where the doctors decide that continuance of pregnancy can affect the health of mother or of unborn child gravely. Some people, however, misuse the technique of surgical termination of pregnancy for ulterior motive to get rid of female foetus (or unborn girl child). In order to have a male child (son), some misguided people in our country get the sex of their unborn child determined by ultrasound technique (though it is illegal to do so), and if it is a female foetus, they get it removed by surgery. This **killing of the unborn girl child is called female foeticide**. Female foeticide is reducing the number of girls drastically in some societies of our country.

Figure 81. Who knows today's girl child may become a great scientist, a famous doctor, a top class engineer, a dedicated administrative officer, a world renowned economist, a wonderful teacher or an unmatched world leader of tomorrow. Stop female foeticide ! Save the girl child.

For a healthy society, the male-female sex ratio must be maintained at almost the same level. Due to reckless female foeticide, the male-female child sex ratio is declining at an alarming rate in some sections of our society. This must be stopped immediately. Female foeticide is a matter of shame for the couples who go for it and also for the doctors who perform such surgical abortions (or rather murder the unborn girl child) for earning some quick money ! Let us not forget that our mother is a female, our sister is a female, and our wife is also a female. Then why not have a female as our daughter ? Remember, daughters are no less than sons. Our Government has already enacted laws to ban prenatal (before-birth) determination of sex of foetuses. These laws must be enforced strictly to save our society from the grave dangers of female foeticide in the long run. Let us not forget the words of Guru Nanak Dev Ji in praise of women (or females). He said *'so kyon manda aakhiye, jit jammein raajaan'* (why should we condemn women who have given birth to emperors of the world !).

Sexually Transmitted Diseases (STD)

The diseases which are spread by sexual contact with an infected person are called sexually transmitted diseases (or STD). Thus, a healthy person can get STD by making sexual contact with an infected person. Some of the common sexually transmitted diseases are :

(*i*) Gonorrhoea,

(*ii*) Syphilis, and

(*iii*) AIDS (Acquired Immune Deficiency Syndrome).

Gonorrhoea and syphilis are caused by bacteria. The bacteria which cause these diseases spread through sexual contact with an infected person. The most common symptoms of the these sexually transmitted

Figure 82. This is Human Immunodeficiency Virus (HIV). The white bood cells (WBCs) of a person destroy disease-causing bacteria and protect the health of a person. HIV infects white blood cells and destroys them gradually. This reduces the immunity (or resistance) of the body to fight diseases. Due to this, diseases which are normally quite mild can kill a person with HIV who develops AIDS disease.

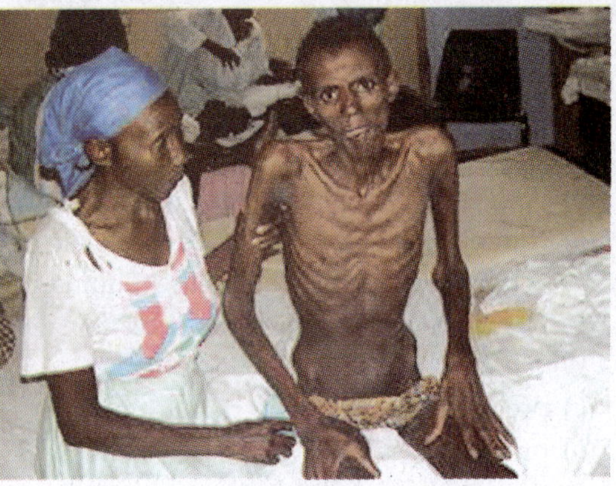

Figure 83. This person is suffering from AIDS disease caused by HIV. The immune system of this person has been damaged making his body so weak that it cannot protect itself against even common infections. This person is just waiting to die.

diseases are burning sensation at urination, passing of urethral discharge (containing pus) and sores in the genitals. Gonorrhoea and syphilis are curable diseases. AIDS disease is caused by a virus called HIV (Human Immunodeficiency Virus). AIDS damages the body's immune system so that the body becomes weak and cannot protect itself against infection. So, AIDS is a very dangerous disease which leads to death. No definite cure has been found for the AIDS disease so far. We are now in a position to **answer the following questions :**

Very Short Answer Type Questions

1. Where are a plant's sex organs located ?
2. What is the function of a flower ?
3. What are the reproductive organs in a flower ?
4. What is the name of :
   (*a*) male part of a flower ?
   (*b*) female part of a flower ?
5. What is the name of female organ of a flower (other than carpel) ?
6. What is the other name of sex cells ?
7. What is the name of sex cells (other than gametes) ?
8. Name the male and female gametes in animals.
9. Where is the male gamete formed :
   (*i*) in humans ?
   (*ii*) in flowering plants ?
10. Where is the female gamete formed :
    (*i*) in humans ?
    (*ii*) in flowering plants ?
11. Name two animals which undergo external fertilisation and two animals which undergo internal fertilisation ?
12. Define sexual reproduction.
13. Do all organisms give birth to individuals like humans ?
14. Write the full forms of the following as they occur in biology :
    (*i*) STD (*ii*) AIDS (*iii*) HIV
15. What is the causative organism for the following diseases ?
    (*i*) Gonorrhoea (*ii*) Syphilis (*iii*) AIDS
16. What are the organs in humans which produce the gametes ?
17. (*a*) What are the male sex cells in humans called ?
    (*b*) Name the organ which produces male sex cells.
18. (*a*) What are the female sex cells in humans called ?
    (*b*) Name the organ which produces female sex cells.
19. Which part of the human body :
    (*a*) produces sperms ?
    (*b*) produces ova ?
    (*c*) passes sperms from a man to a woman ?
20. (*a*) What do the testes in a man produce ?
    (*b*) What do the ovaries in a woman produce ?
21. (*a*) Where in the human body does an ovum get fertilised ?
    (*b*) Where does a fertilised ovum develop into a baby in the human body ?
22. Name the liquid that contains sperms.
23. What is the name of the process in which thickened uterus lining alongwith blood vessels is removed from the body of a human female through vaginal bleeding ?
24. (*a*) For how much time does menstruation last in human females (or women) ?
    (*b*) What is the frequency of menstrual cycle in human females (or women) ?
25. Fill in the following blanks with suitable words :
    (*a*) Pollen grains contain .... gametes of a plant.
    (*b*) Ovules contain .... gametes of a plant.
    (*c*) The ovary of a flower becomes .... after fertilisation.
    (*d*) The ovule becomes a .... after fertilisation.
    (*e*) Flowering plants reproduce by.................method of reproduction.
    (*f*) The female organ of reproduction in the flower is the..................

(*g*) The male organ of reproduction in the flower is the.................... .

(*h*) The name of the structure in the flower in which the male gamete is formed is............

(*i*) The................ at the base of the carpel contains egg cells.

(*j*) The term used to refer to the transfer of pollen from the stamen of one flower to the carpel of another flower of the same species is................

(*k*) The cells involved in sexual reproduction are called ....

(*l*) Fusion of gametes gives rise to a single cell called ....

(*m*) The process of fusion of gametes is called ....

(*n*) A multicellular animal starts its life from a .... through sexual reproduction.

(*o*) The union of a sperm nucleus with an egg nucleus is known as.................... and results in a ....egg.

(*p*) The menstrual cycle is controlled by.....................

Short Answer Type Questions

26. (*a*) What are gametes ?
(*b*) In which sort of reproduction are gametes involved ?
(*c*) What is formed when two gametes fuse ?
(*d*) What is this act of fusion called ?

27. (*a*) Write the names of (*a*) male sex hormone, and (*b*) female sex hormones.
(*b*) What name is given to the fusion of sperm and ovum ?
(*c*) Name the tissue through which the foetus gets all the requirements from the mother's body.

28. (*a*) Draw a neat sketch of the stamen of a flower. Mark in it filament and anther.
(*b*) Draw a neat sketch of the carpel of a flower. Mark in it stigma, style and ovary.
(*c*) What is made in (*i*) anther, and (*ii*) ovary, of a flower ?

29. (*a*) Explain the terms 'self pollination' and 'cross-pollination' ?
(*b*) How do the insects help in cross-pollination ?
(*c*) How is the process of pollination different from fertilization ?

30. (*a*) Explain the term 'fertilisation'.
(*b*) Give some examples of different modes of fertilisation in nature ?
(*c*) What type of fertilisation takes place in (*i*) fish, and (*ii*) birds ?

31. (*a*) What are the male and female gonads in human beings ? Mention their functions.
(*b*) State the advantages of sexual reproduction over asexual reproduction.

32. Describe the various steps involved in the sexual reproduction in animals. Draw labelled diagrams to show the fertilisation of an ovum (or egg) by a sperm to form a zygote.

33. Why does menstruation occur ? Describe the menstrual cycle in human females (or women).

34. (*a*) Write the various steps involved in the sexual reproduction in plants.
(*b*) Name two plants which reproduce by sexual reproduction method and two plants which reproduce by asexual reproduction methods.

35. (*a*) What type of plants reproduce by sexual reproduction method ?
(*b*) What is a seed ? What are the parts of a seed ? Explain with the help of a labelled diagram.

36. (*a*) What is puberty ? Who attains puberty at an earlier age in human beings : male or female (boy or girl) ?
(*b*) Mention two functions each of (*i*) human testes, and (*ii*) human ovaries.

37. (*a*) What is gestation period ? How much is the gestation period in humans ?
(*b*) Name one method of contraception which also protects against sexually transmitted diseases.
(*c*) Name one sexually transmitted disease for which no definite cure has been found so far. What is the causative organism of this disease ?

38. What are the three types of methods used for birth control (or regulating child birth) ? Give one example of each type.

39. (*a*) What is the name of surgical method of birth control in human males in which the sperm ducts are cut and ligated (tied) at both ends ?
(*b*) What is the name of surgical method of birth control in human females in which the oviducts are cut and ligated (tied) at both ends ?

(*c*) Name the contraceptive device used by the human males which acts as a sheath over the male organ and traps the sperms in it.

(*d*) Name the contraceptive device used by human females which is put over the cervix.

40. (*a*) Describe the surgical methods of birth control (*i*) for men, and (*ii*) for women.

(*b*) Name two devices used in the barrier method of birth control.

41. (*a*) What is meant by contraception ? What are the different methods of contraception ?

(*b*) What is done in the contraception method known as (*i*) vasectomy, and (*ii*) tubectomy ?

(*c*) If a woman is using copper-T for contraception, will it protect her from sexually transmitted diseases ?

42. (*a*) What are sexually transmitted diseases ? Give two examples of sexually transmitted diseases.

(*b*) Which method of contraception prevents fertilised egg from being implanted in the uterus ?

43. (*a*) What substances are contained (*i*) in oral pills, and (*ii*) in vaginal pills, used as contraceptives ? How do they work ?

(*b*) How does copper-T prevent pregnancy ?

(*c*) Name the disease caused by HIV.

44. (*a*) What is the name of surgical method of birth control (or preventing pregnancy) which is carried out (*i*) in men, and (*ii*) in women ?

(*b*) Name the part of a seed which (*i*) contains stored food (*ii*) grows into root, and (*iii*) grows into shoot.

45. Explain how, offsprings and parents of organisms reproducing sexually have the same number of chromosomes.

46. In tobacco plant, the male gametes have 24 chromosomes.

(*i*) What is the number of chromosomes in the female gamete ?

(*ii*) What is the number of chromosomes in the zygote ?

47. (*a*) What would be the ratio of chromosome number between an egg and its zygote ?

(*b*) Distinguish between a gamete and a zygote.

48. (*a*) Fertilisation in humans can occur only once in a month. Why ?

(*b*) What is the scientific name of (*i*) womb, and (*ii*) birth canal ?

49. The diagram shows female reproductive system. Name the parts labelled A to D.

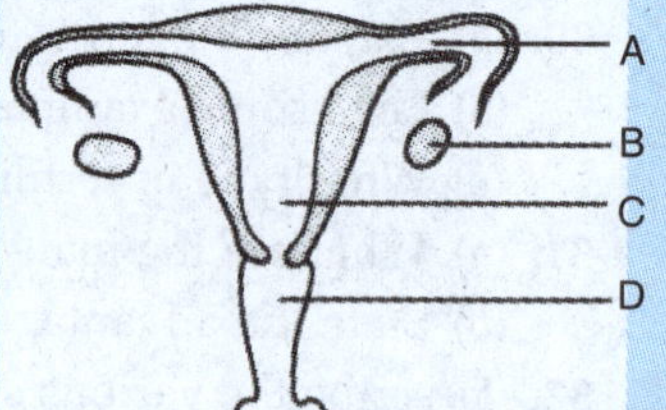

(*a*) In which part do the sperms enter ?

(*b*) Which part releases the egg ?

(*c*) In which part does fertilisation take place ?

(*d*) In which part does the foetus develop ?

50. Why is it an advantage for the testes to be situated in the scrotal sac outside the main body cavity ? Can you think of one disadvantage ?

51. Which structures in human female are equivalent to the following structures in the male ?

(*a*) testes (*b*) vas deferens (*c*) penis

In each case say in what respect the structures are equivalent ?

52. People who die from AIDS are not killed by the virus itself. Explain.

53. (*a*) What is the life support system of a fetus ?

(*b*) How long does a human baby take to develop before birth ?

(*c*) What is the name of the narrow opening between the uterus and the vagina.

Long Answer Type Questions

54. (*a*) What is meant by 'unisexual flowers' and 'bisexual flowers' ? Give two examples of each.

(*b*) What is pollination ? How does pollination occur ?

(*c*) Describe the process of fertilisation in a flower with the help of labelled diagrams.

(*d*) What changes take place in the flower after fertilisation which lead to the formation of seeds and fruit ?

55. (*a*) Draw a neat diagram of a flower showing its various parts. In this diagram mark stem, receptacle, sepals, petals, stamen and carpel.

(*b*) What name is given to (*i*) all the petals of a flower, and (*ii*) all the sepals of a flower ?

(*c*) What are (*i*) stamen, and (*ii*) carpel, in a flower?
(*d*) What is the other name of carpel of a flower ?
(*e*) What is the name of yellow powdery substance present in the anther of a flower ?

56. (*a*) What changes are seen in boys at the time of puberty ?
(*b*) Name the organs which produce sperms in human males.
(*c*) Draw a labelled diagram of the human male reproductive system. With the help of this diagram, describe the working of human male reproductive system ?
(*d*) What is the role of seminal vesicles and prostrate gland in human male reproductive system ?

57. (*a*) What changes are seen in girls at the time of puberty ?
(*b*) Name the organs which produce ova (or egg cells) in human females.
(*c*) Draw a labelled diagram of the human female reproductive system. With the help of this diagram, explain the working of human female reproductive system.
(*d*) Describe the process of fertilisation in humans and development of embryo briefly.

58. (*a*) What is ovulation ? How often does it happen in human females ?
(*b*) Where does fertilisation take place in human females ?
(*c*) Explain why, fertilisation is possible if mating takes place during the middle of menstrual cycle.
(*d*) What is meant by implantation ?
(*e*) What is placenta ? What is its function ?
(*f*) What joins embryo to placenta in mother's body ?

Multiple Choice Questions (MCQs)

59. The anther contains :
(*a*) sepals (*b*) ovules (*c*) carpel (*d*) pollen grains

60. Which of the following is not a part of the female reproductive system in human beings ?
(*a*) ovary (*b*) uterus (*c*) vas deferens (*d*) oviducts

61. One of the following is not a part of the human male reproductive system. This is :
(*a*) testis (*b*) oviduct (*c*) seminal vesicle (*d*) prostrate gland

62. Which of the following is not a sexually transmitted disease ?
(*a*) gonorrhoea (*b*) hepatitis (*c*) syphilis (*d*) AIDS

63. Which of the following method of contraception protects a person from acquiring a sexually transmitted disease ?
(*a*) oral pills (*b*) condom (*c*) copper-T (*d*) surgery

64. In which one of the following birth control methods, a small portion of oviducts of a woman is removed by surgical operation and the cut ends are ligated ?
(*a*) copper-T (*b*) tubectomy (*c*) vasectomy (*d*) diaphragm

65. One of the following is a surgical method which prevents the sperms from reaching the ovum and pregnancy does not occur. This method is :
(*a*) IUCD (*b*) vasectomy (*c*) condom (*d*) tubectomy

66. Fertilisation results immediately in the formation of :
(*a*) a zygote (*b*) an embryo (*c*) a placenta (*d*) a foetus

67. Which one of the following best describes the function of the umbilical cord ? It :
(*a*) feeds the embryo with digested substances.
(*b*) conveys nutrients and wastes to and from the embryo respectively
(*c*) removes waste matter from the embryo to the mother's blood.
(*d*) supplies oxygenated blood from the mother to the embryo.

68. The sexually transmitted disease which is caused by bacteria is :
(*a*) malaria (*d*) diarrhoea (*c*) gonorrhoea (*d*) AIDS

69. AIDS is a deadly disease which is caused by :
(*a*) a protozoan (*b*) a fungus (*c*) a bacterium (*d*) a virus

70. The advantage that internal fertilisation has over external fertilisation is that in internal fertilisation :
(*a*) new off-springs are exactly like the parent
(*b*) production of large numbers of gametes is unnecessary
(*c*) copulation and fusion of gametes is passive
(*d*) fewer individuals are produced

71. The figure given alongside shows the human male reproductive organs. Which structures make sperms and seminal fluid ? 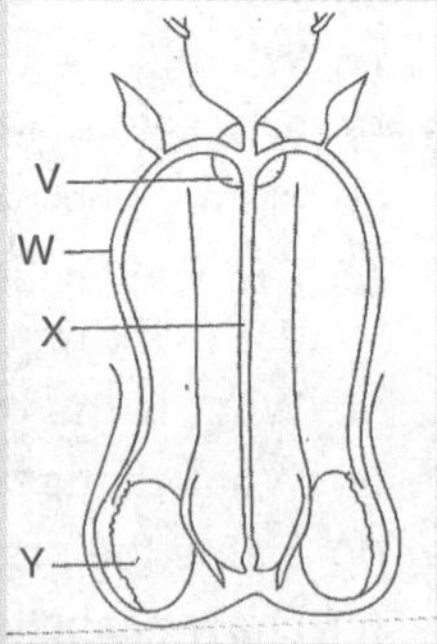
(*a*) V makes sperms and X makes seminal fluid
(*b*) W makes sperms and Y makes seminal fluid
(*c*) X makes sperms and W makes seminal fluid
(*d*) Y makes sperms and V makes seminal fluid

V
W
X
Y

72. In a flower, the parts that produce male and female gametes are respectively :
(*a*) sepal and anther (*b*) filament and stigma (*c*) anther and ovary (*d*) stamen and style

73. Which of the following is the correct sequence of events of sexual reproduction in a flower ?
(*a*) pollination, fertilisation, seed, embryo (*b*) seed, embryo, fertilisation, pollination
(*c*) pollination, fertilisation, embryo, seed (*d*) embryo, seed, pollination, fertilisation

74. The characteristics transmitted from parents to offspring are present in :
(*a*) cytoplasm (*b*) ribosome (*c*) golgi bodies (*d*) genes

75. Characters that are transmitted from parents to offspring during sexual reproduction show :
(*a*) only similarities with parents (*b*) only variations with parents
(*c*) both similarities and variations with parents (*d*) neither similarities nor variations with parents

76. The number of chromosomes in parents and offsprings of a particular species remains constant due to :
(*a*) doubling of chromosomes after zygote formation
(*b*) halving of chromosomes during gamete formation
(*c*) doubling of chromosomes after gamete formation
(*d*) halving of chromosomes after gamete formation

77. The length of pollen tube depends on the distance between :
(*a*) pollen grain and upper surface of stigma
(*b*) pollen grain on upper surface of stigma and ovule
(*c*) pollen grain in anther and upper surface of stigma
(*d*) upper surface of stigma and lower part of style

78. Which of the following statements are true for flowers ?
(*i*) flowers are always bisexual
(*ii*) they contain sexual reproductive organs
(*iii*) they are produced in all groups of plants
(*iv*) after fertilisation they give rise to fruits
(*a*) (*i*) and (*iv*) (*b*) (*ii*) and (*iii*) (*c*) (*i*) and (*iii*) (*d*) (*ii*) and (*iv*)

79. The correct sequence of organs in the male reproductive system for the transport of sperms is :
(*a*) testis ⟶ vas deferens ⟶ urethra
(*b*) testis ⟶ ureter ⟶ urethra
(*c*) testis ⟶ urethra ⟶ ureter
(*d*) testis ⟶ vas deferens ⟶ ureter

80. In human males, the testes lie in the scrotam outside the body because it helps in the :
(*a*) process of mating (*b*) formation of sperms (*c*) easy transfer of sperms (*d*) all the above

81. Which among the following are not the functions of testes at puberty ?
(*i*) formation of germ cells (*ii*) secretion of testosterone
(*iii*) development of placenta (*iv*) secretion of estrogen
(*a*) (*i*) and (*ii*) (*b*) (*i*) and (*iii*) (*c*) (*ii*) and (*iv*) (*d*) (*iii*) and (*iv*)

82. During adolescence, several changes occur in the human body. Mark one change from the following associated with sexual maturation in boys :
(*a*) loss of milk teeth (*b*) increase in height (*c*) cracking of voice (*d*) weight gain

83. In human females, an event that indicates the onset of reproductive phase is :
(*a*) growth of body (*b*) change in hair pattern (*c*) change in voice (*d*) menstruation

84. The offsprings formed as a result of sexual reproduction exhibit more variations because :
(*a*) sexual reproduction is lengthy process
(*b*) genetic material comes from two parents of different species
(*c*) genetic material comes from two parents of same species
(*d*) genetic material comes from many parents

85. One of the following occurs in the reproductive system of flowering plants as well as that of humans. This is :
(*a*) vas deferens (*b*) anther (*c*) ovary (*d*) style

86. Which among the following statements are true for unisexual flowers ?
(*i*) They possess both stamen and pistil
(*ii*) They possess either stamen or pistil
(*iii*) They exhibit cross pollination
(*iv*) Unisexual flowers possessing only stamens cannot produce fruits
(*a*) (*i*) and (*iv*) (*b*) (*ii*), (*iii*) and (*iv*) (*c*) (*ii*) and (*iii*) (*d*) (*i*), (*iii*) and (*iv*)

87. Which of the following statements are true for sexual reproduction in flowering plants ?
(*i*) it requires two types of gametes
(*ii*) fertilisation is a compulsory event
(*iii*) it always results in the formation of zygote
(*iv*) offsprings formed are clones
(*a*) (*i*) and (*iv*) (*b*) (*i*), (*ii*) and (*iv*) (*c*) (*i*), (*ii*) and (*iii*) (*d*) (*ii*), (*iii*) and (*iv*)

88. One of the following process does not lead to the formation of clones. This is :
(*a*) fission (*b*) fertilisation (*c*) fragmentation (*d*) tissue culture

89. In the figure given alongside, the parts marked A, B and C are sequentially :
(*a*) cotyledon, plumule and radicle
(*b*) plumule, radicle and cotyledon
(*c*) plumule, cotyledon and radicle
(*d*) radicle, cotyledon and plumule

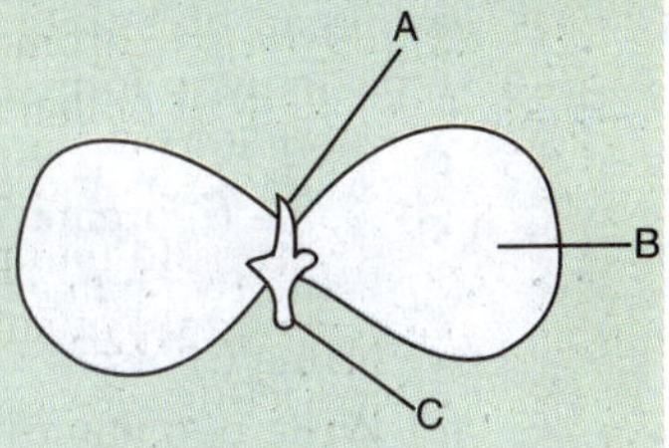

90. The correct sequence of reproductive stages occurring in flowering plants is :
(*a*) gametes, zygote, embryo, seed (*b*) zygote, gametes, embryo, seed
(*c*) seed, embryo, zygote, gametes (*d*) gametes, embryo, zygote, seed

91. The part of a seed which grows and develops into root on germination is :
(*a*) cotyledon (*b*) plumule (*c*) follicle (*d*) radicle

92. The male gametes in a flower and in a human are produced respectively in :
(*a*) stigma and ovary (*b*) anther and style (*c*) ovary and testes (*d*) anther and testes

93. The ratio of number of chromosomes in a human zygote and a human sperm is :
(*a*) 2 : 1 (*b*) 3 : 1 (*c*) 1 : 2 (*d*) 1 : 3

94. The normal body cell of an organism contains 28 pairs of chromosomes. The number of chromosomes present in its germ cell will be :
(*a*) 28 (*b*) 14 (*c*) 56 (*d*) 42

Questions Based on High Order Thinking Skills (HOTS)

95. The flask-shaped organ A at the centre of a flower is surrounded by a number of little stalks B having swollen tops which lie just inside the ring of petals.
(*a*) Name A. What are the various parts of A ?
(*b*) Which part of A contains gametes ?
(*c*) Name B. What is the swollen top of B known as ?

(*d*) What does the swollen top of B contain ?

(*e*) Out of A and B, which one is (*i*) male part, and (*ii*) female part of the flower ?

96. When an insect sits on the flower of a plant then some particles A present in the top of little stalks in the flower attach to its body hair. When this insect now sits on the flower of another similar plant, then particles A attached to the hair of insect are put on the top of a flask-shaped organ at the centre of flower. The particle A grows a long tube B from the top of flask-shaped organ through which C moves down and reaches the bottom part of flask-shaped organ. Here C fuses with the nucleus of D contained in structure E. The fusion of C and D forms a new cell F which grows and develops into a seed of the plant.

(*a*) What are particles A ? What is the process of transferring A from one flower to another flower of similar plant by the insect known as ?

(*b*) What is the name of tube B ?

(*c*) What is C which moves down through the tube B ?

(*d*) Name D and E.

(*e*) What is F ?

97. When a human female reaches a certain age then vaginal bleeding occurs for a few days after regular time intervals.

(*a*) What is this process known as (*i*) in scientific terms, and (*ii*) in everyday language ?

(*b*) At what approximate age this process starts in human females ? What is the human female said to have attained at this stage ?

(*c*) After how much time is this process repeated ? For how many days this process usually lasts ?

(*d*) What does the onset of this process in human females signify ?

(*e*) At which particular event in the life of a human female this process stops temporarily but starts again ?

(*f*) At which approximate age of human female this process stops permanently ?

98. X and Y are two human beings. The organ A in the reproductive system of X releases a mature gamete B once a month which goes into a tube-like structure C through a funnel-like opening. The organ D in the reproductive system of Y makes and releases gametes E which pass through a duct F and are introduced by an organ of Y, into the body of X. B and E fuse together in C to form a new cell G. The cell G divides repeatedly to form a ball of cells H which gets embedded in the lining of organ I of reproductive system of X where it grows and develops into a baby.

(*a*) Name (*i*) organ A, and (*ii*) gamete B.

(*b*) Write two names of tube-like structure C.

(*c*) Name (*i*) organ D, and (*ii*) gamete E.

(*d*) Write two names of duct F.

(*e*) Name (*i*) cell G (*ii*) ball of cells H, and (*iii*) organ I.

(*f*) Out of X and Y, which one is (*i*) male, and (*ii*) female ?

99. When a fertilised egg E formed in the oviduct of a human female divides repeatedly to form an embryo, the embryo gets implanted in the thick and soft lining of the uterus. After this a disc-like special tissue T develops between the uterus wall and embryo through which all the requirements of the developing embryo (and foetus) are met from the mother's body. The embryo is connected to the tissue T through a string like structure S.

(*a*) What is the other name of fertilised egg cell E ?

(*b*) What is the name of tissue T ?

(*c*) Name the string-like structure S .

(*d*) Name two substances which pass from mother's blood to embryo through tissue T and, one type of substance which passes from embryo to mother's blood.

(*e*) What happens to S when the baby is born ? Why ?

100. When a female child is born, her ovaries already contain thousands of immature eggs (or ova) contained in immature structures A. On maturing, A bursts open and an egg shoots out of the ovary in a process called B. The process B starts in the females at puberty and occurs again and again after a time period x. Before every occurrence of process B, the inner lining of uterus becomes thick and soft with lots of blood vessels in it. When the egg cell gets fertilised by a sperm, then an event C occurs in the life of mature human female which lasts for time period y leading to the birth of baby. If, however, the egg cell released by the ovary does not get a sperm to fuse with, then the thick and soft inner lining of uterus breaks down and comes out of the female's body in an event called D. The occurrence of event D is controlled by chemical substances E.

(*a*) What are A ?
(*b*) What is process B ?
(*c*) What is the time period x ?
(*d*) Name the event C.
(*e*) How much is the time period y ?
(*f*) What is the name of process D ?
(*g*) Name the chemical substances E.

101. In the surgical method of birth control available for males, the structures A in the reproductive system are cut and ligated (tied up) at both ends. This prevents the reproductive cells B from coming out from the organs C where they are made in the male body. Since B cannot come out from the male body, they cannot fuse with cell D in the body of a female and hence pregnancy is prevented.

(*a*) What are structures A ?
(*b*) What are cells B ?
(*c*) Name the organs C.
(*d*) What is cell D ?
(*e*) What is the name of this surgical procedure for birth control available to males ?

102. In the surgical method of birth control available for human females, the structures P in the reproductive system are cut and ligated (tied up) properly at both ends. This prevents the reproductive cell Q released by an organ R from entering the structures P so that Q is not available to fuse with another reproductive cell S coming from the male reproductive system. In this way, pregnancy is prevented.

(*a*) What are structures P ?
(*b*) What is cell Q ?
(*c*) Name the organ R.
(*d*) What is the reproductive cell S ?
(*e*) What is the name of this surgical method of birth control available to females ?

103. The human males use a device X made of a very thin rubber sheet as a covering on the male organ to prevent pregnancy. This device traps the gametes Y in it. In order to prevent pregnancy, the human females use a device Z which is a circle of rubber with a metal spring around it. The device Z is put inside the vagina to cover the cervix. It stops Y from going into the uterus.

(*a*) What is device X ?
(*b*) What are Y ?
(*c*) Name the device Z.
(*d*) What is the general name of these methods of birth control (or preventing pregnancy) ?
(*e*) The use of which contraceptive device, X or Z, can protect the persons from sexually transmitted diseases ?

104. A woman uses pills A as a method of birth control (or preventing pregnancy). The pills A stop the ovaries from releasing ovum into oviducts. Another woman uses pills B as a method of birth control. The pills B kill the sperms and prevent pregnancy.

(*a*) What do the pills A contain ?
(*b*) What is the common name of pills A ?
(*c*) What do the pills B contain ?
(*d*) What is the common name of pills B ?
(*e*) What is the general name of these methods of birth control ?

105. A woman uses a device X made of a common metal for preventing pregnancy. This device works by preventing the implantation of fertilised egg cell (or embryo) in the female organ Y.

(*a*) What are the two names of device X ?
(*b*) Name the organ Y.
(*c*) Can this method of contraception protect a woman from acquiring a STD ?

106. A, B and C are three common STDs. A and C are caused by bacteria whereas B is caused by a virus D. The virus D reduces the immunity of the infected person to such a low level that the person can die of even very mild diseases.

(*a*) What could A and C be ?

(*b*) What is B ?

(*c*) Name the virus D ?

(*d*) How can A, B and C be caused ?

(*e*) Out of A, B and C, which one does not have a definite cure as yet ?

107. The germ cell A produced by a person X is round in shape and it fuses with another germ cell B having a long tail and produced by a person Y. The fusion of A and B produces a new cell C. The cell C divides repeatedly and grows inside the organ D of person X to form E in which the body features of the unborn baby are not much developed. E grows further to form F in which the various body features of the unborn baby (like hands, legs, head, eyes, and ears, etc.) can be identified. F grows further and ultimately forms a baby. What are A, B, C, D, E and F ? Out of the two persons X and Y, which one is male and which one female ?

108. Explain why, a human zygote is more likely to grow into an adult than a frog zygote.

109. In a bisexual flower, inspite of the young stamens being removed artificially, the flower produces fruit. Explain.

110. In what ways is fertilisation in a plant :

(*a*) similar to fertilisation in a human ?

(*b*) different from fertilisation in a human ?

ANSWERS

1. In flowers **5.** Pistil **6.** Gametes **7.** Germ cells **9.** (*i*) Testes (*ii*) Anther **10.** (*i*) Ovary (*ii*) Ovary **11.** External fertilisation : Frog and Fish ; Internal fertilisation : Dogs and Cows **13.** No **15.** (*i*) Bacteria (*ii*) Bacteria (*iii*) Virus **19.** (*a*) Testes (*b*) Ovaries (*c*) Penis **21.** (*a*) Oviduct (or Fallopian tube) (*b*) Uterus (or Womb) **22.** Semen **23.** Menstruation **24.** (*a*) 3 to 5 days (*b*) Once every 28 days **25.** (*a*) male (*b*) female (*c*) fruit (*d*) seed (*e*) sexual (*f*) carpel (*g*) stamen (*h*) anther (*i*) ovary (*j*) cross-pollination (*k*) gametes (*l*) zygote (*m*) fertilisation (*n*) single cell (zygote) (*o*) fertilisation ; fertilised (*p*) hormones **27.** (*c*) Placenta **28.** (*c*) (*i*) Male gametes (inside pollens) (*ii*) Female gametes (inside ovules) **29.** (*c*) In pollination, the pollens (containing male gametes) are transferred from anther to stigma of carpel ; In fertilisation, the male gamete fuses with the female gamete present in ovule inside the ovary of flower to form a fertilised egg or zygote **30.** (*c*) (*i*) External fertilisation (*ii*) Internal fertilisation **34.** (*b*) Sexual reproduction : Wheat plant and Sunflower plant ; Asexual reproduction : Ferns and Mosses **35.** (*a*) Flowering plants **37.** (*b*) Use of condom (*c*) AIDS, Virus (HIV) **39.** (*a*) Vasectomy (*b*) Tubectomy (*c*) Condom (*d*) Diaphragm (or Cap) **41.** (*c*) No **42.** (*b*) IUCD (or Copper-T) **43.** (*c*) AIDS **44.** (*a*) (*i*) Vasectomy (*ii*) Tubectomy (*b*) (*i*) Cotyledons (*ii*) Radicle (*iii*) Plumule **45.** Reduction division (meiosis) during gamete formation halves the number of chromosomes in both male and female gametes. Since male and female gametes fuse during fertilisastion, the original number of chromosomes (as in the parent) is restored in the offspring **46.** (*i*) 24 (*ii*) 48 **47.** (*a*) 1 : 2 (*b*) Gamete represents the sex cell or germ cell in sexual reproduction and it is of two types : male gamete and female gamete ; Zygote is the product of fertilisation in which a male gamete and a female gamete fuse with each other **48.** (*a*) Because ovulation takes place once every month, that is, an egg is released once every month by ovary **49.** A is oviduct (or fallopian tube) ; B is ovary ; C is uterus (or womb) ; D is vagina (*a*) Part D (vagina) (*b*) Part B (ovary) (*c*) Part A (oviduct) (*d*) Part C (uterus) **50.** Because the formation of sperms requires a lower temperature than the normal body temperature which is possible due to testes being outside the main body cavity ; Being outside the main body cavity, testes are more prone to injury **51.** (*a*) Ovaries in female ; Both make gametes (*b*) Oviducts in female ; Both transport gametes (*c*) Vagina in female ; Penis discharges sperms and vagina receives sperms **53.** (*a*) Placenta (*b*) About nine months (*c*) Cervix **59.** (*d*) **60.** (*c*) **61.** (*b*) **62.** (*b*) **63.** (*b*) **64.** (*b*) **65.** (*b*) **66.** (*a*) **67.** (*b*) **68.** (c) **69.** (*d*) **70.** (*d*) **71.** (*d*) **72.** (*c*) **73.** (*c*) **74.** (*d*) **75.** (*c*) **76.** (*b*) **77.** (*b*) **78.** (*d*) **79.** (*a*) **80.** (*b*) **81.** (*d*) **82.** (*c*) **83.** (*d*) **84.** (*c*) **85.** (*c*) **86.** (*b*) **87.** (*c*) **88.** (*b*) **89.** (*c*) **90.** (*a*) **91.** (*d*) **92.** (*d*) **93.** (*a*) **94.** (*a*) **95.** (*a*) A is carpel (or pistil) ; Stigma, Style and Ovary (*b*) Ovary (*c*) B is stamen ; Anther (*d*) Pollen grains (*e*) (*i*) B (*ii*) A **96.** (*a*)A are pollen grains ; Cross-pollination (*b*) Pollen tube (*c*) C is male gamete (*d*) D is female gamete (ovum or egg) ; E is ovule (*e*) F is fertilised egg (zygote) **97.** (*a*) (*i*) Menstruation (*ii*) Periods (*b*) 10 to 12 years ; Puberty (*c*) 28 days ; About 3 to 5 days (*d*) That the reproductive system of human female has started working (*e*) Beginning of pregnancy (*f*) About 45 to 50 years **98.** (*a*) (*i*) Ovary (*ii*) Ovum (or Egg) (*b*) Fallopian tube ; Oviduct (*c*) (*i*) Testis (*ii*) Sperm (*d*) Sperm duct ; Vas deferens (*e*) (*i*) Zygote (Fertilised egg) (*ii*) Embryo (*iii*) Uterus (or Womb) (*f*) (*i*) Y is male (*ii*) X is female **99.** (*a*) Zygote (*b*) Placenta (*c*) Umbilical cord (*d*) From mother's blood to embryo : Oxygen and Nutrients ; From embryo to mother's blood : Wastes (*e*) S (umbilical cord) is tied and then cut ; To separate the new born baby from the mother **100.** (*a*) Follicles (*b*) Ovulation (*c*) 28 days (*d*) Conception (or Pregnancy) (*e*) About nine months (*f*) Menstruation (*g*) Hormones **101.** (*a*) Sperm ducts (or Vas deferens) (*b*) Sperms (*c*) Testes (*d*) Egg cell (or Ovum) (*e*) Vasectomy **102.** (*a*) Oviducts (or Fallopian tubes) (*b*) Ovum (or Egg cell) (*c*) Ovary (*d*) Sperms (*e*) Tubectomy **103.** (*a*) Condom (*b*) Sperms (*c*) Diaphragm (or Cap) (*d*) Barrier methods (*e*) X **104.** (*a*) Hormones (*b*) Oral pills (*c*) Spermicides (*d*) Vaginal pills (*e*) Chemical methods **105.** (*a*) Copper-T and IUCD (*b*) Uterus (or Womb) (*c*) No **106.** (*a*) Syphilis and Gonorrhoea (*b*) AIDS (*c*) HIV (*d*) By sexual contact with an infected person (*e*) B (AIDS) **107.** A is ovum (or egg cell); B is sperm ; C is zygote (fertilised egg) ; D is uterus ; E is embryo ; F is foetus; Y is male ; X is female **108.** The human zygote grows inside the uterus of mother so it can grow safely into an adult. On the other hand , a frog zygote grows in the water of pond or stream where it is very unsafe because it may be eaten up by other aquatic animals **109.** Though stamens have been removed but the female organ 'carpel' of the flower is intact. Cross-pollination has occurred in this flower leading to the formation of fruit **110.** (*a*) Similarities : (*i*) The fusion of gametes occurs in the female part in a plant as well as in a human (*ii*) the male gamete moves (or is moved) to the female gamete in a plant as well as in a human (*iii*) A zygote is produced which develops into an embryo in a plant as well as in a human (*b*) Differences : (*i*) There is pollination in a plant but copulation (or mating) in a human to bring the male and female gametes together (*ii*) There is no equivalent in a plant to the oviducts in a human (*iii*) In a human, the male gametes (sperms) swim but in a plant self-fertilisation is possible (The fertilisation of a plant with its own pollen is called self-fertilisation)

Heredity and Evolution

A recognisable feature of a human being (or any other organism) like height, complexion, shape of hair, colour of eyes, and shape of nose and chin, etc, are called 'characters' or 'traits'. **The transmission of characters (or traits) from the parents to their offsprings is called heredity.** In most simple terms, heredity means continuity of features from one generation to the next.

Two parents, a male and a female, are involved in sexual reproduction. The sexually reproducing organisms produce sex cells or gametes. The male gamete called sperm fuses with a female gamete called ovum (or egg) to form a zygote which gradually develops into a young one (or offspring), showing some

(*a*) Male parent (Father)

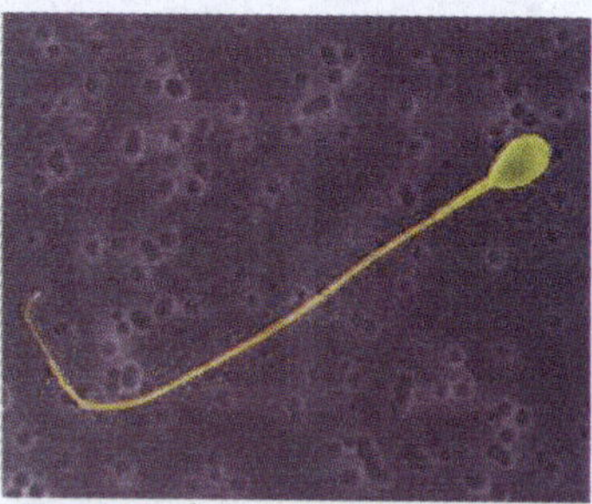

(*b*) Male gamete (male sex cell or sperm)

(*c*) Female parent (Mother)

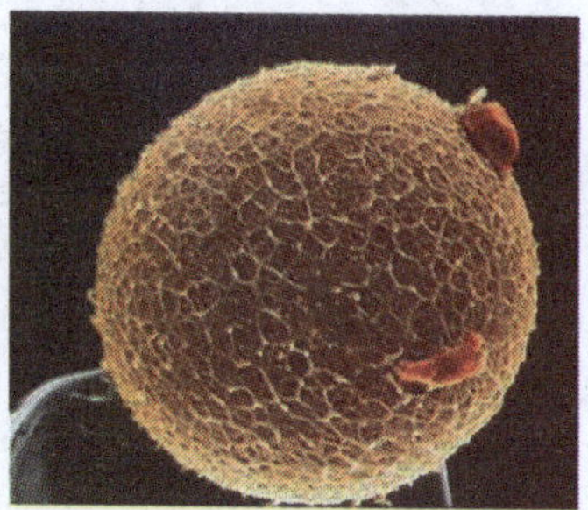

(*d*) Female gamete (female sex cell or ovum or egg)

Figure 1. The heredity information is present on the gametes (or sex cells) of the parents. So, gametes constitute the link between one generation and the next and pass on parents' traits to their children.

similarities with the parents. Actually, **the hereditary information is present in the sex cells (or gametes) of the parents. Thus, gametes constitute the link between one generation and the next, and pass on the paternal (father's) and maternal (mother's) characters or traits to the offspring.** This relation that continues to exist between successive generations is referred to as heredity.

Variations

Although the offsprings inherit the characters (or traits) of the parents and resemble them very closely, but the resemblance is not complete in all respects. The offsprings are never a true copy of the parents. In fact, no two individuals are exactly alike and the members of any one species differ from one another in some characters (or traits) or the other. These differences are known as variations. So, from the biological point of view, variation is the occurrence of differences among the individuals of a species. For example, people have different heights. Their complexion, type of hair, colour of eyes, shape of nose and shape of chin also show differences. **The differences in the characters (or traits) among the individuals of a species is called variation.** For example, human height is a trait which shows variation. This is because some people are very tall, some are less tall, some have medium height, some have short height whereas others are very short.

Here is another example of variations in human beings which involves our ears. The lowest part of our ear is called earlobe. **In most of the people, the earlobe is 'hanging' and it is called free earlobe** [see Figure 2(*a*)]. **In some people, however, the earlobe is closely attached to the side of the head and it is called attached earlobe** [see Figure 2(*b*)]. Thus, most people have free earlobes whereas some people have attached earlobes. So, **the free earlobes and attached earlobes are the two variations found in human population.**

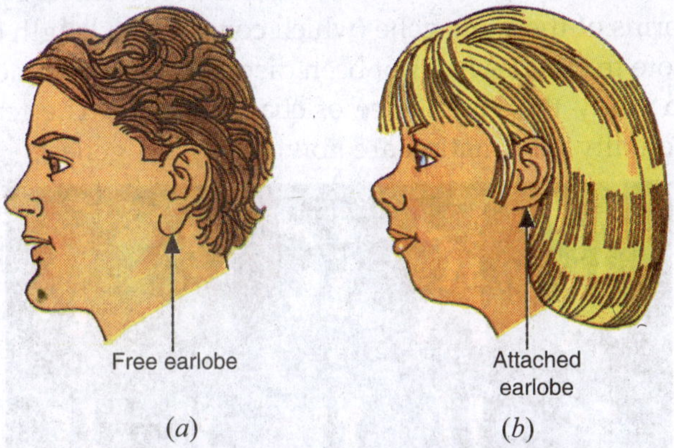

Figure 2. Free earlobe or attached earlobe is a variation found in human population.

Some amount of variations is produced even during asexual reproduction but it is very small. The number of variations produced during sexual reproduction is, however, very large. For example, the sugar cane plants reproduce by the process of asexual reproduction, so if we observe a field of sugar cane, we will find very little variations in various sugar cane plants. All the sugar cane plants almost look alike. But in animals (including human beings) which reproduce by the process of sexual reproduction, a large number of variations are produced. It is due to these variations that no two human beings look alike (except identical twins). From this discussion we conclude that the number of successful variations is maximised by the process of sexual reproduction. **The variation is a necessity for organic evolution.**

Accumulation of Variations

The reproduction of organisms produces variations. The variations produced in organisms during successive generations get accumulated in the organisms. **The significance of a variation shows up only if it continues to be inherited by the offspring for several generations.** This will become clear from the following example. Suppose a bacterium produces two bacteria by asexual reproduction. Again suppose that one of the offspring bacterium has a variation due to which it can tolerate a little higher temperature (or little more heat) than the other one. Now, this variation of little more heat resistance will go on accumulating in the offsprings of successive generations of this bacterium. And this will ultimately give rise to a variant of bacteria which will be highly heat resistant and able to survive even at very high temperatures.

The great advantage of variation to a species is that it increases the chances of its survival in a changing environment. For example, the accumulation of 'heat resistant' variation (or trait) in some bacteria will ensure its survival even when the temperature in its environment rises too much due to a heat wave or some other reasons. On the other hand, the bacteria which did not have this variation to withstand heat would not survive under these circumstances and die.

Before we describe Mendel's experiments for explaining the transmission of characteristics (or traits) from parents to their offsprings or progeny, we should know the meaning of some terms such as chromosome, gene, dominant gene, recessive gene, genotype, phenotype, F_1 generation and F_2 generation. These are described on the next page.

Chromosome is a thread-like structure in the nucleus of a cell formed of DNA which carries the genes (see Figure 3). Different organisms have different number of chromosomes in their nuclei. **A gene is a unit of DNA on a chromosome which governs the synthesis of one protein that controls a specific characteristic (or trait) of an organism** (see Figure 4). There are thousands of genes on a chromosome which control various characteristics of an organism. **Genes are actually units of heredity which transfer characteristics (or traits) from parents to their offsprings during reproduction.** Genes work in pairs. In diagrams and in explanations of heredity, genes are represented by letters. Genes controlling the same characteristics are given the same letters. For example, the gene for tallness is represented by the letter T whereas the gene for dwarfness is represented by the letter t. The letters T and t actually represent two forms of the same gene (which controls the length of an organism, say the length of stem of a plant). Please note that genes had not been discovered at the time when Mendel conducted his experiments on pea plants to study the inheritance of characteristics. The term 'factors' which were used by Mendel as carriers of heredity information are now known as 'genes'.

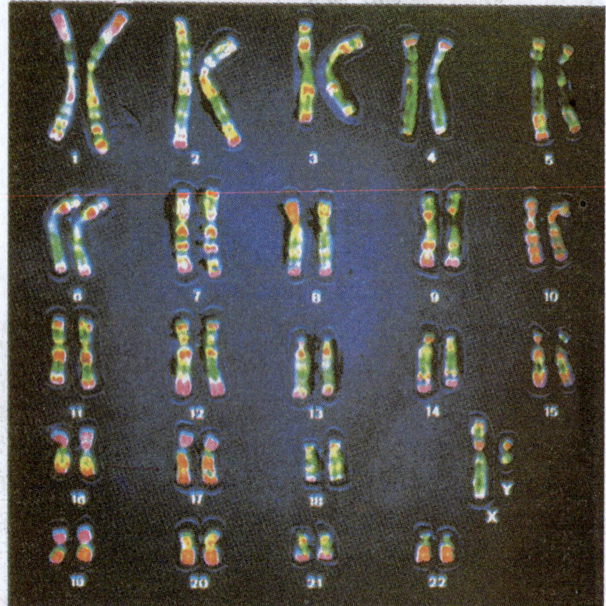

Figure 3. This is a full set of chromosomes present in a human cell. A normal cell of human body contains 23 pairs of chromosomes. 22 pairs of chromosomes match in males and females but 23rd pair is different. X and Y are the sex chromosomes in a male (as shown above) but a female has two X chromosomes.

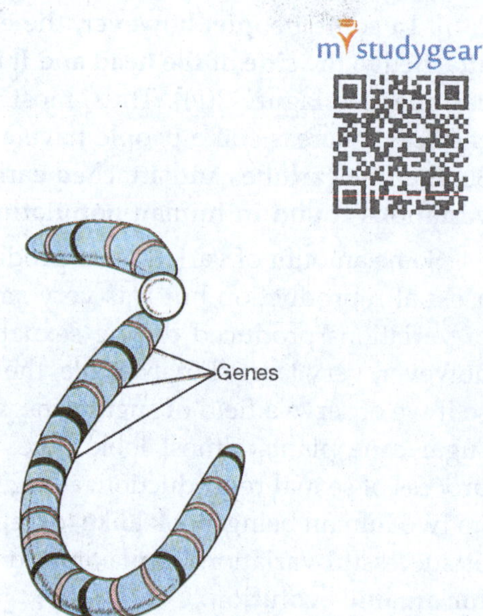

Figure 4. Every chromosome has small parts called genes. Genes control the development of inherited characteristics such as hair colour, eye colour and skin colour, etc, in humans.

Genes for controlling the same characteristic of an organism can be of two types : dominant or recessive. **The gene which decides the appearance of an organism even in the presence of an alternative gene is known as a dominant gene.** It dominates the recessive gene for the same characteristic on the other chromosome of the pair. **The gene which can decide the appearance of an organism only in the presence of another identical gene is called a recessive gene.** A single recessive gene cannot decide the appearance of an organism. **The dominant gene is represented by a capital letter and the corresponding recessive gene is represented by the corresponding small letter.** For example, in pea plants, the dominant gene for tallness is T and the recessive gene for dwarfness is t. Thus, when we write the genetic cross for pea plant, then the capital 'T' represents 'tall' and small 't' represents 'dwarf'.

Genotype shows the genetic constitution of an organism. In simple words, **genotype is the description of genes present in an organism.** Genotype is always a pair of letters such as TT, Tt or tt (where T and t are the different forms of the same gene). Thus, the genotype of a tall plant could be TT or Tt whereas that of

Figure 5. This picture shows a tall pea plant on the left side and a short pea plant on the right side. The genes present in the tall plant are TT or Tt whereas the genes present in the short plant (or dwarf plant) are tt.

Figure 6. This picture shows red and white flowered Busy Lizzie plants. Just like other characteristics of plants (like tallness or dwarfness, etc.) the colour of flowers is also controlled by genes.

a dwarf plant is tt. **The characteristic (or trait) which is visible in an organism is called its phenotype.** For example, being 'tall' or 'dwarf' (short) are phenotypes of a plant because these traits can be seen by us or they are visible to us. The phenotype of an organism is actually its physical characteristic which is determined by its genotype. For example, genotype TT or Tt results in a tall phenotype and the genotype tt results in a dwarf phenotype.

Figure 7. Gregor Mendel : The first scientist to make a systematic study of heredity. He is known as the Father of Genetics.

When two parents cross (or breed) to produce progeny (or offsprings), then their progeny is called first filial generation or F_1 generation (where F stands for Filial which denotes progeny of a cross). **When the first generation progeny cross (or breed) among themselves to produce second generation progeny, then this progeny is called second filial generation or F_2 generation.** In other words, the generation produced by crossing two F_1 progeny is called F_2 generation. An example will make it more clear. Mother and father are parental generation. Their children are F_1 generation, and the grandchildren are F_2 generation.

Gregor Mendel was the first scientist to make a systematic study of patterns of inheritance which involved the transfer of characteristics from parents to progeny (see Figure 7). He did this by using different varieties of pea plants (*Pisum sativum*) which he grew in his garden. Some of the characteristics (or traits) of the pea plants whose transmission to progeny was investigated by Mendel were height of pea plant or length of stem of pea plant (tall or dwarf), shape of seeds (round or wrinkled) and colour of seeds (yellow or green) (see Figure 8). A yet another contrasting characteristics (or traits) investigated were colours of flowers (white or violet).

Mendel chose pea plants for studying inheritance because pea plants had a number of clear cut differences which were easy to tell apart. For example, some pea plants were *'tall'* (having long stem) whereas others were *'dwarf'* (having short stem). Some pea plants produced *round-yellow* seeds whereas others produced *wrinkled-green* seeds, etc. Another reason for choosing pea plants was that they were *self pollinating* (which enabled them to produce next generation of plants easily). And finally, Mendel chose pea

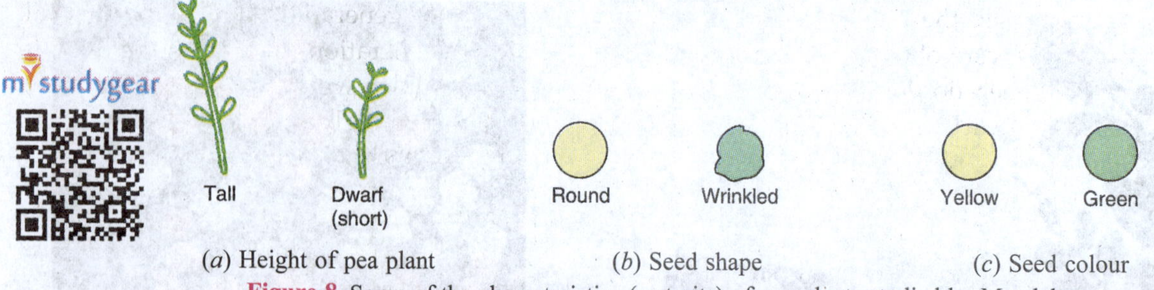

Figure 8. Some of the characteristics (or traits) of pea plants studied by Mendel.

plants to study inheritance (and not animals including human beings) because many generations of pea plants can be produced in a comparatively short time span and their study is much simpler than that of animals.

A new form of plant resulting from a cross (or breeding) of different varieties of a plant is known as a hybrid. When we breed two pea plants having one contrasting characteristic each (or one trait each) to obtain new plants, then it is called a monohybrid cross. **In monohybrid cross we will study the inheritance of one pair of contrasting characteristics 'tallness' and 'dwarfness' of the pea plants by their first generation and second generation progeny.** On the other hand, if we breed two pea plants having two contrasting characteristics each (or two traits each) to obtain new plants, then it is called a dihybrid cross. **In the dihybrid cross we will study the inheritance of two pairs of contrasting characteristics of pea plants such as round-yellow seeds and wrinkled-green seeds.**

RULES FOR THE INHERITANCE OF TRAITS : MENDEL'S CONTRIBUTION

Inheritance is the transmission of genetically controlled characteristics (or traits) from one generation to the next. We will now describe how Mendel studied the inheritance of characters or traits in various generations of pea plants cultivated by him. First we will discuss 'monohybrid inheritance' which concerns the inheritance of a single characteristic (or single trait) such as plant height. After that we will describe the dihybrid inheritance which involves the inheritance of two characteristics (or two traits) such as seed shape and seed colour.

1. Monohybrid Inheritance and the Law of Segregation

In order to trace the inheritance of a single pair of contrasting characteristics among the pea plants (like tall stem and short stem), Mendel crossed (cross-bred) the pure-bred pea plants differing in these traits and noted their occurrence in the progeny of succeeding generations.

(*i*) Mendel first crossed pure-bred tall pea plants with pure-bred dwarf pea plants and found that only tall pea plants were produced in the first generation or F_1 generation (see Figure 9). No dwarf pea plants (or short pea plants) were obtained in the first generation of progeny. From this Mendel concluded that

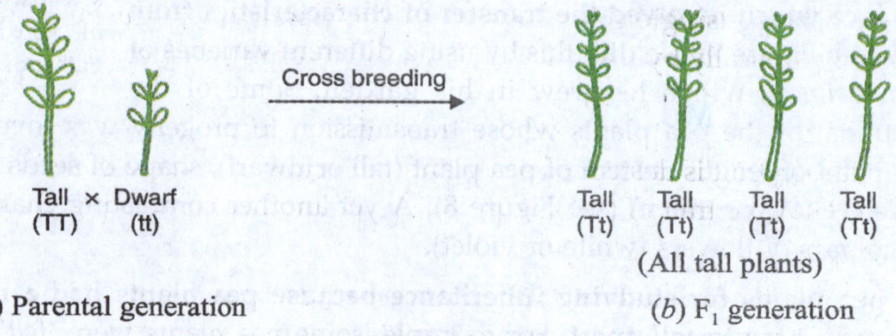

Figure 9. A cross of pure-bred tall and dwarf pea plants.

the first generation (or F_1 cross) showed the traits of only one of the parent plants : tallness. The trait of other parent plant, dwarfness, did not show up in the progeny of first generation.

(*ii*) Mendel then crossed the tall pea plants of the first generation (F_1 generation) and found that tall plants and dwarf plants were obtained in the second generation (or F_2 generation) in the ratio of 3 : 1. In other words in the F_2 generation, three-fourth plants were tall and one-fourth were dwarf (see Figure 10). Mendel noted that the dwarf trait of the parent pea plant which had seemingly disappeared in the first

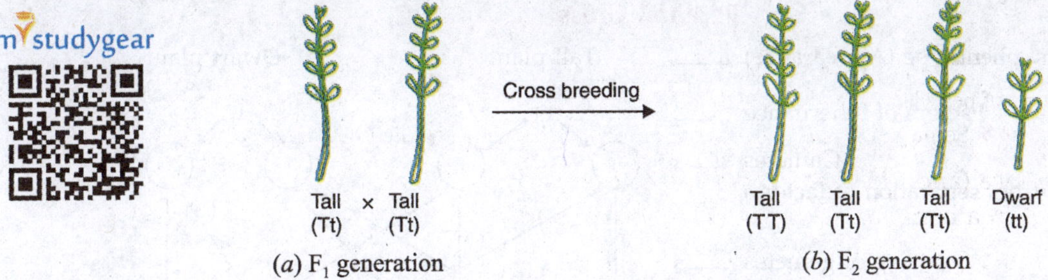

Figure 10. A cross of tall plants of F_1 generation produces tall and dwarf plants in the ratio of 3 :1.

generation progeny, reappeared in the second generation. Mendel said that the trait of dwarfness of one of the parent pea plant had not been lost, it was merely concealed or supressed in the first generation to re-emerge in the second generation. **Mendel called the repressed trait of 'dwarfness' as 'recessive trait' and the expressed trait of 'tallness' as the 'dominant trait'.** In this way, Mendel's experiments with tall and dwarf pea plants showed that the traits may be *dominant* or *recessive*.

Mendel also noted that all the pea plants produced from the hybrid tall parents of F_1 generation, were either tall or dwarf. There were no plants with intermediate height (or medium height) in-between the tall and dwarf plants. In this way, Mendel's experiment showed that the traits (like tallness and dwarfness) are inherited independently. This is because if the traits of tallness or dwarfness had blended (or mixed up), then medium sized pea plants would have been produced.

Out of a total 1064 pea plants of F_2 generation, Mendel found that there were 787 tall pea plants and 277 dwarf pea plants. The ratio of tall plants to dwarf plants comes to be 787 : 277 = 2.84 : 1, which is approximately equal to 3 : 1. Thus, a yet another result obtained from Mendel's monohybrid inheritance experiment is that the ratio of tall plants to dwarf plants in the F_2 generation is 3 : 1. Since tallness is a dominant trait and dwarfness is a recessive trait, so we can also say that the contrasting progeny in the F_2 generation occur in the ratio of 3 dominant to 1 recessive. **The ratio 3 : 1 is known as the monohybrid ratio.**

The results of monohybrid cross enabled Mendel to formulate his first law of inheritance which is called the law of segregation. **According to Mendel's first law of inheritance : The characteristics (or traits) of an organism are determined by internal 'factors' which occur in pairs. Only one of a pair of such factors can be present in a single gamete.** We will now explain the results of monohybrid cross of tall and dwarf pea plants theoretically by using Mendel's first law of inheritance.

Explanation of Results of Monohybrid Inheritance

(*i*) Mendel said that each trait is determined by a pair of 'factors'. This means that the pure-bred tall pea plant has two factors TT for the trait of tallness, and the pure-bred dwarf pea plant also has two factors tt for the trait of dwarfness.

(*ii*) The factors of inheritance of tallness TT separate into two gametes T and T, and the factors for inheritance of dwarfness tt separate into two other gametes t and t (The traits are transmitted to progeny through these gametes).

(*iii*) The gametes of tall pea plant then cross with the gametes of the dwarf pea plant by the process of fertilisation to form zygotes which then produce various progeny in the F_1 generation (or first generation) which consists of all tall plants. Thus, the F_1 generation possesses one factor of inheritance from each parent plant which were carried in gametes. The parental cross is shown clearly in the following chart :

Parental Cross

Parents' phenotype (Appearance) ⟶ Tall plant × Dwarf plant

Factors of inheritance ⟶ TT tt

Gametes (Formed from separation of factors) ⟶ T T t t

Crossing of gametes during fertilisation ⟶

F_1 generation genotype ⟶ Tt Tt Tt Tt

F_1 generation phenotype ⟶ Tall Tall Tall Tall

(All tall plants)

In the F_1 generation shown above, all the progeny plants have factors Tt in which T is the factor for tallness which is a dominant trait. Since all the plants in the F_1 generation have the factors Tt, so all of them are tall. **The small letter t represents recessive trait of dwarfness, which does not show up in first generation in the presence of dominant trait T.**

(*iv*) When two hybrid, tall pea plants (Tt) produced in the first generation (F_1) are now cross-bred with each other, then they will produce second generation (F_2) pea plants. This again happens by the separation of factors of inheritance of these tall plants into individual gametes and then crossing of the gametes during fertilisation as shown below :

F_1 Cross

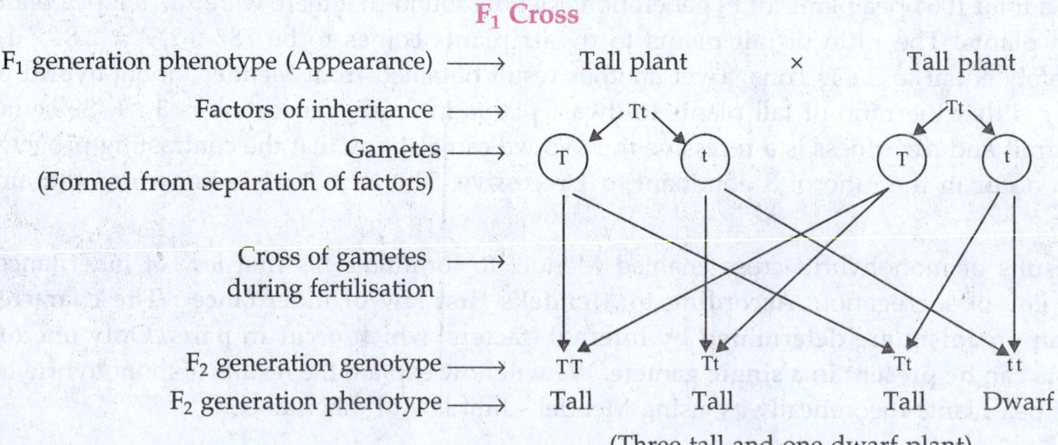

(Three tall and one dwarf plant)

We can see from the above chart that in the F_2 generation (or second generation), the pea plants produced have genotype or inheritance factors TT, Tt, Tt and tt. Now, the plants having genotype TT, Tt and Tt all contain the factor T for dominant trait 'tallness', so all the three plants (TT, Tt and Tt) are tall. The plant having the genotype tt has both factors t for the recessive trait 'dwarfness', so it is a dwarf plant. **Please note that though a single copy of factor T is enough to make a plant tall but both copies of factor t (that is tt) are necessary to make a plant dwarf (or short).**

In the F_2 generation, we get 1 plant having genotype TT, 2 plants having genotype Tt and 1 plant having genotype tt. So, the genotypic ratio in monohydrid cross will be :

$$TT : Tt : tt = 1 : 2 : 1$$

Again, in the F_2 generation, we get 3 tall plants and 1 dwarf plant, so the phenotypic ratio in monohybrid cross will be :

Tall plants : Dwarf plants = 3 : 1

This result is the same as that obtained by Mendel through experiments.

mystudygear

2. Dihybrid Inheritance and the Law of Independent Assortment

Dihybrid inheritance involves the inheritance of two pairs of contrasting characteristics (or contrasting traits) at the same time. **The two pairs of contrasting characteristics chosen by Mendel were shape and colour of seeds : round-yellow seeds, and wrinkled-green seeds** (see Figures 11 and 12). In order to trace the inheritance of two pairs of contrasting traits, Mendel crossed pea plants having round-yellow seeds with pea plants having wrinkled-green seeds and noted their occurrence in the succeeding generations of pea plants. Mendel made the following observations :

Figure 11. Round-yellow pea seeds.

Figure 12. Wrinkled-green pea seeds.

(*i*) Mendel first crossed pure-bred pea plants having round-yellow seeds with pure-bred pea plants having wrinkled-green seeds and found that only round-yellow seeds were produced in the first generation. No wrinkled-green seeds were obtained in the F_1 generation. From this it was concluded that **round shape and yellow colour of the seeds were dominant traits over the wrinkled shape and green colour of the seeds.**

(*ii*) When the F_1 generation pea plants having round-yellow seeds were cross-bred by self pollination, then four types of seeds having different combinations of shape and colour were obtained in second generation or F_2 generation. These were **round-yellow, round-green, wrinkled-yellow and wrinkled-green seeds**. Mendel collected a total of 556 F_2 seeds and counted them shape wise and colour wise. He got the following result :

Round-yellow seeds	315
Round-green seeds	108
Wrinkled-yellow seeds	101
Wrinkled-green seeds	32

The phenotypic ratio of different type of seeds can be written as :

Round yellow seeds : Round green seeds : Wrinkled yellow seeds : Wrinkled green seeds = 315 : 108 : 101 : 32

= 9 : 3 : 3 : 1

Thus, **the ratio of each phenotype (or appearance) of the seeds in the F_2 generation is 9 : 3 : 3 : 1.** This is known as the **dihybrid ratio.**

Mendel observed that he had started with two combinations of characteristics in seeds : round-yellow and wrinkled-green, and two new combinations of characteristics had appeared in the F_2 generation : round-green and wrinkled-yellow (see Figure 13). On the basis of this observation, Mendel concluded that though the two pairs of original characteristics (seed shape and colour) combine in the F_1 generation but they separate and behave independently in subsequent generations.

The results of dihybrid cross enabled Mendel to formulate his second law of inheritance which is called the law of independent assortment. **According to Mendel's second law of inheritance : In the inheritance**

(a) Round-yellow pea seeds

(b) Wrinkled-green pea seeds

(c) Round-green pea seeds

(d) Wrinkled-yellow pea seeds

Figure 13. Mendel started with round-yellow and wrinkled green pea seeds and found that two new combinations of characteristics, round-green and wrinkled yellow seeds, appeared in the F_2 generation.

of more than one pair of traits in a cross simultaneously, the factors responsible for each pair of traits are distributed independently to the gametes.

Explanation of Results of Dihybrid Inheritance

In the dihybrid cross, the parent plants having the phenotype round-yellow seeds have the factors of inheritance or gene combination RRYY (in which RR are the dominant genes for round shape whereas YY are the dominant genes for yellow colour). On the other hand, the parent plants having the phenotype wrinkled-green seeds have the factors of inheritance or gene combination rryy (in which rr are the recessive genes for wrinkled shape and yy are the recessive genes for green colour). Keeping these points in mind, we can now show the dihybrid cross by drawing a chart as we did in the case of a monohybrid cross. The chart showing the dihybrid cross between pea plants having round-yellow seeds and wrinkled-green seeds is given below.

Figure 14. RRYY are the factors of inheritance or genes for the round-yellow seeds (these are dominant genes). On the other hand, rryy are the factors of inheritance or genes for the wrinkled-green seeds (which are recessive genes).

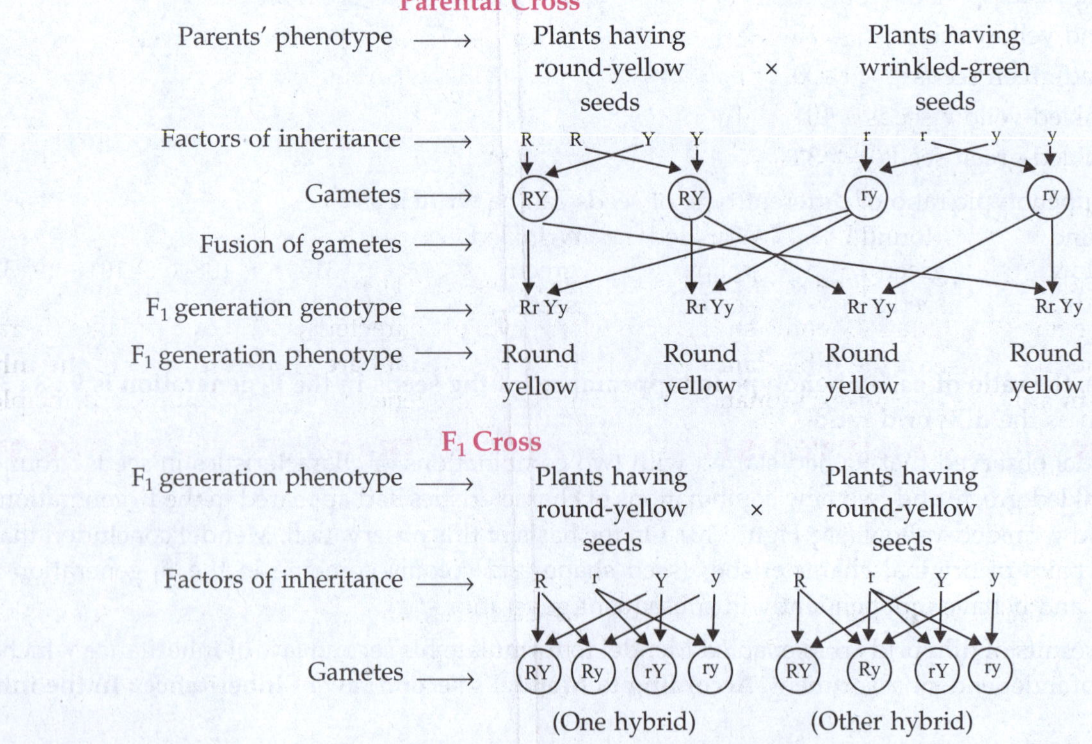

Fusion of gametes (shown in the table) →

Gametes from other hybrid ↓ / Gametes from one hybrid →	(RY)	(Ry)	(rY)	(ry)
(RY)	RRYY Round yellow	RRYy Round yellow	RrYY Round yellow	RrYy Round yellow
(Ry)	RRYy Round yellow	RRyy Round green	RrYy Round yellow	Rryy Round green
(rY)	RrYY Round yellow	RrYy Round yellow	rrYY Wrinkled yellow	rrYy Wrinkled yellow
(ry)	RrYy Round yellow	Rryy Round green	rrYy Wrinkled yellow	rryy Wrinkled green

F_2 ratio : Round-yellow = 9 ; Round-green = 3
Wrinkled-yellow = 3 ; Wrinkled-green = 1

This result is the same as that obtained by Mendel through experiments.

An amazing thing about Mendel's work is that he worked out the underlying rules of inheritance before any knowledge of DNA, chromosomes or genes became available. Let us answer one question now.

Sample Problem. (*a*) What do the progeny of a tall plant with round seeds and a short plant with wrinkled seeds look like ? Why ?

(*b*) What happens when the F_1 progeny obtained above are used to produce F_2 progeny by self pollination ?

Answer. (*a*) The progeny of a *tall* plant having *round* seeds crossed with *short* plants having wrinkled seeds are all *tall* plants having *round* seeds. This is because 'tallness' and 'round shape' of seeds are dominant traits. On the other hand, 'shortness' and 'wrinkled shape' of seeds are recessive traits.

(*b*) When F_1 progeny are cross-bred by self-pollination, then we will get four types of progeny in the F_2 generation. Of these four types of progeny, two types will have traits like parents and the other two will have new combinations of traits. Thus,

(*i*) Some F_2 progeny will be *tall* plants with *round* seeds (9).

(*ii*) Some F_2 progeny will be *tall* plants with *wrinkled* seeds (3).

(*iii*) Some F_2 progeny will be *short* plants with *round* seeds (3).

(*iv*) Some F_2 progeny will be *short* plants with *wrinkled* seeds (1).

Please note that though Mendel studied the inheritance of characteristics by using plants (or rather pea plants) but **the rules for the inheritance of traits given by Mendel are also applicable to the inheritance of traits in animals (including human beings)**. Thus, human genetic follows Mendelian principles.

HOW ARE CHARACTERISTICS (OR TRAITS) TRANSMITTED TO PROGENY

Genes are responsible for the characteristic features (or traits) of an organism : plant or animal. **The characteristics or traits of parents are transmitted to their progeny (offsprings) through genes present on their chromosomes during the process of sexual reproduction**. This happens as follows.

Genes work in pairs. There is a pair of genes for each characteristic of an organism (one is dominant gene and the other is recessive gene). Each parent possesses a pair of genes for each characteristic on a pair of chromosomes. However, each parent passes only one of the two genes of the pair for each characteristic to its progeny through gametes. Thus, the male gamete and female gamete carry one gene for each characteristic from the gene pairs of parents (which are located on the pair of chromosomes). But when a male gamete fuses with a female gamete during fertilisation, they make a new cell called zygote with a full set of genes (on a full set of chromosomes). This zygote grows and develops to form a new organism having characteristics (or traits) from both the parents which it has inherited through genes.

The two genes (or pair of genes) responsible for a particular characteristic are always present on the corresponding positions of the pair of chromosomes. For example, in Figure 15 the two genes for the same characteristic (length of plant stem), are present on the corresponding positions of the pair of chromosomes. One gene of the pair is for 'tallness' and the other is for 'dwarfness'. **Please note that though the progeny inherits two genes (or a pair of genes) for each trait from its parents but the trait shown by the progeny depends on which inherited gene is dominant of the two.** For example, if a pea plant progeny (or hybrid) inherits the gene for tallness (T) from one parent and the gene for dwarfness (t) from the other parent, then it will show the trait of 'tallness' and become a tall plant because the gene for tallness is dominant over the gene for dwarfness. So, although the gene for dwarfness (t) is present in all the cells of the hybrid plants, it does not show its effect (because it is a recessive gene). If , however, both the parent plants pass on one copy each of the recessive gene for dwarfness (t) making the genotype (tt), then the traits of dwarfness will appear in the progeny plant.

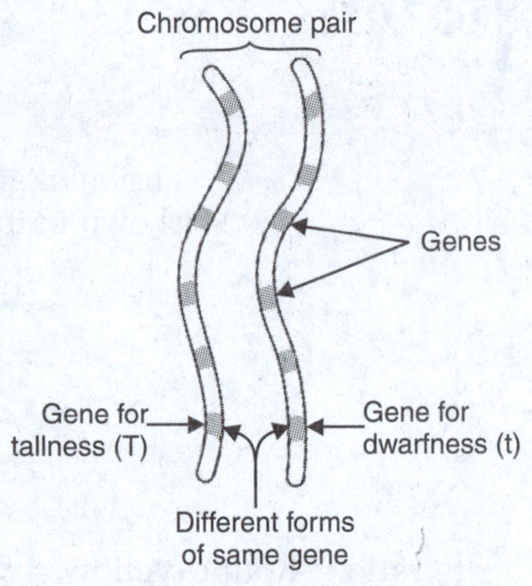

Figure 15. Genes work in pairs.

Please note that the genes for 'tallness' and 'dwarfness' are not to be considered two different genes. They are just the two forms of the same gene which controls only one characteristic feature of a plant : length of its stem. But there can be increase in length of stem making the plant tall or decrease in the length of stem, making the plant dwarf.

How do Genes Control the Characteristics (or Traits)

A gene is the section of DNA on a chromosome which codes for the formation of a protein controlling a specific characteristic (or trait) of the organism. Suppose a plant progeny has gene for the characteristic called 'tallness'. Now, the gene for tallness will give instructions to the plant cells to make a lot of plant growth hormones. And due to the formation of excess of plant growth hormones, the plant will grow too much and hence become tall. On the other hand, if the plant has the gene set for dwarfness, then less plant growth hormones will be produced due to which the plant will grow less, remain short and hence become a dwarf plant.

Just like plants, the characteristics (or traits) in animals (including human beings) are also transmitted from the parents through genes by the process of sexual reproduction. We will now give an example of the transmission of colour of hair from the parents (father and mother) to the child. Before we do that please keep in mind that **black hair is a phenotype produced by the genotype HH or Hh**. On the other hand, **blonde hair (pale yellow hair) is a phenotype produced by the genotype hh**. Let us give the example now.

A mother has black hair, the father has blonde hair (pale yellow hair), and the child has black hair (see Figures 16, 17 and 18). This can be explained on the basis of transmission of genes for 'hair colour' from the mother and father to the child as follows : Mother's cell contain two genes HH for black hair. Both the genes HH are dominant genes, so the mother has black hair (see Figure 16). Father's cells contain two genes (hh) for blonde hair. The two genes hh are recessive genes, so the father has blonde hair (or pale yellow hair) (see Figure 17). Now, during the process of reproduction, the mother transmits one of the dominant genes H for black hair to the child and the father transmits one of his recessive genes h for blonde hair to the child. Due to this, the child has the genes Hh for her hair. Now, the gene H for black hair

Figure 16. Mother's cells contain two dominant genes HH for black hair, so she has black hair.

Figure 17. Father's cells contain two recessive genes hh for blonde hair, so he has blonde hair.

Figure 18. Child has one dominant gene H for black hair (from mother) and one recessive gene h for blonde hair (from father), so her genotype is Hh and phenotype is black hair.

is the dominant gene but the gene h for blonde hair is the recessive gene. The dominant gene H for black hair shows its effect due to which the child has black hair (see Figure 18). The recessive gene h for blonde hair cannot show its effect in the presence of dominant gene H for black hair. *Please note that the genes which dominate other genes are called dominant genes, and the genes which get dominated are called recessive genes.*

We will now describe the inheritance of blood groups by the children from their parents. Please note that the gene which controls the blood groups is represented by the letter I. This gene has three different forms (called alleles) which are represented as I^A, I^B and I^O.

How Blood Groups are Inherited

A person has one of the four blood groups : A, B, AB or O. This blood group system is controlled by a gene which has three different forms denoted by the symbols I^A, I^B and I^O. The genes I^A and I^B show no dominance over each other, that is, they are codominant. However, genes I^A and I^B both are dominant over the gene I^O. In other words, the blood gene I^O is recessive in relation to genes I^A and I^B.

Although there are three gene forms (called alleles) for blood, but any one person can have only two of them. So, the blood group of a person depends on which two forms of the genes he possesses.

(*i*) If the genotype (gene combination) is $I^A I^A$, then the blood group of the person is A. And if the genotype is $I^A I^O$ even then the blood group is A (because I^O is a recessive gene).

(*ii*) If the genotype is $I^B I^B$, then the blood group of the person is B. And if the genotype is $I^B I^O$ even then the blood group is B (because I^O is a recessive gene).

(*iii*) If the genotype is $I^A I^B$, then the blood group of the person is AB.

(*iv*) If the genotype is $I^O I^O$, then the blood group of the person is O.

Figure 19. There are four blood groups : A, B, AB, O.

Let us solve one problem now.

Sample Problem. A man having blood group A marries a woman having blood group O and they have a child. What will be the blood group of the child ?

Answer. The answer to this question depends on whether the blood group A of the man has gene combination $I^A I^A$ or $I^A I^O$.

(*i*) When the blood group A has genotype $I^A I^A$. In this case the genotype of man's blood is $I^A I^A$ and that of woman's blood is $I^O I^O$. So, the child will have blood group A (because the gene I^A is dominant over gene I^O).

(ii) **When the blood group A has genotype I^AI^O.** Here the genotype of man's blood is I^AI^O and that of woman's blood is I^OI^O. So, in this case there is an equal chance that the genotype of child's blood can be either I^AI^O or I^OI^O. Due to this, there is an equal chance of the child acquiring blood group A or blood group O.

Just as the blood group is inherited by a child from its parents, in the same way the sex of a child (boy or girl) is also inherited from the parents : mother and father. We will now describe the inheritance of sex by a child from the parents. Inheritance of sex is also known as sex determination. Please note that while discussing the determination of sex of a child, we use letter symbols to describe whole sex chromosomes rather than individual genes. **The sex chromosomes are :**

XX for a female (girl)
XY for a male (boy)

Sex Determination

A person can have a male sex or a female sex. **The process by which the sex of a person is determined is called sex determination.** Genetics is involved in the determination of the sex of a person. This can be explained as follows.

The chromosomes which determine the sex of a person are called sex chromosomes. There are two types of sex chromosomes, one is called X chromosome and the other is called Y chromosome.

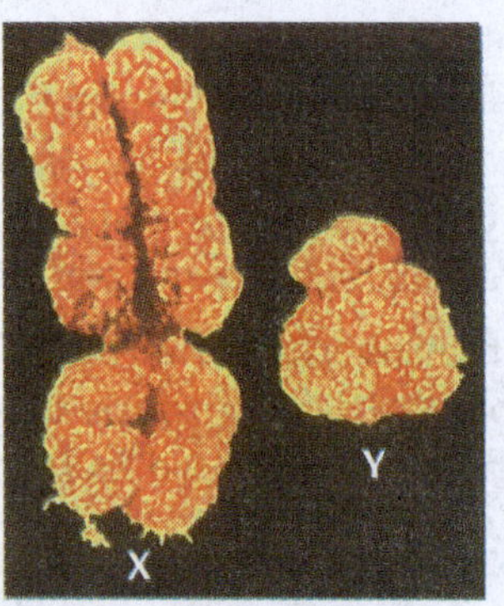

(*a*) The human male (man or father) has one X chromosome and one Y chromosome

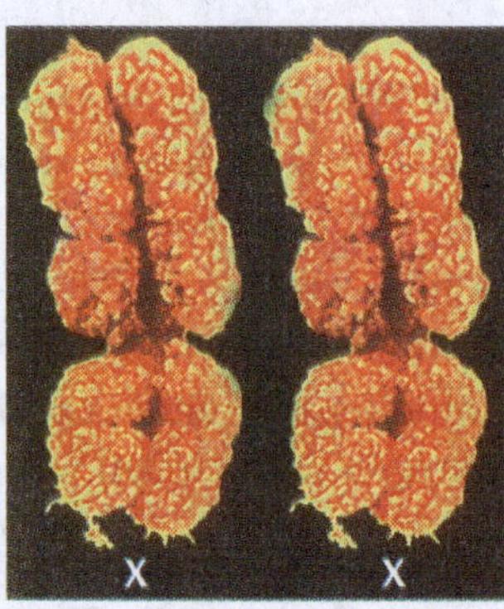

(*b*) The human female (woman or mother) has two X chromosomes.

Figure 20. The sex chromosomes.

(*i*) A male (man or father) has one X chromosome and one Y chromosome [see Figure 20(*a*)]. This means that half the male gametes or half the sperms will have X chromosomes and the other half will have Y chromosomes.

(*ii*) A female (woman or mother) has two X chromosomes (but no Y chromosomes) [see Figure 20(*b*)]. This means that all the female gametes called ova (or eggs) will have only X chromosomes.

The sex of a child depends on what happens at fertilisation : (*a*) If a sperm carrying X chromosome fertilises an ovum (or egg) which carries X chromosome, then the child born will be a girl (or female). This is because the child will have XX combination of sex chromosomes (see Figure 21).

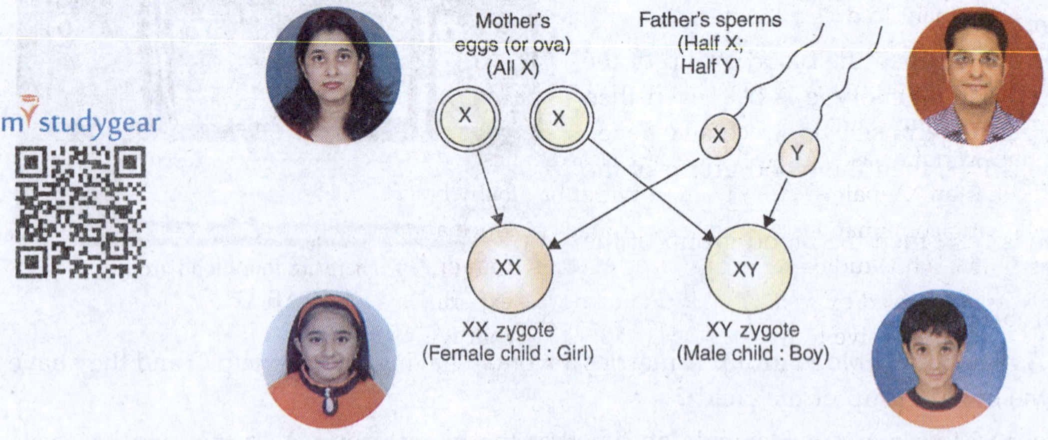

Figure 21. Inheritance of sex in humans.

(*b*) If a sperm carrying Y chromosome fertilises an ovum (or egg) which carries X chromosome, then the child born will be a boy (or male). This is because the child will have XY combination of sex chromosomes (see Figure 21).

Please note that **it is the sperm which determines the sex of the child.** This is because half of the sperms have X chromosomes and the other half have Y chromosomes. Thus, there is a 50 per cent chance of a boy and a 50 per cent chance of a girl being born to the parents. This is why the human population is roughly half males and half females.

From the above discussion we conclude that if the father (man or husband) contributes X sex chromosome at fertilisation through his sperm, the baby born will be a girl. On the other hand, if the father (man or husband) contributes a Y sex chromosome at fertilisation through his sperm, then the baby born will be a boy. This means that it is the sex chromosome contributed by father (man or husband) which decides the sex of the baby which the mother (woman or wife) will give birth to. Thus, **father (man or husband) is responsible for the sex of the baby (boy or girl) which is born**. The belief that mother (woman or wife) is responsible for the sex of her baby is absolutely wrong. In many ignorant Indian families, the mother (woman or wife) is held responsible for the birth of a girl child and unnecessarily harassed by her in-laws (*sasural*). Such people should understand that it is the husband who is responsible for the birth of a girl child (and not his wife). Moreover, a girl is no less than a boy.

In some of the animals, sex determination is also controlled by the environmental factors. For example, in some reptiles, the temperature at which the fertilised egg is incubated before hatching, plays a role in determining the sex of the offspring. It has been found that in a turtle (*Chrysema picta*) , high incubation temperature leads to the development of female offsprings (or female progeny). On the other hand, in the case of a lizard (*Agama agama*), high incubation temperature results in male offsprings (or male progeny). In some animals, such as snails, individuals can change sex, indicating that sex is not determined genetically in such animals. Before we go further and discuss acquired and inherited traits of organisms, **please answer the following questions :**

Very Short Answer Type Questions

1. Which of the processes, sexual reproduction or asexual reproduction, brings about maximum variations in the offsprings ?
2. Name one variation in humans connected with ears.
3. What constitutes the link between one generation and the next ?
4. If the trait A exists in 10% of a population of an asexually reproducing species and a trait B exists in 60% of the same population, which trait is likely to have arisen earlier ?
5. Mendel said that the characteristics or traits of organisms are carried from one generation to the next by internal factors which occur in pairs. What is the modern name for these factors ?
6. Some plants occur in one of the two sizes : tall or dwarf. This characteristic is controlled by one pair of genes. Tallness is dominant to dwarfness. Choose suitable letters for this gene pair.
7. What are the chromosomes XY and XX known as ?
8. Which of the two, sperm or ovum, decides the sex of the child ?
9. State whether the following statement is true or false :
   The sex of an infant is not a case of inheritance of characteristics.
10. A new born child has an XY pair of chromosmes. Will it be a baby boy or a baby girl ?
11. Which of the following combinations of sex chromosomes produce a male child : XX or XY ?
12. Name the first scientist who studied the inheritance of traits from one generation to the next.
13. What type of plants were used by Mendel for conducting his experiments on inheritance ?
14. The gene for red hair is recessive to the gene for black hair. What will be the hair colour of a person if he inherits a gene for red hair from his mother and a gene for black hair from his father ?
15. What are the four blood groups in humans ?
16. Name one reptile in each case where higher incubation temperature leads to the development of : (*a*) male progeny, (*b*) female progeny.
17. Fill in the following blanks with suitable words :
   (*a*) Genes always work in ....
   (*b*) In pea plants, the gene for dwarfness is ....whereas that for tallness is ....

(*c*) Most people have ....earlobes but some have ....earlobes.

(*d*) A human gamete contains................. chromosomes whereas a normal body cell has .... chromosomes in it.

(*e*) All races of man have............blood groups.

(*f*) The................chromosomes for a ....are XX whereas that for a ....are XY.

Short Answer Type Questions

18. Which of the following represent tall plants and which represent short plants (or dwarf plants) ?
(*a*) Tt (*b*) tt (*c*) TT
Give reason for your choice (The symbols have their usual meaning).

19. A man having blood group O marries a woman having blood group B and they have a daughter. What will be the blood group of the daughter ?

20. (*a*) Name the scientist who gave the laws of inheritance.
(*b*) Name an animal in which individuals can change sex. What does this indicate ?

21. Explain with an example, how genes control the characteristics (or traits).

22. (*a*) State one advantage of variation to a species.
(*b*) What are sex chromosomes ? How many sex chromosomes are there ? Name them.

23. Explain how, sex is determined in human babies.

24. What do the following symbols used in the topic on heredity represent ?
(*a*) TT (*b*) tt (*c*) XX (*d*) XY

25. (*a*) What will you get in the F_1 and F_2 generations in the following cross ?
Pure tall pea plant × Pure dwarf pea plant
(*b*) Is it an example of monohybrid cross or dihybrid cross ?

26. In the F_2 generation of a cross, progeny having different traits are produced in the ratio 3 : 1. State whether it is a monohybrid cross or a dihybrid cross ? Give one example of such a cross.

27. (*a*) What is the genotype of dwarf plants which always produced dwarf offspring ?
(*b*) What is the genotype of tall plants which always produced tall offspring ?
(*c*) What is the genotype of (*i*) dwarf plants, and (*ii*) tall plants, whose parental cross always produces tall offspring ?

28. (*a*) If a normal human cell has 46 chromosomes, how many chromosomes will be there in a human (*i*) sperm cell, and (*ii*) zygote ?
(*b*) What sizes of plants are produced if both parents have genes Tt ?

29. In a human, how many chromosmes are present in :
(*a*) a brain cell ?
(*b*) a sperm in the testes ?
(*c*) an egg which has just been produced by the ovary ?
(*d*) a skin cell ?
(*e*) a fertilised egg ?

30. Gregor Mendel's first law of genetics states "Of a pair of contrasted characters, only one can be represented in a gamete by its internal 'factor'.
(*a*) Give the modern name for this 'factor'.
(*b*) State where these factors are found in gametes.

31. Does genetic combination of mother play a significant role in determining the sex of a new born baby ?

32. Give the contrasting traits of the following characters in pea plant and mention which is dominant and which is recessive :
(*a*) Yellow seed (*b*) Round seed

Long Answer Type Questions

33. (*a*) What is meant by 'heredity' ? What are the units of heredity.
(*b*) State Mendel's first law of inheritance.

34. (*a*) Why did Mendel choose pea plants for conducting his experiments on inheritance ?
(*b*) State Mendel's second law of inheritance.

35. (*a*) What do you understand by the term 'variation' ?
(*b*) Name two human traits which show variation.
(*c*) How does the creation of variation in a species ensure its survival ?

36. (*a*) What are genes ? Where are they located in our body ?
(*b*) What is meant by dominant genes and recessive genes ? Give one example of each.
(*c*) Explain how, characteristics (or traits) are inherited through genes.

37. (*a*) How do Mendel's experiments show that traits may be dominant or recessive ?
(*b*) How do Mendel's experiments show that traits are inherited independently ?

Multiple Choice Questions (MCQs)

38. When two parents are crossed, the offspring are referred to as :
(*a*) recessives (*b*) test cross (*c*) F_1 generation (*d*) F_2 generation

39. A cross between two individuals results in a ratio of 9 : 3 : 3 : 1 for four possible phenotypes of progeny. This is an example of a :
(*a*) dihybrid cross (*b*) monohybrid cross (*c*) test cross (*d*) none of these

40. For his experiments on heredity, Mendel used :
(*a*) papaya plants (*b*) potato plants (*c*) pea plants (*d*) pear plants

41. The human animal which has an XY pair of chromosomes is called :
(*a*) male (*b*) hybrid (*c*) female (*d*) doomed

42. The science of heredity is known as :
(*a*) biology (*b*) embryology (*c*) genetics (*d*) biochemistry

43. A gene is a :
(*a*) hybrid (*b*) heritable trait
(*c*) pure breed (*d*) part of a chromosome that transmits a trait

44. A normal cell of human body contains 23 pairs of chromosomes. The number of chromosomes in a sex cell (sperm or ovum) of a human being is most likely to be :
(*a*) 46 (*b*) 23 (*c*) 21 (*d*) 42

45. In order to ensure that he had pure-breeding plants for his experiments, Mendel :
(*a*) cross-fertilised each variety with each other
(*b*) let each variety self fertilise for several generations
(*c*) removed the female parts of the plants
(*d*) removed the male parts of the plants.

46. In the human blood grouping, the four basic blood types are type A, type B, type AB, and type O. The blood proteins A and B are :
(*a*) simple dominant and recessive traits (*b*) incomplete dominant traits
(*c*) codominant traits (*d*) sex-linked traits

47. A plant with two 'small' genes breeds with a plant with two 'tall' genes to produce :
(*a*) small plants and tall plants in the ratio 1 : 3 (*b*) all small plants
(*c*) all tall plants (*d*) tall plants and small plants in the ratio 3 : 1

48. A pregnant woman has an equal chance of her baby being blood group A or blood group AB. Which one of the following shows the possible genotypes of the woman and the father of her child ?
(*a*) $I^A I^A$ and $I^B I^O$ (*b*) $I^A I^B$ and $I^B I^O$ (*c*) $I^A I^O$ and $I^B I^O$ (*d*) $I^A I^B$ and $I^A I^O$

49. The palisade cells of a species of plant contain 28 chromosomes. How many chromosomes will there be in each gamete produced by the plant ?
(*a*) 56 (*b*) 28 (*c*) 14 (*d*) 4

50. Which of the following may be used to obtain an F_2 generation ?
(*a*) allowing flowers on a parent plant to be self-pollinated

(*b*) allowing flowers on an F_1 plant to be self-pollinated
(*c*) cross-pollinating an F_1 plant with a parent plant
(*d*) cross-pollinating two parent plants

51. The following results were obtained by a scientist who crossed the F_1 generation of pure-breeding parents for round and wrinkled seeds.

Dominant trait	*Recessive trait*	*No. of F_2 offspring*
Round seeds	Wrinkled seeds	7524

From these results, it can be concluded that the actual number of round seeds he obtained was :
(*a*) 1881 (*b*) 22572 (*c*) 2508 (*d*) 5643

52. The visible characteristic in an organism is known as :
(*a*) prototype (*b*) stereotype (*c*) phenotype (*d*) genotype

53. The exchange of genetic material takes place in :
(*a*) vegetative reproduction (*b*) asexual reproduction (*c*) sexual reproduction (*d*) budding

54. A cross between a tall plant (TT) and short plant (tt) resulted in progeny that were all tall plants because :
(*a*) tallness is the dominant trait (*b*) shortness is the dominant trait
(*c*) tallness is the recessive trait (*d*) height of plant is not governed by gene T or t

55. The number of pair(s) of sex chromosomes in the zygote of humans is :
(*a*) one (*b*) two (*c*) three (*d*) four

56. In peas, a pure tall plant (TT) is crossed with a pure short plant (tt). The ratio of pure tall plants to pure short plants in F_2 generation will be :
(*a*) 1 : 3 (*b*) 3 : 1 (*c*) 1 : 1 (*d*) 2 : 1

57. The two versions of a trait (character) which are brought in by the male and female gametes are situated on :
(*a*) copies of the same chromosome (*b*) sex chromosomes
(*c*) two different chromosomes (*d*) any chromosomes

58. Select the statements that describe characteristics of genes :
(*i*) genes are specific sequence of bases in a DNA molecule
(*ii*) a gene does not code for proteins
(*iii*) in individuals of a given species, a specific gene is located on a particular chromosome
(*iv*) each chromosome has only one gene
(*a*) (*i*) and (*ii*) (*b*) (*i*) and (*iii*) (*c*) (*i*) and (*iv*) (*d*) (*ii*) and (*iv*)

59. Select the group which shares the maximum number of common characters :
(*a*) two individuals of a species (*b*) two species of a genus
(*c*) two genera of a family (*d*) two genera of two families

60. A trait in an organism is influenced by :
(*a*) paternal DNA only (*b*) maternal DNA only
(*c*) both maternal and paternal DNA (*d*) neither by paternal nor by maternal DNA.

61. In human males all the chromosomes are paired perfectly except one. This/these unpaired chromosomes is/are :
(*i*) large chromosome (*ii*) small chromosome (*iii*) Y chromosome (*iv*) X chromosome
(*a*) (*i*) and (*ii*) (*b*) (*iii*) only (*c*) (*iii*) and (*iv*) (*d*) (*ii*) and (*iv*)

62. The sex of a child is determined by which of the following ?
(*a*) the length of the mother's pregnancy
(*b*) the length of time between ovulation and copulation
(*c*) the presence of an X chromosome in an ovum
(*d*) the presence of a Y chromosome in a sperm

63. A zygote which has inherited an X chromosome from the father will develop into :
(*a*) baby boy (*b*) baby girl (*c*) adult (*d*) either boy or girl

64. Which of the following statement is incorrect ?
(*a*) for every hormone there is a gene
(*b*) for every protein there is a gene
(*c*) for production of every enzyme there is a gene
(*d*) for every type of fat there is a gene

65. If the ratio of each phenotype of the seeds of pea plants in the F_2 generation is 9 : 3 : 3 : 1, it is known as :
(*a*) tetrahybrid ratio (*b*) monohybrid ratio (*c*) dihybrid ratio (*d*) trihybrid ratio

Questions Based on High Order Thinking Skills (HOTS)

66. In humans, if gene B gives brown eyes and gene b gives blue eyes. What will be the colour of eyes of the persons having the following combination of genes ?
(*a*) Bb (*b*) bb (*c*) BB

67. Pure-bred pea plants A are crossed with pure-bred pea plants B. It is found that the plants which look like A do not appear in F_1 generation but re-emerge in F_2 generation. Which of the plants A and B are : (*i*) tall, and (*ii*) dwarf ? Give reason for your answer.

68. Pure-bred tall pea plants are first crossed with pure-bred dwarf pea plants. The pea plants obtained in F_1 generation are then cross-bred to produce F_2 generation of pea plants.
(*a*) What do the plants of F_1 generation look like ?
(*b*) What is the ratio of tall plants to dwarf plants in F_2 generation ?
(*c*) Which type of plants were missing in F_1 generation but reappeared in F_2 generation ?

69. A plant has two varieties, one with red petals and the other with white petals. When these two varieties are cross-pollinated, all the offsprings have red petals ?
(*a*) Which gene is dominant ?
(*b*) Choose suitable letters to represent the two genes.

70. A red-haired woman marries a brown-haired man, and all the children are brown haired. Explain this genetically.

71. A black mouse mates with a brown mouse, and all the offsprings are black.
(*a*) Why are no brown offsprings produced ?
(*b*) If two of the black offpsrings mate with each other what kind of offspring would you expect and in what proportions ? Give reason for your answer.

72. (*a*) E is the gene for brown eye colour and and e is the gene for blue eye colour. Which gene is (*i*) recessive, and (*ii*) dominant ?
(*b*) Both father and mother have the genes Ee in their cells. What colour are their eyes ?
(*c*) Which combination of genes in the zygote will produce children with blue eyes ?
(*d*) Which combinations of genes in the zygote will produce children with brown eyes ?

73. What are the possible blood groups likely to be inherited by children born to a group A mother and a group B father ? Explain your reasoning.

74. A couple with a newborn baby is troubled that the child does not resemble either of them. Suspecting that a mixup occurred at the hospital, they check the blood type of the infant. It is type O. Because the father is type A and the mother type B, they conclude that a mixup has definitely occurred. Are they correct ? Give reason for your answer.

75. A man with blood group A marries a woman with blood group O and their daughter has blood group O. Is this information enough to tell you which of the traits—blood group A or O — is dominant ? Why or why not ?

76. A Mendelian experiment consisted of breeding tall pea plants bearing violet flowers with short pea plants bearing white flowers. The progeny all bore violet flowers, but almost half of them were short. This suggested that the genetic make up (or genotype) of the tall parent can be depicted as :
(*a*) TTWW (*b*) TTww (*c*) TtWW (*d*) TtWw
Give reason for your choice.

77. A person first crossed pure-bred pea plants having round-yellow seeds with pure-bred pea plants having wrinkled-green seeds and found that only A-B type of seeds were produced in the F_1 generation. When F_1 generation pea plants having A-B type of seeds were cross-bred by self-pollination, then in addition to the original round-yellow and wrinkled-green seeds, two new varieties A-D and C-B type of seeds were also obtained.
(*a*) What are A-B type of seeds ?
(*b*) State whether A and B are dominant traits or recessive traits.
(*c*) What are A-D type of seeds ?

(*d*) What are C-B type of seeds ?

(*e*) Out of A-B and A-D types of seeds, which one will be produced in (*i*) minimum numbers, and (*ii*) maximum numbers, in the F_2 generation ?

78. The person A has only B chromosomes in all its gametes. On the other hand, another person C has chromosome D in half of gametes and chromosome E in the other half of gametes. When chromosomes B and D combine during fertilisation, a female zygote results. On the other hand, combination of B and E chromosomes produces a male zygote.

(*a*) What are chromosomes (*i*) B (*ii*) D, and (*iii*) E ?

(*b*) Out of B, D and E, which two chromosomes are of the same type ?

(*c*) Which chromosome is smaller in size ?

(*d*) What is the general name of chromosomes such as B and E ?

(*e*) Out of the two persons A and C, which one is (*i*) male, and (*ii*) female ?

79. Mendel first crossed pure-bred pea plants having round-yellow seeds with pure-bred pea plants having wrinkled-green seeds and found that only round-yellow seeds were produced in the F_1 generation. When F_1 generation pea plants having round-yellow seeds were cross-bred by self pollination, then peas having round-yellow seeds, round green seeds, wrinkled-yellow seeds and wrinkled-green seeds were produced. Mendel collected a total of 2160 seeds.

(*a*) What will be the number of (*i*) round green seeds (*ii*) wrinkled green seeds (*iii*) round yellow seeds, and (*iv*) wrinkled-yellow seeds ?

(*b*) Which 'ratio' as established by Mendel have you made use of in answering the part (*a*) above ?

80. Pure-bred round-yellow pea seeds have genotype RRYY and the pure-bred wrinkled-green pea seeds have genotype rryy. Keeping this in mind, write the phenotypes of the following genotypes of hybrid pea seeds :

(*a*) Rryy (*b*) rrYy (*c*) rrYY (*d*) RrYy (*e*) RRyy

ANSWERS

1. Sexual reproduction **4.** B **5.** Genes **6.** Tt **9.** False **10.** Baby boy **13.** Pea plants **14.** Black hair **17.** (*a*) pairs (*b*) recessive ; dominant (*c*) free ; attached (*d*) 23; 46 (*e*) same (*f*) sex ; female ; male **18.** Tall plants : Tt and TT ; Short plants : tt **19.** Equal chance of having blood group O or blood group B **26.** Monohybrid cross **27.** (*a*) tt (*b*) TT (*c*) (*i*) tt (*ii*) TT **28.** (*a*) (*i*) 23 (*ii*) 46 (*b*) 3 tall plants and 1 dwarf plant **29.** (*a*) 46 (*b*) 23 (*c*) 23 (*d*) 46 (*e*) 46 **30.** (*a*) Genes (*b*) Chromosomes **31.** No, because mother has a pair of X chromosomes. All new born babies will inherit an X chromosome from mother regardless of whether they are baby boys or baby girls. **32.** (*a*) Green seed ; Yellow is dominant; Green is recessive (*b*) Wrinkled seed ; Round is dominant ; Wrinkled is recessive **38.** (*c*) **39.** (*a*) **40.** (*c*) **41.** (*a*) **42.** (*c*) **43.** (*d*) **44.** (*b*) **45.** (*b*) **46.** (*c*) **47.** (*c*) **48.** (*a*) **49.** (*c*) **50.** (*b*) **51.** (*d*) **52.** (*c*) **53.** (*c*) **54.** (*a*) **55.** (*a*) **56.** (*c*) **57.** (*a*) **58.** (*b*) **59.** (*a*) **60.** (*c*) **61.** (*c*) **62.** (*d*) **63.** (*b*) **64.** (*d*) **65.** (*c*) **66.** (*a*) Brown (*b*) Blue (*c*) Brown **67.** (*i*) B (*ii*) A ; Dwarf pea plants do not appear in F_1 generation **68.** (*a*) All tall plants (*b*) 3 : 1 (*c*) Dwarf plants **69.** (*a*) Red colour (*b*) Rr **70.** The brown hair colour genes are dominant to the red hair colour genes ; The genotype of brown hair can be represented as BB and that of red hair as bb **71.** (*a*) Because black colour genes are dominant over brown colour genes (*b*) Three black mice and one brown mouse will be obtained in F_2 generation ; It is a monohybrid cross **72.** (*a*) (*i*) *e* (blue colour) (*ii*) E (brown colour) (*b*) Brown eyes (*c*) ee (*d*) EE and Ee **73.** Possible genotypes are $I^A I^B$, $I^A I^O$, $I^B I^O$ and $I^O I^O$. So, the possible phenotypes or blood groups are : AB, A, B and O **74.** No, the parents are not correct. The baby born to father having blood groups A and mother having blood group B can have any one of the four possible blood groups : A, B , AB and O. **75.** No (**Case I :** If father's blood group A is dominant trait, his genotypes will be I^AI^A and I^AI^O; and mother's blood group O being recessive trait, her genotype will be I^OI^O. So, daughter can receive one recessive allele I^O from father and another recessive allele I^O from mother to have genotype I^OI^O and hence blood group O. **Case II :** If father's blood group A is recessive trait, his genotype will be I^AI^A; and mother's blood group O being dominant trait, her genotypes will be I^OI^O and I^OI^A. In this case, daughter can receive a dominant allele I^O from mother and a recessive allele I^A from father to have genotype I^OI^A and hence blood group O) **76.** (*c*) TtWW (*Hint.* T is the gene form for tallness, t for dwarfness, W for violet colour and w for white colour. T and W are dominant genes whereas t and w are recessive genes) **77.** (*a*) Round yellow (*b*) A (round) and B (yellow) are dominant traits (*c*) Round-green (*d*) Wrinkled-yellow (*e*) (*i*) A–D (*ii*) A–B **78.** (*a*) (*i*) X chromosomes (*ii*) X chromosome (*iii*) Y chromosome (*b*) B and D (both are X chromosomes) (*c*) E (*d*) Sex chromosomes (*e*) (*i*) C (*ii*) A **79.** (*a*) (*i*) 405 (*ii*) 135 (*iii*) 1215 (*iv*) 405 (*b*) Dihybrid ratio **80.** (*a*) Round-green (*b*) Wrinkled-yellow (*c*) Wrinkled-yellow (*d*) Round-yellow (*e*) Round-green

ACQUIRED AND INHERITED TRAITS

A trait (or characteristic) of an organism which is 'not inherited' but develops in response to the environment is called an acquired trait. For example, if a beetle does not get sufficient food for a considerable time, its weight will be reduced due to starvation. The 'low weight' of this beetle is an acquired trait of the beetle which has been acquired in response to the environment which contained insufficient food. Again, suppose the tail of a mouse gets cut. The 'cut tail' of this mouse is also an acquired trait which has been been brought about by some agent in its environment. A man may know how to swim or roller skate or speak French or may have a scar on the face from a cut he got in an accident. All these are acquired traits (or characteristics) which the man has picked up (or acquired) himself as he goes through life. The man is not born with these traits and he cannot pass on these traits to his children. **The acquired traits of organisms cannot be passed on to their future generations.** The reason for this is discussed below.

Figure 22. Swimming is an acquired trait (or characteristic). It is not present by birth. In other words, the technique of swimming is not inherited from parents. It is learnt by the person himself (or herself).

We have already studied that the traits (or characteristics) of parents are passed to their offsprings through genes in reproductive cells (or gametes) during the process of reproduction. So, for the trait of an organism to be passed on, it must have been caused by a change in the genes (or DNA) present in the reproductive cells of the organism. In other words, **only those traits can be transmitted to future generations in which changes have occurred in the genes (or DNA) present in the reproductive cells (or gametes) of parent organisms.** *The changes in the non-reproductive body cells of an organism cannot be inherited by its offsprings.* This will become clear from the following examples.

When the weight of a beetle is reduced too much due to starvation, then though there is a change in the normal body cells of the beetle but no change takes place in the genes (or DNA) present in its reproductive cells (or gametes). And since there is *no change* in the genes (or DNA) of gametes, this acquired trait (of low weight) of beetle cannot be inherited by its offsprings. So, if some generations of beetles are low in body weight because of the availability of less food, then this is not an example of evolution because this change cannot be inherited over generations. Whenever these beetles will get sufficient food, they will become healthy again and the trait of 'low body weight' will disappear.

Let us discuss the other example now. If we breed some mice, all the progeny of mice will have tails, just like their parents. Now, if we cut the tails of these first generation mice surgically and breed them, we will get new mice, all with full tails. It has been observed that even after cutting the tails of mice for a

(*a*) These are first generation mice. All these mice have full tails

(*b*) The tails of all the mice are cut surgically so that they become tail-less mice.

(*c*) All the second generation mice produced by breeding cut-tail mice have full tails. No tail-less mouse is born

Figure 23. The cut-tail of mice is an acquired trait which cannot be passed on to their progeny in future generations through the process of reproduction.

number of generations, a tail-less mouse is never born. Actually, **the cut tail of mice is an acquired trait which is never passed on to their progeny. This is because cutting the tails of mice does not change the genes of their reproductive cells (or gametes).** And since the acquired trait of 'cut tails' does not bring about a change in the genes of mice, this trait cannot be passed on to their next generations. From this discussion we conclude that the experiences of an individual during its life time (called acquired traits) cannot be passed on to its progeny, and hence cannot lead to evolution (because they are not caused by the change in genes).

A trait (or characteristic) of an organism which is caused by a change in its genes (or DNA) is called an inherited trait. Inherited traits can be passed on to the progeny of the organism because they have produced changes in the genes (or DNA) of the organism. Suppose there is a population of red beetles in the green bushes. Again suppose that a colour variation arises during reproduction so that there is one beetle which is green in colour (instead of red). This change of green colour in the beetle has been brought

(*a*) Red beetle (*b*) Green beetle

Figure 24. The colour change of beetle form red to green has been brought about by a change in the genes (or DNA) of its reproductive cells. So, the green colour of bettle is an inherited trait which can be passed on to its progeny.

about by a change in the genes (or DNA) of the reproductive cells. The green colour of this beetle is an inherited trait which can be passed on to the next generations. The change from red beetle to green beetle can be considered to be an example of evolution because it helps in its survival by mixing with green bushes.

Inherited traits actually mean the characteristics which we receive from our parents. This point will become more clear from the following example. Suppose a father has red curly hair, brown eyes, a snub nose and a cleft chin [see Figure 25(*a*)]. Again suppose that the mother has straight black hair, blue eyes, a

(*a*) Father (*b*) Mother

(*c*) Children

Figure 25. This picture shows some of the characteristics which the children inherit from their parents. The development of these characteristics is controlled by the genes on the chromosomes.

long thin nose and a pointed chin [see Figure 25 (*b*)].

The children in the family inherit some characteristics from each of their parents. For example, two children have red hair like father but one of them has straight red hair while the other one has curly red hair. The two children have black hair like the mother. Again, two children have brown eyes like father but the other two have blue eyes like the mother. And finally, two children have snub nose and cleft chin like father whereas the other two have a long thin nose and a pointed chin.

EVOLUTION

There is an enormous 'number' and 'types' of living organisms (plants and animals) on this earth. In addition to this wide variety of living organisms, the remains of the dead organisms which lived in the remote past (called fossils) are also known. An important question now arises : How and from where has such a great variety of living organisms come to exist on this earth ? Also, how the human beings have evolved on this earth ? All these things are studied in the branch of biology called 'evolution'. The word 'evolution' has been derived from the Latin word *'evolvere'* which means to 'unroll' or 'unfold'. Evolution is a kind of gradual unfolding (or formation) of the new organisms from the pre-existing primitive organisms through slow and steady changes. We can now define evolution as follows : **Evolution is the sequence of gradual changes which take place in the primitive organisms over millions of years in which new species are produced.** Since the evolution is of the living organisms, so it is also called 'organic evolution'. It is through the constant process of evolution taking place in the organisms since the origin of life that such an enormous variety of plants and animals have come to exist on this earth at present. All the plants and animals (or organisms) which we see today around us have evolved from some or the other ancestors that lived on this earth long, long ago.

The process of evolution will become clear from the following example of 'pterosaur'. Pterosaur is an anicient flying reptile which lived on the earth about 150 million years ago. The development of pterosaur is an example of evolution. It began life as a big lizard which could just crawl on land [see Figure 26(*a*)]. Over millions of years, small folds of skin developed between its feet which enabled it to glide from tree to tree [see Figure 26(*b*)]. Over many, many generations, spread over millions of years, the folds of skin, and

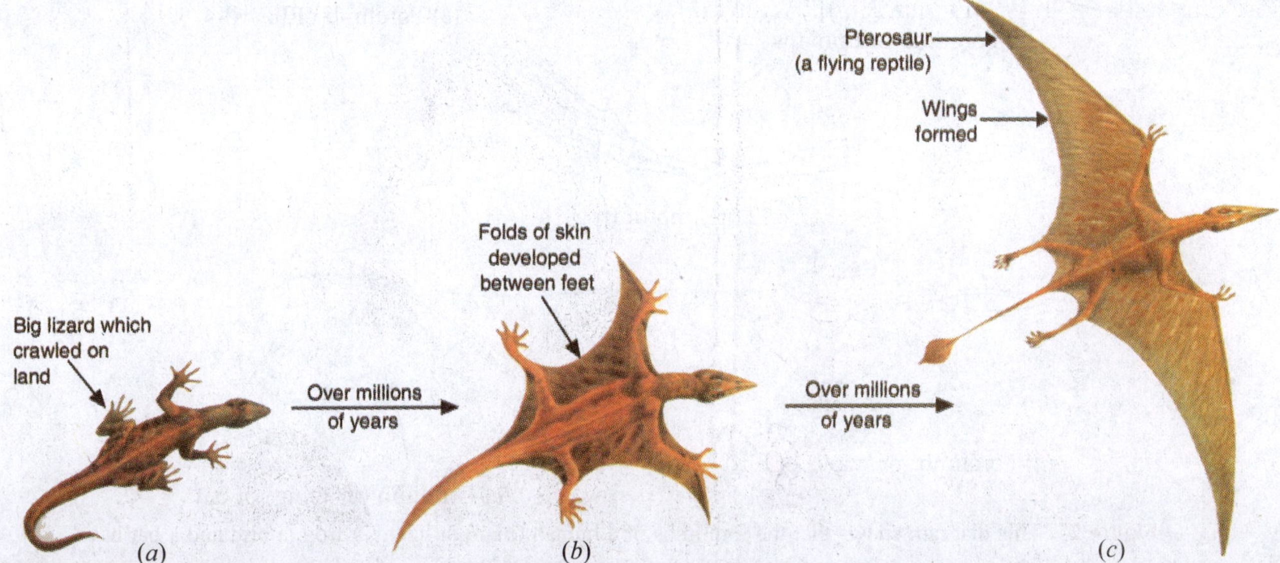

Figure 26. The development of 'pterosaur' (an ancient flying reptile) from a big lizard is an example of evolution.

the bones and muscles supporting them grew to form wings which could make it fly [see Figure 26(c)]. In this way, an animal which crawled on ground evolved into a flying animal. This evolution led to the formation of a new species (of a flying reptile).

EVIDENCES FOR EVOLUTION

Various biological studies tell us that since their origin, living organisms have been undergoing changes in their organisation to evolve into new forms. A number of common features of different kinds of organisms provide evidence in favour of evolution because they can be considered to have evolved from the common ancestor. **The more characteristics (or features) two species have in common, the more closely they will be related**. And the more closely they are related, the more recently they will have had a common ancestor. We will now give some of the evidences which indicate the occurrence of evolution. These evidences reinforce the view that the living organisms have evolved from common ancestors. **Some of the important sources which provide evidences for evolution are :**

(*i*) Homologous organs,
(*ii*) **Analogous organs,** and
(*iii*) Fossils.

We will now discuss all these evidences for evolution briefly.

1. Homologous Organs Provide Evidence for Evolution

If we look at the way in which living organisms are made, we can often see quite striking similarities in their construction. One of these is the presence of homologous organs. **Those organs which have the same basic structure (or same basic design) but different functions are called homologous organs.** The homologous organs of different animals provide evidence for evolution. This will become clear from the following examples.

There are many organs in different groups of animals (or plants) which all seem to be built from the same basic design but are used for many different purposes. These are called homologous organs. For example, the forelimbs of a man, a lizard (reptile), a frog (amphibian), a bird and a bat (mammal) seem to be built from the *same basic design of bones* (as shown in Figure 27), but they *perform different functions*. The

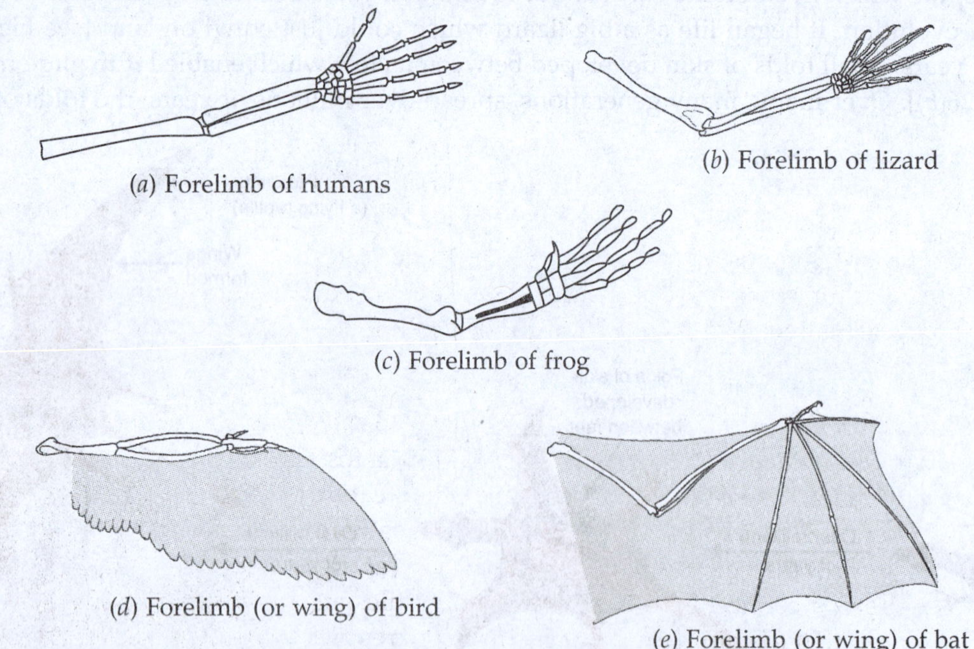

Figure 27. This diagram shows that the forelimbs of a human (man), a lizard, a frog, a bird and a bat have the same basic design of bones. They are homologous organs.

forelimbs of a human (man) are used for grasping; the forelimbs of a lizard are used for running; the forelimbs of a frog are used to *prop up* the front end of its body when at rest, and also act as *shock absorbers* when the frog lands back on the ground after a leap; whereas the forelimbs of a bird and a bat are modified for *flying*. Since the forelimbs of a human, a lizard, a frog, a bird and a bat have similar structures (or design) but perform different functions, they are the homologous organs.

The presence of homologous forelimbs in humans (man), a lizard, a frog, a bird and a bat indicate that all these forelimbs have evolved from a common ancestral animal which had a 'basic design' limb. In other words, it tells us that a human, a lizard, a frog, a bird and a man, all have evolved from a common ancestor. Thus, the presence of homologous organs in different animals provides evidence for evolution by telling us that they are derived from the same ancestor who had the 'basic design' of the organ on which all the homologous organs are based. Please note that the wings of a butterfly (which is an insect) and the wings of a bat *cannot* be considered to be homologous organs because they have different basic designs (though they are used for the same purpose of flying).

2. Analogous Organs Provide Evidence for Evolution

Those organs which have different basic structure (or different basic design) but have similar appearance and perform similar functions are called analogous organs. The analogous organs provide the evidence for evolution. This point will become clear from the following discussion.

There are many organs in different groups of animals which seem to be built from different basic structure but appear to be similar in shape and perform similar functions. These are called analogous organs. For example, the wings of an insect and a bird have different structures (the insects have a fold of membranes as wings which are associated with a few muscles whereas a skeleton, flesh and feathers support bird's wings) but they perform the same function of flying (see Figure 28). Since the wings of insects and birds have different structures (or different designs) but perform similar functions, they are analogous organs. Now, since the analogous organs have different basic design, so they do not indicate a common ancestor for the organism. The analogous organs provide evidence for the evolution in another way. The presence of analogous organs indicates that even the organisms having organs with different structures can adapt to perform similar functions for their survival under hostile environmental conditions. Thus, the presence of analogous organs in different animals provide evidence for evolution by telling us that though they are not derived from common ancestors, they can still evolve to perform similar functions to survive, flourish and keep on evolving in the prevailing environment. The analogous organs actually provide a mechanism for evolution.

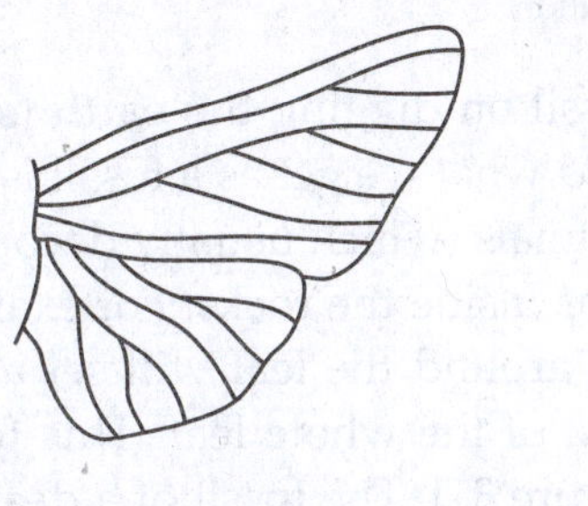

(*a*) Wing of insect

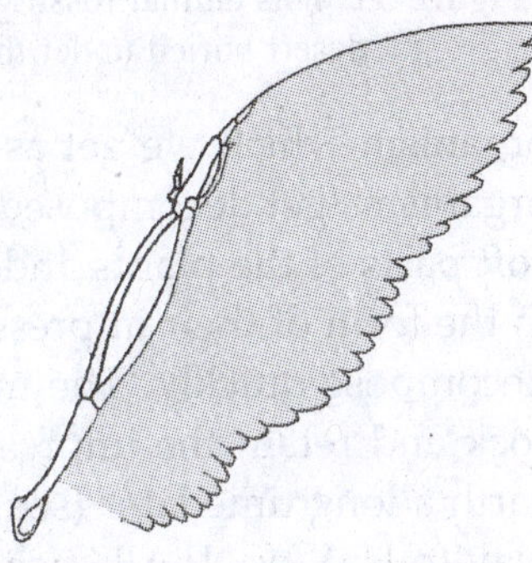

(*b*) Wing of bird

Figure 28. The wings of an insect and a bird have different structures but similar functions. They are analogous organs.

3. Fossils Provide Evidence for Evolution

The remains (or impressions) of dead animals or plants that lived in the remote past are known as fossils. The fossils provide evidence for evolution. For example, a fossil bird called *Archaeopteryx* looks like a bird but it has many other features which are found in reptiles. This is because *Archaeopteryx* has feathered wings like those of birds but teeth and tail like those of reptiles. *Archaeopteryx* is, therefore, a connecting link between the reptiles and birds, and hence suggests that the birds have evolved from the reptiles. Thus, fossils provide the evidence that the present animals (and plants) have originated from the previously existing ones through the process of continuous evolution.

Figure 29. *Archaeopteryx* is a connecting link between reptiles and birds.

We will now describe **how fossils are formed.** Usually, when organisms (plants or animals) die, their bodies will decompose by the action of micro-organisms in the presence of oxygen, moisture, etc.

Sometimes, however, the conditions in the environment are such (like absence of oxygen or moisture, etc), which do not let the body of the organism to decompose completely. It is such body (or body part) of an

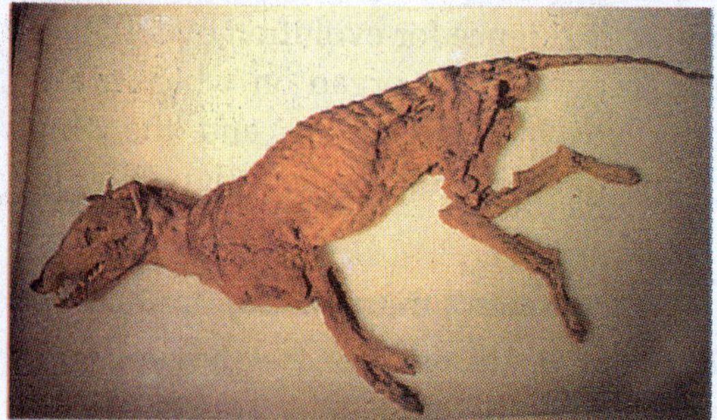

Figure 30. This animal fossil was found in the desert buried under the sand.

Figure 31. This leaf fossil was found in rocks.

organism which we get as fossil on digging the earth (see Figure 30). In many cases the soft parts of the organisms get decomposed and what we get as a fossil is a skeleton of hard parts (like bones, etc). Even the soft parts of the plants and animals (which usually decompose quickly) are sometimes preserved as fossils in the form of their impressions inside the rocks. For example, if a dead leaf gets caught in mud, it will not decompose quickly. The mud around the leaf will set around it as a mould, gradually harden to form a rock and retain the impression of the whole leaf. This forms a leaf fossil which can be dug out from the earth a long time later (see Figure 31). The fossil of a dead insect caught in mud is also formed in a similar way to leaf fossil. All such preserved impressions of the body parts of the once living organisms are also called fossils.

Fossils are obtained by digging into the earth. The age of fossils can be estimated in two ways : by the relative method, and by the carbon dating method. The relative method works like this : When we dig into the earth, we find fossils at different depths. The fossils which we find in layers closer to the surface of the earth are more recent; the fossils which are found in deeper layers are older; whereas the fossils found in the deepest layers of earth are the oldest ones. Fossils which we find today were once living objects. All the living objects contain some carbon-14 atoms which are radioactive. When a living object dies and forms fossil, its carbon-14 radioactivity goes on decreasing gradually. In the carbon dating method, the age of fossils is found by comparing the carbon-14 radioactivity left in fossils with the carbon-14 radioactivity present in living objects today.

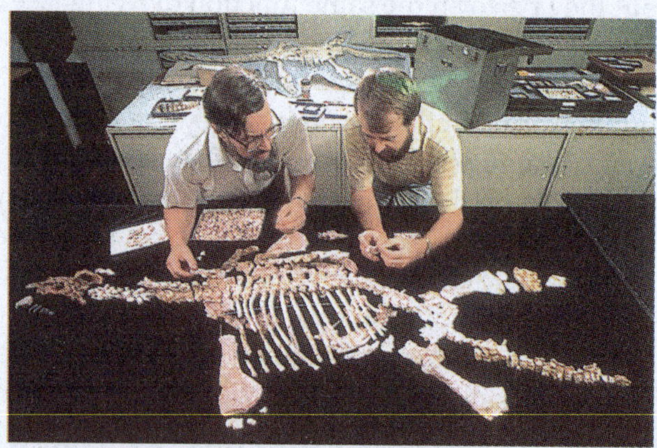

Figure 32. The scientists who study fossils are called palaeontologists. This picture shows the fossilised remains of a dinosaur being studied by palaeontologists.

There are various kinds of fossils. Some of the important fossils which have been studied are those of **ammonite, trilobite** and **dinosaur.** Ammonites were the invertebrate animals (molluscs) with a flat, coiled, spiral shell which lived in the sea [Figure 33(*a*)]. The estimation of the age of ammonite fossils have told us that they are about 180 million years old. This means that ammonites lived in the sea about 180 million years ago. Another invertebrate animal fossil which has been studied is that of trilobite [Figure 33(*b*)]. Trilobites were marine arthropods which were common between 400 to 600 million years ago. Dinosaurs are extinct carnivorous or herbivorous reptiles (The word 'dinosaur' means 'terrible lizard'). The estimation of the age of dinosaur fossils [Figure 33(*c*)] have told us that they first appeared on earth about 250 million years ago and became extinct about 65 million years ago. It is clear from the above discussion that **we can**

(*a*) Fossil of ammonite

(*b*) Fossil of trilobite

(*c*) Fossil of dinosaur skull

Figure 33. Various kinds of fossils.

even study about those species which are extinct (no longer exist), by studying their fossils which are found during the digging of earth.

Darwin's Theory of Evolution

Charles Robert Darwin gave the theory of evolution in his famous book 'The Origin of Species'. The theory of evolution proposed by Darwin is known as 'The Theory of Natural Selection'. This theory is called the theory of natural selection because it suggests that the best adapted organisms are selected by nature to pass on their characteristics (or traits) to the next generation. Darwin's theory of evolution applies to plants as well as animals.

Darwin's theory of evolution can be described as follows :

1. Within any population, there is natural *variation*. Some individuals have more favourable variations than others.
2. Even though all species produce a large number of offsprings, populations remain fairly constant naturally.
3. This is due to the struggle between members of the same species and different species for food, space and mate.
4. The struggle for survival within populations eliminates the unfit individuals. The fit individuals possessing favourable variations survive and reproduce. This is called natural selection (or survival of the fittest).
5. The individuals having favourable variations pass on these variations to their progeny from generation to generation.
6. These variations when accumulated over a long period of time, lead to the origin of a new species.

Figure 34. Charles Darwin : The scientist who gave the theory of evolution.

We will now understand Darwin's theory of evolution by 'natural selection' by taking an example. No two animals are ever exactly alike. So some changes always appear when animals produce their progeny by sexual reproduction. For example, one of the progeny may be tall (having long legs) than the other progeny. Thus, there may be a variation of height in the progeny [see Figure 35(*a*)]. Now, the advantage of long legs to the progeny is that when no food (grass, etc.) is available on the ground, then this progeny having long legs can reach the leaves on tall trees, eat them as food and survive [see Figure 35(*b*)]. On the other hand, the progeny which have short height (due to short legs) cannot reach the leaves on tall trees, they will not get any food, they will starve and hence die [see Figure 35(*b*)]. Thus, nature has selected the animal with long legs to survive (because it is the fittest animal under these circumstances). Now, since long legs help in survival, the long-legged animals will live long enough to produce their offsprings. The offspring will inherit long legs. So, all the future generations will have long-legged animals [see Figure 35(*c*)]. In this way, the animals having short legs have evolved into animals having long legs due to variation. This is an example of evolution.

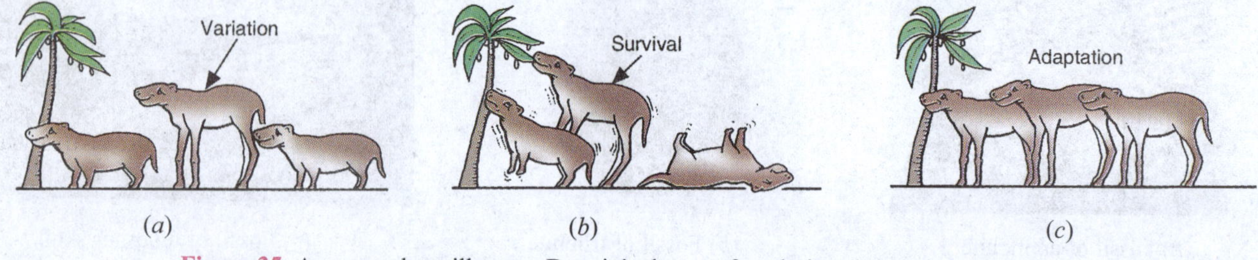

Figure 35. An example to illustrate Darwin's theory of evolution (by natural selection).

We can now define natural selection as follows : **Natural selection is the process of evolution of a species whereby characteristics which help individual organisms to survive and reproduce are passed on to their offspring, and those characteristics which do not help are not passed on.**

Though Darwin's theory was widely accepted, but it was criticised on the ground that it could not explain 'how the variations (which lead to origin of new species) arise'. With the progress in genetics, the source of variations was explained to be the 'genes'. Genes vary in natural population. **Genetic variation is the raw material of evolution.** So, the Darwin's theory was modified accordingly. These days, the most accepted theory of evolution is the **Synthetic Theory of Evolution** in which the origin of species is based on the interaction of 'genetic variation' and 'natural selection'.

Sometimes, a species (a type of animal or plant) may completely die out. It may become **extinct.** Dodo was a large flightless bird which has become extinct (see Figure 36). Once a species is extinct, its genes are lost for ever. It cannot re-emerge at all. The small numbers of surviving tigers are a cause of worry from the point of view of genetics because if they all die out and become extinct, their genes will be lost for ever (see Figure 37). Our coming generations will not be able to see tigers at all. We should, therefore, make all out efforts to protect tigers (and other endangered species) to prevent them from extinction.

Figure 36. Dodo (a large flightless bird) found in Mauritius is no longer alive. It has become extinct.

Figure 37. Only a small number of tigers are alive today. Tigers are threatened with extinction in the near future.

SPECIATION

A species is a population of organisms consisting of similar individuals which can breed together and produce fertile offspring. Species can be of plants or of animals. Wheat, paddy, sunflower, lotus, mango, *neem*, humans, tiger, dog and cat, etc., are all examples of various types of species. The human beings who look so different from each other in terms of size, colour and looks are said to belong to the same species (*Homo sapiens*) because they can interbreed to produce fertile offsprings (sons and daughters). **The process by which new species develop from the existing species is known as speciation.** In simple words, *the formation of new species is called speciation.* We will now explain how new species are formed from the existing species of various populations.

In most of the cases, new species are formed when the population of same species splits into two separate groups which then get isolated from each other geographically by the barriers such as mountain ranges, rivers or the sea. The geographical isolation of the two groups of population leads to their reproductive isolation due to which no genes are exchanged between them. However, breeding continues within the isolated populations producing more and more generations. Over the generations, the processes of genetic drift (random change in gene frequency), and natural selection operate in different ways in the two isolated groups of population and make them more and more different from each other. After thousands of years, the individuals of these isolated groups of population become so different that they will be incapable of reproducing with each other even if they happen to meet again. We say that two new species have been formed.

From the above discussion we conclude that **the important factors which could lead to the rise (or formation) of a new species are the following :**

(*i*) Geographical isolation of a population caused by various types of barriers (such as mountain ranges, rivers and sea). The geographical isolation leads to reproductive isolation due to which there is no flow of genes between separated groups of population.

(*ii*) Genetic drift caused by drastic changes in the frequencies of particular genes by chance alone.

(*iii*) Variations caused in individuals due to natural selection.

It should be noted that **geographical isolation is the major factor in the speciation of sexually reproducing animals because it interrupts the flow of genes between their isolated populations through the gametes.** The geographical isolation, however, *cannot* be a major factor in the speciation of a self-pollinating plant species because it does not have to look to other plants for its process of reproduction to be carried out. Geographical isolation also *cannot* be a major factor in the speciation of an asexually reproducing organism because it does not require any other organism to carry out reproduction.

Evolution of Eyes

The eye is a very important organ for animals. The eye is a complicated organ which cannot be generated by a single DNA change. **The complex body organs of animals such as eyes have been created in 'stages' over many generations.** First of all the rudimentary eye (basic eye) like that of a flatworm (*Planaria*) was formed (see Figure 38). The eyes of flatworm are very simple that are actually just 'eye-spots' which can detect light. Even these rudimentary eyes provide a survival advantage to flatworm. Starting from this basic design, more and more complex eyes were then evolved in various organisms. Most of the animals have eyes. For example, the insects, octopus and invertebrates, all have eyes. The structure of eyes in each of these organisms is, however, different which suggests their separate evolutionary origins. **The evolution of eye is an example of evolution by stages.**

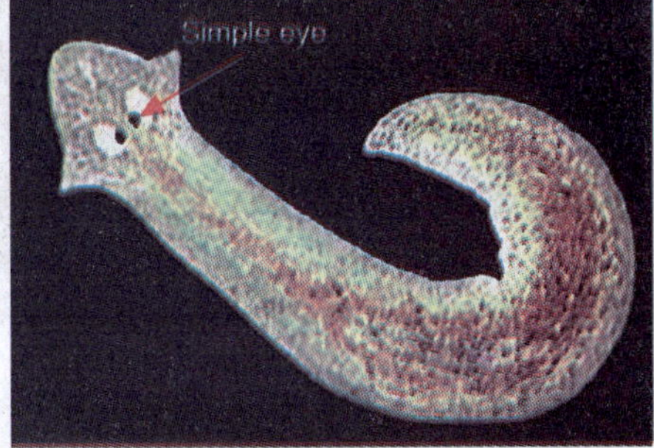

Figure 38. A flatworm (*Planaria*) has very simple eyes called rudimentary eyes.

Evolution of Feathers

Sometimes an evolutionary change produced in an organism for one purpose later on becomes more useful for an entirely different function. For example, birds evolved feathers as a means of providing insulation to their bodies in cold weather but later on these feathers became more useful for the purpose of flying. Even some dinosaurs had feathers though they could not fly by using these feathers. Birds, however, adapted feathers for flying. The presence of feathers on birds tells us that the birds are very closely related to reptiles because dinosaurs (which had feathers) were reptiles.

(*a*) Birds evolved feathers as a means of providing insulation to their bodies in cold weather.

(*b*) Later on, feathers become more useful to the birds for the purpose of flying

Figure 39. Evolution of feathers.

Evolution by Artificial Selection

In the evidence for evolution we have studied that very dissimilar looking structures can evolve from a common ancestral body design. But that was all guesswork about what happened in history long time ago. **We will now give an example from the present time which will show that different looking organisms can in fact be created from the same basic design of the ancestor.**

The wild cabbage plant is a good example to prove that entirely different looking organisms can evolve from the same organism by the process of evolution. The only difference is that here we are using artificial selection for evolution in place of natural selection. This will become clear from the following discussion.

The farmers have been cultivating **wild cabbage** as a food plant for over two thousand years and have produced (or evolved) entirely different looking vegetables like **cabbage, broccoli, cauliflower, kohlrabi** and **kale** from it by artificial selection (see Figure 40).

(*a*) Wild cabbage (*b*) Cabbage (*c*) Broccoli (*d*) Cauliflower (*e*) Kohlrabi (*f*) Kale

Figure 40. The production of vegetables like cabbage, broccoli, cauliflower, kohlrabi and kale from wild cabbage by the farmers is a case of evolution by artificial selection.

(*i*) Some farmers wanted to have very short distances between the leaves of wild cabbage and produced the common variety of 'cabbage'.

(*ii*) When farmers opted for the arrested flower development of wild cabbage plant, it led to the production of another variety of cabbage called 'broccoli'.

(*iii*) Some farmers went in for sterile flowers of wild cabbage and developed another variety of cabbage called 'cauliflower'.

(*iv*) When farmers opted for the swollen parts of wild cabbage, it led to the evolution of a yet another variety of cabbage called 'kohlrabi'.

(*v*) And finally, the farmers wanted to grow large leaves of wild cabbage and ended up producing a leafy vegetable called 'kale' which is also a variety of wild cabbage.

Now, wild cabbage is the ancestor and cabbage, broccoli, cauliflower, kohlrabi and kale are all its varieties which have been obtained by evolution 'induced artificially' by the farmers. The ordinary cabbage, broccoli, cauliflower, kohlrabi and kale look so different from their ancestor wild cabbage that if people had not seen it being done with their own eyes, they would never have believed that vegetables having such different structures can be evolved from the same ancestral vegetable plant.

Evolution Should Not be Equated With Progress

There is no real progress in the concept of evolution. Evolution is just the production of diversity of life forms and shaping of this diversity by the environmental selection. The only progress in evolution appears to be that more and more complex body designs of organisms have emerged over the ages. This will become clear from the following examples.

When a new species is formed, it is not necessary that the old species will disappear (or get eliminated) from earth. It will all depend on the environment. Also it is not as if the newly formed species are in any way better than the older ones. It is simply that genetic drift and natural selection processes have combined to form a population having different body design which cannot interbreed with the older population. It is a common belief that chimpanzees are the ancestors of human beings. It is, however, not true that human beings have evolved from chimpanzees. Actually, both chimpanzees and human beings had a common ancestor long time ago. The two offsprings of that ancestor evolved in their own separate ways to form the modern day chimpanzees and human beings.

(*a*) Chimpanzee

(*b*) Human being

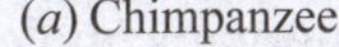

Figure 41. Human beings have not evolved from chimpanzees. Actually, both human beings and chimpanzees had a common ancestor a long time ago.

Again, it is not as if the body designs of older organisms were inefficient. This is because many of the older and simpler forms of organisms still survive on earth. For example, one of the simplest and primitive life forms called 'bacteria' still inhabit some of the most inhospitable (or unfavourable) habitats such as hot springs, deep-sea thermal vents and the ice in Antarctica. Most other organisms cannot survive in such harsh environments.

Human Evolution

Human evolution has been studied by using the various tools of tracing evolutionary relationships like excavating (digging earth), carbon-dating, studying fossils and determining DNA sequences. There is so much diversity of human body and features on the earth that for a long time people used to talk about different 'races' of human beings. The human races were even identified on the basis of their skin colour and named as white, black, yellow or brown. It is now known that the so called human races have not evolved differently. In fact, there is no biological basis for dividing human beings into different 'races'. All human beings (whether, white, black, yellow or brown) are a single species (called *Homo sapiens*).

It has now been established by research that the earliest members of the human species (*Homo sapiens*) came from Africa. So, irrespective of where we have lived for the past few thousand years, we all come from Africa. In other words, our genetic footprints tell us that we have African roots. About hundred thousand years ago, some of our ancestors left Africa while others stayed back. Those who left Africa slowly spread across the whole earth.

Mendel's experiments tell us the mode of inheritance of traits from one generation to the next and Darwin's theory of evolution tells us how organisms develop from simple to more complex forms. But neither tells us anything about how life originated on earth (or began on earth). We will now discuss the origin of life on earth briefly.

Origin of Life on Earth

A British scientist J.B.S. Haldane suggested in 1929 that life must have developed from the simple inorganic molecules (such as methane, ammonia, hydrogen sulphide, etc.) which were present on the earth soon after it was formed. He said that the conditions on earth at that time (including frequent lightning) could have converted simple inorganic molecules into complex organic molecules which were necessary for life. These complex organic molecules must have joined together to form first primitive living organisms. Haldane also suggested from theoretical considerations that **life (or living organisms) originated in the sea water.**

Figure 42. Scientists have come to the conclusion that life (or living organisms) originated in the sea water.

The theory of origin of life on earth proposed by Haldane was confirmed by experiments conducted by Stanley L. Miller and Harold C. Urey in 1953. They assembled an apparatus to create an early earth atmosphere which was supposed to consist of gases like methane, ammonia and hydrogen sulphide, etc., (but no oxygen), over water. This was maintained at a temperature just below 100°C and electric sparks were then passed through the mixture of gases (to simulate lightning) for about one week. At the end of one week, it was found that about 15 per cent of carbon (from methane) had been converted into simple compounds of carbon including 'amino acids' which make up protein molecules found in living organisms. This experiment provides the evidence that the life originated from inanimate matter (or lifeless matter) like inorganic molecules. We are now in a position to **answer the following questions :**

Very Short Answer Type Questions

1. What name is given to the sequence of gradual changes over millions of years in which new species are produced ?
2. Name the scientist who gave the theory of evolution.
3. State whether the following statement is true or false :
   Human beings have evolved from chimpanzees.
4. State one characteristic which shows that the birds are very closely related to dinosaurs.
5. Name an animal having rudimentary eyes.
6. Name the ancestor of the following :
   Broccoli, Kohlrabi, Kale
7. Where did life originate on the earth ?

8. Write the names of at least three inorganic molecules which helped in the origin of life on the earth.
9. Name the famous book written by Charles Robert Darwin.
10. The forelimbs of a frog, a bird and a man show the same basic design (or basic structure) of bones. What name is given to such organs ?
11. Name two organisms which are now extinct and studied from their fossils.
12. Out of the wing of a bird, wing of an insect and the wing of a bat :
    (*a*) which two are homologous organs ?
    (*b*) which two are analogous organs ?
13. Why are human beings who look so different from each other in terms of size, colour and looks said to belong to the same species ?
14. Name five varieties of vegetables which have been produced from 'wild cabbage' by the process of artificial selection.
15. Choose the one term from the following which includes the other three :
    broccoli, wild cabbage, cauliflower, cabbage
16. Fill in the following blanks with suitable words :
    (*a*) The human forelimb and bat's forelimb are an example of .... organs whereas an insect's wing and a bat's wing are an example of .... organs.
    (*b*) The evolution of eye is an example of evolution by ....
    (*c*) The scientific name of all human beings is ....
    (*d*) Broccoli has evolved from .... by the process of artificial selection.
    (*e*) The theory of natural selection for evolution was proposed by ....

Short Answer Type Questions

17. Match the terms given in column I with those given in column II :

Column I	*Column II*
(*i*) Fossil	(*a*) A famous evolutionist
(*ii*) A theory of evolution	(*b*) Survival of the fittest
(*iii*) Probable ancestor of birds	(*c*) Petrified remains of prehistoric life
(*iv*) Charles Darwin	(*d*) Father of genetics
(*v*) Gregor Mendel	(*e*) *Archaeopteryx*

18. What is meant by acquired and inherited traits ? Explain with one example each.
19. Why are the traits acquired during the lifetime of an individual not inherited ?
20. Can the wing of a butterfly and the wing of a bat be considered homologous organs ? Why or why not ?
21. Name two animals having homologous organs and two having analogous organs. Name these organs.
22. What are fossils ? Giving one example, explain how fossils provide evidence for evolution.
23. Give an example of characteristics being used to determine how close two species are in evolutionary terms.
24. In what way are homologous organs evidence for evolution ?
25. Why are the small numbers of surviving tigers a cause of worry from the point of view of genetics ?
26. Will geographical isolation be a major factor in the speciation of an organism that reproduces asexually ? Give reason for your answer.
27. Name the various tools of tracing evolutionary relationships which have been used for studying human evolution.
28. Out of bacteria, spider, fish and chimpanzee, which organism has a better body design in evolutionary terms ? Give reason for your answer.
29. With the help of an example, explain how variation leads to evolution.
30. (*a*) What is meant by a species ? Give two examples of plant species and two of animals.
    (*b*) State the various factors which could lead to the formation of new species.
31. What evidence do we have for the origin of life from inanimate matter (lifeless matter) ?
32. Does geographical isolation of individuals of a species lead to the formation of a new species ? Provide a suitable explanation for your answer.

33. Bacteria have a simpler body plan when compared with human beings. Does it mean that human beings are more evolved than bacteria ? Explain your answer.

Long Answer Type Questions

34. (*a*) Name the scientist who gave the theory of origin of life on earth. What is this theory ?
(*b*) How are those species which are now 'extinct' studied ?

35. What do you understand by the term 'evolution' ? State Darwin's theory of evolution.

36. (*a*) Explain the terms 'analogous organs' and 'homologous organs' with examples.
(*b*) In what way are analogous organs evidence for evolution ?

37. (*a*) Define 'speciation'. Explain how speciation occurs.
(*b*) Will geographical isolation be a major factor in the speciation of a self-pollinating plant species ? Give reason for your answer.

38. (*a*) Define 'natural selection'.
(*b*) "Only variations that confer an advantage to an individual organism will survive in a population". Do you agree with this statement ? Give reason for your answer.

Multiple Choice Questions (MCQs)

39. In evolutionary terms, we have more in common with :
(*a*) a chinese school boy (*b*) a chimpanzee (*c*) a spider (*d*) a bacterium

40. The human species has genetic roots in :
(*a*) America (*b*) Africa (*c*) Australia (*d*) Antarctica

41. Which of the following gas was not present in early earth atmosphere ?
(*a*) Ammonia (*b*) Oxygen (*c*) Hydrogen sulphide (*d*) Methane

42. A gradual change, over a long period, in a form of life is known as :
(*a*) erosion (*b*) evolution (*c*) revolution (*d*) evaluation

43. Scientists believe that all life originated in :
(*a*) the sea (*b*) the soil (*c*) the ground (*d*) the air

44. According to scientists, aves have evolved from :
(*a*) mammals (*b*) amphibians (*c*) reptiles (*d*) arthropods

45. The theory of evolution of species by natural selection was given by :
(*a*) Mendel (*b*) Darwin (*c*) Dalton (*d*) Lamarck

46. The term 'father of genetics' is used for the scientist :
(*a*) Morgan (*b*) Mendel (*c*) Darwin (*d*) Marie Curie

47. One of the following traits cannot be inherited. This one is :
(*a*) colour of eyes (*b*) colour of skin (*c*) size of body (*d*) nature of hair

48. Only one of the following characteristic of the parents can be inherited by their children. This one is :
(*a*) deep scar on chin (*b*) snub nose (*c*) technique of swimming (*d*) cut nose

49. The organs which perform different functions but have the same basic structure are known as :
(*a*) homologous organs (*b*) analogous organs (*c*) homolytic organs (*d*) analytic organs

50. The organs which perform similar functions but have different basic structure are called :
(*a*) asymmetric organs (*b*) analogous organs (*c*) homologous organs (*d*) homophonic organs

51. Wing of an insect and forelimb of a bird are :
(*a*) analogous organs (*b*) analeptic organs (*c*) homologous organs (*d*) homophobic organs

52. If the fossil of an organism is found in the deeper layers of earth, then we can predict that :
(*a*) the extinction of organism has occurred recently
(*b*) the extinction of organism has occurred thousands of years ago
(*c*) the fossil position in the layers of earth is not related to its time of extinction
(*d*) time of extinction cannot be determined.

53. Which of the following statement is incorrect with respect to variations ?
(*a*) all variations in a species have equal chance of survival

(*b*) change in genetic composition results in variations
(*c*) selection of variations by environmental factors forms the basis of evolutionary process
(*d*) variations are the minimum in asexual reproduction

54. One of the following traits of the parents cannot be passed on to their future generations. This trait is :
(*a*) cleft chin (*b*) pointed chin (*c*) scarred chin (*d*) broad chin

55. Some dinosaurs had feathers although they could not fly but birds have feathers that help them to fly. In the context of evolution, this means that :
(*a*) reptiles have evolved from birds
(*b*) there is no evolutionary connection between reptiles and birds
(*c*) feathers are homologous structures in both the organisms
(*d*) birds have evolved from reptiles

56. Select the incorrect statement from the following :
(*a*) frequency of certain genes in a population changes over several generations resulting in evolution
(*b*) reduction in the weight of an organism due to starvation is genetically controlled
(*c*) low weight parents can have heavy weight progeny
(*d*) traits which are not inherited over generations do not cause evolution.

57. New species may be formed if :
(*i*) DNA undergoes significant changes in germ cells
(*ii*) chromosome number changes in the gamete
(*iii*) there is no change in the genetic material
(*iv*) mating does not take place
(*a*) (*i*) and (*ii*) (*b*) (*i*) and (*iii*) (*c*) (*ii*), (*iii*) and (*iv*) (*d*) (*i*), (*ii*) and (*iii*)

58. According to the evolutionary theory, formation of a new species is generally due to :
(*a*) sudden creation by nature
(*b*) accumulation of variations over several generations
(*c*) clones formed during asexual reproduction
(*d*) movement of individuals from one habitat to another.

59. The presence of which of the following types of organs in two animals indicates that they are not derived from a common ancestor ?
(*a*) homologous organs (*b*) excretory organs (*c*) analogous organs (*d*) reproductive organs

60. The presence of which of the following types of organs in two organisms indicates that they are derived from the same ancestor ?
(*a*) analogous organs (*b*) respiratory organs (*c*) digestive organs (*d*) homologous organs

61. One of the following has not been produced from wild cabbage by the process of artificial selection. This one is :
(*a*) kohlrabi (*b*) cabbage (*c*) spinach (*d*) kale

62. The fossil trilobite was originally :
(*a*) an arthropod (*b*) an invertebrate (*c*) a reptile (*d*) an ave

63. One pair of organs in the following animals are not homologous. This is :
(*a*) forelimbs in humans and lizard (*b*) forelimbs in lizard and frog
(*c*) wings in butterfly and bat (*d*) wings in bat and bird

64. The wings of a housefly and the wings of a sparrow are an example of :
(*a*) analogous organs (*b*) vestigial organs (*c*) respiratory organs (*d*) homologous organs

Questions Based on High Order Thinking Skills (HOTS)

65. Some of the important fossils which have been studied are those of organisms X, Y and Z. X were marine arthropods which were common between 400 to 600 million years ago. Y were the invertebrate animals (molluscs) with a flat, coiled, spiral shell which lived in the sea about 180 million years ago. Z are the extinct carnivorous or herbivorous reptiles which appeared on the earth about 250 million years ago and became extinct about 65 million years ago. What are X, Y and Z ?

66. The farmers have been cultivating a food plant X for over two thousand years and have produced as many as five entirely different looking vegetables A, B, C, D and E from it.

(*a*) What could the plant X be ?

(*b*) What are A, B, C, D and E ?

(*c*) What is the process of evolution involved in this example known as ?

67. There are five animals A, B, C, D and E. The animal A uses its modified forelimbs for flying. The animal B uses its forelimbs for running whereas the animal C uses its forelimbs for grasping. The animal D can live on land as well as in water and uses its forelimbs to prop up the front end of its body when at rest. The animal E which respires by using spiracles and tracheae uses wings for flying but its wings are analogous to the modified forelimbs of animal A.

(*a*) What could the animals A, B, C, D and E be ?

(*b*) Why are the forelimbs of animals A, B, C and D called homologous organs ?

(*c*) What does the existence of homologous organs in animals A, B, C and D tell us about their ancestors ?

(*d*) Why are the modified forelimbs of animal A and the wings of animal E called analogous organs ?

(*e*) State whether animals A and E have a common ancestor or not.

68. X, Y, and Z are three animals. The animal X can fly but animal Y can only run on ground or walls. The forelimbs of animals X and Y have the same basic design but they are used for different purposes such as flying and running respectively. The animal Z became extinct a long time ago. The study of fossils of Z tells us that it had some features like those of X and some like those of Y. In fact, Z is said to form a connecting link in the evolutionary chain of X and Y.

(*a*) What could the animals X, Y and Z be ?

(*b*) What name is given to the forelimbs like those of X and Y which have the same basic design but different functions ?

(*c*) Name one feature in which Z resembled X.

(*d*) Name one feature in which Z resembled Y.

(*e*) Which is the correct evolutionary chain involving X, Y and Z : $X \rightarrow Z \rightarrow Y$ or $Y \rightarrow Z \rightarrow X$?

69. A population of red beetles lives in green bushes in a garden. Once during the process of breeding, a green beetle is produced.

(*a*) State whether the change in colour of beetle is a process of evolution or not.

(*b*) Can the new colour of green beetle be passed on to its next generations ?

(*c*) What will be the advantage (if any) of the green colour to the beetle ?

(*d*) State whether the production of green colour involved a change in genetic material or not.

70. The organs P and Q of two animals have different structures but similar functions. On the other hand, the two organs R and S of two other animals have the same basic structure but different functions.

(*a*) What are the organs like P and Q known as ?

(*b*) Name the organs like P and Q. Also name the animals which have such organs.

(*c*) What are the organs like R and S called ?

(*d*) Name the organs like R and S. Also name the animals which have such organs.

ANSWERS

1. Evolution **3.** False **10.** Homologous organs **12.** (*a*) Wings of bird and wings of bat (*b*) Wings of birds and wings of insect **15.** Wild cabbage **16.** (*a*) homologous ; analogous (*b*) stages (*c*) *Homo sapiens* (*d*) wild cabbage (*e*) Darwin **17.** (*i*) *c* (*ii*) *b* (*iii*) *e* (*iv*) *a* (*v*) *d* **39.** (*b*) **40.** (*b*) **41.** (*b*) **42.** (*b*) **43.** (*a*) **44.** (*c*) **45.** (*b*) **46.** (*b*) **47.** (*c*) **48.** (*b*) **49.** (*a*) **50.** (*b*) **51.** (*a*) **52.** (*b*) **53.** (*a*) **54.** (*c*) **55.** (*d*) **56.** (*b*) **57.** (*a*) **58.** (*b*) **59.** (*c*) **60.** (*d*) **61.** (*c*) **62.** (*a*) **63.** (*c*) **64.** (*a*) **65.** X : Trilobites ; Y : Ammonites ; Z : Dinosaurs **66.** (*a*) Wild cabbage (*b*) Cabbage, Broccoli, Cauliflower, Kohlrabi and Kale (c) Artificial selection **67.** (*a*) A : Bird ; B : Lizard ; C : Human ; D : Frog ; E : Insect (*b*) Because they have the same basic design but perform different functions (*c*) They are derived from the same ancestor (*d*) Because they have different basic design but perform similar functions (*e*) No **68.** X : Bird ; Y : Lizard ; Z : Dinosaur (*b*) Homologous organs (*c*) Both Z and X had feathered wings like those of birds (*d*) Both Z and Y had tail like those of reptiles (*e*) $Y \rightarrow Z \rightarrow X$ **69.** (*a*) Yes (*b*) Yes (*c*) The green colour of beetle allows it to mix up with green bushes and helps in its survival (because then it cannot be seen easily by the predators) (*d*) Yes **70.** (*a*) Analogous organs (*b*) Wings ; Insect and Bird (*c*) Homologous organs (*d*) Forelimbs; Lizard and Frog

5 Our Environment

The physical and biological world where we live is called our environment. **The environment includes our physical surroundings like air (or atmosphere), water bodies, soil (land) and all the organisms such as plants, animals, human beings and micro-organisms like bacteria and fungi (called decomposers).** All these constituents of the environment are dependent on one another. So, all the constituents of environment interact with one another and maintain a balance in the environment in a natural way.

Human beings are the only organisms who change the natural environment to fulfil their needs of food, clothing, housing, transport and industry, etc. In fact, the uncontrolled activities of human beings are damaging the balanced and healthy environment more and more.

Biodegradable and Non-biodegradable Wastes

All the waste materials produced by the various activities of man and animals are poisonous to some extent and can be divided into two main groups :

1. Biodegradable wastes, and
2. Non-biodegradable wastes.

Those waste materials which can be broken down to non-poisonous substances in nature in due

Figure 1. Paper is a biodegradable waste.

Figure 2. Plastic is a non-biodegradable waste.

course of time by the action of micro-organisms like certain bacteria, are called biodegradable wastes. A biodegradable waste decays (decomposes) naturally and becomes harmless after some time. **Cattle dung and compost are common examples of biodegradable wastes.** [Compost is the manure made from decayed vegetable-stuff (plants)]. Other examples of biodegradable materials are: **Animal bones ; Leather ; Tea-leaves ; Wool ; Paper ; Wheat ; Wood ; Hay ; Cotton ; Jute ; Grass ; Fruit and Vegetable peels ; Leaves, Flowers, and Cake, etc.** Biodegradable wastes usually do not pollute the environment. Biodegradable wastes pollute the environment only when their amount is large which cannot be degraded (or decomposed) into harmless substances in nature at the right time.

The waste materials which cannot be broken down into non-poisonous or harmless substances in nature are called non-biodegradable wastes. The examples of non-biodegradable wastes are: **D.D.T. (Dichloro Diphenyl Trichloroethane); Plastics; Polythene bags; Ball-point pen refill; Synthetic fibres; Glass objects; Metal articles like Aluminium cans; Iron nails; Silver foil and Radioactive wastes.** All these non-biodegradable wastes cannot be made less toxic (less poisonous) easily and hence they are major pollutants of the environment. The non-biodegradable wastes cannot be decomposed by micro-organisms like bacteria. **D.D.T. is a non-biodegradable waste so it can be passed along the food chain from crops to man or other animals and birds and harm them.** For this reason, D.D.T. has been banned from use in most countries. **Non-biodegradable wastes are the major pollutants of the environment.** For example, the discarded plastic articles, glass articles and metal objects are the non-biodegradable waste materials which cause a lot of pollution in our surroundings. We will now describe a simple experiment to find out whether a given material is biodegradable or non-biodegradable.

We take a piece of paper, a piece of an old cotton cloth and a plastic bag (polythene bag). Dig the ground to about 15 centimetres depth and place the pieces of paper, cotton cloth and plastic bag in the dug up ground separately. We cover them with soil. Leave these buried materials in the ground for about a month. After a month, we dig up the buried materials and observe them. We will find that the piece of paper and the piece of cotton cloth have been partially eaten up (or decomposed) but the plastic bag has remained unaffected, it has not been eaten up (or decomposed). This means that paper and cotton cloth have been decomposed by the micro-organisms present in the soil. So, paper and cotton cloth are biodegradable. On the other hand, the plastic bag has not been decomposed by the micro-organisms present in the soil, therefore, plastic is non-biodegradable. So, the decomposer organisms are not able to decompose plastic into simpler harmless substances.

We will now explain **why some materials are biodegradable whereas others are non-biodegradable.** The micro-organisms like bacteria and other decomposer organisms (called saprophytes) present in our environment are 'specific' in their action. They break down the natural materials or products made from natural materials (say, paper) but do not break down man-made materials such as plastics. So, **it is due to the property of decomposer organisms of being specific in their action that some waste materials are biodegradable whereas others are non-biodegradable.**

We should use the shopping bags (or carry bags) made of paper, cotton cloth or jute because these are

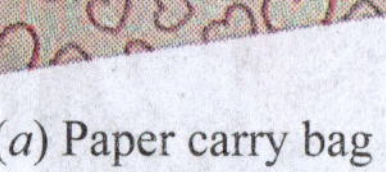

(*a*) Paper carry bag

(*b*) Cloth carry bag

(*c*) Jute carry bag

(*d*) Plastic carry bag

Figure 3. We should use shopping bags (carry bags) made of paper, cotton cloth or jute. Don't use shopping bags made of plastic (polythene). Say NO to plastic carry bags !

biodegradable materials. On the other hand, plastic bags (or polythene bags) should be avoided because plastic is a non-biodegradable material.

ECOSYSTEM

The various communities of living organisms (plants and animals) interact among themselves as well as with their physical environment like soil, air and water. The living organisms interact with one another through their food chains in which one organism consumes another organism. The living organisms like plants interact with soil to get essential nutrients like nitrogen, phosphorus, etc.; with air to get carbon dioxide and also with water bodies, for carrying out the process of photosynthesis. Thus, the various communities of living organisms (called biotic communities) like plants and animals alongwith soil, air and water of that region form a self-sustaining or functional unit of the living world. This 'functional unit' or 'system' made up of living and non-living components which is capable of independent existence is called an ecosystem. The ecosystem includes all the communities of an area (all the plants and animals of an area) functioning with their non-living environment like soil, air and water. We can now define an ecosystem as follows.

An ecosystem is a self-contained unit of living things (plants, animals and decomposers), and their non-living environment (soil, air and water). An ecosystem needs only the input of *sunlight energy* for its functioning. **The examples of ecosystems are : a grassland (meadow); a forest; a desert; a mountain; a**

Figure 4. The pond is an ecosystem.

pond; a lake; a river; and sea. When we say that a pond or lake is an ecosystem, then the word pond also includes all the aquatic life (plants and animals) which occurs in this pond water. This is because the living organisms are found everywhere. Similarly, when we say that a forest is an ecosystem then it means the physical environment of the forest like soil, air and water alongwith all the plants and animals which occur in the forest. The desert, grassland, forest, cropfield and mountains represent *terrestrial* ecosystems (land-based ecosystems) whereas ponds, lakes, river, sea and aquarium represent *aquatic* ecosystems (water-based ecosystems). Most of the ecosystems in the world are *natural* ecosystems but some of them are also *man-made* ecosystems or *artificial* ecosystems. The examples of *artificial* ecosystems are crop-fields (agricultural lands); gardens; parks and aquarium.

Components of an Ecosystem

All the ecosystems are made up of two main components: Abiotic components, and Biotic components. *Abiotic* components mean *non-living* components and *biotic* components mean *living* components. Thus, we can now say that an ecosystem consists of non-living environment and the living biological community.

1. Abiotic Components of an Ecosystem. The abiotic components of an ecosystem (or the non-living components of an ecosystem) include the physical environment like soil, water and air alongwith the inorganic substances like carbon dioxide, nitrogen, oxygen, water, phosphorus, sulphur, sodium, potassium, calcium and other elements present in them. The physical factors or climatic factors like light, temperature, pressure and humidity are also considered abiotic components of the ecosystem.

2. Biotic Components of an Ecosystem. The biotic component of an ecosystem (or the living component of an ecosystem) is a community of organisms (like plants and animals), which is made up of many different inter-dependent populations. The biotic community (or living community) of an ecosystem includes *three* types of organisms :

(*i*) **Producer organisms (or Autotrophs)** which synthesize their own food. All the green plants are producers.

(*ii*) **Consumer organisms (or Heterotrophs)** which are dependent on others for food. All the animals are consumers.

(*iii*) **Decomposer organisms (or Saprotrophs)** which consume the dead remains of other organisms. Certain bacteria and fungi are decomposers.

The Functioning of an Ecosystem

We will now describe how an ecosystem functions as a self-sufficient or independent unit in nature. We have just discussed that an ecosystem has non-living components like soil, water and air which contain inorganic nutrient elements, and the living components called producers, consumers and decomposer organisms. All these components make the ecosystem function as follows: From the nutrient pool of the earth (soil, water and air), carbon dioxide and water are absorbed by the producer organisms (green plants). With the help of sunlight energy, the producer organisms convert these inorganic substances into organic compounds like carbohydrates which act as a food. Thus, **producers trap the solar energy and then provide the basic food or energy for all other life forms in the ecosystem.** The consumers (animals) derive their energy needs, directly or indirectly, from producers (plants). When the producers (plants) and consumers (animals) die, then the decomposer organisms act on their dead bodies to return the various elements back to the nutrient pool (soil, water and air). Thus, an ecosystem involves input of energy and matter which are exchanged between living and non-living components in a cyclic process.

Producers, Consumers and Decomposers

According to the manner in which they obtain their food from the environment, all the organisms can be divided into three groups : producers, consumers and decomposers.

1. Producers

Those organisms which produce food are called producers. **Producers are the organisms which can prepare their own food from simple inorganic substances like carbon dioxide and water by using sunlight energy in the presence of chlorophyll.** The examples of producers are **green plants** and **certain blue-green algae.** The green plants synthesize their food during photosynthesis by taking raw materials from the earth and energy from the sun.

Figure 5. Green plants are called producers. This picture shows a maize plant which produces maize (*makka*) as food.

The green plants produce carbohydrates by photosynthesis and also synthesize proteins and fats. Thus, **the green plants are called producers in the living world.** Producers are the autotrophic organisms (self-feeder organisms) in the ecosystem upon which other organisms depend for food. Thus, producers (like green plants) are autotrophs.

2. Consumers

Those organisms which consume food (eat food) prepared by producers are called consumers. The consumers depend on producers for food, directly or indirectly. The consumers get their food by eating other organisms or their products. In most simple words, consumers are the organisms that eat other organisms. **All the animals are consumers.** Even the microscopic animal life of the water called protozoa are consumer organisms. The examples of common consumer organisms are man, goat, deer, fish, lion, cow and buffalo, etc. The cow and buffalo eat green grass and other green fodder because green grass and other green plants are producers of food. The bio-mass of grass and plants supplies food and energy to these animals like cow and buffalo. It should be noted that the consumer organisms like animals cannot prepare food from simple inorganic substances through photosynthesis. The consumers need ready-made food for their survival which they get from producers (green plants), either directly or indirectly. **If an animal eats grass or other green plants or their products itself we say that it gets the food from producers directly.** For example, a goat gets the food from producers directly when it eats grass. On the other hand, **if an animal eats the meat of another animal (which eats grass), then we say that it gets the food from producer indirectly.** For example, a lion gets food by eating goat which in turn eats grass. So, in this case the lion gets its food indirectly from producer grass (through the goat). Consumer organisms are also called heterotrophs. **Consumers can be further divided into three groups : herbivores, carnivores and omnivores.**

Figure 6. All the animals (including human beings) are consumers of food. This goat is a consumer which is eating plants as food.

(*i*) Herbivores

Some animals eat only plants (or their products). **Those animals which eat only plants are called herbivores.** The herbivores may eat grasses, leaves, grains, fruits or the bark of trees. Some of the examples of herbivores are : **Cow, Buffalo, Goat, Sheep, Horse, Deer, Camel, Ass, Ox, Elephant, Monkey, Squirrel, Rabbit and Hippopotamus.** Cow is called a herbivore because it eats only plants (or plant products) as food. Herbivores are also known as herbivorous animals. The animals which get their food by eating the producers (plants) directly are called primary consumers. Since herbivores obtain their food directly from plants (or producers), therefore, **herbivores (like cattle, deer, goat, etc.) are primary consumers.**

Figure 7. Cow is a herbivore because it eats only plants or plant products (such as grains) as food.

(*ii*) Carnivores

Some animals eat only other animals. They do not eat plant food at all. **Those animals which eat only other animals as food are called carnivores.** The carnivores eat the meat (or flesh) of other animals. So, we can also say that *those animals which eat only the meat (or flesh) of other animals are called carnivores.* Some of the examples of the carnivores are : **Lion, Tiger, Frog, Vulture, Kingfisher, Lizard, Wolf, Snake and Hawk.** Lion is called a carnivore because it eats only the meat (or flesh) of other animals like deer, rabbit and goat, etc. Carnivores are also known as carnivorous animals. The carnivores are usually of two types : *small* carnivores and *large* carnivores. **The small carnivores which feed on herbivores (primary consumers) are called secondary consumers.** For example, a frog, lizard, bird and fox, etc., are secondary consumers. **The large carnivores (or top carnivores) which feed upon the small carnivores (secondary consumers) are called tertiary consumers.** For example, lion, tiger and birds of prey (such as hawk) are some of the tertiary consumers. Please note that humans (man) can be primary, secondary or tertiary consumers depending on the food which they eat.

Figure 8. Lion is a carnivore which eats only the flesh of other animals. This picture shows a lion eating a zebra that it has killed.

(iii) Omnivores

Some animals eat both, plants as well as other animals. **Those animals which eat both, plants and animals, are called omnivores.** In other words, *the omnivores eat plant food as well as the meat (or flesh) of other animals.* Some of the examples of omnivores are : **Man (human beings), Dog, Crow, Sparrow, Bear, Mynah and Ant.** Man is called an omnivore because he eats both, plant food (such as grains, pulses, fruits and vegetables) as well as meat of animals (such as goat, chicken and fish). Omnivores are also called omnivorous animals.

Figure 9. Dog is an omnivore because it eats both, plant food (such as bread) as well as meat.

We will now describe another type of producers and consumers which are extremely small. These are called planktons. **Planktons are very minute or microscopic organisms freely floating on the surface of water in a pond, lake, river or ocean.** Planktons are of two types : Phytoplanktons and Zooplanktons. **The microscopic aquatic plants freely floating on the surface of water are called phytoplanktons.** The free-floating *algae* is an example of phytoplankton. Phytoplanktons are capable of producing food by the process of photosynthesis. **The microscopic aquatic animals freely floating on water are called zooplanktons.** The freely-floating **protozoa** are an example of zooplankton. A very, very small fish is also a zooplankton. Planktons float near the surface of water and provide food for many fish and other aquatic animals.

(*a*) The green layer floating on the surface of water in this lake is that of tiny free-floating plants called 'algae' which are phytoplanktons

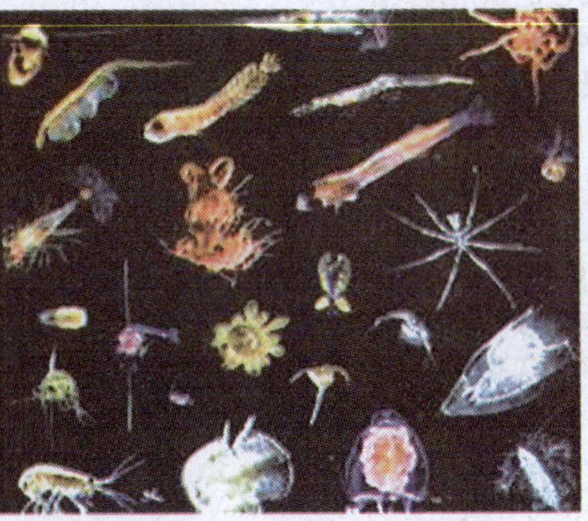

(*b*) This picture shows tiny aquatic animals freely floating on water which are called zooplanktons

Figure 10. Phytoplanktons and zooplanktons.

3. Decomposers

The non-green micro-organisms like some bacteria and fungi, which are incapable of producing their food, live on the dead and decaying (rotting) plants and animal bodies and are consumers of a special type called decomposers. We can now say that: **The micro-organisms which break down the complex organic compounds present in dead organisms like dead plants and animals and their products like faeces, urine, etc., into simpler substances are called decomposers.** The examples of decomposers are ***certain bacteria*** and ***fungi***. The bacteria which act as decomposers are called putrefying bacteria. The bacteria and fungi act as decomposers by the secretions of their body surfaces which decompose the organic matter present in dead plants and animals into simpler substances and liberate ammonia, carbon dioxide, etc. They absorb some of these simpler substances for their own maintenance and release the remaining into the soil, water and air to be used by the producers again In this way, decomposers help in the recycling of materials in ecosystem. The decomposers are also known as micro-consumers or saprotrophs.

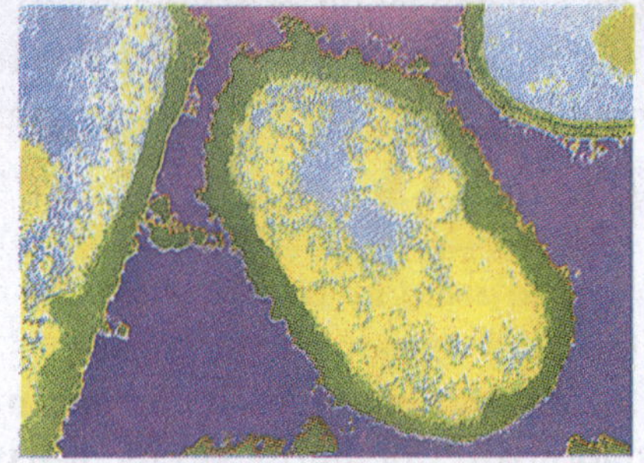

(*a*) Bacteria (magnified 85000 times) which decompose dead plants and animals, and help in the recycling of materials.

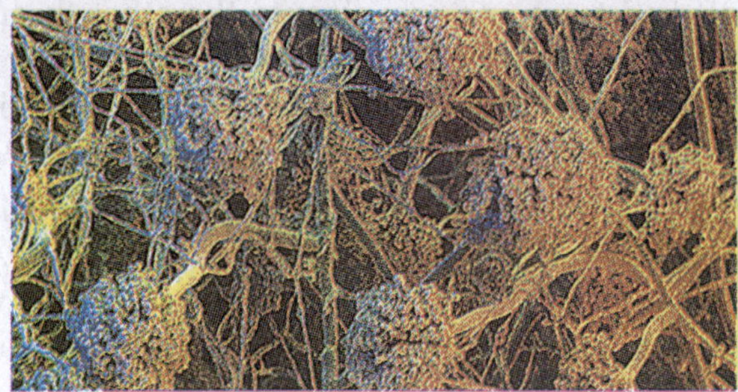

(*b*) Fungi (magnified 300 times) which decompose dead plants and animals, and help in the recycling of materials.

Figure 11. Certain bacteria (called putrefying bacteria) and fungi act as decomposers.

Importance of Decomposers

The decomposers help in decomposing the dead bodies of plants and animals, and hence act as cleansing agents of environment. The decomposers also help in putting back the various elements of which the dead plants and animals are made, back into the soil, air and water for re-use by the producers like crop-plants. This maintains the fertility of soil and the soil would continue to support crops again and again. For example, the decomposers like putrefying bacteria and fungi decompose the dead plants and animal bodies into ammonia (and other simpler substances). This ammonia is converted into nitrates by the nitrifying bacteria present in soil. These nitrates act as fertilizer in the soil and are again absorbed by the plants for their growth. Thus, **it is only due to the presence of decomposers that the various nutrient elements which were initially taken by plants from the soil, air and water are returned to the soil, air and water, after the death of plants and animals.** If, however, there were no decomposers, then the dead bodies of plants and animals would keep lying as such and the elements of which plant and animal bodies are made, would never be returned to their original pools like soil, air and water. In that case, the cyclic process of life and death would be disrupted. This is because in the absence of decomposers the soil, air and water would not be replenished by elements from the bodies of dead organisms. All the nutrients present in soil, air and water would soon

Figure 12. Decomposers at work : This picture shows the rotting of apples by the action of decomposer organisms called bacteria present in the soil. We cannot see the decomposer organisms in this picture because they are too small to be seen with naked eyes. We can, however, see the effect they are producing on these apples.

be exhausted and evolution of life would come to an end. Thus, **the decomposer organisms help in recycling the materials in the ecosystem so that the process of life may go on and on like an unending chain.**

FOOD CHAINS

Anything which we eat to live is called food. Food contains energy. **The food (or energy) can be transferred from one organism to the other through food chains.** The starting point of a food chain is a category of organisms called **producers.** Producers are, in fact, plants. So, we can say that **all the food chains begin with a green plant (or grass) which is the original source of all food.** Let us take an example to understand the meaning of food chain.

Suppose there is a field having a lot of green plants (or producers of food). Now, plants can be eaten up by a rat. The rat, in turn, can be eaten up by a cat. And finally, the cat can be eaten up by a dog. So, we find that there is a sequence (or order) in which one organism eats up the other organism (or consumes the other organism) to fill its belly. **The sequence of living organisms in a community in which one organism consumes another organism to transfer food energy, is called a food chain.** In simple words, **a list of organisms (living beings) showing "who eats whom" is called a food chain.** Let us make this point more clear by taking the example of a simple food chain operating in a grassland or forest. In a grassland or forest, there is a lot of grass (which are green plants). This grass is eaten up by animals like deer. And this deer is then consumed (eaten up) by a lion. This simple food chain operating in a grassland or forest can be represented as :

Grass ⟶ **Deer** ⟶ **Lion**
(Producer) (Herbivore) (Carnivore)

This food chain tells us that grass is the starting point of this food chain. The grass is eaten up by deer and the deer is then eaten up by a lion. In this food chain, grass is the *producer* organism which uses sunlight energy to prepare food like carbohydrates by the process of photosynthesis. This grass is then consumed by a *herbivore* called deer. And the deer is consumed by a *carnivore* called lion. The above food chain can be represented more clearly with the help of a diagram as follows (see Figure 13).

Figure 13. A food chain operating in a grassland or forest.

A food chain represents a single directional (or unidirectional) transfer of energy. For example, the above food chain tells us that the transfer of energy takes place from grass to deer and then to lion. It cannot take place in the reverse direction from lion to deer to grass. **The study of food chains in an area or habitat helps us in knowing various interactions among the different organisms and also their interdependence.**

More Examples of Food Chains

In the food chain that we have discussed above, there are three organisms involved in it : grass, deer and lion, so it is said to be a food chain having three steps or three links. The same grassland has many other food chains operating in it which can have different number of steps. Let us take the example of a grassland food chain having four steps or four links. In a grassland ecosystem, grass is eaten by insects; the insects are eaten by frog; and the frog is then eaten by birds. This is a grassland food chain involving four organisms (or four steps) which can be represented as follows :

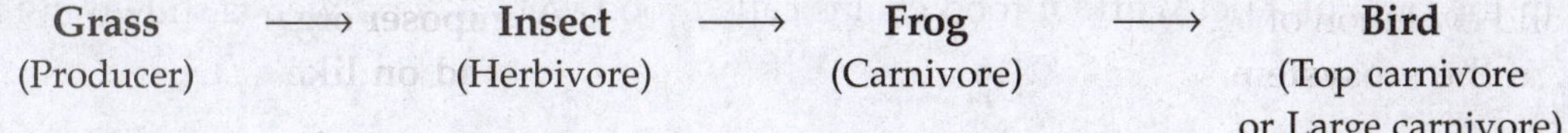

Grass ⟶ **Insect** ⟶ **Frog** ⟶ **Bird**
(Producer) (Herbivore) (Carnivore) (Top carnivore or Large carnivore)

The above food chain can be represented more clearly with the help of pictures of all the organisms involved as follows :

Figure 14. Another food chain occurring in a grassland or forest.

Please note that in this food chain grass is the *producer*. The insect (herbivore) is the *primary consumer*, the frog (small carnivore) is the *secondary consumer* whereas the bird (top carnivore or large carnivore) is the *tertiary consumer*.

Another four-step food chain operating in a grassland is :

Plants ⟶ **Worms** ⟶ **Birds** ⟶ **Cat**
(Producer) (Herbivore) (Carnivore) (Top carnivore)

We will now discuss **the food chain operating in an aquatic ecosystem** (water ecosystem) like a pond, lake, or sea (ocean). In a pond, lake or sea ecosystem, the algae are eaten up by protozoa; the protozoa are eaten up by small fish; and the small fish is eaten up by big fish. This aquatic food chain can be represented as :

Algae ⟶ **Protozoa** ⟶ **Small Fish** ⟶ **Big Fish**
(Phytoplankton) (Zooplankton) (Carnivore) (Large carnivore)
(Producer) (Herbivore)

Please note that in a pond, lake or ocean ecosystem, the producer is a minute organism called algae and protozoa is the minute herbivore.

Figure 15. This picture shows a cat eating a bird (pigeon) as a part of the food chain.

Each organism (or living being) occupies a specific position in the food chain. For example, grass, deer and lion occupy specific positions in the food chain :

Grass ⟶ **Deer** ⟶ **Lion**

Another point to be noted is that one organism (or same organism) can occur in more than one food chains. For example, in the forest food chains, a deer may be consumed by a lion as well as by a jackal :

Grass ⟶ **Deer** ⟶ **Jackal**

So, the same organism, deer, occurs in the food chains of lion as well as that of jackal. The organisms representing producers and consumers in a food chain give a definite structure to an ecosystem.

FOOD WEB

A large number of food chains exist in a community of living organisms in an ecosystem such as a grassland, a forest, a pond or a crop-field. Many of these food chains are inter-connected by species (organisms) which occur in more than one food chain. **The inter-connected food chains operating in an ecosystem which establish a network of relationships between various species, is called a food web.** In simple words, **the network of a large number of food chains existing in an ecosystem is called a food web.** The food web has many intercrosses and linkages among the various species (producers and consumers) present in it. This means that the various food chains in an ecosystem do not operate in isolation (or alone).

They operate in the form of a net-work of food chains called food web. A food web is shown in Figure 16.

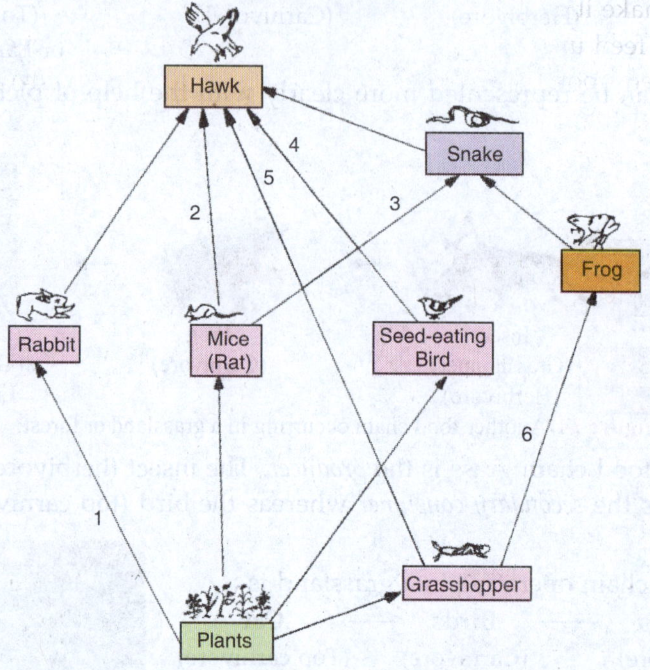

Figure 16. This is a food web. A food web consists of many inter-connected food chains.

In this food web, we can see a network of numerous pathways along which the food (or energy) flows within grassland community. This food web starts from the plants which is a producer and ends in top carnivore hawk (*baaz*). There are as many as six food chains operating in the food web shown above which have been marked 1, 2, 3, 4, 5 and 6 (see Figure 16).

1. In the 1st food chain, plants are eaten by rabbit and then rabbit is eaten by hawk :

   Plants ⟶ Rabbit ⟶ Hawk

2. In the 2nd food chain, plants are eaten by mice (or rats) and the mice are eaten by hawks :

   Plants ⟶ Mice ⟶ Hawk

3. In the 3rd food chain, plants are eaten by mice; mice are eaten by snakes and then snakes are consumed by hawks :

   Plants ⟶ Mice ⟶ Snake ⟶ Hawk

4. In the 4th food chain, plants are eaten by seed-eating birds and the seed-eating birds are consumed by hawks :

   Plants ⟶ Seed-eating Bird ⟶ Hawk

5. In the 5th food chain, plants are eaten up by grasshopper and the grasshopper is consumed by hawks:

   Plants ⟶ Grasshopper ⟶ Hawk

6. In the 6th food chain, plants are eaten by grasshopper, grasshopper is eaten by frog, frog is eaten by snake and then snake is consumed by hawk :

   Plants ⟶ Grasshopper ⟶ Frog ⟶ Snake ⟶ Hawk

TROPHIC LEVELS

A food chain represents the flow of food (or energy) in a given set of organisms or living beings. **The various steps in a food chain at which the transfer of food (or energy) takes place are called trophic levels.** In fact, **in a food chain, each step representing an organism forms a trophic level.** In most simple terms, 'trophic level' means 'feeding level' of the organism.

(i) The plants are **producers** (or autotrophs) and constitute the **first trophic level**. They fix up the sun's energy and make it available for consumers (or heterotrophs).

(ii) **Herbivores** (which feed upon plants) constitute the **second trophic level.**

(iii) **Carnivores** (that feed upon herbivores) constitute the **third trophic level.**

(iv) **Large carnivores** or **Top carnivores** (which feed upon small carnivores), constitute the **fourth trophic level.**

The various trophic levels in a food chain can be represented diagrammatically as shown in Figure 17.

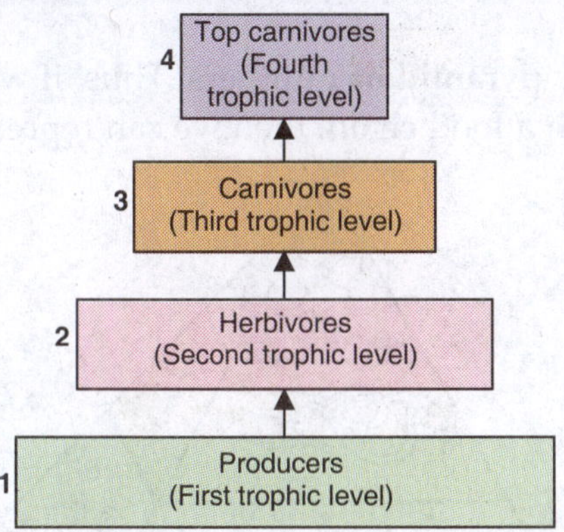

Figure 17. Diagram to show the various trophic levels in a food chain

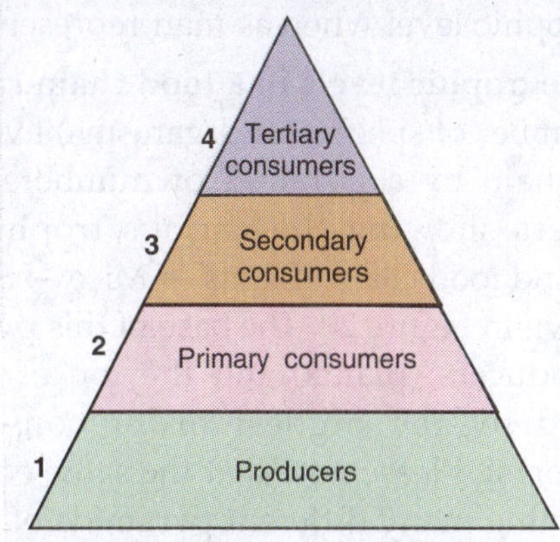

Figure 18. Another way to show the various trophic levels in a food chain.

Herbivores are called primary consumers, small carnivores are called secondary consumers whereas top carnivores or large carnivores are called tertiary consumers. So, we can draw another diagram to represent various trophic levels by using the terms producers, primary consumers, secondary consumers and tertiary consumers as shown in Figure 18. Please note that both, secondary consumers and tertiary consumers are carnivores, the only difference being that *secondary* consumers are *small* carnivores (though we usually do not write the word small), whereas *tertiary* consumers are *large* carnivores which are usually called top carnivores. Please note that the diagram shown in Figure 18 is tapering upwards because as we go up towards higher trophic levels, the number of organisms in them decreases gradually.

The simplest food chain that we have already studied is :

Grass ⟶ Deer ⟶ Lion

Now, this food chain involves three trophic levels. Grass (being producer) represents the 1st trophic level. Deer (being herbivore) represents the 2nd trophic level, and lion (being carnivore) represents the third trophic level.

We have also studied another food chain operating in the grassland, which is :

Grass ⟶ Insect ⟶ Frog ⟶ Bird

In this food chain, grass represents the 1st trophic level; insects represent the 2nd trophic level; frog represents the 3rd trophic level, whereas birds represent 4th trophic level. This is shown more clearly in Figure 19.

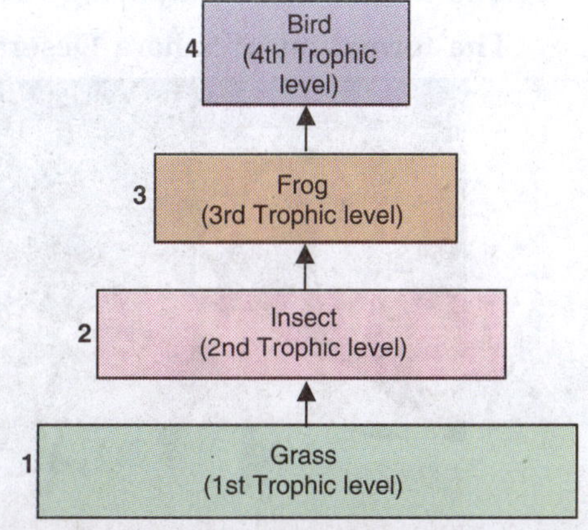

Figure 19. This diagram shows trophic levels in food chain :
Grass ⟶ Insect ⟶ Frog ⟶ Bird

We will now consider some of the food chains involving man (human beings). Now, when man eats plants (or plant products), then the food chain involves only producer and consumer :

Plants ⟶ Man
(Producer) (Consumer)

This food chain has only two trophic levels. Plants being the first trophic level and the man representing second trophic level. But in the case of man who also eats meat (of animals like goat), the food chain involves producer and two consumers, the primary consumer and the secondary consumer :

Plants	$\longrightarrow$	**Goat**	$\longrightarrow$	**Man**
(Producer)		(Herbivore)		(Omnivore)
		(Primary consumer)		(Secondary consumer)

This food chain involving man has three trophic levels. Plants represent 1st trophic level, goat represents 2nd trophic level whereas man represents the 3rd trophic level.

The trophic levels in a food chain can also be represented by pyramid of numbers. Thus, if we count the number of species (or organisms) living at each trophic level in a food chain, then we can represent the food chain by a pyramid of numbers. A pyramid of numbers showing the various trophic levels in the grassland food chain : Plants → Mice → Snakes → Hawks is shown in Figure 20. The base of this pyramid is formed by producers (plants) and the top of this pyramid is formed by the highest order consumers (or top carnivores). Please note that the same ecosystem may be supporting many different pyramids of organisms, each starting with plants at the base but ending in a different organism at the top. Another point to be noted is that there is a greater number of organisms at the lower trophic levels of an ecosystem (the greatest number being at the producer level). As we go to higher and higher trophic levels, the number of organisms in each trophic level goes on decreasing (as shown in Figure 20).

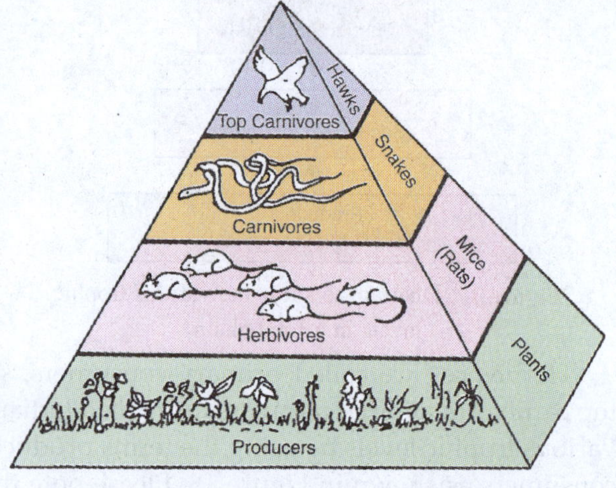

Figure 20. Pyramid of numbers showing the various trophic levels in a food chain.

Effect of Man's Activities on the Ecosystem

Man or for that matter, any other living organism must interact properly with the rest of the ecosystem because he is an integral part of that ecosystem. Some of the man's activities like hunting of various animals disrupt the food chains in which these animals normally take part. This disruption of one food chain affects the numerous other food chains operating in the food web. **The shortening of food chains due to man's activities like hunting leads to an imbalance in the functioning of an ecosystem and ultimately in the functioning of the whole biosphere.** The effect of man's activities on the functioning of an ecosystem will become clear from the following examples.

The formation of Sahara Desert is an example of the ill effect of man's activities on the delicately

Figure 21. This lion has been hunted down and killed just for the sake of misplaced sense of adventure. But the damage it will cause to the environment in the long run is irreparable (impossible to repair !).

Figure 22. This is Sahara Desert. Can you see even a speck of vegetation (plants) in this picture ? This desert is the result of prolonged hunting of lions by man.

balanced ecosystem. When the Romans started capturing lions, the population of lions in the forest was reduced to a large extent. Lion is a predator which kills the herbivorous animals like deer, sheep, goat, buffalo, etc. Now, since the population of predator lion decreased, there was no one to kill the herbivorous animals. Due to this the population of herbivorous animals increased rapidly. The large population of these herbivorous animals ate up all the vegetation (plant materials) in that region, turning the lush-green forests into vast desert called Sahara Desert. Our own Rajasthan Desert was formed as a result of overgrazing of vegetation by progressively increasing tribes of herbivorous animals which occurred due to the reduction in the predator population of lions because of excessive hunting and capturing.

Let us take the example of ***Grass*** $\longrightarrow$ ***Deer*** $\longrightarrow$ ***Lion*** food chain to study the effect of man's activities on the ecosystem. A natural ecosystem is a delicately balanced system. If the man does not disturb this ecosystem, then the organisms like grass, deer and lion in a forest keep a natural balance which benefits them all and gives us a healthy environment. We will now discuss the effect of removing all the three organisms from this food chain, one at a time.

(*i*) If All the Lions are Removed

If all the lions in a forest are removed by killing or capturing, then there will be no predator control over the population of deer. Due to this the population of deer will increase greatly. Deer eat grass. So, an increase in deer population will lead to excessive grazing of grass. The density of producers like grass will be very much reduced. Overgrazing may even eliminate the grass and other green plants completely and turn the lush-green forest into a desert area having no vegetation at all.

(*ii*) If All the Deer are Removed

Deer is a food (or prey) for lion. Now, if somehow, all the deer population from a forest is removed, then there will not be sufficient food for the lions. Some of the lions will die because of starvation and hence the population of lions will decrease. The decrease in population of lions will disturb other food chains in which lions operate. The hungry lions of the forest can come out of the forest in search of food and may even kill domestic animals or human beings for obtaining food. If the lion and deer are operating in other food chains of the food web, the removal of deer population and the subsequent reduction in lion population will disturb the balance of ecosystem.

(*iii*) If All the Producers are Removed

If all the producers like grass and other plants are removed, then no deer or lion (or any other organism) will be able to exist. This is because the food and energy necessary for sustaining life is derived from the producer organisms like grass, plants and their products.

From the above examples we conclude that if we kill all the organisms in one trophic level, it will cause too much damage to the environment. So, we cannot remove all the organisms of a trophic level without causing any damage to the ecosystem. The impact of removing all the organisms of a trophic level will be different for different trophic levels (as explained in the above given examples). We will now answer some questions based on trophic levels.

Sample Problem 1. Which of the following belong to the same trophic level ?

Grass; Hawk; Rabbit; Frog; Deer

Solution. Here, grass is a producer, hawk is a top carnivore, rabbit is a herbivore, frog is a carnivore and deer is a herbivore. Since rabbit and deer are both herbivores, so they belong to the same trophic level (2nd trophic level).

Sample Problem 2. Which of the following belong to the same trophic level ?

Frog; Grasshopper; Grass; Snake; Algae

Solution. Here, frog is a carnivore, grasshopper is a herbivore, grass is a producer, snake is a top carnivore, and algae is producer. Since grass and algae are both producers, so they belong to the same trophic level (1st trophic level).

Before we go further, **please answer the following questions :**

Very Short Answer Type Questions

1. What is the functional unit of the environment comprising of the living and non-living components called ?
2. Name two natural ecosystems and two artificial ecosystems.
3. Which one of the following is not a terrestial ecosystem ?
   Forest, Grassland, Aquarium, Desert
4. Why are plants called producers ?
5. What name has been given to those organisms which break down the complex organic compounds present in dead animals and plants ?
6. What are planktons ?
7. State whether the following statements are true or false :
   (*a*) In biology, human beings are called producers.
   (*b*) Secondary consumers and tertiary consumers, both are carnivores.
8. Which category of organisms forms the starting point of a food chain ?
9. Which of the following belong to the same trophic level ?
   Goat ; Spider ; Plants ; Hawk ; Rat
10. Which of the following belong to the same trophic level ?
    Tree ; Frog ; Snake ; Grass ; Lizard
11. Write an aquatic food chain.
12. Name the organisms belonging to the second and the fourth trophic levels in the food chain comprising the following :
    Frogs, Plants, Snakes, Hawk, Insects
13. What are the various steps of food chain called ?
14. Construct a food chain comprising the following :
    Snakes, Hawk, Rats, Plants
15. Arrange the following in a food chain :
    Fish, Algae, Small animals, Big Fish
16. Which organisms belong to third and fourth trophic levels in the food chain comprising the following ?
    Rats, Plants, Hawk, Snakes
17. Which one term in the following includes the others ?
    air, flora, fauna, environment, water, sunlight, soil
18. A food chain represents a unidirectional flow of X. What is X ?
19. Fill in the following blanks with suitable words :
    (*a*) Decomposer organisms are................in their action.
    (*b*) In nature, all green plants are..................... whereas animals are consumers.
    (*c*) A series of organisms, each of which feeds on the next organism, the beginning of which is a green plant, is called a ....
    (*d*) The science that deals with the inter-relationships of living things with one another and their environment is called.....................
    (*e*) Plastic is a ....material whereas paper is a..................material.

Short Answer Type Questions

20. Explain the terms 'producer' and 'consumer'. Give two examples of producers and two of consumers.
21. (*a*) Define decomposers. Name one decomposer.
    (*b*) What is the role of decomposers in the ecosystem ?
22. What is meant by a primary consumer, secondary consumer and a tertiary consumer ? Give one example of each.

23. Give an example of a four step food chain operating in grassland. Name the secondary consumer in this food chain

24. (*a*) Define trophic level. Draw the food chain with four trophic levels.

(*b*) What will happen if we kill all the organisms in one trophic level ?

25. What is the difference between the food habits of organisms belonging to the first and the third trophic levels ? Give one example each of the organisms belonging to these two trophic levels.

26. Can the organisms of any trophic level be removed without causing any damage to the ecosystem ? Will the impact of removing all the organisms in a trophic level be different for different trophic levels ?

27. Consider the food chain :

Grass ⟶ Deer ⟶ Lion

What will happen if all the lions are removed from the above food chain ?

28. The number of malaria patients in a village increased tremendously when large number of frogs were exported from the village. What could be the cause for it ?

29. How does a biodegradable waste differ from a non-biodegradable waste ? Give two examples of non-biodegradable wastes which pollute our environment.

30. Which of the following are biodegradable and which non-biodegradable ?

Glass bottle, Paper, Ball point pen refill, Hay, DDT, Wheat, Cake, Wood, Polythene bag, Jute bag, Cotton cloth, Grass, Vegetable peels

31. (*a*) Describe an activity to show that while paper is biodegradable but plastic (say, polythene) is non-biodegradable.

(*b*) Explain why, some materials are biodegradable but some are non-biodegradable.

32. Write down a food chain :

(*a*) in the sea

(*b*) which ends with humans

(*c*) with five links in it.

33. At which trophic level a person is feeding when he is eating :

(*a*) roasted chicken (*b*) bread (*c*) eggs (*d*) apple (*e*) fish

34. A student went to study a local pond. In one part of the pond she noticed tadpoles scraping at some pond weed. In another part she saw a water beetle holding a tadpole in its jaws.

(*a*) Construct a food chain for the pond.

(*b*) How many links are there in this chain ?

35. Construct (*a*) a long food chain, and (*b*) a short foodchain, ending with man.

36. (*a*) State one advantage of using jute bags over plastic bags for shopping.

(*b*) Write a common food chain of a pond ecosystem having four links.

37. We do not clean ponds or lakes but an aquarium needs to be cleaned periodically. Why ?

38. What will be the consequence of the absence of decomposers in the ecosystem ?

39. Give two differences between food chain and food web.

40. Write one or two words for each of the following statements/definitions :

(*a*) Each level of food chain where transfer of energy takes place

(*b*) The physical factors like temperature, rainfall, light, soil, air and water of an ecosystem

(*c*) Organisms which depend on the producers for food either directly or indirectly

(*d*) The physical and biological world where we live in

(*e*) Selfcontained unit of living things and their non-living environment needing only sunlight for its functioning

Long Answer Type Questions

41. (*a*) What is meant by biodegradable waste materials ? Give two examples of biodegradable wastes.

(*b*) Which of the following materials are non-biodegradable ?

Aluminium wire, Tea leaves, Synthetic fibre, Wool

42. (*a*) What is meant by non-biodegradable waste materials ? Give two examples of non-biodegradable wastes.

(*b*) Which of the following materials are biodegradable ?
Animal bones, Iron nails, Plastic mugs, Leather belts, Silver foil

43. (*a*) Define an ecosystem. Give examples of any two ecosystems.
(*b*) List the biotic and abiotic components of an ecosystem.

44. (*a*) What is a food chain ? Give one example of a simple food chain.
(*b*) What is a 'food web' ? Show its formation.

45. (*a*) What is meant by 'environment' ?
(*b*) What type of substances are the major pollutants of the environment ? Name two such substances.
(*c*) Name the organisms whose uncontrolled activities are damaging the environment.
(*d*) Explain why, it is better to use paper bags than plastic bags.

Multiple Choice Questions (MCQs)

46. Which of the following constitutes a food chain ?
(*a*) Grass, Wheat and Mango (*b*) Grass, Goat and Human
(*c*) Goat, Cow and Elephant (*d*) Grass, Fish and Goat

47. In a food chain, the initial organism is usually :
(*a*) photosynthetic (*b*) herbivore (*c*) saprophytic (*d*) parasitic

48. Which of the following represents a possible food chain found in a pond :

Primary producers	*Primary consumers*	*Secondary consumers*
(*a*) green algae	fish	mosquito larvae
(*b*) fish	green algae	mosquito larvae
(*c*) mosquito larvae	fish	green algae
(*d*) green algae	mosquito larvae	fish

49. Which of the following are decomposers of dead organisms ?

Bacteria	*Fungi*	*Viruses*
(*a*) no	yes	yes
(*b*) yes	no	yes
(*c*) yes	yes	no
(*d*) yes	yes	yes

50. Which of the following is an artificial ecosystem ?
(*a*) pond (*b*) crop field (*c*) lake (*d*) forest

51. Disposable plastic plates should not be used because :
(*a*) they are made of light weight materials (*b*) they are made of toxic materials
(*c*) they are made of biodegradable materials (*d*) they are made of non-biodegradable materials

52. In a food chain, the third trophic level is always occupied by :
(*a*) carnivores (*b*) herbivores (*c*) decomposers (*d*) producers

53. Accumulation of non-biodegradable pesticides in the food chain in increasing amount at each higher trophic level is known as :
(*a*) eutrophication (*b*) pollution (*c*) biomagnification (*d*) accumulation

54. If a grasshopper is eaten by a frog, then the energy transfer will be from :
(*a*) producer to decomposer (*b*) producer to primary consumer
(*c*) primary consumer to secondary consumer (*d*) secondary consumer to tertiary consumer

55. An ecosystem includes :
(*a*) all living organisms (*b*) non-living objects
(*c*) both living organisms and non-living objects (*d*) all living organisms and input of sun's energy

56. The decomposers in an ecosystem :
(*a*) convert inorganic material to simpler forms (*b*) convert organic material to inorganic forms
(*c*) convert inorganic material into organic compounds (*d*) do not break down organic compounds

57. What will happen if deer is missing in the food chain given below ?

Grass ⟶ Deer ⟶ Tiger

(*a*) The population of tigers increases
(*b*) The population of grass decreases
(*c*) Tigers will start eating grass
(*d*) The population of tigers decreases and the population of grass increases.

58. Organisms which synthesise carbohydrates from inorganic compounds by using radiant energy are called :
(*a*) decomposers (*b*) producers (*c*) herbivores (*d*) carnivores

59. Organisms of a higher trophic level which feed on several types of organisms belonging to a number of lower trophic levels constitute the :
(*a*) ecosystem (*b*) food web (*c*) ecological pyramid (*d*) food chain

60. In the following groups of materials, which group/groups contain only non-biodegradable materials ?
(*i*) wood, paper, leather (*ii*) polythene, detergent, PVC
(*iii*) plastic, detergent, grass (*iv*) plastic, bakelite, DDT
(*a*) (*iii*) (*b*) (*iv*) (*c*) (*i*) and (*iii*) (*d*) (*ii*) and (*iv*)

61. Which of the following statement is incorrect ?
(*a*) all green plants and blue green algae are producers
(*b*) green plants get their food from readymade organic compounds
(*c*) producers prepare their own food from inorganic compounds
(*d*) plants convert solar energy into chemical energy

62. Which of the following group of organisms are not constituents of a food chain ?
(*i*) grass, lion, rabbit, wolf (*ii*) plankton, man, fish, grasshopper
(*iii*) wolf, grass, snake, tiger (*iv*) frog, snake, eagle, grass, grasshopper
(*a*) (*i*) and (*iii*) (*b*) (*iii*) and (*iv*) (*c*) (*ii*) and (*iii*) (*d*) (*i*) and (*iv*)

63. In the figure given alongside, the various trophic levels are shown in the form of a pyramid. At which trophic level the maximum energy is available ?
(*a*) T_4 (*b*) T_2 (*c*) T_1 (*d*) T_3

T_4
T_3
T_2
T_1

64. One of the following is not a biodegradable material. This one is :
(*a*) cotton (*b*) animal bones (*c*) aluminium foil (*d*) wood

65. Which of the following is not a non-biodegradable material ?
(*a*) nylon socks (*b*) plastic school bag (*c*) jute carry bag (*d*) polyester clothes

66. The use of one of the following will pollute the environment. This one is :
(*a*) paper carry bags (*b*) cotton cloth carry bags
(*c*) nylon cloth carry bags (*d*) jute carry bags

67. One of the following is not a consumer. This one is :
(*a*) giraffe (*b*) antelope (*c*) algae (*d*) alligator

68. Which of the following is not a producer ?
(*a*) grass (*b*) zooplankton (*c*) phytoplankton (*d*) paddy

69. One of the following is a micro-consumer. This one is :
(*a*) ant (*b*) lice (*c*) fungi (*d*) mosquito

70. Which of the following act as decomposers in an ecosystem ?
(*a*) *Lactobacillus* bacteria (*b*) *Cyanobacteria* (*c*) *Putrefying* bacteria (*d*) *Rhizobium* bacteria

71. One of the following helps in the recycling of materials in an ecosystem. This one is :
(*a*) autotrophs (*b*) saprotrophs (*c*) omnivores (*d*) carnivores

72. In the food chain comprising of a snake, grass, insect, and frog, the secondary consumer is :
(*a*) insect (*b*) snake (*c*) frog (*d*) grass

73. Sahara Desert was formed over a period of time due to one of the following uncontrolled activities of man :
(*a*) excessive cutting down of forest plants and trees
(*b*) excessive killing of large herbivores
(*c*) excessive killing of large carnivores
(*d*) excessive use of poisonous chemicals called herbicides

Questions Based on High Order Thinking Skills (HOTS)

74. The sea water contains water beetles, tadpole, fish and weeds.
(*a*) Write a food chain comprising all the given organisms.
(*b*) Which organisms in the food chain are (*i*) herbivore, and (*ii*) carnivores ?
(*c*) Which organisms are (*i*) predators, and (*ii*) prey ?
(*d*) Which organisms can trap solar energy to make food ?
(*e*) Which organism is a secondary consumer ?

75. The following is a food chain that ends with human :
plants ⟶ bee ⟶ human
(*a*) Explain how plants provide food for bees.
(*b*) How do bees provide food for humans ?
(*c*) How does this food chain differ from a usual food chain involving human such as : plants → goat → human ?
(*d*) Do you think that the food chain given in this question can really be regarded as a food chain ? Explain your answer.

76. A food chain occurring in the sea which provides food for many people can be written as :
phytoplankton ⟶ zooplankton ⟶ X ⟶ Y
(*a*) Name one phytoplankton.
(*b*) Name two zooplanktons.
(*c*) What could be X ?
(*d*) Name the organism which Y could be.
(*e*) Which organism in the above food chain is a (*i*) primary consumer, and (*ii*) tertiary consumer ?

77. Some hunters are roaming in the plush green forest of Africa. They spot a deer and kill it. They decide to roast the deer there and then and eat it. When the hunters had just finished enjoying the feast of roasted deer, a lion attacks them. The lion kills one of the hunters and eats his flesh.
(*a*) Write a food chain which provides food to lion in this case.
(*b*) Which animal (other than deer) the lion could look for food if he did not get the hunter as prey ?
(*c*) Which other animal in the forest could have been in place of lion ?
(*d*) How does the above food chain differ from the food chain such as : plants ⟶ goat ⟶ man ?

Humans are at the end of most of the food chains in which they occur (as this picutre of man taking home a fish for food shows)

But sometimes luck runs out and humans are forced to become food for others (as this picture of lion eating a man shows). Here the human is no longer at the end of food chain. Look at the miracle of GOD : hunter has become hunted !

78. What would happen to the number of rabbits and grass plants if the number of foxes :
(*a*) increased ?
(*b*) decreased ?

79. What would happen to the number of grass plants and foxes if the number of rabbits :
(*a*) increased ?
(*b*) decreased ?

80. (*a*) Match the terms given in column I with the terms given in column II and column III having the same meaning :

Column I	*Column II*	*Column III*
(*i*) Secondary consumer	Herbivore	1st trophic level
(*ii*) Primary consumer	Autotroph	3rd trophic level
(*iii*) Producer	Carnivore	4th trophic level
(*iv*) Tertiary consumer	Large carnivore	2nd trophic level

(*b*) Give one example of a food chain having four organisms. Below each organism write the three appropriate terms from the part (*a*) above which you think it represents.

ANSWERS

1. Ecosystem **3.** Aquarium **7.** (*a*) False (*b*) True **9.** Goat and Rat (both are herbivores) **10.** Tree and Grass (both are producers) **12.** Second trophic level : Insects ; Fourth trophic level : Snakes **16.** Third trophic level : Snakes ; Fourth trophic level : Hawk **17.** Environment **18.** Energy **19.** (*a*) specific (*b*) producers (*c*) food chain (*d*) ecology (*e*) non-biodegradable ; biodegradable **25.** First trophic level : Autotrophs like green plants ; Third trophic level : Carnivores like frog **28.** Frogs eat up moquitoes. In the absence of frogs, the number of mosquitoes increased too much. Mosquitoes spread malaria **33.** (*a*) 3rd trophic level (*b*) 2nd trophic level (*c*) 3rd trophic level (*d*) 2nd trophic level (*e*) 4th trophic level **34.** (*a*) Weed ⟶ Tadpole ⟶ Water beetle (*b*) Three **35.** (*a*) Algae ⟶ Protozoa ⟶ Small fish ⟶ Big fish ⟶ Man (*b*) Plants ⟶ Man **37.** Pond is a complete ecosystem having decomposer organisms which are the cleansing agents themselves. Aquarium is a sort of incomplete ecosystem in the sense that it does not have decomposer organisms for cleansing purposes. **39.** (*i*) A food chain contains a few organisms feeding on one another whereas a food web contains a large number of organisms in the form of interconnected food chains (*ii*) In a food chain, the organism at higher trophic levels feeds only upon a single organism of the lower trophic level but in a food web, the organism at higher trophic levels can feed upon organisms of lower trophic levels of many food chains **40.** (*a*) Trophic level (*b*)Abiotic components (*c*) Consumers (or Heterotrophs) (*d*) Environment (or Biosphere) (*e*) Ecosystem **45.** (*c*) Humans **46.** (*b*) **47.** (*a*) **48.** (*d*) **49.** (*c*) **50.** (*b*) **51.** (*d*) **52.** (*a*) **53.** (*c*) **54.** (*c*) **55.** (*c*) **56.** (*b*) **57.** (*d*) **58.** (*b*) **59.** (*b*) **60.** (*d*) **61.** (*b*) **62.** (*c*) **63.** (*c*) **64.** (*c*) **65.** (*c*) **66.** (*c*) **67.** (*c*) **68.** (*b*) **69.** (*c*) **70.** (*c*) **71.** (*b*) **72.** (*c*) **73.** (*c*) **74.** (*a*) Weeds ⟶ Tadpole ⟶ Water beetles ⟶ Fish (*b*) (*i*) Tadpole (*ii*) Water beetles ; Fish (*c*) (*i*) Water beetles; Fish (*ii*) Tadpole; Water beetles (*d*) Weed (*e*) Water beetles **75.** (*a*) Bees suck nectar from flowers of plants (*b*) Bees provide honey as food (*c*) In this food chain, human eats the product obtained (honey) from bees, he does not eat the bees *directly*. On the other hand, in the food chain, plants ⟶ goat ⟶ human, the human eats the meat of goat directly (*d*) No. Because the human does not obtain food by eating the bees directly **76.**(*a*) Algae (*b*) Protozoa ; Tadpole (*c*) Fish (*d*) Man (*e*) (*i*) Zooplankton (*ii*) Man **77.** (*a*) Plants ⟶ Deer ⟶ Man ⟶ Lion (*b*) Rabbit (*c*) Tiger (*d*) In the above case, man is not at the end of food chain but in the case of plants ⟶ goat ⟶ man, the man is at the end of food chain. **80.** (*a*) (*i*) Secondary consumer ; Carnivore ; 3rd trophic level (*ii*) Primary consumer ; Herbivore ; 2nd trophic level (*iii*) Producer ; Autotroph ; 1st trophic level (*iv*) Tertiary consumer ; Large carnivore ; 4th trophic level

(*b*)

Plants ⟶	Insect ⟶	Frog ⟶	Snake
Autotroph	Herbivore	Carnivore	Large carnivore
(Producer)	(Primary consumer)	(Secondary consumer)	(Tertiary consumer)
(1st trophic level)	(2nd trophic level)	(3rd trophic level)	(4th trophic level)

THE SUN PROVIDES ENERGY FOR MAINTAINING ALL LIFE ON EARTH

All the organisms (plants and animals) depend on the sun for their constant need of energy, and upon earth for the materials which enter into their body. We will now describe how energy received from the sun flows in the various trophic levels of an ecosystem in the form of chemical energy of food.

TRANSFER OF ENERGY IN FOOD CHAINS

The food chain in a community actually represents a stepwise transfer of food and the energy contained in food. The food and energy enter the living components of the ecosystem through the process of photosynthesis. This is because photosynthesis is a process which combines the substances like carbon dioxide, water and sunlight energy to form food like carbohydrates and converts light energy of the sun into chemical energy of carbohydrates. This food and energy is then transferred from the producer organisms to herbivores and from herbivores to carnivores, through the food chain. Let us discuss this flow of energy in detail.

First Step

The green plants (or producers) have a mechanism for trapping solar energy (sun's energy) with the help of their green pigment called chlorophyll. The green plants after trapping the solar energy, convert it into chemical energy which is stored as carbohydrates in the plants. Thus, the initial point where energy from the environment enters into the living components of ecosystem (like plants and animals) is the process of preparation of food by green plants through photosynthesis. On an average, **about 1% of the sun's energy falling on the leaves is used by the plants in the process of photosynthesis and stored as chemical energy of food.** The plants utilise the energy stored in them for their metabolic activities like respiration and growth (tissue building). Some of the energy is, however, not utilized and it is released as unusable heat into the community environment (see Figure 23).

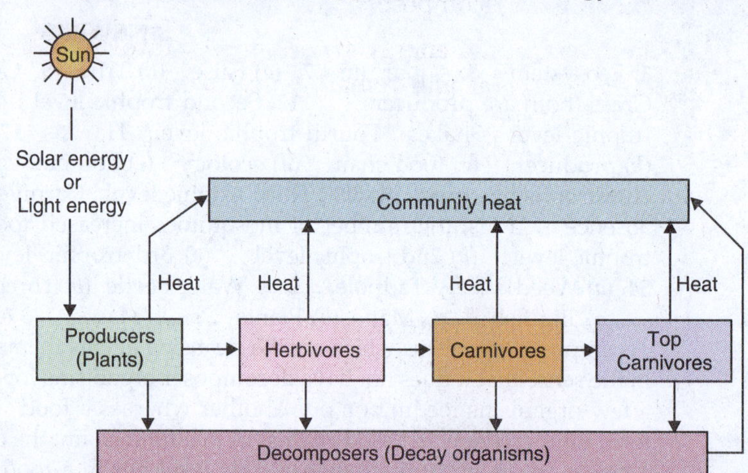

Figure 23. Diagram to show the transfer of energy in a food chain.

Second Step

The plants (or producers) are eaten up by herbivores. The chemical energy stored in plant food is transferred with food to herbivores. The herbivores utilize this energy for their various metabolic activities like respiration and also for their growth. Some of the energy, however, remains unutilized which is released by the herbivores as heat energy to the environment (see Figure 23).

Third Step

The herbivores are eaten up or consumed by carnivores. The chemical energy stored in the flesh of herbivores is transferred with food (or flesh) to the carnivores. The carnivores utilize this energy for their various metabolic activities like respiration and also for their growth. Some of the energy, however, remains unutilized by the carnivores and it is released as heat energy into the environment (see Figure 23). This process of the transfer of energy is repeated with large carnivores or top carnivores (who eat small carnivores), and so on.

It should be noted that some of the energy from producers and consumers (like plants, herbivores and carnivores) is also utilized for the life processes of micro-organisms called decomposers. The decomposers, in turn, release the unutilized energy as heat into the environment (see Figure 23). It is obvious from the above discussion that the energy which remains unutilized by producers, consumers (herbivores and carnivores) and decomposers is lost into the environment as heat. It is called community heat.

We should remember the following points about the transfer of energy in the ecosystem :

1. Energy is not created in the ecosystem. Energy is only converted from one form to another. For example, light energy coming from the sun is converted into chemical energy of food like carbohydrates by the process of photosynthesis. Thus, *photosynthesis converts light energy into chemical energy.*

2. There is a continuous transfer of energy from one trophic level of organisms to the next trophic level in a food chain. For example, producers like plants transfer energy to the herbivorous animals like deer, and the herbivorous animals like deer transfer energy to carnivorous animals like lion, so that there is a continuous transfer of energy in the food chain : Plants → Deer → Lion. This transfer of energy takes place in the form of chemical energy of food.

3. At each trophic level of organisms, some of the energy is utilized by the organisms for their metabolic activities like respiration, and for growth.

4. A part of the energy at each trophic level (like producers, herbivores and carnivores) is utilized for the functioning of decomposers.

5. There is a loss of energy at each energy transfer in various trophic levels of organisms which goes into the environment and remains unutilized. In other words, we can say that the amount of energy available at each successive trophic level is less than the energy available at the producer level. Thus, ***when we move from the first trophic level of producers (plants) to second trophic level of herbivores and third trophic level of carnivores, the amount of energy available gradually decreases.*** This is because at each trophic level, energy is lost as heat energy which goes into the environment.

Flow of Materials in Ecosystem is Cyclic but Flow of Energy is Unidirectional

The materials like water, carbon (as carbon dioxide) and nitrogen (as minerals) are taken up by the plants from soil, air and water bodies, etc., and made into food. This food is then passed on to the animals like herbivores and carnivores in a food chain. After the death and decay of plants and animals, the materials like water, carbon and nitrogen present in their bodies are returned to soil, air and water, from where they were taken originally. These materials can then be reused for the growth of new plants. In this way, **the same materials are used again and again, the materials are not lost from the environment. So, the flow of materials like water, carbon and nitrogen, etc., in the ecosystem is said to be cyclic.** *This is not so in the case of energy.*

The flow of energy in the ecosystem is unidirectional (or one-directional). The energy enters the plants (from the sun) through photosynthesis during the making of food. This energy is then passed on from one organism to another in a food chain. Energy given out by the organisms as heat is lost to the environment, it does not return to be used by the plants again. This makes the flow of energy in ecosystem 'unidirectional'. Thus, **the flow of energy in the ecosystem is said to be unidirectional because the energy lost as heat from the living organisms of a food chain cannot be reused by plants in photosynthesis.**

Ten Per Cent Law

During the transfer of energy through successive trophic levels in an ecosystem, there is a loss of energy all along the path. No transfer of energy is 100 per cent. The studies of transfer of energy in different food chains in a large number of ecosystems has revealed a uniform pattern of transfer of energy, which is given by 10 per cent law. The 10 per cent law which was given by Lindeman in the year 1942, is one of the most useful generalisations about the magnitude of loss of energy in food chains. **According to ten per cent law, only 10 per cent of the energy entering a particular trophic level of organisms is available for transfer to the next higher trophic level.** All the energy transfers in food chains follow the 10% law which in simple terms means that **the energy available at each successive trophic level is 10 per cent of the previous level.** Thus, there is a progressive decline (gradual reduction) in the amount of energy available as we go from producer level to the higher trophic levels of organisms. Let us take one example to understand the 10 per cent law more clearly.

Figure 24. Raymond Lindeman : The scientist who gave ten per cent law for energy transfers in food chains.

Suppose 1000 joules of light energy emitted by the sun falls on the plants (called producers). We know that the plants convert only one per cent (1%) of the light energy falling on them into chemical energy of food. So, the energy which will be available in plant matter as food will be only 1% of 1000 joules, which comes to 10 joules. The remaining 1000 − 10 = 990 joules of light energy or solar energy which is not utilized by the plants is reflected back into the environment (see Figure 25). **Please note that the ten per cent law will *not* apply at this stage.** It will apply only in the transfer of energy in the food chain.

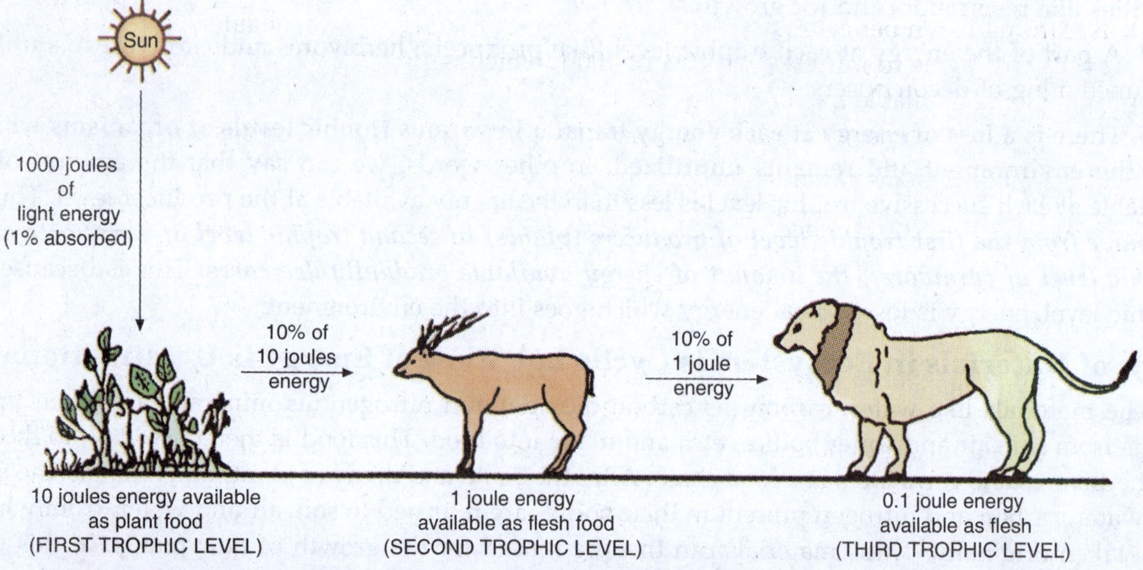

Figure 25. Diagram to illustrate the 10 per cent law for the transfer of energy in a food chain.

We will now apply the 10 per cent law to the food chain : Plants → Herbivores → Carnivores (represented by plants, deer and lion in Figure 25). The plants or first trophic level has 10 joules of energy in it. Now, according to ten per cent law, only 10% of 10 joules of energy (which is 1 joule) will be available for transfer at the next trophic level, so that the herbivore (deer) will have only 1 joule of energy stored as food at the second trophic level (see Figure 25). Applying the ten per cent law again we find that 10% of the remaining 1 joule (which is 0.1 joule) will be transferred to third trophic level of carnivore (lion). So, the energy available in the lion as food will be only 0.1 joule (see Figure 25). We will now solve some problems based on ten per cent law.

Sample Problem 1. Calculate the amount of energy available to lion in the following food chain if plants have 20000 J of energy available from the sun :

Plants ⟶ Deer ⟶ Lion

Solution. (*i*) Plants can trap only 1% of the sun's energy falling on them. Now, 1% of 20000 J is 200 J, so the plants have actually 200 J of energy available in them as food (The 10 per cent law does not apply at this stage).

(*ii*) The plants are eaten up by deer. Now, according to 10 per cent law, 10% of 200 J, that is, 20 J of energy will be available in deer as flesh food.

(*iii*) The deer will transfer 10% of its 20 J energy to the lion. Thus, the food energy available to the lion will be 10% of 20 J which comes to 2 J.

The above results can be shown more clearly as follows :

Sun
20,000 J ↓ (1 % absorbed)

$$\underset{200\text{ J}}{\text{Plants}} \xrightarrow{10\%\text{ of }200\text{ J}} \underset{20\text{ J}}{\text{Deer}} \xrightarrow{10\%\text{ of }20\text{ J}} \underset{2\text{ J}}{\text{Lion}}$$

Sample Problem 2. Consider the following food chain :

Grass ⟶ Mice ⟶ Snakes ⟶ Peacocks

If in this chain, 100 J of energy is available at the producer level, then calculate the energy transferred to the peacocks as food. State the law used in the calculations.

Solution. The producer level in this food chain is grass, so 100 J of energy is available in grass as food. We have now to apply 10 per cent law to the above food chain :

(*i*) According to ten per cent law, 10% of the energy of grass will be available as food in mice. Thus, the energy available to mice will be 10% of 100 J, which is 10 J.

(*ii*) The energy available to snakes will be 10% of 10 J which is 1 J.

(*iii*) And finally, the energy available to peacocks will be 10% of 1 J, which is 0.1 J.

The above conclusions can now be depicted as follows :

$$\underset{100\ J}{\text{Grass}} \xrightarrow{10\%} \underset{10\ J}{\text{Mice}} \xrightarrow{10\%} \underset{1\ J}{\text{Snakes}} \xrightarrow{10\%} \underset{0.1\ J}{\text{Peacocks}}$$

Why the Number of Trophic Levels in a Food Chain is Limited

At each trophic level in a food chain, a large portion of the energy is utilized for the maintenance of organisms which occur at that trophic level and lost as heat. As a result of this, organisms in each trophic level pass on less and less energy to the next trophic levels, than they receive. The longer the food chain, the less is the energy available to the final member of food chain. **Food chains generally consist of three or four steps (three or four organisms)** because after that the energy available for the next organism will be so small that it will be insufficient to sustain the life of that organism. **There are, however, some food chains containing five steps (or five organisms) but there are rarely more than five steps (or five organisms) in a food chain.** We will now discuss the accumulation of harmful chemicals in food chains.

Accumulation of Harmful Chemicals in Food Chains

The accumulation of harmful chemicals such as pesticides in the living organisms like plants, animals and humans (men) unknowingly, through the food chain, is called bioconcentration of pesticides. This happens as follows.

Pesticides are poisonous chemical substances which are sprayed over crop plants to protect them from pests (harmful small animals) and diseases. These chemical pesticides mix up with soil and water. From

Figure 26. DDT is a common pesticide.

Figure 27. Pesticide being sprayed over standing crop in the fields.

soil and water, these pesticides are absorbed by the growing plants alongwith water and other minerals. When herbivorous animals eat plant food, then these poisonous chemical pesticides go into their bodies through the food chain. And when the carnivorous animals eat herbivores, then the pesticides get transferred to their bodies. Man being an omnivore, eats plant food as well as herbivores. So, the pesticides present in plant food and herbivores also get transferred to the man's body through food. Thus, **pesticides enter the food chain at the producer level (plant level)** and in the process of transfer of food through food chains these harmful chemicals get concentrated at each trophic level. **The increase in concentration of harmful chemical substances like pesticides in the body of living organisms at each trophic level of a food chain is called biological magnification.**

Pesticides are *non-biodegradable* chemicals, so they get accumulated at each trophic level. Since humans occupy the top level in any food chain, so the maximum amount of harmful chemical pesticides gets accumulated in our bodies. This damages our health gradually. Tests have shown that the most commonly used pesticide DDT is accumulating in our bodies through the food chains. Please note that the pesticides present in our food grains (like wheat, rice), fruits, vegetables, and meat cannot always be removed by washing, etc. Let us solve one problem now.

Sample Problem. Which of the following will have the maximum concentration of harmful chemicals in its body ?

Peacock, Frog, Grass, Snake, Grasshopper

Solution. In order to answer such questions, we should first write the food chain involving the given organisms. The organism which occurs at the highest trophic level (on the extreme right side) in the food chain will have the maximum concentration of harmful chemicals in its body. In this case, grass is eaten by grasshopper; grasshopper is eaten by frog; frog is eaten by snake and finally snake is eaten by peacock. So, the food chain will be :

Grass ⟶ Grasshopper ⟶ Frog ⟶ Snake ⟶ Peacock

In this food chain, since peacock occurs at the highest trophic level (on the extreme right side), therefore, peacock will have the maximum concentration of harmful chemicals in its body.

How do Our Activities Affect the Environment

We (human beings) are an important part of the environment. Our activities change the environment around us. And the changes in environment then affect us. We will now discuss two environmental problems caused by our activities : depletion of ozone layer, and disposal of domestic wastes (or household garbage).

DEPLETION OF OZONE LAYER

We know that oxygen is O_2. Oxygen molecule is made up of 2 atoms of oxygen combined together. Oxygen gas is essential for life because it is needed in respiration. Ozone is O_3. Ozone molecule is made up of 3 atoms of oxygen combined together. Ozone is also a gas but it is poisonous in nature (if inhaled). Let us see how ozone is formed. Ozone is formed high up in the atmosphere by the action of ultraviolet radiation on oxygen gas. This happens as follows : The high energy ultraviolet radiation (UV radiation) coming from the sun splits oxygen gas into free oxygen atoms.

$$\underset{\text{Oxygen molecule}}{O_2} \xrightarrow[\text{(From sun)}]{\text{UV radiation}} \underset{\text{Oxygen atom}}{O} + \underset{\text{Oxygen atom}}{O}$$

The free oxygen atoms thus produced are very reactive. One oxygen atom reacts with an oxygen molecule to form an ozone molecule :

$$\underset{\text{Oxygen molecule}}{O_2} + \underset{\text{Oxygen atom}}{O} \longrightarrow \underset{\text{Ozone molecule}}{O_3}$$

At a height between 15 kilometres and 60 kilometres, there is a layer of ozone gas (O_3) in the upper atmosphere. This **ozone layer is very important for the existence of life on earth because it absorbs most of the harmful ultraviolet radiations coming from the sun and prevents them from reaching the earth.** The ultraviolet radiations have extremely harmful effects on human beings, other animals as well as plants.

For example, **ultraviolet rays can cause skin cancer.** They also damage the eyes by causing an eye disease called cataract. Ultraviolet rays damage immune system by lowering the body's resistance to diseases.

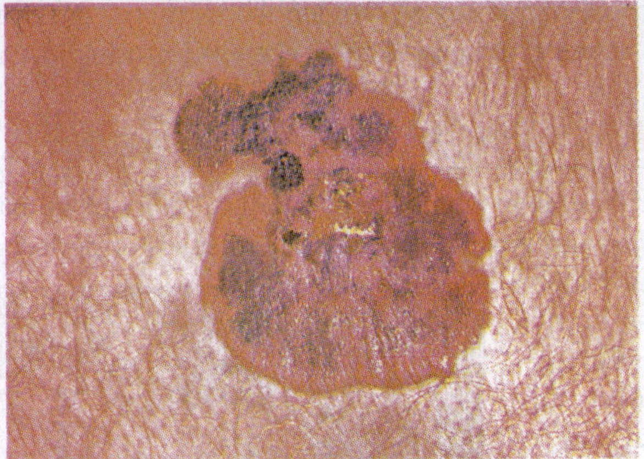

Figure 28. This type of skin cancer can be caused by ultraviolet radiations (or ultraviolet rays) coming from the sun.

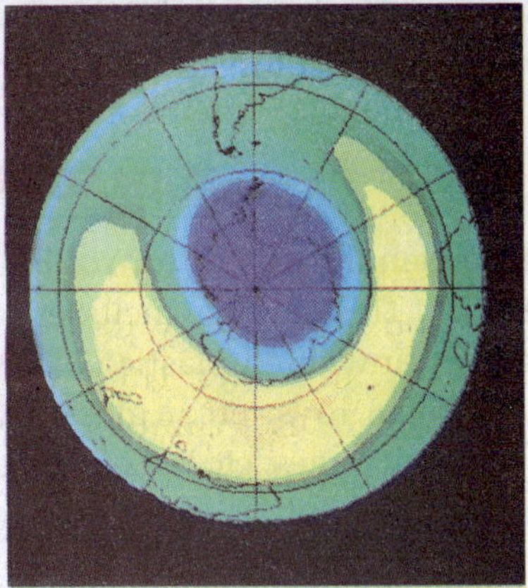

Figure 29. This satellite picture shows that a hole has already been formed in ozone layer over Antarctica. The blue area in the above picture is the hole in the ozone layer where there is virtually no ozone at all.

Thus, it is the ozone layer in the upper atmosphere which protects us from these diseases by absorbing ultraviolet rays coming from the sun.

It has now been found that the amount of ozone is getting depleted (or reduced) due to which the ozone layer in the upper atmosphere is becoming thinner and thinner day by day. **The depletion of ozone layer is due to the use of chemicals called chlorofluorocarbons.**

Figure 30. Chlorofluorocarbons (CFCs) are used in refrigerators. The CFC refrigerant circulates through pipes at the back of refrigerator.

Figure 31. This aerosol 'can' contains a mixture of CFC and liquid 'air freshener' under pressure. When pressure is released, the CFC acts as a propellant and pushes out air freshner in the form of a spray.

This happens as follows : Chlorofluorocarbons (CFC) are the chemicals which are widely used in refrigeration (refrigerators and air conditioners) as a coolant; in fire extinguishers and in aerosol sprayers. Chlorofluorocarbons released into the air react with ozone gas present in the ozone layer and destroy it gradually. Due to this, the ozone layer in the upper atmosphere has become thinner, allowing more ultraviolet rays to pass through it to the earth. Thus, due to the depletion of ozone layer caused by chlorofluorocarbons, more ultraviolet radiations reach the earth.

If the ozone layer in the atmosphere disappears completely, then all the extemely harmful ultraviolet radiations coming from the sun would reach the earth. These ultraviolet radiations would cause skin cancer and other ailments in men and animals, and also damage the plants. All the life on the earth would be destroyed gradually. In 1987, in an attempt to protect ozone layer, the United Nations Environment Programme (UNEP) forged an agreement among its member countries to freeze CFC production at 1986 levels.

MANAGING THE GARBAGE WE PRODUCE

The household wastes (or rubbish) is called garbage. Every household produces a lot of garbage (or wastes) daily. This garbage includes left-over food, fruit and vegetable peels, fallen leaves of potted plants, waste paper, unwanted plastic objects (such as plastic bottles, polythene bags, toys, etc.), glass articles (like glass bottles, broken window panes, etc.), metal objects (like aluminium foils, rusted iron grills, etc.), old wooden objects, rags (old, torn clothes), discarded shoes, and sewage. Some of the garbage (or waste) is biodegradable whereas a major part of it is non-biodegradable. If the household garbage or waste is not disposed of properly, it can pollute the environment like soil, water and air.

Figure 32. Household wastes (or rubbish).

'Disposal of waste' means 'to get rid of waste'. The disposal of waste should be done in a scientific way. There are different methods of waste disposal. The method to be used depends on the nature of the waste. **Some of the important modes of waste disposal are :**

(*i*) Recycling (*ii*) Preparation of compost (*iii*) Incineration (*iv*) Landfill (*v*) Sewage treatment

We will now describe all these methods of waste disposal (or garbage disposal) briefly, one by one. Let us start with recycling.

1. Recycling

The solid wastes like paper, plastics and metals, etc., are recycled. For example, waste paper is sent to paper mills where it is reprocessed to form new paper once again. The broken plastic articles like plastic

(*a*) These greeting cards are made of recycled paper

(*b*) These household articles are made of recycled plastic

(*c*) These hanging lampshades are made of recycled metal

Figure 33. Wastes like paper, plastic and metal should be recycled to be used again.

bags, buckets, bowls, cups, plates, etc., are sent to plastic processing factories where they are melted and remoulded to make new articles. Similarly, waste metal articles are sent to metal industries where they are melted and recycled as solid metal for various purposes.

2. Preparation of Compost

Biodegradable domestic wastes such as left-over food, fruit and vegetable peels, and leaves of potted plants, etc., can be converted into compost by burying in a pit dug into ground, and used as manure.

Figure 34. This is compost. It has been prepared by burying domestic wastes such as left-over food, fruit and vegetable peels, and leaves of potted plants in a pit dug into the ground.

Figure 35. This is an incinerator. The solid waste is burned at a high temperature in the incinerator. The organic matter in waste burns away and only a little ash is left behind.

3. Incineration

'Incineration' means 'reducing to ashes'. The burning of a substance at high temperature (of more than 1000°C) to form ash is called incineration. Incineration is used to destroy household waste, chemical waste and biological waste (like that from hospitals). Incineration greatly reduces the volume of the waste. This is because when the large volume of waste material is burned, then only a small amount of ash is left behind which can be disposed of by landfill. Incineration is carried out in an incinerator (which is a kind of furnace). The waste disposal on large scale by using incinerators is done by the Municipality of a City. The solid waste is burned at a high temperature in the incinerator. All the organic matter present in waste is removed as carbon dioxide and water vapour. The ash left behind is removed from time to time.

4. Landfill

The disposal of wastes by putting it in low-lying areas of ground and covering it with earth is called landfill. Most of the solid waste in urban areas (which cannot be disposed of by other methods) is dumped in low-lying areas of ground and covered with earth to level the uneven ground. A big landfill site can be used to dispose of waste materials (or garbage) for a considerable time.

Figure 36. A landfill site where solid wastes are dumped in low-lying area of ground and covered with earth (or soil).

Figure 37. A sewage treatment plant where dirty drain water is treated to convert it into clean water which is then discharged into a river.

5. Sewage Treatment

The dirty drain water containing urine and faeces which is carried from our homes by the underground pipes (called sewers) is called sewage. If untreated sewage is dumped into a river, it can pollute the river water. Thus, sewage is disposed of by treating it at the sewage treatment plant (or sewage works). The treatment of sewage produces clean water which is discharged into the river. The organic matter present in sewage is 'digested' in the digesters of sewage treatment plant to produce 'sewage gas' (which is a kind of biogas), and 'manure'.

We will now give an example to illustrate how the use of biodegradable and non-biodegradable materials can make a difference to our environment. There was a time when tea in trains was served in plastic glasses which had to be returned to the vendor. This was, however, not a hygienic thing to do. Later on disposable plastic cups were introduced (which are used 'once' and then 'thrown away'). Though it was hygienic to use a disposable plastic cup for drinking tea but the disposal of millions of plastic cups on daily basis posed a big problem. Sometime back *'kulhads'* (disposable cups made of clay) were introduced for serving tea in trains. It was, however, soon realised that the use of a lot of clay for making millions of *kulhads* daily led to the loss of fertile top soil from fields (which was used for making *kulhads*). So, the practice of using *'kulhads'* has also been discontinued. These days, disposable paper cups are being used. **The use of disposable paper cups has the following advantages over the plastic cups :**

(*i*) Paper cups are *biodegradable.* So, even if paper cups are thrown away after use, they will decompose (break down) automatically by the action of micro-organisms in due course of time. On the other hand, plastic cups are *non-biodegradable.* They will remain as such and pollute the environment.

(*ii*) Paper cups can even be disposed of by burning without causing much air pollution. On the other hand, burning of plastic cups produces toxic gases (poisonous gases) which cause too much air pollution.

We are now in a position to **answer the following questions :**

Very Short Answer Type Questions

1. What percentage of the solar energy is trapped and utilised by the plants ?
2. What percentage of energy available at the producer level is transferred at successive trophic levels in a food chain ?
3. Name the process in which a harmful chemical enters the food chain and gets concentrated at each trophic level.
4. In a food chain consisting of grass, frog, bird and insects, where will the concentration of the harmful chemicals be maximum ?
5. If a harmful chemical enters a food chain comprising cat, mice and plants, which one of these organisms is likely to have the maximum concentration of the harmful chemical in its body ?
6. Which radiations are absorbed by ozone layer ?
7. Name the group of chemical compounds which damages the ozone layer.
8. Name two waste materials which can be recycled.
9. Name the process by which the volume of solid wastes can be reduced.
10. If 5 joules of energy is available at producer level (plants), then how much energy will be transferred to the lion in the following food chain ?

    Plants ⟶ Goat ⟶ Lion
11. State whether the following statement is true or false :

    Only 10 per cent of the light energy given by the sun is available for transfer at each higher trophic level in a food chain.
12. Where does all the energy in living organisms originate from ?
13. Why are there rarely more than five links (or five organisms) in a food chain ?
14. Name two predators of snakes in a food web operating in a forest ecosystem.
15. Fill in the following blanks with suitable words :

    (*a*) Ultraviolet rays can cause skin................

    (*b*) Pesticides enter the food chain at the ....level

(c) Grass ⟶ .... ⟶ Human
(d) Lettuce ⟶ .... ⟶ Fox
(e) Plants ⟶ Antelope ⟶ ....

Short Answer Type Questions

16. What is ten per cent law ? Explain with an example.
17. Write the full form of CFC. Give its one harmful effect.
18. Explain how, harmful ultraviolet radiations of sunlight are prevented from reaching the earth's surface.
19. What are the causes of depletion of ozone layer ? Which diseases are likely to be caused if the ozone layer will become thinner ?
20. Explain how harmful chemicals enter our bodies.
21. 'If we excessively use pesticides to protect the crops from diseases, then it may cause long-term damage to mankind'. Justify this statement.
22. What is meant by biological magnification ? With the help of a food chain, explain how biological magnification of harmful chemicals can occur.
23. What is meant by bioconcentration of pesticides ? Which common pesticide has accumulated in human body in considerable amounts ?
24. What is garbage ? What does garbage consist of ?
25. Name the various modes of waste disposal.
26. How can the wastes such as paper, plastic and metal objects be disposed of ?
27. Give a method for the disposal of household wastes such as left-over food, fruit and vegetable peels, and leaves of potted plants.
28. What is meant by incineration ? For what purpose is it used ?
29. How are most of the solid wastes in urban areas disposed of ?
30. State two advantages of using disposable paper cups over disposable plastic cups.
31. What is sewage ? How is sewage disposed of ?
32. Write the harmful effects of ozone depletion.
33. What would happen if the ozone layer in the atmosphere completely disappears ?

Long Answer Type Questions

34. (a) With the help of a flow diagram, describe how energy from the sun flows through various trophic levels.
(b) Explain why, the flow of energy in the ecosystem is said to be unidirectional.

35. (a) What is ozone ? How is it formed ?
(b) How does ozone layer protect us from harmful effects in the environment ?
(c) What is UNEP ? What step has been taken by UNEP in 1987 to prevent too much damage to the ozone layer ?

36. (a) How is energy introduced into the ecosystem ?
(b) Consider the following food chains :
(i) Plants ⟶ Mice ⟶ Snakes ⟶ Hawks
(ii) Plants ⟶ Mice ⟶ Hawks
If energy available at the producer level in both the food chains is 100 J, in which case will hawks get more energy as food and by how much ? Justify your answer.

37. (a) Explain why, a food chain usually cannot have more than three or four steps.
(b) Calculate the amount of energy that will be available to big fish in the following food chain, if 10,000 J of energy is available to small algae from the sun :
Small algae ⟶ Zooplankton ⟶ Fish ⟶ Big fish

38. (a) Name and state the law given by Lindeman which tells us how much energy entering a particular trophic level of organisms is available for trasnsfer to the next higher trophic level.
(b) How much energy will be available to hawks in the food chain comprising hawk, snake, paddy and mice, if 10,000 J of energy is available to paddy from the sun ?

Multiple Choice Questions (MCQs)

39. What provides the energy which then flows through a food chain ?
(*a*) glucose (*b*) oxygen (*c*) respiration (*d*) sunlight

40. Which pollutant released into the air during refrigeration and airconditioning is the greatest contributor to the depletion of ozone layer ?
(*a*) BHC (*b*) DDT (*c*) CFC (*d*) UNEP

41. In the food chain given below, if the amount of energy available at fourth trophic level is 5 kJ, what was the energy available at the producer level ?

Grass ⟶ Grasshopper ⟶ Frog ⟶ Snake ⟶ Hawk

(*a*) 500 kJ (*b*) 50 kJ (*c*) 5000 kJ (*d*) 5 kJ

42. Which of the following limits the number of trophic levels in a food chain ?
(*a*) insufficient food supply from producer level
(*b*) decrease in energy at higher trophic levels
(*c*) increase in the number of organisms at higher trophic levels
(*d*) accumulation of harmful chemicals at higher trophic levels

43. What percentage of sun's energy falling on the leaves of green plants is utilised by the plants in the process of photosynthesis and stored as chemical energy of food ?
(*a*) 99 per cent (*b*) 10 per cent (*c*) 1 per cent (*d*) 20 per cent

44. The depletion of ozone layer in the upper atmosphere is mainly due to the emission of :
(*a*) unburnt hydrocarbons (*b*) chlorofluorocarbons
(*c*) greenhouse gases (*d*) ultraviolet radiations

45. In an ecosystem, the ten per cent energy available for transfer from one trophic level to the next is in the form of :
(*a*) heat energy (*b*) light energy (*c*) chemical energy (*d*) mechanical energy

46. The flow of energy in an ecosystem is always :
(*a*) unidirectional (*b*) bidirectional (*c*) cyclic (*d*) multidirectional

47. The excessive exposure of humans to ultraviolet rays results in :
(*i*) damage to immune system (*ii*) damage to lungs
(*iii*) skin cancer (*iv*) peptic ulcers
(*a*) (*i*) and (*ii*) (*b*) (*ii*) and (*iv*) (*c*) (*i*) and (*iii*) (*d*) (*iii*) and (*iv*)

48. Which of the following gets the minimum energy through the food chain in an ecosystem ?
(*a*) carnivore (*b*) large carnivore (*c*) producer (*d*) herbivore

49. A food chain comprises of cat, seed-eating bird, plants, and dog. The organism which will have the maximum concentration of harmful pesticides coming through the food chain is most likely to be :
(*a*) cat (*b*) plants (*c*) dog (*d*) seed-eating bird

50. An aquatic food chain comprises of the organisms like tadpoles, weeds, fish and water beetles. The organism which gets the minimum energy through this food chain is :
(*a*) water beetles (*b*) tadpoles (*c*) weeds (*d*) fish

51. Most of the water surface of a lake is covered with algae. This algae is part of the food chain which also includes small fish, bird, larvae and big fish. Which of the following will obtain the maximum energy ?
(*a*) big fish (*b*) bird (*c*) larvae (*d*) small fish

52. If the energy available at the producer level in a food chain is 150 J, how much energy will be transferred to : tertiary consumer ?
(*a*) 15 J (*b*) 10 J (*c*) 1.50 J (*d*) 0.15 J

53. If the energy transferred to a tertiary consumer in a food chain is 10 J, how much energy was available to the primary consumer ?
(*a*) 100 J (*b*) 500 J (*c*) 1000 J (*d*) 5000 J

54. In addition to wheat plants, a crop field ecosystem has organisms such as snake, peacock, eagle and mice. If the wheat plants are sprayed with pesticides periodically, which of the following will have the minimum concentration of pesticides in the body ?

(*a*) snake (*b*) eagle (*c*) mice (*d*) peacock

55. Which of the following is the best method to dispose of biological wastes from hospitals ?

(*a*) landfill (*b*) recycling (*c*) incineration (*d*) composting

56. In an ecosystem :

(*i*) the flow of energy is unidirectional

(*ii*) the flow of materials is unidirectional

(*iii*) the flow of materials is cyclic

(*iv*) the flow of energy is cyclic.

(*a*) (*i*) and (*ii*) (*b*) (*ii*) and (*iii*) (*c*) (*i*) and (*iv*) (*d*) (*i*) and (*iii*)

57. The ten per cent law is associated with

(*a*) transfer of energy from various trophic levels to decomposers in a food chain

(*b*) transfer of ATP energy into muscular energy

(*c*) transfer of chemical energy from one organism to another

(*d*) transfer of sun's energy to the organisms called producers.

58. The harmful chemical which is accumulating in human beings through food chain is :

(*a*) benzenehexachloride (*b*) dichlorodiphenyltrichloroethane

(*c*) chlorofluorocarbon (*d*) abscisic acid

59. O_2 is converted into O_3 by the action of :

(*a*) infrared radiations (*b*) ultraviolet radiations

(*c*) gamma radiations (*d*) cosmic radiations

60. Which of the following cannot be added in a composting pit to prepare compost ?

(*a*) sunflower plants (*b*) fruit and vegetable peels

(*c*) flowers of plastic (*d*) red worms

Questions Based on High Order Thinking Skills (HOTS)

61. The gas A is used by most of the animals to obtain energy from food by the process of respiration. When A is acted upon by radiation X, it gets converted into another gas B which is an allotrope of A but poisonous when inhaled. B forms a kind of layer C in the upper atmosphere which absorbs radiations X coming from a source Y and prevent them from reaching the earth. Some chemicals Z released from the various devices on the earth are destroying the layer C slowly. In fact, a hole has already been formed in layer C over the area D of the earth.

(*a*) What are gases (*i*) A, and (*ii*) B ? Write their molecular formulae.

(*b*) Name the layer C.

(*c*) What are (*i*) X, (*ii*) Y, and (*iii*) Z ?

(*d*) Name the area D.

(*e*) Name any two human ailments which may be caused by X.

62. The surface of water in a lake appears green due to a layer of tiny free-floating organisms X on its surface. The lake water also contains organisms like water beetle, fish and tadpole. The sun shines over the lake water and provides energy for the functioning of this lake ecosystem.

(*a*) What could organisms X be ?

(*b*) Write a food chain comprising of all the four organisms mentioned.

(*c*) What is the general name of the food chains like the one written above ?

(*d*) Name (*i*) secondary consumer (*ii*) producer (*iii*) tertiary consumer, and (*iv*) primary consumer, in the above food chain.

(*e*) If the tertiary consumer gets 0.2 J of energy from the secondary consumer, then how much energy was radiated by the sun to the producer ?

63. A forest ecosystem having a lot of green plants has some foxes, lions and rabbits in it.

(*a*) Write a food chain comprising all the four organisms mentioned above.

(*b*) Name (*i*) one herbivore, and (*ii*) two carnivores, in this food chain.

(*c*) Name the link which is a predator as well as a prey.

(*d*) Name (*i*) second trophic level, and (*ii*) third trophic level.

(*e*) Which link of this food chain can feed on second trophic level as well as third trophic level, independently ?

(*f*) If the sun provides 1000 J of energy to the plants, then how much energy will be transferred to fox through the food chain.

64. A food chain consists of fish, larvae, phytoplanktons and birds. The level of pesticides in water in which the fish, larvae and phytoplanktons live is quite high.

(*a*) In which organisms the pesticides enter from the polluted water ? What is this level of organisms known as ?

(*b*) Which organism will have the maximum amount of pesticides accumulated through the food chain ? What is this process known as ?

(*c*) Write the food chain comprising all the organisms mentioned above.

(*d*) Which other organism you could write in place of bird in the above food chain ?

65. Every household produces a lot of material A daily. In one of the methods of disposal B, material A is burned at a very high temperature of about 1000°C in a structure called C. During this process, the organic matter present is removed as D and E whereas F is left behind (which can be dumped in a landfill site).

(*a*) What is material A ?

(*b*) Name the method of disposal B.

(*c*) What is structure C known as ?

(*d*) What are (*i*) D (*ii*) E, and (*iii*) F ?

(*e*) This method is especially suitable for the disposal of materials produced by certain institutions. Name such institutions.

ANSWERS

4. Bird **5.** Cat **8.** Paper and Plastics **10.** 0.05 J **11.** False **12.** Sun **14.** Peacock and Hawk **15.** (*a*) cancer (*b*) producer (*c*) Goat (*d*) Rabbit (*e*) Lion **36.** (*b*) Second case ; 0.9 J **37.** (*b*) 0.1 J **38.** (*b*) 0.1 J **39.** (*d*) **40.** (*c*) **41.** (*c*) **42.** (*b*) **43.** (*c*) **44.** (*b*) **45.** (*c*) **46.** (*a*) **47.** (*c*) **48.** (*b*) **49.** (*c*) **50.** (*d*) **51.** (*c*) **52.** (*d*) **53.** (*c*) **54.** (*c*) **55.** (*c*) **56.** (*d*) **57.** (*c*) **58.** (*b*) **59.** (*b*) **60.** (*c*) **61.** (*a*) (*i*) Oxygen, O_2 (*ii*) Ozone, O_3 (*b*) Ozone layer (*c*) (*i*) Ultraviolet radiations (*ii*) Sun (*iii*) Chlorofluorocarbons (CFCs) (*d*) Antarctica (*e*) Skin cancer ; Cataract **62.** (*a*) Algae (*b*) Algae ⟶ Tadpole ⟶ Water beetle ⟶ Fish (*c*) Aquatic food chains (*d*) (*i*) Water beetle (*ii*) Algae (*iii*) Fish (*iv*) Tadpole (*e*) 20000 J **63.** (*a*) Green plants ⟶ Rabbit ⟶ Fox ⟶ Lion (*b*) (*i*) Rabbit (*ii*) Fox and Lion (*c*) Fox (*d*) (*i*) Rabbit (*ii*) Fox (*e*) Lion (*f*) 0.1 J **64.** (*a*) Phytoplanktons ; Producer level (*b*) Bird ; Biological magnification (*c*) Phytoplanktons ⟶ Larvae ⟶ Fish ⟶ Bird (*d*) Man **65.** (*a*) Garbage (*b*) Incineration (*c*) Incinerator (*d*) (*i*) Carbon dioxide (*ii*) Water (*iii*) Ash (*e*) Hospitals

Management of Natural Resources

Anything in the environment 'which can be used' is called a 'natural resource'. Some of our important natural resources are : Forests and Wildlife, Water, Coal and Petroleum. **A system of controlling the use of natural resources in such a way as to avoid their wastage and to use them in the most effective way, is called management of natural resources.** The natural resources are a 'tool' of development (or advancement) for human beings but it should be 'sustainable development'. **The development which meets the current basic human needs and also preserves the resources for the needs**

(*a*) Forests and Wildlife

(*b*) Water

(*c*) Coal

(*d*) Petroleum

Figure 1. Some of our important natural resources are forests and wildlife, water, coal and petroleum.

of future generations, is called sustainable development. And to protect the environment from harm or destruction is said to 'conserve' the environment. In this chapter we will describe how to use our natural resources so as to achieve sustainable development as well as to conserve our environment.

Why do We Need to Manage Our Resources

All the things which we use (or consume) such as food, clothes, furniture, fuels, vehicles, water, etc., are obtained from the resources on this earth. **We need to manage our natural resources because of the following reasons :**

1. **The resources of the earth are limited.** Because of the rapid increase in human population, the

demand for resources is increasing day by day. The proper management can ensure that the natural resources are used judiciously so that they fulfil the needs of present generation and also last for the generations to come.

2. The proper management of natural resources takes into consideration long-term perspective (or view) and prevents their exploitation to the hilt for short-term gains.

3. The proper management can ensure equitable distribution of natural resources so that all the people can benefit from the development of these resources.

4. The proper management will take into consideration the damage caused to the environment during the 'extraction' or 'use' of the natural resources and find ways and means to minimise this damage. For example, if some forest trees have to be cut for various purposes, then the damage to the environment can be minimised by planting new saplings in place of cut down trees.

FORESTS AND WILDLIFE

A large area of land on which trees and other plants grow naturally is called a forest. And **the wild animals (like lion, tiger, elephants, deer, snakes, etc.) and birds which live in a forest, are called wildlife.**

Figure 2. Forests and Wildlife

The 'plants' and 'animals' of a forest are called 'flora' and 'fauna' respectively. Due to the presence of a large number of species (of plants and animals), forests are said to be 'biodiversity hotspots'. **One of the main aim of the management of forests and wildlife is to conserve the biodiversity which we have inherited.** This is because the loss of biodiversity leads to the loss of ecological stability of the forest ecosystem. We will now discuss the various stakeholders in the management of forests and their aspirations.

A person with an interest or concern in something is called a stakeholder. When we consider the management (or conservation) of forests, we find that there are four stakeholders in it. These are :

1. **The people** who live in and around the forest and are dependent to some extent on forest produce (forest products) to lead their life.
2. **The Forest Department** of the Government which owns the forest land and controls the resources from the forest.
3. **The industrialists** who use various forest products for their factories, such as wood for making paper and furniture, and *tendu* leaves for making *bidis*, etc.
4. **The forest and wildlife activists** who want to see the forests in their pristine form (original condition).

We will now describe what each of these stakeholder groups needs or gets out of the forests. The people who live in villages around the forests take firewood (fuel) from the forest trees. They usually lop (cut) the branches of the trees and pluck their leaves but do not cut down the whole trees. They take

Figure 3. Villagers taking away firewood from the forest trees.

bamboo from the forest to make their huts and baskets for collecting and storing food materials. The local people take wood for making agricultural implements and gather fruits, nuts and medicinal herbs from the forest. They also collect green fodder and graze their cattle in the forest. On the whole, **people living near the forests usually use the resources of the forests in a way that much damage is not done to the environment.** In fact, the people living near forests had developed practices to ensure that the forest resources were used in a sustainable manner. So, the damage caused to forests cannot be attributed to only the local people living around the forests.

The Forest Department has a major stake in the resources of forests and wildlife because it is a good source of revenue for the Government. Most of the forest revenue comes from the sale of cut down forest trees for timber (which is wood used in buildings and furniture). In order to plant trees for timber such as pine, teak, and eucalyptus, etc., huge areas of forests are cleared of all vegetation. This destoys a large amount of biodiversity in the area which harms the environment. The management of protected forest areas by keeping the local people out completely has some ill effects too. This will become clear from the following example. The great Himalayan National Park is a protected forest area which contains alpine meadows that were earlier grazed by outside sheep in summer. So, nomadic shepherds (having no permanent home) drove their flock of sheep up from the valley to this area every summer. After the formation of Himalayan National Park, the grazing by sheep was not allowed. This has a harmful effect on the growth of vegetation because, without regular grazing by sheep, the grass first grows very tall and then falls over, preventing fresh growth from below. The developmental projects like building roads through the forest area and construction of dams are also damaging the forests. Even the large inflow of tourists to the forests for observing wildlife, building rest-houses for tourists within the forest and dumping of waste materials (like plastic bottles, etc.) by the tourists in the forest, are damaging the forest environment.

Industrialists have a major vested interest in forest resources. They consider the forests as merely a source of raw material for their industry (or factories). Some of the major industries which are based on

Figure 4. Forest trees are cut down to obtain wood for use in buildings, furniture, making paper and sports goods. Forests are the most rapidly dwindling resource in the world.

Figure 5. A cut down forest should be replenished by planting more trees. This picture shows a forest being replanted.

forest produce are : Timber industry, Paper manufacturing industry (or Paper mills), Lac industry and Sports equipment industry. In fact, most of the deforestation is caused by industrial needs. It is true that wood from the forest trees is needed for manufacturing various types of goods required for development but at the same time efforts should be made to make up the loss of trees cut down from the forest. This can be done by planting saplings in the forest in place of cut down trees. It should be noted that **the destruction of forests affects not just the availability of forest products but also the quality of soil and the sources of water.**

A major programme called silviculture has been started to replenish the forests by growing more trees and plants. Thus, silviculture is a major programme started to replenish depleting forests. The silviculture programme has many advantages :

(*i*) It produces a large quantity of raw materials for industry (like timber and paper industry)
(*ii*) It increases the area of earth under forests (which is good for the conservation of wildlife)
(*iii*) It maintains a perfect water cycle in nature
(*iv*) It prevents soil erosion
(*v*) It prevents floods

There are certain people (called activists) who are not dependent on the forests (or wildlife) in any way but who want forests and wildlife to be conserved to prevent undue damage to the environment. They started by working for the conservation of large wild animals such as tigers, lions, elephants, and rhinoceros but they now recognise the need to preserve forests as well. This is because without preserving forests, we cannot conserve wildlife (wild animals and birds). We will now give two instances where ordinary people have played a great role in the conservation of forests by preventing them from being cut down indiscriminately.

(*i*) The Case of Khejri Trees

There is a Bishnoi community in Rajasthan state of our country for whom conservation of forests and wildlife has been a religious belief. In 1731, Amrita Devi Bishnoi led a group of 363 persons who sacrificed their lives for the protection of khejri trees in khejrali village near Jodhpur in Rajasthan. This shows the determination of some people to work for the conservation of their natural environment. The Government has recently instituted an 'Amrita Devi Bishnoi National Award for Wildlife Conservation' in the memory of Amrita Devi Bishnoi.

Figure 6. Khejri tree in Rajasthan.

Figure 7. Amrita Devi Bishnoi National Award for Wildlife Conservation being presented to a woman for her contribution to the conservation of wildlife.

Figure 8. This picture shows the women activists of *Chipko Andolan* (Hug the Trees Movement) clasping the tree trunk to prevent it from being cut down.

(ii) The Chipko Andolan

Another example of the contribution of common people towards the conservation of forests is the *Chipko Andolan* (Hug the Trees Movement). The *Chipko Andolan* originated from an incident in a remote village called 'Reni' in Garhwal, high up in the Himalayas in the early 1970s. A logging contractor had been allowed to cut down trees in a forest close to a village. The people of the village did not want this forest to be cut down because it would have spoiled their healthy environment. One day, when the men folk of the village were out for work, the contractor's workers came in the forest to cut down the trees. In the absence of men, the women of the village reached the forest quickly and clasped the tree trunks with their arms, preventing the workers from cutting down the trees. The forest trees were thus saved. The *Chipko* Movement quickly spread across all the communities and helped in the conservation of forests.

Participation of Local People in the Management of Forests

People's participation in the management of forests can help in increasing forest produce as well as in their conservation. An example of how local people's participation in the management of forests led to the revival of degraded forests is like this : In 1972, the West Bengal Forest Department formulated a novel scheme to revive the degraded sal forests by involving the local people. A beginning was made in the Arabari forest range of Midnapore district. A far-sighted forest officer A.K. Banerjee involved the villagers of the area around the forest in the protection of 1272 hectares of badly degraded sal forest. In return for help in protecting the forest, the villagers were given employment in both silviculture and harvesting operations of the forest, 25 per cent of the final harvest produce, and were allowed to collect firewood and fodder from the forest area on a nominal payment. **With the active and willing participation of local people living around the forest, the degraded sal forest of Arabari became thick and green within ten years.** This is how participation of local people can lead to efficient management of forests.

Conservation of Wildlife

The large scale poaching (killing) of wild animals residing in the forests by man is a serious threat to the survival of many animal and bird species. This also disturbs the food chains in which these animals occur resulting in undesirable consequences for the whole ecosystem. This point will become more clear from the following example. Snake is a wild animal. The skin of snakes is in great demand for making fancy leather goods, so the snake skin sells at a high price in the market. Now, to make some easy money, some people kill the snakes indiscriminately in large numbers to obtain their skin. This **large scale killing of snakes disrupts the food chains in which snakes occur and creates an imbalance in nature.** For example, snake is a friend of the farmer in the sense that it eats vermins like rats and mice which are pests and damage the crops. Now, when the snakes are killed in large numbers to obtain their skin, the population of snakes is reduced greatly. Now, due to the lesser number of 'predator' snakes, the population of pests like rats and mice in crop-fields increases. The increased number of rats and mice in the fields damages the

Figure 9. This handbag is made from skin of snake.

Figure 10. Snake is a friend of the farmer because it eats up rats from the fields which damage the crops.

Figure 11. Natural habitats of wild animals and birds should be preserved by establishing National Parks and Bird Sanctuaries.

standing crops leading to loss in the production of food-grains.

It is very important to conserve wildlife to maintain the ecological balance in nature and to preserve the gene pool. **Some of the measures (or steps) to be taken for the conservation of wildlife are given below :**

1. Laws should be made to impose a total ban on poaching (killing) or capturing of any animal or bird belonging to an endangered species. The poaching of an endangered species of animals and birds should be made a punishable offence. Such laws should not remain on paper only, they should be enforced strictly.

2. Even if some type of wild animals and birds are in abundance today, their indiscriminate killing should not be allowed by the forest authorities.

3. The natural habitats of wild animals and birds should be preserved by establishing National Parks and Sanctuaries throughout the country.

4. The Government Department connected with the conservation of wildlife should conduct a periodic survey in all the forests, National Parks and Sanctuaries to have a knowledge of the population of all species of wild animals and birds, so that these animals can be helped in the times of distress like floods and famines.

5. Special attention should be paid to the conservation of endangered species of wild animals and birds to prevent their extinction altogether.

6. The unauthorised felling (cutting) of forest trees for timber trade and fuel-wood should be curbed (stopped) immediately. This is because depletion of forests destroys the natural habitat of wild animals and birds, and exposes them to the cruelty of man as well as nature.

7. In the case of Government authorised felling of forest trees, for every acre of forest cut down, an equal area of land should be planted with saplings of trees to make up for the loss in the long run.

WATER FOR ALL

Water is the basic necessity for all forms of life, human beings, other animals as well as plants. Some parts of our country have good resources of water whereas other parts suffer from chronic water shortage. **The regions having good availability of water are flourishing because they have good crops but the regions having shortage of water are in the thick of poverty because of poor crop growth.** It is, therefore, necessary to have proper management of available water resources so that there is an equitable distribution of water for all the people in all the parts of the country. **The various sources of water which are available to us are: Rains, Rivers, Lakes, Ponds, Wells, Oceans and Glaciers (Snow mountains).** We will discuss the management of water from some of these sources of water in detail. Let us start with rains.

Rain is a very important source of water. Rains in India are largely due to monsoon which lasts for a few months. This means that most of the rainwater falls on the earth in a few months of the year. This rainwater fills the lakes and ponds, and also flows into rivers. Some rainwater also seeps into the ground and becomes available as ground water (or rather underground water). Though most of the parts of our country get a good rainfall during monsoon but due to the loss of vegetation cover, much water does not seep into the ground, it rather flows into rivers. Rainwater is stored in lakes for use over a long period of time. There are some natural lakes in our country. Some artificial lakes have also been made at various places to store rainwater to meet the increasing

Figure 12. Water controls our lives. Our crops, our food and our health depend on good supply of water. Many of our people still cannot obtain sufficient quantity of clean water easily. Long queues for collecting water can be seen at many places. We should not waste water. Every drop counts. Remember : *jal hi jeevan hai* (water gives life)

demand for water. In fact, many cities of our country depend on such lakes for their water supply during the year.

Despite good rains, we are not able to meet the demand for water of all the people because :

(*i*) our population is increasing rapidly.

(*ii*) due to lack of sufficient vegetation cover on ground, only a little rain water seeps into the ground and gets stored as ground water.

(*iii*) the high yielding varieties of crops require much more water for irrigation.

(*iv*) discharge of untreated sewage and industrial wastes into rivers and lakes reduces the availability of usable water.

(*v*) the changing life-style of people, especially in urban areas, is consuming more water.

Rivers are another important source of water. Rivers get their water supply from the melting of snow lying on the peaks of snow mountains (or glaciers) as well as from rains. The management of river-water is done by constructing dams on rivers.

Dams

In order to make proper use of river water, dams are constructed across the rivers to regulate the flow of water. In our country dams have been built across many rivers. The large reservoir of a dam stores a huge amount of water (brought in by the flowing river). This stored water is then allowed to flow downstream at the desired rate. Bhakra Dam is one such dam which has been built across the river Satluj in the state of Punjab in our country. Dams built across the rivers are big storehouses of river water.

Figure 13. A dam built across a river is a big storehouse of water.

Dams are useful for the society in the following ways :

1. Water from a dam is used for irrigation in fields through a network of canals. Dams ensure round the year water supply to the crop fields and help raise agricultural production. For example, Indira Gandhi Canal originating from Bhakra Dam has brought greenery to considerable areas of Rajasthan.

2. Water from a dam is supplied to the people in towns and cities through pipelines after suitable treatment. In this way, construction of dams ensures continuous water supply in the region.

3. The falling water (or flowing water) from the dam is used for generating electricity. The water rushing down the dam turns turbines which run electric generators. The electricity thus produced is called hydroelectricity.

The construction of high-rise dams for the management of river water and generation of electricity has certain problems associated with it. The public opposition to the construction of large dams on rivers is mainly due to the following three problems likely to be created by them :

(*i*) Social Problems

Due to the construction of high-rise dams, a large number of human settlements (or villages) are submerged in the water of large reservoir formed by the dam and many people are rendered homeless. This creates a social problem. It is, therefore, necessary that all the people who are displaced from the dam site are given adequate compensation by the Government for rehabilitation so as to start their life afresh.

(*ii*) Environmental Problems

The construction of high-rise dams on the rivers contributes to deforestation and loss of biodiversity. This is because a vast variety of flora and fauna (plants and animals) get submerged in the water of large reservoir formed by the dam and disturb the ecological balance.

(*iii*) Economic Problems

Some people say that the construction of high-rise dams involves the spending of huge amount of public money without the generation of proportionate benefits. On the other hand, others say that there can be no real progress without building dams because they allow us to manage our water resources properly and at the same time give us much needed electricity (without causing any air pollution). So, whether the construction of dams on rivers is an economic problem or not is a debatable question.

The opposition to the construction of Tehri Dam on the river Ganga and raising the height of Sardar Sarovar Dam on the river Narmada are due to such problems. We have all heard about the protests by the *Narmada Bachao Andolan* (Save the Narmada Movement) against the raising of height of Sardar Sarovar Dam. So, before taking a decision to construct high-rise dams on rivers, or raising the height of existing dams, it is necessary to consider its long term effects on social life and environment carefully.

Pollution of River Water

The water in most of our rivers is highly polluted. **The pollution of river water is caused by the dumping of untreated sewage and industrial wastes into it.** For example, the river Ganga which flows for over 2500 kilometres from Gangotri in the Himalayas to Ganga Sagar in the Bay of Bengal is being turned into a dirty water drain by the discharge of untreated sewage and industrial wastes emanating from more than a hundred towns and cities which lie along its way. In addition to sewage and industrial wastes, the pollution of river Ganga is also caused by other human activities like bathing, washing of clothes, immersion of ashes of the dead and dumping of unburnt corpses in its water. The industries also discharge chemical effluents into the river water. The toxicity of these chemical effluents kills the fish in many parts of the river.

Figure 14. Industrial wastes are polluting the river water.

The contamination of river water can be usually found from two factors: (*i*) the presence of coliform bacteria in river water, and (*ii*) measurement of pH of river water. Coliform is a group of bacteria found in human intestines. The presence of coliform in the river water indicates its contamination by disease-causing micro-organisms. This is because though coliform itself is harmless but its presence in river water indicates that other, more harmful, intestinal bacteria might also be present. The pH of river water is measured by using universal indicator paper. If the pH of river water is found to be below 7, then the river water will be acidic and hence polluted. A multicrore 'Ganga Action Plan' (GAP) project was launched in 1985 to clean the river Ganga and make its water pollution free.

Wells and tube-wells (bore-wells) are yet another source of water. Some of the rainwater which falls on earth seeps through the soil and goes down under the surface of the earth. Ultimately this water is stopped by some hard rocks and collects there. This underground water is taken out by digging a 'well' into the ground. This is called well water. Such wells are a common sight in village areas. The deep tube-wells called 'bore-wells' are also dug into the earth which are much deeper than the ordinary wells and their water is drawn out by using water pumps. This water is used for the irrigation of crops and for drinking purposes.

When too much water is pumped out through deep tube-wells then the water table (level of water below the earth's surface) gets lowered too much. This lowering of water table decreases the amount of available underground water. In order to maintain the water table at a proper depth, it is necessary to ensure better percolation of rainwater into the soil. A scheme called 'rainwater harvesting' is recommended to stop flowing rainwater and make it percolate into the soil more efficiently.

Rainwater Harvesting

The people in rural India have used a large number of water collecting methods to capture as much rainwater as possible which had fallen on their land. Some of the methods used for water harvesting by the rural people (or farmers) were : Digging of small pits and lakes ; Building of small earthen dams (or embankments); Construction of dykes (long walls of earth to trap water); Construction of sand and limestone reservoirs; and setting up of roof-top water collecting units. All these methods of collecting and saving rain water have recharged the depleting groundwater levels.

Rainwater harvesting is an age-old practice in India. Water-harvesting techniques used depend on the location where it is to be used. Some of the ancient 'water harvesting structures' used in different rural regions of our country (which are still in use) are given below :

Region	Ancient water harvesting structure
1. Rajasthan	*Khadin*, Tanks, *Nadis*
2. Maharashtra	*Bandharas*, *Tals*
3. Madhya Pradesh and Uttar Pradesh	*Bhundhis*
4. Bihar	*Ahars* and *Pynes*
5. Himachal Pradesh	*Kulhs*
6. Jammu region	Ponds
7. Tamil Nadu	*Eris* (Tanks)
8. Kerala	*Surangams*
9. Karnataka	*Kattas*

We will now describe a traditional rainwater harvesting system for agriculture called *khadin* which is used in Rajasthan. The main feature of *khadin* system of rainwater harvesting is a very long (100 m to 300 m long) earthen embankment called *'bund'* built across the lower edge of the sloping farmland (see Figure 15). The rainwater from catchment area flows down the slopes and stopped by the *bund* to form a

Figure 15. The traditional rainwater harvesting system for agriculture called '*khadin*' used in Rajasthan.

reservoir. The excess water flows across the *bund* through sluiceways (or pathways) provided for this purpose and goes into shallow wells dug behind the *bund*. The rainwater which collects in the reservoir formed by the *bund*, and in the well, seeps slowly into the land (or ground). This water-saturated land is subsequently used for growing crops.

Please note that **the main purpose of water harvesting is not to hold rainwater on the surface of the earth but to make rainwater percolate under the ground so as to recharge 'groundwater'.** The various **advantages** of water stored in the ground are as follows :

(*i*) The water stored in ground does not evaporate.

(*ii*) The water stored in ground spreads out to recharge wells and provides moisture for crops over a wide area.

(*iii*) The water stored in ground does not promote breeding of mosquitoes (unlike stagnant water collected in ponds or artificial lakes).

(*iv*) The water stored in ground is protected from contamination by human and animal wastes.

(*v*) The water stored in ground is utilised for the benefit of local population.

Rainwater harvesting in rural areas not only increases the agricultural production and income of the farmers but also mitigates (makes less severe) the effect of droughts and floods, and increases the life of downstream dams and reservoirs.

Rainwater Harvesting in Urban Areas (City Areas)

In rural areas (village areas), most of the ground has open soil due to which rainwater can seep into the ground naturally to make up for the loss in groundwater due to excessive use. In urban areas (city areas), however, most of the ground is covered with buildings, concrete pavements and metalled roads due to which only very little rainwater seeps into the ground naturally. Most of the rainwater which falls in cities flows into dirty water drains and goes away. So, rainwater harvesting is necessary in city areas. Rainwater harvesting by making more water percolate into the ground is usually done in those areas of a city where tube-wells for supplying water are located. This is to make sure that the tube-wells will never go dry.

The rainwater harvesting from open spaces around the buildings in a city is done by constructing percolation pits covered with concrete slabs having holes in them, and connected to a recharge well through

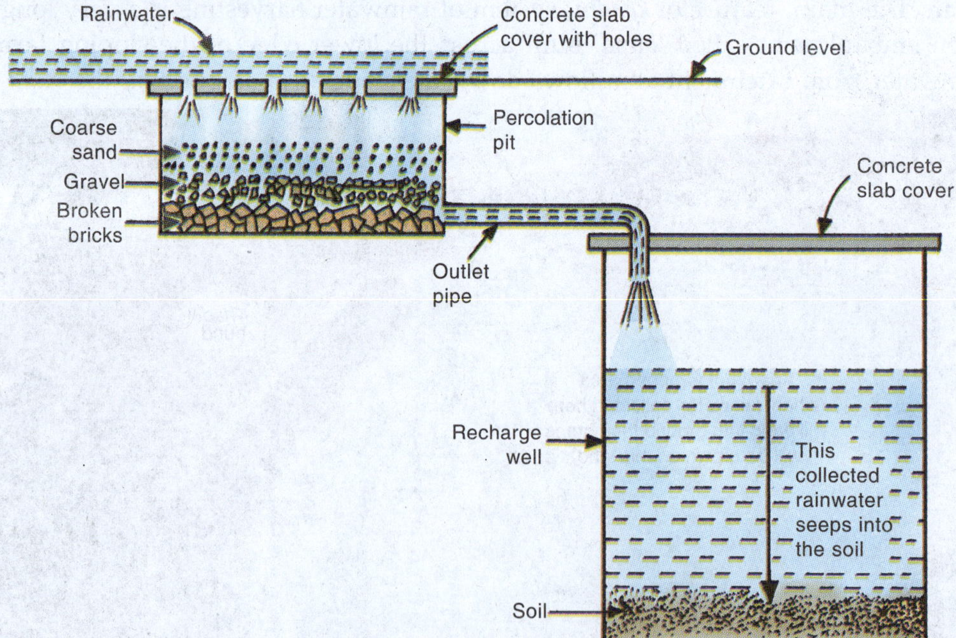

Figure 16. Rainwater harvesting in open spaces around buildings to recharge groundwater.

a pipe (see Figure 16). The recharge well is about 1 metre in diameter and 3 metres deep. The rainwater falling in the open spaces around buildings goes into the percolation pit through the holes in its concrete slab cover. After filtration in percolation pit, rainwater enters the recharge well through the outlet pipe and gradually seeps into the soil. Please note that the purpose of recharge well is to collect the vast amount of water falling on the ground quickly when it rains and then make it seep into soil gradually. This groundwater can then be taken out through tube-wells as and when required. The advantage of rainwater harvesting is that it increases the availability of groundwater and helps in overcoming water shortage.

COAL AND PETROLEUM

Coal and petroleum are called fossil fuels. Coal and petroleum are the natural resources which are important 'sources' of energy for us. Coal is used as a fuel as such in homes and in industry, or it is used to generate electricity at Thermal Power Plants. Petroleum products such as petrol and diesel are used as fuels in transport to run scooters, motorcycles, cars, buses, trucks, trains, ships and aeroplanes. Kerosene and LPG (Liquefied Petroleum Gas) obtained from petroleum are used as domestic fuels for cooking food, etc. Since the industrial revolution, we have been using increasing amounts of energy to meet our basic needs (like cooking food) and for the manufacture of goods upon which our life depends. All these energy needs have so far been met mostly by coal and petroleum reserves of the earth.

Coal and Petroleum in the Earth are Limited

Coal and petroleum were formed from the degradation of biomass of plants and animals respectively, buried deep under the earth millions of years ago. We obtain coal from the 'coal mines' dug into the earth and petroleum is obtained by digging 'oil wells' deep in the earth. The crude petroleum oil obtained from

(*a*) Coal

(*b*) Petroleum (Crude oil)

Figure 17. Coal and petroleum deposits inside the earth are limited. They may get exhausted soon. It is, therefore, necessary to conserve (or save) coal and petroleum by reducing their consumption.

oil wells is then separated into fuels such as LPG, petrol, diesel and kerosene. We have been using coal and petroleum resources at such a rapid rate in the past that they will get exhausted in the near future. It has been estimated that at the present rate of consumption, the known petroleum reserves of the earth will last us for just about 40 years more and the coal will last for about another 200 years only. Once exhausted, coal and petroleum will not be available to us in near future (because they are formed extremely slowly over a very, very long time). It is, therefore, necessary to conserve (or save) coal and petroleum resources of the earth by *reducing* their consumption so that they may last for as long as possible.

Steps to Reduce the Consumption of Coal and Petroleum

Coal is used mainly to produce electricity. So, if we can save electricity, then the consumption of coal will be automatically reduced. Similarly, the petroleum products kerosene and LPG are used for cooking food, and petrol and diesel are used as fuel in motor vehicles, so if we can save on kerosene, LPG, petrol and diesel, then the consumption of petroleum will also get reduced. **Some of the steps which can be**

taken to conserve energy resources (like coal and petroleum) are as follows :

1. Switch off the lights, fans, television and other electrical appliances when not needed. This will save a lot of electricity.
2. Use energy efficient electrical appliances to save electricity. This can be done by using Compact Fluorescent Lamps (CFL) and fluorescent tube-lights instead of traditional filament-type electric bulbs (because CFL and tube-lights consume much less electric energy as compared to filament-type electric bulbs for producing the same amount of light).

Figure 18. On the left side is filament-type electric bulb which uses much more electric energy. On the right side is the energy efficient CFL which uses much less electric energy for providing the same amount of light. This is because CFL wastes much less electric energy as heat.

Figure 19. Solar cookers should be used to cook food whenever possible. The use of solar cookers will save precious fuels such as coal, kerosene and LPG.

3. Use stairs to climb at least up to three floors of a building instead of taking a lift. This will save electricity.
4. Pressure cookers should be used for cooking food to save fuels like kerosene and LPG.
5. Good quality stoves should be used to burn fuels like kerosene and cooking gas (LPG) so as to obtain maximum heat.
6. Solar cookers should be used to cook food whenever possible.
7. The use of biogas as domestic fuel should be encouraged in rural areas.
8. Bicycles should be used for covering short distances to save precious fuel like petrol (which is used in cars, scooters and motorcycles).
9. Public transport system (local bus and train service) in the cities should be improved so that people do not commute in their personal vehicles. This will save a lot of petrol and diesel.
10. Fuel efficient engines of motor vehicles should be designed to reduce the consumption of petrol and diesel.

Pollution Caused by Burning Coal and Petroleum Based Fuels

Since coal and petroleum have been formed from biomass (plant and animal material), therefore, in addition to carbon and hydrogen, they also contain nitrogen and sulphur elements. When coal, and petroleum based fuels (like petrol and diesel) are burnt, the products of combustion are : **Carbon dioxide, Water, Sulphur dioxide** and **Nitrogen oxides.** And if combustion takes place in an *insufficient* supply of air (or oxygen), then some **carbon monoxide** is also produced. Out of all the products of combustion of these fuels, only water is harmless and does not affect the environment. All other products are harmful and hence pollute the environment. For example :

(*i*) Sulphur dioxide attacks the lungs causing bronchitis and other diseases. Sulphur dioxide also dissolves in rainwater making it acidic. The acid rain thus produced damages trees, plants, aquatic organisms, buildings and metal structures.

(*ii*) Just like sulphur dioxide, nitrogen oxides attack the breathing system and also cause acid rain.

(*iii*) Carbon monoxide is a very poisonous gas. If carbon monoxide gets into our blood stream, it stops red blood cells from carrying oxygen from lungs to the rest of the body causing suffocation. Too much carbon monoxide causes death.

(*iv*) Though carbon dioxide is not a poisonous gas but it is a greenhouse gas which traps sun's heat energy falling on the earth. The burning of more and more of fossil fuels is increasing the amount of carbon dioxide in the atmosphere causing increased greenhouse effect leading to global warming.

Figure 20. The upper branches of this tree have been damaged by acid rain produced mainly by sulphur dioxide and nitrogen oxides present in polluted air.

From the above discussion we conclude that : **We need to use fossil fuels (coal and petroleum) judiciously because :**

(*i*) fossil fuels (coal and petroleum) left in the earth are limited which will get exhausted soon, and

(*ii*) the products of combustion of fossil fuels (coal and petroleum) pollute the environment.

The three R's to Save the Environment

The excessive and indiscriminate use of various types of natural resources is spoiling our healthy environment day by day. We can save our environment by practising three R's : Reduce, Recycle and Reuse. This is explained below.

1. Reduce

Reduce means that we use less of the natural resources by cutting down on those practices which lead to their wastage. For example, we can reduce the wastage of electricity by switching off unnecessary lights and fans. Saving electricity means that we are reducing the use of coal (because coal is used to produce electricity). We can reduce the wastage of water by repairing the leaking taps. We can reduce the use of LPG by making use of solar cooker for cooking food. We can reduce the use of petrol by walking or cycling for short distances. And we can reduce the use of water resources and fertilisers by preventing the wastage of food (because a lot of water and fertilisers are utilised for the production of food).

Figure 21. The wastage of water can be reduced by repairing leaking taps immediately.

Figure 22. The use of petrol can be reduced by cycling for short distances. It will also keep us physically fit.

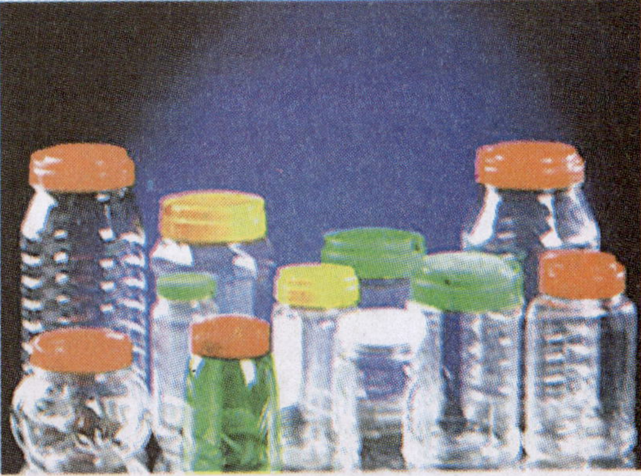

Figure 23. These plastic jars can be reused for storing things like salt, spices, sugar, tea-leaves, and pulses, etc., in the kitchen.

2. Recycle

Recycling means that we should collect the used and discarded items of paper, plastic, glass and metals, and send them to the respective industries for making fresh paper, plastic, glass or metal objects. In order to recycle materials, we should first segregate (separate) our domestic wastes properly so that the materials which can be recycled do not get dumped alongwith other household wastes which are to be thrown away.

3. Reuse

Reuse means that, if possible, we should use the same things again. For example, the plastic jars in which we buy various food items like jams and pickles, etc., can be used later on for storing things like salt, spices, sugar, tea-leaves and pulses, etc. And paper envelopes can be reversed inside out and used again. The process of 'reuse' is better than that of 'recycling' because some *energy* is used to recycle old objects but *no energy* is required during reuse. The items which can be reused are, however, very limited.

We are now in a position to **answer the following questions :**

Very Short Answer Type Questions

1. Name two fossil fuels.
2. Name the major programme started to replenish forests.
3. Apart from the availability of forest products, name two other things which are affected by the destruction of forests.
4. Name the rivers with which the following dams are associated :
   (*a*) Tehri Dam (*b*) Sardar Sarovar Dam (*c*) Bhakra Dam
5. Name two factors which can be used to find whether river water has been contaminated.
6. Name the bacteria whose presence in water indicates the contamination with disease-causing micro-organisms.
7. With which process are the following ancient structures associated ?
   Kulhs, Eris, Surangams, Kattas, Pynes
8. Which fossil fuel is conserved :
   (*a*) when we save on electricity ?
   (*b*) when we use bicycle for covering short distances instead of a motorbike ?
9. What is the main purpose of rainwater harvesting ?
10. What is the name of the process in which rainwater falling on the earth is stopped from flowing and made to percolate into the ground ?
11. Name the most common practice of recharging ground water.
12. The pH of a river water sample as measured by pH paper is found to be 6. What does it tell us about water ?
13. Name the person who is most remembered for the protection of *Khejri* trees in Rajasthan.
14. State whether the following statement is true or false :
    Chipko Andolan was associated with the conservation of wild animals such as tigers and lions.
15. Write the full names of (*a*) CFL, and (*b*) CFC.
16. Choose one term from the following which include all others :
    coal, natural gas, fossil fuels, petroleum
17. Why is the process of 'reuse' better than that of 'recycling' ?
18. Name a clean gaseous fuel other than LPG and natural gas.
19. Fill in the following blanks with suitable words :
    (*a*) LPG is a .... fuel but biogas is not a..............fuel.
    (*b*) Glaciers are a source of ....
    (*c*) One of the main aim of management of forests and wildlife is to conserve the .... which we have inherited.
    (*d*) *Khadin* is a traditional .... harvesting system in Rajasthan.
    (*e*) When a fuel burns in an insufficient supply of air, then some poisonous gas called .... is also produced.

Short Answer Type Questions

20. What is meant by "sustainable development" ?
21. What is silviculture ? What are its advantages ?
22. Write a short note on *'Chipko Andolan'* (Hug the Trees Movement).
23. Why should we conserve forests and wildlife ?
24. Describe briefly the *'khadin'* system of rainwater harvesting practised in Rajasthan.
25. What measures would you take to conserve electricity in your house ?
26. Although coal and petroleum are produced by the degradation of biomass, even then we need to conserve them. Why ?
27. Is water conservation necessary ? Give reasons.
28. Name the products of combustion of fossil fuels like coal and petroleum products. How do they affect us and our environment ?
29. Why should fossil fuels like coal and petroleum be used judiciously ?
30. What are the three R's to save the environment ? Explain with one example of each.
31. What are the main uses of coal and petroleum products ?
32. State any five steps to reduce the consumption of coal and petroleum products.
33. Explain why, despite good rains, we are not able to meet the demand for water of all the people in our country.
34. Give one example to show how the participation of local people can lead to the efficient management of forests.
35. Explain briefly, how rainwater harvesting is done from open spaces around the buildings in city areas.

Long Answer Type Questions

36. (*a*) What is a natural resource ? Name three important natural resources.
    (*b*) Why do we need to manage our natural resources ?
37. (*a*) State the advantages of constructing dams across the rivers.
    (*b*) Describe some of the problems associated with the construction of dams.
38. (*a*) Name any five sources of water (other than rivers)
    (*b*) Describe how, the water of river Ganga has been highly polluted.
39. (*a*) Name the major industries which are based on forest produce.
    (*b*) State the main aim of the management of forests and wildlife.
    (*c*) Name the four main stakeholders in the management of forest resources.
40. (*a*) What is meant by rainwater harvesting ? Name some of the ancient structures used for rainwater harvesting by the rural people.
    (*b*) What are the various advantages of water stored in ground ?

Multiple Choice Questions (MCQs)

41. The Bishnoi community of Rajasthan is associated with the conservation of :
    (*a*) coal and petroleum (*b*) forests and wildlife (*c*) water resources (*d*) abiotic environment
42. The *Chipko Andolan* is associated with :
    (*a*) Tigers (*b*) Turtles (*c*) Trees (*d*) Tomatoes
43. Amrita Devi Bishnoi was associated with :
    (*a*) preventing the custom of child marriage in Rajasthan (*b*) campaign to save the girl child
    (*c*) conservation of cultural heritage of Rajasthan (*d*) conservation of forests and wildlife
44. One of the following is not a direct stakeholder in the management (or conservation) of forests. This is :
    (*a*) the people who have paper mills. (*b*) the people who run the forest department
    (*c*) the people who campaign for the conservation of forests (*d*) the people who live in urban areas
45. The river water is said to be polluted with acidic wastes if the pH of river water is :
    (*a*) zero (*b*) above 7 (*c*) below 7 (*d*) exactly 7

46. The major programme started to replenish the damaged forests is called :
(a) horticulture (b) tissue culture (c) agriculture (d) silviculture

47. With which tree Amrita Devi Bishnoi is associated ?
(a) *khajoor* (b) *khejrali* (c) *khejri* (d) *keekar*

48. One of the following does not contribute in producing acid rain. This one is :
(a) sulphur dioxide (b) carbon dioxide (c) nitrogen oxides (d) carbon monoxide

49. The poisonous gas which reduces the oxygen-carrying capacity of blood to a large extent is :
(a) SO_2 (b) NO (c) CO (d) CO_2

50. Which of the following is not an ancient water harvesting structure ?
(a) *kattas* (b) *sargam* (c) *kulhs* (d) *surangams*

51. Snakes are killed in large numbers because :
(a) they are very poisonous (b) they kill rats
(c) their skin is expensive (d) they damage the crops

52. Which of the following is not a fossil fuel ?
(a) LPG (b) natural gas (c) biogas (d) CNG

53. Which of the following is not a natural resource ?
(a) soil (b) water (c) electricity (d) natural gas

54. The most rapidly dwindling natural resource in the world is :
(a) water (b) soil (c) sunlight (d) forests

55. Which of the following is not a natural resource ?
(a) snake (b) wind (c) wooden house (d) mango tree

56. The three R's which can help us to conserve natural resources for long term use are :
(a) recycle, regenerate, reuse (b) reduce, regenerate, reuse
(c) reduce, reuse, redistribute (d) reduce, recycle, reuse

57. The main reason for the abundant coliform bacteria in the water of river Ganga is :
(a) immersion of ashes of the dead into the river (b) washing of clothes on the banks of river
(c) discharge of industrial wastes into river water (d) disposal of unburnt corpses into river water

58. The pH of a sample of water collected from a river is found to be in the range of 3.5 to 4.5. The most likely reason for this is the waste being discharged into the river from a :
(a) soap and detergent manufacturing factory (b) car battery manufacturing factory
(c) alcohol manufacturing factory (d) plastic cups moulding factory

59. Which of the following statement is incorrect ?
(a) economic development is linked to environmental conservation
(b) sustainable development meets the current basic human needs and also preserves resources for future generations
(c) sustainable development does not take into consideration the viewpoints of all stakeholders
(d) sustainable development is a long planned and persistent development

60. Arabari forest of Bengal is dominated by :
(a) Teak (b) Sal (c) Bambooo (d) Mangroove

61. Groundwater will not be depleted due to :
(a) process of afforestation (b) establishing thermal power plants
(c) process of deforestation (d) cultivation of high yielding varieties of crops

62. *Ahars, Kattas, Bhundhis* and *Khadins* are the modes of :
(a) grain storage (b) soil conservation (c) water harvesting (d) cold storage

63. Which of the following combination of terms has no fossil fuel ?
(a) wind, ocean, coke (b) kerosene, tide, wind (c) wood, wind, sun (d) petrol, wood, sun

64. The use of one of the following is eco-friendly. This one is :
(a) cars for transportation (b) polybags for shopping
(c) windmills for generating power (d) dyes for colouring clothes

65. *Khadins* are used in Rajasthan to :
(a) hold water for irrigation (b) recharge groundwater
(c) promote soil erosion (d) trap wild animals

Questions Based on High Order Thinking Skills (HOTS)

66. In a village, farmers started cultivating crops all around a lake which was always filled with water. They added lot of materials W to the soil in their fields to increase the yield of crops. Soon they found that the whole surface of water in the lake was covered with a green layer made up of tiny organisms X. After some time, the fish present in the lake started dying in large numbers because they could not get sufficient Y due to a process Z which had occurred in lake water and drained out all the Y present in the water of lake.

(*a*) What do you think materials W are ?
(*b*) Name (*i*) X, and (*ii*) Y.
(*c*) What is the process Z known as ?
(*d*) What happens during the process Z which uses up all the Y present in lake water ?
(*e*) What does this example tell us about the use of materials like W ?

67. There were lot of organisms A in the crop fields in an area. These organisms used to feed on organisms B also present in the crop fields but which damaged the standing crops. One day some people arrived in the fields and killed all the organisms A so that they could remove their C for making fancy items which were in great demand. Due to large scale killing of A, the population of B increased too much damaging all the crops in the area and causing a famine-like situation. Apart from A, there is another organism D which can also kill and eat B. Name A, B, C and D.

68. There are two important fuels A and B both of which are extracted from deep inside the earth. Fuel A is a thick, dark, foul smelling liquid whereas fuel B is a black solid. Combustion of both the fuels produces products, C, D, E and F. The product C makes the rainwater only slightly acidic but it is mainly responsible for causing global warming. The product D is neither acidic nor basic. It is harmless and does not affect the environment in any way. Both E and F attack breathing system of humans and are mainly responsible for causing acid rain. In addition to combustion of fuels A and B, the product F is also formed when lightning occurs in the sky.

(*a*) What are (*i*) fuel A, and (*ii*) fuel B ?
(*b*) Name (*i*) C (*ii*) D (*iii*) E, and (*iv*) F
(*c*) What is the process of formation of F during lightning known as ?
(*d*) Which fuel is supposed to be exhausted sooner : A or B ?
(*e*) Which fuel is mostly used for generating electricity at thermal power plants ?

69. A man bought a device X which could cook pulses, vegetables and rice without using any fuel like wood, coal, kerosene or LPG, etc. This device did not work at night. It also took a lot of time for cooking.

(*a*) Name the device X.
(*b*) What is the source of energy which cooks food in this device ?
(*c*) What is the name of the process which traps energy in this device ?
(*d*) State one advantage (other than saving on fuel) of using such a device for cooking food.

70. A person buys two electrical devices P and Q for lighting purposes in his house. The device P consumes only 5 units of electricity in a month but device Q consumes 15 units of electricity in a month when used for the same number of hours daily. The device Q wastes a lot of electricity by radiating energy C but P does not do so.

(*a*) What type of device is (*i*) P, and (*ii*) Q ?
(*b*) Name one component which is present in Q but not in P.
(*c*) Name the energy C.
(*d*) Which device is more energy efficient : P or Q ?
(*e*) Which fossil fuel is most likely to be conserved if all of us switch over to devices like P ?

ANSWERS

8. (*a*) Coal (*b*) Petroleum **10.** Rainwater harvesting **11.** Rainwater harvesting **12.** Water is polluted with acidic wastes **14.** False **16.** Fossil fuels **18.** Biogas **19.** (*a*) fossil ; fossil (*b*) water (*c*) biodiversity (*d*) water (*e*) carbon monoxide **41.** (*b*) **42.** (*c*) **43.** (*d*) **44.** (*d*) **45.** (*c*) **46.** (*d*) **47.** (*c*) **48.** (*d*) **49.** (*c*) **50.** (*b*) **51.** (*c*) **52.** (*c*) **53.** (*c*) **54.** (*d*) **55.** (*c*) **56.** (*d*) **57.** (*d*) **58.** (*b*) **59.** (*c*) **60.** (*b*) **61.** (*a*) **62.** (*c*) **63.** (*c*) **64.** (*c*) **65.** (*b*) **66.** (*a*) Fertilisers (*b*) (*i*) Algae (*ii*) Oxygen (*c*) Eutrophication (*d*) When algae die, bacteria use all the oxygen dissolved in water to decompose dead algae (*e*) Excessive use of fertilisers in fields is not good for the environment **67.** A : Snakes ; B : Rats ; C : Skin ; D : Cat **68.** (*a*) (*i*) Petroleum (*ii*) Coal (*b*) (*i*) Carbon dioxide (*ii*) Water (*iii*) Sulphur dioxide (*iv*) Nitrogen oxides (*c*) Natural fixation of nitrogen (*d*) A (Petroleum) (*e*) B (Coal) **69.** (*a*) Solar cooker (*b*) Sun (*c*) Greenhouse effect (*d*) It does not cause air pollution **70.** (*a*) (*i*) Compact Fluorescent Lamp (CFL)(*ii*) Filament type bulb (or lamp) (*b*) Filament (*c*) Heat energy (*d*) P (*e*) Coal

Multiple Choice Questions (MCQs)
(Based on Practical Skills in Science)

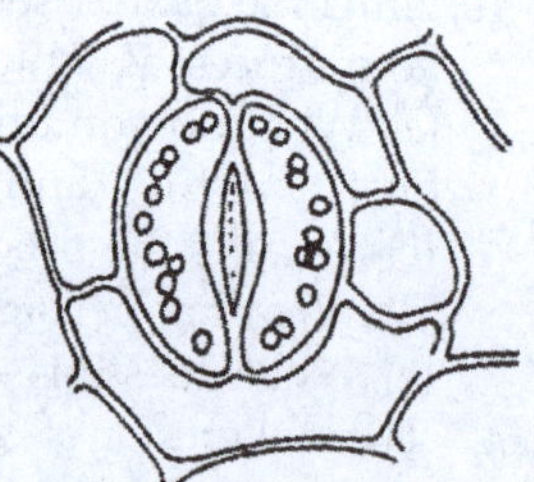

1. In the sketch of the stomatal apparatus given alongside, which one of the following is missing ?

(1) Cell membranes of the cells (2) Cell walls of the cells

(3) Nuclei in the guard cells (4) Chloroplasts in the guard cells

2. A student focussed the leaf epidermal peel under the low power of microscope but could not see all the parts. He should :

(1) use the coarse adjustment knob again to focus the slide.

(2) use the fine adjustment knob to increase magnification.

(3) focus under high power using coarse adjustment knob.

(4) focus under high power using fine adjustment knob.

3. The temporary mount of the leaf epidermal peel which looked pinkish red under the microscope was :

(1) stained in acetocarmine and mounted in glycerine

(2) stained in iodine and mounted in water

(3) stained in safranin and mounted in glycerine

(4) stained in methylene blue and mounted in water

4. A well stained leaf peel mount when observed under the high power of a microscope shows nuclei in :

(1) only epidermal cells (2) only guard cells

(3) guard cells and epidermal cells (4) guard cells, epidermal cells and stoma

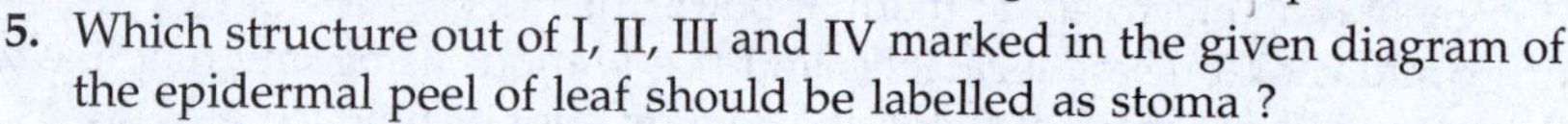

5. Which structure out of I, II, III and IV marked in the given diagram of the epidermal peel of leaf should be labelled as stoma ?

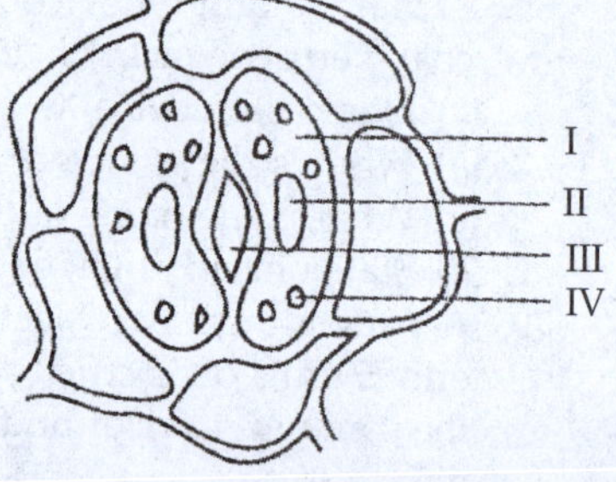

(1) I

(2) II

(3) III

(4) IV

6. A student had drawn the diagram of stomata in a hurry, as shown alongside. He could not be given full marks as he :

Stoma

(1) forgot to draw nuclei in guard cells and also to label the diagram.

(2) did not draw nuclei in guard cells and other cells.

(3) should have drawn nuclei and chloroplasts in guard cells and nuclei in all epidermal cells.

(4) did not label the stoma in its correct position.

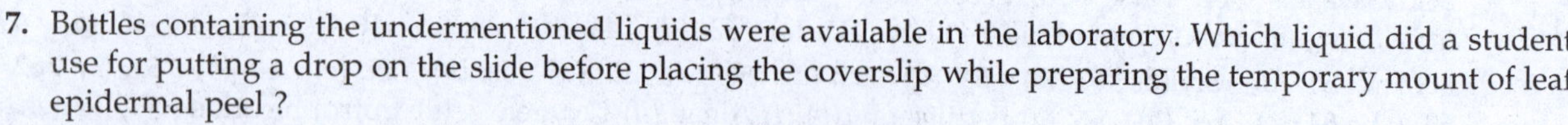

7. Bottles containing the undermentioned liquids were available in the laboratory. Which liquid did a student use for putting a drop on the slide before placing the coverslip while preparing the temporary mount of leaf epidermal peel ?

(1) Water (2) Safranin (3) Glycerine (4) Iodine

8. To prepare a good temporary mount of the petunia leaf peel showing many stomata, the student has to get the peel from the :

(1) tip of the leaf (2) upper surface of the leaf

(3) lower surface of the leaf (4) point of attachment of leaf to its petiole

9. While preparing a good temporary mount of leaf peel to observe stomata, care should be taken to avoid :
(1) adding glycerine to the slide (2) using water to wash the slide
(3) having air bubbles in the slide (4) staining the peel with safranin

10. In the sketch of stomatal apparatus given alongside, the parts I, II, III and IV were labelled differently by four students. The correct labelling is shown in :

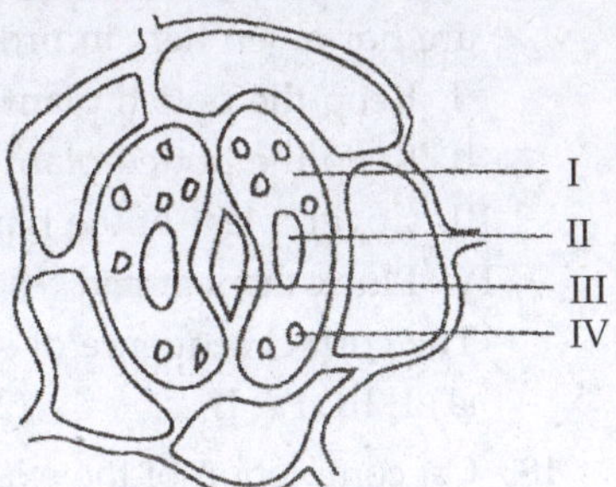

(1) (I) guard cells, (II) stoma, (III) starch granule, (IV) nucleus
(2) (I) cytoplasm, (II) nucleus, (III) stoma, (IV) chloroplast
(3) (I) guard cells, (II) starch, (III) nucleus, (IV) stoma
(4) (I) cytoplasm, (II) chloroplast, (III) stoma, (IV) nucleus

11. In the slide of an epidermal peel, the parts which appear pink coloured after staining with safranin are :
(1) stomata only (2) nuclei only
(3) cell membrane and cytoplasm (4) all parts in the peel

12. Four students, A, B, C and D, make the records given below, for the parts marked X and Y in this diagram.

Student	X	Y
A	Stoma	Guard cell
B	Guard cell	Stoma
C	Epidermal cell	Stoma
D	Stoma	Epidermal cell

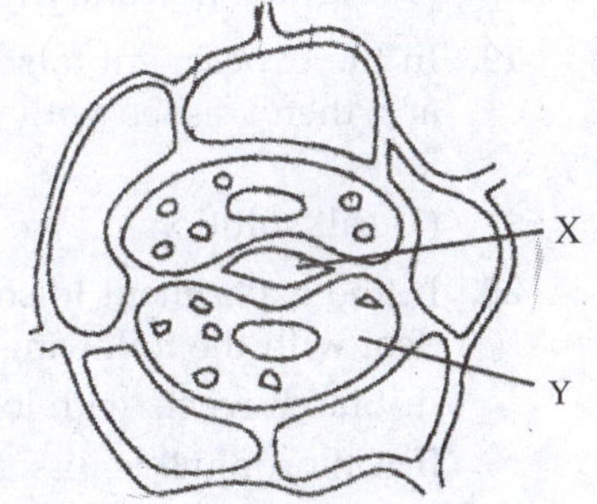

The correct record, out of these, is that of student :
(1) A (2) B (3) C (4) D

13. The steps involved in making a slide of epidermal peel of leaf are given as follows :
I. Pull out a thin peel from the lower surface of the leaf
II. Place a drop of glycerine on the slide
III. Stain the peel in safranin
IV. Place the stained peel on the glycerine
V. Remove the extra stain by washing with water
VI. Place the coverslip over the peel
Which one is the correct sequence of steps to be followed ?
(1) I, II, III, IV, V, VI (2) I, III, V, II, IV, VI (3) I, III, IV, II, V, VI (4) I, II, IV, III, V, VI

14. Given alongside is a sketch of a leaf partially covered with black paper and which is to be used in the experiment to show that light is compulsory for the process of photosynthesis. At the end of the experiment, which one of the leaf parts labelled I, II and III will become blue black when dipped in iodine solution ?

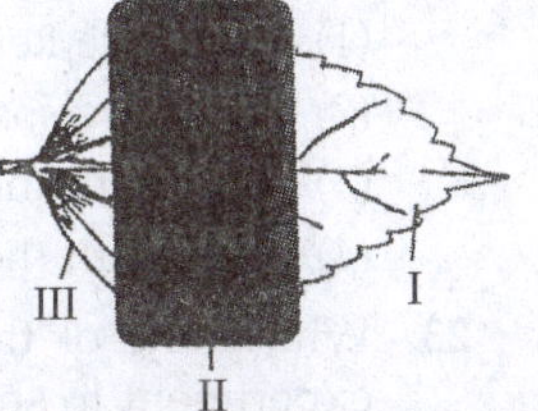

(1) I only (2) II only (3) I and III (4) II and III

15. Before testing the leaf for starch at the end of the experiment, 'light is necessary for photosynthesis', the experimental leaf should be boiled in :
(1) Water (2) Alcohol (3) KOH solution (4) Hydrochloric acid

16. Given below are the steps to be followed for performing 'starch test' on a green leaf.
(A) Boil the leaf in alcohol (B) Boil the leaf in water
(C) Dip the leaf in iodine solution (D) Wash the leaf in water

Which one of the following sequences should the students follow to get the correct result ?

(1) (A), (D), (B), (C) (2) (D), (A), (B), (C) (3) (B), (D), (A), (C) (4) (B), (A), (D), (C)

17. The steps necessary for setting up the experiment, 'To demonstrate that light is necessary for photosynthesis' are not given here in proper sequence :

I. Keep the potted plant in sunlight for 3 to 4 hours.

II. Keep the potted plant in darkness for about 48 hours.

III. Cover a leaf of the plant with a strip of black paper.

IV. Pluck the leaf and test it for starch.

The correct sequence of steps is :

(1) I, III, IV, II (2) I, IV, III, II (3) II, IV, III, I (4) II, III, I, IV

18. On completion of the experiment to demonstrate that 'Light is necessary for photosynthesis', four students reported the inference as follows. Identify the correct inference :

(1) Part of the leaf covered with strip can only undergo photosynthesis.

(2) Uncovered part of the leaf cannot synthesise starch

(3) Photosynthesis takes place only in the presence of sunlight

(4) Light is necessary for the synthesis of starch in green plants.

19. In the experiment to show that light is necessary for photosynthesis, the plucked leaf is boiled in ethanol and then washed with water. After this, it is tested for the presence of a carbohydrate by a chemical which is :

(1) salt solution (2) sugar solution (3) iodine solution (4) starch solution

20. In the experiment to show that light is necessary for photosynthesis, some of the steps of the experiment deal with the following activities :

I. Starch reacts with iodine and gives blue-black colour

II. Chlorophyll is dissolved in ethanol

III. Hot water makes leaf tissue soft

The correct sequence of these steps is :

(1) I–II–III (2) II–III–I (3) III–II–I (4) I–III– II

21. A portion of each of four destarched leaves of a plant was covered with paper strips of various kinds. The plant was exposed to sunlight for 5 hours. Thereafter, the strips were removed and the leaves tested for starch in the covered portion. Which one out of the four leaves gave the starch test in the covered portion ?

(1) that covered with black paper strip

(2) that covered with green paper strip

(3) that covered with white paper strip

(4) that covered with transparent paper strip

22. In order to destarch the leaves for an experiment to show that sunlight is necessary for photosynthesis, the :

(1) leaves are kept in alcohol and boiled in a water bath

(2) leaves are soaked in iodine for two hours

(3) plant with the leaves is kept in dark room for 48 hours

(4) plant with the leaves is exposed to light of a lamp, a night before the experiment

23. Which one of the following is the correct combination of relevant materials required for setting up an experiment to show that light is necessary for photosynthesis ?

(1) destarched leaves, strips of black paper, starch solution, and iodine crystals

(2) a potted plant, strips of coloured paper, starch solution, iodine and potassium iodide

(3) destarched leaves, strips of black paper, starch solution and potassium iodide

(4) destarched leaves, strips of black paper and iodine solution

24. A portion of destarched leaf of a potted plant was covered with a black strip of paper. The plant was then exposed to sunlight for six hours and then tested for starch. It was observed that :

(1) both covered and uncovered parts of leaf turned blue-black

(2) both covered and uncovered parts of leaf turned yellowish-brown

(3) only the uncovered part of leaf turned blue-black
(4) only the covered part of leaf turned blue-black

25. A star-shaped figure was cut in the black paper strip used for covering the leaf of a destarched plant used for demonstrating that light is necessary for photosynthesis. At the end of the experiment when the leaf was tested for starch with iodine, the star-shaped figure on the leaf was found to be :

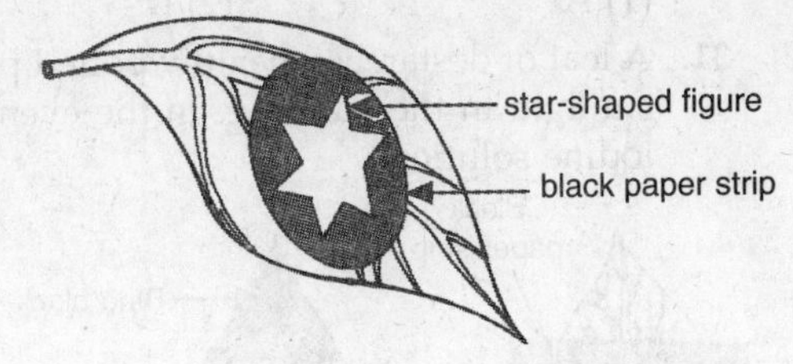

(1) colourless (2) green in colour
(3) brown in colour (4) blue-black in colour

26. In an experiment to test the presence of starch in a leaf, the leaf is boiled in alcohol for a few minutes using a water bath. This is an essential step in the experiment because alcohol :
(1) softens the leaf (2) disinfects the leaf
(3) allows iodine to enter the leaf (4) dissolves chlorophyll from leaf

27. For the experiment 'Light is necessary for photosynthesis', the potted plant was first kept in darkness for a day. This is to :
(1) deactivate chloroplasts (2) destarch leaves
(3) activate chloroplasts (4) prepare leaves for photosynthesis

28. When asked to set up an experiment to show that 'light is necessary for photosynthesis', a student ran to the school garden and set up the experiment by using a plant growing in the school garden. The experiment failed. His classmates made the following suggestions to get success in the experiment :
Student A : Safranin should be used instead of iodine
Student B : The leaf should not be boiled in alcohol to remove chlorophyll before testing for starch
Student C : Transparent paper should be used instead of black paper strip
Student D : The leaf should be destarched before starting the experiment
The correct suggestion is given by :
(1) student A (2) student B (3) student C (4) student D

29. The steps taken for setting up an experiment to demonstrate that 'light is necessary for photosynthesis', were as follows :
- A strip of black paper was clipped on the leaf of a potted plant
- The plant was kept in the sun for four hours
- The strip was removed and the leaf was placed in boiling alcohol in a water bath
- The leaf was washed and tested for starch

The result was not as expected. Identify the step which had been missed out :
(1) The plant was kept in the dark for 24 hours before starting the experiment
(2) The leaf was boiled in water after placing it in boiling alcohol
(3) The leaf was sprinkled with water before placing the black paper strip
(4) A transparent strip was used to cover the black paper strip

30. Out of the following figures, choose the one showing the correct procedure for removing chlorophyll from the leaf in the experiment 'light is necessary for photosynthesis' :

Leaf in boiling water
(A)

Leaf in boiling alcohol
(B)

Leaf in ethanol, heated in a water bath
(C)

Leaf in water, heated in a water bath
(D)

The correct procedure is :

(1) A (2) B (3) C (4) D

31. A leaf of destarched healthy potted plant was covered by black paper strip as shown in Figure I, and kept in sunlight in the morning. In the evening, it was plucked off and tested for the presence of starch by using iodine solution.

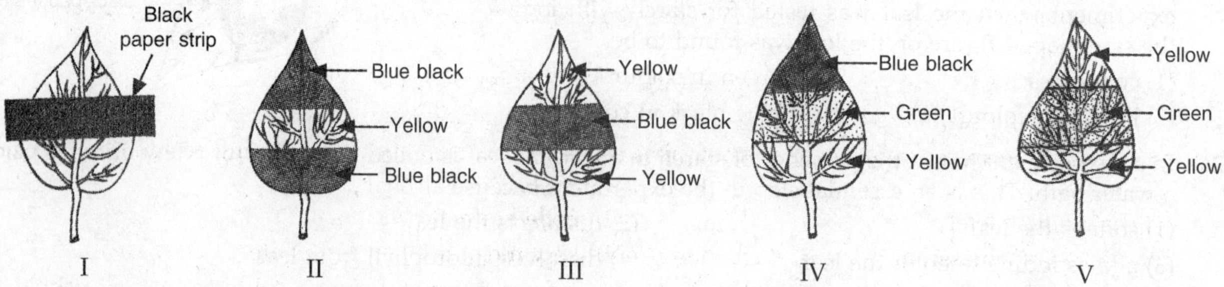

The observation is matched with the Figure No. :

(1) II (2) III (3) IV (4) V

32. In an experiment to test the presence of starch in a leaf, the plucked leaf is first boiled in water for a few minutes. This is an important step in the experiment because it :

(1) converts glucose made in the leaf into starch
(2) dissolves chlorophyll present in the green leaf
(3) extracts starch to destarch the leaf
(4) makes the leaf more permeable to iodine solution

33. Why is some KOH placed in a small test tube in the flask with germinating seeds in the experiment to demonstrate occurrence of respiration in germinating seeds ?

(1) To provide oxygen required by the seeds for respiration.
(2) To absorb carbon dioxide and create partial vacuum in the flask.
(3) To absorb water from the seeds to make them dry.
(4) To make the air present in the flask alkaline.

34. Which one of the following is the correct set of three precautions for setting up the experiment to demonstrate that carbon dioxide is evolved during respiration ?

(1) Air tight set up; delivery tube dips in water in beaker; flask has seeds which have just germinated.
(2) Thread holding KOH test tube; air tight flask; delivery tube above surface of water in the beaker.
(3) Germinated seeds under water in the flask; experimental set up not air tight; delivery tube above water level.
(4) Delivery tube touching bottom of water; KOH test tube held by a thick wire; seeds covered by water.

35. The experimental set up shown here to demonstrate that 'CO$_2$ is given out during respiration', did not yield expected results because :

(1) the flask was not air tight
(2) there was no KOH in a test tube in the flask
(3) the delivery tube was dipped in water
(4) the germinating seeds were not immersed in water

Rubber cork

Germinating seeds Water

36. The following experimental set-ups were kept in the laboratory to show that 'CO$_2$ is given out during respiration'.

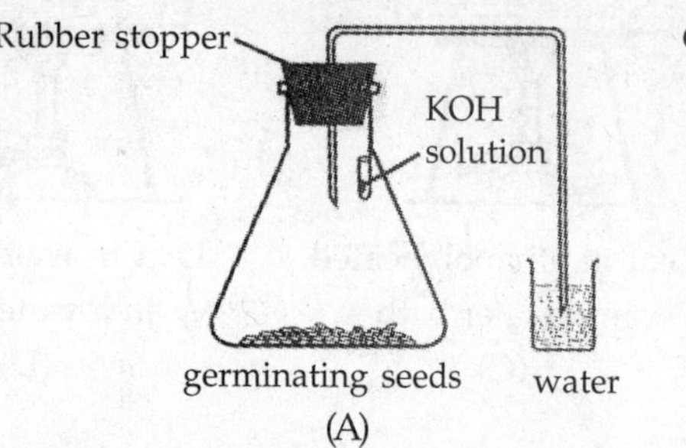

(A)

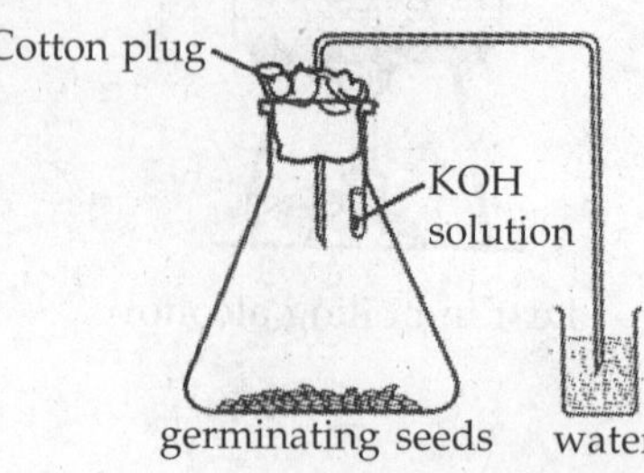

(B)

After two hours, students observed that water rises in the delivery tube :

(1) only in set up (A) (2) only in set up (B)

(3) in both (A) and (B) (4) neither in set up (A) nor in set up (B)

37. In the experiment to show that CO_2 is given out during respiration by germinating seeds, the student uses :

(1) Lime water (2) Alcohol (3) KOH solution (4) Iodine solution

38. The most appropriate reason for taking germinating seeds in the experiment to show that carbon dioxide is produced during respiration, is :

(1) germinating seeds create high temperature (2) germinating seeds are easy to handle

(3) germinating seeds are living things (4) germinating seeds are in dormant state

39. Before setting up an experiment to show that seeds release carbon dioxide during respiration, the seeds should be :

(1) dried completely (2) boiled to make them soft

(3) soaked in potassium hydroxide solution (4) kept moist till they germinate

40. Which of the following precautions are to be taken for a successful run of the experiment to show that carbon dioxide is given out during respiration ?

A. Cork should be air-tight

B. Seeds in the flask should be totally dry

C. A small tube with freshly prepared KOH solution should be placed in the flask

D. The end of the delivery tube should be above water level

The correct answer is :

(1) A and B (2) A and C (3) A, B and C (4) A, B and D

41. The chemical required in the experiment to show that carbon dioxide gas is released during respiration is :

(1) potassium bicarbonate (2) potassium dichromate

(3) potassium permanganate (4) potassium hydroxide

42. In the experiment to demonstrate that CO_2 is given out during respiration, what would you observe in the delivery tube dipped in water ?

(1) Water level rises in the delivery tube

(2) Water turns milky and rises in the delivery tube

(3) Water turns milky but does not rise in the delivery tube

(4) Water level in the delivery tube remains unchanged

43. An experimental set-up to demonstrate respiration in germinating seeds is shown here. It is observed that water from the beaker has not risen into the delivery tube (bent tube). This is because :

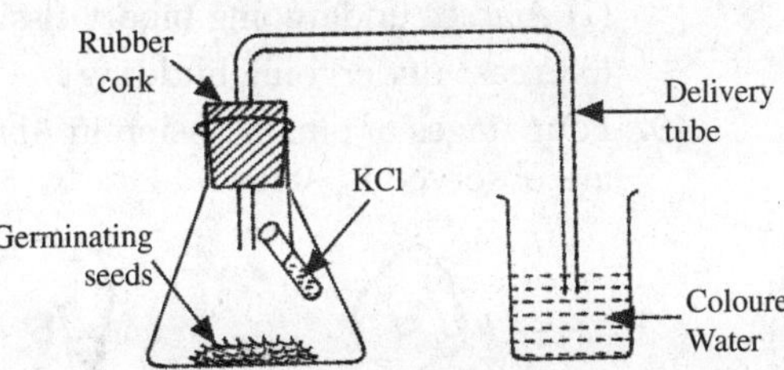

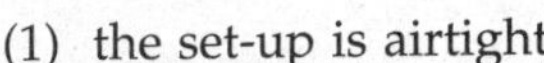

(1) the set-up is airtight

(2) the beaker has coloured water

(3) carbon dioxide is not being absorbed

(4) no oxygen is available to seeds for respiration

44. In the experiment to show that carbon dioxide is given out during respiration in humans, the student uses :

(1) lime water (2) alcohol

(3) potassium hydroxide solution (4) iodine solution

45. An experimental set-up is given here to demonstrate that CO_2 is given out during respiration. Four students made the following observations marked as I, II, III and IV.

I. Level of water remained the same in both the beaker and the delivery tube

II. Level of water increased in the delivery tube

III. Level of water reduced in both the beaker and the delivery tube

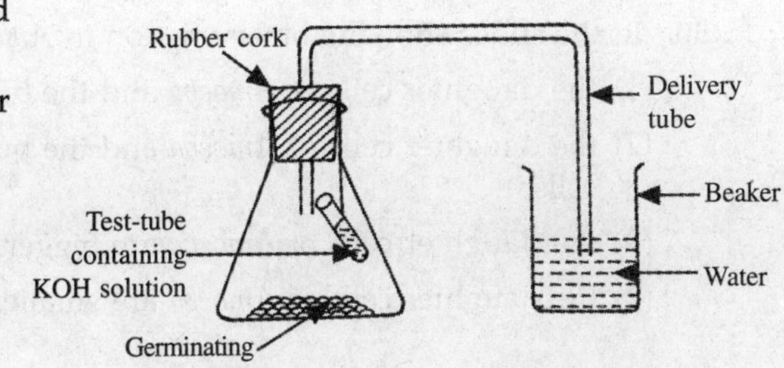

IV. Water ascends into the delivery tube and back flows into the beaker.

Which one of the above is the correct observation ?

(1) I (2) II (3) III (4) IV

46 The given slides A and B were identified by four students I, II, III and IV as stated below :

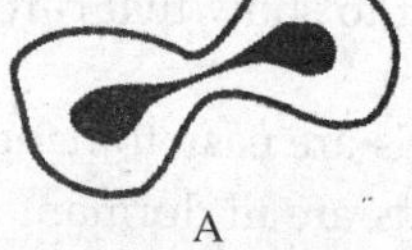

A B

	Slide A	Slide B
I.	Binary fission in *Amoeba*	Daughter cells of *Amoeba*
II.	Budding in yeast	Buds of yeast
III.	Binary fission in *Amoeba*	Buds of yeast
IV	Budding in yeast	Daughter cells in *Amoeba*

Of the above mentioned identifications of slides A and B, which one is correct ?

(1) I (2) II (3) III (4) IV

47. The correct diagram showing an *Amoeba* undergoing binary fission is :

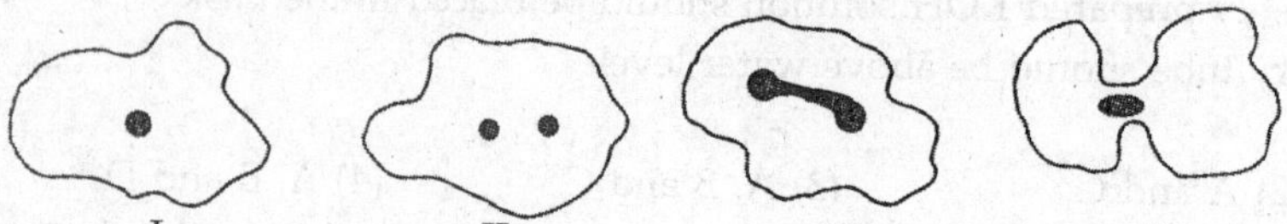

I II III IV

(1) I (2) II (3) III (4) IV

48. The figure given here shows :

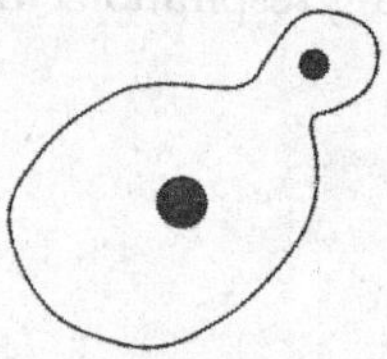

(1) *Amoeba* undergoing binary fission (2) Yeast undergoing binary fission

(3) Yeast undergoing budding (4) *Amoeba* undergoing budding

49. Four stages of binary fission in *Amoeba* are shown below. The stage at which nuclear fission and cytokinesis are observed is, stage :

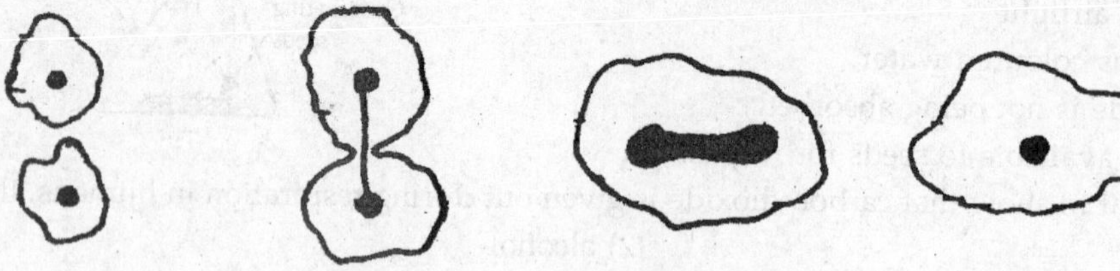

I II III IV

(1) I (2) II (3) III (4) IV

50. In the slides showing binary fission in *Amoeba* and budding in yeast, the correct observations are :

(1) the daughter cells of *Amoeba* and the bud of yeast are smaller than their respective parental cells

(2) the daughter cells of *Amoeba* and the bud of yeast are of the same size as their respective parental cells

(3) the daughter cells of *Amoeba* are bigger than the parent but the bud of yeast is smaller than the parent

(4) the daughter cells of *Amoeba* are smaller than the parent but the bud of yeast is larger than the parent

51. In the figure of budding in yeast given here, the structures A, B, C and D should be labelled respectively as :
(1) nucleus of bud, bud, yeast, nucleus
(2) dividing nucleus of bud, bud, yeast, nucleus
(3) nucleus of bud, bud, yeast, dividing nucleus of yeast
(4) dividing nucleus of yeast, yeast, bud, nucleus of bud

52. The diagram given alongside illustrates :
(1) bud formation in yeast
(2) binary fission in amoeba
(3) formation of daughter cells in yeast
(4) formation of pseudopodia in amoeba

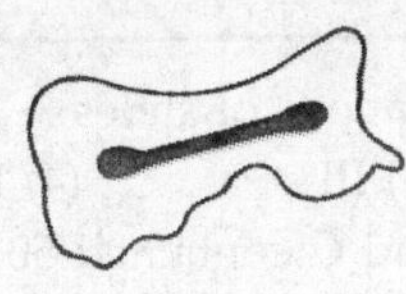

53. Which stage out of those marked I, II, III and IV is showing the binary fission in *Amoeba* ?

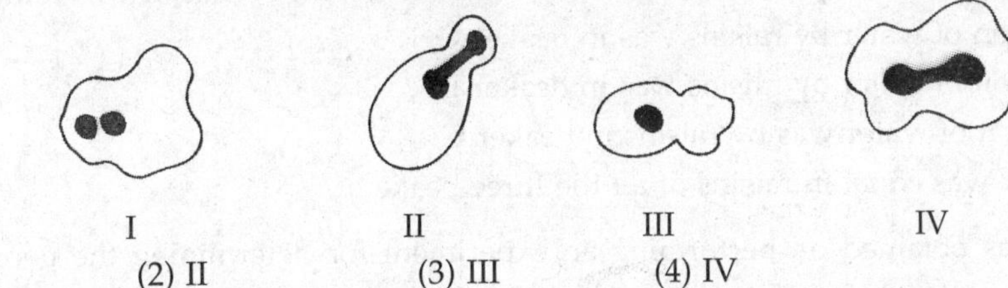

(1) I (2) II (3) III (4) IV

54. The following figures illustrate the binary fission in *Amoeba* in an incorrect sequence :

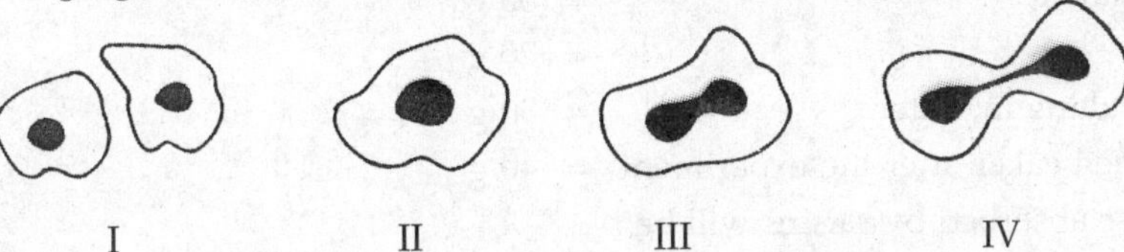

The correct sequence is :
(1) I, III, IV, II (2) II, III, IV, I (3) IV, III, II, I (4) III, IV, II, I

55. Which one of the following sketches does not illustrate budding in yeast ?

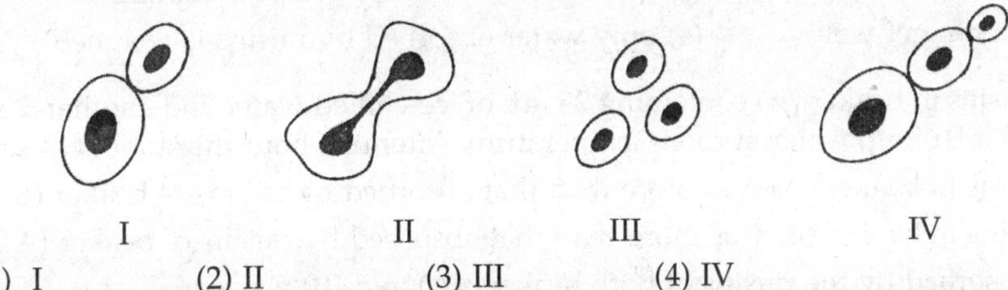

(1) I (2) II (3) III (4) IV

56. Slides A and B show stages of asexual reproduction in two different organisms :

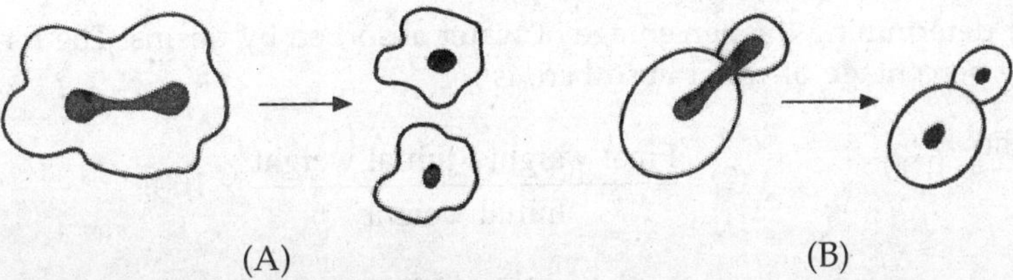

The slides A and B are depicting :
(1) binary fission in both *Amoeba* and Yeast
(2) budding in both *Amoeba* and Yeast
(3) binary fission in yeast and budding in *Amoeba*
(4) binary fission in *Amoeba* and budding in *Yeast*

57. The given slides A and B were identified by four students I, II, III and IV as stated below :

(A) (B)

Slide A	Slide B
I. Binary fission in *Amoeba*	Daughter cells of *Amoeba*
II. Budding in Yeast	Buds of Yeast
III. Binary fission in *Amoeba*	Buds of Yeast
IV. Budding in Yeast	Daughter cells in *Amoeba*

Of the above mentioned identifications of slides A and B, which one is correct ?

(1) I (2) II (3) III (4) IV

58. Each of the three beakers A, B and C contained 50 mL of distilled water. A student placed five raisins in each beaker. The raisins for each beaker weighed the same. The beakers were kept at room temperature. The raisins were removed from beaker A after 10 minutes, from beaker B after 20 minutes and from beaker C after one hour. On calculating the percentage of water absorbed by the raisins, it was found that :

(1) maximum absorption of water by raisins was in beaker C
(2) maximum absorption of water by raisins was in beaker B
(3) minimum absorption of water was by raisins in beaker C
(4) absorption of water was equal in raisins of all the three beakers

59. The following data was obtained on performing an experiment for determining the percentage of water absorbed by raisins :

Mass of water in the beaker = 50 g
Mass of dry raisins = 20 g
Mass of raisins after soaking in water = 30 g
Mass of water left in the beaker after the experiment = 40 g

The percentage of water absorbed by raisins will be :

(1) 10% (2) 25% (3) 45 % (4) 50%

60. At the end of the experiment, 'to determine the percentage of water absorbed by raisins', the raisins are wiped just before weighing. This is to ensure that :

(1) hands do not get wet
(2) the raisins lose water before weighing
(3) the weighing scale does not get wet
(4) only water absorbed by raisins is weighed.

61. A student soaked 5 g of raisins in beaker (A) containing 25 mL of ice-chilled water and another 5 g of raisins in beaker (B) containing 25 mL of tap water at room temperature. After one hour the student observed that :

(1) water absorbed by raisins in beaker (A) was more than that absorbed by raisins of beaker (B)
(2) water absorbed by raisins in beaker (B) was more than that absorbed by raisins of beaker (A).
(3) the amount of water absorbed by the raisins of both beakers (A) and (B) was equal.
(4) no water was absorbed by raisins in either of the beakers (A) and (B).

62. Raisins are soaked in water for determining the percentage of water absorbed by raisins. The formula used by a student for calculating the percentage of water absorbed, is :

(1) $\frac{\text{Initial weight} - \text{Final weight}}{\text{Initial weight}} \times 100$
(2) $\frac{\text{Final weight} - \text{Initial weight}}{\text{Initial weight}} \times 100$
(3) $\frac{\text{Final weight} - \text{Initial weight}}{\text{Final weight}} \times 100$
(4) $\frac{\text{Initial weight} - \text{Final weight}}{\text{Final weight}} \times 100$

63. A student soaked 10 g of raisins in 50 mL of distilled water in two beakers A and B each. She maintained beaker A at 25°C and beaker B at 50°C. After an hour, the percentage of water absorbed will be :

(1) the same in both A and B
(2) more in A than in B
(3) more in B than in A
(4) exactly twice in B than in A.

64. A student dissolved 5 g of sugar in 100 mL of distilled water in beaker A. He dissolved 100 g of sugar in 100 mL of distilled water in beaker B. Then he dropped a few raisins of equal weight in each beaker. After two hours he found the raisins in A swollen and those in B shrunken. The inference drawn is that :

(1) sugar concentration of raisins is lower than that of solution A and higher than that of solution B.

(2) sugar concentration of raisins is higher than that of solution A and lower than that of solution B.

(3) in B the cell membrane of raisins was damaged resulting in bleaching

(4) in A the permeability of water of the cell membrane of raisins was enhanced

65. Which of the following set of materials is required to set up an experiment to determine the percentage of water absorbed by raisins ?

(1) raisins, beaker of water, filter paper, petri dish, weight box, balance

(2) raisins, petri dish, beaker, filter paper, weight box, balance

(3) raisins, beaker of water, blotting paper, physical balance, weight box

(4) raisins, beaker, blotting paper, petri dish, weight box, balance

66. An experiment was set up to determine the percentage of water absorbed by raisins. If the mass of dry raisins was 40 g, and the mass of wet raisins was 45 g, then the percentage of water absorbed would be :

(1) $\frac{45\,g}{40\,g}\times 100$ (2) $\frac{40\,g}{45\,g}\times 100$

(3) $\frac{(45-40)\,g}{40\,g}\times 100$ (4) $\frac{(45-40)\,g}{45\,g}\times 100$

67. 5 dry raisins were placed in each of the two beakers containing 50 mL of water. After four hours, the raisins were taken out and wiped. For calculating the percentage of water absorbed by raisins, the raisins should have been weighed :

(1) only before placing in water (2) only after four hours of their being in water

(3) both before and after placing in water (4) before and at intervals of every hour

68. Raisins swell up after being placed in a beaker containing water for some time because :

(1) the concentration of water in the cell sap is higher than the water in the beaker

(2) the concentration of water in the cell sap is lower than the water in the beaker

(3) the concentration of water in the cell sap is the same as that of water in the beaker

(4) water inside the raisins passed out of them when placed in a beaker of water

69. A group of students performed an experiment to determine the percentage of water absorbed by raisins. The initial weight of raisins is 5 grams and final weight is 8 grams. The percentage of water absorbed will be :

(1) 62.5 (2) 160 (3) 60 (4) 20

70. If the weight of dry raisins is W_1 and that of soaked raisins is W_2, then the correct equation for calculating the percentage of water absorbed by raisins will be :

(1) $W_1 - W_2$ (2) $W_2 - W_1$ (3) $\frac{W_2 - W_1}{W_1}\times 100$ (4) $\frac{W_1 - W_2}{W_2}\times 100$

71. In the experiment to show that carbon dioxide is produced during respiration by germinating seeds, the alkali solution kept in a small test-tube absorbs :

(1) only O_2 gas (2) only CO_2 gas

(3) both O_2 and CO_2 gases (4) neither O_2 nor CO_2 gases

72. During the preparation of slide, a drop of glycerine is used so that :

(1) material sticks on the slide

(2) bacteria may not attack the material

(3) material may not dry up

(4) visibility of material through the microscope may improve

73. During the preparation of a temporary mount of leaf peel, the excess glycerine is removed by :

(1) dipping slide in water (2) a blotting paper
(3) a cotton cloth (4) tilting the slide

74. The apparatus required to perform the experiment to show the evolution of carbon dioxide during respiration includes :

(1) flat-bottom flask, rubber cork, small glass tube, water, KOH solution, delivery tube, germinating seeds, thread, vaseline, small beaker

(2) round-bottom flask, rubber cork, boiling tube, water, NaOH solution, delivery tube, dry seeds, thread, vaseline, small beaker

(3) measuring-flask, rubber cork, small glass tube, water, Na_2CO_3 solution , delivery tube, germinating seeds, thread, vaseline, small beaker

(4) flat-bottom flask, rubber cork, small glass tube, water, KOH solution, delivery tube, dry seeds, thread, vaseline, small beaker

75. In the experiment to demonstrate that starch is made as food by the process of photosynthesis, the plucked leaf is first boiled in water for about 3 to 5 minutes in order to :

(1) remove chlorophyll from leaf cells
(2) break down the cell membranes of leaf cells
(3) soften the brittle leaf
(4) convert starch into glucose so that it can be tested easily

ANSWERS

1. 3	**2.** 4	**3.** 3	**4.** 3	**5.** 3
6. 3	**7.** 3	**8.** 3	**9.** 3	**10.** 2
11. 4	**12.** 1	**13.** 2	**14.** 3	**15.** 2
16. 4	**17.** 4	**18.** 4	**19.** 3	**20.** 2
21. 4	**22.** 3	**23.** 4	**24.** 3	**25.** 4
26. 4	**27.** 2	**28.** 4	**29.** 1	**30.** 3
31. 1	**32.** 4	**33.** 2	**34.** 1	**35.** 2
36. 1	**37.** 3	**38.** 3	**39.** 4	**40.** 2
41. 4	**42.** 1	**43.** 3	**44.** 1	**45.** 2
46. 1	**47.** 3	**48.** 3	**49.** 2	**50.** 1
51. 1	**52.** 2	**53.** 4	**54.** 2	**55.** 2
56. 4	**57.** 1	**58.** 1	**59.** 4	**60.** 4
61. 2	**62.** 2	**63.** 3	**64.** 2	**65.** 3
66. 3	**67.** 3	**68.** 2	**69.** 3	**70.** 3
71. 2	**72.** 3	**73.** 2	**74.** 1	**75.** 2

NCERT BOOK QUESTIONS AND EXERCISES (with answers)

Chapter : LIFE PROCESSES

NCERT Book, Page 95

Q. 1. Why is diffusion insufficient to meet the oxygen requirements of multicellular organisms like humans ?

Ans. In large multicellular organisms like humans, the oxygen of air will have to travel large distances inside the human body to reach each and every cell of the body. Now, since diffusion is a very, very slow process, it will take a very long time to make oxygen available to all the body cells. Thus, diffusion is insufficient to meet the oxygen requirements of multicellular organisms like humans because the volume of human body is so big that oxygen (of air) cannot diffuse into all the internal cells of the human body quickly. So, when the size of the multicellular organism is large, then respiratory pigments (such as haemoglobin) present in blood take up the oxygen from the air in the lungs and carry it quickly to all the body cells.

Q. 2. What criteria do we use to decide whether something is alive ?

Ans. We can decide whether something is alive (or living) by using the following characteristics of livings things :

(*i*) Living things can move by themselves.
(*ii*) Living things need food, air and water.
(*iii*) Living things can grow
(*iv*) Living things can respond to changes around them. They are sensitive.
(*v*) Living things respire (release energy from food).
(*vi*) Living things excrete (get rid of waste materials from their body).
(*vii*) Living things can reproduce. They can have young ones.

Q.3. What are outside raw materials used by an organism ?

Ans. (*i*) An autotrophic organism (like a green plant) uses outside raw materials such as carbon dioxide, water and minerals alongwith sunlight to make its own food by the process of photosynthesis.

(*ii*) A heterotrophic organism (like an animal) uses outside raw material such as readymade organic food to grow, develop, synthesise proteins and other substances needed in the body.

(*iii*) Most of the organisms use oxygen (of air) as outside material for breaking down food and releasing energy for themselves in a process called respiration.

Q.4. What processes would you consider essential for maintaining life ?

Ans. The various processes essential for maintaining life are : Nutrition, Respiration, Transport, Excretion, Control and Coordination, Growth, Movement and Reproduction.

NCERT Book, Page 101

Q. 1. What are the differences between autotrophic nutrition and heterotrophic nutrition ?

Ans. (*i*) In autotrophic nutrition, an organism synthesises its own organic food from simple inorganic materials like carbon dioxide, water and minerals present in the surroundings by using sunlight energy. In heterotrophic nutrition, an organism cannot synthesise its own food, it depends on other organisms for food.

(*ii*) Autotrophic nutrition takes place in green plants and certain bacteria which can carry out photosynthesis. Heterotrophic nutrition occurs in all animals, and non-green plants which cannot carry out photosynthesis.

Q.2. Where do plants get each of the raw materials required for photosynthesis ?

Ans. The two raw materials required by the plants for photosynthesis are : Carbon dioxide and Water. The plants get carbon dioxide gas from the air (or atmosphere). The plants get water from the soil.

Q.3. What is the role of the acid in our stomach ?

Ans. The role of acid in the stomach is to make the medium of gastric juice acidic so that the enzyme pepsin can break down proteins of the food effectively. This is because the enzyme pepsin can digest proteins effectively only in the acidic medium. Another role of acid is that it kills any bacteria which may enter the stomach with our food.

Q.4. What is the function of digestive enzymes ?

Ans. Digestive enzymes are the biological catalysts which break down the complex food molecules (like carbohydrates, proteins and fats) into such small particles which can be absorbed from the alimentary canal into the blood stream.

Q.5. How is the small intestine designed to absorb digested food ?

Ans. The inner surface of small intestine has millions of tiny, finger-like projections called villi. The presence of villi gives the inner walls of the small intestine a very large surface area. And the large inner surface area of small intestine helps in the rapid absorption of the digested food.

NCERT Book, Page 105

Q.1. What advantage over an aquatic organism does a terrestrial organism have with regard to obtaining oxygen for respiration ?

Ans. The aquatic organisms use the oxygen dissolved in water for carrying out respiration. The amount of oxygen dissolved in water is, however, limited. The terrestrial organisms take oxygen from air which contains much higher amount of oxygen. Thus, a terrestrial organism has an advantage over an aquatic organism in regard to obtaining oxygen because it is surrounded by an oxygen-rich air from which it can take any amount of oxygen.

Q.2. What are the different ways in which glucose is oxidised to provide energy in various organisms ?

Ans. There are two different ways in which glucose is oxidised to provide energy in various organisms : aerobic respiration, and anaerobic respiration. Aerobic respiration uses oxygen (of air) whereas anaerobic respiration takes place without oxygen.

(*i*) In aerobic respiration, the glucose food is completely broken down by the oxygen (of air) inhaled during breathing to form carbon dioxide and water, and a lot of energy is released.

(*ii*) In anaerobic respiration, the glucose food is incompletely broken down by micro-organisms like yeast in the absence of oxygen (of air) to form ethanol and carbon dioxide, but much less energy is released.

Q.3. How are oxygen and carbon dioxide transported in human beings ?

Ans. In human beings, oxygen is carried from the lungs by the respiratory pigment haemoglobin which is present in red blood corpuscles. Haemoglobin has a very high affinity for oxygen. Carbon dioxide is more soluble in water than oxygen. So, most of the carbon dioxide produced during respiration in the human body is transported in the dissolved form in our blood.

Q.4. How are the lungs designed in human beings to maximise the area for exchange of gases ?

Ans. There are millions of alveoli in the lungs. The presence of millions of alveoli in the lungs provides a very large area for the exchange of gases. And the availability of large surface area maximises the exchange of gases. For example, if all alveoli from the two human lungs are unfolded, they would give an area of about 80 square metres (which is nearly the size of a tennis court !).

NCERT Book, Page 110

Q.1. What are the components of transport system in human beings ? What are the functions of these components ?

Ans. The components of transport system in human beings are blood and lymph. The functions of blood and lymph are as follows :

(*i*) Red blood cells carry oxygen from the lungs to all the cells of the body. Blood plasma carries digested food, proteins, common salt, waste products (like carbon dioxide and urea) and hormones from one part to another part in the body.

(*ii*) Lymph puts into circulation large protein molecules by carrying them from the tissues into the blood stream (which could not be absorbed by blood capillaries due to their large size). Lymph also carries digested fat from intestine to other tissues, and excess fluid from the extra-cellular space back into blood.

Q.2. Why is it necessary to separate oxygenated and deoxygenated blood in mammals and birds ?

Ans. The mammals and birds are warm-blooded animals which have high energy needs because they constantly require energy to maintain their body temperature. It is necessary to separate oxygenated blood and deoxygenated blood in mammals and birds because such a separation allows a highly efficient supply of oxygen to the body cells which is required for producing a lot of energy needed by them.

Q.3. What are the components of the transport system in highly organised plants ?

Ans. The two components of transport in highly organised plants are xylem and phloem.

(*i*) Xylem tissue is made of dead cells in the form of xylem vessels and tracheids. It transports water and dissolved minerals from roots to all the parts of the plant.

(*ii*) Phloem tissue is made of living cells in the form of sieve tubes and companion cells. It transports food made in leaves by photosynthesis to all the parts of a plant.

Q.4. How are water and minerals transported in plants ?

Ans. Water and the minerals dissolved in it are transported in plants by xylem tissue. In xylem tissue, the xylem vessels and tracheids of the roots, stems and leaves are interconnected to form a continuous water conducting channel which reaches all the parts of the plant. The mechanism of transport of water in plants is as follows: The leaves of plants have tiny pores called stomata. The water brought in by xylem to the leaves is constantly being lost by evaporation through stomata. The loss of water in the form of water vapour from the leaves of a plant is called transpiration. The continuous evaporation of water (or transpiration) from the cells of leaves creates a kind of suction which pulls up water from the roots through the xylem (just as a cold drink moves up the straw when we suck at the upper end of the straw). Thus, transpiration helps in the upward movement of water and dissolved minerals from the roots to the leaves.

Q.5. How is food transported in plants ?

Ans. The transport of food (made by photosynthesis) in the plant leaves takes place through 'phloem tissue'. The phloem tissue consists of sieve tubes alongwith their companion cells. The mechanism of movement of food in phloem (or translocation) by utilising energy is described below : The sugar (food) made in leaves is loaded into the sieve tubes of phloem tissue by using energy from ATP. Water now enters into sieve tubes containing sugar by the process of osmosis due to which the pressure in the phloem tissue rises. This high pressure produced in the phloem tissue moves the food to all the parts of the plant having less pressure in their tissues. This allows the phloem to transport food according to the needs of the plant. The movement of food in phloem can be upwards or downwards depending on the requirements of the plant.

NCERT Book, Page 112

Q.1. Describe the structure and functioning of nephrons.

Ans. The nephron has a cup-shaped bag at its upper end which is called Bowman's capsule. The lower end of Bowman's capsule is tube-shaped and it is called a tubule. The Bowman's capsule and the tubule taken together make a nephron (Each kidney has about 1 million nephrons). One end of the tubule is connected to

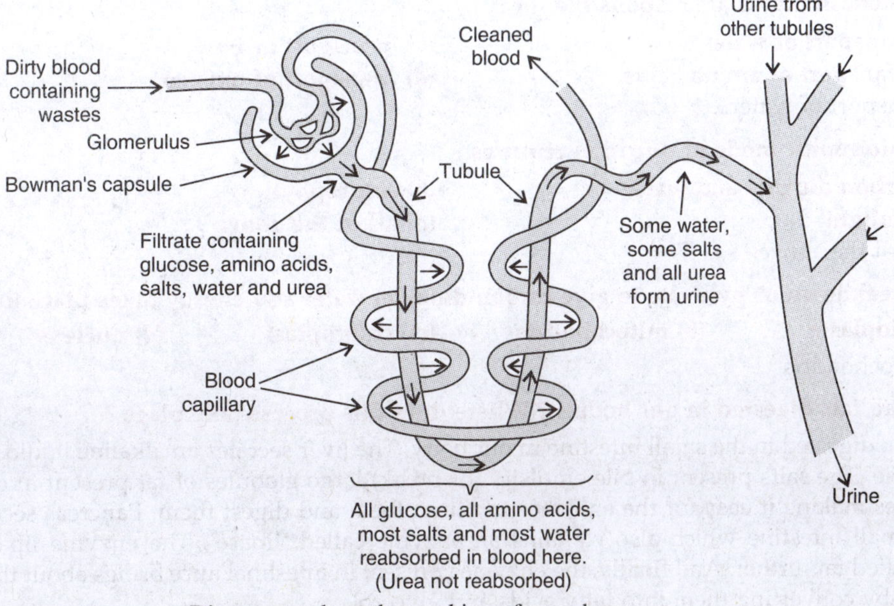

Diagram to show the working of a nephron.

Bowman's capsule and its other end is connected to a urine-collecting duct of the kidney. The Bowman's capsule contains a bundle of capillaries which is called glomerulus. One end of glomerulus is attached to renal artery which brings the dirty blood containing the urea waste in it. The other end of glomerulus comes out of Bowman's capsule as a blood capillary, surrounds the tubule of nephron and finally joins a renal vein (putting urea-free clean blood into it). The function of glomerulus is to filter the blood passing through it. The dirty blood containing waste like urea (brought by renal artery) enters the glomerulus. The glomerulus filters this blood. During filtration, the substances like glucose, amino acids, salts, water and urea, etc., present in the blood pass into Bowman's capsule and then enter the tubule of nephron. When the filtrate containing useful substances as well as the waste substances passes through the tubule, then the useful substances like all glucose, all amino acids, most salts, and most water, etc., are reabsorbed into the blood through blood capillaries surrounding the tubule. Only the waste substances urea, some unwanted salts and excess water remain behind in the tubule. The liquid left behind in the tubule of nephron is urine. The nephron carries this urine into the collecting duct of the kidney from where it is carried to ureter. From the ureter, urine passes into urinary bladder. Urine is stored in the bladder for some time and ultimately passed out of the body through urethra.

Q.2. What are the methods used by plants to get rid of excretory products ?

Ans. (*i*) The plants produce carbon dioxide as a waste product during respiration and oxygen as a waste product during photosynthesis. The plants get rid of gaseous waste products through stomata in their leaves and lenticels in stems.

(*ii*) The plants store some of the solid and liquid wastes in their body parts such as leaves, bark and fruits. The plants get rid of stored solid and liquid wastes by the shedding of leaves, peeling of bark and felling of fruits.

(*iii*) The plants get rid of their wastes by secreting them in the form of gums and resins. The plants also secrete some waste substances into the soil around them.

Q.3. How is the amount of urine produced regulated ?

Ans. The amount of urine produced is regulated by reabsorption of water and some of the dissolved substances into the blood through blood capillaries surrounding the tubules of nephrons. The amount of urine produced depends on how much excess water is present in the body and how much of dissolved wastes are to be excreted.

NCERT Book, Page 113

Q. 1 The kidneys in human beings are a part of the system for :

(*a*) nutrition **(*b*) respiration** **(*c*) excretion** **(*d*) transportation**

Ans. (*c*) excretion.

Q.2. The xylem in plants are responsible for :

(*a*) transport of water **(*b*) transport of food**
(*c*) transport of amino acids **(*d*) transport of oxygen**

Ans. (*a*) transport of water.

Q.3. The autotrophic mode of nutrition requires :

(*a*) carbon dioxide and water **(*b*) chlorophyll**
(*c*) sunlight **(*d*) all of the above**

Ans. (*d*) all of the above

Q.4. The breakdown of pyruvate to give carbon dioxide, water and energy takes place in :

(*a*) cytoplasm **(*b*) mitochondria** **(*c*) chloroplast** **(*d*) nucleus**

Ans. (*b*) mitochondria

Q.5. How are fats digested in our bodies ? Where does this process take place ?

Ans. Fats are digested in the small intestine in our body. The liver secretes an alkaline liquid called bile into small intestine. The salts present in bile emulsify (or break) large globules of fat present in our food into smaller globules making it easy for the enzymes to act on them and digest them. Pancreas secretes pancreatic juice into small intestine which also contains an enzyme called 'lipase'. The enzyme lipase breaks down the emulsified fat further. And finally, the enzymes present in intestinal juice brings about the complete digestion of fats by converting them into fatty acids and glycerol.

Q.6. What is the role of saliva in the digestion of food ?

Ans. Saliva contains an enzyme called salivary amylase. The enzyme salivary amylase present in saliva breaks down the complex 'starch' carbohydrate present in food into a simpler sugar.

Q.7. What are the conditions necessary for autotrophic nutrition and what are its by-products ?

Ans. Autotrophic mode of nutrition involves the making of food by green plants by the process of photosynthesis. The conditions necessary for autotrophic nutrition are the presence of : Carbon dioxide, Water, Chlorophyll and Sunlight. Carbon dioxide combines with water in the presence of sunlight energy (absorbed by chlorophyll) to form food like glucose. This glucose carbohydrate is used for providing energy to the plant. A part of glucose is stored in plants as starch which can be used as a source of energy whenever the plant needs it. The major by-product of autotrophic nutrition (or photosynthesis) is oxygen gas which goes into the air.

Q.8. (*a*) What are the differences between aerobic and anaerobic respiration ?

(*b*) Name some organisms that use the anaerobic mode of respiration.

Ans. (*a*) See Table on page 36 of this book.

(*b*) Anaerobic mode of respiration is used by certain micro-organisms such as yeast and some bacteria known as anaerobic bacteria.

Q.9. How are the alveoli designed to maximise the exchange of gases ?

Ans. There are millions of alveoli (thin-walled air-sacs) in the lungs. The presence of millions of alveoli in the lungs provides a very large area for the exchange of gases. And the availability of large surface area maximises the exchange of gases. For example, if all alveoli from the two human lungs are unfolded, they would give an area of about 80 square metres (which is nearly the size of a tennis court !).

Q.10. What would be the consequences of a deficiency of haemoglobin in our bodies ?

Ans. The oxygen required for breathing and respiration (release of energy) is carried by haemoglobin present in our blood. The deficiency of haemoglobin in the blood of a person reduces the oxygen-carrying capacity of blood resulting in breathing problems, tiredness and lack of energy. The person looks pale and loses weight.

Q.11. Describe double circulation in human beings. Why is it necessary ?

Ans. A circulatory system in which the blood travels twice through the heart in one complete cycle of the body is called double circulation. In the human circulatory system, the pathway of blood from the heart to the rest of the body and back to the heart is called systemic circulation ; and the pathway of blood from the heart to the lungs and back to the heart is called pulmonary circulation. These two types of circulation taken together make double circulation. The double circulation is necessary to supply oxygenated blood to the whole body (except lungs), and then to get deoxygenated blood reoxygenated in the lungs. (For detailed description of double circulation in human beings, see page 61 of this book).

Q.12. What are the differences between the transport of materials in xylem and phloem ?

Ans. (*i*) Xylem tissue transports water and dissolved minerals in plants whereas phloem tissue transports the food (made by photosynthesis) to all the parts of the plant.

(*ii*) Xylem tissue carries the water and dissolved minerals only upwards from the roots of the plant but the movement of food from the leaves through phloem can be upwards as well as downwards depending on the requirements of the plant.

(*iii*) The upward movement of water and dissolved minerals in xylem tissue is caused by a suction force produced by the continuous evaporation of water (or transpiration) from the cells of leaves of the plant which pulls up water from the roots. On the other hand, the food made in leaves is transported through phloem tissue by utilising energy from ATP.

Q.13. Compare alveoli in the lungs and nephrons in the kidneys with respect to their structure and functioning.

Ans. (*i*) **Structure.** Alveoli in the lungs and nephrons in the kidneys, both possess an elaborate network of blood capillaries.

(*ii*) **Functioning.** Alveoli purify the deoxygenated blood by removing carbon dioxide from it and making it oxygenated by introducing oxygen in it (during the gaseous exchange). Similarly, nephrons purify the dirty blood by filtering out waste products like urea from it in the form of urine.

Chapter : CONTROL AND COORDINATION

NCERT Book, Page 119

Q.1. What is the difference between a reflex action and walking ?

Ans. Reflex action is a rapid, automatic response to a stimulus which is not under the voluntary control of the brain. It is a kind of involuntary action which involves only the spinal cord. A reflex action is not based on our thinking. On the other hand, walking is a voluntary action which we undertake knowingly. The action of walking involves thinking by the brain. The central nervous system (brain and spinal cord) takes part in the action of walking.

Q.2. What happens at the synapse between two neurons ?

Ans. The synapse is a microscopic gap between any two adjacent neurons. Electrical impulses (or nerve impulses) carrying messages pass over the synapse when going from one neuron to another. Actually, synapse between two neurons acts as a one-way valve which allows electrical impulses to pass in one direction only. This happens as follows : When an electrical impulse coming from the receptor reaches the end of the axon of sensory neuron, then the electrical impulse releases tiny amount of a chemical substance (called neuro-transmitter substance) into the synapse (or gap) between two adjacent neurons. This chemical substance crosses the synapse (or gap) and starts a similar electrical impulse in the dendrite of the next neuron. In this way, the electrical impulses (or messages) are passed from one neuron to the next across the synapse.

Q.3. Which part of the brain maintains posture and equilibrium of the body ?

Ans. Cerebellum.

Q.4. How do we detect the smell of an *agarbatti* (incense stick) ?

Ans. When the *agarbatti* burns, it produces vapours having a characteristic pleasant smell. This smell is detected by the olfactory receptors present inside our nose. The action of smell of *agarbatti* on receptors sets off chemical reactions which generate electrical impulses. The sensory neurons carry these electrical impulses to the sensory area of forebrain (called cerebrum). This makes us detect the smell of burning *agarbatti.*

Q.5. What is the role of the brain in reflex action ?

Ans. Reflex action takes place in the spinal cord. Only the information that a reflex action has taken place goes on to reach the brain.

NCERT Book, Page 122

Q.1. What are plant hormones ?

Ans. The organic chemical substances produced in plants which control growth, development and responses in plants, are called plant hormones. The examples of plant hormones are : Auxins, Gibberellins, Cytokinins and Abscisic acid.

Q.2. How is the movement of leaves of the sensitive plant different from the movement of a shoot towards light ?

Ans. See Sample Problem 3 on page 92 of this book.

Q.3. Give an example of a plant hormone that promotes growth.

Ans. Auxin.

Q.4. How do auxins promote the growth of a tendril around a support ?

Ans. See Sample Problem 2 on page 92 of this book.

Q.5. Design an experiment to demonstrate hydrotropism.

Ans. See page 87 of this book.

NCERT Book, Page 125

Q.1. How does the chemical coordination take place in animals ?

Ans. The chemical coordination in animals takes place through the action of chemicals called 'hormones'. Hormones are the chemicals which are made inside the animal body in very small amounts by certain glands. Hormones are released directly into the blood. They are carried by the blood circulatory system to other parts of the body. Hormones travel all over the body but affect only particular organs at particular places. The organs which they affect are called target organs. The hormones control and coordinate several functions of the animal body such as growth, development, metabolism, behaviour and secondary sexual characteristics, etc.

Q.2. Why is the use of iodised salt advisable ?

Ans. Iodine is necessary for the thyroid gland to make thyroxine hormone. Thyroxine hormone regulates the metabolism of carbohydrates, fats and proteins so as to produce the best balance for growth. If there is deficiency of iodine in our diet, the formation of thyroxine hormone will be reduced and lead to a disease called goitre. One of the symptoms of goitre disease is that the neck of the person appears to be swollen. Iodised salt contains appropriate amounts of iodine compounds. Iodised salt can provide all the iodine needed by the thyroid gland to make sufficient thyroxine hormone for the body. So, if we take iodised salt, there can be no deficiency of iodine (or thyroxine) in the body and hence goitre disease can be prevented.

Q.3. How does our body respond when adrenaline is secreted into the blood ?

Ans. The adrenaline hormone prepares our body to function at maximum efficiency during emergency situations like danger, anger, excitement, etc. This happens as follows : When we are faced with a dangerous situation (like being chased by a ferocious dog), then our nervous system stimulates the adrenal glands to secrete more adrenaline hormone into our blood. This adrenaline hormone increases our 'heart beats', 'breathing rate', 'blood flow into muscles' and causes liver 'to put more stored glucose into our blood'. All these actions of adrenaline hormone produce a lot of energy in our body very, very quickly. And this energy helps us to cope up with emergency situations (like running away very fast from a ferocious dog or fighting an enemy, etc.).

Q.4. Why are some patients of diabetes treated by giving injections of insulin ?

Ans. Insulin is a hormone which is produced and secreted by a gland called pancreas. The function of insulin hormone is to lower the blood sugar level. Deficiency of insulin hormone in the body raises the blood sugar level causing a disease known as diabetes. The high sugar level in the blood of a diabetic person can lead to many harmful effects. Some persons having diabetes are treated by giving injections of insulin because addition of insulin hormone to blood lowers the blood sugar level.

NCERT Book, Pages 125 and 126

Q.1. Which of the following is a plant hormone ?

(*a*) Insulin **(*b*) Thyroxin** **(*c*) Oestrogen** **(*d*) Cytokinin**

Ans. (*d*) Cytokinin.

Q.2. The gap between two neurons is called a :

(*a*) dendrite **(*b*) synapse** **(*c*) axon** **(*d*) impulse**

Ans. (*b*) synapse.

Q.3. The brain is responsible for :

(*a*) thinking **(*b*) regulating the heart beat**

(*c*) balancing the body **(*d*) all of the above**

Ans. (*d*) all of the above.

Q.4. What is the function of receptors in our body ? Think of situations where receptors do not work properly. What problems are likely to arise ?

Ans. Receptors are the special cells present in our sense organs. Receptors detect all the information from our environment and feed it to the nervous system. For example, gustatory receptors present in our tongue detect taste of our food whereas olfactory receptors present in our nose detect smell. Now, if the gustatory receptors of our tongue do not work properly, we will not be able to know the taste of different types of foods (whether sweet, salty, sour or bitter, etc.). And if the olfactory receptors present in our nose do not work properly, we will not be able to smell things (like the flavour of a food or the fragrance of a perfume).

Q.5. Draw the structure of a neuron and explain its function.

Ans. A neuron consists of three parts : cell body, dendrites and axon (see Figure on next page). The cell body of a neuron is like a typical animal cell which contains cytoplasm and a nucleus. A number of long and thin fibres stretch out from the cell body of a neuron. They are called nerve fibres. The shorter fibres on the cell body of a neuron are called dendrites. The longest fibre on the cell body of a neuron is called axon. The axon

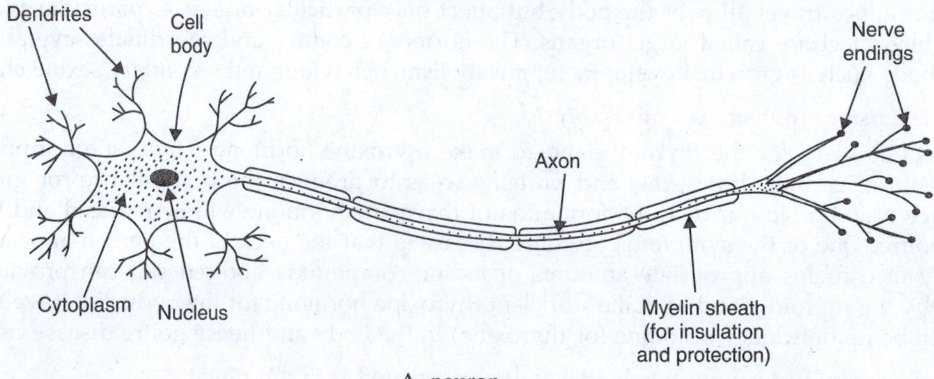

A neuron.

has an insulating and protective sheath (or cover) of myelin around it. The function of neurons is to carry messages over long distances in the body of a person quickly. The messages which neurons transmit in nervous system are in the form of electrical impulses (also called nerve impulses). Actually, neurons make the whole nervous system work efficiently. For example, the sensory neurons transmit impulses from the sensory cells or receptors (present in sense organs) towards the central nervous system (spinal cord and brain). And the motor neurons transmit impulses from the central nervous system towards the muscle cells (or effectors) for taking appropriate action.

Q.6. How does phototropism occur in plants ?

Ans. The bending of a plant stem towards light is an example of phototropism. The plant stem responds to light and bends towards it due to the action of 'auxin hormone'. This happens as follows : The auxin hormone is present in the tip of the stem of the growing plant. The auxin hormone prefers to stay in shade, away from light. So, when sunlight falls on the stem from one side, auxin hormone gets concentrated on the side of the stem which is away from light. Auxin promotes growth. So, due to more auxin, the shady side of stem (which is away from light) grows to be longer than the side of stem which is facing light, and makes the stem bend towards light. For example, in Figure given here, the left side A of the stem (which is away from light) has more auxin hormone and grows faster than right side B which is towards light. Since side A of stem becomes longer than side B, the stem bends towards right side (in the direction of light).

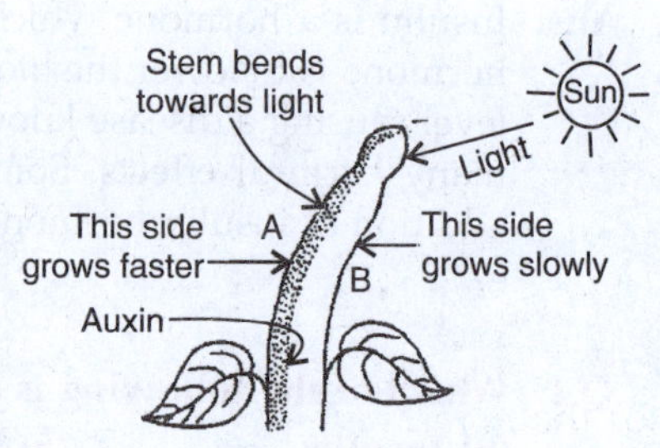

Mechanism of phototropism.

Q.7. Which signals will get disrupted in case of a spinal cord injury ?

Ans. Reflex actions and involuntary actions will get disrupted in case of a spinal cord injury.

Q.8. How does chemical coordination occur in plants ?

Ans. The plants do not have nervous system but they can still sense things. The plants can sense the presence of stimuli such as light, gravity, chemicals, water, and touch, etc., and respond to them by the action of hormones. Thus, the plants coordinate their behaviour against environmental changes by using organic chemicals called hormones. This is called 'chemical coordination'. The hormones in plants coordinate their behaviour by affecting the growth of a part of the plant resulting in the movement of that plant part in response to a stimulus. For example, when sunlight falls on a shoot from one side, the auxin hormone causes the shady side of shoot to grow faster, making the shoot bend towards sunlight.

Q.9. What is the need for a system of control and coordination in an organism ?

Ans. An organism needs a system of control and coordination for its survival in this world. The system of control and coordination is necessary in plants as well as animals (including human beings).

(*i*) The plants need carbon dioxide, water and sunlight. It is due to the presence of a hormonal system of control and coordination in plants that the stomata in their leaves open to allow in carbon dioxide gas, the roots bend towards water and the shoots grow towards sunlight. It is also due to control and coordination that tendrils in plants having weak stems make them climb on to neighbouring supports.

(*ii*) In human beings, the system of control and coordination is needed for all our actions, thinking and behaviour. The human nervous system receives information from the surroundings, processes it and then responds accordingly. Our heart beats, breathing, reading, writing, cycling, dancing and various reflex actions are all because of the nervous system. The hormonal system (endocrine system) helps in controlling and coordinating activities like metabolism, development, reproduction and preparing our body to cope up with grave situations.

Q.10. How are involuntary actions and reflex actions different from each other ?

Ans. Involuntary actions are those which we cannot control even if we want to. There is no stimulus involved in the involuntary actions. They take place on their own. For example, our heart beats all the time without our thinking about it. So, the beating of heart is a purely involuntary action. Involuntary actions are regulated by the brain. The reflex actions are also a kind of involuntary actions but they take place in response to a stimulus. For example, the decrease in the size of the pupil of our eye on stepping out in bright light is a reflex action which takes place in response to a stimulus 'light'. Reflex actions are usually regulated by the spinal cord.

Q.11. Compare and contrast nervous and hormonal mechanisms for control and coordination in animals.

Ans. See Table on page 114 of this book.

Q.12. What is the difference between the manner in which movement takes place in a sensitive plant and the movement in your legs ?

Ans. See Sample Problem 4 on page 92 of this book.

Chapter : HOW DO ORGANISMS REPRODUCE

NCERT Book, Page 128

Q.1. What is the importance of DNA copying in reproduction ?

Ans. (*i*) The chromosomes in the nucleus of a cell contain information for the inheritance of features from the parents to next generation in the form of DNA (Deoxyribo Nucleic Acid) molecules. So, the first importance of DNA copying is that the characteristics of the parent organism are transmitted to its offsprings.

(*ii*) When the DNA already present in the nucleus of a parent cell is copied by making more of DNA by certain biochemical reactions, then slight variations come in the two copies formed. These slight variations in the copying of DNA molecules lead to slight variations in the offspring produced. Thus, another importance of DNA copying is that some variations are produced in the offsprings during reproduction which form the basis for evolution.

Q.2. Why is variation beneficial to the species but not necessarily for the individual ?

Ans. Variation is useful for the survival of a species even in adverse environmental conditions. This happens as follows : There may be some drastic changes like excessive heat or cold or shortage of water (drought), etc., in the habitat of a species of organisms. Now, if all the organisms of a population living in that habitat are exactly identical, then there is danger that all of them may die and no one would survive under those conditions. This will eliminate the species from that habitat completely. However, if some variations are present in some individual organisms to tolerate excessive heat or cold or survive on meagre water supply, then there is a chance for them to survive and flourish even in adverse environment. For example, if there is a population of certain bacteria living in temperate water (which is neither very hot nor very cold) and the temperature of water increases too much due to global warming, then most of these bacteria will not be able to tolerate excessive heat and hence die. But some bacteria which had variations to resist heat would survive and grow further.

NCERT Book, Page 133

Q.1. How does binary fission differ from multiple fission ?

Ans. In binary fission, the parent organism splits (or divides) to form two new organisms. On the other hand, in multiple fission the parent organism splits (or divides) to form many new organisms simultaneously. *Amoeba* reproduces by the process of binary fission whereas the malarial parasite *Plasmodium* reproduces by the process of multiple fission.

Q.2. How will an organism be benefitted if it reproduces through spores ?

Ans. The reproduction by spores takes place in plants. Spores are covered by hard protective coat which enables them to survive under unfavourable conditions like lack of food, lack of water and extreme temperatures. But when the conditions become favourable (food and water are available, and temperature is suitable), then the spores can grow to produce new plants. Thus, the reproduction by spores benefits the plants because by surviving under adverse conditions, the spores make these plants live for ever.

Q.3. Can you think of reasons why more complex organisms cannot give rise to new individuals through regeneration ?

Ans. In complex multicellular organisms, specialised cells make up tissues; tissues make up organs; organs make up organ systems; and finally organ systems make up organisms. Since complex multicellular organisms have a very high degree of organisation in their body, they cannot be reproduced from their cut body parts by the process of regeneration. For example, a dog is a complex multicellular organism which cannot be regenerated from its cut body part say, a cut tail. This is because the cells present in the cut tail of a dog cannot produce dog's organs like heart, brain, lungs, stomach, intestines and limbs, etc., needed for the making of a complete dog. The complex multicellular organisms need more complex ways of reproduction like sexual reproduction.

Q.4. Why is vegetative propagation practised for growing some types of plants ?

Ans. Vegetative propagation is practised for growing some type of plants because it has the following advantages :

(*i*) All the plants produced by vegetative propagation are genetically similar enough to the parent plant to have all its characteristics.

(*ii*) The fruit trees grown from seeds may take many years before they start to bear fruits. But the fruit trees grown by vegetative propagation methods like cuttings or by grafting start to bear fruits much earlier (only after a few growing seasons).

(*iii*) The plants grown by vegetative propagation usually need less attention in their early years than the plants grown from seeds.

(*iv*) Many plants can be grown from just one parent plant by artificial propagation.

(*v*) Vegetative propagation makes possible the propagation of plants such as banana, rose, jasmine and orange that have lost the capacity to produce viable seeds.

Q.5. Why is DNA copying an essential part of the process of reproduction ?

Ans. DNA contains information for the inheritance of characteristics from the parents to the next generation. DNA copying is an essential part of the process of reproduction because it makes possible the transmission of characteristics of the parents to its offsprings in the next generation.

NCERT Book, Page 140

Q.1. How is the process of pollination different from fertilisation ?

Ans. Pollination is the transfer of pollen grains from the anther of stamen of a flower to the stigma of a carpel in the same flower or another flower of the same species. On the other hand, fertilisation occurs when the male gamete present in the pollen grain joins with the female gamete (or egg) present in ovule to form a zygote.

Q.2. What is the role of seminal vesicles and prostrate gland ?

Ans. Seminal vesicles and prostrate gland occur in male reproductive system. The seminal vesicles and prostrate gland add their secretions to the vas deferens which carries sperms from the testes. The secretions of seminal vesicles and prostrate gland provide nutrition to the sperms and also make their further transport easier.

Q.3. What are the changes seen in girls at the time of puberty ?

Ans. The various changes which occur in girls at puberty are : Hair grow under armpits and pubic region. Mammary glands (or breasts) develop and enlarge. The hips broaden. Extra fat is deposited in various parts of the body like hips and thighs. Fallopian tubes, uterus and vagina enlarge. Ovaries start to release eggs. Menstruation (monthly periods) starts. Feelings and sexual drives associated with adulthood begin to develop.

Q. 4. How does the embryo get nourishment inside the mother's body ?

Ans. The embryo gets nutrition from the mother's blood with the help of a special tissue called placenta. Placenta is a disc-shaped tissue which is embedded in the uterus wall (uterine wall). It has villi on the embryo side of the tissue. On the mother's side are blood spaces which surround the villi. Placenta provides a large surface area for glucose and oxygen to pass from the mother to the embryo. The developing embryo also produces waste substances which can be removed by transferring them into the mother's blood through the placenta.

Q.5. If a woman is using a copper-T, will it help in protecting her from sexually transmitted diseases ?

Ans. No, the use of copper-T for contraception will not protect a woman from sexually transmitted diseases.

NCERT Book, Page 141

Q.1. Asexual reproduction takes place through budding in :

(*a*) amoeba **(*b*) yeast** **(*c*) plasmodium** **(*d*) leishmania**

Ans. (*b*) yeast

Q.2. Which of the following is not a part of the female reproductive system in human beings ?

(*a*) ovary **(*b*) uterus** **(*c*) vas deferens** **(*d*) fallopian tube**

Ans. (*c*) vas deferens

Q.3. The anther contains :

(*a*) sepals **(*b*) ovules** **(*c*) carpel** **(*d*) pollen grains**

Ans. (*d*) pollen grains

Q.4. What are the advantages of sexual reproduction over asexual reproduction ?

Ans. (*i*) Sexual reproduction combines DNA from two individuals (male and female) due to which the offspring has a lot of variations. On the other hand, in asexual reproduction, only the DNA of one individual is copied due to which the variations in the offspring are extremely small.

(*ii*) Due to lot of variations sexual reproduction allows species to change to more advanced forms from one generation to the next and speed up evolution. On the other hand, asexual reproduction does not allow a species to change much from one generation to the next and hence evolution becomes very, very slow.

Q. 5. What are the functions performed by testes in human beings ?

Ans. The function of testes is to make male sex cells (or male gametes) called sperms and also to make the male sex hormone called testosterone. The testosterone hormone brings about changes seen in the appearance of boys at the time of puberty such as deeper voice, beard, moustache, and more body hair (than girls).

Q. 6. Why does menstruation occur ?

Ans. Since the ovary of a woman releases one egg (or ovum) every month, therefore, the uterus also prepares itself every month to receive a fertilised egg (if formed). In this process, the inner lining of the uterus becomes thick and soft with lots of blood capillaries (blood vessels) in it. This preparation in uterus is necessary because in case the egg is fertilised by a sperm, then the uterus has to keep this fertilised egg and nourish it to develop it into a baby. If, however, the egg released by the ovary is not fertilised, then the thick lining of the uterus is not needed. So, the uterus lining breaks down and comes out through the vagina in the form of blood and mucous. This is called menstruation.

Q.7. Draw a labelled diagram of the longitudinal section of a flower.

Ans. See Figure 43 on page 150 of this book.

Q.8. What are the different methods of contraception ?

Ans. The various methods of contraception (preventing pregnancy in woman) are : Barrier methods, Chemical methods, use of Loop or Copper–T, and Surgical methods.

(*i*) In the barrier methods of preventing pregnancy, the physical devices such as condoms and diaphragm (or cap) are used. Condoms are used by males (by putting them as a covering on the penis). Diaphragm (or cap) is used by females (by putting it in the vagina to cover the cervix). Condom as well as diaphragm prevent the sperms from meeting the ovum (or egg) by acting as a barrier between them.

(*ii*) In the chemical methods of preventing pregnancy, the females use oral pills. The oral pills contain hormones which stop the ovaries from releasing ovum (or eggs) into the oviduct.

(*iii*) The loop or copper–T are also very effective in preventing pregnancy. A loop or copper–T is placed inside the uterus by a doctor or a trained nurse. The loop or copper–T prevents the implantation of fertilised egg in the uterus. Loop and copper–T are called intra-uterine contraceptive devices (IUCD).

(*iv*) Surgical methods of birth control are available for males as well as females. In males, a small portion of the sperm duct (or vas deferens) is removed by surgical operation and both the cut ends are ligated (or tied) properly. This prevents the sperms from coming out. The surgical procedure carried out in males is called 'vasectomy'. In females, a small portion of the oviducts is removed by surgical operation and the cut ends are ligated (or tied). This prevents the ovum (or egg) from entering into the oviducts. The surgical procedure carried out in females is called tubectomy.

Q. 9. How are the modes of reproduction different in unicellular and multicellular organisms ?

Ans. (*a*) Most of the unicellular organisms (such as protozoa and bacteria) reproduce by the asexual process of 'fission'. In this process, mere cell division leads to the creation of new individuals.

(*b*) In simple multicellular organisms, reproduction occurs by asexual methods such as budding, spore formation, fragmentation and regeneration, etc. But in complex multicellular organisms, reproduction takes place by sexual methods involving gametes (sex cells) from two parents — a male and a female.

Q. 10. How does reproduction help in providing stability to populations of species ?

Ans. The process of reproduction introduces some variations in the individual organisms of a species. The variations introduced in some individual organisms may enable them to survive even in adverse environmental conditions such as excessive heat or cold or shortage of water, etc. (when most other members of the species will die). In this way, the introduction of variations during reproduction provides stability to the populations of various species by preventing some of their individuals from getting wiped out during adverse environmental conditions.

Q.11. What could be the reasons for adopting contraceptive methods ?

Ans. (*i*) The use of contraceptive methods helps in family planning (birth control). By adopting contraceptive methods, a couple can avoid unwanted pregnancy. They can choose how many children to have and when to have them. A couple can also space the birth of children properly by using contraceptive methods.

(*ii*) Some of the contraceptive methods (like the use of condom) also provide protection to a person from sexually transmitted diseases.

Chapter : HEREDITY AND EVOLUTION

NCERT Book, Page 143

Q.1. If a trait A exists in 10% of a population of an asexually reproducing species and a trait B exists in 60% of the same population, which trait is likely to have arisen earlier ?

Ans. The trait B which exists in 60% of the population is likely to have arisen earlier. This is because the traits (or variations) produced in an organism during successive generations get accumulated in the populations of the species.

Q.2. How does the creation of variations in a species promote its survival ?

Ans. Due to the creation of variations, a species can adjust to the changing environment around it. And this promotes the survival of the species in the changing environment. For example, the accumulation of 'heat resistant' variation (or trait) in some bacteria will ensure its survival even when the temperature in its environment rises too much due to a heat wave or some other reasons. On the other hand, the bacteria which did not have this variation to withstand heat would not survive under these circumstances and die.

NCERT Book, Page 147

Q. 1. How do Mendel's experiments show that traits may be dominant or recessive ?

Ans. Mendel first crossed pure-bred tall pea plants with pure-bred dwarf pea plants and found that only tall pea plants were produced in the first generation or F_1 generation (see Figure 1). No dwarf pea plants (or short

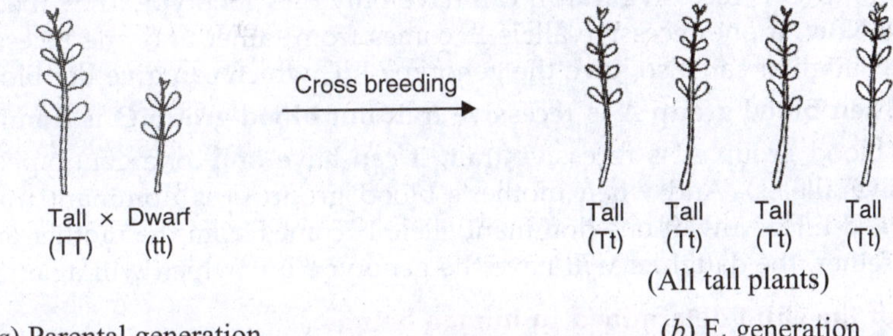

Figure 1. A cross of tall and dwarf pea plants.

pea plants) were obtained in the first generation of progeny. From this Mendel concluded that the first generation (or F_1 cross) showed the traits of only one of the parent plants : tallness. The trait of other parent plant, dwarfness, did not show up in the progeny of first generation.

Mendel then crossed the tall pea plants of the first generation (F_1 generation) and found that tall plants and dwarf plants were obtained in the second generation (or F_2 generation) in the ratio of 3 : 1. In other words, in the F_2 generation, three-fourth plants were tall and one-fourth were dwarf (see Figure 2). Mendel noted that the dwarf trait of the parent pea plant which had seemingly disappeared in the first generation progeny,

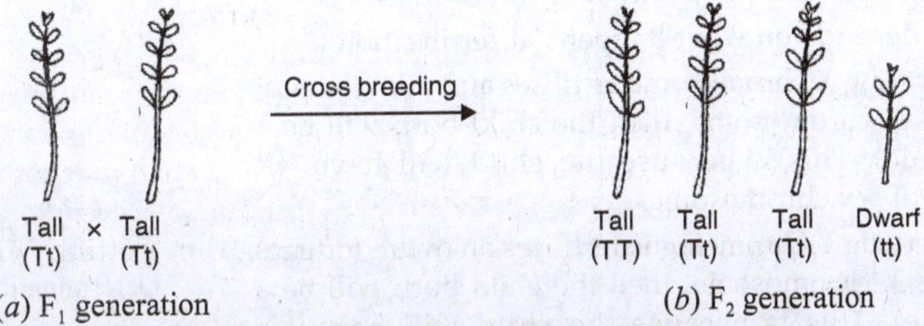

Figure 2. A cross of tall plants of F_1 generation.

reappeared in the second generation. Mendel said that the trait of dwarfness of one of the parent pea plant had not been lost, it was merely concealed or supressed in the first generation to re-emerge in the second generation. Mendel called the repressed trait of 'dwarfness' as 'recessive trait' and the expressed trait of 'tallness' as the 'dominant trait'. In this way, Mendel's experiments with tall and dwarf pea plants showed that the traits may be *dominant* or *recessive*.

Q. 2. How do Mendel's experiments show that traits are inherited independently ?

Ans. When Mendel crossed pure-bred tall pea plants with pure-bred dwarf pea plants, he found that only tall pea plants were produced in the F_1 generation. Now, when Mendel further crossed the tall pea plants of the F_1 generation, he found that tall plants and dwarf plants were obtained in the ratio 3 : 1 in the F_2 generation. Mendel noted that all the pea plants produced in the F_2 generation were either tall or dwarf. There were no plants with intermediate height (or medium height) in-between the tall and dwarf plants. In this way, Mendel's experiment showed that the traits (like tallness and dwarfness) are inherited independently. This is because if the traits of tallness and dwarfness had blended (or mixed up), then medium sized pea plants would have been produced.

Q.3. A man with blood group A marries a woman with blood group O and their daughter has blood group O. Is this information enough to tell you which of the traits — blood group A or O — is dominant ? Why or why not ?

Ans. No, this information is not enough to tell us which of the traits, blood group A or blood group O, is dominant. This is because :

(*i*) if the blood group A is dominant trait and blood group O is recessive trait, the daughter can have blood group O, and

(*ii*) even if the blood group A is recessive trait but blood group O is dominant trait, the daughter can still have blood group O.

Let us discuss these two possibilities in detail.

***Possibility 1 :* When blood group A is dominant trait but blood group O is recessive trait**

When father's blood group A is dominant trait, it can have two genotypes : I^AI^A and I^AI^O. And when mother's blood group O is recessive trait it can have only one genotype : I^OI^O (because it should have two recessive alleles). Now, if one recessive allele I^O comes from father and one recessive allele I^O comes from mother, then the daughter can also have the genotype I^OI^O which can give her blood group O.

***Possibility 2 :* When blood group A is recessive trait but blood group O is dominant trait**

When father's blood group A is recessive trait, it can have only one genotype: $I^A I^A$ (because it should have two recessive alleles). And when mother's blood group O is dominant trait, then it can have two genotypes : I^OI^O and I^OI^A. Now, if one dominant allele I^O comes from the mother and one recessive allele I^A comes from the father, the daughter will have the genotype I^OI^A which will again give her blood group O.

Q.4. How is the sex of the child determined in human beings ?

Ans. Genetics is involved in the determination of the sex of a child. This can be explained as follows : The chromosomes which determine the sex of a child are called sex chromosomes. There are two types of sex chromosomes, one is called X chromosome and the other is called Y chromosome.

(*i*) A male (man or father) has one X chromosome and one Y chromosome. This means that half the male gametes or half the sperms will have X chromosomes and the other half will have Y chromosomes.

(*ii*) A female (woman or mother) has two X chromosomes (but no Y chromosomes). This means that all the female gametes called ova (or eggs) will have only X chromosomes.

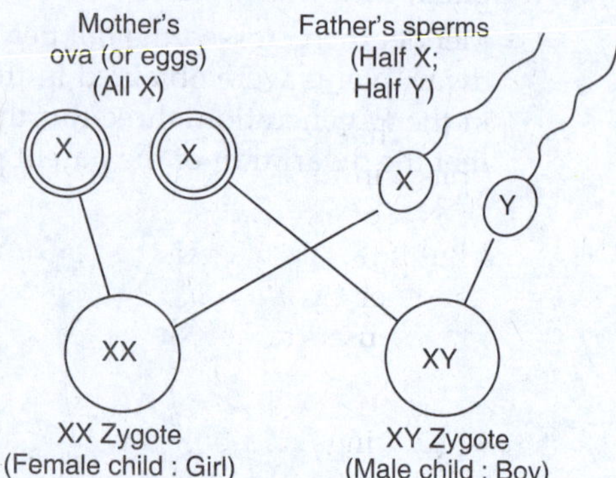

Determination of sex of a child.

The sex of a child depends on what happens at fertilisation :

(*a*) If a sperm carrying X chromosome fertilises an ovum (or egg) which carries X chromosome, then the child born will be a girl (or female). This is because the child will have XX combination of sex chromosomes.

(*b*) If a sperm carrying Y chromosome fertilises an ovum (or egg) which carries X chromosome, then the child born will be a boy (or male). This is because the child will have XY combination of sex chromosomes.

NCERT Book, Page 150

Q.1. What are the different ways in which individuals with a particular trait may increase in a population ?

Ans. The various ways in which individuals with a particular trait may increase in a population are :

(i) By the process of natural selection in which the characteristics that help individual organisms to survive and reproduce are passed on to their offsprings, and those characteristics which do not help are not passed on.

(ii) By the process of genetic drift caused by drastic changes in the frequencies of particular genes by chance alone.

Q.2. Why are the traits acquired during the life-time of an individual not inherited ?

Ans. For a trait of an organism to be inherited, it should bring about a change in the genes (or DNA) present in the reproductive cells or gametes of that organism. The traits acquired during the life-time of a person do not bring about a change in the genes (or DNA) present in its reproductive cells or gametes and hence they are not inherited by the offsprings.

Q. 3. Why are the small number of surviving tigers a cause of worry from the point of view of genetics ?

Ans. Sometimes a species (a type of animal or plant) may completely die out. It may become extinct. Once a species is extinct, its genes are lost for ever. It cannot re-emerge at all. The small numbers of surviving tigers are a cause of worry from the point of view of genetics because if they all die out and become extinct, their genes will be lost for ever. Our coming generations will not be able to see tigers at all.

NCERT Book, Page 151

Q.1. What factors could lead to the rise of a new species ?

Ans. The important factors which could lead to the rise (or formation) of a new species are the following :

(i) Geographical isolation of a population caused by various types of barriers (such as mountain ranges, rivers and sea). The geographical isolation leads to reproductive isolation due to which there is no flow of genes between separated groups of population.

(ii) Genetic drift caused by drastic changes in the frequencies of particular genes by chance alone.

(iii) Variations caused in individuals due to natural selection.

Q. 2. Will geographical isolation be a major factor in the speciation of a self-pollinating plant species ? Why or why not ?

Ans. Geographical isolation will not be a major factor in the speciation of a self-pollinating plant because it does not depend on other plants for its process of reproduction to be carried out.

Q. 3. Will geographical isolation be a major factor in the speciation of an organism that reproduces asexually ? Why or why not ?

Ans. Geographical isolation cannot be a major factor in the speciation of an asexually reproducing organism because it does not require any other organism to carry out reproduction.

NCERT Book, Page 156

Q. 1. Give an example of the characteristics being used to determine how close two species are in evolutionary terms.

Ans. The changes in DNA during reproduction are mainly responsible for evolution. The changes which take place in the DNA of species go on accumulating from one generation to the next. So, if the changes in the DNA of any two species are less, then the two species are quite close to one another in evolutionary terms. But if the changes in the DNA of two species are much more, then the two species will be far apart from one another in evolutionary terms. Thus, it is the characteristic of the extent of change in the DNA which is being used to determine how close two species are in evolutionary terms.

Q.2. Can the wings of a butterfly and the wings of a bat be considered homologous organs ? Why or why not ?

Ans. The wings of a butterfly and the wings of a bat cannot be considered homologous organs because though the function of wings in both cases is the same (flying) but they have different basic design. The butterfly (which is an insect) has a fold of membranes as wings which are associated with a few muscles but no bones are present. On the other hand, a skeleton made of bones supports the bat's wings.

Q.3. What are fossils ? What do they tell us about the process of evolution ?

Ans. The remains (or impressions) of dead animals or plants that lived in the remote past are known as fossils. The fossils provide evidence for evolution. For example, a fossil bird called *Archaeopteryx* looks like a bird but it has many other features which are found in reptiles. This is because *Archaeopteryx* has feathered wings like those of birds but teeth and tail like those of reptiles. *Archaeopteryx* is, therefore, a connecting link between the reptiles and birds, and hence suggests that the birds have evolved from the reptiles. Thus, fossils provide the evidence that the present animals (and plants) have originated from the previously existing ones through the process of continuous evolution.

NCERT Book, Page 158

Q.1. Why are human beings who look so different from each other in terms of size, colour and looks said to belong to the same species ?

Ans. The human beings who look so different from each other in terms of size, colour and looks are said to belong to the same species (*Homo sapiens*) because they can interbreed to produce fertile offsprings (sons and daughters).

Q.2. In evolutionary terms can we say which among bacteria, spiders, fish and chimpanzees have a 'better' body design? Why or why not ?

Ans. In evolutionary terms, we can say that bacteria has a 'better' body design than spiders, fish, and chimpanzees. This is because though bacteria is one of the simplest and primitive life forms but it still inhabits and survives in some of the most inhospitable (most unfavourable) habitats such as hot springs, deep-sea thermal vents and ice in Antarctica. Most other organisms (including spider, fish and chimpanzees) cannot survive in such harsh environments.

NCERT Book, Page 159

Q.1. A Mendelian experiment consisted of breeding tall pea plants bearing violet flowers with short pea plants bearing white flowers. The progeny all bore violet flowers, but almost half of them were short. This suggests that the genetic make up of the tall parent can be depicted as :

(*a*) TTWW (*b*) TTww (*c*) TtWW (*d*) TtWw

Give reason for your choice.

Ans. (*c*) TtWW.

Explanation : T is the gene for tallness, t is the gene for shortness (or dwarfness), W is the gene for violet colour and w is the gene for white colour. Now, in this case, all the progeny bore violet flowers, so the parent tall plant must contain only the dominant genes for colour (which is violet colour). That is, the parent plant should have the gene pair WW. Again, since almost half of progeny plants were short, this means that the parent tall plant should contain genes for tallness as well as shortness. That is, the parent plant should have genes Tt in it. Now, combining Tt and WW, the genetic make up of the parent plant becomes TtWW.

Q.2. An example of homologous organs is :

(*a*) Our arm and a dog's foreleg

(*b*) Our teeth and an elephants' tusks

(*c*) potato and runners of grass

(*d*) all of the above

Ans. (*d*) all of the above

Q.3. In evolutionary terms, we have more in common with :

(*a*) a Chinese school boy (*b*) a chimpanzee (*c*) a spider (*d*) a bacterium

Ans. (*a*) a Chinese school boy.

Q.4. A study found that children with light coloured eyes are likely to have parents with light coloured eyes. On this basis, can we say anything about whether the light eye colour trait is dominant or recessive ? Why or why not ?

Ans. Just on the basis of the statement that children with light-coloured eyes are likely to have parents with light-coloured eyes, we cannot say whether the light eye colour trait is dominant or recessive. This is because two copies of a trait (say eye colour) are inherited from both parents (one from father and the other from mother) and unless we know the nature of the two eye-colour traits, we cannot tell which is dominant and which is recessive. Recessive traits appear only when both the parents contribute recessive genes. So, from the statement given here we can only presume that both the parents are contributing recessive genes.

Q.5. How are the areas of study–evolution and classification–interlinked ?

Ans. The classification of organisms is a reflection of their evolutionary relationships. Classification is based on similarities and differences amongst organisms :

(*i*) The more characteristics two organisms have in common, the more closely they are related. And the more closely they are related, the more recently they will have had a common ancestor in the evolutionary chain.

(*ii*) The more different characteristics two organisms have, the more remotely they are related. And the more remotely they are related, they will have had a common ancestor in the more remote past.

Q.6. Explain the terms analogous and homologous organs with examples.

Ans. Those organs which have different basic structure (or different basic design) but have similar appearance and perform similar functions are called analogous organs. The wings of an insect and the wings of a bird are analogous organs. The wings of an insect and a bird have different structures (the insects have a fold of membranes as wings which are associated with a few muscles whereas a skeleton of bones, flesh and feathers support bird's wings) but they perform the same function of flying.

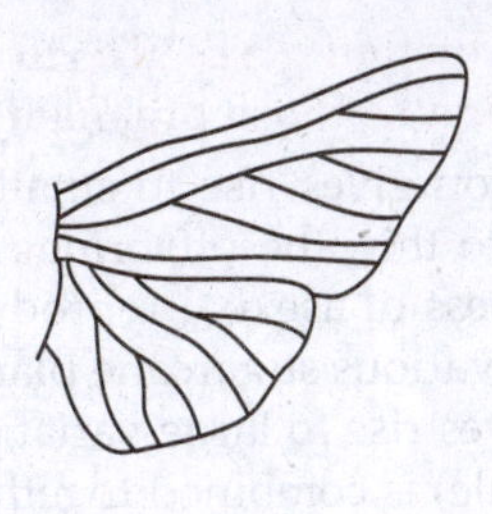

(*a*) Wing of insect

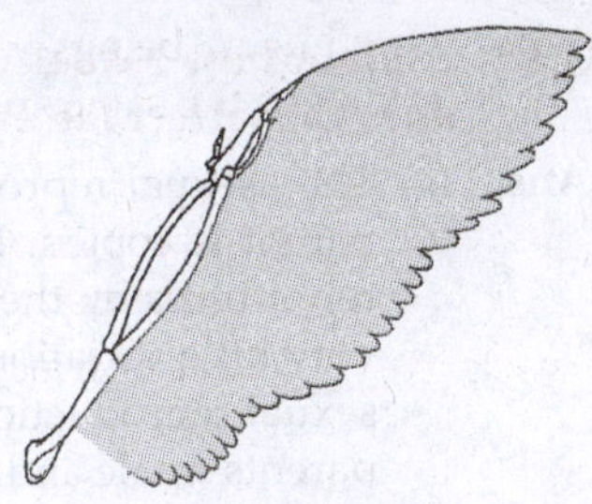

(*b*) Wing of bird

Analogous organs.

Those organs which have the same basic structure (or same basic design) but different functions are called homologous organs. The forelimbs of humans (man) and a lizard are homologous organs. Both these organs

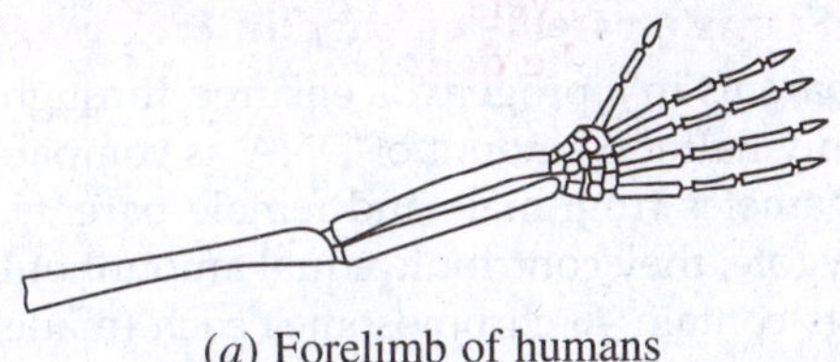

(*a*) Forelimb of humans

(*b*) Forelimb of lizard

Homologous organs.

have the same basic design of bones but they perform different functions.The forelimbs of a human (man) are used for grasping whereas the forelimbs of a lizard are used for running.

Q.7. Outline a project which aims to find the dominant coat colour in dogs.

Ans. In order to find the dominant coat colour (or dominant hair colour) in dogs, we should first select pure-bred male and female dogs having black colour and pure-bred male and female dogs having brown colour. Then :

(*i*) cross the pure-bred black male dog with pure-bred brown female dog

(*ii*) also, cross the pure-bred brown male dog with pure-bred black female dog

Observe the coat colour (or hair colour) of progeny (or puppies) produced.

(*a*) If all the progeny (or puppies) are black in colour, then black will be the dominant coat colour in dogs.

(*b*) If, however, all the progeny (or puppies) are brown in colour, then brown will be the dominant coat colour in dogs.

Q.8. Explain the importance of fossils in deciding evolutionary relationships.

Ans. The importance of fossils in deciding evolutionary relationships is that they provide evidence that the present animals (and plants) have originated from the previously existing animals (and plants) through the process of continuous evolution. For example, a fossil bird called *Archaeopteryx* looks like a bird but it has many other features which are found in reptiles. This is because *Archaeopteryx* has feathered wings like those of birds but teeth and tail like those of reptiles. *Archaeopteryx* is, therefore, a connecting link between the reptiles and birds, and hence suggests that the birds have evolved from the reptiles.

Q.9. What evidence do we have for the origin of life from inanimate matter (lifeless matter) ?

Ans. The British Scientist J.B.S. Haldane suggested in 1929 that life must have originated from inanimate matter (lifeless matter) consisting of simple inorganic molecules such as methane, ammonia and hydrogen sulphide, etc., which were present on the earth soon after it was formed. The evidence for the origin of life from inanimate matter was provided by the experiments conducted by Stanley L. Miller and Harold C. Urey in

1953. They assembled an apparatus to create an early earth atmosphere which was supposed to consist of gases like methane, ammonia and hydrogen sulphide, etc., (but no oxygen), over water. This was maintained at a temperature just below 100°C and electric sparks were then passed through the mixture of gases (to simulate lightning) for about one week. At the end of one week, it was found that about 15 per cent of carbon (from methane) had been converted into simple compounds of carbon including 'amino acids' which make up protein molecules found in living organisms. This experiment provides the evidence that the life originated from inanimate matter (or lifeless matter) like inorganic molecules.

Q.10. Explain how sexual reproduction gives rise to more viable variations than asexual reproduction. How does this affect the evolution of those organisms that reproduce sexually ?

Ans. (*a*) The asexual reproduction gives rise to small variations because in this process the DNA of only one parent is copied. Due to this, the offsprings produced look almost the same. For example, sugarcane reproduces by the process of asexual reproduction, so if we observe a field of sugarcane, we will find very little variations in various sugarcane plants. All the sugarcane plants look alike. On the other hand, sexual reproduction gives rise to large variations because in this process DNA from the gametes of two parents (male and female) is combined together. For example, it is due to the large variations produced by sexual reproduction that no two human beings look alike (except identical twins).

(*b*) The large genetic variations produced during sexual reproduction lead to the continuous evolution of those organisms which reproduce sexually. In fact, sexual reproduction plays an important role in the origin of new species having different characteristics. All this is not possible in the case of asexual reproduction.

Q.11. How is the equal genetic contribution of male and female parents ensured in the progeny ?

Ans. The equal genetic contribution of male and female parents in a progeny is ensured through the special type of reproductive cells (called gametes) which have only half the amount of DNA as compared to other body cells (called non-reproductive cells). So, when the gametes from male and female parents combine during sexual reproduction to form a fertilised egg called zygote, they contribute equal amount of DNA (half each). For example, the normal body cells of human beings contain 46 chromosomes each (made of DNA). Now, the human sperm cell (or male gamete) has 23 chromosomes and the human egg cell (or female gamete) has also 23 chromosomes. So, the combination of 23 chromosomes from male and an equal number of 23 chromosomes from female during sexual reproduction ensures equal genetic contribution of male and female parents in the progeny (to give 23 + 23 = 46 chromosomes).

Q.12. Only variations that confer advantage to an individual organism will survive in a population. Do you agree with this statement ? Why or why not ?

Ans. Yes, only those variations that confer advantage to an individual organism will survive in a population. This will become clear from the following example. Suppose there is a population of red beetles in the green bushes and a colour variation arises during reproduction so that one beetle is now green in colour (instead of red). This variation offers advantage of survival because the green beetle can mix up with green bushes, it cannot be spotted and eaten up by a crow and hence its population will increase. If, however, the variation had produced a blue coloured beetle, then this colour could not offer any survival advantage because blue beetle in green bushes could be easily spotted by a crow and eaten by it.

Chapter : OUR ENVIRONMENT

NCERT Book, Page 257

Q.1. Why are some substances biodegradable and some non-biodegradable ?

Ans. The micro-organisms like bacteria and other decomposer organisms (called saprophytes) present in our environment are 'specific' in their action. They break down the natural substances or products made from natural substances (like dead remains of plants and animals, and their waste products, paper, etc.) but do not break down man-made substances such as plastics, metals and glass objects, etc. So, it is due to the property of decomposer organisms of being specific in their action that some waste substances are biodegradable whereas some are non-biodegradable.

Q.2. Give any two ways in which biodegradable substances would affect the environment.

Ans. (*i*) The rotting biodegradable wastes (like rotting plant and animal wastes) act as breeding grounds for flies and cockroaches. These flies and cockroaches carry germs and spread various diseases to people living in that area.

(*ii*) The rotting biodegradable wastes emit foul smell in the environment which makes the life of people in the area miserable.

Q.3. Give any two ways in which non-biodegradable substances would affect the environment.

Ans. (*i*) Some of the non-biodegradable wastes (such as pesticides like DDT and metals like mercury) enter the food chain of humans. These non-biodegradable wastes get concentrated in human beings and damage their health in the long run.

(*ii*) The excessive use of non-biodegradable fertilisers in agriculture makes the soil either too much acidic or too much alkaline. When the soil becomes too acidic or too alkaline, the crop yield is reduced.

(*iii*) The dumping of non-biodegradable wastes like plastic, glass and metal objects here and there acts as an eyesore and spoils the environment.

NCERT Book, Page 261

Q.1. What are trophic levels ? Give an example of a food chain and state the different trophic levels in it.

Ans. A food chain represents the flow of food (or energy) in a given set of organisms or living beings. The various steps in a food chain at which the transfer of food (or energy) takes place are called trophic levels. In fact, in a food chain, each step representing an organism forms a trophic level. Consider a food chain operating in a grassland which consists of four organisms :

Grass ⟶ Insects ⟶ Frog ⟶ Birds

In this food chain, grass is the producer and represents the first trophic level. Insects are the herbivores (which eat grass) and represent second trophic level. Frog is the carnivore (which eats insects) and represents third trophic level. And birds are the top carnivores (which eat frogs) and represent fourth trophic level.

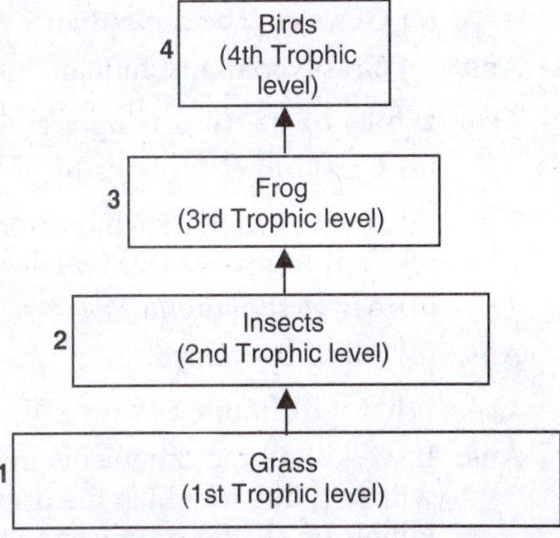

Q.2. What is the role of decomposers in the ecosystem ?

Ans. The decomposers help in decomposing the dead bodies of plants and animals, and hence act as cleansing agents of environment. The decomposers also help in putting back the various elements of which the dead plants and animals are made, back into the soil, air and water for re-use by the producers like crop-plants. This maintains the fertility of soil and the soil would continue to support crops again and again. For example, the decomposers like putrefying bacteria and fungi decompose the dead plants and animal bodies into ammonia (and other simpler substances). This ammonia is converted into nitrates by the nitrifying bacteria present in soil. These nitrates act as fertilizer in the soil and are again absorbed by the plants for their growth.

NCERT Book, Page 264

Q.1. What is ozone and how does it affect any ecosystem ?

Ans. Ozone is a gas made up of three atoms of oxygen joined together. The molecular formula of ozone is O_3. Ozone is formed high up in the atmosphere by the action of ultraviolet radiations (coming from the sun) on the oxygen gas. The ozone layer present high up in the atmosphere protects all forms of life on earth by absorbing harmful ultraviolet radiations coming from the sun. Certain chemicals like chlorofluorocarbons (CFCs) which are widely used in refrigeration, fire extinguishers and aerosol sprayers reach the upper atmosphere and react with ozone gas present in ozone layer and destroy it gradually. Due to this the ozone layer in the upper atmosphere is becoming thinner, allowing more harmful ultraviolet rays to pass through it and reach the earth. Thus, due to the depletion of ozone layer caused by chlorofluorocarbons, more ultraviolet rays reach the earth. These ultraviolet rays can cause skin cancer, cataract in the eyes and damage immune system of human beings. They also harm animals and plants.

Q.2. How can you help in reducing the problem of waste disposal ? Give any two methods.

Ans. The two methods which can help in reducing the problem of waste disposal are : recycling, and preparation of compost. These are described below.

(*i*) The solid wastes like paper, plastics, glass and metals, etc., are recycled. For example, waste paper is sent to paper mills where it is reprocessed to form new paper once again. The broken plastic articles like plastic bags, buckets, bowls, cups, plates, etc., are sent to plastic processing factories where they are melted and remoulded to make new articles. Similarly, waste metal articles are sent to metal industries where they are melted and recycled as solid metal for various purposes.

(*ii*) Biodegradable domestic wastes such as left-over food, fruit and vegetable peels, and leaves of potted plants, etc., can be converted into compost by burying in a pit dug into ground, and used as manure.

NCERT Book, Pages 264 and 265

Q.1. Which of the following groups contain only biodegradable items ?

(*a*) Grass, flowers and leather **(*b*) Grass, wood and plastic**

(*c*) Fruit peels, cake and lime juice **(*d*) Cake, wood and grass**

Ans. (*a*), (*c*) and (*d*).

Q.2. Which of the following constitute a food chain ?

(*a*) Grass, wheat and mango **(*b*) Grass, goat and human**

(*c*) Goat, cow and elephant **(*d*) Grass, fish and goat**

Ans. (*b*) Grass, goat and human

Q.3. Which of the following are environment-friendly practices ?

(*a*) Carrying cloth bags to put purchases in while shopping

(*b*) Switching off unnecessary lights and fans

(*c*) Walking to school instead of getting your mother to drop you on her scooter

(*d*) All of the above

Ans. (*d*) All of the above.

Q.4. What will happen if we kill all the organisms in one trophic level ?

Ans. If we kill all the organisms in one trophic level, then transfer of food (and energy) to the next trophic level will stop due to which the organisms of next trophic level will starve and die or migrate to other areas. The killing of all the organisms in one trophic level will also lead to the overpopulation of organisms in the previous trophic level. These effects will cause an imbalance in the ecosystem. For example, if we kill all the herbivorous animals like deer, rabbits, etc., in a forest, then the carnivorous animals like lions, tigers, etc., will not get food. Due to this, the lions and tigers, etc., will starve and die or migrate from forest and go towards human settlements and attack people. Moreover, in the absence of herbivores like deer, rabbits, etc., the population of the previous trophic level 'plants' (or vegetation) will increase too much (because there are no deer or rabbits to eat them). All these effects will create an imbalance in the ecosystem.

Q.5. Will the impact of removing all the organisms in a trophic level be different for different trophic levels ? Can the organisms of any trophic level be removed without causing any damage to the ecosystem ?

Ans. (*a*) Yes, the impact of removing all the organisms in a trophic level will be different for different trophic levels. For example, in the food chain : Grass ⟶ Deer ⟶ Lion :

(*i*) If we remove all the lions at the third trophic level, then the number of deer will increase too much. All these deer will eat up all the grass and other plants turning the forest into a desert.

(*ii*) If we remove all the deer at the second trophic level, then lions will not get sufficient food, they will starve and die. Deer eat grass and other green plants, so the amount of grass and other green plants will increase too much.

(*b*) No, all the organisms of any trophic level cannot be removed without causing any damage to the ecosystem.

Q.6. What is biological magnification ? Will the level of this magnification be different at different levels of the ecosystem ?

Ans. (*a*) The harmful chemicals like pesticides enter the food chain at the producer level (plant level) and in the process of transfer of food through food chains these harmful chemicals get concentrated at each trophic level. The increase in concentration of harmful chemical substances like pesticides in the body of living organisms at each trophic level of a food chain is called biological magnification. Pesticides are non-biodegradable chemicals, so they get accumulated at each trophic level.

(*b*) Yes, the level of biological magnification is different for different trophic levels of an ecosystem. For example, in the food chain : Plants → Goat → Man, the harmful chemicals enter into plants from soil and water. When goat eats these plants, the chemicals enter into goat's body. And ultimately when a non-vegetarian man eats the goat meat, the harmful chemicals are transferred to his body. The level or concentration of the harmful chemicals increases with increasing trophic level. In the above given food chain, the concentration of harmful chemicals is minimum in the plants, higher in the goat and maximum in man.

Q.7. What are the problems caused by the non-biodegradable wastes that we generate ?

Ans. The non-biodegradable wastes cannot be made less toxic easily, so they cause a lot of problems for us as well as the environment. For example :

(*i*) Some of the non-biodegradable wastes (such as pesticides like DDT and metals like mercury) enter the food chain of humans. These non-biodegradable wastes get concentrated in human beings and damage their health in the long run.

(*ii*) The excessive use of non-biodegradable fertilisers in agriculture makes the soil either too much acidic or too much alkaline. When the soil becomes too acidic or too alkaline, the crop yields is reduced.

Q.8. If all the waste we generate is biodegradable, will this have no impact on the environment ?

Ans. Even if all the waste we generate is biodegradable, it will have an impact on the environment. This is because too much biodegradable waste cannot be broken down into harmless simpler substances by the decomposers like micro-organisms at the right time. Due to this, the biodegradable wastes will go on accumulating in the environment and act as pollutants resulting in harmful effects on the environment. For example, the rotting biodegradable wastes act as breeding grounds for flies and cockroaches, etc., which spread diseases. Moreover, the rotting biodegradable wastes emit foul smell in the environment which makes the life of people miserable.

Q.9. Why is the damage to the ozone layer a cause for concern ? What steps are being taken to limit this damage ?

Ans. The ozone gas layer high up in the atmosphere is very important for the existence of life on earth because it absorbs most of the harmful ultraviolet radiations coming from the sun and prevents them from reaching the earth. The damage to the ozone layer is a cause for concern because damage to ozone layer will make it thinner which will allow much more harmful ultraviolet radiations (coming from the sun) to reach the earth. These ultraviolet radiations can then cause skin cancer in humans. They can also damage the eyes by causing an eye disease called cataract. Ultraviolet rays damage immune system by lowering the body's resistance to diseases. They also damage crop plants. In fact, if too much damage occurs to the ozone layer and it disappears completely, then all the life on the earth would be destroyed gradually. The depletion of ozone layer is due to the use of chemicals called chlorofluorocarbons (CFCs) in refrigeration, fire extinguishers and aerosol sprayers. So, in 1987, in an attempt to protect ozone layer, the United Nations Environment Programme (UNEP) forged an agreement among its member countries to freeze CFC production at 1986 levels. The chlorofluorocarbons (CFCs) are now being replaced by hydroflurorocarbons (HFCs) which do not damage the ozone layer.

Chapter : MANAGEMENT OF NATURAL RESOURCES

NCERT Book, Page 269

Q.1. What changes can you make in your habits to become more environment friendly ?

Ans. We can make the following changes in our habits to become more environment friendly :

(*i*) Switch off the lights, fans, TV, geyser and other electrical appliances when not needed.

(*ii*) Stop using polythene bags and start using bags made of cloth or jute.

(*iii*) Start going to nearby school on bicycle instead of asking parents to drop us on scooter or car.

(*iv*) Stop using any products made of animal skin, fur or ivory.

(*v*) Collect used articles made of paper, plastic, glass and metals, and send them for recycling.

Q.2. What would be the advantages of exploiting resources with short-term aims ?

Ans. If the resources are exploited to the hilt with short-term aims, then the present generation will benefit too much. For example, the exploitation of resources with short-term aims would provide more than sufficient food, water, and energy to all the people in the present generation.

Q.3. How would these advantages differ from the advantages of using a long-term perspective in managing our resources ?

Ans. Exploiting the natural resources with short-term aims would be too much beneficial for the present generation but no resources will be left for the needs of future generations. On the other hand, the management of natural resources on a long-term perspective will meet the basic needs of the present generation and also ensure that sufficient natural resources are left for the needs of future generations.

Q.4. Why do you think there should be equitable distribution of natural resources ? What forces would be working against an equitable distribution of resources ?

Ans. At present, the rich and powerful people are cornering a major share of the country's natural resources (such as irrigation water from canals). There should be an equitable distribution of natural resources so that even poor people may benefit more by using them. Some vested interests with money and influence are working against the equitable distribution of natural resources.

NCERT Book, Page 273

Q.1. Why should we conserve forests and wildlife ?

Ans. (*i*) We should conserve forests because they provide raw materials for a number of industries like timber industry, paper industry, lac industry and sports equipment industry. Forests prevent floods and soil erosion. Forests help in bringing sufficient rainfall by maintaining a perfect water cycle in nature. Forests also provide natural habitat to wild animals and birds, and help in their conservation. Forests are essential for maintaining the ecological balance by preserving the biodiversity (large number of species of plants and animals).

(*ii*) The wild animals and birds which live in a forest are called 'wildlife'. We should conserve wildlife to maintain ecological balance in nature. For example, it is necessary to conserve wild animals like lions and tigers to maintain the forest ecosystem because they keep the population of herbivorous animals (like deer) under control and save the vegetation from overgrazing and its ill effects on environment. This is because overgrazing destroys the green plants and reduces the rainfall in that area. Due to less rainfall, the lush green forest environment can turn into a desert over a period of time. Wildlife should also be conserved to prevent the extinction of rare varieties of animals and birds from this earth.

Q.2. Suggest some approaches towards the conservation of forests.

Ans. Some of the measures which can be taken for the conservation of forests are as follows :

(*i*) The indiscriminate and unauthorised felling (cutting) of forest trees for timber trade and firewood should be curbed immediately.

(*ii*) In case of Government authorised felling of forest trees, for every acre of forest cut down, an equal area of land should be planted with saplings of trees to make up for the loss in the long run.

(*iii*) Overgrazing of forest vegetation by the cattle of local people should be prevented.

(*iv*) Measures should be taken to prevent and control forest fires.

(*v*) The local people of villages in and around the forest should be involved in the conservation of forests by giving employment in silviculture and harvesting operations of the forest.

NCERT Book, Page 276

Q.1. Find out about the traditional systems of water harvesting/management in your region.

Ans. The traditional systems of water harvesting in our region are ponds and lakes where rainwater is stored.

Q.2. Compare the above systems with the probable systems in hilly/mountainous areas or plains or plateau regions.

Ans. Dams are built over rivers in hilly/mountainous areas. They are more advantageous because they store running river water which can be used to generate electricity. Moreover, since the water stored in dam keeps flowing to turn the turbines, it does not act as a breeding ground for mosquitoes (which spread malaria). The stagnant water in ponds and lakes, however, becomes a breeding ground for mosquitoes.

Q.3. Find out the source of water in your region/locality. Is water from this source available to all people living in that area ?

Ans. In our region, the source of water is a river flowing through the city and some tube-wells dug at various places in the area. The river water and tube-well water is supplied to the homes through taps after suitable treatment. Though water from these sources is available to all the people living in this area but it is not available in sufficient quantity everywhere. There is usually some shortage of water which becomes very severe during hot summer season. Some villages on the outskirts of the city also obtain their water supply directly from the wells.

NCERT Book, Pages 278 and 279

Q.1. What changes would you suggest in your home in order to be environment friendly ?

Ans. (*i*) Use energy efficient compact fluorescent lamps (CFLs) instead of traditional filament-type electric bulbs.

(*ii*) Install solar cell panels to generate as much electricity as possible.

(*iii*) Use solar cooker to cook food whenever possible.

(*iv*) Use solar water heater for getting hot water instead of electric geyser.

(*v*) Reuse the empty plastic and glass containers for storage purposes in the kitchen, and send the useless papers, plastic, glass and metal objects for recycling.

Q.2. Can you suggest some changes in your school which would make it environment friendly ?

Ans. (*i*) School buses should be run on CNG instead of diesel.

(*ii*) Rainwater harvesting should be done to recharge ground water.

(*iii*) Trees should be planted along the school boundary.

(*iv*) The fallen leaves of trees should be collected and made into compost. This compost can be used in school garden.

(*v*) Install solar cell panels to produce electricity.

Q.3. We saw in this chapter that there are four main stakeholders when it comes to forests and wildlife. Which among these should have the authority to decide the management of forest produce ? Why do you think so ?

Ans. The four main stakeholders in the management of forests and wildlife are :

(*i*) The local people who live in and around the forest,

(*ii*) The Forest department of the Government,

(*iii*) The industrialists who use various forest products for their factories, and

(*iv*) The forest and wildlife activists who want to save forests.

The local people who live in and around the forest area should have the authority to decide the management of forest produce. This is because the local people are well versed in the practices to use the forest produce in a sustainable manner as they have been using the forest and wildlife resources since the ancient times without causing any damage to the environment.

Q.4. How can you as an individual contribute or make a difference to the management of (a) forests and wildlife (b) water resources, and (c) coal and petroleum ?

Ans. (*a*) Cutting of trees will not be allowed. The products made from animal skin, fur or ivory will not be used.

(*b*) Running tap water will not be used for brushing the teeth or taking bath. Water will be taken in a mug and bucket for these purposes to prevent its wastage. Leaking taps will be repaired immediately.

(*c*) Switch off unnecessary lights and fans, etc., and use bicycle to cover short distances instead of a scooter or car.

Q.5. What can you as an individual do to reduce your consumption of the various natural resources ?

Ans. (*i*) Use energy efficient CFLs instead of filament-type electric bulbs to save electricity (and reduce the consumption of coal).

(*ii*) Switch off unnecessary lights and fans, and use stairs instead of using lift to save electricity.

(*iii*) Use solar cooker to cook food whenever possible and solar heater to obtain hot water (so as to reduce the consumption of coal, kerosene or LPG).

(*iv*) Use bicycle to cover short distances instead of scooter or car to reduce the consumption of petrol.

(*v*) Prevent wastage of water by getting the leaking taps repaired.

Q.6. List five things you have done over the last one week to :

(*a*) conserve our natural resources.

(*b*) increase the pressure on our natural resources.

Ans. (*a*) The five things done by me over the last one week to conserve our natural resources were :

(*i*) Replaced all the filament-type bulbs in my house by CFLs.

(*ii*) Bought a pressure cooker to cook the food to save fuel.

(*iii*) Cooked rice and pulses (*dal*) for lunch by using a solar cooker.

(*iv*) Installed a solar water heater to obtain hot water.

(*v*) Went to school by bicycle when I missed the school bus.

(*b*) The five things done by me over the last one week which increased the pressure on our natural resources were :

(*i*) Forgot to switch off light in my room once before going to sleep.

(*ii*) Did not close the tap while brushing the teeth one day.

(*iii*) Asked my father to drop me to school on his car one day when I missed the school bus.

(*iv*) Wasted two big paper sheets while performing a science experiment in the laboratory.

(*v*) Threw away a used plastic container which could have been reused to store salt or sugar in the kitchen.

Q.7. On the basis of the issues raised in this chapter, what changes would you incorporate in your life-style in a move towards a sustainable use of our resources ?

Ans. (*i*) Walking on foot or riding a bicycle to go to nearby market or other nearby places.

(*ii*) Using stairs in a building up to at least three floors instead of using a lift.

(*iii*) Put on an extra sweater on a cold day rather than use a room heater.

(*iv*) Stop using any products made of animal skin, fur or ivory.

(*v*) Switch off the lights, fans, TV, geyser and other electrical appliances when not needed.

(*vi*) Use compact fluorescent lamps (CFLs) instead of filament-type bulbs.

(*vii*) Use solar cooker and solar water heater.

(*viii*) Stop using polythene bags and start using bags made of cloth or jute.

(*ix*) Recycle products made of paper, plastics, glass and metals.

Value Based Questions
(with Answers)

Q.1. Suman purchased a number of earthen flower pots (*gamle*) and planted beautiful plants in them by adding proper fertiliser to the soil. She started watering these plants everyday by putting lots of water in the earthen flower pots. After about one month, Suman noticed that though most of the potted plants were growing well and appeared to be healthy, but one of the plants was on the verge of dying (though it was being watered daily alongwith other potted plants). Suman told about this problem to her friend Geeta. Geeta examined the earthen flower pot of this dying plant carefully including its bottom and immediately understood what the problem was. She advised Suman to change the earthen pot of this plant. Suman then shifted this plant to another earthen pot and watered it. The same plant now started growing normally and became a healthy plant after some time.

(*a*) What defect do you think could have been observed by Geeta at the bottom of earthen pot of this plant ?

(*b*) How was this defect affecting the growth of plant and making it almost die ?

(*c*) Which life process could not be performed efficiently by the roots of this plant under these conditions ?

(*d*) What special term is used for the condition which existed in this particular earthen flower pot ?

(*e*) Why did Suman use another earthen pot for this plant ?

(*f*) What values are displayed by Geeta in this incident ?

Ans. (*a*) Geeta could have observed that there was no hole at the bottom of this earthen flower pot (*gamla*) for the excess water to be drained out.

(*b*) Since there was no hole at the bottom of this earthen pot, too much water collected in it. This too much water expelled all the air from in-between the soil particles in the earthen flower pot. Due to this, oxygen was not available to the roots of this plant for aerobic respiration. Under these conditions, the roots respire anaerobically, producing alcohol. And this was killing the plant gradually.

(*c*) Aerobic respiration.

(*d*) Waterlogging.

(*e*) Suman used another earthen pot for this plant which had a hole at its bottom (to drain off the excess water).

(*f*) The values displayed by Geeta in this incident are (*i*) Awareness (or knowledge) that plant roots require air for respiration (*ii*) Curiosity to get at the bottom of the problem, and (*iii*) Helping nature.

Q.2. Abhinav was participating in a marathon (long distance race). He was running at position two right from the beginning. Just when he was nearing the finishing line, he started running even faster so as to stand first. And when he was about to win the marathon, he got a severe muscle cramp in his leg. This cramp prevented Abhinav from running any further and shattered his dream of winning the marathon.

(*a*) Which process provides most of the energy to Abhinav for running the marathon ?

(*b*) Which process provides a little extra energy to Abhinav for running very, very fast towards the end of race ?

(*c*) Which substance gets accumulated in the leg muscles of Abhinav that causes muscle cramp ?

(*d*) Why does this substance get accumulated in the leg muscles of Abhinav ?

(*e*) What advice will you give to Abhinav so as to get relief from this cramp ? How will it help ?

Ans. (*a*) Most of the energy in the leg muscles of Abhinav for running the marathon is provided by aerobic respiration (which breaks down food like glucose with oxygen to produce large amount of energy).

(*b*) The little extra energy in the leg muscles for running very, very fast is provided by the process of anaerobic respiration (which breaks down food like glucose without oxygen to produce small amount of energy).

(*c*) Lactic acid.

(*d*) The lactic acid gets accumulated in the leg muscles of Abhinav because during very fast running, oxygen gets used faster in the muscles than can be supplied by the blood. So, anaerobic respiration (without oxygen) takes place in muscle cells causing partial oxidation of glucose food to form lactic acid (and releasing some energy). This lactic acid gets accumulated in leg muscles.

(*e*) Abhinav should take a hot water bath or a massage. Hot water bath and massage improve the circulation of blood. Due to improved blood flow, the supply of oxygen to the leg muscles increases. This oxygen breaks down lactic acid accumulated in leg muscles and gives relief from cramp.

Q.3. One day Mohan had a severe toothache. His father took Mohan to a dentist. The dentist examined all the teeth of Mohan very carefully and said that he had tiny holes in his two teeth. He also told Mohan that all his teeth were covered with a sticky, yellowish layer. The dentist performed a certain procedure on his two teeth having tiny holes and also gave him some medicines. Mohan's toothache disappeared gradually.

(*a*) What are the tiny holes in the teeth known as ?

(*b*) How are the tiny holes formed in the teeth ?

(*c*) What kind of procedure was performed by dentist on Mohan's two teeth ?

(*d*) What is the sticky, yellowish layer on Mohan's teeth known as ?

(*e*) How is the sticky, yellowish layer formed on the teeth ?

(*f*) What advice will you give to Mohan to avoid such dental problems in future ?

Ans. (*a*) The tiny holes formed in the teeth are known as 'cavities' or 'dental caries'.

(*b*) When a person eats sugary food (sugar-containing food), then the bacteria present in mouth act on sugar present in food to produce acids. These acids first dissolve the calcium salts from tooth enamel and then from dentine forming tiny holes (or cavities) in the tooth over a period of time.

(*c*) Mohan's dental cavities (or holes) were first cleaned by the dentist and then 'filled' with appropriate filling material.

(*d*) The sticky, yellowish layer on the teeth is known as 'dental plaque'.

(*e*) If the teeth are not cleaned regularly, they become covered with a stickly, yellowish layer of food particles and bacteria cells called 'dental plaque'.

(*f*) (*i*) Mohan should eat less of sugary food such as toffees, chocolates and sweets, etc. He should also avoid drinking too much of sweetened drinks such as Coca-Cola, Pepsi, etc.

(*ii*) Mohan should brush his teeth regularly with a toothpaste (after eating food). This will remove the dental plaque before bacteria produce acids.

(*iii*) Mohan should get his teeth examined by a dentist at least once in three months.

Q.4. Abhishek's house is very near to a main road crossing having traffic signals. It was a Diwali night and there was a big traffic jam on the main road just outside his house. All the neighbours of Abhishek and other colony residents were also bursting crackers and enjoying many other types of fireworks. Abhishek's 70 year old grandmother, who was watching the fireworks, was taken ill suddenly. She complained of difficulty in breathing and also felt nausea and headache. Abhishek's grandmother was rushed to a nearby hospital where the doctors made her inhale some medicine and then put her on oxygen for some time. Abhishek's grandmother recovered fairly quickly. The doctor advised his grandmother to remain inside the house for that night with all the doors and windows closed. The doctor also asked her to buy a small, portable oxygen gas cylinder and use it to breathe at home if she felt suffocated again.

(*a*) What made Abhishek's grandmother suddenly ill ?

(*b*) Which system/body part of grandmother got affected ? Why was only Abhishek's grandmother affected ?

(*c*) Give two reasons for this condition of Abhishek's grandmother.

(*d*) What deficiency was caused in the body of Abhishek's grandmother ?

(*e*) Why was grandmother advised to remain inside the house all the time with doors and windows closed ?

(*f*) What advice would you give to others to avoid such a situation ?

Ans. (*a*) Abhishek's grandmother became ill because she had inhaled air polluted with toxic gases emitted by vehicles on the nearby road and Diwali fireworks.

(*b*) Respiratory system (including lungs) got affected. Only Abhishek's grandmother was affected because her lungs had become very weak due to old age.

(*c*) (*i*) Air pollution caused by the exhaust gases of vehicles on the road just outside the house.

(*ii*) Air pollution caused by Diwali fireworks.

(*d*) The deficiency of oxygen was caused in the body of grandmother.

(*e*) Abhishek's grandmother was advised to remain inside the house to avoid breathing too much polluted air outside.

(*f*) (*i*) Avoid fireworks on Diwali day to prevent too much air pollution.

(*ii*) Use less polluting fuels (such as CNG) in motor vehicles.

(*iii*) Use public transport (such as buses, metro, etc.) to travel within the city instead of individual vehicles.

(*iv*) If possible, take a house away from main road and traffic signals.

Q.5. Shyam had just recovered from dengue fever for which he was confined to bed for many days. He was really fed up and wanted to go out with his friend Ram. So, Ram and Shyam went out into city forest for a walk. While walking in the city forest, Shyam fell down and got a cut on his leg from barbed wire lying nearby. The leg started bleeding. Shyam thought that the bleeding from cut would stop automatically after some time. But this did not happen. The bleeding from cut went on continuously. After some time, Shyam also started having breathing difficulty and he now wanted to go back home. Ram held Shyam firmly by the arm to give support and both came out of the city forest. Ram then hailed a taxi and took Shyam straight to the hospital. He told everything to doctors. After performing some tests quickly, doctors gave blood transfusion to Shyam. His parents were also informed.

(*a*) Which component was deficient in the blood of Shyam which led to too much bleeding from the cut ?

(*b*) Could the deficiency of this component of blood have been caused by dengue ?

(*c*) What is the function of this component in our body ?

(*d*) What could be the probable reason for the breathing difficulty of Shyam ? Explain.

(*e*) What is the cause of dengue disease : virus, bacteria or protozoa ? Name the carrier which spreads dengue.

(*f*) What values are displayed by Ram in this episode ?

Ans. (*a*) Shyam's blood was deficient in platelets.

(*b*) Yes, dengue reduces the blood platelet count of a person drastically.

(*c*) Platelets help in the coagulation of blood (or clotting of blood) in a cut. It is due to the presence of platelets that the blood coming out of a cut becomes semi-solid and plugs the cut (or seals the cut) due to which bleeding stops.

(*d*) The deficiency of haemoglobin could be the probable cause of Shyam's breathing difficulty. This can be explained as follows : Haemoglobin present in blood carries oxygen and hence is essential for breathing. When a lot of blood was lost by Shyam through the cut, then the amount of blood and hence that of haemoglobin in the body became less. This less amount of haemoglobin carried less oxygen into the lungs and caused breathing difficulty.

(*e*) The cause of dengue disease is a virus (called dengue virus). It is spread by *Aedes* mosquitoes.

(*f*) The values displayed by Ram in this episode are (*i*) Awareness or knowledge (that too much blood loss from the body could endanger the life of Shyam) (*ii*) Concern to save life of his friend (by taking him straight to hospital), and (*iii*) Correct decision-making skill (of not wasting precious time in going back home first).

Q.6. Meena is always in a hurry. She just gulps her food quickly and rushes out to play badminton with her friend. Moreover, she is fond of eating junk food such as burgers and pizzas. Meena hates to eat fresh green vegetables and prefers only pulses (*dal*). Meena usually complains of stomach ache while playing. Meena looks pale, feels very weak and tires easily. Her nails are turning white and she has also started losing weight.

(*a*) What could probably be the reason for Meena's stomach ache while playing ?

(*b*) What is the harm of eating too much junk food ?

(*c*) Name the disease Meena is suffering from which makes her look pale, feel very weak and tired, and lose weight.

(*d*) What is the cause of Meena's disease ?

(*e*) How does this disease affect Meena ? Explain.

(*f*) What advice would you give to Meena to get rid of all the ailments described above ?

Ans. (*a*) One of the probable reasons for the stomach ache of Meena while playing could be that she gulps her food in big chunks (without chewing) just before going to play. The big chunks of food could hit the stomach wall while playing and cause stomach ache.

(*b*) Junk food does not make a balanced diet. Junk food lacks many essential nutrients leading to some deficiency diseases.

(*c*) Meena is suffering from a disease called 'anaemia'.

(*d*) The cause of Meena's disease anaemia is the deficiency of haemoglobin in her blood which comes from the deficiency of iron mineral in her diet (because iron mineral is essential for making haemoglobin).

(*e*) The function of haemoglobin is to carry oxygen in the body. Due to deficiency of haemoglobin (caused by lack of iron in diet), the blood of Meena is not able to carry sufficient oxygen to all the body cells to meet their requirements of oxidation of food and production of energy. In this way, deficiency of haemoglobin results in the production of less energy for Meena. Since she has less energy than needed, she feels weak, tired and loses weight. The deficiency of red coloured haemoglobin also makes her look pale and turns her nails white (instead of red).

(*f*) (*i*) Meena should chew her food properly while eating and convert it into as small particles as possible. This will also help in mixing saliva with food for proper digestion. In this way, her stomach ache may disappear.

(*ii*) Meena should avoid eating too much of junk food. It may cause deficiency diseases and also lead to obesity.

(*iii*) Meena should include spinach (*palak, saag*), other green leafy vegetables, apples, etc., in her diet because all these food items contain a good amount of iron mineral. This will cure anaemia.

Q.7. Raman's 50 year old ailing uncle Vinod was admitted to a hospital. The doctors performed many blood tests and found that the blood of Vinod contained some unwanted wastes in it. These wastes had accumulated in blood due to non-functioning of a pair of vital organs in the body of Vinod. The doctors suggested two options for the treatment of Vinod so as to save his life. Raman is a student of class X who has studied various life processes in detail. So, he could easily make out the ailment his uncle was suffering from.

(*a*) What could be the pair of organs of Vinod which were not functioning properly ? Where are these organs located in the body ?

(*b*) What is the function of these organs ?

(*c*) Name the major waste which is removed by these organs from the blood.

(*d*) Name the ailment (or disease) Vinod is suffering from.

(*e*) What could be the two options for the treatment of Vinod ?

(*f*) What advice Raman could give to others so as to prevent such an ailment ?

Ans. (*a*) The pair of organs of Vinod which were not functioning properly are the two kidneys. The kidneys are bean-shaped organs towards the back of our body, just above the waist.

(*b*) The function of kidneys is to remove the poisonous substance urea, other waste salts, and excess water from the blood and excrete them in the form of a yellowish liquid called urine.

(*c*) Urea.

(*d*) Vinod is suffering from 'kidney failure'.

(*e*) The two options available to Vinod for the treatment of his ailment are :

(*i*) Dialysis (in which the dirty blood of kidney patient containing unwanted wastes is cleaned periodically by passing through a kidney machine), and

(*ii*) Kidney transplant (in which the matching kidney donated by a healthy person is transplanted in place of damaged kidney by surgical operation).

(*f*) Kidneys can usually be damaged by continued high blood pressure (called hypertension), and also by very high blood sugar (called diabetes). So, the general advice given by Raman to others so as to prevent kidney ailment would be :

(*i*) Keep your blood pressure under control.

(*ii*) Keep your blood sugar (diabetes) under control.

(*iii*) Get the kidney functioning test done from time to time.

Q.8. Rashmi lives alone in Delhi. Her house is near a main road where heavy traffic plies all day and night. The construction activities for building a huge commercial complex are also in full swing near her house. Rashmi had to go to America for six months. She was worried about her beautiful houseplants kept on terrace. She gave the keys of her house to a neighbour and requested her to water the plants daily. The neighbour kept her promise and watered the plants daily (because there was no rain at all during those six months). When Rashmi returned after six months, she found that most of the plants had pest

infestations and diseases. The plants had become very weak and unhealthy. Rashmi could not understand why, even after regular watering, the plants were in a very bad shape. One day Rashmi's niece Laxmi, who is a student of class X, came to meet her. Rashmi told her problem to Laxmi. Laxmi examined the plants carefully and came to know what the problem was. She explained everything to Rashmi and gave advice to restore the good health of these plants.

(*a*) What had happened to the plants kept on the terrace when Rashmi was away for six months ?

(*b*) Which process in plants could not take place at optimal level due to the above happening ? Explain.

(*c*) Why had the plants become weak and caught pests and diseases ?

(*d*) What advice was given by Laxmi to Rashmi to restore the good health of these plants ?

(*e*) Which natural process/processes perform the similar functions which Rashmi was told to perform ?

Ans. (*a*) A lot of dust had deposited on both sides of leaves of plants and covered them.

(*b*) The process of photosynthesis (food making) could not take place at optimal level due to thick layer of dust on the leaves. This happened as follows : The layer of dust on the leaves blocks the sunlight and reduces the leaves' ability to carry out photosynthesis to make food for the plant. Even the stomata on the surface of leaves get blocked reducing the intake of carbon dioxide from surrounding air. This further retards photosynthesis.

(*c*) Photosynthesis is the process by which plants make their own food. Since photosynthesis was reduced, the plants did not get sufficient food to remain healthy. The plants became weak and hence prone to pests and diseases.

(*d*) Laxmi advised Rashmi to wash the leaves of houseplants by spraying water on them, so as to remove the thick layer of dust from them.

(*e*) (*i*) The rain usually washes away the dust from the leaves of plants and trees and makes them dust-free.

(*ii*) The fast blowing wind shakes the leaves of plants and trees and also helps in removing dust from them.

Q.9. John is a 50 year old man. He was complaining of pain in the abdominal area for the last few days. He went to a hospital where doctors performed an ultrasound scan on him. The ultrasound scan showed the presence of a number of tiny stones in the sac-shaped organ on the underside of the liver. The doctors performed a keyhole surgery on John and removed the sac-shaped organ from his body alongwith tiny stones. John got immediate relief from pain.

(*a*) What is the sac-shaped organ beneath the liver known as ?

(*b*) What liquid does this sac-shaped organ contain ?

(*c*) What are the functions of the liquid contained in this sac-shaped organ ?

(*d*) Why do you think it is possible to remove this sac-shaped organ containing stones but the kidneys having stones cannot be removed ?

(*e*) What advice would you give to John regarding his diet ?

Ans. (*a*) The sac-shaped organ beneath the liver is known as 'gall bladder'.

(*b*) Gall bladder stores bile (until needed for digestion). Bile is a greenish-yellow liquid made and secreted by the liver.

(*c*) Bile is alkaline and contains salts which help to emulsify or break the fats (or lipids) present in food. Bile performs two functions :

(*i*) Bile makes the partially digested acidic food coming from the stomach alkaline so that pancreatic enzymes can act on it.

(*ii*) Bile salts break the fats (or oils) present in food into small globules making it easy for the enzymes to act and digest them.

(*d*) Gall bladder is not a vital organ of our body, so our body can cope well without it. But kidneys are vital organs of our body, so our body cannot function properly without them.

(*e*) John should avoid eating oily food (or fried food). He should also avoid eating spicy food.

Q.10 Bhushan noticed that his sister Seema had developed swollen neck. Being a science student of class 10, Bhushan knew the reason that causes the neck of a person to swell up. Bhushan asked his mother which type of common salt she purchases from the market for cooking food. The mother told Bhushan that she never checked the brand or contents of the common salt packet. She purchased whatever common salt shopkeeper gave her. Bhushan then went to the market himself and purchased a special type of common

salt. He asked his mother to always use this salt in preparing food for the whole family. When Bhushan's sister was taken to a doctor, he confirmed what Bhushan had in mind. The doctor also advised his sister and everyone else in the family to use a special type of salt to prevent such a condition.

(*a*) Name the disease which Seema is suffering from ?

(*b*) What causes this disease ?

(*c*) Which part of endocrine system is involved in this disease ? What happens to this part during the occurrence of this disease ?

(*d*) What type of salt was recommended by Bhushan and doctor for the whole family ? Why was this salt recommended ?

(*e*) Why does this disease occur more in hilly areas but not at all in coastal areas ?

(*f*) What values are displayed by Bhushan in this episode ?

Ans. (*a*) Seema is suffering from a disease called 'goitre'.

(*b*) Goitre disease is caused by the deficiency of iodine mineral in the diet.

(*c*) Thyroid gland of the endocrine system is involved in this disease. Due to the deficiency of iodine in the diet, thyroid gland is not able to make sufficient amount of iodine-containing hormone called 'thyroxine'. And due to the deficiency of thyroxine hormone, thyroid gland present in the neck of Seema enlarges too much, causing the neck to swell too much.

(*d*) Bhushan and the doctor both recommended iodised common salt or iodised salt (which contains an appropriate amount of iodine mineral). This was done to make up for the deficiency of iodine (and that of thyroxine hormone) in the body to prevent goitre.

(*e*) Goitre disease occurs more in hilly areas because the soil (in which food is grown), and water in hilly areas is deficient in iodine mineral. Goitre disease does not occur at all in coastal areas (or sea-side areas) because the people of coastal areas eat a lot of sea food (sea fish, etc.) which contains a good amount of iodine.

(*f*) The values displayed by Bhushan in this episode are (*i*) Awareness (or knowledge) that goitre disease develops due to the deficiency of iodine in the diet and can be prevented by using iodised salt, and (*ii*) Concern to protect his family from goitre disease by using iodised salt in cooking food.

Q.11. Ahmad is a 50 year old man who is mainly a sedentary worker. He always gets his medical check up done once in a year. Till last year all his blood reports were normal. This year his blood (and even urine) tests showed the presence of large quantities of sugar. The doctor gave him some medicines to control sugar. The doctor also asked him to avoid certain food items and adopt a healthy life-style.

(*a*) Name the disease which Ahmad is suffering from.

(*b*) Name the gland whose malfunctioning causes this disease.

(*c*) How does the malfunctioning of this gland cause this disease ?

(*d*) What is done if this disease does not get controlled by taking oral medicines ?

(*e*) Name one vital organ which gets damaged if this disease persists uncontrolled for a long time.

(*f*) What life-style changes would you suggest for Ahmad which can help him control this 'disease' ?

Ans. (*a*) Ahmad is suffering from 'diabetes'.

(*b*) Malfunctioning of pancreas causes diabetes.

(*c*) Pancreas makes and secretes insulin hormone into the blood. The function of insulin hormone is to lower the blood sugar level (or blood glucose level). If due to malfunctioning, pancreas does not produce and secrete sufficient amount of insulin hormone into blood, then the sugar level in blood rises too much leading to diabetes.

(*d*) The persons having severe diabetes which cannot be controlled by medicines are given insulin injections.

(*e*) If uncontrolled diabetes persists for a long time, it may damage kidneys.

(*f*) Ahmad can control diabetes :

(*i*) by controlling diet (by avoiding sweet food items containing sugar such as chocolates, sweets, soft drinks, etc.),

(*ii*) by taking regular physical exercise (including brisk walk, etc.), and

(*iii*) by reducing weight.

Q.12. Dodi is the only child of his rich parents. He insisted on getting a new motorbike on his 16th birthday. Though Dodi was underage by two years for obtaining a driving licence but he started driving motorbike without a driving licence. He even did not wear any protective equipment while driving the motorbike. Neighbours usually saw Dodi driving the motorbike very fast and rashly. He did not obey any traffic rules while driving. One day Dodi was driving his motorbike very fast on the main road with a friend seated behind him. He was trying to show off his misplaced sense of adventure by performing some dangerous stunts. Just then a heavily loaded truck appeared on the road in front of him. When this truck applied brakes suddenly to save a dog crossing the road, Dodi could not stop his speeding motorbike in time. The motorbike went under the truck banging Dodi's head against the rear side of truck. Dodi was hurt badly. Dodi was rushed to the nearby hospital where he was declared brought dead. Dodi's friend was lucky to escape with minor injuries.

The sad story of a motorbike fan

(*a*) What type of injury do you think Dodi could have received that led to his immediate death ?

(*b*) Which protective equipment Dodi was not wearing at the time of the accident ?

(*c*) Which body part/vital organ of Dodi could have been protected by wearing the above protective equipment that could have perhaps saved Dodi's life ?

(*d*) Do you think it is good to perform stunts on a running motorbike ? Give two reasons for your answer.

(*e*) What advice would you give to young children to avoid such unfortunate incidents ?

(*f*) What advice would you give to the parents of such children ?

Ans. (*a*) Dodi must have received a serious head injury.

(*b*) Dodi was not wearing a helmet at the time of accident.

(*c*) Wearing helmet could have protected the head of Dodi during the accident. It could have prevented or minimised the head injury. Helmet also protects the vital organ 'brain' which is inside the skull.

(*d*) No, it is not. Performing stunts on running motorbikes endanger the life of biker himself as well as that of other road users. Performing stunts on motorbike is like attempting to commit suicide.

(*e*) The children should drive motorbikes (and other vehicles like cars, etc.) on attaining the age of 18 years after learning all the traffic rules and obtaining a proper driving licence. They must wear helmet while driving motorbike and obey traffic rules. They must not attempt any risky stunts and keep the speed under control. Remember : speed thrills but kills.

(*f*) The parents should not gift (or lend) vehicles like motorbikes and cars to their underage children out of misplaced sense of love and affection or to show off their riches to the society. Those parents who do such things are actually the biggest enemies of their own children.

Q.13. Seeta and Geeta are neighbours in the same colony where they live. Seeta's father and Geeta's father both work in the same company and earn equal salary (or equal money). Seeta has one brother whereas Geeta has four brothers and sisters. Geeta is very bright in her studies. Earlier Geeta used to study in one of the top city schools alongwith Seeta but now her father has shifted Geeta to an ordinary school. Seeta's family has a new car whereas Geeta's family has an old scooter. Seeta and her brother wear beautiful clothes whereas Geeta's siblings wear ordinary clothes. Seeta's mother is very healthy whereas Geeta's mother usually suffers from one ailment or another. Seeta's home atmosphere is relaxed and happy whereas there is always some tension in Geeta's house.

(*a*) What do you think is the main reason for the lower living standard of Geeta's family than Seeta's family (though their incomes are equal) ?

(*b*) What is the most probable reason for shifting Geeta from one of the top schools to an ordinary school (though she is very bright in studies) ?

(*c*) What type of measures do you think were not taken by Geeta's parents at appropriate times in the past for limiting the size of their family ?

(*d*) What factor is responsible for the poor health of Geeta's mother (whereas Seeta's mother is very healthy) ?

(*e*) What values are displayed by Seeta's parents in this episode ?

Ans. (*a*) The main reason for the comparatively lower living standard of Geeta's family is their large family consisting of 7 persons (father, mother and 5 children) whereas Seeta's family has only 4 persons (father, mother and 2 children). Due to this, in Geeta's family, the father's income is used for the upkeep of 7 persons whereas in Seeta's family, an equal income is available for just 4 persons.

(*b*) The most probable reason for shifting Geeta from a top school to an ordinary school is that due to large number of children, her father cannot afford much higher school fee in a top school.

(*c*) Geeta's parents did not take family planning measures (or birth control measures) to control the size of their family by having less number of children at the appropriate times in the past.

(*d*) Every pregnancy puts a lot of demands (nutritional, physical and emotional) on the body of the mother. So, the frequent pregnancies (to have a large number of children) have spoiled the health of Geeta's mother. On the other hand, just two pregnancies (to have only two children) have kept Seeta's mother in good health.

(*e*) Seeta's parents displayed the values of (*i*) Awareness of birth control measures (to limit the size of their family) (*ii*) Concern for the health of mother of children (*iii*) Desire to provide best possible education and facilities to children, and (*iv*) National responsibility (of not adding too much to country's population).

Q.14. Mamta is a married woman having two children. She does not want to have any more children. Her husband also supports her decision not to have more children. They are both happy with just two children, both of whom are daughters.

(*a*) Suggest any two types of birth control methods which Mamta and her husband can make use of to avoid pregnancy. Explain how these methods work to prevent pregnancy.

(*b*) Which birth control method has additional advantage of giving protection from sexually transmitted diseases (STDs) ?

(*c*) What values are displayed by Mamta and her husband in not wanting to have any more children ?

Ans. (*a*) The two common type of birth control methods which can be followed by Mamta and her husband are :

(*i*) **Barrier Methods.** In these methods, a condom (*nirodh*) is used by the husband or a diaphragm (cap) is used by the wife to prevent the meeting of sperms with ovum (or egg) and prevent pregnancy.

(*ii*) **Chemical Methods.** In these methods, oral pills and vaginal pills can be used by the wife. Oral pills contain hormones which stop ovaries from releasing the ovum (or egg) into oviduct. Vaginal pills contain the chemicals called spermicides which kill the sperms.

(*b*) The use of condom (*nirodh*) is a birth control method which provides additional advantage of protection from sexually transmitted diseases.

(*c*) The values displayed by Mamta and her husband are :

(*i*) Awareness (or knowledge) that various birth control methods are available to prevent pregnancy and limit the size of family.

(*ii*) Concern for the health of woman (because too many pregnancies spoil the health of woman or mother).

(*iii*) Concern for the future of children (because good facilities and best education can be provided only if the number of children is less).

(*iv*) Responsible citizens (because they do not want to increase country's population too much and put pressure on its limited resources).

Q.15. Vidya is a married woman who has a cleft chin (a deep hollow in her chin). Vidya has recently been blessed with a baby girl who has also a cleft chin. Anita is a close friend of Vidya. When she learnt that Vidya's baby girl also has a cleft chin like Vidya, she got worried. This is because Anita has a huge scar on her left cheek which remained permanently after she got a cut on the cheek during an accident which took place in her school days. Anita is worried that her baby (which is due shortly), may also have a scar on her left cheek just like her. One day, Anita's niece Radha, who is a science student of class X, came to see her. Anita shared her apprehension with Radha. Radha could understand her problem. She told Anita that her case is entirely different from that of Vidya. Radha explained everything to Anita clearly. Anita was now very much relaxed.

(*a*) What is an acquired trait ?

(*b*) What is an inherited trait ?

(*c*) What type of trait is (*i*) cleft chin, and (*ii*) cheek scar ?

(*d*) Explain why, Vidya's cleft chin has been passed on to her baby but Anita's cheek scar cannot be passed on to her baby.

(*e*) What values are displayed by Radha in this episode ?

Ans. (*a*) A trait (or characteristic) of an organism which is 'not inherited' but develops in response to the environment, is called an acquired trait. Acquired trait involves changes only in the non-reproductive cells of an organism and hence cannot be passed on to the next generation.

(*b*) A trait (or characteristic) of an organism which is caused by a change in the genes (or DNA) present in the reproductive cells (or gametes) of parent organism is called inherited trait. Inherited trait can be passed on to the next generation.

(*c*) (*i*) Cleft chin is an inherited trait.

(*ii*) Cheek scar is an acquired trait.

(*d*) Vidya's cleft chin trait has been passed on to her baby because it is an inherited trait involving reproductive cells (or gametes). Anita's cheek scar cannot be passed on to her baby because it is an acquired trait involving only non-reproductive body cells.

(*e*) The values displayed by Radha in this episode are (*i*) Awareness (or knowledge) of acquired traits and inherited traits (*ii*) Application of knowledge in real-life situations, and (*iii*) concern for the health of Anita during pregnancy (by reducing her tension).

Q.16. Mohan and Radha are husband and wife who live in a village. They are going to have their first baby. Mohan has blonde hair (pale yellow hair) with genotype hh whereas Radha has black hair with genotype HH. A discussion started between Mohan and Radha whether their baby would have blonde hair (pale yellow hair) like father or black hair like mother. Bikram is Mohan's nephew. He had come to meet his uncle (*mama ji*) Mohan in the village. Bikram, who is a science student of class 10 in a city school, was listening to their discussion. When Mohan and Radha could not come to a conclusion about the hair colour of their would-be baby, Bikram said that the baby would have black hair colour. He explained the reason for this to Mohan and Radha.

(*a*) What are the factors which transmit characteristics (or traits) from the parents to their baby ?

(*b*) Name the process through which these factors are transmitted from parents to their baby.

(*c*) Explain how Bikram could tell in advance that the baby to be born would have black hair colour like mother (and not blonde hair like father).

(*d*) What values are exhibited by Bikram in this episode ?

Ans. (*a*) The characteristics (or traits) are transmitted from the parents to their baby through genes present on their sex chromosomes.

(*b*) Sexual reproduction.

(*c*) (*i*) Mother's (Radha's) cells contain two dominant genes HH for black hair, so she has black hair.

(*ii*) Father's (Mohan's) cells contain two recessive genes hh for blonde hair, so he has blonde hair.

(*iii*) Baby will get one dominant gene H for black hair (from mother) and one recessive gene h for blonde hair (from father), so its genotype will be Hh and phenotype will be black hair.

(*d*) The values exhibited by Bikram in this episode are (*i*) Awareness (or knowledge) of the transmission of characteristics (or traits) from parents to progeny, and (*ii*) Application of knowledge in solving real-life problems.

Q. 17. Rahul and his classmates toured some of the villages in North Indian States during the summer holidays. They found that in this area there were many more boys than girls in the age group of up to 6 years. Rahul and his friends then went to a small Government Hospital just outside a village. The doctor told them that in this area the birth of a girl child is considered a burden on the family. So, every family in the village wants to have only boys (or sons). He said that people of the village are going to private clinics in cities for getting the pre-natal (before birth) determination of sex done on pregnant women and if the foetus is of a girl child, it is aborted. Due to this illegal practice of selective abortions, child sex ratio is declining at an alarming rate and has created many social problems. The doctor also told that in many households, the women are harassed and tortured for giving birth to a girl child. The village elders blame only the woman for bearing the girl child. The doctor said that they are trying to change the mind set of village people at great personal risk but it will take a lot of time to get rid of this social evil.

(*a*) What term is used for the act of deliberately aborting the foetus if it is of a girl child ?

(*b*) What is child sex ratio ? Why is it declining rapidly ?

(*c*) Why is the birth of a girl child considered a burden in the family ?

(*d*) In our society, the woman (or wife) is blamed for giving birth to a girl child. Prove scientifically that it is actually the man (or husband) who is responsible for the birth of a girl child.

(*e*) State an ill effect of this horrific practice of selective abortions in the long run.

(*f*) How can this evil of killing girl child even before her birth can be prevented ?

Ans. (*a*) The act of deliberately aborting the foetus if it is of a girl child, is called female foeticide. (The deliberate termination of a woman's pregnancy is called abortion).

(*b*) Child sex ratio is the number of girls per thousand boys in human population of an area between the age group of 0 to 6 years. Child sex ratio is declining rapidly due to female foeticide.

(*c*) The demand of dowry during the marriage of a girl is the main reason for thinking that the birth of a girl child is burden on the family.

(*d*) Half of the man's sperms have X sex chromosomes whereas the other half sperms have Y sex chromosomes. On the other hand, all the ova (or eggs) of woman have only X sex chromosomes. Now, a girl child is conceived when the sperm of man carrying X chromosome fertilises the ovum (or egg) of woman carrying X chromosome. It is clear that man (or husband) is responsible for the birth of a girl child and not the wife (because only man has Y sex chromosome in half of his sperms which is required to have a male child or boy).

(*e*) An ill effect of female foeticide in the long run is that sufficient number of young girls is not available in the area to marry off all the boys in this age group. Due to this shortage of girls, brides are even bought and sold for this purpose.

(*f*) Female foeticide can be prevented :

(*i*) by strict implementation of laws to prohibit pre-natal determination of sex, to stop female foeticide and dowry system.

(*ii*) by spreading awareness that no society can run or flourish without girls.

(*iii*) by providing free and compulsory education to girls and reservation in certain professions (such as teaching) so that they can become financially independent.

Q.18. Mr. Sharma had a complete medical check-up a few days back. The doctors diagnosed him to be HIV-positive (HIV+ve). This news spread like wildfire in the colony where he lives and also in the office where he works. The neighbours and colleagues who used to greet him with handshakes and warm hugs now tried to shun him (avoid him). They were reluctant to shake hands with him or hug him. Even Mr. Sharma's own family became indifferent towards him and started treating him badly. Mr. Sharma felt neglected and isolated by all the people around him. He went into depression. A good neighbour, Mr. Mukesh, noted that Mr. Sharma was under a lot of depression because of HIV infection. So, Mr. Mukesh met the family of Mr. Sharma and explained them all about HIV infection. He told them that HIV infection can be treated with drugs and kept under control. He also clarified various myths about HIV and AIDS.

(*a*) What is HIV ? What is meant by saying that Mr. Sharma is HIV-positive (HIV+ve) ?

(*b*) **What are the various ways in which HIV can be transmitted ?**

(*c*) **Can HIV be contracted by shaking hands with or hugging a person infected with HIV ? Do you think HIV is the same as AIDS ?**

(*d*) **What are the various ways of protection from HIV infection ?**

(*e*) **Do you think people's indifference towards HIV infected person Mr. Sharma is justified ? How should we behave with such persons ?**

(*f*) **What values are displayed by Mr. Mukesh in this episode ?**

Ans. (*a*) HIV stands for Human Immunodeficiency Virus. HIV-positive means that the person has HIV infection.

(*b*) HIV can be transmitted :

(*i*) by having unprotected sex (without condom) with an HIV infected person.

(*ii*) by the transfusion of HIV infected blood.

(*iii*) by using HIV infected needles and syringes for injections.

(*iv*) from HIV infected mother to child during pregnancy and breastfeeding.

(*c*) No, HIV infection cannot be contracted by shaking hands or hugging a person infected with HIV. There is no harm in staying and working with an HIV-positive person. HIV is not the same as AIDS. HIV is the virus that leads to AIDS. A person can have HIV virus for many, many years without having AIDS disease. Being HIV positive does not mean that the person has AIDS disease.

(*d*) A person can protect himself from HIV infection :

(*i*) by having safe sex by using a condom.

(*ii*) by ensuring that any blood needed by him is tested for HIV infection.

(*iii*) by using new and disposable needles and syringes for getting injections.

(*iv*) by getting tested for sexually transmitted diseases (including HIV).

(*e*) The people's indifference (or rudeness) towards the HIV-positive Mr. Sharma is highly unjustified. Our behaviour towards an HIV+ve person should be full of sympathy and concern for his suffering and misfortune. We should help him to come out of depression and encourage him to lead a normal life by taking all the available drugs to control this infection.

(*f*) The values displayed by Mr. Mukesh are (*i*) Awareness (or knowledge) that HIV infection can be treated with drugs and kept under control, and that being HIV positive is not the same as having AIDS disease, and (*ii*) Compassion (sympathy and concern for the sufferings of others).

Q.19. Budh Ram and Satto are husband and wife who live in a village. They already have two children in the form of two lovely daughters. During third pregnancy, Budh Ram and Satto went to a city clinic and, after paying a hefty bribe, got the pre-natal scan done on the foetus. After knowing the sex of foetus, they went to a famous lady doctor who specialises in gynaecology and requested her to carry out the medical termination of pregnancy. They offered her big money for doing this job. The lady doctor said a firm 'No'. When the couple insisted, the doctor threatened to call the police and get them arrested.

(*a*) **What type of scan was done to know the pre-natal (before birth) sex of foetus illegally ?**

(*b*) **What do you think this scan showed ?**

(*c*) **Why did Budh Ram and Satto want to terminate this pregnancy ?**

(*d*) **What term is used specifically for such type of termination of pregnancy ?**

(*e*) **What values were displayed by the lady doctor ?**

Ans. (*a*) An ultrasound scan was done to know the sex of foetus.

(*b*) The ultrasound scan showed that it was a female foetus.

(*c*) Budh Ram and Satto wanted to terminate this pregnancy so as to abort the female foetus (foetus of the girl child). This is because they wanted to try again for having a boy child (or son).

(*d*) Female foeticide.

(*e*) The values displayed by the lady doctor are :

(*i*) Awareness (or knowledge) that it is against the law to abort a female foetus (foetus of the girl child).

(*ii*) Concern for the girl child.

(*iii*) Responsibility towards society (to maintain healthy child sex ratio).

(*iv*) Honesty (in not accepting bribe).

Q.20. Shivani visited her village with her parents during the winter holidays. When she went to the fields outside the village, she saw a farmer spraying pesticides over the standing crops in the fields. When she looked at the container of pesticide lying on the ground, she knew that it was a pesticide which had been banned from use in most of the countries. The farmer was spraying pesticide without taking any precautions. Shivani asked the farmer to cover his nose and mouth properly with a cloth while spraying the pesticide. She also asked him not to spray too much pesticide on the crops because it is harmful to human beings, other animals and aquatic life in the long run. Shivani educated the farmer about the various harmful effects of this pesticide.

(*a*) What are pesticides ? Why are pesticides sprayed over the crops ? Which pesticide was being sprayed by the farmer on the crops ?

(*b*) (*i*) At which trophic level pesticides enter a food chain ?

(*ii*) At which trophic level of food chain, the concentration of pesticides is the maximum ?

(*c*) What name is given to the process of concentration of pesticides in the body of living organisms at each trophic level of a food chain ?

(*d*) Why do pesticides get accumulated at each trophic level in a food chain ?

(*e*) What are the harmful effects of the pesticide being sprayed by this farmer ?

(*f*) What values are displayed by Shivani in this episode ?

Ans. (*a*) Pesticides are the poisonous chemical substances which are sprayed over the standing crop plants to protect them from pests (harmful small animals) and diseases. The farmer was spraying DDT pesticide on the crops.

(*b*) (*i*) The pesticides enter a food chain at the first trophic level called producer level (which are the plants).

(*ii*) The concentration of pesticides is the maximum at the highest trophic level of organisms in a food chain (which occurs on the extreme right side in a food chain).

(*c*) Biological magnification.

(*d*) Pesticides get accumulated at each trophic level in a food chain because they are non-biodegradable chemical substances (which cannot be decomposed naturally by various micro-organisms present in soil and water bodies).

(*e*) DDT damages liver, nervous system and reproductive system in human beings. DDT can also cause various types of cancers, including liver cancer.

(*f*) The values displayed by Shivani are (*i*) Awareness (that DDT is harmful to human beings and other animals) (*ii*) Concern for the farmer (that DDT may not enter his respiratory system and damage it), and (*iii*) Concern for the environment (because DDT is non-biodegradable pesticide and persists in the soil and water bodies for a very long time).

Q.21. Diya has just moved into a new house in another colony alongwith her parents. Diya is a keen observer of all the human activities going around her in the colony. She noticed that in the colony people threw the left-over food, and fruit and vegetable peels into overflowing garbage bins to be taken away by the staff of Municipal Corporation. She also saw that the gardener of the colony collected all the fallen leaves of houseplants and garden plants in one corner of the park, let them dry, and ultimately burnt them. It was brought to her knowledge that Residents Welfare Association of the colony spent a lot of money every year in purchasing chemical fertiliser for the garden plants and grass lawns. Keeping all this in view, Diya presented a plan of action to the President of Welfare Association. On the successful completion of this plan after a few months, there was no need to purchase chemical fertiliser anymore. The environment also looked very neat and clean.

(*a*) What do you think was Diya's plan of action ?

(*b*) How did Diya's plan of action help the environment ?

(*c*) How did Diya's plan of action help the Residents Welfare Association ?

(*d*) What values of Diya are displayed by this plan of action ?

Ans. (*a*) Diya used the left-over food, fruit and vegetable peels and fallen leaves collected from the whole colony for making compost.

(*b*) The left-over food, and fruit and vegetable peels which used to rot in garbage bins and emit foul smell were now buried in the compost pit. Similarly, the fallen plant leaves which used to remain scattered here and there, and produced lot of smoke on burning, were now buried in compost pit. These actions helped in keeping the environment neat and clean.

(*c*) A lot of money which was earlier spent by Residents Welfare Association in purchasing the chemical fertiliser for the garden plants and grass lawns was saved. This is because the compost made in the colony itself was now used as manure to grow plants in the garden as well as in lawns.

(*d*) The values displayed by Diya are (*i*) Awareness (that waste materials such as left-over food, fruit and vegetable peels, and fallen leaves of plants can be converted into a useful material called compost) (*ii*) Concern for the environment (to keep it clean and protect it from the harmful effects of using chemical fertilisers), and (*iii*) Desire to help Residents Welfare Association (by saving money spent on fertilisers).

Q.22. Mr. Bhatia wanted to buy a new refrigerator and a new air conditioner in place of old ones which were purchased ten years ago. When Mr. Bhatia went to the market to buy these items his son Ankit, who is a student of tenth standard, also went with him. Before buying the new refrigerator and air conditioner, Ankit asked the various details from the shopkeeper and made sure that they did not contain old refrigerant which was not environment-friendly. The shopkeeper told him that these items now work with the new, eco-friendly refrigerant. Mr. Bhatia was puzzled by all this discussion. When they reached home, Ankit explained everything to his father. Ankit's father was happy at his choice.

(*a*) What do you think were the old refrigerants used in earlier refrigerator and air conditioner ?

(*b*) What was the harmful effect of old refrigerants to the environment if they leaked out ?

(*c*) What diseases could have been caused if people of the whole world had continued to use old refrigerants ? Why ?

(*d*) Name the new refrigerant which is being used increasingly in place of old one.

(*e*) Why is the new refrigerant being used these days not harmful to the environment ?

(*f*) What values are displayed by Ankit in this episode ?

Ans. (*a*) CFCs (Chloro-Fluoro-Carbons).

(*b*) CFCs are ozone depleting substances. So, if CFCs leaked out from refrigerators or air conditioners, they would attack the protective ozone layer high up in the atmosphere and destroy it gradually.

(*c*) If the people of whole world continued to use CFCs, then more and more of protective ozone layer in the upper atmosphere could be damaged, allowing more and more harmful ultraviolet radiations coming from the sun to pass through it and reach the earth. These ultraviolet radiations could cause diseases such as skin cancer, eye cataract, and damage the immune system by lowering the body's resistance to diseases.

(*d*) HFCs (Hydro-Fluoro-Carbons).

(*e*) The new refrigerants (HFCs) do not attack or destroy the protective ozone layer in the upper atmosphere. So, they are not harmful to the environment.

(*f*) The values displayed by Ankit are (*i*) Awareness (or knowledge) that ozone-friendly refrigerants (HFCs) are now available which can be used in place of harmful CFCs, and (*ii*) Desire to protect the useful ozone layer and prevent the harmful effects of ozone depletion.

Q.23. The teacher had just finished the chapter on environment in her class X lecture. She then placed four types of carry bags on the table in the classroom. These were cloth carry bag, paper carry bag, polythene carry bag and jute carry bag. The teacher asked Anushka to choose any two bags which she thinks are the most environment-friendly. Anushka thought for a while and then picked up cloth carry bag and jute carry bag.

(*a*) Explain why, Anushka did not choose the polythene carry bag though it is long lasting and water-proof ?

(*b*) What is the reason for not choosing the paper bag ?

(*c*) Why did Anushka choose only cotton cloth bag and jute bag ?

(*d*) What values are displayed by Anushka in making her choices ?

Ans. (*a*) Anushka did not choose a polythene carry bag because polythene is a plastic which is a non-biodegradable material. Polythene bags lie scattered here and there and cause a lot of pollution. It is also not possible to dispose of old polythene bags by burning because they produce extremely harmful gases on burning.

(*b*) Anushka did not choose the paper bag because though paper is biodegradable material but it is made from wood for which many forest trees have to be cut down regularly. So, Anushka did not choose paper bag to save trees by preventing deforestation.

(*c*) Anushka chose cloth bag and jute bag because cloth bag is made of cloth which comes from cotton crop grown in fields. Similarly, jute for making jute bag is obtained from jute crop grown in fields by the farmers. Since both cotton and jute are grown as crops in fields and they are biodegradable too, therefore, making of cloth bag and jute bag does not harm the environment in any way.

(*d*) The values displayed by Anushka are (*i*) Awareness (or knowledge) of biodegradable and non-biodegradable materials, and (*ii*) Concern for the environment.

Q.24. Apoorva is a student of tenth class. She has asked her father to replace all the old filament-type bulbs in her house by CFLs. She herself uses a bicycle for going to her school. Apoorva has a habit of writing on both the sides of her notebook pages and never tears away pages from notebooks. One day when Apoorva went to the village fields alongwith her father, she saw two snakes in the standing crops. The farmers wanted to kill these snakes but Apoorva requested them not to do so. While at home or school, Apoorva is very particular to get the leaking taps repaired by the plumber immediately.

(*a*) What really is conserved when Apoorva uses CFLs in her house instead of filament-type bulbs ?

(*b*) What really is conserved when Apoorva goes to her school on bicycle ?

(*c*) What really is conserved when Apoorva writes on both sides of the pages in her notebook ?

(*d*) What really is conserved when Apoorva does not allow the snakes in standing crop fields to be killed ?

(*e*) What is conserved when Apoorva gets the leaking taps repaired immediately ?

(*f*) What are the things conserved by Apoorva commonly known as ?

(*g*) What values are displayed by Apoorva by her actions ?

Ans. (*a*) Coal (because coal is used to produce electricity).

(*b*) Petroleum (because a petroleum product 'petrol' is used in going to school by car or scooter).

(*c*) Forests (because paper used in making notebook is obtained from wood of forest trees).

(*d*) Wildlife (because snake is a part of wildlife which is a friend of the farmer).

(*e*) Water (because leaking taps waste water).

(*f*) Natural resources.

(*g*) The values displayed by Apoorva are (*i*) Management of natural resources (or conservation of natural resources) because coal, petroleum, forests and wildlife, and water are all natural resources, and (*ii*) Concern for a healthy environment.

Q.25. Mohan, Rohan and Sohan are three classmates. They have three different habits. Mohan is fond of taking bread and apple jam. Whenever all the jam of the container is eaten up by him, Mohan cleans the container thoroughly and puts iodised salt in it which his mother keeps on the kitchen rack. Rohan has a habit of putting old notebooks, newspapers and magazines at one place and sell it to *Kabadiwala* after a month to make some extra pocket money. Sohan has also a unique habit of going from room to room in his big house and switch off the lights and fans when no one is in the rooms. Actually, Mohan, Rohan and Sohan are collectively trying to practise three R's taught by their teacher in their own ways.

(*a*) What is meant by three R's ? In which context are they used ?

(*b*) Which of the three R's is exemplified by Mohan's action ?

(*c*) Which of the three R's is exemplified by Rohan's action ?

(*d*) Which of the three R's is exemplified by Sohan's action ?

(*e*) Why is the R exemplified by Mohan's action better than the R exemplified by Rohan's action ?

(*f*) What values are displayed by Mohan, Rohan and Sohan in this episode ?

Ans. (*a*) The three R's stand for Reduce, Recycle and Reuse. These are used in the context of natural resources.

(*b*) Mohan reuses the empty jam container for storing iodised salt, so the R exemplified by Mohan's action is 'Reuse'.

(*c*) Rohan sells old paper products such as old notebooks, newspapers and magazines to *kabadiwala* for being sent to paper mills for recycling (making new paper), so the R exemplified by Rohan's action is 'Recycle'.

(*d*) Sohan switches off lights and fans when not needed to avoid wastage of electricity and reduces the consumption of coal (which is usually used to produce electricity), so the R exemplified by Sohan's action is 'Reduce'.

(*e*) We have just seen that Mohan practises 'reuse' and Rohan practises 'recycle'. The process of 'reuse' is better than that of recycling because though some energy is used to recycle old objects but no energy is required during reuse.

(*f*) The values displayed by Mohan, Rohan and Sohan are : (*i*) Awareness (or knowledge) of 3 R's to save the environment, and (*ii*) Ability to use their knowledge in everyday situations.

MODEL TEST PAPER 1

(As per the latest marking scheme)

SCIENCE

CLASS – X

Time allowed: 03 Hours **Maximum Marks: 80**

General Instructions:*

(i) The question paper comprises two sections, A and B. You are to attempt both the sections.

(ii) All questions are compulsory.

(iii) All questions of Section-A and B are to be attempted separately.

(iv) Question numbers 1 and 2 in Section-A are one mark questions. They are to be answered in one word or in one sentence.

(v) Question numbers 3 to 5 in Section-A are two marks questions. These are to be answered in 30 words each.

(vi) Question numbers 6 to 15 in Section-A are three marks questions. These are to be answered in about 50 words each.

(vii) Question numbers 16 to 21 in Section-A are 5 marks questions. These are to be answered in 70 words each.

(viii) Question numbers 22 to 27 in Section-B are based on practical skills. Each question is a two marks question. These are to be answered in brief.

SECTION-A

1. From amongst the metals sodium, calcium, aluminium, copper and magnesium, name the metal: 1

   (a) which reacts with water only on boiling, and

   (b) another which does not react even with steam.

2. To an astronaut, why does the sky appear dark instead of blue? 1

3. Explain with the help of a diagram, why a pencil partly immersed in water appears to be bent at the water surface. 2

4. What is an oxidation reaction? Identify in the following reaction (a) the substance oxidized, and (b) the substance reduced: 2

$$ZnO + C \rightarrow Zn + CO$$

* The general instructions are valid for all the Model Test Papers.

5. What is 'reproduction'? Mention the importance of DNA copying in reproduction. 2

6. What physical and chemical properties of elements were used by Mendeleev in creating his periodic table? List two observations which posed a challenge to Mendeleev's Periodic Law. 3

7. (a) Show the formation of NaCl from sodium and chlorine atoms by the transfer of electron(s). 3

(b) Why has sodium chloride a high melting point?

(c) Name the anode and the cathode used in the electrolytic refining of impure copper metal.

8. (a) What happens chemically when quicklime is added to water? Write chemical equation of the reaction involved. 3

(b) What is 'Baking Powder'? How does it make the cake soft and spongy?

9. (a) The refractive index of diamond is 2.42. What is the meaning of this statement in relation to speed of light? 3

(b) Describe an activity to draw a magnetic field line outside a bar magnet from one pole to another pole.

10. For the circuit shown in the diagram given below: 3

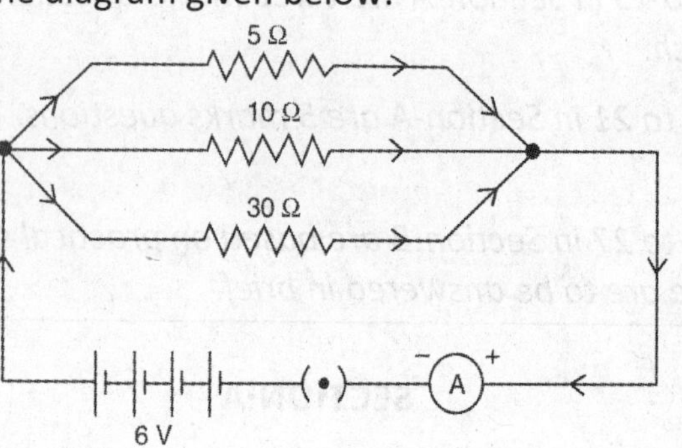

Calculate:

(a) the value of current through each resistor.

(b) the total current in the circuit.

(c) the total effective resistance of the circuit.

11. (a) Draw a diagram to show the formation of image of a distant object by a myopic eye. How can such an eye defect by remedied? 3

(b) State two reasons due to which this eye defect may be caused.

(c) A person with a myopic eye cannot see objects beyond a distance of 1.5 m. What would be the power of the corrective lens used to restore proper vision?

12. (a) Distinguish between the terms 'overloading' and 'short-circuiting' as used in domestic circuits. 3

(b) Why are the coils of electric toasters made of an alloy rather than a pure metal?

13. "Damage to the ozone layer is a cause for concern". Justify this statement. Suggest any two steps to limit this damage. 3

14. Define 'hormones'. Name the hormone secreted by thyroid. Write its function. Why is the use of iodised salt advised to us? 3

15. (a) State any one difference between pollination and fertilization. 3

(b) A man with blood group A marries a woman with blood group O and their daughter has blood group O. Is this information enough to tell you which of the traits—blood group A or O is dominant? Why?

16. (a) Why does carbon form compounds mainly by covalent bonding? 5

(b) List any two reasons for carbon forming a very large number of compounds.

(c) An organic acid 'X' is a liquid which often freezes during winter time in cold countries, has the molecular formula $C_2H_4O_2$. On warming it with ethanol in the presence of a few drops of concentrated sulphuric acid, a compound 'Y' with a sweet smell is formed.

(i) Identify 'X' and 'Y'.

(ii) Write a chemical equation for the reaction involved.

17. (a) What is a homologous series of compounds? List any two characteristics of a homologous series. 5

(b) (i) What would be observed on adding a 5% alkaline potassium permanganate solution drop by drop to some warm ethanol in a test tube?

(ii) Write the name of the compound formed during the chemical reaction.

(c) How would you distinguish experimentally between an alcohol and a carboxylic acid on the basis of a chemical property?

18. (a) What is meant by saying that the potential difference between two points is 1 volt? Name a device that helps to measure the potential difference across a conductor. 5

(b) Why does the connecting cord of an electric heater not glow hot while the heating element does?

(c) Electrical resistivities of some substances at 20°C are given below:

Silver	1.60×10^{-8} Ωm
Copper	1.62×10^{-8} Ωm
Tungsten	5.20×10^{-8} Ωm
Iron	10.0×10^{-8} Ωm
Mercury	94.0×10^{-8} Ωm
Nichrome	100×10^{-6} Ωm

Answer the following questions in relation to them:

(i) Among silver and copper, which one is a better conductor? Why?

(ii) Which material would you advise to be used in electrical heating devices? Why?

19. (a) Name an instrument that measures electric current in a circuit. Define the unit of electric current. 5

(b) What do the following symbols mean in circuit diagrams?

(i) (ii)

(c) An electric circuit consisting of a 0.5 m long nichrome wire XY, an ammeter, a voltmeter, four cells of 1.5 V each and a plug key was set up.

(i) Draw a diagram of this electric circuit to study the relation between the potential difference maintained between the points 'X' and 'Y' and the electric current flowing through XY.

(ii) Following graph was plotted between V and I values:

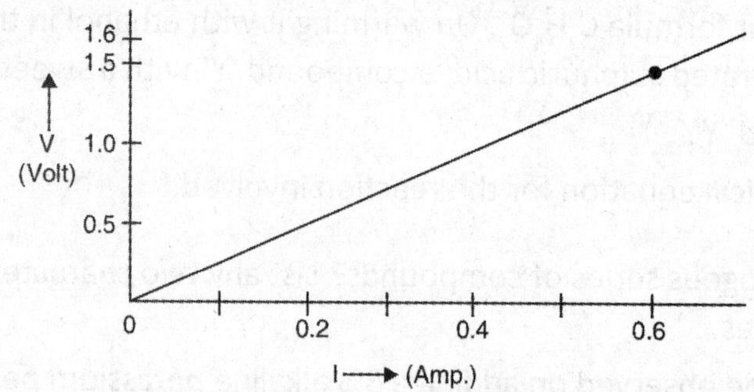

What would be the values of $\frac{V}{I}$ ratios when the potential difference is 0.8 V, 1.2 V and 1.6 V, respectively? What conclusion do you draw from these values?

20. (a) Draw a diagram depicting Human Alimentary Canal and label on it Gall Bladder, Liver and Pancreas. 5

(b) State the roles of Liver and Pancreas.

(c) Name the organ which performs the following functions in humans:

(i) Absorption of digested food.

(ii) Absorption of water.

21. (a) Draw a sectional view of the human heart and label on it Aorta, Right Ventricle and Pulmonary Vein. 5

(b) State the functions of the following components of transport system:

(i) Blood (ii) Lymph

SECTION B

22. A metal is treated with dilute sulphuric acid. The gas evolved is collected by the method shown in the figure. Answer the following: 2

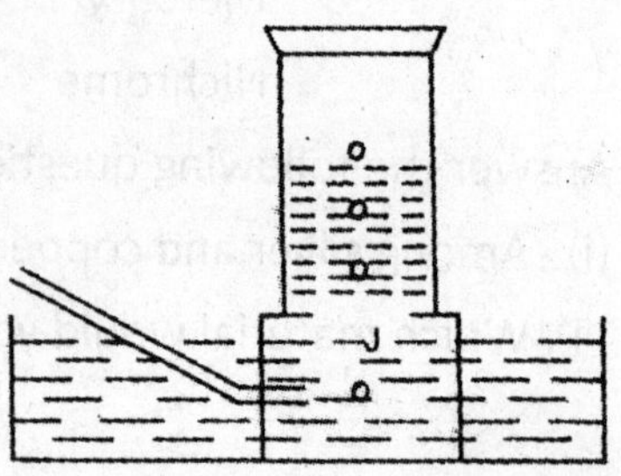

(a) Name the gas.

(b) Name the method of collection of the gas.

(c) Is the gas soluble or insoluble in water?

(d) Is the gas lighter or heavier than air?

23. Ashwini has been given four test-tubes containing the following: 2

(a) Universal indicator

(b) Distilled water

(c) Sodium hydrogencarbonate

(d) Phenolphthalein

What will be observed by Ashwini when he adds a few drops of acetic acid to each test-tube, one by one?

24. A beam of white light falling on a glass prism gets split up into seven colours marked 1 to 7 as shown in the diagram. 2

Which two positions correspond closely to the colour of:

(a) a solution of potassium permanganate?

(b) 'danger' or stop signal lights?

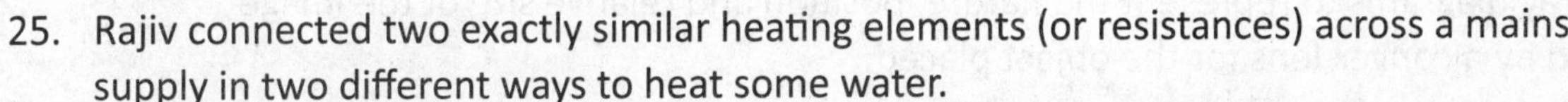

25. Rajiv connected two exactly similar heating elements (or resistances) across a mains supply in two different ways to heat some water. 2

(a) Is more heat obtained when the heating elements are connected in series or when they are connected in parallel?

(b) Give reasons for your answer.

26. A student observed a permanent slide showing asexual reproduction in yeast. 2

(a) Draw diagrams of the observations the student must have made from the slide.

(b) Name the process of asexual reproduction of yeast.

27. Given below is a sketch of a leaf partially covered with black paper and which is to be used in the experiment to show that light is compulsory for the process of photosynthesis: 2

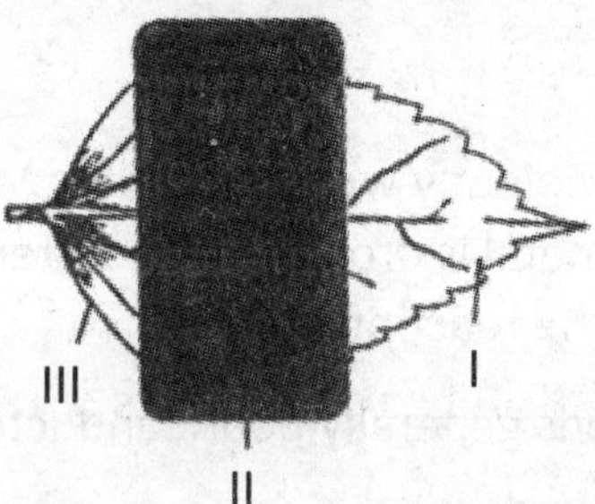

(a) At the end of the experiment, which of the leaf part/leaf parts labelled I, II and III will become blue-black when dipped in iodine solution?

(b) Which substance will be missing in the leaf part/leaf parts which will not become blue-black when dipped in iodine solution?

MODEL TEST PAPER 2

(As per the latest marking scheme)

SCIENCE

CLASS – X

Time allowed: 03 Hours **Maximum Marks: 80**

SECTION A

1. How is the increase in demand for energy affecting our environment adversely? 1

2. Balance the following chemical equation: 1

$$FeSO_4 \xrightarrow{\text{Heat}} Fe_2O_3 + SO_2 + SO_3$$

3. Draw ray diagrams to represent the nature, position and relative size of the image formed by a convex lens for the object placed: 2

   (a) at $2F_1$

   (b) between F_1 and the optical centre O of lens

4. Give an example of a decomposition reaction. Describe an activity to illustrate such a reaction by heating. 2

5. Write one function each of the following components of the transport system in human beings: 2

   (a) Blood vessels

   (b) Blood platelets

   (c) Lymph

   (d) Heart

6. Name two metals which react violently with cold water. Write any three observations you would make when such a metal is dropped into water. How would you identify the gas evolved, if any, during the reaction? 3

7. (a) Why are covalent compounds generally poor conductors of electricity? 3

   (b) Name the following compound:

```
    H       H
    |       |
H — C — C — C — H
    |   ||  |
    H   O   H
```

   (c) Name the gas evolved when ethanoic acid is added to sodium carbonate. How would you prove the presence of this gas?

8. (a) What is the difference between washing soda and baking soda? 3

(b) Write the chemical formula for bleaching powder. How is bleaching powder prepared? For what purpose is it used in paper factories?

9. In the electrolysis of acidified water: 3

(a) Name the gas collected at (i) anode, and (ii) cathode

(b) Why is the volume of gas collected at one electrode double than that at the other electrode?

(c) What would happen if dilute sulphuric acid is not added to water?

10. Two lamps, one rated 40 W at 220 V and the other 60 W at 220 V, are connected in parallel to the electric supply at 220 V. 3

(a) Draw a circuit diagram to show the connections.

(b) Calculate the current drawn from the electric supply.

(c) Calculate the total energy consumed by the two lamps together when they operate for one hour.

11. (a) Why is a series arrangement not used for connecting domestic electrical appliances in a circuit? 3

(b) Draw a diagram to show the magnetic field lines around a bar magnet. List any two properties of magnetic field lines.

12. Name the electric device which converts mechanical energy into electrical energy. Draw the labelled diagram and explain the principle involved in this device. 3

13. Write any three differences between aerobic and anaerobic respiration. 3

14. How is ozone formed in the upper atmosphere? Why is damage to ozone layer a cause of concern to us? What causes this damage? 3

15. (a) State one difference between arteries and veins. 3

(b) Name any two sexually transmitted diseases. What advice is given to prevent them?

16. (a) What is meant by dispersion of white light? Describe the formation of rainbow in the sky with the help of a diagram. 5

(b) What is hypermetropia? Draw ray diagrams to show the image formation of an object by:

(i) Hypermetropic eye

(ii) Correction made with a suitable lens for hypermetropic eye.

17. (a) Give reasons for the following: 5

(i) Colour of the clear sky is blue.

(ii) The sun can be seen about two minutes before actual sunrise.

(iii) We cannot see an object clearly if it is placed very close to the eyes.

(b) What is Presbyopia? Write two causes of this defect.

18. (a) Why do we classify elements? 5

(b) What were the two criteria used by Mendeleev in creating his Periodic Table?

(c) Why did Mendeleev leave some gaps in his Periodic Table?

(d) In Mendeleev's Periodic Table, why was there no mention of Noble gases such as Helium, Neon and Argon?

(e) Would you place the two isotopes of chlorine, Cl-35 and Cl-37 in different slots because of their different atomic masses or in the same slot because their chemical properties are the same? Justify your answer.

19. (a) Show the formation of Na_2O by the transfer of electrons between the combining atoms. 5

(b) Why are ionic compounds usually hard?

(c) How is it that ionic compounds in the solid state do not conduct electricity but they do so when in molten state?

(d) What type of chemical bonds are present in CCl_4?

(e) What type of chemical bonds are present in $MgCl_2$?

20. (a) Draw the structure of a neuron and label the following on it: 5

Nucleus, Dendrite, Cell body and Axon

(b) Name the part of neuron:

(i) where information is acquired.

(ii) through which information travels as an electrical impulse.

21. (a) What is (i) phototropism, and (ii) geotropism? With labelled diagrams, describe an activity to show that light and gravity change the direction that plant parts grow in. 5

(b) Mention the role of each of the following plant hormones:

(i) Auxin

(ii) Abscisic acid

SECTION B

22. (a) How will you test for the gas which is liberated when hydrochloric acid reacts with an active metal? 2

(b) Name any two active metals which can be used with hydrochloric acid to liberate the same gas.

23. Sunita performs two sets of experiments to study the formation of lather (foam) by using liquid soap. 2

Set 1: She takes 10 ml of distilled water in test tube 'A', adds 5–6 drops of liquid soap in it and shakes the test tube vigorously.

Set 2: She takes 10 ml of distilled water in test tube 'B', adds 5–6 drops of liquid soap in it alongwith half spoonful of $CaSO_4$, and shakes the test tube vigorously.

(a) In which test tube, A or B, less lather is formed? Why?

(b) In which test tube, A or B, more lather is formed? Why?

24. (a) Copy this figure in your answer-book and show the direction of the light ray after reflection: 2

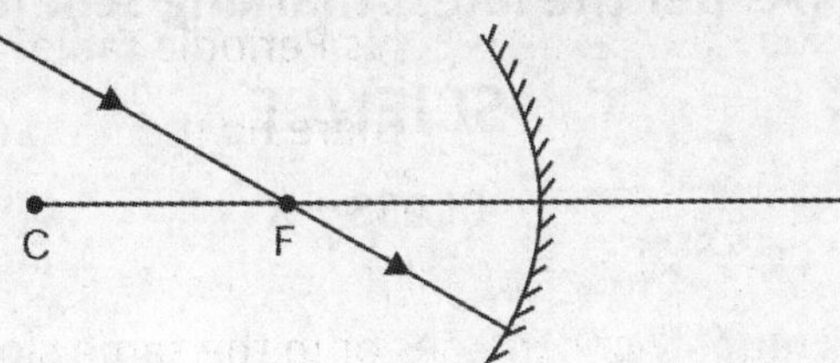

(b) What type of mirror is shown in the above figure: a converging mirror or a diverging mirror?

25. A student is performing an experiment to verify Ohm's Law in the laboratory. The ammeter given to him for this purpose has 10 divisions between 0 and 0.5A on its scale. If the pointer shows 22 divisions on the ammeter scale while taking a reading, what is the value of current according to this position of pointer? 2

26. In the test tubes A and B shown below, yeast was kept in sugar solution. Which products of respiration would you expect in tubes A and B? 2

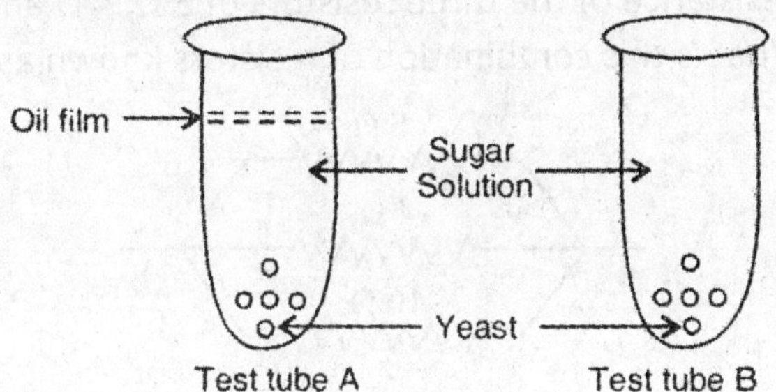

Give reason for your answer.

27. Before testing the leaf for starch at the end of the experiment "Light is necessary for photosynthesis": 2

(a) In which liquid the leaf should be boiled?

(b) Why should the leaf be boiled in this liquid?

MODEL TEST PAPER 3

(As per the latest marking scheme)

SCIENCE

CLASS – X

Time allowed: 03 Hours **Maximum Marks: 80**

SECTION A

1. Why is red colour selected for danger signal lights? 1

2. Balance the following chemical equation: 1

$$MnO_2 + HCl \rightarrow MnCl_2 + Cl_2 + H_2O$$

3. What is the common name of $CaSO_4 . \frac{1}{2} H_2O$? Also name the compound from which it is prepared. 2

4. What is the resultant resistance of the three resistors of 5 Ω, 4 Ω and 10 Ω connected as shown in the figure? What is this combination of resistors known as? 2

5 Ω

4 Ω

10 Ω

5. Define variation in relation to a species. Why is variation beneficial to the species? 2

6. (a) Show on a diagram the transfer of electrons between the atoms in the formation of MgO. 3
   (b) Name the solvent in which ionic compounds are generally soluble.
   (c) Why are aqueous solutions of ionic compounds able to conduct electricity?

7. Explain why, the blue colour of copper sulphate solution fades when an iron nail is kept dipped in it. Write chemical equation of the reaction involved. What does this reaction tell us about the relative reactivities of copper and iron? 3

8. Why are decomposition reactions called the opposite of combination reactions? Explain by giving one example (with equation) of each type of reaction. 3

9. The atom of an element has the electron structure 2, 7. 3
   (a) What is the atomic number of the element?
   (b) To which of the following would it be chemically similar?

$${}_{7}N, \quad {}_{15}P, \quad {}_{17}Cl, \quad {}_{18}Ar$$

(c) Why would you expect it to be similar?

10. The position of hand shown in the figure corresponds to one of the Fleming's rules. 3
 (a) Which Fleming's rule is illustrated by this hand?
 (b) In this figure of hand, what is indicated:
  (i) by the direction of forefinger?
  (ii) by the direction of centre finger?
  (iii) by the direction of thumb?

11. Two resistors, with resistances 5 Ω and 10 Ω respectively are to be connected to a battery of emf 6 V so as to obtain: (i) minimum current flowing (ii) maximum current flowing. 3
 (a) How will you connect the resistances in each case?
 (b) Calculate the strength of the total current in the circuit in two cases.

12. What is hypermetropia? State the two causes of hypermetropia. With the help of ray diagrams, show: 3
 (a) the eye-defect hypermetropia
 (b) correction of hypermetropia by using a lens

13. Distinguish between biodegradable and non-biodegradable substances. List two effects of each of them on our environment. 3

14. Why are bacteria and fungi called decomposers? List any two advantages of decomposers to the environment. 3

15. (a) Name two different ways in which glucose is oxidized to provide energy in various organisms. 3
 (b) Write any two differences between the two ways of oxidation of glucose in organisms.

16. (a) Which two criteria did Mendeleev use to classify the elements in his periodic table? 5
 (b) State Mendeleev's periodic law.
 (c) Why could no fixed position be given to hydrogen in Mendeleev's periodic table?
 (d) How and why does the atomic size vary as you go:
  (i) from left to right along a period?
  (ii) down a group?

17. Write the names and symbols of the two most reactive metals belonging to the Group I of the periodic table. Explain by drawing electronic structure how either one of the two metals reacts with a halogen. With which name is the bond formed between these elements known and what is the class of the compound so formed known? State any four physical properties of such compounds. 5

18. (a) What is a solenoid? Draw a sketch of the pattern of field lines of the magnetic field through and around a current carrying solenoid. 5

(b) Consider a circular loop of wire lying in the plane of the table. Let the current pass through the loop clockwise. Apply the right hand rule to find out the direction of the magnetic field inside and outside the loop.

19. Derive the expression for the heat produced due to a current '*I*' flowing for a time interval '*t*' through a resistor '*R*' having a potential difference '*V*' across its ends. With which name is the relation known? How much heat will an instrument of 12 W produce in one minute if it is connected to a battery of 12 V? 5

20. (a) Draw a diagram of human alimentary canal and label on it: Oesophagus, Gall bladder, Liver and Pancreas 5

(b) Explain the statement, 'Bile does not contain any enzyme but it is essential for digestion.'

21. (a) Draw a diagram of excretory system in human beings and label on it: Aorta, vena cava, urinary bladder, urethra. 5

(b) List two vital functions of the kidney.

SECTION B

22. Draw the following diagram in your answer-book and show the formation of image of the object AB with the help of suitable rays. 2

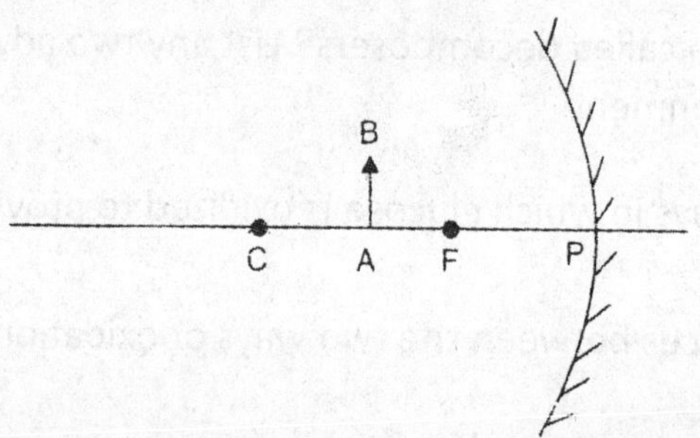

What type of reflecting surface is shown in the above diagram?

23. A student was given three resistors of 2 ohms, 3 ohms and 5 ohms by his teacher. The teacher asked him to connect these three resistors in such a way so as to obtain the minimum resistance. 2

(a) In what way should the student connect the resistors?

(b) Draw a diagram of the combination of resistors.

24. When a student adds some dilute hydrochloric acid to baking soda taken in a test-tube, a gas is evolved. 2

(a) Name the gas evolved.

(b) How can this gas be tested?

25. A student was given two test-tubes A and B each containing a colourless solution. When a few drops of universal indicator were added to the two test-tubes, one by one, then the colour of solution in test-tube A changed to blue whereas the colour of solution in test-tube B changed to orange. 2

(a) Which test-tube has a solution of pH higher than 7 ?

(b) Which test-tube has a solution of pH lower than 7 ?

(c) Which test-tube has an acidic solution?

(d) Which test-tube has an alkaline solution?

26. A student conducted an experiment to show that carbon dioxide is released during respiration. State two precautions that the student must take for obtaining correct observations. 2

27. A star-shaped figure was cut in the black paper strip used for covering a part of the leaf of a destarched plant used for demonstrating that light is necessary for photosynthesis. At the end of the experiment (after the removal of chlorophyll), the leaf was tested for starch with iodine solution. 2

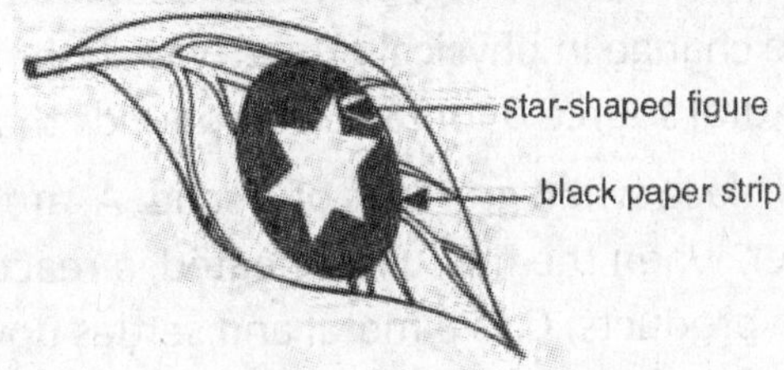

(a) What colour, if any, will be produced on the part of leaf under the star-shaped figure?

(b) Give reason for your answer.

MODEL TEST PAPER 4

(As per the latest marking scheme)

SCIENCE

CLASS – X

Time allowed: 03 Hours **Maximum Marks: 80**

SECTION A

1. Name a reducing agent that may be used to obtain manganese from manganese dioxide. 1
2. Why does a ray of light bend when it travels from one medium into another? 1
3. A compound which is prepared from gypsum has the property of hardening when mixed with a proper quantity of water. Identify the compound. Write the chemical equation for its preparation. For what purpose is it used in hospitals? 2
4. What is the minimum number of rays required for locating the image formed by a concave mirror for an object. Draw a ray diagram to show the formation of a virtual image by a concave mirror. 2
5. Name the type of respiration in which the end products are: 2
   (a) ethanol, carbon dioxide and energy.
   (b) carbon dioxide, water and energy.
6. Name the functional group of organic compounds that can be hydrogenated. With the help of suitable example, explain the process of hydrogenation mentioning the conditions of the reaction and any one change in physical property with the formation of the product. Name any one natural source of organic compounds that are hydrogenated. 3
7. No chemical reaction takes place when granules of a solid, A, are mixed with the powder of another solid, B. However, when the mixture is heated, a reaction takes place between its components. One of the products, C, is a metal and settles down in the molten state while the other product, D, floats over it. It was observed that the reaction was highly exothermic. 3
   (a) Based on the given information, make an assumption about A and B and write a chemical equation for the chemical reaction indicating the conditions of reaction, physical state of reactants and products and thermal status of the reaction.
   (b) Mention any two types of reactions under which above chemical reaction can be classified.
8. Atoms of eight elements A, B, C, D, E, F, G and H have the same number of electronic shells but different number of electrons in their outermost shells. It was found that elements A and G combine to form an ionic compound which can also be extracted from sea water. Oxides of the elements A and B are basic in nature while those of E and F are acidic. The oxide of element D is almost neutral. Answer the following questions based on the information given herein: 3
   (a) To which group or period of the periodic table do the listed elements belong?
   (b) Which one of the eight elements is likely to be a noble gas?

(c) Which one of the eight elements would have the largest atomic radius?

(d) Which two elements amongst these are likely to be non-metals?

(e) Which one of these eight elements is likely to be a semi-metal or metalloid?

9. State, giving reasons, which of the following reactions will occur and which will not: 3

(a) $MgSO_4$ (aq) + Cu (s) $\rightarrow$ $CuSO_4$ (aq) + Mg (s)

(b) $CuSO_4$ (aq) + Fe (s) $\rightarrow$ $FeSO_4$ (aq) + Cu (s)

(c) $MgSO_4$ (aq) + Fe (s) $\rightarrow$ $FeSO_4$ (aq) + Mg (s)

10. Draw three labelled ray-diagrams to show the defect of vision called hypermetropia and how it is corrected by using a lens. Also name the lens used. 3

11. At what distance should an object be placed from a convex lens of focal length 18 cm to obtain an image at 36 cm from it on the other side? What will be the magnification produced in this case? 3

12. The magnetic field associated with a current carrying straight conductor is in anticlockwise direction. If the conductor was held along the east-west direction, what will be the direction of current through it? Name and state the rule applied to determine the direction of current. 3

13. Explain analogous organs and homologous organs. Identify the analogous and homologous organs amongst the following: 3

Wings of an insect, wings of a bat, forelimbs of frog, forelimbs of a human.

14. (a) Explain the terms: 3

(i) implantation (ii) placenta

(b) What is the average duration of human pregnancy?

15. Explain the mechanism of reflex action with a suitable example. 3

16. (a) Why did Mendeleev leave gaps in his periodic table? 5

(b) State any three limitations of Mendeleev's classification.

(c) How does electronic configurations of atoms change in a period with increase in atomic number?

17. What is meant by refining of a metal? Name the most widely used method of refining impure metals produced by various reduction processes. Describe with the help of a labelled diagram how this method may be used for refining of copper. 5

18. Explain the process of digestion of food in mouth, stomach and small intestine in human body. 5

19. (a) Define 'Photosynthesis'. Apart from sunlight, what other conditions are necessary for the process of photosynthesis. 5

(b) Describe an experiment to show that "sunlight is essential for photosynthesis".

20. (a) What is a magnetic field? How can the direction of magnetic field lines at a place be determined? 5

(b) State the rule for the direction of the magnetic field produced around a current-carrying conductor. Draw a sketch of the pattern of field lines due to a current flowing through a straight conductor.

21. Explain with the help of a labelled circuit diagram how will you find the resistance of a combination of three resistors, of resistance R_1, R_2 and R_3 joined in parallel. Also mention how you will connect the ammeter and the voltmeter in the circuit when measuring the current in the circuit and the potential difference across one of the three resistors of the combination. 5

SECTION B

22. Draw the given diagram in your answer book and complete it for the path of ray of light beyond the lens. 2

(a) What type of lens is shown in this diagram?

(b) Is it a converging lens or a diverging lens?

2F F O F 2F

23. A student connects a coil of insulated wire to a galvanometer. What would be seen if a bar magnet with its north pole towards one face of the coil is: 2

(a) moved quickly towards it?

(b) moved quickly away from the coil?

(c) placed near the face of the coil?

Name the phenomenon involved.

24. A student was working in a chemistry laboratory. He found that a bottle contained a white powdery substance but half of the label on the bottle was torn. The part of label still sticking to the bottle had NaH written on it. The student took this powdery substance in a test-tube and added dil. HCl to it. A gas was evolved which extinguished a burning match-stick. 2

(a) Name the gas evolved.

(b) Write the formula of white powdery substance.

25. Ravi placed a zinc plate in a glass container having a blue coloured solution of a metal sulphate MSO_4 for a considerable time. He found that the blue colour of solution got lighter and lighter, and finally the solution became colourless. A red-brown deposit was also formed on the zinc plate. 2

(a) Which metal, zinc or M, occurs lower in the reactivity series?

(b) Name the substance which forms colourless solution.

26. A student is performing an experiment to show that sunlight is necessary for photosynthesis. In the first stage, he keeps a potted plant with green leaves in a dark place for about 3 days. Towards the end of the experiment, he boils one leaf in alcohol before using iodine for testing starch. 2

(a) Why is the plant kept in a dark place for about 3 days?

(b) Why is the leaf boiled in alcohol before testing for starch with iodine?

27. Pure-bred pea plants A are crossed with pure-bred pea plants B. It is found that the plants which look like A do not appear in F_1 generation but re-emerge in F_2 generation. 2

(a) Which of the plants A and B are: (i) tall, and (ii) dwarf?

(b) Give reason for your answer.